# WOMEN
# IN AMERICA

ISSN 2332-3876

# WOMEN IN AMERICA

Erin Brown

**INFORMATION PLUS® REFERENCE SERIES**
Formerly Published by Information Plus, Wylie, Texas

GALE
A Cengage Company

Farmington Hills, Mich • San Francisco • New York • Waterville, Maine
Meriden, Conn • Mason, Ohio • Chicago

**Women in America**

Erin Brown

Kepos Media, Inc.: Steven Long and
Janice Jorgensen, Series Editors

Project Editor: Laura Avery

Rights Acquisition and Management:
Ashley Maynard, Carissa Poweleit

Composition: Evi Abou-El-Seoud, Jeff Sumner,
Mary Beth Trimper

Manufacturing: Rita Wimberley

Product Design: Kristin Julien

For product information and technology assistance, contact us at
**Gale Customer Support, 1-800-877-4253.**
For permission to use material from this text or product,
submit all requests online at **www.cengage.com/permissions.**
Further permissions questions can be emailed to
**permissionrequest@cengage.com**

Cover photograph: © Victorpr/Shutterstock.com.

While every effort has been made to ensure the reliability of the information presented in this publication, Gale, a Cengage Company, does not guarantee the accuracy of the data contained herein. Gale accepts no payment for listing; and inclusion in the publication of any organization, agency, institution, publication, service, or individual does not imply endorsement of the editors or publisher. Errors brought to the attention of the publisher and verified to the satisfaction of the publisher will be corrected in future editions.

Gale
27500 Drake Rd.
Farmington Hills, MI 48331-3535

ISBN-13: 978-0-7876-5103-9 (set)
ISBN-13: 978-1-4103-2563-1

ISSN 2332-3876

This title is also available as an e-book.
ISBN-13: 978-1-4103-2595-2
Contact your Gale sales representative for ordering information.

Printed in the United States of America
1 2 3 4 5      22 21 20 19 18

# TABLE OF CONTENTS

presented. The chapter ends with a discussion of women as presidential and vice presidential candidates and as cabinet members.

# CHAPTER 10

Women are less likely than men to be victims of violent crime, but they outnumber men as victims of certain types of crimes, including rape and sexual assault. This chapter provides detailed statistics on the who, what, where, when, and why of female crime victims. Intimate partner crime (the most common form of domestic violence), the prevalence of sexual assault and harassment, and hate crimes are also examined.

# CHAPTER 11

Women commit about 20% of crimes, but in many categories their arrest rates are rising, as compared with men's. This chapter presents and interprets statistics on violent crimes committed by women, female prisoners, and the death sentence as applied to women.

# PREFACE

*Women in America* is part of the *Information Plus Reference Series*. The purpose of each volume of the series is to present the latest facts on a topic of pressing concern in modern American life. These topics include the most controversial and studied social issues of the 21st century: abortion, capital punishment, care for senior citizens, crime, education, the environment, health care, immigration, national security, social welfare, sports, and many more. Although this series is written especially for high school and undergraduate students, it is an excellent resource for anyone in need of factual information on current affairs.

By presenting the facts, it is the intention of Gale, a Cengage Company, to provide its readers with everything they need to reach an informed opinion on current issues. To that end, there is a particular emphasis in this series on the presentation of scientific studies, surveys, and statistics. These data are generally presented in the form of tables, charts, and other graphics placed within the text of each book. Every graphic is directly referred to and carefully explained in the text. The source of each graphic is presented within the graphic itself. The data used in these graphics are drawn from the most reputable and reliable sources such as the various branches of the US government and private organizations and associations. Every effort has been made to secure the most recent information available. Readers should bear in mind that many major studies take years to conduct and that additional years often pass before the data from these studies are made available to the public. Therefore, in many cases the most recent information available in 2018 is dated from 2014 or 2015. Older statistics are sometimes presented as well if they are derived from landmark studies or of particular interest and no more-recent information exists.

Although statistics are a major focus of the *Information Plus Reference Series*, they are by no means its only content. Each book also presents the widely held posi-tions and important ideas that shape how the book's subject is discussed in the United States. These positions are explained in detail and, where possible, in the words of their proponents. Some of the other material to be found in these books includes historical background, descriptions of major events related to the subject, relevant laws and court cases, and examples of how these issues play out in American life. Some books also feature primary documents or have pro and con debate sections that provide the words and opinions of prominent Americans on both sides of a controversial topic. All material is presented in an evenhanded and unbiased manner; readers will never be encouraged to accept one view of an issue over another.

## HOW TO USE THIS BOOK

As American women marry later in life, have fewer children, attain more education, and participate in the labor force in growing numbers, their roles are changing. Nevertheless, in terms of caregiving responsibility, earnings and assets, and gender-linked jobs, many women have experienced little change. These conflicting developments are illuminated by information on women's demographic trends, educational achievements, employment, financial status, health issues, parental and elder care responsibilities, political roles, victimization, and criminal behavior, which are all presented and explained in this book.

*Women in America* consists of 11 chapters and 3 appendixes. Each chapter is devoted to a particular aspect of American women. For a summary of the information that is covered in each chapter, please see the synopses that are provided in the Table of Contents. Chapters generally begin with an overview of the basic facts and background information on the chapter's topic, then proceed to examine subtopics of particular interest. For example, Chapter 6: Women's Health begins by presenting differences between women and men in terms of life expectancy and death rates. The chapter then describes women's particular health care needs and the various options they have for accessing health care and health insurance coverage. Next, the chapter examines the leading causes of death among women, including heart disease and various cancers. Other health issues that affect women are also covered, including sexually transmitted diseases, osteoporosis, and mental health challenges such as depression and eating disorders. Finally, the chapter considers the health consequences of substance use, including tobacco, alcohol, and illicit drugs, indicating how lifestyle choices such as exercise and maintaining healthy body weight can be instrumental in disease prevention. Readers can find their way through a chapter by looking for the section and subsection headings, which are clearly set off from the text. They can also refer to the book's extensive Index if they already know what they are looking for.

## Statistical Information

The tables and figures featured throughout *Women in America* will be of particular use to readers in learning about this issue. These tables and figures represent an extensive collection of the most recent and important statistics on women and related issues—for example, graphics cover changes in the median age at first marriage, college enrollment rates, the number of master's degrees earned by women and men, the employment status of women, median weekly earnings of men and women, the most common occupations for employed women, child care arrangements for grade school children with employed mothers, and the number of women in Congress since 1917. Gale, a Cengage Company, believes that making this information available to readers is the most important way to fulfill the goal of this book: to help readers understand the issues and controversies surrounding women in American society and to reach their own conclusions.

Each table or figure has a unique identifier appearing above it for ease of identification and reference. Titles for the tables and figures explain their purpose. At the end of each table or figure, the original source of the data is provided.

To help readers understand these often complicated statistics, all tables and figures are explained in the text. References in the text direct readers to the relevant statistics. Furthermore, the contents of all tables and figures are fully indexed. Please see the opening section of the Index at the back of this volume for a description of how to find tables and figures within it.

## Appendixes

Besides the main body text and images, *Women in America* has three appendixes. The first is the Important Names and Addresses directory. Here, readers will find contact information for a number of government and private organizations that can provide further information on women. The second appendix is the Resources section, which can also assist readers in conducting their own research. In this section, the author and editors of *Women in America* describe some of the sources that were most useful during the compilation of this book. The final appendix is the detailed Index. It has been greatly expanded from previous editions and should make it even easier to find specific topics in this book.

## COMMENTS AND SUGGESTIONS

The editors of the *Information Plus Reference Series* welcome your feedback on *Women in America*. Please direct all correspondence to:

Editors
*Information Plus Reference Series*
27500 Drake Rd.
Farmington Hills, MI 48331-3535

# CHAPTER 1
# AMERICAN WOMEN: WHO ARE THEY?

For American women, the problem of gender inequality dates back to the colonial era when, in keeping with English law, women were prohibited from owning property in their own name or keeping their own earnings. Over the course of US history, women's struggle for equality with men has been particularly focused in the political arena, in the workplace, and in the realm of reproductive rights—that is, women's freedom to make their own decisions about whether and when to become pregnant and bear children. Historians generally describe two waves of feminism (activism on behalf of women's rights) in the United States: the first during the mid- to late 19th century, which emerged as an outgrowth of the antislavery movement, and the second during the 1960s and 1970s following the African American civil rights movement.

The first women's rights convention in the United States was held in 1848 at Seneca Falls, New York. Organized by abolitionists Lucretia Mott (1793–1880) and Elizabeth Cady Stanton (1815–1902), the event featured the reading of Stanton's "Declaration of Sentiments and Grievances," a treatise that enumerated the injustices suffered by American women and called for various improvements to their legal rights—most notably the right to vote. Although Seneca Falls marked the advent of the women's suffrage movement, it was not until 1920, with the ratification of the 19th Amendment, that women's right to vote was finally enshrined in the US Constitution.

During the second wave of American feminism, women achieved a number of major legal milestones, beginning with the passage of the Civil Rights Act of 1964, under which Title VII prohibits workplace discrimination on the basis of race, color, religion, sex, or national origin. Signed into law in 1972, Title IX of the Education Amendments prohibits sex discrimination in all aspects of education programs that receive federal support. In 1973 the US Supreme Court issued a landmark ruling in *Roe v. Wade* (410 US 113), establishing women's legal right to abortion.

In the decades that followed, women increasingly demonstrated their ability to compete with men in every sphere of American life, from Capitol Hill, to the boardroom, to the military. Yet, in 2018 American women continued to face a range of gender-based disparities, discrimination, and challenges to their reproductive rights. The chapters that follow examine these issues and the impact they have on women's economic security, their health, their families, and the larger social fabric.

## POPULATION

In 2014 the US Census Bureau estimated that 313.4 million people were living in the United States. (See Table 1.1.) More than half (51%), or 159.8 million, were female, and 153.6 million were male. By 2060, according to the Census Bureau, in *2014 National Population Projections* (March 13, 2018, https://www2.census.gov/programs-surveys/popproj/tables/2017/2017-summary-tables/np2017-t2.xlsx), the US population is expected to reach 403.7 million, of which 203.2 million (50.3%) will be female.

### Age and Sex

Table 1.1 shows the distribution of the US population according to age and sex. In 2014 there were approximately equal numbers of US residents (varying from 19.4 million to 22.4 million) in each of the following age groups: under five years, five to nine years, 10 to 14 years, 15 to 19 years, 20 to 24 years, 25 to 29 years, 30 to 34 years, 35 to 39 years, 40 to 44 years, 45 to 49 years, 50 to 54 years, and 55 to 59 years. At age 60 and beyond, the numbers for each five-year subset dropped significantly as a result of mortality. There were 18.4 million Americans between the ages of 60 and 64 years, 15 million between 65 and 69 years, 10.8 million between

**TABLE 1.1**

## Population by age and sex, 2014

[Numbers in thousands. Civilian noninstitutionalized population.*]

| | Both sexes | | Male | | Female | |
|---|---|---|---|---|---|---|
| Age | Number | Percent | Number | Percent | Number | Percent |
| All ages | 313,401 | 100.0 | 153,595 | 100.0 | 159,806 | 100.0 |
| Under 5 years | 19,865 | 6.3 | 10,154 | 6.6 | 9,711 | 6.1 |
| 5 to 9 years | 20,522 | 6.5 | 10,483 | 6.8 | 10,039 | 6.3 |
| 10 to 14 years | 20,642 | 6.6 | 10,545 | 6.9 | 10,097 | 6.3 |
| 15 to 19 years | 20,807 | 6.6 | 10,585 | 6.9 | 10,221 | 6.4 |
| 20 to 24 years | 22,278 | 7.1 | 11,243 | 7.3 | 11,035 | 6.9 |
| 25 to 29 years | 21,474 | 6.9 | 10,822 | 7.0 | 10,653 | 6.7 |
| 30 to 34 years | 20,974 | 6.7 | 10,377 | 6.8 | 10,598 | 6.6 |
| 35 to 39 years | 19,407 | 6.2 | 9,555 | 6.2 | 9,852 | 6.2 |
| 40 to 44 years | 20,382 | 6.5 | 10,037 | 6.5 | 10,345 | 6.5 |
| 45 to 49 years | 20,668 | 6.6 | 10,148 | 6.6 | 10,520 | 6.6 |
| 50 to 54 years | 22,355 | 7.1 | 10,908 | 7.1 | 11,447 | 7.2 |
| 55 to 59 years | 21,109 | 6.7 | 10,193 | 6.6 | 10,916 | 6.8 |
| 60 to 64 years | 18,440 | 5.9 | 8,812 | 5.7 | 9,627 | 6.0 |
| 65 to 69 years | 14,986 | 4.8 | 7,093 | 4.6 | 7,893 | 4.9 |
| 70 to 74 years | 10,805 | 3.4 | 4,980 | 3.2 | 5,825 | 3.6 |
| 75 to 79 years | 7,804 | 2.5 | 3,374 | 2.2 | 4,429 | 2.8 |
| 80 to 84 years | 5,627 | 1.8 | 2,383 | 1.6 | 3,244 | 2.0 |
| 85 years and over | 5,255 | 1.7 | 1,901 | 1.2 | 3,354 | 2.1 |
| Median age | 37.6 | X | 36.4 | X | 38.8 | X |

*Plus armed forces living off post or with their families on post.
Note: Details may not sum to totals because of rounding.
The 2014 CPS ASEC included redesigned questions for income and health insurance coverage. All of the approximately 98,000 addresses were selected to receive the improved set of health insurance coverage items. The improved income questions were implemented using a split panel design. Approximately 68,000 addresses were selected to receive a set of income questions similar to those used in the 2013 CPS ASEC. The remaining 30,000 addresses were selected to receive the redesigned income questions.
CPS ASEC = Current Population Survey Annual Social and Economic Supplement.

SOURCE: Adapted from "Table 1. Population by Age and Sex: 2014," in *Age and Sex Composition in the United States: 2014*, US Census Bureau, August 2017, https://www.census.gov/data/tables/2014/demo/age-and-sex/2014-age-sex-composition.html (accessed January 17, 2018)

70 and 74 years, 7.8 million between 75 and 79 years, 5.6 million between 80 and 84 years, and 5.3 million over the age of 85 years in 2014.

In 2014 the US population between the ages of zero and 49 years was approximately half male and half female, with males slightly outnumbering females in all age groups between zero and 29 years of age and with females slightly outnumbering males in all age groups between 30 and 49 years of age. (See Table 1.1.) Beginning with the subset of Americans aged 50 to 54 years, females outnumbered males more significantly, and the gap between female and male numbers widened among those over the age of 65 years. This was a reflection of a mortality gap between women and men; women tend to live longer than men and to account for a significantly larger proportion of the total elderly population.

### Race and Hispanic Origin

In 2014 whites remained a majority in the United States, but their numbers were shrinking relative to other groups, including the fast-growing Hispanic and Asian American populations. Approximately 195.5 million of the total US population of 313.4 million consisted of non-Hispanic whites, and non-Hispanic white females outnumbered non-Hispanic white males 99.4 million to 96.1 million. (See Table 1.2.) There were 54.3 million

people of Hispanic origin living in the United States in 2014, and Hispanic males outnumbered Hispanic females 27.4 million to 26.9 million. There were an estimated 40.6 million African Americans in 2014, of which 21.6 million were female and 19 million were male. (See Table 1.3.) The population of Asian Americans stood at 17 million, with females outnumbering males 8.9 million to 8.1 million. (See Table 1.4.)

### Life Expectancy

The National Center for Health Statistics (NCHS) indicates in *Health, United States, 2016* (May 2017, https://www.cdc.gov/nchs/data/hus/hus16.pdf) that male life expectancy in the United States increased from 68.8 years in 1975 to 76.3 years in 2015. Female life expectancy increased less but remained well above that of males, growing from 76.6 years to 81.2 years during the same time span. Among both males and females there were racial and ethnic disparities in life expectancy. (See Figure 1.1.) Hispanic males and females both had higher life expectancies than did their counterparts among non-Hispanic whites and non-Hispanic African Americans. The life expectancy for a Hispanic female born in the United States in 2015 was 84.3 years, compared with 81.1 years for a non-Hispanic white female and 78.1 years for a non-Hispanic African American female. Although non-Hispanic African American females had

**TABLE 1.2**

**Population by sex, Hispanic origin, and race, 2014**

[Numbers in thousands. Civilian noninstitutionalized population.[a]]

| | | | Hispanic origin and race[b] | | |
| | Total | Hispanic | Non-Hispanic | | |
| | | | Total | White alone | All other races |
| Sex and age | Number | Number | Number | Number | Number |
|---|---|---|---|---|---|
| Both sexes | 313,401 | 54,268 | 259,134 | 195,489 | 63,644 |
| Male | 153,595 | 27,382 | 126,212 | 96,134 | 30,078 |
| Female | 159,806 | 26,885 | 132,921 | 99,355 | 33,566 |

[a]Plus armed forces living off post or with their families on post.
[b]Hispanic refers to people whose origin is Mexican, Puerto Rican, Cuban, Spanish-speaking Central or South American countries, or other Hispanic/Latino, regardless of race.
Note: Details may not sum to totals because of rounding.
The 2014 CPS ASEC included redesigned questions for income and health insurance coverage. All of the approximately 98,000 addresses were selected to receive the improved set of health insurance coverage items. The improved income questions were implemented using a split panel design. Approximately 68,000 addresses were selected to receive a set of income questions similar to those used in the 2013 CPS ASEC. The remaining 30,000 addresses were selected to receive the redesigned income questions.
CPS ASEC = Current Population Survey Annual Social and Economic Supplement.

SOURCE: Adapted from "Table 1. Population by Sex, Age, Hispanic Origin, and Race: 2014," in *The Hispanic Population in the United States: 2014*, US Census Bureau, August 2017, https://www2.census.gov/programs-surveys/demo/tables/hispanic-origin/2014/cps-2014-hispanic-tab1.xls (accessed January 17, 2018)

**TABLE 1.3**

**Population by sex for black alone and white alone, 2014**

[Numbers in thousands. Civilian noninstitutionalized population.[a]]

| | | Race and Hispanic origin[b] | | |
| | Total | Black alone | White alone, not Hispanic | Other[c] |
| Sex and age | Number | Number | Number | Number |
|---|---|---|---|---|
| Both sexes | 313,401 | 40,647 | 195,489 | 77,265 |
| Male | 153,595 | 19,021 | 96,134 | 38,439 |
| Female | 159,806 | 21,626 | 99,355 | 38,825 |

[a]Plus armed forces living off post or with their families on post.
[b]Hispanic refers to people whose origin is Mexican, Puerto Rican, Cuban, Spanish-speaking Central or South American countries, or other Hispanic/Latino, regardless of race.
[c]Includes American Indian and Alaska Native; Asian alone; Native Hawaiian and other Pacific Islander alone; white alone, Hispanic; and two or more races.
Note: Details may not sum to totals because of rounding.
The 2014 Current Population Survey, The Annual Social and Economic Supplement (CPS ASEC) included redesigned questions for income and health insurance coverage. All of the approximately 98,000 addresses were selected to receive the improved set of health insurance coverage items. The improved income questions were implemented using a split panel design. Approximately 68,000 addresses were selected to receive a set of income questions similar to those used in the 2013 CPS ASEC. The remaining 30,000 addresses were selected to receive the redesigned income questions. The source of data for this table is the CPS ASEC sample of 98,000 addresses.

SOURCE: Adapted from "Table 1. Population by Sex and Age, for Black Alone and White Alone, Not Hispanic: 2014," in *The Black Alone Population in the United States: 2014*, US Census Bureau, August 2017, https://www2.census.gov/programs-surveys/demo/tables/race/2014/ppl-ba14/ba14tab1.xlsx (accessed January 17, 2018)

**TABLE 1.4**

**Population by sex for Asian alone and white alone, 2014**

[Numbers in thousands. Civilian noninstitutionalized population.[a]]

| | | Race and Hispanic origin[b] | | |
| | Total | Asian alone | White alone, not Hispanic | Other[c] |
| Sex and age | Number | Number | Number | Number |
|---|---|---|---|---|
| Both sexes | 313,401 | 17,008 | 195,489 | 100,903 |
| Male | 153,595 | 8,112 | 96,134 | 49,349 |
| Female | 159,806 | 8,897 | 99,355 | 51,554 |

[a]Plus armed forces living off post or with their families on post.
[b]Hispanic refers to people whose origin is Mexican, Puerto Rican, Cuban, Spanish-speaking Central or South American countries, or other Hispanic/Latino, regardless of race.
[c]Includes American Indian and Alaska Native alone; black alone; Native Hawaiian and other Pacific Islander alone; white alone, Hispanic; and two or more races.
Note: Details may not sum to totals because of rounding.
The 2014 Current Population Survey, the Annual Social and Economic Supplement (CPS ASEC) included redesigned questions for income and health insurance coverage. All of the approximately 98,000 addresses were selected to receive the improved set of health insurance coverage items. The improved income questions were implemented using a split panel design. Approximately 68,000 addresses were selected to receive a set of income questions similar to those used in the 2013 CPS ASEC. The remaining 30,000 addresses were selected to receive the redesigned income questions. The source of data for this table is the CPS ASEC sample of 98,000 addresses.

SOURCE: Adapted from "Table 1. Population by Sex and Age, for Asian Alone and White Alone, Not Hispanic: 2014," in *The Asian Alone Population in the United States: 2014*, US Census Bureau, August 2017, https://www2.census.gov/programs-surveys/demo/tables/race/2014/ppl-aa14/aa14tab1.xlsx (accessed January 17, 2018)

a lower life expectancy than non-Hispanic white females, non-Hispanic African American females had a higher life expectancy than non-Hispanic white males (76.3 years).

**Foreign-Born Women**

In *Modern Immigration Wave Brings 59 Million to U.S., Driving Population Growth and Change through 2065* (September 28, 2015, http://assets.pewresearch.org/ wp-content/uploads/sites/7/2015/09/2015-09-28_modern-immigration-wave_REPORT.pdf), the Pew Research Center notes that between 1960 and 2013 the United States' foreign-born population increased from 9.7 million to 41.3 million. The foreign-born population was much younger in 2013 than in 1960, with the median age (the middle value; half of all people were younger and half were older) falling from 57 years to 43 years. Whereas immigrants in 1960 came primarily from Europe and settled in the

FIGURE 1.1

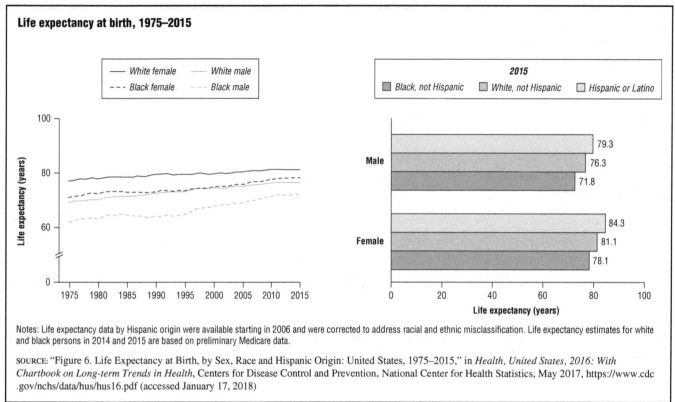

**Life expectancy at birth, 1975–2015**

Notes: Life expectancy data by Hispanic origin were available starting in 2006 and were corrected to address racial and ethnic misclassification. Life expectancy estimates for white and black persons in 2014 and 2015 are based on preliminary Medicare data.

SOURCE: "Figure 6. Life Expectancy at Birth, by Sex, Race and Hispanic Origin: United States, 1975–2015," in *Health, United States, 2016: With Chartbook on Long-term Trends in Health*, Centers for Disease Control and Prevention, National Center for Health Statistics, May 2017, https://www.cdc.gov/nchs/data/hus/hus16.pdf (accessed January 17, 2018)

Northeast and the Midwest, immigrants in 2013 came primarily from Latin America and Asia and often settled in the West and South.

Elizabeth M. Grieco et al. of the Census Bureau note in *The Foreign-Born Population in the United States: 2010* (May 2012, https://www.census.gov/prod/2012pubs/acs-19.pdf), the most recent report on this topic as of April 2018, that the gender balance among the foreign born in 2010 closely resembled that of the native born, with females constituting approximately 51% of the total for both groups. Among certain age and demographic groups, however, foreign-born males outnumbered females. Among the foreign born who were between the ages of 18 and 44 years, only 49% were female. Only 47% of foreign-born residents who came from Africa were female, and only 46% of those from Mexico were female. By contrast, 55% of the foreign-born populations from Europe and North America were female, and 54% of the foreign-born populations from the Caribbean and South America were female.

The United States is home to millions of undocumented foreign-born women. Because many of these women risk deportation if they publicize their status, it is believed that they may not be adequately counted by the Census Bureau. According to Bryan Baker of the US Department of Homeland Security, in *Estimates of the Unauthorized Immigrant Population Residing in the United States: January 2014* (July 2017, https://www.dhs.gov/sites/default/files/publications/Unauthorized%20Immigrant%20Population%20Estimates%20in%20the%20US%20January%202014_1.pdf), as of 2014 there were an estimated 12.1 million undocumented people living in the United States, of which 5.7 million were female.

## MARITAL STATUS
### Married Women

The marriage rate has declined since 1980. The NCHS reports in "Annual Summary of Births, Deaths, Marriages, and Divorces: United States, 1981" (*Monthly Vital Statistics Report*, vol. 30, no. 13, December 20, 1982) that the marriage rate was 10.6 per 1,000 people in 1980. By 2016, according to the NCHS, in "Marriages and Divorces" (December 2017, https://www.cdc.gov/nchs/data/dvs/national_marriage_divorce_rates_00-16.pdf), the rate had dropped to 6.9 marriages per 1,000 people. In 2017 an estimated 63.3 million American women aged 15 years and older were married and living with a spouse. (See Table 1.5.) Additionally, 1.9 million women were married but living apart from their spouse and 2.9 million women were legally separated from their spouse. In 2017 a greater percentage of women (10.9%) than men (8.7%) were divorced; however, men were more likely than women to have never married (34.9% and 29.3%, respectively).

In *America's Families and Living Arrangements: 2012* (August 2013, https://www.census.gov/prod/2013pubs/p20-570.pdf), Jonathan Vespa, Jamie M. Lewis, and Rose M.

**TABLE 1.5**

## Marital status of people aged 15 years and over, by sex and age, 2017

[Numbers in thousands, except for percentages]

| | Total Number | Married spouse present Number | Married spouse absent Number | Widowed Number | Divorced Number | Separated Number | Never married Number | Total Percent | Married spouse present Percent | Married spouse absent Percent | Widowed Percent | Divorced Percent | Separated Percent | Never married Percent |
|---|---|---|---|---|---|---|---|---|---|---|---|---|---|---|
| **Both sexes** | | | | | | | | | | | | | | |
| **Total 15+** | **259,063** | **126,650** | **3,956** | **14,919** | **25,482** | **5,144** | **82,912** | **100.0** | **48.9** | **1.5** | **5.8** | **9.8** | **2.0** | **32.0** |
| 15–17 years | 13,077 | 30 | 102 | 10 | 25 | 103 | 12,808 | 100.0 | 0.2 | 0.8 | 0.1 | 0.2 | 0.8 | 97.9 |
| 18–19 years | 7,731 | 102 | 39 | 14 | 34 | 56 | 7,485 | 100.0 | 1.3 | 0.5 | 0.2 | 0.4 | 0.7 | 96.8 |
| 20–24 years | 21,534 | 2,178 | 156 | 40 | 165 | 186 | 18,809 | 100.0 | 10.1 | 0.7 | 0.2 | 0.8 | 0.9 | 87.3 |
| 25–29 years | 22,730 | 7,115 | 372 | 61 | 594 | 432 | 14,156 | 100.0 | 31.3 | 1.6 | 0.3 | 2.6 | 1.9 | 62.3 |
| 30–34 years | 21,499 | 10,976 | 396 | 69 | 1,345 | 498 | 8,214 | 100.0 | 51.1 | 1.8 | 0.3 | 6.3 | 2.3 | 38.2 |
| 35–39 years | 20,752 | 12,591 | 362 | 182 | 1,874 | 596 | 5,146 | 100.0 | 60.7 | 1.7 | 0.9 | 9.0 | 2.9 | 24.8 |
| 40–44 years | 19,269 | 12,470 | 341 | 213 | 2,229 | 552 | 3,465 | 100.0 | 64.7 | 1.8 | 1.1 | 11.6 | 2.9 | 18.0 |
| 45–49 years | 20,650 | 13,340 | 409 | 324 | 2,989 | 666 | 2,922 | 100.0 | 64.6 | 2.0 | 1.6 | 14.5 | 3.2 | 14.2 |
| 50–54 years | 21,353 | 13,557 | 358 | 589 | 3,405 | 662 | 2,781 | 100.0 | 63.5 | 1.7 | 2.8 | 15.9 | 3.1 | 13.0 |
| 55–64 years | 41,308 | 26,417 | 692 | 2,141 | 6,819 | 866 | 4,373 | 100.0 | 64.0 | 1.7 | 5.2 | 16.5 | 2.1 | 10.6 |
| 65–74 years | 29,174 | 18,550 | 424 | 3,712 | 4,186 | 401 | 1,901 | 100.0 | 63.6 | 1.5 | 12.7 | 14.3 | 1.4 | 6.5 |
| 75–84 years | 14,185 | 7,494 | 213 | 4,219 | 1,545 | 108 | 605 | 100.0 | 52.8 | 1.5 | 29.7 | 10.9 | 0.8 | 4.3 |
| 85+ years | 5,801 | 1,828 | 91 | 3,346 | 272 | 16 | 248 | 100.0 | 31.5 | 1.6 | 57.7 | 4.7 | 0.3 | 4.3 |
| 15–17 years | 13,077 | 30 | 102 | 10 | 25 | 103 | 12,808 | 100.0 | 0.2 | 0.8 | 0.1 | 0.2 | 0.8 | 97.9 |
| 18+ years | 245,986 | 126,620 | 3,854 | 14,910 | 25,457 | 5,041 | 70,105 | 100.0 | 51.5 | 1.6 | 6.1 | 10.3 | 2.0 | 28.5 |
| 15–64 years | 209,902 | 98,777 | 3,229 | 3,642 | 19,478 | 4,618 | 80,159 | 100.0 | 47.1 | 1.5 | 1.7 | 9.3 | 2.2 | 38.2 |
| 65+ years | 49,160 | 27,873 | 727 | 11,277 | 6,004 | 525 | 2,754 | 100.0 | 56.7 | 1.5 | 22.9 | 12.2 | 1.1 | 5.6 |
| **Male** | | | | | | | | | | | | | | |
| **Total 15+** | **125,660** | **63,325** | **2,088** | **3,277** | **10,891** | **2,254** | **43,825** | **100.0** | **50.4** | **1.7** | **2.6** | **8.7** | **1.8** | **34.9** |
| 15–17 years | 6,642 | 17 | 56 | 5 | 10 | 54 | 6,499 | 100.0 | 0.3 | 0.8 | 0.1 | 0.2 | 0.8 | 97.8 |
| 18–19 years | 3,932 | 35 | 16 | 8 | 11 | 35 | 3,827 | 100.0 | 0.9 | 0.4 | 0.2 | 0.3 | 0.9 | 97.3 |
| 20–24 years | 10,845 | 847 | 75 | 13 | 56 | 97 | 9,756 | 100.0 | 7.8 | 0.7 | 0.1 | 0.5 | 0.9 | 90.0 |
| 25–29 years | 11,397 | 3,002 | 185 | 16 | 225 | 157 | 7,812 | 100.0 | 26.3 | 1.6 | 0.1 | 2.0 | 1.4 | 68.5 |
| 30–34 years | 10,708 | 5,101 | 202 | 14 | 626 | 184 | 4,581 | 100.0 | 47.6 | 1.9 | 0.1 | 5.8 | 1.7 | 42.8 |
| 35–39 years | 10,270 | 6,128 | 200 | 31 | 849 | 232 | 2,829 | 100.0 | 59.7 | 2.0 | 0.3 | 8.3 | 2.3 | 27.5 |
| 40–44 years | 9,452 | 6,235 | 175 | 44 | 916 | 231 | 1,849 | 100.0 | 66.0 | 1.9 | 0.5 | 9.7 | 2.4 | 19.6 |
| 45–49 years | 10,111 | 6,437 | 241 | 91 | 1,337 | 336 | 1,670 | 100.0 | 63.7 | 2.4 | 0.9 | 13.2 | 3.3 | 16.5 |
| 50–54 years | 10,442 | 6,794 | 187 | 124 | 1,496 | 277 | 1,564 | 100.0 | 65.1 | 1.8 | 1.2 | 14.3 | 2.7 | 15.0 |
| 55–64 years | 19,735 | 13,267 | 364 | 470 | 2,993 | 389 | 2,252 | 100.0 | 67.2 | 1.8 | 2.4 | 15.2 | 2.0 | 11.4 |
| 65–74 years | 13,652 | 9,888 | 210 | 808 | 1,687 | 194 | 867 | 100.0 | 72.4 | 1.5 | 5.9 | 12.4 | 1.4 | 6.3 |
| 75–84 years | 6,313 | 4,369 | 127 | 935 | 593 | 61 | 228 | 100.0 | 69.2 | 2.0 | 14.8 | 9.4 | 1.0 | 3.6 |
| 85+ years | 2,160 | 1,205 | 50 | 716 | 90 | 7 | 91 | 100.0 | 55.8 | 2.3 | 33.2 | 4.2 | 0.3 | 4.2 |
| 15–17 years | 6,642 | 17 | 56 | 5 | 10 | 54 | 6,499 | 100.0 | 0.3 | 0.8 | 0.1 | 0.2 | 0.8 | 97.8 |
| 18+ years | 119,018 | 63,308 | 2,032 | 3,271 | 10,880 | 2,200 | 37,326 | 100.0 | 53.2 | 1.7 | 2.7 | 9.1 | 1.8 | 31.4 |
| 15–64 years | 103,535 | 47,863 | 1,702 | 818 | 8,520 | 1,993 | 42,639 | 100.0 | 46.2 | 1.6 | 0.8 | 8.2 | 1.9 | 41.2 |
| 65+ years | 22,125 | 15,462 | 387 | 2,459 | 2,370 | 262 | 1,186 | 100.0 | 69.9 | 1.7 | 11.1 | 10.7 | 1.2 | 5.4 |
| **Female** | | | | | | | | | | | | | | |
| **Total 15+** | **133,403** | **63,325** | **1,868** | **11,642** | **14,591** | **2,889** | **39,087** | **100.0** | **47.5** | **1.4** | **8.7** | **10.9** | **2.2** | **29.3** |
| 15–17 years | 6,435 | 13 | 46 | 4 | 15 | 49 | 6,309 | 100.0 | 0.2 | 0.7 | 0.1 | 0.2 | 0.8 | 98.0 |
| 18–19 years | 3,799 | 68 | 23 | 6.0 | 23 | 22 | 3,658 | 100.0 | 1.8 | 0.6 | 0.2 | 0.6 | 0.6 | 96.3 |
| 20–24 years | 10,689 | 1,331 | 81 | 27 | 109 | 89 | 9,053 | 100.0 | 12.5 | 0.8 | 0.2 | 1.0 | 0.8 | 84.7 |
| 25–29 years | 11,333 | 4,113 | 187 | 45 | 369 | 275 | 6,344 | 100.0 | 36.3 | 1.6 | 0.4 | 3.3 | 2.4 | 56.0 |
| 30–34 years | 10,790 | 5,875 | 194 | 55 | 719 | 314 | 3,633 | 100.0 | 54.4 | 1.8 | 0.5 | 6.7 | 2.9 | 33.7 |
| 35–39 years | 10,482 | 6,463 | 162 | 151 | 1,025 | 364 | 2,318 | 100.0 | 61.7 | 1.5 | 1.4 | 9.8 | 3.5 | 22.1 |
| 40–44 years | 9,817 | 6,234 | 166 | 169 | 1,312 | 321 | 1,615 | 100.0 | 63.5 | 1.7 | 1.7 | 13.4 | 3.3 | 16.5 |
| 45–49 years | 10,539 | 6,903 | 168 | 233 | 1,651 | 330 | 1,252 | 100.0 | 65.5 | 1.6 | 2.2 | 15.7 | 3.1 | 11.9 |

**TABLE 1.5**

**Marital status of people aged 15 years and over, by sex and age, 2017** [CONTINUED]

[Numbers in thousands, except for percentages]

| | Total | | Married spouse present | | Married spouse absent | | Widowed | | Divorced | | Separated | | Never married | | Total | Married spouse present | Married spouse absent | Widowed | Divorced | Separated | Never married |
|---|---|---|---|---|---|---|---|---|---|---|---|---|---|---|---|---|---|---|---|---|---|
| | Number | | Number | | Number | | Number | | Number | | Number | | Number | | Percent | Percent | Percent | Percent | Percent | Percent | Percent |
| 50–54 years | 10,911 | | 6,764 | | 171 | | 465 | | 1,910 | | 385 | | 1,217 | | 100.0 | 62.0 | 1.6 | 4.3 | 17.5 | 3.5 | 11.2 |
| 55–64 years | 21,573 | | 13,150 | | 329 | | 1,671 | | 3,826 | | 477 | | 2,121 | | 100.0 | 61.0 | 1.5 | 7.7 | 17.7 | 2.2 | 9.8 |
| 65–74 years | 15,522 | | 8,662 | | 214 | | 2,905 | | 2,500 | | 207 | | 1,034 | | 100.0 | 55.8 | 1.4 | 18.7 | 16.1 | 1.3 | 6.7 |
| 75–84 years | 7,872 | | 3,125 | | 86 | | 3,284 | | 952 | | 48 | | 377 | | 100.0 | 39.7 | 1.1 | 41.7 | 12.1 | 0.6 | 4.8 |
| 85+ years | 3,641 | | 623 | | 41 | | 2,630 | | 182 | | 9 | | 156 | | 100.0 | 17.1 | 1.1 | 72.2 | 5.0 | 0.2 | 4.3 |
| 15–17 years | 6,435 | | 13 | | 46 | | 4 | | 15 | | 49 | | 6,309 | | 100.0 | 0.2 | 0.7 | 0.1 | 0.2 | 0.8 | 98.0 |
| 18+ years | 126,968 | | 63,312 | | 1,822 | | 11,638 | | 14,577 | | 2,841 | | 32,778 | | 100.0 | 49.9 | 1.4 | 9.2 | 11.5 | 2.2 | 25.8 |
| 15–64 years | 106,368 | | 50,914 | | 1,527 | | 2,824 | | 10,958 | | 2,626 | | 37,519 | | 100.0 | 47.9 | 1.4 | 2.7 | 10.3 | 2.5 | 35.3 |
| 65+ years | 27,035 | | 12,411 | | 341 | | 8,818 | | 3,634 | | 264 | | 1,568 | | 100.0 | 45.9 | 1.3 | 32.6 | 13.4 | 1.0 | 5.8 |

Note: Prior to 2001, this table included group quarters people.

SOURCE: Adapted from "Table A1. Marital Status of People 15 Years and over, by Age, Sex, and Personal Earnings: 2017," in *America's Families and Living Arrangements: 2017*, US Census Bureau, November 2017, https://www2.census.gov/programs-surveys/demo/tables/families/2017/cps-2017/taba1-all.xls (accessed January 17, 2018)

Kreider of the Census Bureau report that the percentage of married-couple households among all household types has steadily decreased since 1970. In that year, 70.6% of all households were headed by married couples, either with or without children; a decade later, such households accounted for 60.8% of all households. (See Figure 1.2.) By 1990 only 56.1% of households were organized around a husband-wife pair, and the decline in so-called traditional family households continued in the 21st century. In 2000 the percentage of married-couple households was 52.8%, and in 2012 it was 48.7%.

## Single Women

Accompanying the decline in the marriage rate was the growth of the percentage of unmarried individuals who were living alone during the early 21st century. In 2017, 51.1% of females aged 15 years and older were single (widowed, divorced, separated, or never married), as were 48% of males. (See Table 1.5.) Although more men than women never marry, women are more likely to be single because they are less likely than men to remarry following divorce or the death of a spouse.

The reduction in marriage rates among women varies significantly according to race and Hispanic origin. In *America's Families and Living Arrangements: 2014* (April 3, 2017, https://www.census.gov/data/tables/2014/demo/families/cps-2014.html), the Census Bureau notes that in 2014 just 23.6% of non-Hispanic white women, 27.2% of Asian American women (who identified as either Asian alone or Asian in combination with other races), and 35.9% of Hispanic women had never been married. By contrast, 46% of non-Hispanic African American women aged 15 years and older had never been married. The percentages of divorced and widowed women were more similar across demographic categories.

POSTPONING MARRIAGE. The age at which both women and men marry has risen dramatically since the middle of the 20th century. As Figure 1.3 shows, since 1960 the median age at first marriage for women has risen from around age 20 to over 27. These increases are mirrored by the increases for men, whose median age at first marriage was approximately 23 in 1960 and over 29 in 2017. In 2017, 84.7% of women aged 20 to 24 years had never been married, whereas in 1970 only 35.8% of

**FIGURE 1.2**

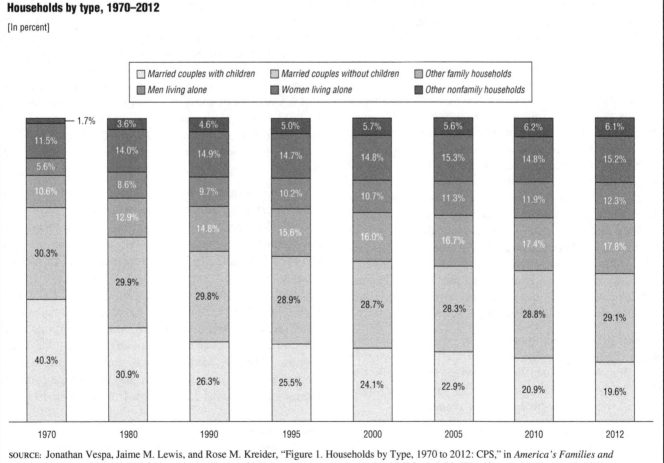

Households by type, 1970–2012

[In percent]

SOURCE: Jonathan Vespa, Jaime M. Lewis, and Rose M. Kreider, "Figure 1. Households by Type, 1970 to 2012: CPS," in *America's Families and Living Arrangements: 2012*, US Census Bureau, August 2013, https://www.census.gov/prod/2013pubs/p20-570.pdf (accessed January 17, 2018)

FIGURE 1.3

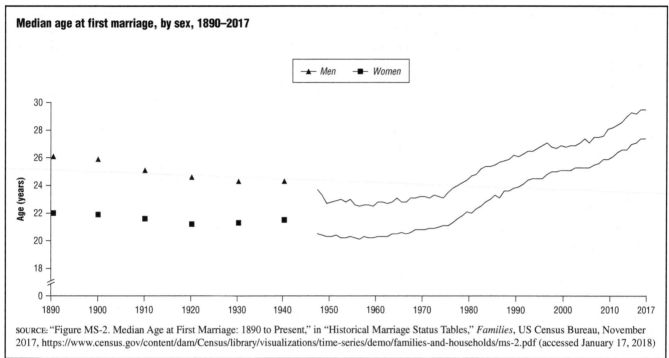

**Median age at first marriage, by sex, 1890–2017**

SOURCE: "Figure MS-2. Median Age at First Marriage: 1890 to Present," in "Historical Marriage Status Tables," *Families*, US Census Bureau, November 2017, https://www.census.gov/content/dam/Census/library/visualizations/time-series/demo/families-and-households/ms-2.pdf (accessed January 17, 2018)

women in this age group had not been married. (See Table 1.5; for 1970 data, see Jason Fields of the Census Bureau, in *America's Families and Living Arrangements: 2003* [November 2004, https://www.census.gov/prod/2004pubs/p20-553.pdf].) Many women now postpone marriage to pursue higher education and careers.

**DIVORCED WOMEN.** In 1969 California became the first state to pass a "no fault" divorce law, allowing divorce by mutual consent. In the years that followed, as many other states followed suit, divorce became much more common in the United States. Abigail Abrams reports in "Divorce Rate in U.S. Drops to Nearly 40-Year Low" (Time.com, December 5, 2016) that the US divorce rate peaked in 1980, when there were nearly 23 divorces per 1,000 married women aged 15 years and older. Since then, divorce rates have declined steadily, reaching a 40-year low in 2015, when there were 16.9 divorces per 1,000 married women aged 15 years and older. Abrams notes, "Divorce and marriage rates vary drastically in different groups of people. The wealthy and well-educated tend to marry and stay together much more than those who are less well-off."

In 2017 approximately 14.6 million American women aged 15 years and older, or 10.9% of all women, were divorced and had not remarried. (See Table 1.5.) More women remain unmarried after divorce than men: 8.7% of men had divorced and not remarried.

**WIDOWHOOD.** Women and men experience and respond to the death of their spouse differently in the aggregate. Approximately 8.7% of women aged 15 years and older were widows in 2017, whereas only 2.6% of

men were widowers. (See Table 1.5.) Among those older Americans most likely to be widowed, women are also far more likely to be widowed than men. Nearly one-third (32.6%) of women aged 65 years and older in 2017 were widows who had not remarried. Of the 11.6 million American women older than age 15 who were widowed and had not remarried, 8.8 million were aged 65 years and older. By contrast, only 3.3 million men aged 15 years and older were widowed and had not remarried, and 2.5 million of these men were over 65 years of age. Only 11.1% of men aged 65 years and older were widowers. These disparities are due to two factors: women, on average, live longer than men do, and men remarry after the death of a spouse more often than women do.

**NEVER-MARRIED WOMEN.** Being unmarried used to be considered a temporary or transitional state for most people. However, after 1970 there was a large increase in the number of individuals who had never been married. Between 1970 and 2017 the percentage of never-married women increased significantly in every age group between 15 and 64 years. (See Table 1.5; for 1970 data, see Fields.) The percentages of never-married males likewise increased significantly in these age groups. The percentages of never-married people in the oldest age groups, however, have declined. For example, among women aged 65 years and older, the percentage of never married in 2017 was 5.8%, down from 7.7% in 1970.

**Cohabitation**

As attitudes change in the United States, marital status may no longer accurately reflect the personal relationships of individuals. Changes in attitudes toward cohabitation have contributed to the rise in the median age for first marriages, as well as to the increasing numbers of individuals who never marry or who do not remarry following divorce or death of a spouse. Among many Americans, marriage is no longer viewed as a prerequisite for living together and raising children.

In *America's Families and Living Arrangements: 2017* (November 15, 2017, https://www.census.gov/data/tables/2017/demo/families/cps-2017.html), the Census Bureau reports that 7.8 million households were headed by unmarried, opposite-sex couples, compared with 60.8 million households headed by married couples. The proportion of all family households headed by unmarried partners has increased from 2.9% of all households in 1996 to 9.4% of all households in 2017. The proportion of unmarried couples living together is probably even higher, as some couples maintain additional households or are reluctant to describe themselves as a cohabitating couple. According to the Census Bureau, a large proportion of unmarried partner households contained children under the age of 18 years (37.1%), as did married-couple households (38.6%).

Women in unmarried partnerships tend to be younger than those in marriages. According to the Census Bureau, in 2017 only 2.2% of married women were aged 24 years and younger, whereas 18.6% of women in unmarried partnerships were in this age group. By contrast, 82% of married women were aged 35 years and older, whereas 44.4% of women in unmarried couples were over the age of 35 years. This age difference is most likely due to two factors: many couples who live together at a young age eventually get married, and people in younger cohorts are more likely to accept cohabitation as an alternative to marriage.

**Same-Sex Marriage**

The Census Bureau's data on same-sex households are rudimentary. Furthermore, these data are complicated by the fact that until the 2000 census data were not collected on such households and by the numerous changes in marriage laws that have altered the legal status of same-sex partnerships since 2000.

Between 2000 and 2013 same-sex couples were increasingly being legally recognized in the United States. In 2000 Vermont was the first state to legalize same-sex civil unions, granting same-sex couples the benefits of marriage. Thereafter, many other states followed suit, or went a step further by legalizing same-sex marriage. Before June 2013 same-sex couples who received state recognition and benefits based on their marriage or civil union were denied federal recognition and benefits. This was a result of the Defense of Marriage Act (DOMA), signed by President Bill Clinton (1946–) in 1996, which excluded same-sex couples from the definition of marriage and barred them from receiving more than 1,000 federal benefits and protections that were afforded to opposite-sex couples. Additionally, by 2013, 35 states had passed laws or amended their constitution to prohibit same-sex marriage.

In June 2013 same-sex marriage advocates at the federal level won an important victory with the US Supreme Court ruling in *United States v. Windsor* (No. 12-307). The case involved Edith Windsor, the surviving member of a same-sex New York couple of 50 years, who had been married in Canada in 2007. When Windsor's partner Thea Spyer died in 2009 and left her estate to Windsor, the Internal Revenue Service denied Windsor the estate tax exemption available to surviving spouses, citing DOMA in its ruling that the exemption did not apply. Windsor was required to pay more than $360,000 because her marriage was not recognized by the federal government. She filed suit in 2010 seeking a refund, and her case made its way to the Supreme Court, where the justices ruled 5–4 in her favor, striking down the portion of DOMA that excluded same-sex partners from the definition of marriage. The ruling effectively extended federal marriage recognition and benefits to those same-sex couples whose states already recognized their unions. The ruling did not, however, affect the prohibition of same-sex marriage in those states where it remained illegal.

In June 2015 the movement for marriage equality won a historic victory with the Supreme Court decision in *Obergefell v. Hodges* (No. 14-556), which made same-sex marriage legal in all 50 states. The main plaintiff in this case, James Obergefell, challenged Ohio's ban on same-sex marriage after being denied the right to put his name on the death certificate of his late husband, John Arthur. In all, the case involved 12 couples and four states—Ohio, Kentucky, Michigan, and Tennessee—where same-sex marriage bans had been upheld in previous federal appeals court decisions. The Supreme Court's landmark 5–4 ruling centered on the 14th Amendment to the US Constitution, which guarantees all US citizens "equal protection" under the law. Ultimately, the court found that the right to marry is among the fundamental liberties protected by the 14th Amendment, and therefore it may not be denied to same-sex couples. With the decision, same-sex marriage bans were nullified in 13 states, and marriage equality became the law of the land.

**LIVING ARRANGEMENTS**

More and more Americans are marrying later, choosing to remain single, divorcing, and cohabitating without marriage. Birth rates among women aged 15 to 29 years declined between 1990 and 2015, whereas birth rates among women aged 30 to 44 years increased during this same period. (See Figure 1.4.) Many women, married or

FIGURE 1.4

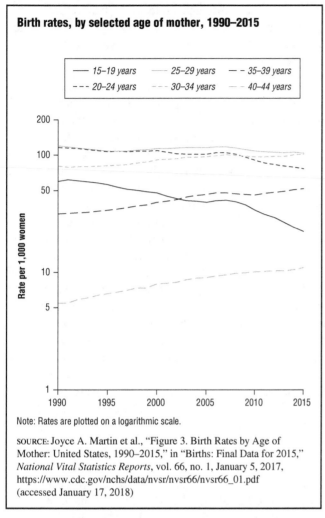

**Birth rates, by selected age of mother, 1990–2015**

Legend:
- 15–19 years
- 20–24 years
- 25–29 years
- 30–34 years
- 35–39 years
- 40–44 years

Rate per 1,000 women

Note: Rates are plotted on a logarithmic scale.

SOURCE: Joyce A. Martin et al., "Figure 3. Birth Rates by Age of Mother: United States, 1990–2015," in "Births: Final Data for 2015," *National Vital Statistics Reports*, vol. 66, no. 1, January 5, 2017, https://www.cdc.gov/nchs/data/nvsr/nvsr66/nvsr66_01.pdf (accessed January 17, 2018)

single, are choosing to remain childless. The Census Bureau (May 16, 2017, https://www.census.gov/data/tables/time-series/demo/fertility/his-cps.html#par_list) indicates that whereas in 1976 only 35.1% of women aged 15 to 44 years were childless, by 2016, 48.6% of women that age were childless. Many people are choosing to raise children in homes other than traditional married-couple households. Lindsay M. Monte and Renee R. Ellis of the Census Bureau explain in *Fertility of Women in the United States: 2012* (July 2014, https://www.census.gov/content/dam/Census/library/publications/2014/demo/p20-575.pdf), the most recent report on this topic as of April 2018, that "recent research suggests that nonmarital births are increasingly occurring to women in cohabiting relationships." According to the researchers, the marital status of women at the time of their first birth has shifted dramatically in recent decades. Between 1990 and 1994, 70% of women were married at the time of their first birth, whereas between 2005 and 2012 this number had decreased to 55%. Significantly, Monte and Ellis point out that the unmarried status of these mothers did not necessarily indicate the lack of a committed parental partnership: "Since 1995,

first births to cohabiting couples have consistently surpassed those to women who were neither married nor cohabiting. These data reinforce others' findings about the rise in cohabitation as a family form."

These and other trends have had enormous effects on the living arrangements of US households. The move away from traditional household models has, for example, been accompanied by a significant decrease in the average household size. Between 1970 and 2017 the average household size decreased from 3.2 to 2.5 (for 1970 data, see Fields; for 2017 data, see the Census Bureau's *America's Families and Living Arrangements: 2017*).

**Types of Households**

The Census Bureau defines a household as everyone who lives in a single housing unit. One of the people who owns, is buying, or rents the housing unit is designated as the householder. Households are categorized by the Census Bureau as either family or nonfamily households. A family household consists of at least two people who are related by birth, adoption, or marriage but may include other individuals who are not related. A nonfamily household consists of either a householder living alone or a householder who is not related to any of the other people who live in the same housing unit. These people may include roommates or unmarried partners. Nonetheless, people other than the householder in a nonfamily household may be related to each other. Most households in the United States remained family households during the second decade of the 21st century, although the proportion of family households had declined dramatically, from 81.2% in 1970 to 65.6% in 2017 (for 1970 data, see Fields; for 2017 data, see the Census Bureau's *America's Families and Living Arrangements: 2017*).

**Family Households**

Between 1970 and 2017 the proportion of households consisting of a married couple with children under the age of 18 years decreased from 40.3% to 19.4% (for 1970 data, see Fields; for 2017 data, see the Census Bureau's *America's Families and Living Arrangements: 2017*). The proportion of households consisting of married couples without children decreased as well, but not as drastically, from 30.3% in 1970 to 30.8% in 2017. This group includes couples who have not yet had children but intend to, couples who do not intend to have children, and older couples whose children are aged 18 years and older.

Historically, the Census Bureau has found that in most married-couple households, both partners tend to come from the same race and ethnic group. According to the Census Bureau, in *America's Families and Living*

*Arrangements: 2017*, in 2017, 65.5% of married couples were non-Hispanic white, 12% were Hispanic, and 6.5% were non-Hispanic African American. The average household size for married-couple households was 3.2 people.

According to the Census Bureau, 9.5 million families with children under the age of 18 years were headed by a single, female householder in 2017. Approximately 50.3% (4.8 million) of single mothers in 2017 had never been married, 29.3% (2.8 million) were divorced, 16.8% (1.6 million) were separated, and 3.6% (341,000) were widowed.

## Women Living Alone

Most nonfamily households consist of women or men living alone. In *America's Families and Living Arrangements: 2017*, the Census Bureau indicates that there were 22.9 million women and 20.5 million men living alone. Women living alone thus accounted for 18.1% of all US households. Many women live alone later in their life after they divorce or are widowed, whereas divorced or widowed men are more likely to remarry. Women's longer life expectancy further predisposes them to spend their later years alone.

# CHAPTER 2

# WOMEN'S EDUCATION

## EDUCATIONAL ATTAINMENT

The average number of years of education an American receives changed drastically during the 20th century. According to the National Center for Education Statistics (NCES; April 2017, https://nces.ed.gov/programs/digest/d16/tables/dt16_104.10.asp), in 1940, among adults aged 25 years and older, 26.3% of women and 22.7% of men had completed high school, and 3.8% of women and 5.5% of men had completed four years of college. Most African Americans had only an elementary school education in 1940; only 8.4% of African American women and 6.9% of African American men had completed high school. By 2016, 89.6% of all women and 88.5% of all men aged 25 years and older had completed high school, and 33.7% of women and 33.2% of men had completed four years of college. African Americans' educational attainment had increased dramatically as well: 88.3% of African American women and 87% of African American men had graduated from high school, and 24.8% of women and 21.8% of men had completed four years of college.

Table 2.1 shows that in 2016, 31.2 million (28%) women aged 25 years and older had completed high school but had not attended college. Another 19 million (17%) women aged 25 years and older had attended some college, 12.2 million (10.9%) women had earned an associate's degree, and 23.5 million (21%) women had earned a bachelor's degree. Another 11.1 million (10%) women had earned a master's degree and 3 million (2.7%) women had received a professional degree or a doctorate. Only 11.8 million (10.6%) women aged 25 years and older had not graduated from high school in 2016, with the highest proportion of these high school dropouts in the older age groups (aged 40 years and older), indicating that the percentage of American women who do not receive a high school diploma will continue to decline in the coming decades.

## The Educational Attainment Level of Women Compared with Men

Table 2.2 shows that of the population over three years old in October 2016, 24.7% of all females were enrolled in school and 25.6% of all males were enrolled. The higher overall percentage of males in school reflects the fact that males slightly outnumber females in the younger age groups and that there are more females in the older, nonschool-age population. There were 4.5 million males enrolled in kindergarten or nursery school, compared with 4.3 million females. Another 16.7 million males and 15.9 million females were enrolled in elementary school, and 8.5 million males and 8.1 million females were enrolled in high school. Only at the college level does the situation reverse. In October 2016, 8.6 million males and 10.6 million females were enrolled in college or graduate school.

In 2015 a smaller proportion of 16- to 24-year-old females (5.4%) than males (6.3%) were high school dropouts. (See Table 2.3.) The female dropout rate fell below the male rate in 1977. The dropout rate for both females and males decreased between 1972 and 2015, and the decrease was larger for females (15.1% to 5.4%) than for males (14.1% to 6.3%). Joel McFarland, Patrick Stark, and Jiashan Cui indicate in *Trends in High School Dropout and Completion Rates in the United States: 2013* (October 2016, https://nces.ed.gov/pubs2016/2016117rev.pdf) that this gender difference held true for all race and ethnic groups, with the exception of Pacific Islanders. Also, both Hispanic females and males have had significantly higher dropout rates than non-Hispanic whites and non-Hispanic African Americans. In 2013, 9.6% of Hispanic females and 13.9% of Hispanic males were high school dropouts.

In most years since 1990, more women than men have enrolled in college immediately following high school graduation. (See Figure 2.1.) According to the

TABLE 2.1

**Number of persons aged 18 and over, by highest level of education attained, age, sex, and race and Hispanic origin, 2016**

[Numbers in thousands.]

| Sex, race/ethnicity, and age | Total | Elementary school (kindergarten–8th grade) | High school | | | Postsecondary education | | | | |
|---|---|---|---|---|---|---|---|---|---|---|
| | | | 1 to 3 years | 4 years, no completion | Completion[a] | Some college, no degree | Associate's degree | Bachelor's degree | Master's degree | First-professional or doctor's degree |
| **Total, 18 and over** | **244,807** | **9,879** | **14,828** | **3,946** | **70,882** | **46,750** | **23,400** | **47,718** | **20,187** | **7,216** |
| 18 and 19 years old | 7,818 | 99 | 2,595 | 718 | 2,144 | 2,122 | 77 | b | b | b |
| 20 to 24 years old | 21,973 | 288 | 1,089 | 411 | 6,736 | 8,626 | 1,666 | 2,880 | 225 | b |
| 25 years old and over | 215,015 | 9,492 | 11,144 | 2,817 | 62,002 | 36,003 | 21,657 | 44,778 | 19,958 | 7,164 |
| 25 to 29 years old | 22,434 | 473 | 1,095 | 306 | 5,708 | 4,509 | 2,250 | 6,027 | 1,674 | 393 |
| 30 to 34 years old | 21,329 | 595 | 997 | 258 | 5,516 | 3,510 | 2,340 | 5,104 | 2,189 | 819 |
| 35 to 39 years old | 20,387 | 802 | 1,022 | 272 | 5,134 | 3,275 | 2,116 | 4,738 | 2,314 | 714 |
| 40 to 49 years old | 40,297 | 1,741 | 2,049 | 556 | 10,620 | 6,320 | 4,295 | 9,023 | 4,205 | 1,489 |
| 50 to 59 years old | 43,722 | 1,790 | 2,165 | 551 | 13,439 | 7,192 | 4,896 | 8,558 | 3,798 | 1,332 |
| 60 to 64 years old | 19,300 | 723 | 874 | 232 | 5,778 | 3,491 | 2,035 | 3,726 | 1,751 | 691 |
| 65 years old and over | 47,547 | 3,369 | 2,942 | 642 | 15,807 | 7,706 | 3,725 | 7,603 | 4,026 | 1,726 |
| **Males, 18 and over** | **118,467** | **4,908** | **7,690** | **2,140** | **35,788** | **22,140** | **10,206** | **22,485** | **8,916** | **4,194** |
| 18 and 19 years old | 4,006 | 59 | 1,433 | 393 | 1,139 | 939 | b | b | b | b |
| 20 to 24 years old | 11,089 | 153 | 617 | 243 | 3,869 | 4,190 | 731 | 1,181 | 84 | b |
| 25 years old and over | 103,372 | 4,696 | 5,640 | 1,504 | 30,780 | 17,011 | 9,457 | 21,281 | 8,829 | 4,173 |
| 25 to 29 years old | 11,287 | 270 | 587 | 174 | 3,253 | 2,286 | 1,024 | 2,876 | 656 | 160 |
| 30 to 34 years old | 10,558 | 314 | 525 | 140 | 3,133 | 1,662 | 1,044 | 2,498 | 852 | 390 |
| 35 to 39 years old | 10,056 | 468 | 534 | 136 | 2,885 | 1,599 | 963 | 2,080 | 998 | 394 |
| 40 to 49 years old | 19,771 | 871 | 1,103 | 336 | 5,688 | 3,120 | 1,824 | 4,106 | 1,962 | 760 |
| 50 to 59 years old | 21,338 | 898 | 1,222 | 297 | 6,940 | 3,340 | 2,094 | 4,066 | 1,698 | 784 |
| 60 to 64 years old | 9,153 | 326 | 434 | 125 | 2,693 | 1,708 | 909 | 1,787 | 727 | 445 |
| 65 years old and over | 21,209 | 1,549 | 1,235 | 295 | 6,189 | 3,298 | 1,599 | 3,868 | 1,935 | 1,241 |
| **Females, 18 and over** | **126,339** | **4,971** | **7,137** | **1,806** | **35,094** | **24,611** | **13,194** | **25,234** | **11,271** | **3,021** |
| 18 and 19 years old | 3,812 | b | 1,162 | 325 | 1,006 | 1,183 | b | b | b | b |
| 20 to 24 years old | 10,884 | 135 | 472 | 168 | 2,866 | 4,436 | 936 | 1,699 | 141 | b |
| 25 years old and over | 111,643 | 4,796 | 5,504 | 1,313 | 31,221 | 18,992 | 12,200 | 23,497 | 11,129 | 2,991 |
| 25 to 29 years old | 11,146 | 202 | 507 | 131 | 2,455 | 2,223 | 1,226 | 3,151 | 1,018 | 233 |
| 30 to 34 years old | 10,771 | 281 | 472 | 118 | 2,383 | 1,848 | 1,296 | 2,606 | 1,338 | 430 |
| 35 to 39 years old | 10,331 | 334 | 489 | 136 | 2,249 | 1,677 | 1,153 | 2,658 | 1,316 | 320 |
| 40 to 49 years old | 20,526 | 870 | 946 | 219 | 4,932 | 3,200 | 2,470 | 4,917 | 2,243 | 729 |
| 50 to 59 years old | 22,384 | 892 | 944 | 254 | 6,500 | 3,852 | 2,802 | 4,492 | 2,100 | 548 |
| 60 to 64 years old | 10,148 | 397 | 439 | 108 | 3,085 | 1,783 | 1,126 | 1,939 | 1,024 | 246 |
| 65 years old and over | 26,337 | 1,820 | 1,707 | 347 | 9,618 | 4,408 | 2,126 | 3,735 | 2,091 | 485 |
| **White, 18 and over** | **157,591** | **2,398** | **7,116** | **1,657** | **44,840** | **30,072** | **16,628** | **34,812** | **14,714** | **5,353** |
| 18 and 19 years old | 4,186 | 49 | 1,437 | 319 | 1,163 | 1,141 | b | b | b | b |
| 20 to 24 years old | 11,991 | 66 | 468 | 131 | 3,406 | 4,747 | 1,027 | 1,983 | 128 | b |
| 25 years old and over | 141,414 | 2,283 | 5,211 | 1,207 | 40,271 | 24,184 | 15,566 | 32,791 | 14,582 | 5,317 |
| 25 to 29 years old | 12,574 | 90 | 413 | 99 | 2,801 | 2,343 | 1,434 | 4,074 | 1,049 | 270 |
| 30 to 34 years old | 12,185 | 75 | 326 | 103 | 2,797 | 1,980 | 1,487 | 3,447 | 1,395 | 576 |
| 35 to 39 years old | 11,654 | 117 | 363 | 73 | 2,713 | 1,866 | 1,366 | 3,183 | 1,492 | 480 |
| 40 to 49 years old | 24,503 | 227 | 735 | 185 | 6,108 | 4,057 | 2,954 | 6,402 | 2,850 | 985 |
| 50 to 59 years old | 29,834 | 322 | 1,033 | 233 | 9,087 | 5,049 | 3,627 | 6,542 | 2,947 | 994 |
| 60 to 64 years old | 13,980 | 127 | 423 | 124 | 4,204 | 2,591 | 1,640 | 2,874 | 1,429 | 568 |
| 65 years old and over | 36,682 | 1,324 | 1,918 | 391 | 12,561 | 6,298 | 3,058 | 6,268 | 3,420 | 1,444 |
| **Black, 18 and over** | **28,983** | **811** | **2,369** | **730** | **9,863** | **6,618** | **2,566** | **3,906** | **1,696** | **424** |
| 18 and 19 years old | 1,077 | b | 388 | 117 | 304 | 236 | b | b | b | b |
| 20 to 24 years old | 3,214 | b | 203 | 103 | 1,210 | 1,253 | 182 | 200 | b | b |
| 25 years old and over | 24,691 | 753 | 1,778 | 510 | 8,348 | 5,128 | 2,381 | 3,692 | 1,675 | 424 |
| 25 to 29 years old | 3,013 | b | 170 | b | 960 | 831 | 269 | 530 | 136 | b |
| 30 to 34 years old | 2,650 | b | 135 | b | 845 | 588 | 305 | 497 | 174 | b |
| 35 to 39 years old | 2,523 | b | 130 | b | 807 | 522 | 295 | 440 | 218 | b |
| 40 to 49 years old | 4,931 | 81 | 300 | 89 | 1,615 | 998 | 540 | 772 | 420 | 116 |
| 50 to 59 years old | 5,222 | 115 | 379 | 129 | 1,917 | 1,053 | 470 | 757 | 322 | 80 |
| 60 to 64 years old | 2,139 | 70 | 187 | b | 719 | 468 | 193 | 285 | 123 | 44 |
| 65 years old and over | 4,214 | 389 | 477 | 116 | 1,486 | 667 | 309 | 411 | 281 | 77 |

NCES (July 2016, https://nces.ed.gov/programs/digest/d16/tables/dt16_302.10.asp), in 2015, 1.5 million (72.5%) recent female high school completers enrolled in either a two- or four-year postsecondary institution, compared with 1.4 million (65.8%) males. More than a quarter (26.2%) of the 1.5 million women who had recently completed high school were enrolled in two-year colleges, and 46.4% were enrolled in four-year institutions. These percentages were up dramatically from 1973, when 43.4% of the 1.6 million women who had recently completed high school were

TABLE 2.1

**Number of persons aged 18 and over, by highest level of education attained, age, sex, and race and Hispanic origin, 2016** [CONTINUED]

[Numbers in thousands.]

| Sex, race/ethnicity, and age | Total | Elementary school (kindergarten–8th grade) | High school 1 to 3 years | 4 years, no completion | Completion[a] | Postsecondary education Some college, no degree | Associate's degree | Bachelor's degree | Master's degree | First-professional or doctor's degree |
|---|---|---|---|---|---|---|---|---|---|---|
| **Hispanic, 18 and over** | **38,549** | **5,893** | **4,415** | **1,244** | **12,015** | **6,670** | **2,740** | **3,845** | **1,284** | **443** |
| 18 and 19 years old | 1,787 | (b) | 535 | 227 | 515 | 448 | b | b | b | b |
| 20 to 24 years old | 4,744 | 169 | 348 | 143 | 1,713 | 1,728 | 326 | 279 | b | b |
| 25 years old and over | 32,019 | 5,694 | 3,531 | 875 | 9,787 | 4,493 | 2,383 | 3,566 | 1,260 | 430 |
| 25 to 29 years old | 4,624 | 318 | 449 | 130 | 1,547 | 933 | 383 | 676 | 158 | b |
| 30 to 34 years old | 4,325 | 482 | 487 | 107 | 1,459 | 674 | 383 | 508 | 186 | 40 |
| 35 to 39 years old | 4,249 | 644 | 485 | 133 | 1,314 | 626 | 321 | 469 | 200 | 57 |
| 40 to 49 years old | 7,401 | 1,332 | 922 | 237 | 2,249 | 875 | 515 | 839 | 328 | 106 |
| 50 to 59 years old | 5,628 | 1,176 | 625 | 149 | 1,654 | 711 | 472 | 549 | 197 | 96 |
| 60 to 64 years old | 1,927 | 436 | 197 | b | 538 | 269 | 122 | 237 | 71 | b |
| 65 years old and over | 3,863 | 1,307 | 367 | 86 | 1,025 | 407 | 187 | 288 | 120 | 76 |
| **Asian, 18 and over** | **14,108** | **667** | **463** | **219** | **2,493** | **1,946** | **894** | **4,319** | **2,197** | **909** |
| 18 and 19 years old | 388 | b | 104 | b | 59 | 186 | b | b | b | b |
| 20 to 24 years old | 1,259 | b | b | b | 149 | 582 | 97 | 339 | b | b |
| 25 years old and over | 12,462 | 657 | 341 | 175 | 2,285 | 1,179 | 793 | 3,976 | 2,149 | 907 |
| 25 to 29 years old | 1,512 | b | b | b | 177 | 206 | 88 | 617 | 304 | 72 |
| 30 to 34 years old | 1,592 | b | b | b | 225 | 142 | 100 | 534 | 391 | 148 |
| 35 to 39 years old | 1,478 | b | b | b | 171 | 140 | 78 | 542 | 371 | 123 |
| 40 to 49 years old | 2,630 | 91 | b | b | 452 | 189 | 178 | 846 | 529 | 258 |
| 50 to 59 years old | 2,247 | 156 | 68 | b | 510 | 214 | 217 | 608 | 290 | 149 |
| 60 to 64 years old | 899 | 85 | b | b | 203 | 89 | 45 | 272 | 93 | b |
| 65 years old and over | 2,103 | 292 | 106 | b | 546 | 199 | 88 | 557 | 170 | 112 |

[a]Includes completion of high school through equivalency programs, such as a GED (General Equivalency Development) program.
[b]Reporting standards not met. Either there are too few cases for a reliable estimate or the coefficient of variation (CV) is 50 percent or greater.
Note: Total includes other racial/ethnic groups not shown separately. Race categories exclude persons of Hispanic ethnicity. Detail may not sum to totals because of rounding.

SOURCE: Adapted from "Table 104.30. Number of Persons Age 18 and over, by Highest Level of Educational Attainment, Sex, Race/Ethnicity, and Age: 2016," in *Digest of Education Statistics: 2016*, US Department of Education, Institute of Education Sciences, National Center for Education Statistics, March 2017, https://nces.ed.gov/programs/digest/d16/tables/dt16_104.30.asp (accessed January 18, 2018).

enrolled in college, 15.2% in two-year and 28.2% in four-year institutions. The percentage of recent male high school completers who were enrolled in college grew more slowly between 1973 (when 50% of 1.5 million were enrolled) and 2015.

### Test Scores

According to the NCES (June 2016, https://nces.ed.gov/programs/digest/d16/tables/dt16_221.10.asp), between 1992 and 2015 girls consistently scored higher than boys in reading exams at each age level tested. On average, female fourth graders scored seven points higher than their male counterparts, and female eighth graders scored 11 points higher than males. Among 12th graders, female students' reading scores averaged 10 points higher than the scores of their male peers in 2013 and 2015.

In general, math scores for both males and females have risen, and then dipped slightly, in parallel fashion since 1990. (See Figure 2.2.) Despite a stereotypical belief that females do not do as well as males in math, the achievement gap is small. In 2015 female fourth graders scored just two points lower than males on average, while female eighth graders scored the same as their male peers. The math achievement gap between boys and

girls, however, tends to increase slightly in high school. Joel McFarland et al. note in *The Condition of Education: 2017* (May 2017, https://nces.ed.gov/pubs2017/2017144.pdf) that the average math scores for 12th graders reflect a two-point difference between male and female achievement in 2005, and a three-point difference in 2013 and 2015. The researchers identify more serious disparities among different racial and ethnic groups. The 2015 achievement gap between African American and white 12th graders was 30 points, and the achievement gap between Hispanic and white 12th graders was 21 points.

The male-female achievement gap is more pronounced in the sciences, and the gap gets larger as students age. (See Table 2.4.) In 2015 among eighth graders males outscored females by an average of three points, while among 12th graders males outscored females by an average five points. These numbers were consistent with those for 2009, when girls scored below boys in science at every age level.

**SAT.** According to the College Board, in *2016 College-Bound Seniors: Total Group Profile Report* (2016, https://reports.collegeboard.org/pdf/total-group-2016.pdf), in 2016 female college-bound high school seniors scored slightly below their male counterparts (493 versus 495)

# TABLE 2.2

## School enrollment of the population three years old and over, by age and sex, October 2016

[Numbers in thousands. Civilian noninstitutionalized population.]

| | Population | Enrolled in school | | | | | | | | | | Not enrolled in school | | | | | |
| | | Total | | Nursery or kindergarten | | Elementary | | High school | | College undergraduate or graduate | | Total | | High school graduate | | Not high school graduate | |
| All races | Number | Number | Percent | Number | Percent | Number | Percent | Number | Percent | Number | Percent | Number | Percent | Number | Percent | Number | Percent |
|---|---|---|---|---|---|---|---|---|---|---|---|---|---|---|---|---|---|
| **Both sexes** | | | | | | | | | | | | | | | | | |
| **Total** | 307,516 | 77,232 | 25.1 | 8,764 | 2.8 | 32,604 | 10.6 | 16,668 | 5.4 | 19,196 | 6.2 | 230,284 | 74.9 | 199,749 | 65 | 30,535 | 9.9 |
| 3 and 4 years old | 7,971 | 4,289 | 53.8 | 4,289 | 53.8 | * | * | * | * | * | * | 3,682 | 46.2 | * | * | 3,682 | 46.2 |
| 5 and 6 years old | 8,050 | 7,507 | 93.3 | 4,415 | 54.8 | 3,092 | 38.4 | * | * | * | * | 543 | 6.7 | * | * | 543 | 6.7 |
| 7 to 9 years old | 12,369 | 12,093 | 97.8 | 60 | 0.5 | 12,033 | 97.3 | * | * | * | * | 276 | 2.2 | * | * | 276 | 2.2 |
| 10 to 13 years old | 16,535 | 16,288 | 98.5 | * | * | 16,008 | 96.8 | 280 | 1.7 | * | * | 246 | 1.5 | * | * | 246 | 1.5 |
| 14 and 15 years old | 8,271 | 8,107 | 98.0 | * | * | 1,343 | 16.2 | 6,739 | 81.5 | 25 | 0.3 | 164 | 2.0 | 34 | 0.4 | 129 | 1.6 |
| 16 and 17 years old | 8,475 | 7,879 | 93.0 | * | * | 55 | 0.6 | 7,608 | 89.8 | 216 | 2.5 | 595 | 7.0 | 172 | 2 | 423 | 5.0 |
| 18 and 19 years old | 8,266 | 5,741 | 69.5 | * | * | 29 | 0.4 | 1,541 | 18.6 | 4,171 | 50.5 | 2,525 | 30.5 | 1,993 | 24.1 | 532 | 6.4 |
| 20 and 21 years old | 8,286 | 4,597 | 55.5 | * | * | 9 | 0.1 | 171 | 2.1 | 4,417 | 53.3 | 3,690 | 44.5 | 3,163 | 38.2 | 527 | 6.4 |
| 22 to 24 years old | 13,340 | 3,841 | 28.8 | * | * | 9 | 0.1 | 99 | 0.7 | 3,733 | 28 | 9,499 | 71.2 | 8,647 | 64.8 | 852 | 6.4 |
| 25 to 29 years old | 22,410 | 2,966 | 13.2 | * | * | 11 | * | 73 | 0.3 | 2,882 | 12.9 | 19,444 | 86.8 | 17,774 | 79.3 | 1,670 | 7.5 |
| 30 to 34 years old | 21,335 | 1,364 | 6.4 | * | * | 6 | * | 23 | 0.1 | 1,336 | 6.3 | 19,971 | 93.6 | 18,139 | 85 | 1,832 | 8.6 |
| 35 to 44 years old | 39,887 | 1,495 | 3.7 | * | * | 4 | * | 66 | 0.2 | 1,425 | 3.6 | 38,392 | 96.3 | 34,382 | 86.2 | 4,010 | 10.1 |
| 45 to 54 years old | 42,291 | 717 | 1.7 | * | * | 4 | * | 40 | 0.1 | 673 | 1.6 | 41,575 | 98.3 | 37,065 | 87.6 | 4,510 | 10.7 |
| 55 years old and over | 90,030 | 349 | 0.4 | * | * | 3 | * | 27 | * | 319 | 0.4 | 89,681 | 99.6 | 78,380 | 87.1 | 11,301 | 12.6 |
| **Male** | | | | | | | | | | | | | | | | | |
| **Total** | 150,027 | 38,351 | 25.6 | 4,487 | 3.0 | 16,682 | 11.1 | 8,538 | 5.7 | 8,644 | 5.8 | 111,676 | 74.4 | 96,156 | 64.1 | 15,520 | 10.3 |
| 3 and 4 years old | 4,067 | 2,201 | 54.1 | 2,201 | 54.1 | * | * | * | * | * | * | 1,866 | 45.9 | * | * | 1,866 | 45.9 |
| 5 and 6 years old | 4,125 | 3,824 | 92.7 | 2,259 | 54.8 | 1,566 | 38.0 | * | * | * | * | 300 | 7.3 | * | * | 300 | 7.3 |
| 7 to 9 years old | 6,300 | 6,141 | 97.5 | 27 | 0.4 | 6,114 | 97.0 | * | * | * | * | 159 | 2.5 | * | * | 159 | 2.5 |
| 10 to 13 years old | 8,435 | 8,294 | 98.3 | * | * | 8,190 | 97.1 | 104 | 1.2 | * | * | 141 | 1.7 | * | * | 141 | 1.7 |
| 14 and 15 years old | 4,212 | 4,159 | 98.7 | * | * | 738 | 17.5 | 3,417 | 81.1 | 3 | 0.1 | 53 | 1.3 | 5 | 0.1 | 48 | 1.1 |
| 16 and 17 years old | 4,296 | 3,981 | 92.7 | * | * | 39 | 0.9 | 3,866 | 90.0 | 76 | 1.8 | 315 | 7.3 | 78 | 1.8 | 237 | 5.5 |
| 18 and 19 years old | 4,192 | 2,860 | 68.2 | * | * | 14 | 0.3 | 903 | 21.5 | 1,944 | 46.4 | 1,332 | 31.8 | 1,028 | 24.5 | 303 | 7.2 |
| 20 and 21 years old | 4,214 | 2,165 | 51.4 | * | * | * | * | 80 | 1.9 | 2,085 | 49.5 | 2,049 | 48.6 | 1,725 | 40.9 | 324 | 7.7 |
| 22 to 24 years old | 6,636 | 1,832 | 27.6 | * | * | 4 | 0.1 | 56 | 0.8 | 1,771 | 26.7 | 4,804 | 72.4 | 4,298 | 64.8 | 506 | 7.6 |
| 25 to 29 years old | 11,142 | 1,311 | 11.8 | * | * | 11 | 0.1 | 36 | 0.3 | 1,264 | 11.3 | 9,831 | 88.2 | 8,906 | 79.9 | 925 | 8.3 |
| 30 to 34 years old | 10,535 | 582 | 5.5 | * | * | 3 | * | 6 | 0.1 | 574 | 5.4 | 9,952 | 94.5 | 8,958 | 85 | 994 | 9.4 |
| 35 to 44 years old | 19,550 | 580 | 3.0 | * | * | 1 | * | 30 | 0.2 | 550 | 2.8 | 18,970 | 97.0 | 16,771 | 85.8 | 2,199 | 11.2 |
| 45 to 54 years old | 20,676 | 277 | 1.3 | * | * | * | * | 20 | 0.1 | 256 | 1.2 | 20,399 | 98.7 | 18,030 | 87.2 | 2,369 | 11.5 |
| 55 years old and over | 41,649 | 144 | 0.3 | * | * | 3 | * | 20 | * | 121 | 0.3 | 41,505 | 99.7 | 36,357 | 87.3 | 5,148 | 12.4 |
| **Female** | | | | | | | | | | | | | | | | | |
| **Total** | 157,489 | 38,881 | 24.7 | 4,277 | 2.7 | 15,923 | 10.1 | 8,130 | 5.2 | 10,551 | 6.7 | 118,608 | 75.3 | 103,593 | 65.8 | 15,015 | 9.5 |
| 3 and 4 years old | 3,904 | 2,088 | 53.5 | 2,088 | 53.5 | * | * | * | * | * | * | 1,816 | 46.5 | * | * | 1,816 | 46.5 |
| 5 and 6 years old | 3,925 | 3,682 | 93.8 | 2,156 | 54.9 | 1,526 | 38.9 | * | * | * | * | 243 | 6.2 | * | * | 243 | 6.2 |
| 7 to 9 years old | 6,069 | 5,951 | 98.1 | 33 | 0.5 | 5,919 | 97.5 | * | * | * | * | 117 | 1.9 | * | * | 117 | 1.9 |
| 10 to 13 years old | 8,100 | 7,994 | 98.7 | * | * | 7,819 | 96.5 | 176 | 2.2 | * | * | 105 | 1.3 | * | * | 105 | 1.3 |
| 14 and 15 years old | 4,059 | 3,948 | 97.3 | * | * | 605 | 14.9 | 3,322 | 81.8 | 21 | 0.5 | 111 | 2.7 | 29 | 0.7 | 82 | 2.0 |
| 16 and 17 years old | 4,178 | 3,899 | 93.3 | * | * | 17 | 0.4 | 3,742 | 89.6 | 140 | 3.3 | 280 | 6.7 | 94 | 2.3 | 186 | 4.4 |
| 18 and 19 years old | 4,075 | 2,881 | 70.7 | * | * | 15 | 0.4 | 638 | 15.7 | 2,227 | 54.7 | 1,193 | 29.3 | 965 | 23.7 | 229 | 5.6 |
| 20 and 21 years old | 4,072 | 2,431 | 59.7 | * | * | 8 | 0.2 | 91 | 2.2 | 2,331 | 57.3 | 1,641 | 40.3 | 1,438 | 35.3 | 203 | 5.0 |
| 22 to 24 years old | 6,705 | 2,009 | 30.0 | * | * | 4 | 0.1 | 43 | 0.6 | 1,962 | 29.3 | 4,695 | 70.0 | 4,349 | 64.9 | 346 | 5.2 |
| 25 to 29 years old | 11,268 | 1,655 | 14.7 | * | * | * | * | 37 | 0.3 | 1,618 | 14.4 | 9,613 | 85.3 | 8,869 | 78.7 | 745 | 6.6 |
| 30 to 34 years old | 10,800 | 782 | 7.2 | * | * | 3 | * | 17 | 0.2 | 762 | 7.1 | 10,018 | 92.8 | 9,180 | 85 | 838 | 7.8 |
| 35 to 44 years old | 20,337 | 914 | 4.5 | * | * | 3 | * | 36 | 0.2 | 876 | 4.3 | 19,423 | 95.5 | 17,611 | 86.6 | 1,811 | 8.9 |

**TABLE 2.2**

**School enrollment of the population three years old and over, by age and sex, October 2016** [CONTINUED]

[Numbers in thousands. Civilian noninstitutionalized population.]

| | Population | Enrolled in school | | | | | | | | | | Not enrolled in school | | | | | |
| | | Total | | Nursery or kindergarten | | Elementary | | High school | | College undergraduate or graduate | | Total | | High school graduate | | Not high school graduate | |
| All races | Number | Number | Percent | Number | Percent | Number | Percent | Number | Percent | Number | Percent | Number | Percent | Number | Percent | Number | Percent |
|---|---|---|---|---|---|---|---|---|---|---|---|---|---|---|---|---|---|
| 45 to 54 years old | 21,615 | 440 | 2.0 | * | * | 4 | * | 19 | 0.1 | 417 | 1.9 | 21,175 | 98.0 | 19,034 | 88.1 | 2,141 | 9.9 |
| 55 years old and over | 48,381 | 205 | 0.4 | * | * | * | * | 7 | — | 198 | 0.4 | 48,176 | 99.6 | 42,023 | 86.9 | 6,153 | 12.7 |

*Represents zero or rounds to zero.

SOURCE: "Table 1. Enrollment Status of the Population 3 Years and over, by Sex, Age, Race, Hispanic Origin, Foreign Born, and Foreign-Born Parentage: October 2016," in *School Enrollment: CPS October 2016— Detailed Tables*, US Census Bureau, August 2017, https://www2.census.gov/programs-surveys/demo/tables/school-enrollment/2016/2016-cps/tab01-01.xlsx (accessed January 18, 2018)

TABLE 2.3

**Percentage of 16- to 24-year-olds who were high school dropouts, by sex and race and Hispanic origin, 1960–2015**

| Year | Total status dropout rate | | | | Male status dropout rate | | | | Female status dropout rate | | | |
|------|-----------|-------|-------|----------|-----------|-------|-------|----------|-----------|-------|-------|----------|
| | All races[a] | White | Black | Hispanic | All races[a] | White | Black | Hispanic | All races[a] | White | Black | Hispanic |
| 1960[b] | 27.2 | — | — | — | 27.8 | — | — | — | 26.7 | — | — | — |
| 1967[c] | 17.0 | 15.4 | 28.6 | — | 16.5 | 14.7 | 30.6 | — | 17.3 | 16.1 | 26.9 | — |
| 1968[c] | 16.2 | 14.7 | 27.4 | — | 15.8 | 14.4 | 27.1 | — | 16.5 | 15.0 | 27.6 | — |
| 1969[c] | 15.2 | 13.6 | 26.7 | — | 14.3 | 12.6 | 26.9 | — | 16.0 | 14.6 | 26.7 | — |
| 1970[c] | 15.0 | 13.2 | 27.9 | — | 14.2 | 12.2 | 29.4 | — | 15.7 | 14.1 | 26.6 | — |
| 1971[c] | 14.7 | 13.4 | 24.0 | — | 14.2 | 12.6 | 25.5 | — | 15.2 | 14.2 | 22.6 | — |
| 1972 | 14.6 | 12.3 | 21.3 | 34.3 | 14.1 | 11.6 | 22.3 | 33.7 | 15.1 | 12.8 | 20.5 | 34.8 |
| 1973 | 14.1 | 11.6 | 22.2 | 33.5 | 13.7 | 11.5 | 21.5 | 30.4 | 14.5 | 11.8 | 22.8 | 36.4 |
| 1974 | 14.3 | 11.9 | 21.2 | 33.0 | 14.2 | 12.0 | 20.1 | 33.8 | 14.3 | 11.8 | 22.1 | 32.2 |
| 1975 | 13.9 | 11.4 | 22.9 | 29.2 | 13.3 | 11.0 | 23.0 | 26.7 | 14.5 | 11.8 | 22.9 | 31.6 |
| 1976 | 14.1 | 12.0 | 20.5 | 31.4 | 14.1 | 12.1 | 21.2 | 30.3 | 14.2 | 11.8 | 19.9 | 32.3 |
| 1977 | 14.1 | 11.9 | 19.8 | 33.0 | 14.5 | 12.6 | 19.5 | 31.6 | 13.8 | 11.2 | 20.0 | 34.3 |
| 1978 | 14.2 | 11.9 | 20.2 | 33.3 | 14.6 | 12.2 | 22.5 | 33.6 | 13.9 | 11.6 | 18.3 | 33.1 |
| 1979 | 14.6 | 12.0 | 21.1 | 33.8 | 15.0 | 12.6 | 22.4 | 33.0 | 14.2 | 11.5 | 20.0 | 34.5 |
| 1980 | 14.1 | 11.4 | 19.1 | 35.2 | 15.1 | 12.3 | 20.8 | 37.2 | 13.1 | 10.5 | 17.7 | 33.2 |
| 1981 | 13.9 | 11.3 | 18.4 | 33.2 | 15.1 | 12.5 | 19.9 | 36.0 | 12.8 | 10.2 | 17.1 | 30.4 |
| 1982 | 13.9 | 11.4 | 18.4 | 31.7 | 14.5 | 12.0 | 21.2 | 30.5 | 13.3 | 10.8 | 15.9 | 32.8 |
| 1983 | 13.7 | 11.1 | 18.0 | 31.6 | 14.9 | 12.2 | 19.9 | 34.3 | 12.5 | 10.1 | 16.2 | 29.1 |
| 1984 | 13.1 | 11.0 | 15.5 | 29.8 | 14.0 | 11.9 | 16.8 | 30.6 | 12.3 | 10.1 | 14.3 | 29.0 |
| 1985 | 12.6 | 10.4 | 15.2 | 27.6 | 13.4 | 11.1 | 16.1 | 29.9 | 11.8 | 9.8 | 14.3 | 25.2 |
| 1986 | 12.2 | 9.7 | 14.2 | 30.1 | 13.1 | 10.3 | 15.0 | 32.8 | 11.4 | 9.1 | 13.5 | 27.2 |
| 1987 | 12.6 | 10.4 | 14.1 | 28.6 | 13.2 | 10.8 | 15.0 | 29.1 | 12.1 | 10.0 | 13.3 | 28.1 |
| 1988 | 12.9 | 9.6 | 14.5 | 35.8 | 13.5 | 10.3 | 15.0 | 36.0 | 12.2 | 8.9 | 14.0 | 35.4 |
| 1989 | 12.6 | 9.4 | 13.9 | 33.0 | 13.6 | 10.3 | 14.9 | 34.4 | 11.7 | 8.5 | 13.0 | 31.6 |
| 1990 | 12.1 | 9.0 | 13.2 | 32.4 | 12.3 | 9.3 | 11.9 | 34.3 | 11.8 | 8.7 | 14.4 | 30.3 |
| 1991 | 12.5 | 8.9 | 13.6 | 35.3 | 13.0 | 8.9 | 13.5 | 39.2 | 11.9 | 8.9 | 13.7 | 31.1 |
| 1992[d] | 11.0 | 7.7 | 13.7 | 29.4 | 11.3 | 8.0 | 12.5 | 32.1 | 10.7 | 7.4 | 14.8 | 26.6 |
| 1993[d] | 11.0 | 7.9 | 13.6 | 27.5 | 11.2 | 8.2 | 12.6 | 28.1 | 10.9 | 7.6 | 14.4 | 26.9 |
| 1994[d] | 11.4 | 7.7 | 12.6 | 30.0 | 12.3 | 8.0 | 14.1 | 31.6 | 10.6 | 7.5 | 11.3 | 28.1 |
| 1995[d] | 12.0 | 8.6 | 12.1 | 30.0 | 12.2 | 9.0 | 11.1 | 30.0 | 11.7 | 8.2 | 12.9 | 30.0 |
| 1996[d] | 11.1 | 7.3 | 13.0 | 29.4 | 11.4 | 7.3 | 13.5 | 30.3 | 10.9 | 7.3 | 12.5 | 28.3 |
| 1997[d] | 11.0 | 7.6 | 13.4 | 25.3 | 11.9 | 8.5 | 13.3 | 27.0 | 10.1 | 6.7 | 13.5 | 23.4 |
| 1998[d] | 11.8 | 7.7 | 13.8 | 29.5 | 13.3 | 8.6 | 15.5 | 33.5 | 10.3 | 6.9 | 12.2 | 25.0 |
| 1999[d] | 11.2 | 7.3 | 12.6 | 28.6 | 11.9 | 7.7 | 12.1 | 31.0 | 10.5 | 6.9 | 13.0 | 26.0 |
| 2000[d] | 10.9 | 6.9 | 13.1 | 27.8 | 12.0 | 7.0 | 15.3 | 31.8 | 9.9 | 6.9 | 11.1 | 23.5 |
| 2001[d] | 10.7 | 7.3 | 10.9 | 27.0 | 12.2 | 7.9 | 13.0 | 31.6 | 9.3 | 6.7 | 9.0 | 22.1 |
| 2002[d] | 10.5 | 6.5 | 11.3 | 25.7 | 11.8 | 6.7 | 12.8 | 29.6 | 9.2 | 6.3 | 9.9 | 21.2 |
| 2003[d, e] | 9.9 | 6.3 | 10.9 | 23.5 | 11.3 | 7.1 | 12.5 | 26.7 | 8.4 | 5.6 | 9.5 | 20.1 |
| 2004[d, e] | 10.3 | 6.8 | 11.8 | 23.8 | 11.6 | 7.1 | 13.5 | 28.5 | 9.0 | 6.4 | 10.2 | 18.5 |
| 2005[d, e] | 9.4 | 6.0 | 10.4 | 22.4 | 10.8 | 6.6 | 12.0 | 26.4 | 8.0 | 5.3 | 9.0 | 18.1 |
| 2006[d, e] | 9.3 | 5.8 | 10.7 | 22.1 | 10.3 | 6.4 | 9.7 | 25.7 | 8.3 | 5.3 | 11.7 | 18.1 |
| 2007[d, e] | 8.7 | 5.3 | 8.4 | 21.4 | 9.8 | 6.0 | 8.0 | 24.7 | 7.7 | 4.5 | 8.8 | 18.0 |
| 2008[d, e] | 8.0 | 4.8 | 9.9 | 18.3 | 8.5 | 5.4 | 8.7 | 19.9 | 7.5 | 4.2 | 11.1 | 16.7 |
| 2009[d, e] | 8.1 | 5.2 | 9.3 | 17.6 | 9.1 | 6.3 | 10.6 | 19.0 | 7.0 | 4.1 | 8.1 | 16.1 |
| 2010[d, e, f] | 7.4 | 5.1 | 8.0 | 15.1 | 8.5 | 5.9 | 9.5 | 17.3 | 6.3 | 4.2 | 6.7 | 12.8 |
| 2011[d, e, f] | 7.1 | 5.0 | 7.3 | 13.6 | 7.7 | 5.4 | 8.3 | 14.6 | 6.5 | 4.6 | 6.4 | 12.4 |
| 2012[d, e, f] | 6.6 | 4.3 | 7.5 | 12.7 | 7.3 | 4.8 | 8.1 | 13.9 | 5.9 | 3.8 | 7.0 | 11.3 |
| 2013[d, e, f] | 6.8 | 5.1 | 7.3 | 11.7 | 7.2 | 5.5 | 8.2 | 12.6 | 6.3 | 4.7 | 6.6 | 10.8 |
| 2014[d, e, f] | 6.5 | 5.2 | 7.4 | 10.6 | 7.1 | 5.7 | 7.1 | 11.8 | 5.9 | 4.8 | 7.7 | 9.3 |
| 2015[d, e, f] | 5.9 | 4.6 | 6.5 | 9.2 | 6.3 | 5.0 | 6.4 | 9.9 | 5.4 | 4.1 | 6.5 | 8.4 |

on the critical reading section of the SAT (formerly called the Scholastic Assessment Test), significantly below males (494 versus 524) on the mathematics section, and significantly higher than males (487 versus 475) on the writing section. These disparities were consistent with the results of previous years' tests. This difference between male and female scores, especially in mathematics, is a subject of much debate and controversy.

The College Board suggests that the larger number of female test takers contributes to females' lower scores because lower average scores are to be expected when more people from a self-selected population take the exam. Since the early 1970s more females than males have taken the SAT; in 2016, 875,342 (53.5%) of the more than 1.6 million students who took the SAT were female. Skeptics suggest that this fails to account for the disparities in test scores, given that 60% of students who described themselves as having an A+ grade point average, 61% of those with an A average, and 57% of those with an A− average were females. By contrast, 59% of students who described themselves as having a C average and 63% of those with a D or F average were male. The question of how to explain the gender gap in SAT performance is a source of ongoing debate.

## TABLE 2.3

**Percentage of 16- to 24-year-olds who were high school dropouts, by sex and race and Hispanic origin, 1960–2015** [CONTINUED]

—Not available.
[a]Includes other racial/ethnic groups not separately shown.
[b]Based on the April 1960 decennial census.
[c]For 1967 through 1971, white and black include persons of Hispanic ethnicity.
[d]Because of changes in data collection procedures, data may not be comparable with figures for years prior to 1992.
[e]White and black exclude persons of two or more races.
[f]Beginning in 2010, standard errors were computed using replicate weights, which produced more precise values than the generalized variance function methodology used in prior years.
Note: "Status" dropouts are 16- to 24-year-olds who are not enrolled in school and who have not completed a high school program, regardless of when they left school. People who have received GED (General Equivalency Development) credentials are counted as high school completers. All data except for 1960 are based on October counts. Data are based on sample surveys of the civilian noninstitutionalized population, which excludes persons in prisons, persons in the military, and other persons not living in households. Race categories exclude persons of Hispanic ethnicity except where otherwise noted. Some data have been revised from previously published figures.

SOURCE: Adapted from "Table 219.70. Percentage of High School Dropouts among Persons 16 to 24 Years Old (Status Dropout Rate), by Sex and Race/ Ethnicity: Selected Years, 1960 through 2015," in *Digest of Education Statistics: 2016*, US Department of Education, Institute of Education Sciences, National Center for Education Statistics, August 2016, https://nces.ed.gov/programs/digest/d16/tables/dt16_219.70.asp (accessed January 18, 2018)

## FIGURE 2.1

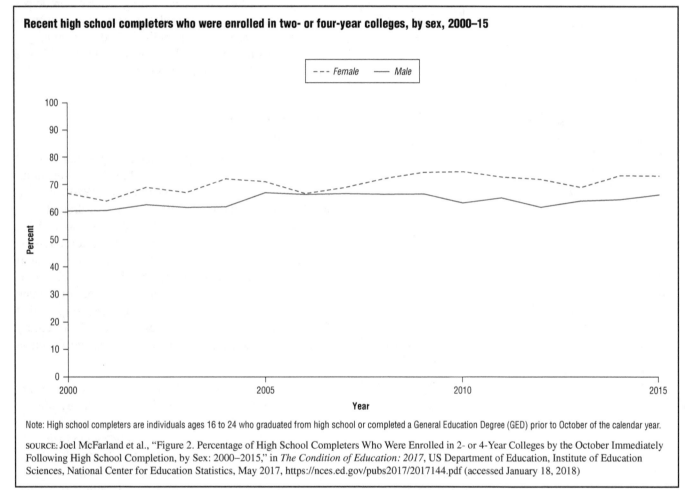

**Recent high school completers who were enrolled in two- or four-year colleges, by sex, 2000–15**

Note: High school completers are individuals ages 16 to 24 who graduated from high school or completed a General Education Degree (GED) prior to October of the calendar year.

SOURCE: Joel McFarland et al., "Figure 2. Percentage of High School Completers Who Were Enrolled in 2- or 4-Year Colleges by the October Immediately Following High School Completion, by Sex: 2000–2015," in *The Condition of Education: 2017*, US Department of Education, Institute of Education Sciences, National Center for Education Statistics, May 2017, https://nces.ed.gov/pubs2017/2017144.pdf (accessed January 18, 2018)

In 2016 the College Board gave the SAT its most significant revamping in a decade. The intention was to make the test more relevant to what high school students were learning in the classroom and make questions more fair to students of different socioeconomic, racial, and gender backgrounds. Still, Anemona Hartocollis reports in "Tutors See Stereotypes and Gender Bias in SAT. Testers See None of the Above" (NYTimes.com, June 26, 2016) that test-prep industry experts identified material on the test that they said were classic examples of "stereotype threat." Hartocollis explains, stereotype threat occurs when test takers are reminded of a negative stereotype about their race or gender, and this triggers "a kind of test anxiety that leads them to underperform" on the test in general. Psychologists and researchers who study stereotype threat maintained that the College Board had more work to do to ensure that girls' performance on the SAT was not being impaired by the content of the test itself.

FIGURE 2.2

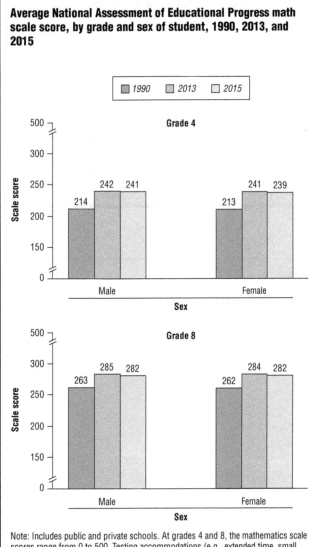

**Average National Assessment of Educational Progress math scale score, by grade and sex of student, 1990, 2013, and 2015**

Note: Includes public and private schools. At grades 4 and 8, the mathematics scale scores range from 0 to 500. Testing accommodations (e.g., extended time, small group testing) for children with disabilities and English language learners were not permitted in 1990. Although rounded numbers are displayed, the figures are based on unrounded estimates.

SOURCE: Joel McFarland et al., "Figure 4. Average National Assessment of Educational Progress (NAEP) Mathematics Scale Scores of 4th- and 8th-Grade Students, by Sex: 1990, 2013, and 2015," in *The Condition of Education: 2017,* US Department of Education, Institute of Education Sciences, National Center for Education Statistics, May 2017, https://nces.ed.gov/pubs2017/2017144.pdf (accessed January 18, 2018)

Gender disparities in math and science education are the focus of intense research among a wide range of experts and organizations, including the Organisation for Economic Co-operation and Development (OECD), an international organization dedicated to promoting global economic development. Among its other activities, the OECD coordinates the Program for International Student Assessment (PISA), a standardized test of reading, mathematics, and science literacy that is administered every three years among 15-year-old students in more than 60 countries. In *PISA 2015 Results (Volume 1): Excellence and Equity in Education* (2016, https://

www.oecd-ilibrary.org/pisa-2015-results-volume-i_5jln6 j3gp9mt.pdf?itemId=%2Fcontent%2Fpublication%2F 9789264266490-en&mimeType=pdf), the OECD finds that gender disparities in science, math, and reading achievement vary considerably from one country to the next. Specifically, it explains, "This indicates that gender disparities in performance do not stem from innate differences in aptitude, but rather from factors that parents, teachers, policy makers and opinion leaders can influence." To help close the gender gap in science achievement, the OECD recommends that educators and employers should provide better career information to expand and improve students' understanding of what it means to pursue a career in science and the range of career opportunities that can follow from training in science and technology. With access to objective and reliable career information, students will begin to disregard the prevailing gender stereotypes about scientists and science-related occupations, such as "computer science is a 'masculine' field and biology a 'feminine' field; scientists achieve success due to brilliance rather than hard work; and scientists are 'mad.'"

## HIGHER EDUCATION

### College Enrollment

During the 1930s approximately equal numbers of men and women attended college, but the overall numbers were quite small. Between 1940 and 1970 the number of men who attended college increased dramatically as a result of the Servicemen's Readjustment Act of 1944 (also known as the G.I. Bill), which offered tuition assistance to service personnel returning from World War II (1939–1945), the Korean War (1950–1953), and the Vietnam War (1954–1975). However, the number of women attending colleges and universities began to surpass that of men during the late 1970s, and by the 21st century women significantly outnumbered men on most college campuses.

According to the US Census Bureau (August 28, 2017, https://www2.census.gov/programs-surveys/demo/tables/school-enrollment/time-series/cps-historical-time-series/tablea-6.xlsx), in 1947 women accounted for only 27% of college enrollments. The decades that followed saw the number of women enrolled in college grow steadily, and by 1979 there were more women than men enrolled in college. (See Figure 2.3.) The growth of the female population of college students continued to outpace that of the male population. In 2016 women accounted for 55% of all college enrollments. (See Table 2.2.) There were 10.6 million female college students, compared with 8.6 million male students. In *Projections of Education Statistics to 2025* (September 2017, https://nces.ed.gov/pubs2017/2017019.pdf), William J. Hussar and Tabitha M. Bailey predict that college enrollment by women will continue to increase at a faster rate than

**TABLE 2.4**

**Average National Assessment of Educational Progress science scale score, by grade level, selected school and student characteristics, and percentile, selected years 2009, 2011, and 2015**

| Selected characteristic, percentile, and achievement level | Grade 4 | | | Grade 8 | | | Grade 12 | | |
|---|---|---|---|---|---|---|---|---|---|
| | 2009 | 2011 | 2015 | 2009 | 2011 | 2015 | 2009 | 2011 | 2015 |
| | Average science scale score[a] | | | | | | | | |
| **All students** | 150 | — | 154 | 150 | 152 | 154 | 150 | — | 150 |
| **Sex** | | | | | | | | | |
| Male | 151 | — | 154 | 152 | 154 | 155 | 153 | — | 153 |
| Female | 149 | — | 154 | 148 | 149 | 152 | 147 | — | 148 |
| Gap between male and female score | 1 | — | 1 | 4 | 5 | 3 | 6 | — | 5 |
| **Race/ethnicity** | | | | | | | | | |
| White | 163 | — | 166 | 162 | 163 | 166 | 159 | — | 160 |
| Black | 127 | — | 133 | 126 | 129 | 132 | 125 | — | 125 |
| Hispanic | 131 | — | 139 | 132 | 137 | 140 | 134 | — | 136 |
| Asian/Pacific Islander | 160 | — | 167 | 160 | 159 | 164 | 164 | — | 166 |
| Asian | — | — | 169 | — | 161 | 166 | — | — | 167 |
| Pacific Islander | — | — | 143 | — | 139 | 138 | — | — | ‡ |
| American Indian/Alaska Native | 135 | — | 139 | 137 | 141 | 139 | 144 | — | 135 |
| Two or more races[b] | 154 | — | 158 | 151 | 156 | 159 | 151 | — | 156 |
| Gap between White and Black score | 36 | — | 33 | 36 | 35 | 34 | 34 | — | 36 |
| Gap between White and Hispanic score | 32 | — | 27 | 30 | 27 | 26 | 25 | — | 24 |
| **English language learner (ELL) status** | | | | | | | | | |
| ELL | 114 | — | 121 | 103 | 106 | 110 | 104 | — | 105 |
| Non-ELL | 154 | — | 158 | 153 | 154 | 157 | 151 | — | 152 |
| Gap between ELL and non-ELL score | 39 | — | 36 | 49 | 48 | 46 | 47 | — | 47 |
| **Disability status[c]** | | | | | | | | | |
| Identified as student with disability (SD) | 129 | — | 131 | 123 | 124 | 124 | 121 | — | 124 |
| Not identified as SD | 153 | — | 157 | 153 | 155 | 158 | 153 | — | 153 |
| Gap between SD and non-SD score | 23 | — | 26 | 31 | 31 | 34 | 31 | — | 29 |
| **Highest education level of either parent** | | | | | | | | | |
| Did not finish high school | — | — | — | 131 | 132 | 137 | 131 | — | 131 |
| Graduated high school | — | — | — | 139 | 140 | 142 | 138 | — | 136 |
| Some education after high school | — | — | — | 152 | 153 | 155 | 147 | — | 148 |
| Graduated college | — | — | — | 161 | 162 | 165 | 161 | — | 162 |
| **Percent of students in school eligible for free or reduced-price lunch** | | | | | | | | | |
| 0–25 percent eligible (low poverty) | 167 | — | 172 | 165 | 167 | 170 | 163 | — | 165 |
| 26–50 percent eligible | 155 | — | 161 | 154 | 157 | 161 | 148 | — | 154 |
| 51–75 percent eligible | 144 | — | 151 | 141 | 146 | 150 | 136 | — | 143 |
| 76–100 percent eligible (high poverty) | 126 | — | 134 | 124 | 129 | 134 | 124 | — | 126 |
| Gap between low- and high-poverty score | 41 | — | 38 | 41 | 38 | 36 | 38 | — | 39 |
| **School locale** | | | | | | | | | |
| City | 142 | — | 148 | 142 | 144 | 148 | 146 | — | 145 |
| Suburban | 154 | — | 157 | 154 | 155 | 158 | 154 | — | 153 |
| Town | 150 | — | 153 | 149 | 153 | 154 | 150 | — | 150 |
| Rural | 155 | — | 157 | 154 | 156 | 156 | 150 | — | 152 |
| **Percentile[d]** | | | | | | | | | |
| 10th | 104 | — | 108 | 103 | 106 | 109 | 104 | — | 103 |
| 25th | 128 | — | 132 | 128 | 131 | 133 | 126 | — | 126 |
| 50th | 153 | — | 157 | 153 | 155 | 157 | 151 | — | 151 |
| 75th | 175 | — | 178 | 175 | 176 | 178 | 174 | — | 176 |
| 90th | 192 | — | 196 | 192 | 193 | 195 | 194 | — | 196 |

—Not available.

[a]Scale ranges from 0 to 300 for all three grades, but scores cannot be compared across grades. For example, the average score of 166 for white 4th-graders in 2015 does not denote higher performance than the score of 160 for white 12th-graders.

[b]Prior to 2011, students in the "two or more races" category were categorized as "unclassified."

[c]The student with disability (SD) variable used in this table includes students who have a 504 plan, even if they do not have an Individualized Education Plan (IEP).

[d]The percentile represents a specific point on the percentage distribution of all students ranked by their science score from low to high. For example, 10 percent of students scored at or below the 10th percentile score, while 90 percent of students scored above it.

Note: In 2011, only 8th-grade students were assessed in science. Includes students tested with accommodations (7 to 14 percent of all students, depending on grade level and year); excludes only those students with disabilities and English language learners who were unable to be tested even with accommodations (1 to 3 percent of all students). Race categories exclude persons of Hispanic ethnicity.

SOURCE: Adapted from "Table 223.10. Average National Assessment of Educational Progress (NAEP) Science Scale Score, Standard Deviation, and Percentage of Students Attaining Science Achievement Levels, by Grade Level, Selected Student and School Characteristics, and Percentile: 2009, 2011, and 2015," in *Digest of Education Statistics: 2016*, US Department of Education, Institute of Education Sciences, National Center for Education Statistics, January 2017, https://nces.ed.gov/programs/digest/d16/tables/dt16_223.10.asp (accessed January 18, 2018)

FIGURE 2.3

**College enrollment by sex and age, selected years 1947–2016**

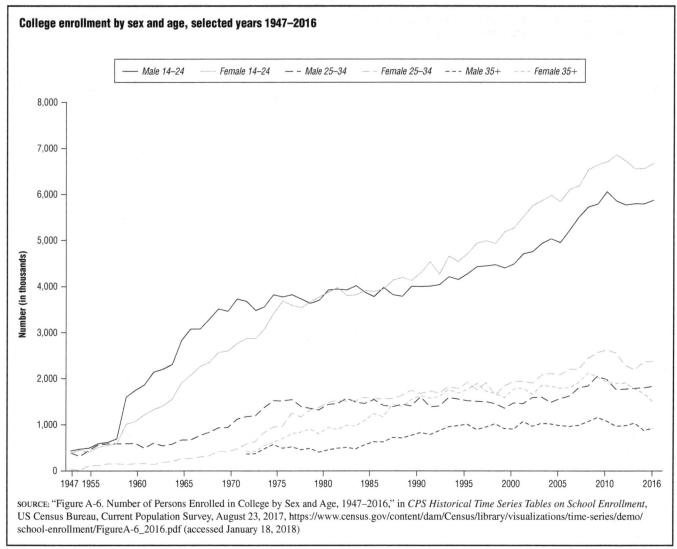

SOURCE: "Figure A-6. Number of Persons Enrolled in College by Sex and Age, 1947–2016," in *CPS Historical Time Series Tables on School Enrollment*, US Census Bureau, Current Population Survey, August 23, 2017, https://www.census.gov/content/dam/Census/library/visualizations/time-series/demo/school-enrollment/FigureA-6_2016.pdf (accessed January 18, 2018)

male enrollment. Between 2014 and 2025 male enrollment is expected to increase 13%, whereas female enrollment is expected to increase 17%.

### Associate's and Bachelor's Degrees

Women not only attend college at higher rates than men but also earn more college degrees than men. According to Hussar and Bailey, between 2000–01 and 2013–14 the number of associate's degrees awarded to women increased 76%, compared with an increase of 69% for men. In 2013–14 women earned 612,559 associate's degrees, or 61% of the total 1,003,364 awarded. (See Figure 2.4.) Between 2013–14 and 2025–26 the number of associate's degrees awarded to women is expected to increase 37%, compared with an increase of 15% for men.

Similar growth in the number of women earning bachelor's degrees occurred during the early years of the 21st century, and comparable increases were projected for the future. Hussar and Bailey indicate that between 2000–01 and 2013–14 the number of bachelor's degrees awarded to women increased 50%, almost equal to the increase of 51% for men. In 2013–14 women earned 1,068,122 bachelor's degrees, or 57% of the total 1,869,814 awarded. (See Figure 2.5.) Between 2013–14 and 2025–26 the number of bachelor's degrees awarded to women is projected to increase 11%, compared with an increase of 6% for men.

**FIELDS OF STUDY.** At the associate level, a majority of women who earned degrees in 2014–15 studied liberal arts and sciences, health professions, or business. (See Table 2.5.) Among the 617,358 associate's degrees awarded to women that year, 226,487 (36.7%) were degrees in liberal arts and sciences, general studies, and humanities, 168,177 (27.2%) were degrees in health professions and related programs, and 81,823 (13.3%) were business degrees. Other popular courses of study for women were homeland security, law enforcement, and firefighting 19,163 degrees), multi/interdisciplinary studies (17,141 degrees), education (15,227 degrees), and the visual and performing arts (12,577 degrees).

**FIGURE 2.4**

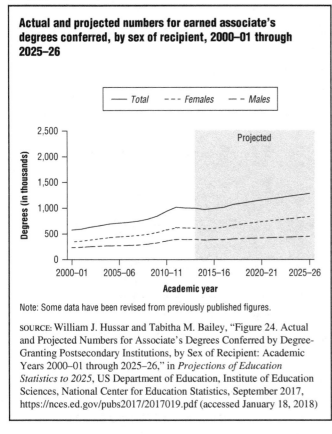

Actual and projected numbers for earned associate's degrees conferred, by sex of recipient, 2000–01 through 2025–26

— Total    - - - Females    — — Males

Note: Some data have been revised from previously published figures.

SOURCE: William J. Hussar and Tabitha M. Bailey, "Figure 24. Actual and Projected Numbers for Associate's Degrees Conferred by Degree-Granting Postsecondary Institutions, by Sex of Recipient: Academic Years 2000–01 through 2025–26," in *Projections of Education Statistics to 2025*, US Department of Education, Institute of Education Sciences, National Center for Education Statistics, September 2017, https://nces.ed.gov/pubs2017/2017019.pdf (accessed January 18, 2018)

**FIGURE 2.5**

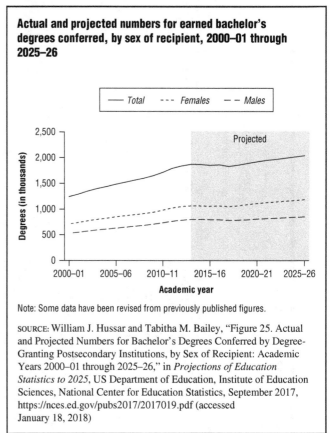

Actual and projected numbers for earned bachelor's degrees conferred, by sex of recipient, 2000–01 through 2025–26

— Total    - - - Females    — — Males

Note: Some data have been revised from previously published figures.

SOURCE: William J. Hussar and Tabitha M. Bailey, "Figure 25. Actual and Projected Numbers for Bachelor's Degrees Conferred by Degree-Granting Postsecondary Institutions, by Sex of Recipient: Academic Years 2000–01 through 2025–26," in *Projections of Education Statistics to 2025*, US Department of Education, Institute of Education Sciences, National Center for Education Statistics, September 2017, https://nces.ed.gov/pubs2017/2017019.pdf (accessed January 18, 2018)

Health professions and business were the leading fields of study at the bachelor's level, accounting, respectively, for 182,570 (16.9%) and 172,489 (15.9%) of the total 1,082,265 degrees awarded in 2014–15. (See Table 2.6.) Other top programs of study among women who earned bachelor's degrees were psychology (90,755 degrees), education (73,150 degrees), social sciences (70,214 degrees), biological and biomedical sciences (64,794 degrees), communication, journalism, and related programs (58,799 degrees), and visual and performing arts (57,812 degrees).

**Master's Degrees**

During the mid-1980s women began outpacing men at the master's level. Hussar and Bailey note that between 2000–01 and 2013–14 the number of master's degrees awarded to women increased 64%, compared with an increase of 53% for men. In 2013–14 women earned 451,668 master's degrees, or 59.9% of the total 754,475 awarded. (See Figure 2.6.) Between 2013–14 and 2025–26 men are expected to regain ground in their share of master's degrees awarded. Over the course of this decade, the number of master's degrees awarded to men is projected to increase 35%, compared with an increase of 27% for women.

**FIELDS OF STUDY.** The fields of study that attracted the most female master's candidates in 2014–15 were similar to those that attracted the most female bachelor's candidates, with one key difference: education was by far the most popular field. Of the total 452,118 master's degrees awarded to women that year, 112,581 (24.9%) were in education. (See Table 2.7.) Another 86,635 (19.2%) were in business and 84,117 (18.6%) were in health professions and related programs. Other popular fields among women who earned master's degrees in 2014–15 were public administration and social services (34,896 degrees), psychology (21,235 degrees), engineering (11,471 degrees), visual and performing arts (10,113 degrees), and social sciences (8,572 degrees).

**Doctor's Degrees**

Women also outpace men in the earning of doctor's degrees, although this is a more recent development than at the other degree levels, and men remain closer to parity with women at this level. (See Figure 2.7.) Thomas D. Snyder, Cristobal de Brey, and Sally A. Dillow indicate in *Digest of Education Statistics: 2016* (February 2018, https://nces.ed.gov/pubs2017/2017094.pdf) that in 1976–77 women earned 19,509 doctor's degrees, or 21.4% of the total 91,218 awarded; in 1990–91 women earned 41,305 doctor's degrees, or 39.1% of the total 105,547 awarded; and in 2000–01 women earned 55,414 doctor's degrees, or 46.3% of the total 119,585 awarded. Women earned slightly less than 50% of all doctor's degrees in

# TABLE 2.5

## Associate's degrees conferred to females by postsecondary institutions, by race/ethnicity and field of study, 2013–14 and 2014–15

| Field of study | 2013–14 Total | White | Black | Hispanic | Asian/Pacific Islander Total | Asian | Pacific Islander | American Indian/Alaska Native | Two or more races | Nonresident alien | 2014–15 Total | White | Black | Hispanic | Asian/Pacific Islander Total | Asian | Pacific Islander | American Indian/Alaska Native | Two or more races | Nonresident alien |
|---|---|---|---|---|---|---|---|---|---|---|---|---|---|---|---|---|---|---|---|---|
| All fields, total | 613,681 | 362,670 | 88,753 | 103,448 | 28,544 | 26,472 | 2,072 | 6,656 | 13,726 | 9,884 | 617,358 | 354,114 | 90,505 | 111,263 | 29,380 | 27,445 | 1,935 | 6,403 | 15,508 | 10,185 |
| Agriculture and natural resources | 2,643 | 2,376 | 27 | 110 | 18 | 15 | 3 | 54 | 41 | 17 | 2,791 | 2,415 | 39 | 166 | 32 | 26 | 6 | 64 | 43 | 32 |
| Architecture and related services | 139 | 49 | 5 | 63 | 12 | 12 | 0 | 0 | 2 | 8 | 149 | 57 | 6 | 52 | 21 | 20 | 1 | 1 | 2 | 10 |
| Area, ethnic, cultural, gender, and group studies | 233 | 49 | 18 | 61 | 25 | 11 | 14 | 52 | 19 | 9 | 234 | 56 | 14 | 51 | 17 | 6 | 11 | 59 | 34 | 3 |
| Biological and biomedical sciences | 3,066 | 1,374 | 262 | 877 | 370 | 360 | 10 | 53 | 66 | 64 | 3,248 | 1,398 | 283 | 981 | 390 | 369 | 21 | 48 | 87 | 61 |
| Business | 81,539 | 45,634 | 13,991 | 11,952 | 4,697 | 4,371 | 326 | 1,008 | 1,760 | 2,497 | 81,823 | 44,507 | 14,317 | 12,667 | 5,002 | 4,723 | 279 | 921 | 1,908 | 2,501 |
| Communication, journalism, and related programs | 2,752 | 1,341 | 289 | 750 | 169 | 160 | 9 | 9 | 89 | 105 | 3,458 | 1,548 | 344 | 1,078 | 193 | 183 | 10 | 21 | 145 | 129 |
| Communications technologies | 1,427 | 905 | 158 | 192 | 66 | 64 | 2 | 17 | 57 | 32 | 1,469 | 900 | 204 | 210 | 58 | 54 | 4 | 12 | 46 | 39 |
| Computer and information sciences | 7,694 | 4,336 | 1,591 | 903 | 410 | 389 | 21 | 105 | 200 | 149 | 7,619 | 4,161 | 1,606 | 904 | 449 | 421 | 28 | 97 | 224 | 178 |
| Construction trades | 252 | 139 | 27 | 23 | 21 | 19 | 2 | 12 | 28 | 2 | 288 | 165 | 43 | 38 | 20 | 14 | 6 | 8 | 12 | 2 |
| Education | 15,479 | 9,260 | 2,441 | 2,727 | 272 | 240 | 32 | 378 | 237 | 164 | 15,227 | 8,656 | 2,580 | 2,891 | 312 | 266 | 46 | 346 | 302 | 140 |
| Engineering | 570 | 284 | 40 | 115 | 69 | 67 | 2 | 9 | 20 | 33 | 672 | 344 | 35 | 133 | 89 | 87 | 2 | 8 | 17 | 46 |
| Engineering technologies and engineering-related fields* | 3,888 | 2,470 | 543 | 478 | 192 | 181 | 11 | 68 | 91 | 46 | 4,072 | 2,404 | 665 | 561 | 192 | 180 | 12 | 75 | 110 | 65 |
| English language and literature/letters | 1,402 | 730 | 136 | 364 | 75 | 71 | 4 | 11 | 61 | 25 | 1,522 | 704 | 141 | 482 | 93 | 90 | 3 | 16 | 63 | 23 |
| Family and consumer sciences/human sciences | 8,307 | 4,012 | 1,655 | 1,945 | 367 | 349 | 18 | 99 | 127 | 102 | 8,347 | 4,038 | 1,596 | 2,052 | 366 | 347 | 19 | 68 | 139 | 88 |
| Foreign languages, literatures, and linguistics | 1,805 | 1,016 | 93 | 520 | 59 | 55 | 4 | 16 | 43 | 58 | 1,597 | 781 | 101 | 548 | 55 | 49 | 6 | 18 | 63 | 31 |
| Health professions and related programs | 175,239 | 117,547 | 24,296 | 20,690 | 7,107 | 6,578 | 529 | 1,675 | 2,934 | 990 | 168,177 | 111,325 | 24,064 | 20,347 | 6,708 | 6,241 | 467 | 1,560 | 3,244 | 929 |
| Homeland security, law enforcement, and firefighting | 20,393 | 9,350 | 4,830 | 5,102 | 344 | 286 | 58 | 223 | 459 | 85 | 19,163 | 8,480 | 4,465 | 5,177 | 313 | 253 | 60 | 210 | 446 | 72 |
| Legal professions and studies | 8,842 | 5,664 | 1,294 | 1,362 | 192 | 171 | 21 | 88 | 196 | 46 | 7,733 | 4,753 | 1,259 | 1,266 | 163 | 144 | 19 | 67 | 172 | 53 |
| Liberal arts and sciences, general studies, and humanities | 217,487 | 125,516 | 30,079 | 40,686 | 9,613 | 8,832 | 781 | 2,094 | 5,525 | 3,974 | 226,487 | 126,839 | 31,699 | 45,422 | 9,853 | 9,169 | 684 | 2,125 | 6,342 | 4,207 |
| Library science | 166 | 126 | 9 | 19 | 8 | 8 | 0 | 9 | 2 | 1 | 145 | 102 | 10 | 27 | 3 | 3 | 0 | 1 | 2 | 0 |
| Mathematics and statistics | 649 | 253 | 14 | 199 | 108 | 108 | 0 | 9 | 23 | 43 | 782 | 329 | 28 | 216 | 142 | 140 | 2 | 3 | 30 | 34 |
| Mechanic and repair technologies/technicians | 1,049 | 643 | 131 | 158 | 48 | 42 | 6 | 30 | 30 | 9 | 1,050 | 667 | 128 | 168 | 24 | 17 | 7 | 22 | 31 | 10 |
| Military technologies and applied sciences | 186 | 106 | 34 | 24 | 10 | 9 | 1 | 0 | 12 | 0 | 214 | 124 | 42 | 27 | 10 | 6 | 4 | 1 | 10 | 0 |
| Multi/interdisciplinary studies | 16,770 | 8,542 | 1,425 | 4,161 | 1,734 | 1,665 | 69 | 125 | 487 | 296 | 17,141 | 8,364 | 1,535 | 4,293 | 1,945 | 1,874 | 71 | 109 | 592 | 303 |
| Parks, recreation, leisure, and fitness studies | 1,538 | 829 | 160 | 380 | 76 | 71 | 5 | 18 | 54 | 21 | 1,728 | 858 | 123 | 524 | 128 | 121 | 7 | 25 | 55 | 15 |
| Philosophy and religious studies | 152 | 56 | 58 | 23 | 11 | 8 | 3 | 0 | 3 | 1 | 358 | 260 | 44 | 23 | 5 | 4 | 1 | 1 | 7 | 18 |
| Physical sciences and science technologies | 2,828 | 1,383 | 377 | 489 | 335 | 324 | 11 | 31 | 76 | 137 | 3,071 | 1,406 | 353 | 596 | 425 | 409 | 16 | 38 | 109 | 144 |
| Precision production | 216 | 164 | 18 | 14 | 2 | 2 | 0 | 8 | 10 | 0 | 233 | 186 | 6 | 17 | 2 | 1 | 1 | 8 | 14 | 0 |
| Psychology | 5,794 | 2,492 | 479 | 2,128 | 337 | 323 | 14 | 94 | 196 | 68 | 6,689 | 2,583 | 574 | 2,672 | 410 | 395 | 15 | 107 | 258 | 85 |
| Public administration and social services | 7,638 | 3,937 | 2,149 | 1,184 | 86 | 71 | 15 | 97 | 137 | 48 | 7,183 | 3,641 | 1,896 | 1,231 | 105 | 87 | 18 | 117 | 151 | 42 |
| Social sciences and history | 10,356 | 4,143 | 945 | 3,612 | 936 | 877 | 59 | 163 | 381 | 176 | 11,242 | 4,285 | 1,069 | 4,089 | 1,062 | 992 | 70 | 136 | 421 | 180 |
| Social sciences | 9,936 | 3,910 | 930 | 3,488 | 922 | 865 | 57 | 158 | 354 | 174 | 10,743 | 4,028 | 1,041 | 3,934 | 1,044 | 977 | 67 | 127 | 391 | 178 |
| History | 420 | 233 | 15 | 124 | 14 | 12 | 2 | 5 | 27 | 2 | 499 | 257 | 28 | 155 | 18 | 15 | 3 | 9 | 30 | 2 |
| Theology and religious vocations | 488 | 317 | 115 | 37 | 1 | 1 | 0 | 8 | 5 | 5 | 582 | 330 | 159 | 67 | 8 | 5 | 3 | 9 | 6 | 3 |
| Transportation and materials moving | 333 | 169 | 31 | 69 | 18 | 16 | 0 | 4 | 16 | 26 | 287 | 149 | 31 | 50 | 13 | 12 | 1 | 2 | 15 | 27 |
| Visual and performing arts | 12,361 | 7,458 | 1,033 | 2,031 | 756 | 716 | 40 | 97 | 339 | 647 | 12,577 | 7,299 | 1,046 | 2,237 | 772 | 737 | 35 | 100 | 408 | 715 |
| Other and not classified | 0 | 0 | 0 | 0 | 0 | 0 | 0 | 0 | 0 | 0 | 0 | 0 | 0 | 0 | 0 | 0 | 0 | 0 | 0 | 0 |

**TABLE 2.5**

**Associate's degrees conferred to females by postsecondary institutions, by race/ethnicity and field of study, 2013–14 and 2014–15** [CONTINUED]

*Excludes "construction trades" and "mechanic and repair technologies/technicians," which are listed separately.

Note: Data are for degree-granting postsecondary institutions, which are institutions that grant associate's or higher degrees and participate in Title IV federal financial aid programs. Race categories exclude persons of Hispanic ethnicity. Reported racial/ethnic distributions of students by level of degree, field of degree, and sex were used to estimate race/ethnicity for students whose race/ethnicity was not reported. To facilitate trend comparisons, certain aggregations have been made of the degree fields as reported in the Integrated Postsecondary Education Data System (IPEDS): "agriculture and natural resources" includes agriculture, agriculture operations, and related sciences and natural resources and conservation; and "business" includes business management, marketing, and related support services and personal and culinary services. Some data have been revised from previously published figures.

SOURCE: "Table 321.50. Associate's Degrees Conferred to Females by Postsecondary Institutions, by Race/Ethnicity and Field of Study: 2013–14 and 2014–15," in *Digest of Education Statistics: 2016*, US Department of Education, Institute of Education Sciences, National Center for Education Statistics, September 2016, https://nces.ed.gov/programs/digest/d16/tables/dt16_321.50.asp (accessed January 18, 2018)

# TABLE 2.6

**Bachelor's degrees conferred to females by postsecondary institutions, by race/ethnicity and field of study, 2013–14 and 2014–15**

Each year block below is ordered: Total, White, Black, Hispanic, then Asian/Pacific Islander (Total, Asian, Pacific Islander), American Indian/Alaska Native, Two or more races, Non-resident alien.

| Field of study | 2013–14 Total | White | Black | Hispanic | A/PI Total | Asian | Pacific Islander | Amer. Indian/Alaska Native | Two or more races | Non-resident alien | 2014–15 Total | White | Black | Hispanic | A/PI Total | Asian | Pacific Islander | Amer. Indian/Alaska Native | Two or more races | Non-resident alien |
|---|---|---|---|---|---|---|---|---|---|---|---|---|---|---|---|---|---|---|---|---|
| All fields, total | 1,068,245 | 682,989 | 123,147 | 122,113 | 71,818 | 68,881 | 2,937 | 6,613 | 27,285 | 34,280 | 1,082,265 | 679,928 | 123,440 | 130,990 | 72,883 | 70,125 | 2,758 | 6,145 | 31,966 | 36,913 |
| Agriculture and natural resources | 17,871 | 14,085 | 608 | 1,294 | 820 | 766 | 54 | 121 | 538 | 405 | 18,692 | 14,513 | 612 | 1,513 | 877 | 828 | 49 | 131 | 604 | 442 |
| Architecture and related services | 3,975 | 2,360 | 237 | 531 | 385 | 379 | 6 | 13 | 87 | 362 | 3,974 | 2,178 | 183 | 571 | 450 | 442 | 8 | 17 | 130 | 445 |
| Area, ethnic, cultural, gender, and group studies | 5,809 | 2,681 | 805 | 1,143 | 579 | 559 | 20 | 133 | 283 | 185 | 5,489 | 2,457 | 836 | 1,131 | 501 | 479 | 22 | 108 | 285 | 171 |
| Biological and biomedical sciences | 61,217 | 36,503 | 5,350 | 5,965 | 9,503 | 9,332 | 171 | 303 | 1,903 | 1,690 | 64,794 | 38,048 | 5,670 | 6,977 | 9,763 | 9,619 | 144 | 264 | 2,356 | 1,716 |
| Business | 169,664 | 97,933 | 22,920 | 19,366 | 13,110 | 12,515 | 595 | 1,112 | 3,447 | 11,776 | 172,489 | 98,864 | 22,562 | 20,536 | 13,215 | 12,704 | 511 | 996 | 3,955 | 12,361 |
| Communication, journalism, and related programs | 56,638 | 38,223 | 6,206 | 6,183 | 2,439 | 2,337 | 102 | 250 | 1,633 | 1,704 | 58,799 | 38,475 | 6,433 | 7,129 | 2,465 | 2,347 | 118 | 217 | 2,026 | 2,054 |
| Communications technologies | 1,572 | 963 | 208 | 145 | 125 | 119 | 6 | 7 | 62 | 62 | 1,768 | 1,083 | 198 | 185 | 130 | 123 | 7 | 11 | 93 | 68 |
| Computer and information sciences | 9,951 | 5,150 | 1,592 | 908 | 1,316 | 1,277 | 39 | 62 | 288 | 635 | 10,741 | 5,354 | 1,579 | 1,001 | 1,592 | 1,542 | 50 | 67 | 365 | 783 |
| Construction trades | 25 | 13 | 1 | 9 | 2 | 2 | | | | | 18 | 9 | 1 | 3 | | | | 1 | | 4 |
| Education | 78,481 | 62,449 | 5,901 | 5,942 | 1,720 | 1,550 | 170 | 597 | 1,211 | 661 | 73,150 | 57,400 | 5,583 | 5,896 | 1,648 | 1,507 | 141 | 534 | 1,402 | 687 |
| Engineering | 18,263 | 10,813 | 963 | 1,716 | 2,510 | 2,474 | 36 | 82 | 530 | 1,649 | 19,603 | 11,453 | 983 | 1,954 | 2,670 | 2,636 | 34 | 75 | 685 | 1,783 |
| Engineering technologies and engineering-related fields* | 1,726 | 1,072 | 266 | 176 | 80 | 76 | 4 | 21 | 32 | 79 | 1,918 | 1,185 | 300 | 192 | 97 | 94 | 3 | 15 | 54 | 75 |
| English language and literature/letters | 34,633 | 24,695 | 2,979 | 3,734 | 1,511 | 1,459 | 52 | 167 | 1,121 | 426 | 31,794 | 22,482 | 2,643 | 3,576 | 1,273 | 1,222 | 51 | 153 | 1,244 | 423 |
| Family and consumer sciences/human sciences | 21,680 | 14,526 | 2,627 | 2,416 | 1,137 | 1,075 | 62 | 164 | 499 | 311 | 21,572 | 14,061 | 2,735 | 2,596 | 1,111 | 1,078 | 33 | 140 | 596 | 333 |
| Foreign languages, literatures, and linguistics | 14,066 | 8,773 | 661 | 3,029 | 799 | 776 | 23 | 44 | 451 | 309 | 13,426 | 8,052 | 676 | 2,989 | 806 | 791 | 15 | 47 | 521 | 335 |
| Health professions and related programs | 167,845 | 114,748 | 20,307 | 14,663 | 12,025 | 11,425 | 600 | 919 | 3,355 | 1,828 | 182,570 | 124,375 | 21,314 | 17,059 | 12,854 | 12,255 | 599 | 965 | 4,231 | 1,772 |
| Homeland security, law enforcement, and firefighting | 29,009 | 14,127 | 7,490 | 5,612 | 658 | 553 | 105 | 217 | 691 | 214 | 29,083 | 13,697 | 7,423 | 6,027 | 669 | 576 | 93 | 239 | 835 | 193 |
| Legal professions and studies | 3,057 | 1,708 | 561 | 452 | 147 | 142 | 5 | 38 | 84 | 67 | 3,072 | 1,751 | 569 | 489 | 114 | 106 | 8 | 25 | 90 | 34 |
| Liberal arts and sciences, general studies, and humanities | 28,786 | 18,105 | 4,245 | 3,833 | 1,027 | 948 | 79 | 270 | 834 | 472 | 27,511 | 17,295 | 3,966 | 3,657 | 1,021 | 956 | 65 | 247 | 822 | 503 |
| Library science | 16 | 11 | | 1 | | | | 1 | 2 | | 83 | 66 | 7 | 4 | 1 | 0 | 1 | 1 | 4 | 0 |
| Mathematics and statistics | 9,017 | 5,558 | 521 | 786 | 864 | 849 | 15 | 27 | 218 | 1,043 | 9,391 | 5,513 | 518 | 879 | 964 | 948 | 16 | 26 | 260 | 1,231 |
| Mechanic and repair technologies/technicians | 21 | 13 | | 4 | 2 | 2 | | 1 | | 1 | 25 | 16 | | 3 | 2 | 2 | | 1 | 1 | 2 |
| Military technologies and applied sciences | 24 | 8 | 8 | 4 | 2 | 1 | 1 | | 2 | | 51 | 37 | 8 | 3 | | | 1 | | 2 | |
| Multi/interdisciplinary studies | 32,266 | 19,908 | 3,977 | 4,723 | 1,905 | 1,822 | 83 | 231 | 852 | 670 | 31,626 | 19,052 | 3,784 | 5,021 | 1,848 | 1,770 | 78 | 195 | 1,012 | 714 |
| Parks, recreation, leisure, and fitness studies | 21,330 | 15,526 | 1,952 | 1,992 | 889 | 825 | 64 | 160 | 515 | 296 | 23,058 | 16,306 | 2,175 | 2,335 | 1,010 | 951 | 59 | 140 | 774 | 318 |
| Philosophy and religious studies | 4,416 | 2,982 | 403 | 431 | 299 | 286 | 13 | 33 | 154 | 114 | 4,068 | 2,728 | 360 | 435 | 248 | 237 | 11 | 17 | 164 | 116 |
| Physical sciences and science technologies | 11,503 | 7,318 | 869 | 873 | 1,406 | 1,382 | 24 | 82 | 361 | 594 | 11,560 | 7,273 | 806 | 1,073 | 1,347 | 1,323 | 24 | 57 | 375 | 629 |
| Precision production | 16 | 11 | 1 | 1 | | | | 1 | 2 | | 15 | 6 | 2 | 2 | | | | | 4 | 1 |
| Psychology | 90,006 | 54,737 | 11,393 | 13,332 | 5,523 | 5,311 | 212 | 513 | 2,674 | 1,834 | 90,755 | 53,916 | 11,597 | 14,329 | 5,497 | 5,276 | 221 | 472 | 3,017 | 1,927 |
| Public administration and social services | 27,567 | 15,423 | 6,235 | 3,938 | 810 | 724 | 86 | 251 | 633 | 277 | 28,218 | 15,738 | 6,335 | 4,045 | 865 | 780 | 85 | 228 | 740 | 267 |
| Social sciences and history | 84,878 | 48,916 | 9,885 | 12,526 | 6,254 | 6,066 | 188 | 464 | 2,882 | 3,951 | 81,466 | 45,108 | 9,601 | 12,678 | 6,109 | 5,919 | 190 | 440 | 3,040 | 4,490 |
| Social sciences | 72,519 | 39,625 | 9,120 | 11,197 | 5,844 | 5,682 | 162 | 388 | 2,508 | 3,837 | 70,214 | 36,753 | 8,903 | 11,441 | 5,720 | 5,538 | 182 | 385 | 2,666 | 4,346 |
| History | 12,359 | 9,291 | 765 | 1,329 | 410 | 384 | 26 | 76 | 374 | 114 | 11,252 | 8,355 | 698 | 1,237 | 389 | 381 | 8 | 55 | 374 | 144 |
| Theology and religious vocations | 3,048 | 2,295 | 334 | 201 | 83 | 79 | 4 | 19 | 53 | 63 | 3,096 | 2,284 | 366 | 206 | 81 | 69 | 12 | 15 | 69 | 75 |
| Transportation and materials moving | 535 | 347 | 52 | 61 | 34 | 28 | 6 | 6 | 13 | 22 | 578 | 380 | 46 | 53 | 39 | 35 | 4 | 1 | 22 | 37 |
| Visual and performing arts | 59,237 | 40,926 | 3,581 | 6,120 | 3,852 | 3,740 | 112 | 304 | 1,876 | 2,578 | 57,812 | 38,773 | 3,568 | 6,443 | 3,613 | 3,507 | 106 | 300 | 2,193 | 2,922 |
| Other and not classified | 0 | 0 | 0 | 0 | 0 | 0 | 0 | 0 | 0 | 0 | 0 | 0 | 0 | 0 | 0 | 0 | 0 | 0 | 0 | 0 |

## TABLE 2.6

**Bachelor's degrees conferred to females by postsecondary institutions, by race/ethnicity and field of study, 2013–14 and 2014–15** [CONTINUED]

*Excludes "Construction trades" and "Mechanic and repair technologies/technicians," which are listed separately.

Note: Data are for postsecondary institutions participating in Title IV federal financial aid programs. Race categories exclude persons of Hispanic ethnicity. Reported racial/ethnic distributions of students by level of degree, field of degree, and sex were used to estimate race/ethnicity for students whose race/ethnicity was not reported. To facilitate trend comparisons, certain aggregations have been made of the degree fields as reported in the Integrated Postsecondary Education Data System (IPEDS): "agriculture and natural resources" includes agriculture, agriculture operations, and related sciences and natural resources and conservation; and "business" includes business management, marketing, and related support services and personal and culinary services. Some data have been revised from previously published figures.

SOURCE: "Table 322.50. Bachelor's Degrees Conferred to Females by Postsecondary Institutions, by Race/Ethnicity and Field of Study: 2013–14 and 2014–15," in *Digest of Education Statistics: 2016*, US Department of Education, Institute of Education Sciences, National Center for Education Statistics, September 2016, https://nces.ed.gov/programs/digest/d16/tables/dt16_322.50.asp (accessed January 18, 2018)

**FIGURE 2.6**

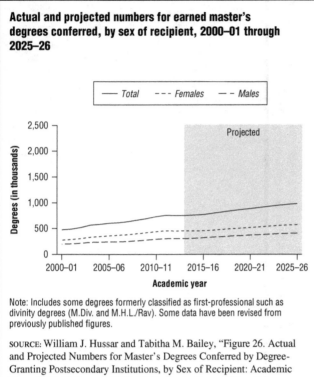

Actual and projected numbers for earned master's degrees conferred, by sex of recipient, 2000–01 through 2025–26

Note: Includes some degrees formerly classified as first-professional such as divinity degrees (M.Div. and M.H.L./Rav). Some data have been revised from previously published figures.

SOURCE: William J. Hussar and Tabitha M. Bailey, "Figure 26. Actual and Projected Numbers for Master's Degrees Conferred by Degree-Granting Postsecondary Institutions, by Sex of Recipient: Academic Years 2000–01 through 2025–26," in *Projections of Education Statistics to 2025*, US Department of Education, Institute of Education Sciences, National Center for Education Statistics, September 2017, https://nces.ed.gov/pubs2017/2017019.pdf (accessed January 18, 2018)

2004–05, before slightly surpassing 50% the following year, when 69,144 women earned doctor's degrees. Each year since then, women have earned more doctor's degrees than men. In 2014–15 women accounted for 93,626 doctor's degrees, or 52.4% of the total 178,547 awarded. Hussar and Bailey note that the number of women earning doctor's degrees increased 66% between 2000–01 and 2013–14, compared with a 33% increase for men. They estimate that between 2013–14 and 2025–26 this growth will slow to 19%, but will continue to outpace the growth among men, whose growth is projected to be 16% for the same period. Women are projected to earn 110,000 (52.6%) of the total 209,000 doctor's degrees projected to be awarded in 2025–26.

**FIELDS OF STUDY.** A majority of the 93,626 doctor's degrees awarded to women in 2014–15 were in the fields of health professions and related programs (41,577, or 44.4%) and legal professions and studies (19,365 degrees, or 20.7% of the total). (See Table 2.8.) Other popular doctor's programs for those women who earned degrees in 2014–15 were education (7,934 degrees), psychology (4,959 degrees), and biological and biomedical sciences (4,290 degrees).

## ACHIEVING EDUCATIONAL EQUITY
### Single-Sex or Coeducational Schools?

Before the late 1960s many private high schools and colleges were single-sex schools. By the end of the 20th century most schools were coeducational. The early 21st century, however, saw renewed interest and an increase in the number of single-sex schools, particularly for girls.

Proponents of single-sex education for girls often cite findings by Linda J. Sax et al. in *Women Graduates of Single-Sex and Coeducational High Schools: Differences in Their Characteristics and the Transition to College* (March 2009, http://www.heri.ucla.edu/PDFs/Sax_FINAL %20REPORT_Sing_1F02B4.pdf), a study based on data from the annual Freshman Survey, which is administered by the Cooperative Institutional Research Program at the Higher Education Research Institute at the University of California, Los Angeles. Comparing survey responses from 6,552 female graduates of single-sex high schools versus 14,684 female graduates of coed high schools, the study concludes that girls' school graduates consistently have better academic outcomes than do their peers who graduate from coeducational institutions. They assess their own abilities, self-confidence, and ambition above that of their coed peers, and more graduates of single-sex high schools plan to go to college than do graduates of coed schools. They have greater confidence in their mathematics and computer abilities and are more likely to consider careers in traditionally male fields such as engineering. They also study longer hours, make more effort to talk with teachers outside of class, and tutor others—in effect, they put more effort into their education than do their peers at coed schools.

The number of single-sex public schools in the United States has increased considerably since 2006, when the US Department of Education eased restrictions that prohibited separating public-school students according to sex. Juliet Williams of the University of California, Los Angeles, estimates in *The Separation Solution?: Single-Sex Education and the New Politics of Gender Equality* (2016) that there were nearly 80 single-sex public schools in the United States in 2016, up from just three in 1990, while approximately 1,000 schools across the country were offering separate instruction for boys and girls in certain academic subjects, such as reading and math. Williams describes the widespread inclination for schools to experiment with single-sex instruction, despite the lack of substantive evidence proving its benefits, as part of a "desperate search for alternatives to the dismal failure of the status quo approach in public education."

As of April 2018, the most exhaustive academic study on the outcomes of single-sex education in the United States was "The Effects of Single-Sex Compared with Coeducational Schooling on Students' Performance and Attitudes: A Meta-analysis" (*Psychological Bulletin*, July 2014) by Erin Pahlke, Janet S. Hyde, and Carlie M. Allison. This report reflects the researchers' meta-analysis of data from 184 previous studies, representing the testing of 1.6 million students in grades kindergarten to 12 from

**TABLE 2.7.**

**Master's degrees conferred to females by postsecondary institutions, by race/ethnicity and field of study, 2013–14 and 2014–15**

| Field of study | 2013–14 | | | | | | | | | | 2014–15 | | | | | | | | | |
|---|---|---|---|---|---|---|---|---|---|---|---|---|---|---|---|---|---|---|---|---|
| | | | | | Asian/Pacific Islander | | | American Indian/Alaska Native | Two or more races | Non-resident alien | | | | | Asian/Pacific Islander | | | American Indian/Alaska Native | Two or more races | Non-resident alien |
| | Total | White | Black | Hispanic | Total | Asian | Pacific Islander | | | | Total | White | Black | Hispanic | Total | Asian | Pacific Islander | | | |
| **All fields, total** | 451,736 | 271,468 | 61,998 | 35,397 | 24,578 | 23,493 | 1,085 | 2,293 | 8,527 | 47,475 | 452,118 | 264,954 | 60,948 | 37,335 | 24,929 | 23,961 | 968 | 2,187 | 9,186 | 52,579 |
| Agriculture and natural resources | 3,578 | 2,522 | 130 | 182 | 126 | 123 | 3 | 12 | 63 | 543 | 3,522 | 2,421 | 122 | 182 | 132 | 124 | 8 | 28 | 81 | 556 |
| Architecture and related services | 3,926 | 1,975 | 173 | 340 | 318 | 313 | 5 | 14 | 89 | 1,017 | 3,859 | 1,812 | 180 | 334 | 283 | 280 | 3 | 8 | 99 | 1,143 |
| Area, ethnic, cultural, gender, and group studies | 1,213 | 531 | 129 | 169 | 83 | 77 | 6 | 31 | 46 | 224 | 1,181 | 555 | 112 | 161 | 85 | 81 | 4 | 25 | 44 | 199 |
| Biological and biomedical sciences | 7,891 | 4,202 | 596 | 493 | 1,050 | 1,039 | 11 | 31 | 184 | 1,335 | 8,401 | 4,360 | 663 | 545 | 1,081 | 1,073 | 8 | 20 | 202 | 1,530 |
| Business | 88,303 | 41,664 | 17,231 | 6,513 | 6,284 | 6,040 | 244 | 433 | 1,437 | 14,741 | 86,635 | 39,857 | 16,324 | 6,904 | 6,293 | 6,024 | 269 | 434 | 1,621 | 15,202 |
| Communication, journalism, and related programs | 6,544 | 3,425 | 834 | 549 | 271 | 267 | 4 | 21 | 189 | 1,255 | 6,765 | 3,502 | 855 | 518 | 275 | 270 | 5 | 22 | 182 | 1,411 |
| Communications technologies | 255 | 88 | 23 | 8 | 13 | 13 | 0 | 1 | 4 | 118 | 259 | 68 | 22 | 27 | 15 | 15 | 0 | 0 | 3 | 124 |
| Computer and information sciences | 7,042 | 1,787 | 763 | 224 | 728 | 715 | 13 | 25 | 95 | 3,420 | 9,582 | 1,949 | 785 | 279 | 855 | 840 | 15 | 15 | 123 | 5,576 |
| Construction trades | 0 | 0 | 0 | 0 | 0 | 0 | 0 | 0 | 0 | 0 | 0 | 0 | 0 | 0 | 0 | 0 | 0 | 0 | 0 | 0 |
| Education | 118,681 | 84,741 | 14,129 | 10,263 | 3,710 | 3,417 | 293 | 628 | 1,838 | 3,372 | 112,581 | 79,420 | 13,071 | 10,624 | 3,529 | 3,300 | 229 | 580 | 1,998 | 3,359 |
| Engineering | 10,214 | 3,113 | 305 | 493 | 1,050 | 1,043 | 7 | 8 | 145 | 5,100 | 11,471 | 3,141 | 316 | 467 | 1,049 | 1,040 | 9 | 16 | 159 | 6,323 |
| Engineering technologies and engineering-related fields* | 1,338 | 530 | 134 | 64 | 81 | 80 | 1 | 7 | 24 | 498 | 1,516 | 613 | 144 | 90 | 87 | 87 | 0 | 10 | 20 | 552 |
| English language and literature/letters | 6,179 | 4,731 | 373 | 434 | 210 | 199 | 11 | 23 | 180 | 228 | 5,876 | 4,384 | 377 | 422 | 216 | 212 | 4 | 33 | 184 | 260 |
| Family and consumer sciences/human sciences | 2,664 | 1,729 | 393 | 183 | 93 | 85 | 8 | 14 | 61 | 191 | 2,719 | 1,703 | 435 | 213 | 127 | 119 | 8 | 24 | 42 | 175 |
| Foreign languages, literatures, and linguistics | 2,260 | 1,186 | 57 | 372 | 93 | 84 | 9 | 9 | 51 | 492 | 2,325 | 1,132 | 44 | 406 | 84 | 84 | 0 | 2 | 46 | 611 |
| Health professions and related programs | 79,665 | 53,820 | 10,462 | 5,328 | 5,692 | 5,453 | 239 | 394 | 1,475 | 2,494 | 84,117 | 56,442 | 11,063 | 5,812 | 6,240 | 6,040 | 200 | 406 | 1,641 | 2,513 |
| Homeland security, law enforcement, and firefighting | 4,645 | 2,416 | 1,356 | 495 | 135 | 121 | 14 | 36 | 113 | 94 | 4,861 | 2,560 | 1,435 | 511 | 118 | 102 | 16 | 30 | 122 | 85 |
| Legal professions and studies | 4,087 | 1,042 | 375 | 222 | 149 | 146 | 3 | 23 | 45 | 2,231 | 4,236 | 982 | 423 | 185 | 147 | 142 | 5 | 32 | 45 | 2,427 |
| Liberal arts and sciences, general studies, and humanities | 1,793 | 1,185 | 257 | 136 | 49 | 45 | 4 | 14 | 35 | 117 | 1,795 | 1,165 | 229 | 156 | 52 | 50 | 2 | 13 | 55 | 125 |
| Library science | 4,780 | 3,866 | 216 | 292 | 196 | 184 | 12 | 30 | 107 | 73 | 4,234 | 3,349 | 233 | 329 | 131 | 126 | 5 | 24 | 105 | 63 |
| Mathematics and statistics | 3,017 | 1,073 | 77 | 88 | 234 | 233 | 1 | 1 | 26 | 1,518 | 3,081 | 988 | 67 | 81 | 224 | 223 | 1 | 4 | 36 | 1,681 |
| Mechanic and repair technologies/technicians | 0 | 0 | 0 | 0 | 0 | 0 | 0 | 0 | 0 | 0 | 0 | 0 | 0 | 0 | 0 | 0 | 0 | 0 | 0 | 0 |
| Military technologies and applied sciences | 8 | 6 | 0 | 0 | 0 | 0 | 0 | 0 | 0 | 2 | 27 | 19 | 5 | 0 | 2 | 2 | 0 | 0 | 2 | 1 |
| Multi/interdisciplinary studies | 5,055 | 3,128 | 485 | 352 | 248 | 235 | 13 | 21 | 161 | 660 | 4,953 | 2,965 | 476 | 382 | 268 | 258 | 10 | 24 | 121 | 717 |
| Parks, recreation, leisure, and fitness studies | 3,271 | 2,316 | 396 | 205 | 81 | 76 | 5 | 17 | 81 | 175 | 3,310 | 2,381 | 382 | 177 | 83 | 69 | 14 | 20 | 96 | 171 |
| Philosophy and religious studies | 783 | 495 | 119 | 47 | 39 | 37 | 2 | 5 | 16 | 62 | 690 | 500 | 54 | 31 | 24 | 24 | 0 | 1 | 16 | 64 |
| Physical sciences and science technologies | 2,672 | 1,492 | 97 | 112 | 152 | 151 | 1 | 3 | 57 | 759 | 2,662 | 1,427 | 102 | 139 | 147 | 146 | 1 | 6 | 57 | 784 |
| Precision production | 5 | 1 | 0 | 0 | 0 | 0 | 0 | 0 | 0 | 3 | 1 | 1 | 0 | 0 | 0 | 0 | 0 | 0 | 0 | 0 |
| Psychology | 22,197 | 14,481 | 3,187 | 2,253 | 907 | 846 | 61 | 136 | 499 | 734 | 21,235 | 13,641 | 3,028 | 2,323 | 836 | 774 | 62 | 112 | 528 | 767 |
| Public administration and social services | 33,674 | 18,825 | 7,031 | 3,894 | 1,265 | 1,194 | 71 | 244 | 887 | 1,528 | 34,896 | 19,412 | 7,286 | 4,330 | 1,272 | 1,212 | 60 | 219 | 899 | 1,478 |
| Social sciences and history | 10,733 | 5,976 | 997 | 850 | 502 | 488 | 14 | 49 | 301 | 2,058 | 10,215 | 5,540 | 972 | 862 | 482 | 472 | 10 | 39 | 285 | 2,035 |
| Social sciences | 8,980 | 4,603 | 906 | 724 | 465 | 453 | 12 | 34 | 251 | 1,997 | 8,572 | 4,240 | 897 | 752 | 448 | 440 | 8 | 26 | 233 | 1,976 |
| History | 1,753 | 1,373 | 91 | 126 | 37 | 35 | 2 | 15 | 50 | 61 | 1,643 | 1,300 | 75 | 110 | 34 | 32 | 2 | 13 | 52 | 59 |
| Theology and religious vocations | 4,883 | 3,039 | 1,095 | 215 | 214 | 202 | 12 | 20 | 75 | 225 | 4,834 | 2,911 | 1,129 | 229 | 216 | 211 | 5 | 14 | 84 | 251 |
| Transportation and materials moving | 223 | 145 | 25 | 21 | 6 | 6 | 0 | 4 | 10 | 12 | 166 | 103 | 13 | 16 | 8 | 7 | 1 | 1 | 5 | 20 |
| Visual and performing arts | 10,157 | 5,938 | 553 | 600 | 599 | 581 | 18 | 39 | 232 | 2,196 | 10,113 | 5,651 | 601 | 600 | 568 | 554 | 14 | 25 | 292 | 2,376 |
| Other and not classified | 0 | 0 | 0 | 0 | 0 | 0 | 0 | 0 | 0 | 0 | 0 | 0 | 0 | 0 | 0 | 0 | 0 | 0 | 0 | 0 |

## TABLE 2.7

**Master's degrees conferred to females by postsecondary institutions, by race/ethnicity and field of study, 2013–14 and 2014–15** [CONTINUED]

*Excludes "construction trades" and "mechanic and repair technologies/technicians," which are listed separately.

Note: Data are for postsecondary institutions participating in Title IV federal financial aid programs. Race categories exclude persons of Hispanic ethnicity. Reported racial/ethnic distributions of students by level of degree, field of degree, and sex were used to estimate race/ethnicity for students whose race/ethnicity was not reported. To facilitate trend comparisons, certain aggregations have been made of the degree fields as reported in the Integrated Postsecondary Education Data System (IPEDS): "agriculture and natural resources" includes agriculture, agriculture operations, and related sciences and natural resources and conservation; and "business" includes business management, marketing, and related support services and personal and culinary services. Some data have been revised from previously published figures.

SOURCE: "Table 323.50. Master's Degrees Conferred to Females by Postsecondary Institutions, by Race/Ethnicity and Field of Study: 2013–14 and 2014–15," in *Digest of Education Statistics: 2016*, US Department of Education, Institute of Education Sciences, National Center for Education Statistics, September 2016, https://nces.ed.gov/programs/digest/d16/tables/dt16_323.50.asp (accessed January 18, 2018)

FIGURE 2.7

**Actual and projected numbers for earned doctor's degrees conferred, by sex of recipient, 2000–01 through 2025–26**

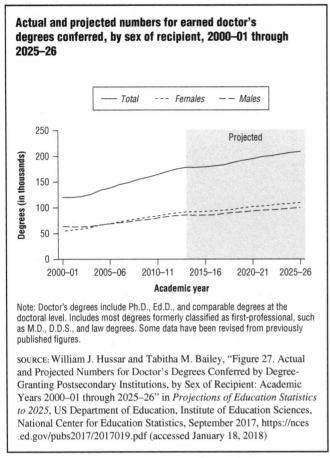

Note: Doctor's degrees include Ph.D., Ed.D., and comparable degrees at the doctoral level. Includes most degrees formerly classified as first-professional, such as M.D., D.D.S., and law degrees. Some data have been revised from previously published figures.

SOURCE: William J. Hussar and Tabitha M. Bailey, "Figure 27. Actual and Projected Numbers for Doctor's Degrees Conferred by Degree-Granting Postsecondary Institutions, by Sex of Recipient: Academic Years 2000–01 through 2025–26" in *Projections of Education Statistics to 2025*, US Department of Education, Institute of Education Sciences, National Center for Education Statistics, September 2017, https://nces.ed.gov/pubs2017/2017019.pdf (accessed January 18, 2018)

21 nations for a range of outcomes, from math and science performance to educational aspirations, self-concept, and gender stereotyping. Ultimately, Pahlke, Hyde, and Allison find no substantive advantages—either academic or social—to single-sex education, either for girls or for boys. Moreover, in "Study Challenges Claims of Single-Sex Schooling Benefits" (Wisc.edu, February 3, 2014), David Tenenbaum quotes Hyde, who explained, "There is a mountain of research in social psychology showing that segregation by race or gender feeds stereotypes, and that's not what we want. The adult world is an integrated world, in the workplace and in the family, and the best thing we can do is provide that environment for children in school as we prepare them for adulthood."

## TITLE IX

Title IX of the Education Amendments of 1972 prohibits sex discrimination in any education program or activity that receives federal funding, including athletics. Since its passage, Title IX has led to dramatic increases in girls' and women's participation in school athletics. The National Coalition for Women and Girls in Education (NCWGE) reports in *Title IX at 45: Advancing Opportunity through Equity in Education* (2017, http://www.ncwge.org/TitleIX45/Title%20IX%20at%2045-Advancing%20Opportunity%20through%20Equity%20in%20Educa

tion.pdf) that girls' participation in high school athletics has risen from fewer than 300,000 during the 1971–72 school year (immediately before the legislation passed) to 3.3 million in 2015–16. Although female participation in high school athletics still lags behind that of males, in 2015–16 girls accounted for 42% of all high school athletes, up from 7% in 1971–72.

Title IX has also increased the number of women's sports teams and the level of female participation in athletics at the college level. The NCWGE reports that the number of women participating in college athletics grew from 29,977 in 1971–72 to 214,086 in 2015–16—an increase of 614%. The coalition cites numerous studies finding that participation in sports is associated with short- and long-term health benefits, including reduced risk of obesity, heart disease, osteoporosis, and breast cancer. Furthermore, girls who play sports indicate higher levels of confidence and self-esteem, more positive body image, and lower levels of depression, compared with their peers who do not play sports. Title IX has also led to dramatic increases in the opportunities for female athletes to earn college scholarships. According to the NCWGE, in 1972 women's teams received only 2% of collegiate athletic budgets, while athletic scholarships for women were "nonexistent"; by 2013–14 women received 47% of the total athletic scholarship dollars at Division I schools (although they continued to receive less than their share of total school athletic spending, despite making up more than 50% of the student body).

In spite of being known as a law applying to athletics, Title IX was also designed to address inequalities in educational opportunity. In 2012 the administration of President Barack Obama (1961–) announced that it would use the law to encourage greater female participation in educational fields from which they had been either intentionally or accidentally excluded—namely, the so-called STEM fields (science, technology, engineering, and mathematics). In October 2012 the Department of Education's Office for Civil Rights released *Title IX and Access to Courses and Programs in Science, Technology, Engineering, and Math* (http://www2.ed.gov/about/offices/list/ocr/presentations/stem-t9-powerpoint.pdf), an updated guideline that explicitly addresses the application of Title IX to STEM in kindergarten to 12th grade and postsecondary institutions. The report explains and illustrates how schools receiving federal funding must ensure equal access to STEM educational programs, such as through their admission and recruitment practices, distribution of scholarships and fellowships, administration of courses, policies toward married students and those with children, and other aspects of educational programming.

Under Title IX, sexual harassment, rape, and sexual assault also amount to sex discrimination, given that these behaviors create a hostile educational environment that can impede access to educational opportunities. As

## TABLE 2.8

**Doctor's degrees conferred to females by postsecondary institutions, by race/ethnicity and field of study, 2013–14 and 2014–15**

| Field of study | 2013–14 Total | White | Black | Hispanic | A/PI Total | Asian | Pacific Islander | American Indian/Alaska Native | Two or more races | Nonresident alien | 2014–15 Total | White | Black | Hispanic | A/PI Total | Asian | Pacific Islander | American Indian/Alaska Native | Two or more races | Nonresident alien |
|---|---|---|---|---|---|---|---|---|---|---|---|---|---|---|---|---|---|---|---|---|
| All fields, total | 92,002 | 56,783 | 8,111 | 5,877 | 10,848 | 10,673 | 175 | 496 | 1,669 | 8,218 | 93,626 | 56,847 | 8,811 | 6,246 | 10,860 | 10,677 | 183 | 474 | 1,993 | 8,395 |
| Agriculture and natural resources | 668 | 323 | 21 | 22 | 29 | 29 | 0 | 2 | 4 | 267 | 750 | 388 | 18 | 28 | 29 | 28 | 1 | 7 | 10 | 270 |
| Architecture and related services | 113 | 35 | 12 | 6 | 11 | 10 | 1 | 0 | 3 | 46 | 127 | 45 | 3 | 9 | 16 | 16 | 0 | 0 | 5 | 49 |
| Area, ethnic, cultural, gender, and group studies | 206 | 88 | 39 | 15 | 17 | 17 | 0 | 6 | 7 | 34 | 192 | 93 | 32 | 20 | 8 | 7 | 1 | 9 | 6 | 24 |
| Biological and biomedical sciences | 4,418 | 2,342 | 195 | 199 | 420 | 410 | 10 | 14 | 60 | 1,188 | 4,290 | 2,205 | 157 | 236 | 445 | 438 | 7 | 15 | 66 | 1,166 |
| Business | 1,317 | 583 | 316 | 53 | 78 | 77 | 1 | 5 | 9 | 273 | 1,400 | 593 | 367 | 54 | 109 | 105 | 4 | 9 | 12 | 256 |
| Communication, journalism, and related programs | 345 | 195 | 21 | 26 | 13 | 13 | 0 | 1 | 3 | 86 | 385 | 218 | 33 | 14 | 16 | 16 | 0 | 0 | 3 | 101 |
| Communications technologies | 2 | 0 | 1 | 0 | 1 | 1 | 0 | 0 | 0 | 0 | 0 | 0 | 0 | 0 | 0 | 0 | 0 | 0 | 0 | 0 |
| Computer and information sciences | 416 | 120 | 21 | 13 | 42 | 42 | 0 | 2 | 1 | 217 | 450 | 121 | 26 | 11 | 38 | 38 | 0 | 0 | 4 | 250 |
| Construction trades | 0 | 0 | 0 | 0 | 0 | 0 | 0 | 0 | 0 | 0 | 0 | 0 | 0 | 0 | 0 | 0 | 0 | 0 | 0 | 0 |
| Education | 7,465 | 4,567 | 1,533 | 569 | 288 | 278 | 10 | 46 | 87 | 375 | 7,934 | 4,745 | 1,714 | 573 | 332 | 307 | 25 | 53 | 105 | 412 |
| Engineering | 2,271 | 680 | 70 | 72 | 235 | 233 | 2 | 2 | 19 | 1,193 | 2,367 | 744 | 56 | 74 | 219 | 219 | 0 | 4 | 35 | 1,235 |
| Engineering technologies and engineering-related fields* | 26 | 15 | 0 | 0 | 0 | 0 | 0 | 1 | 0 | 10 | 37 | 14 | 3 | 1 | 2 | 2 | 0 | 0 | 1 | 16 |
| English language and literature/letters | 836 | 656 | 37 | 28 | 35 | 35 | 0 | 3 | 9 | 68 | 864 | 679 | 27 | 33 | 40 | 40 | 0 | 4 | 11 | 70 |
| Family and consumer sciences/human sciences | 273 | 154 | 33 | 7 | 18 | 18 | 0 | 0 | 2 | 59 | 256 | 141 | 29 | 12 | 13 | 12 | 1 | 1 | 5 | 55 |
| Foreign languages, literatures, and linguistics | 732 | 379 | 12 | 77 | 48 | 48 | 0 | 2 | 6 | 208 | 711 | 351 | 6 | 98 | 33 | 33 | 0 | 1 | 12 | 210 |
| Health professions and related programs | 39,365 | 25,630 | 2,709 | 2,027 | 6,912 | 6,834 | 78 | 176 | 707 | 1,204 | 41,577 | 26,902 | 3,023 | 2,280 | 7,064 | 6,974 | 90 | 150 | 810 | 1,348 |
| Homeland security, law enforcement, and firefighting | 86 | 63 | 16 | 3 | 1 | 1 | 0 | 0 | 1 | 2 | 97 | 64 | 11 | 8 | 2 | 2 | 0 | 1 | 2 | 9 |
| Legal professions and studies | 20,674 | 13,371 | 2,013 | 2,041 | 1,893 | 1,835 | 58 | 174 | 564 | 618 | 19,365 | 11,999 | 2,123 | 2,087 | 1,670 | 1,634 | 36 | 160 | 735 | 591 |
| Liberal arts and sciences, general studies, and humanities | 61 | 48 | 3 | 1 | 3 | 3 | 0 | 1 | 2 | 3 | 48 | 29 | 6 | 2 | 5 | 5 | 0 | 0 | 1 | 5 |
| Library science | 38 | 22 | 3 | 3 | 0 | 0 | 0 | 0 | 0 | 10 | 33 | 23 | 3 | 0 | 2 | 2 | 0 | 0 | 0 | 5 |
| Mathematics and statistics | 538 | 196 | 10 | 8 | 34 | 34 | 0 | 1 | 4 | 285 | 503 | 175 | 7 | 8 | 34 | 34 | 0 | 0 | 3 | 276 |
| Mechanic and repair technologies/technicians | 0 | 0 | 0 | 0 | 0 | 0 | 0 | 0 | 0 | 0 | 0 | 0 | 0 | 0 | 0 | 0 | 0 | 0 | 0 | 0 |
| Military technologies and applied sciences | 0 | 0 | 0 | 0 | 0 | 0 | 0 | 0 | 0 | 0 | 0 | 0 | 0 | 0 | 0 | 0 | 0 | 0 | 0 | 0 |
| Multi/interdisciplinary studies | 447 | 263 | 46 | 17 | 29 | 29 | 0 | 1 | 6 | 85 | 460 | 262 | 56 | 22 | 26 | 25 | 1 | 1 | 10 | 84 |
| Parks, recreation, leisure, and fitness studies | 159 | 113 | 12 | 8 | 3 | 3 | 0 | 0 | 4 | 21 | 127 | 77 | 17 | 0 | 4 | 4 | 0 | 2 | 1 | 27 |
| Philosophy and religious studies | 237 | 166 | 11 | 7 | 10 | 10 | 0 | 4 | 4 | 35 | 240 | 163 | 18 | 12 | 14 | 14 | 0 | 7 | 3 | 28 |
| Physical sciences and science technologies | 1,933 | 901 | 62 | 53 | 122 | 120 | 2 | 8 | 22 | 765 | 1,997 | 918 | 63 | 75 | 130 | 127 | 3 | 0 | 15 | 789 |
| Precision production | 0 | 0 | 0 | 0 | 0 | 0 | 0 | 0 | 0 | 0 | 0 | 0 | 0 | 0 | 0 | 0 | 0 | 0 | 0 | 0 |
| Psychology | 4,954 | 3,420 | 457 | 408 | 313 | 301 | 12 | 22 | 91 | 243 | 4,959 | 3,360 | 511 | 393 | 329 | 319 | 10 | 29 | 80 | 257 |
| Public administration and social services | 701 | 388 | 153 | 32 | 33 | 32 | 1 | 7 | 6 | 82 | 749 | 423 | 169 | 31 | 38 | 37 | 1 | 6 | 9 | 73 |
| Social sciences and history | 2,230 | 1,257 | 117 | 135 | 136 | 136 | 0 | 13 | 31 | 541 | 2,239 | 1,295 | 139 | 125 | 120 | 120 | 0 | 13 | 34 | 513 |
| Social sciences | 1,783 | 947 | 89 | 107 | 116 | 116 | 0 | 12 | 25 | 487 | 1,788 | 977 | 107 | 98 | 105 | 105 | 0 | 12 | 26 | 463 |
| History | 447 | 310 | 28 | 28 | 20 | 20 | 0 | 1 | 6 | 54 | 451 | 318 | 32 | 27 | 15 | 15 | 0 | 1 | 8 | 50 |
| Theology and religious vocations | 581 | 309 | 170 | 17 | 36 | 36 | 0 | 3 | 7 | 39 | 512 | 263 | 166 | 16 | 32 | 29 | 3 | 3 | 5 | 30 |
| Transportation and materials moving | 1 | 1 | 0 | 0 | 0 | 0 | 0 | 0 | 0 | 0 | 1 | 1 | 0 | 0 | 0 | 0 | 0 | 0 | 0 | 0 |
| Visual and performing arts | 909 | 499 | 18 | 29 | 88 | 88 | 0 | 2 | 12 | 261 | 956 | 556 | 28 | 24 | 90 | 90 | 0 | 2 | 10 | 246 |
| Other and not classified | 0 | 0 | 0 | 0 | 0 | 0 | 0 | 0 | 0 | 0 | 0 | 0 | 0 | 0 | 0 | 0 | 0 | 0 | 0 | 0 |

TABLE 2.8

**Doctor's degrees conferred to females by postsecondary institutions, by race/ethnicity and field of study, 2013–14 and 2014–15** [CONTINUED]

*Excludes "construction trades" and "mechanic and repair technologies/technicians," which are listed separately.

Note: Data are for postsecondary institutions participating in Title IV federal financial aid programs. Race categories exclude persons of Hispanic ethnicity. Reported racial/ethnic distributions of students by level of degree, field of degree, and sex were used to estimate race/ethnicity for students whose race/ethnicity was not reported. To facilitate trend comparisons, certain aggregations have been made of the degree fields as reported in the Integrated Postsecondary Data System (IPEDS): "agriculture and natural resources" includes agriculture, agriculture operations, and related sciences and natural resources and conservation; and "business" includes business management, marketing, and related support services and personal and culinary services. Some data have been revised from previously published figures.

SOURCE: "Table 324.35. Doctor's Degrees Conferred to Females by Postsecondary Institutions, by Race/Ethnicity and Field of Study: 2013–14 and 2014–15," in *Digest of Education Statistics: 2016*, US Department of Education, Institute of Education Sciences, National Center for Education Statistics, September 2016, https://nces.ed.gov/programs/digest/d16/tables/dt16_324.35.asp (accessed January 18, 2018)

such, the US Supreme Court has ruled that schools receiving federal funds may be held legally responsible if they neglect to address student complaints of sexual harassment and sexual violence. In 2011, amid growing national concern over the prevalence of sexual harassment and rape on college campuses, the Department of Education's Office for Civil Rights under President Obama issued a guidance document in the form of a Dear Colleague Letter that advised US colleges and universities of their obligation to prevent, investigate, and resolve student sexual misconduct grievances. The letter warned that schools were subject to a loss of federal funding if they failed to take the necessary actions to make students safe from sexual harassment, assault, and rape. Although many women's groups hailed the letter as an important step toward empowering sexual assault victims, critics charged that it unfairly privileged the rights of accusers over those of the accused.

In 2017, under the administration of President Donald Trump (1946–), the US secretary of education Betsy DeVos (1958–) announced plans to rescind and replace the Obama-era directive on grounds that it denied proper legal protections for the accused. In "Education Department Withdraws Obama-Era Campus Sexual Assault Guidance" (September 22, 2017), Sophie Tatum indicates that the Foundation for Individual Rights in Education, a students' rights and free speech organization, applauded the Department of Education's move to end the Obama administration's "destructive policy," which "made it impossible for campuses to serve the needs of victims while also respecting the rights of the accused." Meanwhile, advocates for sexual assault survivors and various women's rights groups strongly denounced the policy change. For example, the American Association of University Women issued a statement (September 7, 2017, https://www.aauw.org/article/aauw-responds-to-title-ix-announcement/) that described the Department of Education's decision as "a blatant intent to roll back protections for students. It is an action that is at direct odds with upholding the civil rights of all Americans."

# CHAPTER 3
# WOMEN IN THE LABOR FORCE

## 20TH-CENTURY CHANGES IN WOMEN'S WORK

Although women have always labored hard, early American women primarily worked in their own home and as domestic servants. With the United States' entry into World War II (1939–1945) in December 1941, a huge number of American men were drafted or volunteered to serve in the military, leaving behind their jobs, and US factories went into overdrive to keep pace with the needs of combat-related products. The need for workers at home became so great that even married women were encouraged to take jobs outside the home. According to the Public Broadcasting Service, in the documentary *The War* (September 2007, http://www.pbs.org/the war), by 1943 an estimated 6 million women who had never worked outside the home were part of the labor force. With the war's end in 1945, women were expected to return to their home to make jobs available for discharged servicemen. The postwar economy, however, was strong enough to support working women, and more educated, middle-class married women began entering the labor force.

The women's movement of the 1960s sparked further lasting changes in attitudes about women in the workplace, and women's participation in the labor force grew steadily in the decades that followed. In 1976, 47.3% of women aged 16 years and older were in the labor force (i.e., they were either employed or unemployed and looking for a job), and by 1999, 60% of women were in the labor force. (See Table 3.1.) Nevertheless, the percentage of women in the labor force showed a gradual decline into the second decade of the 21st century. In 2016, 56.8% of women were in the labor force. Women's lower labor force participation rate hinges on their greater likelihood to drop out of the labor force to care for children and on their longer average life spans. Women are more likely than men to be alive after having retired from the labor force.

Over time, women's earnings have also come closer to parity with men's earnings. According to the US Bureau of Labor Statistics (BLS), in *Women in the Labor Force: A Databook* (April 2017, https://www.bls.gov/opub/reports/womens-databook/2016/pdf/home.pdf), in 1979 women working full time earned 62% of what men earned in the same job. By 2015 women's earnings had reached 81% of men's. The disparity between women's and men's earnings, which is known as the gender pay gap, persists as a result of subtle forms of discrimination that affect how women are valued and the opportunities they have in the workplace. (See Chapter 5.)

### Labor Force Participation and Age

Since 1950 the biggest increase in labor force participation has been among women between the ages of 25 and 54 years. During the early post–World War II era the highest rates of labor force participation were among women under the age of 25 years, the age by which most women had left the labor force to raise their children. As more women enroll in higher education and marry and have children at later ages, the pattern of women's labor force participation has come to resemble that of men. As women complete their education, their presence in the labor force increases steadily, peaking between the ages of 25 and 54 years. According to the BLS, 74.3% of 25- to 54-year-old women were in the labor force in 2016. (See Table 3.2.) There were no significant disparities among individual subgroups of this population: 74.5% of women aged 25 to 34 years, 74.5% of women aged 35 to 44 years, and 73.9% of women aged 45 to 54 years were in the labor force that year.

After the age of 55 years, labor force participation begins to decline, as workers start to retire or are downsized. The BLS indicates that only 15.5% of women aged 65 years and older were in the labor force in 2016, compared with 24% of men aged 65 years and older.

**TABLE 3.1**

**Employment status of the civilian noninstitutional population 16 years and older, by sex,1976–2016**

[Numbers in thousands]

| Sex and year | Civilian noninstitutional population | Civilian labor force | | Employed | | | | Unemployed | | Not in labor force |
|---|---|---|---|---|---|---|---|---|---|---|
| | | Total | Percent of population | Total | Percent of population | Agriculture | Nonagricultural industries | Number | Percent of labor force | |
| **Men** | | | | | | | | | | |
| 1976 | 73,759 | 57,174 | 77.5 | 53,138 | 72.0 | 2,744 | 50,394 | 4,036 | 7.1 | 16,585 |
| 1977 | 75,193 | 58,396 | 77.7 | 54,728 | 72.8 | 2,671 | 52,057 | 3,667 | 6.3 | 16,797 |
| 1978 | 76,576 | 59,620 | 77.9 | 56,479 | 73.8 | 2,718 | 53,761 | 3,142 | 5.3 | 16,956 |
| 1979 | 78,020 | 60,726 | 77.8 | 57,607 | 73.8 | 2,686 | 54,921 | 3,120 | 5.1 | 17,293 |
| 1980 | 79,398 | 61,453 | 77.4 | 57,186 | 72.0 | 2,709 | 54,477 | 4,267 | 6.9 | 17,945 |
| 1981 | 80,511 | 61,974 | 77.0 | 57,397 | 71.3 | 2,700 | 54,697 | 4,577 | 7.4 | 18,537 |
| 1982 | 81,523 | 62,450 | 76.6 | 56,271 | 69.0 | 2,736 | 53,534 | 6,179 | 9.9 | 19,073 |
| 1983 | 82,531 | 63,047 | 76.4 | 56,787 | 68.8 | 2,704 | 54,083 | 6,260 | 9.9 | 19,484 |
| 1984 | 83,605 | 63,835 | 76.4 | 59,091 | 70.7 | 2,668 | 56,423 | 4,744 | 7.4 | 19,771 |
| 1985 | 84,469 | 64,411 | 76.3 | 59,891 | 70.9 | 2,535 | 57,356 | 4,521 | 7.0 | 20,058 |
| 1986 | 85,798 | 65,422 | 76.3 | 60,892 | 71.0 | 2,511 | 58,381 | 4,530 | 6.9 | 20,376 |
| 1987 | 86,899 | 66,207 | 76.2 | 62,107 | 71.5 | 2,543 | 59,564 | 4,101 | 6.2 | 20,692 |
| 1988 | 87,857 | 66,927 | 76.2 | 63,273 | 72.0 | 2,493 | 60,780 | 3,655 | 5.5 | 20,930 |
| 1989 | 88,762 | 67,840 | 76.4 | 64,315 | 72.5 | 2,513 | 61,802 | 3,525 | 5.2 | 20,923 |
| 1990 | 90,377 | 69,011 | 76.4 | 65,104 | 72.0 | 2,546 | 62,559 | 3,906 | 5.7 | 21,367 |
| 1991 | 91,278 | 69,168 | 75.8 | 64,223 | 70.4 | 2,589 | 61,634 | 4,946 | 7.2 | 22,110 |
| 1992 | 92,270 | 69,964 | 75.8 | 64,440 | 69.8 | 2,575 | 61,866 | 5,523 | 7.9 | 22,306 |
| 1993 | 93,332 | 70,404 | 75.4 | 65,349 | 70.0 | 2,478 | 62,871 | 5,055 | 7.2 | 22,927 |
| 1994 | 94,355 | 70,817 | 75.1 | 66,450 | 70.4 | 2,554 | 63,896 | 4,367 | 6.2 | 23,538 |
| 1995 | 95,178 | 71,360 | 75.0 | 67,377 | 70.8 | 2,559 | 64,818 | 3,983 | 5.6 | 23,818 |
| 1996 | 96,206 | 72,087 | 74.9 | 68,207 | 70.9 | 2,573 | 65,634 | 3,880 | 5.4 | 24,119 |
| 1997 | 97,715 | 73,261 | 75.0 | 69,685 | 71.3 | 2,552 | 67,133 | 3,577 | 4.9 | 24,454 |
| 1998 | 98,758 | 73,959 | 74.9 | 70,693 | 71.6 | 2,553 | 68,140 | 3,266 | 4.4 | 24,799 |
| 1999 | 99,722 | 74,512 | 74.7 | 71,446 | 71.6 | 2,432 | 69,014 | 3,066 | 4.1 | 25,210 |
| 2000 | 101,964 | 76,280 | 74.8 | 73,305 | 71.9 | 1,861 | 71,444 | 2,975 | 3.9 | 25,684 |
| 2001 | 103,282 | 76,886 | 74.4 | 73,196 | 70.9 | 1,708 | 71,488 | 3,690 | 4.8 | 26,396 |
| 2002 | 104,585 | 77,500 | 74.1 | 72,903 | 69.7 | 1,724 | 71,179 | 4,597 | 5.9 | 27,085 |
| 2003 | 106,435 | 78,238 | 73.5 | 73,332 | 68.9 | 1,695 | 71,636 | 4,906 | 6.3 | 28,197 |
| 2004 | 107,710 | 78,980 | 73.3 | 74,524 | 69.2 | 1,687 | 72,838 | 4,456 | 5.6 | 28,730 |
| 2005 | 109,151 | 80,033 | 73.3 | 75,973 | 69.6 | 1,654 | 74,319 | 4,059 | 5.1 | 29,119 |
| 2006 | 110,605 | 81,255 | 73.5 | 77,502 | 70.1 | 1,663 | 75,838 | 3,753 | 4.6 | 29,350 |
| 2007 | 112,173 | 82,136 | 73.2 | 78,254 | 69.8 | 1,604 | 76,650 | 3,882 | 4.7 | 30,036 |
| 2008 | 113,113 | 82,520 | 73.0 | 77,486 | 68.5 | 1,650 | 75,836 | 5,033 | 6.1 | 30,593 |
| 2009 | 114,136 | 82,123 | 72.0 | 73,670 | 64.5 | 1,607 | 72,062 | 8,453 | 10.3 | 32,013 |
| 2010 | 115,174 | 81,985 | 71.2 | 73,359 | 63.7 | 1,665 | 71,694 | 8,626 | 10.5 | 33,189 |
| 2011 | 116,317 | 81,975 | 70.5 | 74,290 | 63.9 | 1,698 | 72,592 | 7,684 | 9.4 | 34,343 |
| 2012 | 117,343 | 82,327 | 70.2 | 75,555 | 64.4 | 1,626 | 73,930 | 6,771 | 8.2 | 35,017 |
| 2013 | 118,555 | 82,667 | 69.7 | 76,353 | 64.4 | 1,611 | 74,742 | 6,314 | 7.6 | 35,889 |
| 2014 | 119,748 | 82,882 | 69.2 | 77,692 | 64.9 | 1,685 | 76,007 | 5,190 | 6.3 | 36,865 |
| 2015 | 121,101 | 83,620 | 69.1 | 79,131 | 65.3 | 1,826 | 77,305 | 4,490 | 5.4 | 37,481 |
| 2016 | 122,497 | 84,755 | 69.2 | 80,568 | 65.8 | 1,839 | 78,729 | 4,187 | 4.9 | 37,743 |
| **Women** | | | | | | | | | | |
| 1976 | 82,390 | 38,983 | 47.3 | 35,615 | 43.2 | 588 | 35,027 | 3,369 | 8.6 | 43,406 |
| 1977 | 83,840 | 40,613 | 48.4 | 37,289 | 44.5 | 612 | 36,677 | 3,324 | 8.2 | 43,227 |
| 1978 | 85,334 | 42,631 | 50.0 | 39,569 | 46.4 | 669 | 38,900 | 3,061 | 7.2 | 42,703 |
| 1979 | 86,843 | 44,235 | 50.9 | 41,217 | 47.5 | 661 | 40,556 | 3,018 | 6.8 | 42,608 |
| 1980 | 88,348 | 45,487 | 51.5 | 42,117 | 47.7 | 656 | 41,461 | 3,370 | 7.4 | 42,861 |
| 1981 | 89,618 | 46,696 | 52.1 | 43,000 | 48.0 | 667 | 42,333 | 3,696 | 7.9 | 42,922 |
| 1982 | 90,748 | 47,755 | 52.6 | 43,256 | 47.7 | 665 | 42,591 | 4,499 | 9.4 | 42,993 |
| 1983 | 91,684 | 48,503 | 52.9 | 44,047 | 48.0 | 680 | 43,367 | 4,457 | 9.2 | 43,181 |
| 1984 | 92,778 | 49,709 | 53.6 | 45,915 | 49.5 | 653 | 45,262 | 3,794 | 7.6 | 43,068 |
| 1985 | 93,736 | 51,050 | 54.5 | 47,259 | 50.4 | 644 | 46,615 | 3,791 | 7.4 | 42,686 |
| 1986 | 94,789 | 52,413 | 55.3 | 48,706 | 51.4 | 652 | 48,054 | 3,707 | 7.1 | 42,376 |
| 1987 | 95,853 | 53,658 | 56.0 | 50,334 | 52.5 | 666 | 49,668 | 3,324 | 6.2 | 42,195 |
| 1988 | 96,756 | 54,742 | 56.6 | 51,696 | 53.4 | 676 | 51,020 | 3,046 | 5.6 | 42,014 |
| 1989 | 97,630 | 56,030 | 57.4 | 53,027 | 54.3 | 687 | 52,341 | 3,003 | 5.4 | 41,601 |
| 1990 | 98,787 | 56,829 | 57.5 | 53,689 | 54.3 | 678 | 53,011 | 3,140 | 5.5 | 41,957 |
| 1991 | 99,646 | 57,178 | 57.4 | 53,496 | 53.7 | 680 | 52,815 | 3,683 | 6.4 | 42,468 |
| 1992 | 100,535 | 58,141 | 57.8 | 54,052 | 53.8 | 672 | 53,380 | 4,090 | 7.0 | 42,394 |
| 1993 | 101,506 | 58,795 | 57.9 | 54,910 | 54.1 | 637 | 54,273 | 3,885 | 6.6 | 42,711 |
| 1994 | 102,460 | 60,239 | 58.8 | 56,610 | 55.3 | 855 | 55,755 | 3,629 | 6.0 | 42,221 |
| 1995 | 103,406 | 60,944 | 58.9 | 57,523 | 55.6 | 881 | 56,642 | 3,421 | 5.6 | 42,462 |
| 1996 | 104,385 | 61,857 | 59.3 | 58,501 | 56.0 | 871 | 57,630 | 3,356 | 5.4 | 42,528 |
| 1997 | 105,418 | 63,036 | 59.8 | 59,873 | 56.8 | 847 | 59,026 | 3,162 | 5.0 | 42,382 |

**TABLE 3.1**

**Employment status of the civilian noninstitutional population 16 years and older, by sex, 1976–2016** [CONTINUED]

[Numbers in thousands]

| Sex and year | Civilian noninstitutional population | Civilian labor force | | | | | | | | | Not in labor force |
|---|---|---|---|---|---|---|---|---|---|---|---|
| | | | | | Employed | | | | Unemployed | | |
| | | Total | Percent of population | Total | Percent of population | Agriculture | Nonagricultural industries | Number | Percent of labor force | | |
| **Women** | | | | | | | | | | | |
| 1998 | 106,462 | 63,714 | 59.8 | 60,771 | 57.1 | 825 | 59,945 | 2,944 | 4.6 | | 42,748 |
| 1999 | 108,031 | 64,855 | 60.0 | 62,042 | 57.4 | 849 | 61,193 | 2,814 | 4.3 | | 43,175 |
| 2000 | 110,613 | 66,303 | 59.9 | 63,586 | 57.5 | 602 | 62,983 | 2,717 | 4.1 | | 44,310 |
| 2001 | 111,811 | 66,848 | 59.8 | 63,737 | 57.0 | 591 | 63,147 | 3,111 | 4.7 | | 44,962 |
| 2002 | 112,985 | 67,363 | 59.6 | 63,582 | 56.3 | 587 | 62,995 | 3,781 | 5.6 | | 45,621 |
| 2003 | 114,733 | 68,272 | 59.5 | 64,404 | 56.1 | 580 | 63,824 | 3,868 | 5.7 | | 46,461 |
| 2004 | 115,647 | 68,421 | 59.2 | 64,728 | 56.0 | 546 | 64,182 | 3,694 | 5.4 | | 47,225 |
| 2005 | 116,931 | 69,288 | 59.3 | 65,757 | 56.2 | 544 | 65,213 | 3,531 | 5.1 | | 47,643 |
| 2006 | 118,210 | 70,173 | 59.4 | 66,925 | 56.6 | 543 | 66,382 | 3,247 | 4.6 | | 48,037 |
| 2007 | 119,694 | 70,988 | 59.3 | 67,792 | 56.6 | 490 | 67,302 | 3,196 | 4.5 | | 48,707 |
| 2008 | 120,675 | 71,767 | 59.5 | 67,876 | 56.2 | 518 | 67,358 | 3,891 | 5.4 | | 48,908 |
| 2009 | 121,665 | 72,019 | 59.2 | 66,208 | 54.4 | 496 | 65,712 | 5,811 | 8.1 | | 49,646 |
| 2010 | 122,656 | 71,904 | 58.6 | 65,705 | 53.6 | 541 | 65,164 | 6,199 | 8.6 | | 50,752 |
| 2011 | 123,300 | 71,642 | 58.1 | 65,579 | 53.2 | 556 | 65,023 | 6,063 | 8.5 | | 51,658 |
| 2012 | 125,941 | 72,648 | 57.7 | 66,914 | 53.1 | 560 | 66,353 | 5,734 | 7.9 | | 53,293 |
| 2013 | 127,124 | 72,722 | 57.2 | 67,577 | 53.2 | 519 | 67,058 | 5,146 | 7.1 | | 54,401 |
| 2014 | 128,199 | 73,039 | 57.0 | 68,613 | 53.5 | 552 | 68,061 | 4,426 | 6.1 | | 55,159 |
| 2015 | 129,700 | 73,510 | 56.7 | 69,703 | 53.7 | 597 | 69,106 | 3,807 | 5.2 | | 56,190 |
| 2016 | 131,040 | 74,432 | 56.8 | 70,868 | 54.1 | 621 | 70,247 | 3,564 | 4.8 | | 56,608 |

Note: Revisions to population controls and other changes can affect the comparability of labor force levels over time. In recent years, for example, updated population controls have been introduced annually with the release of January data.

SOURCE: "2. Employment Status of the Civilian Noninstitutional Population 16 Years and over by Sex, 1976 to Date," in *Labor Force Statistics from the Current Population Survey*, US Bureau of Labor Statistics, February 8, 2017, https://www.bls.gov/cps/cpsaat02.pdf (accessed January 19, 2018)

(See Table 3.2.) By contrast, Howard N. Fullerton Jr. of the BLS reports in "Labor Force Participation: 75 Years of Change, 1950–98 and 1998–2025" (*Monthly Labor Review*, December 1999) that in 1950, 9.7% of women and 45.8% of men this age were working. Labor force participation of women aged 65 years and older was up slightly in 1960, but men's labor force participation was down sharply. This decline in labor force participation among older men was largely driven by the increased availability of pensions and disability payments, and the increase in participation among older women reflects the large overall gains in the number of women in the labor force.

### Labor Force Participation and Race and Ethnicity

Among men, there are statistically significant disparities in labor force participation by race and Hispanic origin. According to the BLS (http://www.bls.gov/cps/cpsaat04.htm, http://www.bls.gov/cps/cpsaat05.htm), 75.8% of Hispanic men were in the labor force in 2017, compared with 71.9% of Asian American men, 69.5% of white men, and 64.6% of African American men.

Among women, the disparities were smaller. African American women participated in the labor force at the highest rate (60.3%), while white women, Hispanic women, and Asian American women all participated at a rate of 56.4%. These levels of female labor force participation by race and Hispanic origin are a relatively recent phenomenon, as Fullerton explains. Until the late 1980s African American women had a significantly higher labor force participation rate than did white women. Since then, however, white women's labor participation rates have risen to the point that they have become comparable.

### Marital Status, Labor Force Status, and Employment Status

Women participate in the labor force at different rates depending on their marital status. In 2016, 76% of women who were never married, married with spouse absent, separated, divorced, or widowed participated in the labor force, compared with 67.9% of women who were married and lived with their spouse. (See Table 3.3; note that single women are categorized under the heading "Other marital status.") This greater participation in the labor force does not equate with a higher rate of employment, however. The unemployment rate for single women was 7.8% in 2016, compared with 3.2% for married women. Thus, single women participated in the workforce at a greater rate than married women in 2016; however, they were also more than twice as likely to be unemployed. Even so, the proportion of employed women among all married women (65.7%) remained lower than the proportion of employed women among all single women (70.1%) in 2016.

Married women were far more likely to have additional household sources of income than were single women in 2016. As Table 3.4 shows, nearly half (48%)

**TABLE 3.2**

**Employment status of the civilian noninstitutional population, by age and sex, 2016**

[Numbers in thousands]

| | | 2016 | | | | | | |
|---|---|---|---|---|---|---|---|---|
| | | Civilian labor force | | | | | | |
| | | | | Employed | | Unemployed | | |
| Age and sex | Civilian noninstitutional population | Total | Percent of population | Total | Percent of population | Number | Percent of labor force | Not in labor force |
| **Total** | | | | | | | | |
| 16 years and over | 253,538 | 159,187 | 62.8 | 151,436 | 59.7 | 7,751 | 4.9 | 94,351 |
| 16 to 19 years | 16,714 | 5,889 | 35.2 | 4,965 | 29.7 | 925 | 15.7 | 10,824 |
| 16 to 17 years | 8,994 | 2,127 | 23.6 | 1,747 | 19.4 | 380 | 17.9 | 6,867 |
| 18 to 19 years | 7,720 | 3,763 | 48.7 | 3,218 | 41.7 | 545 | 14.5 | 3,957 |
| 20 to 24 years | 21,721 | 15,313 | 70.5 | 14,027 | 64.6 | 1,286 | 8.4 | 6,408 |
| 25 to 54 years | 125,761 | 102,248 | 81.3 | 98,004 | 77.9 | 4,244 | 4.2 | 23,513 |
| 25 to 34 years | 43,547 | 35,519 | 81.6 | 33,722 | 77.4 | 1,797 | 5.1 | 8,027 |
| 25 to 29 years | 22,265 | 18,100 | 81.3 | 17,088 | 76.7 | 1,012 | 5.6 | 4,165 |
| 30 to 34 years | 21,282 | 17,420 | 81.9 | 16,634 | 78.2 | 786 | 4.5 | 3,862 |
| 35 to 44 years | 39,817 | 32,820 | 82.4 | 31,562 | 79.3 | 1,258 | 3.8 | 6,997 |
| 35 to 39 years | 20,394 | 16,784 | 82.3 | 16,121 | 79.0 | 663 | 4.0 | 3,610 |
| 40 to 44 years | 19,422 | 16,036 | 82.6 | 15,441 | 79.5 | 594 | 3.7 | 3,387 |
| 45 to 54 years | 42,397 | 33,909 | 80.0 | 32,720 | 77.2 | 1,189 | 3.5 | 8,489 |
| 45 to 49 years | 20,703 | 16,910 | 81.7 | 16,298 | 78.7 | 611 | 3.6 | 3,793 |
| 50 to 54 years | 21,694 | 16,999 | 78.4 | 16,421 | 75.7 | 577 | 3.4 | 4,696 |
| 55 to 64 years | 41,308 | 26,465 | 64.1 | 25,524 | 61.8 | 941 | 3.6 | 14,843 |
| 55 to 59 years | 21,804 | 15,584 | 71.5 | 15,031 | 68.9 | 553 | 3.6 | 6,220 |
| 60 to 64 years | 19,504 | 10,881 | 55.8 | 10,493 | 53.8 | 388 | 3.6 | 8,623 |
| 65 years and over | 48,035 | 9,272 | 19.3 | 8,916 | 18.6 | 355 | 3.8 | 38,763 |
| 65 to 69 years | 16,671 | 5,367 | 32.2 | 5,168 | 31.0 | 199 | 3.7 | 11,305 |
| 70 to 74 years | 11,765 | 2,254 | 19.2 | 2,165 | 18.4 | 88 | 3.9 | 9,511 |
| 75 years and over | 19,599 | 1,651 | 8.4 | 1,583 | 8.1 | 68 | 4.1 | 17,947 |
| **Men** | | | | | | | | |
| 16 years and over | 122,497 | 84,755 | 69.2 | 80,568 | 65.8 | 4,187 | 4.9 | 37,743 |
| 16 to19 years | 8,475 | 2,995 | 35.3 | 2,484 | 29.3 | 512 | 17.1 | 5,479 |
| 16 to17 years | 4,509 | 1,028 | 22.8 | 825 | 18.3 | 203 | 19.7 | 3,481 |
| 18 to19 years | 3,966 | 1,967 | 49.6 | 1,659 | 41.8 | 309 | 15.7 | 1,998 |
| 20 to 24 years | 10,897 | 7,954 | 73.0 | 7,212 | 66.2 | 742 | 9.3 | 2,943 |
| 25 to 54 years | 61,811 | 54,726 | 88.5 | 52,514 | 85.0 | 2,212 | 4.0 | 7,085 |
| 25 to 34 years | 21,570 | 19,151 | 88.8 | 18,185 | 84.3 | 966 | 5.0 | 2,420 |
| 25 to 29 years | 11,068 | 9,660 | 87.3 | 9,104 | 82.3 | 557 | 5.8 | 1,407 |
| 30 to 34 years | 10,503 | 9,490 | 90.4 | 9,081 | 86.5 | 409 | 4.3 | 1,012 |
| 35 to 44 years | 19,514 | 17,686 | 90.6 | 17,042 | 87.3 | 644 | 3.6 | 1,828 |
| 35 to 39 years | 10,016 | 9,092 | 90.8 | 8,759 | 87.4 | 334 | 3.7 | 924 |
| 40 to 44 years | 9,497 | 8,593 | 90.5 | 8,283 | 87.2 | 310 | 3.6 | 904 |
| 45 to 54 years | 20,727 | 17,890 | 86.3 | 17,287 | 83.4 | 602 | 3.4 | 2,837 |
| 45 to 49 years | 10,142 | 8,947 | 88.2 | 8,637 | 85.2 | 310 | 3.5 | 1,195 |
| 50 to 54 years | 10,585 | 8,942 | 84.5 | 8,651 | 81.7 | 292 | 3.3 | 1,643 |
| 55 to 64 years | 19,867 | 13,938 | 70.2 | 13,410 | 67.5 | 528 | 3.8 | 5,929 |
| 55 to 59 years | 10,557 | 8,168 | 77.4 | 7,860 | 74.5 | 308 | 3.8 | 2,388 |
| 60 to 64 years | 9,310 | 5,770 | 62.0 | 5,550 | 59.6 | 220 | 3.8 | 3,540 |
| 65 years and over | 21,448 | 5,141 | 24.0 | 4,948 | 23.1 | 193 | 3.8 | 16,306 |
| 65 to 69 years | 7,841 | 2,894 | 36.9 | 2,781 | 35.5 | 113 | 3.9 | 4,946 |
| 70 to 74 years | 5,412 | 1,286 | 23.8 | 1,241 | 22.9 | 46 | 3.5 | 4,126 |
| 75 years and over | 8,195 | 960 | 11.7 | 926 | 11.3 | 35 | 3.6 | 7,234 |
| **Women** | | | | | | | | |
| 16 years and over | 131,040 | 74,432 | 56.8 | 70,868 | 54.1 | 3,564 | 4.8 | 56,608 |
| 16 to19 years | 8,239 | 2,894 | 35.1 | 2,481 | 30.1 | 413 | 14.3 | 5,345 |
| 16 to17 years | 4,485 | 1,099 | 24.5 | 922 | 20.6 | 177 | 16.1 | 3,386 |
| 18 to19 years | 3,754 | 1,795 | 47.8 | 1,559 | 41.5 | 236 | 13.2 | 1,959 |
| 20 to 24 years | 10,823 | 7,359 | 68.0 | 6,815 | 63.0 | 545 | 7.4 | 3,464 |
| 25 to 54 years | 63,950 | 47,522 | 74.3 | 45,490 | 71.1 | 2,032 | 4.3 | 16,428 |
| 25 to 34 years | 21,976 | 16,369 | 74.5 | 15,537 | 70.7 | 832 | 5.1 | 5,608 |
| 25 to 29 years | 11,198 | 8,439 | 75.4 | 7,985 | 71.3 | 455 | 5.4 | 2,758 |
| 30 to 34 years | 10,779 | 7,929 | 73.6 | 7,553 | 70.1 | 377 | 4.8 | 2,850 |
| 35 to 44 years | 20,303 | 15,134 | 74.5 | 14,520 | 71.5 | 614 | 4.1 | 5,169 |
| 35 to 39 years | 10,378 | 7,692 | 74.1 | 7,362 | 70.9 | 330 | 4.3 | 2,686 |
| 40 to 44 years | 9,925 | 7,442 | 75.0 | 7,158 | 72.1 | 284 | 3.8 | 2,482 |
| 45 to 54 years | 21,670 | 16,019 | 73.9 | 15,433 | 71.2 | 586 | 3.7 | 5,651 |
| 45 to 49 years | 10,561 | 7,963 | 75.4 | 7,662 | 72.5 | 301 | 3.8 | 2,598 |
| 50 to 54 years | 11,109 | 8,056 | 72.5 | 7,771 | 70.0 | 285 | 3.5 | 3,053 |
| 55 to 64 years | 21,441 | 12,527 | 58.4 | 12,114 | 56.5 | 413 | 3.3 | 8,914 |
| 55 to 59 years | 11,247 | 7,416 | 65.9 | 7,171 | 63.8 | 245 | 3.3 | 3,831 |

TABLE 3.2

**Employment status of the civilian noninstitutional population, by age and sex, 2016** [CONTINUED]

[Numbers in thousands]

| Age and sex | Civilian noninstitutional population | 2016 Civilian labor force | | | | | | Not in labor force |
|---|---|---|---|---|---|---|---|---|
| | | | | | Employed | | Unemployed | |
| | | Total | Percent of population | Total | Percent of population | Number | Percent of labor force | |
| 60 to 64 years | 10,194 | 5,111 | 50.1 | 4,943 | 48.5 | 168 | 3.3 | 5,083 |
| 65 years and over | 26,587 | 4,130 | 15.5 | 3,968 | 14.9 | 162 | 3.9 | 22,457 |
| 65 to 69 years | 8,831 | 2,472 | 28.0 | 2,386 | 27.0 | 86 | 3.5 | 6,359 |
| 70 to 74 years | 6,352 | 967 | 15.2 | 924 | 14.6 | 43 | 4.4 | 5,385 |
| 75 years and over | 11,404 | 691 | 6.1 | 658 | 5.8 | 33 | 4.8 | 10,713 |

Note: Updated population controls are introduced annually with the release of January data.

SOURCE: Adapted from "3. Employment Status of the Civilian Noninstitutional Population by Age, Sex, and Race," in *Labor Force Statistics from the Current Population Survey*, US Bureau of Labor Statistics, February 8, 2017, https://www.bls.gov/cps/cpsaat03.pdf (accessed January 19, 2018)

of married-couple households were two-earner households. In an additional 19.5% of married-couple households, the husband was the only employed member of the household, and in 7.1% the wife was the only employed member of the household. In 18.9% of married-couple households, no family member was employed. By comparison, in 41.5% of households headed by women with no spouse present, the female householder was the sole breadwinner. In 21% of female-headed households, another household member was employed in addition to the female householder, and in 14.1%, at least one other member of the household was employed while the female householder was unemployed. In 23.4% of female-headed households, no one was employed. The likelihood of female-headed households' being single-earner families or families in which no one was employed points to the far greater likelihood of poverty in these households. (See Chapter 5.)

### Labor Force Participation of Mothers

According to the BLS, in *Women in the Labor Force: A Databook*), the percentage of women without children under the age of 18 years who participate in the labor force has grown appreciably since the 1970s. In 1975, 45.1% of women who did not have children living with them participated in the labor force, and 8.9% of these women were unemployed. By 1990, 52.3% of women without children at home were participating in the labor force and 4.6% were unemployed, and by 2000, 54.8% of these women were in the labor force and 4.3% were unemployed. Labor force participation among women without children at home declined slightly during the early years of the new century and stood at 51.6% in 2016, while unemployment among these women stood at 4.8%. (See Table 3.3.)

Meanwhile, the increase in labor force participation among women with children at home increased dramatically over this same period. According to the BLS, 47.4% of women with children under the age of 18 years were in the labor force in 1975 and 11% were unemployed. By 1990 more than two-thirds (66.7%) of mothers were participating in the labor force and 6% were unemployed, and by 2000, 72.9% were in the labor force and 4.3% were unemployed. By 2016 the labor force participation rate of women with children under the age of 18 years had fallen slightly to 70.5%, and the unemployment rate for these women had increased slightly to 4.8%. (See Table 3.3.) The labor force participation rate was higher for women with children aged six to 17 years (75%) than for women with children under the age of six years (64.7%). The labor force participation rate was also higher among single women with children (76%) than among married women with children (67.9%). Besides being far more likely to be impoverished, single women with children were also significantly more likely to be looking for work than their married counterparts.

### EMPLOYMENT SECTORS

As Table 3.5 shows, only 621,000 women aged 16 years and older were employed in agriculture in 2016, compared with 1.8 million men. Of the nearly 66.8 million female nonagricultural wage and salary workers, 55.1 million (82.4%) were employed in private industry. Of those in private industry, 664,000 worked in private households and the remainder worked in other private industries. The remaining 11.7 million female nonagricultural wage and salary workers were government employees. Another 3.4 million women were self-employed and 43,000 did unpaid work in the family.

Women aged 16 years and older accounted for 30.6 million (51.5%) of the total 59.4 million jobs in management, professional, and related occupations in 2016. (See Table 3.6.) Within this overall subset of occupations women were underrepresented in management, business, and financial operations jobs and overrepresented

**TABLE 3.3**

**Employment status of the population, by sex, marital status, and presence and age of own children under 18, 2015–16**

[Numbers in thousands]

| Characteristic | 2015 | | | 2016 | | |
|---|---|---|---|---|---|---|
| | Total | Men | Women | Total | Men | Women |
| **With own children under 18 years** | | | | | | |
| Civilian noninstitutional population | 65,564 | 29,095 | 36,469 | 65,055 | 28,992 | 36,063 |
| Civilian labor force | 52,476 | 26,978 | 25,498 | 52,321 | 26,902 | 25,419 |
| Participation rate | 80.0 | 92.7 | 69.9 | 80.4 | 92.8 | 70.5 |
| Employed | 50,238 | 26,079 | 24,159 | 50,240 | 26,039 | 24,201 |
| Full-time workers[a] | 43,250 | 24,880 | 18,370 | 43,352 | 24,896 | 18,456 |
| Part-time workers[b] | 6,989 | 1,199 | 5,790 | 6,887 | 1,143 | 5,744 |
| Employment-population ratio | 76.6 | 89.6 | 66.2 | 77.2 | 89.8 | 67.1 |
| Unemployed | 2,238 | 899 | 1,339 | 2,082 | 864 | 1,218 |
| Unemployment rate | 4.3 | 3.3 | 5.3 | 4.0 | 3.2 | 4.8 |
| **Married, spouse present[c]** | | | | | | |
| Civilian noninstitutional population | 49,822 | 25,122 | 24,700 | 49,472 | 25,007 | 24,465 |
| Civilian labor force | 40,226 | 23,532 | 16,694 | 40,016 | 23,409 | 16,607 |
| Participation rate | 80.7 | 93.7 | 67.6 | 80.9 | 93.6 | 67.9 |
| Employed | 39,026 | 22,889 | 16,137 | 38,866 | 22,791 | 16,075 |
| Full-time workers[a] | 34,148 | 21,958 | 12,190 | 34,112 | 21,899 | 12,214 |
| Part-time workers[b] | 4,877 | 931 | 3,947 | 4,754 | 892 | 3,861 |
| Employment-population ratio | 78.3 | 91.1 | 65.3 | 78.6 | 91.1 | 65.7 |
| Unemployed | 1,200 | 643 | 557 | 1,150 | 618 | 532 |
| Unemployment rate | 3.0 | 2.7 | 3.3 | 2.9 | 2.6 | 3.2 |
| **Other marital status[d]** | | | | | | |
| Civilian noninstitutional population | 15,742 | 3,973 | 11,769 | 15,583 | 3,985 | 11,598 |
| Civilian labor force | 12,250 | 3,446 | 8,804 | 12,305 | 3,494 | 8,811 |
| Participation rate | 77.8 | 86.7 | 74.8 | 79.0 | 87.7 | 76.0 |
| Employed | 11,213 | 3,190 | 8,022 | 11,374 | 3,248 | 8,125 |
| Full-time workers[a] | 9,101 | 2,922 | 6,179 | 9,240 | 2,997 | 6,243 |
| Part-time workers[b] | 2,111 | 268 | 1,843 | 2,134 | 251 | 1,883 |
| Employment-population ratio | 71.2 | 80.3 | 68.2 | 73.0 | 81.5 | 70.1 |
| Unemployed | 1,038 | 256 | 782 | 931 | 246 | 686 |
| Unemployment rate | 8.5 | 7.4 | 8.9 | 7.6 | 7.0 | 7.8 |
| **With own children 6 to 17 years, none younger** | | | | | | |
| Civilian noninstitutional population | 36,616 | 16,171 | 20,445 | 36,491 | 16,152 | 20,338 |
| Civilian labor force | 30,057 | 14,840 | 15,218 | 30,088 | 14,836 | 15,252 |
| Participation rate | 82.1 | 91.8 | 74.4 | 82.5 | 91.9 | 75.0 |
| Employed | 28,923 | 14,392 | 14,531 | 28,998 | 14,393 | 14,605 |
| Full-time workers[a] | 25,073 | 13,785 | 11,288 | 25,166 | 13,785 | 11,381 |
| Part-time workers[b] | 3,850 | 607 | 3,243 | 3,831 | 607 | 3,224 |
| Employment-population ratio | 79.0 | 89.0 | 71.1 | 79.5 | 89.1 | 71.8 |
| Unemployed | 1,134 | 448 | 687 | 1,090 | 444 | 646 |
| Unemployment rate | 3.8 | 3.0 | 4.5 | 3.6 | 3.0 | 4.2 |
| **With own children under 6 years** | | | | | | |
| Civilian noninstitutional population | 28,948 | 12,924 | 16,024 | 28,565 | 12,840 | 15,724 |
| Civilian labor force | 22,419 | 12,138 | 10,281 | 22,233 | 12,066 | 10,167 |
| Participation rate | 77.4 | 93.9 | 64.2 | 77.8 | 94.0 | 64.7 |
| Employed | 21,315 | 11,687 | 9,628 | 21,242 | 11,646 | 9,596 |
| Full-time workers[a] | 18,177 | 11,095 | 7,082 | 18,186 | 11,110 | 7,076 |
| Part-time workers[b] | 3,139 | 592 | 2,547 | 3,056 | 536 | 2,520 |
| Employment-population ratio | 73.6 | 90.4 | 60.1 | 74.4 | 90.7 | 61.0 |
| Unemployed | 1,104 | 451 | 652 | 992 | 420 | 572 |
| Unemployment rate | 4.9 | 3.7 | 6.3 | 4.5 | 3.5 | 5.6 |
| **With no own children under 18 years** | | | | | | |
| Civilian noninstitutional population | 185,237 | 92,006 | 93,231 | 188,482 | 93,505 | 94,978 |
| Civilian labor force | 104,654 | 56,643 | 48,011 | 106,866 | 57,852 | 49,014 |
| Participation rate | 56.5 | 61.6 | 51.5 | 56.7 | 61.9 | 51.6 |
| Employed | 98,595 | 53,052 | 45,544 | 101,196 | 54,529 | 46,667 |
| Full-time workers[a] | 78,243 | 44,471 | 33,772 | 80,408 | 45,671 | 34,738 |
| Part-time workers[b] | 20,353 | 8,581 | 11,772 | 20,788 | 8,858 | 11,930 |
| Employment-population ratio | 53.2 | 57.7 | 48.9 | 53.7 | 58.3 | 49.1 |
| Unemployed | 6,058 | 3,591 | 2,468 | 5,670 | 3,323 | 2,346 |
| Unemployment rate | 5.8 | 6.3 | 5.1 | 5.3 | 5.7 | 4.8 |

in professional and related jobs; their overrepresentation in this second category is largely due to the fact that they accounted for 6.5 million (73.1%) of the total 8.9 million jobs in education, training, and library occupations.

More women than men in all age groups work in service industries. In 2016, 15.2 million (56.6%) of the 26.8 million service jobs were held by women aged 16 years and older. (See Table 3.6.) Women especially

**TABLE 3.3**

**Employment status of the population, by sex, marital status, and presence and age of own children under 18, 2015–16** [CONTINUED]

[Numbers in thousands]

[a]Usually work 35 hours or more per week at all jobs.
[b]Usually work less than 35 hours per week at all jobs.
[c]Refers to persons in opposite-sex married couples only.
[d]Includes persons who are never married; widowed; divorced; separated; and married, spouse absent; as well as persons in same-sex marriages.
Note: Own children include sons, daughters, step-children, and adopted children. Not included are nieces, nephews, grandchildren, and other related and unrelated children. Detail may not sum to totals due to rounding. Updated population controls are introduced annually with the release of January data.

SOURCE: "Table 5. Employment Status of the Population by Sex, Marital Status, and Presence and Age of Own Children under 18, 2015–2016 Annual Averages," in *Employment Characteristics of Families—2016*, US Bureau of Labor Statistics, April 20, 2017, https://www.bls.gov/news.release/pdf/famee.pdf (accessed January 19, 2018)

**TABLE 3.4**

**Families, by presence and relationship of employed members and family type, 2015–16**

[Numbers in thousands]

| Characteristic | Number 2015 | Number 2016 | Percent distribution 2015 | Percent distribution 2016 |
|---|---|---|---|---|
| **Married-couple families[a]** | | | | |
| Total | 59,217 | 59,747 | 100.0 | 100.0 |
| With at least one family member employed | 48,205 | 48,440 | 81.4 | 81.1 |
| Husband only | 11,726 | 11,649 | 19.8 | 19.5 |
| Wife only | 4,209 | 4,253 | 7.1 | 7.1 |
| Husband and wife | 28,434 | 28,693 | 48.0 | 48.0 |
| Other employment combinations | 3,837 | 3,845 | 6.5 | 6.4 |
| With no family member employed | 11,012 | 11,307 | 18.6 | 18.9 |
| **Families maintained by women[b]** | | | | |
| Total | 15,693 | 15,669 | 100.0 | 100.0 |
| With at least one family member employed | 11,765 | 12,001 | 75.0 | 76.6 |
| Householder only | 6,451 | 6,502 | 41.1 | 41.5 |
| Householder and other member(s) | 3,181 | 3,293 | 20.3 | 21.0 |
| Other member(s), not householder | 2,133 | 2,205 | 13.6 | 14.1 |
| With no family member employed | 3,928 | 3,668 | 25.0 | 23.4 |
| **Families maintained by men[b]** | | | | |
| Total | 6,499 | 6,676 | 100.0 | 100.0 |
| With at least one family member employed | 5,389 | 5,582 | 82.9 | 83.6 |
| Householder only | 2,517 | 2,577 | 38.7 | 38.6 |
| Householder and other member(s) | 1,932 | 2,050 | 29.7 | 30.7 |
| Other member(s), not householder | 940 | 955 | 14.5 | 14.3 |
| With no family member employed | 1,110 | 1,094 | 17.1 | 16.4 |

[a]Refers to opposite-sex married-couple families only.
[b]No opposite-sex spouse present.
Note: Detail may not sum to totals due to rounding. Updated population controls are introduced annually with the release of January data.

SOURCE: "Table 2. Families by Presence and Relationship of Employed Members and Family Type, 2015–2016 Annual Averages," in *Employment Characteristics of Families—2016*, US Bureau of Labor Statistics, April 20, 2017, https://www.bls.gov/news.release/pdf/famee.pdf (accessed January 19, 2018)

predominated in health care support and personal care and service occupations; 3.1 million (87.7%) of the 3.6 million health care support jobs and 4.5 million (77.3%) of the 5.8 million personal care and service jobs were held by women. Women also predominated in sales and office occupations as a whole, but this was because they dominated the subcategory of office and administrative support occupations, holding 12.8 million (72.1%) of 17.7 million positions.

In 2016 women were dramatically underrepresented in natural resources, construction, and maintenance occupations, where they held 657,000 (4.7%) of the 13.9 million jobs; and in production, transportation, and material moving occupations, where they held 3.9 million (22.1%) of the 17.7 million positions. (See Table 3.6.)

## UNION REPRESENTATION

The BLS (January 19, 2018, http://www.bls.gov/cps/cpsaat40.htm) reports that in 2017, 10% of employed female wage and salary workers were union members and 11.3% were represented by unions (this latter figure includes workers who were not union members themselves but worked in jobs that were covered by union contracts). Slightly higher percentages of male wage and salary workers were union members (11.4%) or had union representation (12.5%).

In "Union Membership Remained Steady in 2017. The Trend May Not Hold" (WashingtonPost.com, January 19, 2018), Christopher Ingraham notes that a number of factors have contributed to the precipitous decline in union membership since the mid-20th century, when about one-third of all American workers were union members. One of the main factors was the steady loss of American manufacturing and other blue-collar jobs (where union representation was historically strong) due to automation and outsourcing overseas. Organized labor has also been hindered by a hostile political climate and the enactment of right-to-work laws, which place checks on collective bargaining rights that typically undermine union power and make membership less attractive for workers. As of 2018, 28 states had right-to-work laws. Most of these states were in the South and West, where union membership has historically been low. The adoption of right-to-work laws in midwestern states that had once been union strongholds, such as Indiana (which enacted such a law in 2012), Wisconsin (2012), and Michigan (2013), cut more deeply into overall union membership. Union membership fell 18% in Indiana and 13% in Wisconsin in 2012 as a result of the laws' implementation that year.

In spite of the decline in union membership, union representation continued to confer significant financial

TABLE 3.5

**Employed persons in agriculture and related industries and in nonagricultural industries by age, sex, and class of worker, 2016**

[In thousands]

| | | | | | 2016 | | | | | | | |
|---|---|---|---|---|---|---|---|---|---|---|---|---|
| | | | | | | Nonagricultural industries | | | | | | |
| | | | | | | | Wage and salary workers* | | | | | |
| | | Agriculture and related industries | | | | | Private industries | | | | | |
| Age and sex | Total | Wage and salary workers* | Self-employed workers, unincorporated | Unpaid family workers | Total | Total | Total | Private household workers | Other private industries | Government | Self-employed workers, unincorporated | Unpaid family workers |
| Total, 16 years and over | 2,460 | 1,583 | 853 | 23 | 148,976 | 140,161 | 119,530 | 724 | 118,807 | 20,630 | 8,751 | 65 |
| 16 to 19 years | 100 | 84 | 7 | 9 | 4,865 | 4,788 | 4,543 | 42 | 4,501 | 245 | 71 | 6 |
| 16 to 17 years | 51 | 43 | 2 | 7 | 1,695 | 1,662 | 1,590 | 17 | 1,573 | 72 | 31 | 3 |
| 18 to 19 years | 48 | 41 | 5 | 2 | 3,169 | 3,126 | 2,953 | 26 | 2,928 | 173 | 40 | 3 |
| 20 to 24 years | 166 | 149 | 14 | 4 | 13,861 | 13,602 | 12,476 | 99 | 12,376 | 1,126 | 252 | 7 |
| 25 to 34 years | 433 | 335 | 95 | 3 | 33,289 | 32,011 | 28,030 | 126 | 27,904 | 3,981 | 1,269 | 9 |
| 35 to 44 years | 420 | 302 | 116 | 1 | 31,143 | 29,348 | 24,752 | 122 | 24,630 | 4,597 | 1,787 | 8 |
| 45 to 54 years | 492 | 355 | 135 | 1 | 32,228 | 30,086 | 24,744 | 154 | 24,590 | 5,342 | 2,128 | 13 |
| 55 to 64 years | 468 | 243 | 223 | 2 | 25,056 | 22,999 | 18,826 | 124 | 18,703 | 4,173 | 2,044 | 13 |
| 65 years and over | 381 | 114 | 264 | 4 | 8,535 | 7,326 | 6,160 | 57 | 6,103 | 1,167 | 1,200 | 9 |
| Men, 16 years and over | 1,839 | 1,211 | 614 | 14 | 78,729 | 73,342 | 64,452 | 60 | 64,392 | 8,890 | 5,366 | 22 |
| 16 to 19 years | 72 | 61 | 6 | 5 | 2,412 | 2,368 | 2,253 | 5 | 2,249 | 114 | 41 | 4 |
| 16 to 17 years | 34 | 30 | 1 | 4 | 791 | 771 | 738 | 2 | 736 | 33 | 18 | 1 |
| 18 to 19 years | 37 | 31 | 5 | 1 | 1,621 | 1,597 | 1,515 | 2 | 1,513 | 82 | 22 | 2 |
| 20 to 24 years | 132 | 118 | 10 | 4 | 7,081 | 6,912 | 6,410 | 8 | 6,402 | 502 | 164 | 5 |
| 25 to 34 years | 331 | 259 | 70 | 2 | 17,854 | 17,079 | 15,283 | 6 | 15,277 | 1,796 | 771 | 4 |
| 35 to 44 years | 319 | 234 | 85 | 0 | 16,723 | 15,643 | 13,656 | 9 | 13,648 | 1,987 | 1,079 | 1 |
| 45 to 54 years | 361 | 269 | 92 | 0 | 16,926 | 15,635 | 13,412 | 9 | 13,403 | 2,223 | 1,290 | 1 |
| 55 to 64 years | 333 | 184 | 149 | 1 | 13,076 | 11,804 | 10,081 | 16 | 10,065 | 1,723 | 1,268 | 5 |
| 65 years and over | 291 | 86 | 203 | 2 | 4,657 | 3,900 | 3,357 | 8 | 3,349 | 544 | 754 | 2 |
| Women, 16 years and over | 621 | 372 | 239 | 10 | 70,247 | 66,819 | 55,079 | 664 | 54,415 | 11,740 | 3,385 | 43 |
| 16 to 19 years | 28 | 23 | 1 | 4 | 2,453 | 2,421 | 2,290 | 38 | 2,252 | 131 | 30 | 2 |
| 16 to 17 years | 17 | 13 | 1 | 3 | 905 | 891 | 851 | 14 | 837 | 40 | 12 | 1 |
| 18 to 19 years | 11 | 10 | 0 | 1 | 1,548 | 1,530 | 1,438 | 24 | 1,415 | 91 | 18 | 1 |
| 20 to 24 years | 35 | 31 | 3 | 0 | 6,780 | 6,689 | 6,066 | 91 | 5,974 | 624 | 89 | 2 |
| 25 to 34 years | 103 | 76 | 26 | 1 | 15,434 | 14,931 | 12,747 | 119 | 12,627 | 2,185 | 498 | 5 |
| 35 to 44 years | 101 | 68 | 32 | 1 | 14,419 | 13,705 | 11,096 | 113 | 10,982 | 2,609 | 708 | 7 |
| 45 to 54 years | 131 | 86 | 44 | 1 | 15,302 | 14,451 | 11,332 | 145 | 11,188 | 3,119 | 839 | 12 |
| 55 to 64 years | 134 | 60 | 74 | 1 | 11,980 | 11,195 | 8,745 | 108 | 8,637 | 2,450 | 776 | 8 |
| 65 years and over | 91 | 28 | 60 | 2 | 3,878 | 3,426 | 2,803 | 49 | 2,754 | 623 | 446 | 6 |

*Includes self-employed workers whose businesses are incorporated.
Note: Updated population controls are introduced annually with the release of January data.

SOURCE: "15. Employed Persons in Agriculture and Nonagricultural Industries by Age, Sex, and Class of Worker," in *Labor Force Statistics from the Current Population Survey*, US Bureau of Labor Statistics, February 8, 2017, https://www.bls.gov/cps/cpsaat15.pdf (accessed January 19, 2018)

advantages. According to the BLS (January 19, 2018, http://www.bls.gov/news.release/union2.t02.htm), union members saw median weekly earnings (the middle value; half made more money and half made less money) of $1,041 in 2017, compared with a median of $829 for nonunion workers. Female workers on the whole earned less than men in 2017, but unionized female workers enjoyed substantially higher median weekly earnings ($970) than either their nonunion counterparts ($746) or nonunionized male workers ($914).

## ALTERNATIVE WORK ARRANGEMENTS
### Part-Time Work

In 2016, 17.7 million women aged 16 years and older worked part time and 53.2 million worked full time. (See

Table 3.7.) In other words, 25% of all women workers worked only part time. The likelihood that a woman worked part time varied by race and Hispanic origin: 14.2 million, or 26% of all employed white women worked part time, compared with 2.8 million (26.2%) employed Hispanic women, 897,000 (20.9%) employed Asian American women, and 1.9 million (20.2%) employed African American women. Men were much less likely than women to work part time. Only 10 million (12.4%) of 80.6 million employed men worked part time.

In 2016 most people who worked part time did so for noneconomic reasons, such as caring for a child or other family member. About 7.3 million male part-time workers, or 73% of all male part-time workers, worked shorter hours for noneconomic reasons, as did 14.1 million (80%) female

TABLE 3.6

**Employed persons by occupation, sex, and age, 2015 and 2016**

[In thousands]

| Occupation | Total 16 years and over | | Men 16 years and over | | Men 20 years and over | | Women 16 years and over | | Women 20 years and over | |
|---|---|---|---|---|---|---|---|---|---|---|
| | 2015 | 2016 | 2015 | 2016 | 2015 | 2016 | 2015 | 2016 | 2015 | 2016 |
| Total | 148,834 | 151,436 | 79,131 | 80,568 | 76,776 | 78,084 | 69,703 | 70,868 | 67,323 | 68,387 |
| Management, professional, and related occupations | 57,960 | 59,438 | 28,090 | 28,846 | 27,918 | 28,662 | 29,871 | 30,593 | 29,658 | 30,381 |
| Management, business, and financial operations occupations | 24,108 | 24,941 | 13,589 | 14,019 | 13,548 | 13,973 | 10,519 | 10,922 | 10,476 | 10,881 |
| Management occupations | 16,994 | 17,418 | 10,340 | 10,611 | 10,309 | 10,576 | 6,654 | 6,807 | 6,624 | 6,777 |
| Business and financial operations occupations | 7,114 | 7,523 | 3,249 | 3,408 | 3,238 | 3,397 | 3,866 | 4,115 | 3,851 | 4,103 |
| Professional and related occupations | 33,852 | 34,498 | 14,501 | 14,827 | 14,371 | 14,689 | 19,351 | 19,671 | 19,183 | 19,500 |
| Computer and mathematical occupations | 4,369 | 4,601 | 3,291 | 3,428 | 3,277 | 3,407 | 1,078 | 1,173 | 1,072 | 1,165 |
| Architecture and engineering occupations | 2,954 | 3,106 | 2,508 | 2,665 | 2,495 | 2,649 | 446 | 441 | 444 | 439 |
| Life, physical, and social science occupations | 1,404 | 1,367 | 750 | 765 | 743 | 762 | 654 | 602 | 650 | 599 |
| Community and social service occupations | 2,596 | 2,612 | 900 | 901 | 895 | 892 | 1,696 | 1,711 | 1,685 | 1,701 |
| Legal occupations | 1,803 | 1,808 | 897 | 871 | 896 | 870 | 905 | 936 | 902 | 934 |
| Education, training, and library occupations | 8,908 | 8,948 | 2,368 | 2,410 | 2,331 | 2,373 | 6,540 | 6,538 | 6,457 | 6,464 |
| Arts, design, entertainment, sports, and media occupations | 3,051 | 3,097 | 1,599 | 1,596 | 1,558 | 1,552 | 1,452 | 1,502 | 1,413 | 1,457 |
| Healthcare practitioner and technical occupations | 8,766 | 8,960 | 2,186 | 2,190 | 2,176 | 2,182 | 6,580 | 6,769 | 6,558 | 6,741 |
| Service occupations | 25,896 | 26,811 | 11,209 | 11,625 | 10,295 | 10,657 | 14,686 | 15,186 | 13,637 | 14,084 |
| Healthcare support occupations | 3,514 | 3,554 | 436 | 438 | 425 | 422 | 3,079 | 3,116 | 2,995 | 3,050 |
| Protective service occupations | 3,109 | 3,117 | 2,447 | 2,423 | 2,387 | 2,358 | 662 | 694 | 621 | 645 |
| Food preparation and serving related occupations | 8,142 | 8,542 | 3,702 | 3,969 | 3,083 | 3,319 | 4,440 | 4,573 | 3,778 | 3,876 |
| Building and grounds cleaning and maintenance occupations | 5,716 | 5,804 | 3,368 | 3,478 | 3,233 | 3,336 | 2,348 | 2,326 | 2,291 | 2,266 |
| Personal care and service occupations | 5,415 | 5,795 | 1,257 | 1,318 | 1,166 | 1,223 | 4,157 | 4,477 | 3,951 | 4,247 |
| Sales and office occupations | 33,598 | 33,539 | 12,939 | 13,023 | 12,314 | 12,358 | 20,659 | 20,516 | 19,667 | 19,499 |
| Sales and related occupations | 15,700 | 15,848 | 7,960 | 8,088 | 7,565 | 7,673 | 7,741 | 7,761 | 7,023 | 7,045 |
| Office and administrative support occupations | 17,897 | 17,691 | 4,980 | 4,936 | 4,749 | 4,685 | 12,918 | 12,755 | 12,645 | 12,454 |
| Natural resources, construction, and maintenance occupations | 13,733 | 13,904 | 13,091 | 13,247 | 12,822 | 12,959 | 642 | 657 | 618 | 628 |
| Farming, fishing, and forestry occupations | 1,073 | 1,096 | 813 | 852 | 752 | 795 | 260 | 244 | 243 | 224 |
| Construction and extraction occupations | 7,652 | 7,929 | 7,445 | 7,693 | 7,307 | 7,548 | 207 | 236 | 203 | 230 |
| Installation, maintenance, and repair occupations | 5,008 | 4,879 | 4,833 | 4,703 | 4,763 | 4,617 | 175 | 177 | 173 | 174 |
| Production, transportation, and material moving occupations | 17,647 | 17,743 | 13,801 | 13,826 | 13,427 | 13,448 | 3,846 | 3,916 | 3,742 | 3,795 |
| Production occupations | 8,522 | 8,459 | 6,070 | 6,073 | 5,965 | 5,964 | 2,452 | 2,385 | 2,402 | 2,333 |
| Transportation and material moving occupations | 9,125 | 9,284 | 7,731 | 7,753 | 7,463 | 7,484 | 1,394 | 1,531 | 1,341 | 1,462 |

Note: Updated population controls are introduced annually with the release of January data.

SOURCE: "9. Employed Persons by Occupation, Sex, and Age," in *Labor Force Statistics from the Current Population Survey*, US Bureau of Labor Statistics, February 8, 2017, https://www.bls.gov/cps/cpsaat09.pdf (accessed January 19, 2018)

part-time workers. (See Table 3.7.) In addition, many people who usually worked full time were temporarily working part time in 2016; 4.8 million male full-time workers, or 6.9% of all male full-time workers, and 4.7 million female workers, or 8.8% of all female full-time workers, did so. Some of these people may have temporarily reduced their working hours to meet the needs of family, although it is likely that the lingering effects of the so-called Great Recession (which officially lasted from late 2007 to mid-2009 but which was still being felt in the labor market in 2018) led to the underemployment of some of these usual full-time workers.

Relatively few part-time workers have access to retirement, health care, and other benefits. In the press release "Employee Benefits in the United States—March 2017" (July 21, 2017, http://www.bls.gov/news.release/ebs2.htm), the BLS reports that in 2017, 38% of part-time employees in private industry had access to retirement benefits, 19% had access to medical care benefits, and 36% had paid sick leave. These percentages were drastically lower than for full-time workers. The federal government is the largest employer of part-time workers as a result of the Federal Employees Part-Time Career

Employment Act of 1978. This act gives part-time federal employees benefits and permanent status. Both private companies and the federal government now use part-time status as a way to recruit talented women who do not want to work full time or are unable to do so because of other commitments.

**Flextime and Telecommuting**

Changes in the structure of the American family, along with technological advances that have changed the nature of the workplace, have led many businesses to offer alternatives to the traditional 40-hour, nine-to-five workweek. Flextime is an arrangement whereby employees are allowed to vary their work hours, so long as they are present for a core part of the workday and accomplish all assigned tasks. Telecommuting involves working from home via computer and phone. Both have become significant new features of contemporary professional life, and they are especially attractive to employees seeking to balance professional and family life. Many employers offer flexible schedules and/or the ability to work part of the week from home in an effort to bolster employee morale and retention.

TABLE 3.7

**Employed and unemployed full- and part-time workers by age, sex, race, and Hispanic origin, 2016**

[In thousands]

| Age, sex, race, and Hispanic or Latino ethnicity | 2016 | | | | | | | | | |
|---|---|---|---|---|---|---|---|---|---|---|
| | Employed[a] | | | | | | | | Unemployed | |
| | Full-time workers | | | | Part-time workers | | | | | |
| | | At work | | | | At work[b] | | | | |
| | Total | 35 hours or more | 1 to 34 hours for economic or noneconomic reasons | Not at work | Total | Part time for economic reasons | Part time for noneconomic reasons | Not at work | Looking for full-time work | Looking for part-time work |
| **Total** | | | | | | | | | | |
| Total, 16 years and over | 123,761 | 110,540 | 9,507 | 3,713 | 27,675 | 4,684 | 21,421 | 1,571 | 6,345 | 1,406 |
| 16 to 19 years | 1,397 | 1,189 | 176 | 32 | 3,567 | 285 | 3,142 | 141 | 464 | 461 |
| 16 to 17 years | 226 | 188 | 31 | 7 | 1,521 | 39 | 1,416 | 66 | 104 | 276 |
| 18 to 19 years | 1,171 | 1,002 | 145 | 25 | 2,046 | 245 | 1,726 | 75 | 360 | 185 |
| 20 years and over | 122,363 | 109,351 | 9,332 | 3,681 | 24,108 | 4,399 | 18,279 | 1,430 | 5,881 | 945 |
| 20 to 24 years | 9,258 | 8,306 | 765 | 187 | 4,769 | 932 | 3,654 | 184 | 1,057 | 229 |
| 25 years and over | 113,106 | 101,045 | 8,567 | 3,494 | 19,339 | 3,467 | 14,625 | 1,246 | 4,824 | 716 |
| 25 to 54 years | 86,194 | 77,500 | 6,194 | 2,500 | 11,810 | 2,696 | 8,426 | 688 | 3,826 | 418 |
| 55 years and over | 26,912 | 23,545 | 2,372 | 994 | 7,529 | 771 | 6,199 | 558 | 998 | 299 |
| **Men, 16 years and over** | 70,567 | 63,943 | 4,841 | 1,782 | 10,002 | 2,194 | 7,305 | 502 | 3,607 | 580 |
| 16 to 19 years | 820 | 702 | 101 | 17 | 1,664 | 155 | 1,448 | 61 | 278 | 234 |
| 20 years and over | 69,747 | 63,242 | 4,740 | 1,765 | 8,337 | 2,039 | 5,857 | 441 | 3,329 | 346 |
| 20 to 24 years | 5,140 | 4,654 | 394 | 93 | 2,072 | 486 | 1,521 | 66 | 637 | 104 |
| 25 years and over | 64,607 | 58,588 | 4,347 | 1,672 | 6,265 | 1,554 | 4,336 | 375 | 2,691 | 242 |
| 25 to 54 years | 49,235 | 44,941 | 3,146 | 1,148 | 3,279 | 1,199 | 1,931 | 149 | 2,089 | 123 |
| 55 years and over | 15,372 | 13,647 | 1,201 | 524 | 2,986 | 355 | 2,405 | 226 | 602 | 120 |
| **Women, 16 years and over** | 53,194 | 46,597 | 4,666 | 1,931 | 17,674 | 2,490 | 14,115 | 1,069 | 2,739 | 826 |
| 16 to 19 years | 578 | 488 | 75 | 15 | 1,903 | 130 | 1,693 | 80 | 186 | 227 |
| 20 years and over | 52,616 | 46,109 | 4,591 | 1,916 | 15,770 | 2,360 | 12,422 | 989 | 2,553 | 599 |
| 20 to 24 years | 4,118 | 3,652 | 371 | 94 | 2,697 | 446 | 2,133 | 118 | 420 | 125 |
| 25 years and over | 48,499 | 42,457 | 4,220 | 1,821 | 13,074 | 1,913 | 10,289 | 871 | 2,133 | 474 |
| 25 to 54 years | 36,959 | 32,559 | 3,049 | 1,352 | 8,531 | 1,497 | 6,495 | 539 | 1,737 | 295 |
| 55 years and over | 11,540 | 9,898 | 1,172 | 470 | 4,543 | 417 | 3,794 | 332 | 396 | 179 |
| **White** | | | | | | | | | | |
| **Men, 16 years and over** | 56,735 | 51,333 | 3,941 | 1,460 | 7,877 | 1,598 | 5,873 | 407 | 2,526 | 426 |
| 16 to 19 years | 663 | 570 | 80 | 14 | 1,373 | 118 | 1,205 | 50 | 183 | 175 |
| 20 years and over | 56,071 | 50,764 | 3,861 | 1,447 | 6,504 | 1,480 | 4,668 | 356 | 2,344 | 250 |
| 20 to 24 years | 4,064 | 3,687 | 303 | 74 | 1,534 | 346 | 1,137 | 50 | 411 | 73 |
| 25 years and over | 52,007 | 47,076 | 3,558 | 1,372 | 4,970 | 1,133 | 3,531 | 306 | 1,933 | 178 |
| 25 to 54 years | 38,997 | 35,558 | 2,522 | 918 | 2,388 | 855 | 1,421 | 113 | 1,460 | 84 |
| 55 years and over | 13,010 | 11,519 | 1,037 | 455 | 2,582 | 279 | 2,111 | 193 | 473 | 94 |
| **Women, 16 years and over** | 40,477 | 35,331 | 3,640 | 1,506 | 14,225 | 1,784 | 11,560 | 881 | 1,781 | 613 |
| 16 to 19 years | 439 | 377 | 52 | 10 | 1,491 | 95 | 1,334 | 62 | 129 | 164 |
| 20 years and over | 40,037 | 34,955 | 3,587 | 1,495 | 12,733 | 1,689 | 10,226 | 819 | 1,652 | 448 |
| 20 to 24 years | 3,078 | 2,738 | 269 | 71 | 2,046 | 316 | 1,638 | 91 | 265 | 82 |
| 25 years and over | 36,959 | 32,216 | 3,319 | 1,424 | 10,688 | 1,372 | 8,588 | 727 | 1,387 | 366 |
| 25 to 54 years | 27,646 | 24,281 | 2,331 | 1,034 | 6,765 | 1,050 | 5,285 | 431 | 1,091 | 219 |
| 55 years and over | 9,313 | 7,935 | 988 | 390 | 3,922 | 323 | 3,303 | 296 | 296 | 147 |
| **Black or African American** | | | | | | | | | | |
| **Men, 16 years and over** | 7,279 | 6,616 | 490 | 173 | 1,192 | 375 | 764 | 53 | 751 | 94 |
| 16 to 19 years | 87 | 71 | 14 | 2 | 155 | 27 | 122 | 6 | 77 | 32 |
| 20 years and over | 7,192 | 6,545 | 476 | 171 | 1,036 | 348 | 642 | 47 | 675 | 62 |
| 20 to 24 years | 606 | 544 | 52 | 10 | 299 | 96 | 198 | 6 | 167 | 18 |
| 25 years and over | 6,586 | 6,001 | 424 | 161 | 737 | 252 | 444 | 41 | 507 | 44 |
| 25 to 54 years | 5,298 | 4,843 | 332 | 123 | 503 | 207 | 276 | 19 | 429 | 26 |
| 55 years and over | 1,288 | 1,158 | 92 | 38 | 234 | 45 | 168 | 22 | 78 | 18 |
| **Women, 16 years and over** | 7,591 | 6,722 | 622 | 247 | 1,920 | 474 | 1,342 | 104 | 674 | 136 |
| 16 to 19 years | 85 | 71 | 12 | 2 | 207 | 22 | 176 | 9 | 44 | 43 |
| 20 years and over | 7,506 | 6,651 | 609 | 245 | 1,713 | 452 | 1,166 | 95 | 630 | 94 |
| 20 to 24 years | 638 | 565 | 60 | 13 | 386 | 98 | 272 | 16 | 116 | 27 |
| 25 years and over | 6,867 | 6,086 | 549 | 232 | 1,327 | 354 | 894 | 79 | 514 | 66 |
| 25 to 54 years | 5,543 | 4,914 | 441 | 188 | 959 | 299 | 601 | 59 | 446 | 45 |
| 55 years and over | 1,324 | 1,172 | 108 | 45 | 368 | 55 | 293 | 20 | 68 | 21 |

Flextime and telecommuting are particularly attractive to professional working mothers. According to Kim Parker and Wendy Wang of the Pew Research Center, in *Modern Parenthood: Roles of Moms and Dads Converge*

**TABLE 3.7**

**Employed and unemployed full- and part-time workers by age, sex, race, and Hispanic origin, 2016** [CONTINUED]

[In thousands]

| | 2016 | | | | | | | | | |
| | Employed[a] | | | | | | | | Unemployed | |
| | Full-time workers | | | | Part-time workers | | | | | |
| | | At work | | | | At work[b] | | | | |
| Age, sex, race, and Hispanic or Latino ethnicity | Total | 35 hours or more | 1 to 34 hours for economic or noneconomic reasons | Not at work | Total | Part time for economic reasons | Part time for noneconomic reasons | Not at work | Looking for full-time work | Looking for part-time work |
|---|---|---|---|---|---|---|---|---|---|---|
| **Asian** | | | | | | | | | | |
| Men, 16 years and over | 4,386 | 4,055 | 234 | 97 | 529 | 119 | 387 | 24 | 152 | 25 |
| 16 to 19 years | 29 | 26 | 3 | 0 | 50 | 5 | 43 | 2 | 4 | 9 |
| 20 years and over | 4,357 | 4,030 | 231 | 96 | 479 | 114 | 344 | 22 | 148 | 16 |
| 20 to 24 years | 206 | 186 | 15 | 4 | 142 | 22 | 115 | 5 | 21 | 6 |
| 25 years and over | 4,151 | 3,843 | 216 | 92 | 337 | 91 | 229 | 17 | 127 | 10 |
| 25 to 54 years | 3,352 | 3,111 | 170 | 70 | 227 | 72 | 145 | 9 | 99 | 6 |
| 55 years and over | 800 | 732 | 46 | 22 | 111 | 19 | 84 | 8 | 27 | 4 |
| Women, 16 years and over | 3,401 | 3,065 | 222 | 114 | 897 | 117 | 729 | 51 | 140 | 32 |
| 16 to 19 years | 14 | 10 | 3 | 1 | 67 | 2 | 62 | 3 | 1 | 6 |
| 20 years and over | 3,387 | 3,055 | 219 | 114 | 830 | 114 | 667 | 49 | 139 | 26 |
| 20 to 24 years | 184 | 165 | 17 | 3 | 136 | 10 | 121 | 5 | 17 | 5 |
| 25 years and over | 3,203 | 2,890 | 202 | 111 | 694 | 105 | 546 | 43 | 122 | 21 |
| 25 to 54 years | 2,541 | 2,300 | 152 | 88 | 514 | 77 | 404 | 33 | 100 | 14 |
| 55 years and over | 663 | 590 | 50 | 23 | 180 | 28 | 143 | 10 | 22 | 7 |
| **Hispanic or Latino ethnicity** | | | | | | | | | | |
| Men, 16 years and over | 12,932 | 11,756 | 916 | 260 | 1,631 | 548 | 1,029 | 55 | 724 | 109 |
| 16 to 19 years | 210 | 181 | 26 | 3 | 298 | 33 | 257 | 8 | 66 | 48 |
| 20 years and over | 12,722 | 11,575 | 890 | 257 | 1,333 | 514 | 772 | 47 | 659 | 61 |
| 20 to 24 years | 1,268 | 1,147 | 101 | 20 | 409 | 106 | 294 | 9 | 144 | 27 |
| 25 years and over | 11,454 | 10,428 | 789 | 237 | 924 | 408 | 478 | 38 | 514 | 34 |
| 25 to 54 years | 9,801 | 8,946 | 664 | 191 | 703 | 334 | 343 | 27 | 425 | 22 |
| 55 years and over | 1,653 | 1,482 | 125 | 46 | 221 | 74 | 136 | 11 | 89 | 12 |
| Women, 16 years and over | 7,882 | 7,002 | 640 | 239 | 2,805 | 597 | 2,092 | 116 | 552 | 163 |
| 16 to 19 years | 124 | 107 | 14 | 3 | 346 | 33 | 304 | 9 | 35 | 52 |
| 20 years and over | 7,758 | 6,895 | 627 | 236 | 2,459 | 564 | 1,788 | 107 | 516 | 111 |
| 20 to 24 years | 854 | 749 | 85 | 20 | 556 | 100 | 438 | 17 | 97 | 30 |
| 25 years and over | 6,904 | 6,146 | 542 | 216 | 1,903 | 463 | 1,350 | 90 | 419 | 81 |
| 25 to 54 years | 5,857 | 5,225 | 454 | 178 | 1,517 | 379 | 1,068 | 70 | 363 | 66 |
| 55 years and over | 1,047 | 921 | 88 | 38 | 387 | 84 | 282 | 21 | 56 | 15 |

[a]Employed persons are classified as full- or part-time workers based on their usual weekly hours at all jobs regardless of the number of hours they are at work during the reference week. Persons absent from work also are classified according to their usual status. Full time is 35 hours or more per week; part time is less than 35 hours.
[b]Includes some persons at work 35 hours or more classified by their reason for usually working part time.
Note: Estimates for the above race groups (white, black or African American, and Asian) do not sum to totals because data are not presented for all races. Persons whose ethnicity is identified as Hispanic or Latino may be of any race. Updated population controls are introduced annually with the release of January data.

SOURCE: "8. Employed and Unemployed Full- and Part-Time Workers by Age, Sex, Race, and Hispanic or Latino Ethnicity," in *Labor Force Statistics from the Current Population Survey*, US Bureau of Labor Statistics, February 8, 2017, https://www.bls.gov/cps/cpsaat08.pdf (accessed January 19, 2018)

*as They Balance Work and Family* (March 14, 2013, http://assets.pewresearch.org/wp-content/uploads/sites/3/2013/03/FINAL_modern_parenthood_03-2013.pdf), mothers and fathers are roughly equal in their stated desire to have more time at home raising their children, but "when it comes to what they value most in a job, working fathers place more importance on having a high-paying job, while working mothers are more concerned with having a flexible schedule." A growing body of research also suggests that employers benefit from flexible arrangements in the form of improved worker loyalty and productivity. In *The 2015 Workplace Flexibility Study* (February 17, 2015, https://workplacetrends.com/the-2015-workplace-flexibility-study/), WorkplaceTrends.com, a research and advisory membership portal for human resources professionals, and CareerArc, a global recruitment and outplacement firm, indicate that employers offering flexibility programs reported improved employee satisfaction (87%), increased productivity (71%), and better ability to retain current talent (65%). Meanwhile, 75% of employees surveyed (and 74% of unemployed survey respondents) ranked workplace flexibility as their most important benefit.

Access to flextime varies considerably from one industry to the next. The White House Council of Economic Advisers cites in *Work-Life Balance and the Economics of Workplace Flexibility* (June 2014, https://obamawhite house.archives.gov/sites/default/files/docs/updated_work place_flex_report_final_0.pdf) findings from the 2011 American Time Use Survey, which indicated that although about 65% of workers in the information services industry had the freedom to alter their working hours in 2011, less than one-third of full-time workers in the construction, transportation, and utility industries enjoyed the same benefit.

Telecommuting, like flextime, is a workplace perk usually reserved for professionals. The BLS reports in the press release "American Time Use Survey—2016 Results" (June 27, 2017, https://www.bls.gov/news.release/pdf/atus.pdf) that 22% of all employed people did some work at home on an average workday in 2016. Among workers aged 25 years and older, 43.1% of those with an advanced degree did some work from home on an average day, compared with 31.6% of those with a bachelor's degree and 12% of those with only a high school diploma. About one-third of those working in management, business, and financial operations (34.1%) and in professional and related occupations (33.3%) worked from home. Those working in production (7.7%), installation, maintenance, and repair (6.4%), and transportation and material moving (5.4%) were the least likely to work from home. Those who were self-employed were far more likely to telecommute than those who worked on a wage or salary basis. More than half (53.8%) of self-employed workers spent time working from home on an average day, averaging 4.3 hours of work from home. By comparison, 19.2% of wage and salary workers spent time working from home, averaging 2.9 hours per day.

According to the BLS, women who were employed full time were somewhat more likely than men who were employed full time to have worked from home on an average day in 2016 (23.2% of women versus 21.8% of men). Among part-time workers, the difference was more pronounced, as 24.7% of women worked from home, compared with 17.3% of men. It should also be noted that certain occupations have always involved some amount of at-home work. For example, those in education, training, and library occupations, the overwhelming majority of whom are schoolteachers, frequently plan lessons and grade assignments at home. The BLS reports in "Work-at-Home Patterns by Occupation" (March 2009, http://www.bls.gov/opub/ils/pdf/opbils72.pdf), the most recent year for which government data were available as of April 2018, that individuals in education-oriented jobs typically accomplished 11.8% of their weekly workload at home in 2009, the highest percentage among all wage and salary workers. Among self-employed workers, those who worked in personal care operations accomplished 42.6% of an average weekly workload at home in 2009, second only to those in arts, design, entertainment, sports, and media occupations (55.2%).

## Multiple Jobholders

In 2016, 5.5% of employed women aged 16 years and older held more than one job, as did 4.5% of employed men. (See Table 3.8.) Among women, those between the ages of 20 and 24 years (7.5%) were the most likely to hold more than one job, whereas women aged 65 years and older (4%) were the least likely. A larger proportion of white women (5.6%) than African American (5.4%), Asian American (3.8%), or Hispanic (3.6%) women held multiple jobs. Married women living with their spouse were less likely (4.7%) than widowed, divorced, or separated (6.2%) or never married (6.4%) women to hold more than one job, reflecting the greater economic security of married women.

Etienne Lalé of the University of Bristol notes in "Multiple Jobholding over the Last Two Decades" (*Monthly Labor Review*, April 2015) that multiple jobholding rates have been gradually declining since the mid-1990s. Having peaked at 6.8% during the summer of 1995, the proportion of multiple jobholders among all employed workers was down to 5% at the end of 2013. Lalé indicates that although moonlighting (multiple job holding) has declined among both men and women, the downward trend among men became visible in 2002, while the rate among women remained steady until about 2009. Overall, widowed, divorced, or separated individuals of both sexes are more likely to hold multiple jobs than either their married or single counterparts. Married men moonlight more than men who are widowed, divorced, or separated, while single women moonlight more than married women.

## UNEMPLOYMENT
### Unemployment Rates

The labor force includes both people who are employed and people who are looking for work. The unemployment situation in the United States became critical during the Great Recession, when unemployment reached record levels in some states. An unemployment rate of approximately 5% is considered normal even in times of economic growth; the unemployment rate in the wake of the recession reached a peak of 10% overall in October 2009. Recovery was slow after the official end of the recession, with unemployment levels remaining high for years.

By 2018 the national economy appeared to be back to a state of steady growth. In the press release "The Employment Situation—March 2018" (April, 2018, http://www.bls.gov/news.release/pdf/empsit.pdf), the BLS reports that in March 2018 the overall unemployment rate had dipped to 4.1%, with even lower rates for adult women (3.7%) and men (3.7%). Young people were the most likely to be unemployed; teens aged 16 to 19 years had an unemployment rate of 13.5%. Among racial and

**TABLE 3.8**

**Multiple jobholders by selected characteristics, 2016**

[Numbers in thousands]

| Characteristic | Total | | | | Men | | | | Women | | | |
|---|---|---|---|---|---|---|---|---|---|---|---|---|
| | Number | | Rate[a] | | Number | | Rate[a] | | Number | | Rate[a] | |
| | 2015 | 2016 | 2015 | 2016 | 2015 | 2016 | 2015 | 2016 | 2015 | 2016 | 2015 | 2016 |
| **Age** | | | | | | | | | | | | |
| Total, 16 years and over[b] | 7,262 | 7,531 | 4.9 | 5.0 | 3,571 | 3,645 | 4.5 | 4.5 | 3,692 | 3,887 | 5.3 | 5.5 |
| 16 to 19 years | 199 | 205 | 4.2 | 4.1 | 73 | 81 | 3.1 | 3.3 | 126 | 124 | 5.3 | 5.0 |
| 20 years and over | 7,063 | 7,326 | 4.9 | 5.0 | 3,498 | 3,563 | 4.6 | 4.6 | 3,565 | 3,763 | 5.3 | 5.5 |
| 20 to 24 years | 799 | 848 | 5.7 | 6.0 | 329 | 335 | 4.6 | 4.6 | 470 | 514 | 6.9 | 7.5 |
| 25 years and over | 6,264 | 6,478 | 4.8 | 4.9 | 3,169 | 3,229 | 4.6 | 4.6 | 3,095 | 3,249 | 5.1 | 5.3 |
| 25 to 54 years | 4,783 | 4,961 | 4.9 | 5.1 | 2,408 | 2,460 | 4.6 | 4.7 | 2,375 | 2,501 | 5.3 | 5.5 |
| 55 years and over | 1,481 | 1,516 | 4.4 | 4.4 | 761 | 769 | 4.3 | 4.2 | 720 | 747 | 4.6 | 4.6 |
| 55 to 64 years | 1,162 | 1,161 | 4.7 | 4.5 | 587 | 571 | 4.5 | 4.3 | 575 | 589 | 4.8 | 4.9 |
| 65 years and over | 319 | 356 | 3.8 | 4.0 | 174 | 198 | 3.7 | 4.0 | 145 | 158 | 3.8 | 4.0 |
| **Race and Hispanic or Latino ethnicity** | | | | | | | | | | | | |
| White | 5,881 | 5,999 | 5.0 | 5.0 | 2,917 | 2,926 | 4.6 | 4.5 | 2,964 | 3,072 | 5.5 | 5.6 |
| Black or African American | 869 | 958 | 5.0 | 5.3 | 410 | 449 | 5.0 | 5.3 | 459 | 510 | 4.9 | 5.4 |
| Asian | 271 | 308 | 3.1 | 3.3 | 121 | 143 | 2.6 | 2.9 | 150 | 165 | 3.7 | 3.8 |
| Hispanic or Latino ethnicity | 782 | 820 | 3.2 | 3.2 | 430 | 433 | 3.0 | 3.0 | 352 | 387 | 3.4 | 3.6 |
| **Marital status** | | | | | | | | | | | | |
| Married, spouse present[c] | 3,702 | 3,761 | 4.6 | 4.7 | 2,121 | 2,114 | 4.7 | 4.7 | 1,581 | 1,647 | 4.5 | 4.7 |
| Widowed, divorced, or separated[d] | 1,243 | 1,307 | 5.2 | 5.4 | 423 | 442 | 4.3 | 4.4 | 820 | 865 | 5.9 | 6.2 |
| Never married | 2,318 | 2,463 | 5.1 | 5.3 | 1,027 | 1,089 | 4.2 | 4.3 | 1,291 | 1,374 | 6.2 | 6.4 |
| **Full- or part-time status** | | | | | | | | | | | | |
| Primary job full time, secondary job part time | 3,909 | 4,084 | — | — | 2,128 | 2,235 | — | — | 1,781 | 1,849 | — | — |
| Primary and secondary jobs both part time | 1,951 | 2,075 | — | — | 662 | 703 | — | — | 1,288 | 1,372 | — | — |
| Primary and secondary jobs both full time | 242 | 278 | — | — | 156 | 167 | — | — | 86 | 112 | — | — |
| Hours vary on primary or secondary job | 1,114 | 1,038 | — | — | 600 | 512 | — | — | 514 | 526 | — | — |

[a]Multiple jobholders as a percent of all employed persons in specified group.
[b]Includes a small number of persons who work part time on their primary job and full time on their secondary jobs(s), not shown separately.
[c]Refers to persons in opposite-sex married couples only.
[d]Separated includes persons who are married, spouse absent.
Note: Full time is 35 hours or more per week; part time is less than 35 hours. Estimates for the above race groups (white, black or African American, and Asian) do not sum to totals because data are not presented for all races. Persons whose ethnicity is identified as Hispanic or Latino may be of any race. Updated population controls are introduced annually with the release of January data. Dash indicates no data or data that do not meet publication criteria (values not shown where base is less than 35,000).

SOURCE: "36. Multiple Jobholders by Selected Characteristics," in *Labor Force Statistics from the Current Population Survey*, US Bureau of Labor Statistics, February 8, 2017, http://www.bls.gov/cps/cpsaat36.pdf (accessed January 19, 2018)

ethnic groups, Asian Americans had the lowest unemployment rate (3.1%), followed by whites (3.6%), Hispanics (5.1%), and African Americans (6.9%).

## Unemployed Mothers

The BLS notes in *Women in the Labor Force* that in 2015, 75.1% of single women with children under the age of 18 years were in the civilian labor force; 9.5% of these single mothers were unemployed, which was more than three times the unemployment rate of married women with children under the age of 18 years (2.8%). Among Asian American single mothers, the unemployment rate was 2.7%, compared with 7.7% among white single mothers, 9.7% among Hispanic single mothers, and 13.3% among African American single mothers. Many unmarried mothers have a lower socioeconomic status, lack job skills, and have limited access to child care. More financially well-off mothers often choose to remain at home until their children reach school age, either because of inadequate child care or because of a desire

to spend more time with their children during the formative years. Many of these women return to work when their children are older.

## Duration of Unemployment

Since the beginning of the Great Recession, the duration of spells of unemployment rose steadily. According to the BLS, in "Employment Situation—March 2018," the number of long-term unemployed (those jobless for 27 weeks or longer) was 1.3 million in March 2018, representing 20.3% of all unemployed workers. Although this number was significantly down from its record high of 6.7 million in 2010, it was still high by historical standards. Over the course of 2016, 30.5% (2.4 million of 7.8 million) of all unemployed people were out of work for less than five weeks, 28.7% (2.2 million of 7.8 million) were out of work from five to 14 weeks, and 40.8% (3.2 million of 7.8 million) had been out of work for 15 weeks or longer. (See Table 3.9.) Men and women experienced comparable periods of

TABLE 3.9

## Unemployed persons by age, sex, race and Hispanic origin, marital status, and duration of unemployment, 2016

[Numbers in thousands]

| | 2016 | | | | | | Weeks | |
|---|---|---|---|---|---|---|---|---|
| | Unemployed | | | | | | | |
| | | | | 15 weeks and over | | | Average (mean) duration | Median duration |
| Characteristic | Total | Less than 5 weeks | 5 to 14 weeks | Total | 15 to 26 weeks | 27 weeks and over | | |
| **Age and sex** | | | | | | | | |
| Total, 16 years and over | 7,751 | 2,362 | 2,226 | 3,163 | 1,158 | 2,005 | 27.5 | 10.6 |
| 16 to 19 years | 925 | 385 | 300 | 240 | 117 | 122 | 14.3 | 6.8 |
| 20 to 24 years | 1,286 | 444 | 398 | 444 | 192 | 252 | 21.0 | 9.0 |
| 25 to 34 years | 1,797 | 532 | 529 | 737 | 281 | 456 | 25.3 | 10.9 |
| 35 to 44 years | 1,258 | 355 | 372 | 531 | 186 | 344 | 27.9 | 11.3 |
| 45 to 54 years | 1,189 | 311 | 302 | 576 | 189 | 387 | 35.4 | 13.8 |
| 55 to 64 years | 941 | 224 | 240 | 478 | 150 | 328 | 38.5 | 15.0 |
| 65 years and over | 355 | 112 | 86 | 157 | 42 | 115 | 39.3 | 11.7 |
| **Men, 16 years and over** | 4,187 | 1,245 | 1,181 | 1,761 | 625 | 1,136 | 29.3 | 11.2 |
| 16 to 19 years | 512 | 201 | 174 | 137 | 64 | 73 | 15.5 | 7.4 |
| 20 to 24 years | 742 | 242 | 219 | 280 | 116 | 165 | 23.0 | 9.9 |
| 25 to 34 years | 966 | 288 | 274 | 405 | 149 | 255 | 26.6 | 11.1 |
| 35 to 44 years | 644 | 183 | 189 | 271 | 96 | 175 | 27.6 | 11.5 |
| 45 to 54 years | 602 | 153 | 149 | 300 | 92 | 209 | 40.0 | 14.4 |
| 55 to 64 years | 528 | 123 | 133 | 273 | 86 | 187 | 39.2 | 15.6 |
| 65 years and over | 193 | 56 | 43 | 94 | 23 | 71 | 48.0 | 13.7 |
| **Women, 16 years and over** | 3,564 | 1,117 | 1,046 | 1,402 | 533 | 869 | 25.4 | 10.1 |
| 16 to 19 years | 413 | 184 | 126 | 103 | 54 | 49 | 12.9 | 6.0 |
| 20 to 24 years | 545 | 202 | 179 | 164 | 77 | 87 | 18.2 | 7.9 |
| 25 to 34 years | 832 | 244 | 255 | 332 | 131 | 201 | 23.8 | 10.6 |
| 35 to 44 years | 614 | 172 | 183 | 259 | 90 | 169 | 28.3 | 11.2 |
| 45 to 54 years | 586 | 158 | 153 | 276 | 98 | 178 | 30.8 | 13.2 |
| 55 to 64 years | 413 | 101 | 107 | 205 | 64 | 141 | 37.4 | 14.3 |
| 65 years and over | 162 | 56 | 43 | 63 | 20 | 44 | 28.9 | 9.9 |
| **Race and Hispanic or Latino ethnicity** | | | | | | | | |
| White, 16 years and over | 5,345 | 1,717 | 1,555 | 2,073 | 784 | 1,289 | 26.3 | 10.0 |
| Men | 2,952 | 921 | 828 | 1,203 | 443 | 760 | 28.6 | 10.6 |
| Women | 2,393 | 796 | 727 | 870 | 341 | 529 | 23.5 | 9.4 |
| Black or African American, 16 years and over | 1,655 | 422 | 451 | 782 | 257 | 525 | 31.8 | 13.4 |
| Men | 845 | 213 | 233 | 400 | 121 | 278 | 33.2 | 13.4 |
| Women | 810 | 209 | 219 | 382 | 136 | 247 | 30.4 | 13.3 |
| Asian, 16 years and over | 349 | 100 | 100 | 149 | 55 | 94 | 27.9 | 11.4 |
| Men | 176 | 48 | 53 | 76 | 26 | 49 | 28.0 | 11.6 |
| Women | 172 | 52 | 47 | 73 | 29 | 44 | 27.8 | 11.3 |
| Hispanic or Latino ethnicity, 16 years and over | 1,548 | 517 | 447 | 583 | 230 | 354 | 24.3 | 9.6 |
| Men | 833 | 290 | 234 | 309 | 119 | 190 | 23.7 | 9.4 |
| Women | 715 | 228 | 213 | 274 | 110 | 164 | 25.0 | 9.9 |
| **Marital status** | | | | | | | | |
| **Men, 16 years and over** | | | | | | | | |
| Married, spouse present[a] | 1,259 | 369 | 339 | 552 | 192 | 360 | 30.3 | 11.8 |
| Widowed, divorced, or separated[b] | 600 | 157 | 175 | 268 | 96 | 172 | 34.1 | 12.5 |
| Never married | 2,328 | 720 | 667 | 940 | 337 | 604 | 27.5 | 10.5 |
| **Women, 16 years and over** | | | | | | | | |
| Married, spouse present[a] | 1,093 | 343 | 318 | 433 | 169 | 264 | 25.7 | 10.1 |
| Widowed, divorced, or separated[b] | 757 | 205 | 211 | 341 | 111 | 229 | 30.1 | 12.4 |
| Never married | 1,715 | 569 | 517 | 629 | 253 | 376 | 23.1 | 9.4 |

[a]Refers to persons in opposite-sex married couples only.
[b]Separated includes persons who are married, spouse absent.
Note: Estimates for the above race groups (white, black or African American, and Asian) do not sum to totals because data are not presented for all races. Persons whose ethnicity is identified as Hispanic or Latino may be of any race. Updated population controls are introduced annually with the release of January data.

SOURCE: "31. Unemployed Persons by Age, Sex, Race, Hispanic or Latino Ethnicity, Marital Status, and Duration of Unemployment," in *Labor Force Statistics from the Current Population Survey*, US Bureau of Labor Statistics, February 8, 2017, https://www.bls.gov/cps/cpsaat31.pdf (accessed January 19, 2018)

unemployment. On average, men aged 16 years and older stayed unemployed for 29.3 weeks, whereas women of the same age stayed unemployed for an average of 25.4 weeks. Among unemployed women, white women had the lowest average duration of unemployment (23.5 weeks), followed by Hispanic women (25 weeks), Asian American women (27.8 weeks), and African American women (30.4 weeks). For all these demographic groups, the average period of unemployment had gone down by between six to nine weeks since 2014, suggesting that the struggle to find jobs was beginning to abate, even for the long-term unemployed.

In 2008, as the Great Recession gathered steam, Congress sought to offset the effects on workers by creating the Emergency Unemployment Compensation program, which provided a temporary extension of benefits to unemployed people who had already exhausted their state-level benefits. Unemployment benefits vary by state, but they are usually available for up to 26 weeks. The Emergency Unemployment Compensation program, together with state and other programs, allowed people to draw benefits for up to 46 weeks; those in the hardest hit states could draw benefits for up to 99 weeks. Even with these extensions, people laid off when the recession began were facing the prospect of their unemployment aid running out, given that high unemployment lasted far beyond the recession's official end in mid-2009. The temporary program was extended numerous times as the unemployment crisis lingered. Congress ultimately allowed the Emergency Unemployment Compensation program to expire on January 1, 2014, cutting off unemployment benefits for roughly 1.3 million unemployed Americans. During the months that followed, the unemployment rate continued to decrease. In "The Employment Situation—March 2018," the BLS indicates that as of March 2018 the number of long-term unemployed had declined by 345,000 over the preceding 12 months.

### Reasons for Unemployment

According to the BLS (January 19, 2018, http://www.bls.gov/cps/cpsaat27.htm), of the 2.9 million unemployed women aged 20 years and older in 2017, 1.3 million (47% of all unemployed women over the age of 20 years) had lost their job or had completed a temporary job and 378,000 (13.2%) had been laid off only temporarily. Approximately 996,000 (34.7%) unemployed women over the age of 20 years were trying to reenter the labor force after having left for a time, and 375,000 (13.1%) had left their job. Another 149,000 (5.2%) unemployed women were trying to enter the labor force for the first time.

Displaced workers are people aged 20 years and older who lost their job because their company either closed or moved to a new location or because their job was eliminated. According to the BLS, in the press release "Worker Displacement, 2013–15" (August 25, 2016, http://www.bls.gov/news.release/disp.nr0.htm), female displaced workers in 2016 were less likely to be reemployed than were males. As of January 2016, the reemployment rate for men was 66.5% (up slightly from 64% in January 2014), while the reemployment rate for women was 64.1% (up from 58% in January 2014). Additionally, displaced women workers were more likely than displaced men workers to leave the labor force altogether; they did so at a rate of 19.6%, compared with 17.8% for men.

### Out of the Labor Force

Discouraged workers are those who have stopped looking for work or who want to work but are unable to apply for jobs because they lack child care or transportation. Discouraged workers are not part of the official labor force. According to the BLS (January 19, 2018, http://www.bls.gov/cps/cpsaat35.htm), 3 million (5.3%) of the 56.6 million women who were not in the labor force in 2017 wanted to be working. Of these 3 million women, 575,000 were unable to work because of school, family, ill health, or other problems (including a lack of child care or transportation), and another 177,000 were not currently looking for work because they were discouraged about their job prospects. These women may have been discouraged by the continued high unemployment, they may have looked and been unable to find a job, or they may have lacked training or education. This category also includes women who may have been discriminated against, perhaps for being a single mother or for being a member of a particular age group or race.

### EDUCATION AND THE LABOR FORCE

There is a strong correlation between a woman's education and her labor force status. In 1970 only 11.2% of women in the workforce were college graduates, and another 10.9% had attended college but not taken a degree or had an associate's degree. (See Table 3.10.) Women whose highest level of educational attainment was a high school diploma made up 44.3% of all females in the labor force in 1970, and those without a high school diploma accounted for another 33.5% of all females in the labor force. By 2015 more than seven out of 10 women in the labor force had either graduated from college (41.1%) or had attended college but not taken a degree or had an associate's degree (29.6%). Women who had graduated from high school but not attended college made up 23.2% of the female labor force, and women without a high school degree accounted for only 6.1% of the female labor force. This shift in the percent distribution of women in the labor force speaks to the increasing necessity of postsecondary education in the labor market and to the increasing difficulty faced by those without a high school diploma. These trends are expected to continue, with most future job growth coming in professions that require an associate's degree or higher.

### LABOR FORCE PROJECTIONS

Labor force growth was rapid from the 1970s to the 1990s, driven in part by the large size of the baby boom generation (people born between 1946 and 1964), an expanding economy, and the rapid growth of the female labor force. According to Mitra Toossi of the BLS, in *A Look at the Future of the U.S. Labor Force to 2060* (September 2016, https://www.bls.gov/spotlight/2016/a-look-at-the-future-of-the-us-labor-force-to-2060/pdf/a-look-at-the-future-of-the-us-labor-force-to-2060.pdf),

TABLE 3.10

**Percentage distribution of women in the civilian labor force, aged 25–64 years, by educational attainment, 1970–2015**

| Year | Civilian labor force (thousands) | Total | High school | | College | |
|------|------|------|------|------|------|------|
| | | | Less than 4 years | 4 years, no college | 1 to 3 years | 4 years or more |
| 1970 | 22,462 | 100.0 | 33.5 | 44.3 | 10.9 | 11.2 |
| 1971 | 22,804 | 100.0 | 32.2 | 44.2 | 11.9 | 11.8 |
| 1972 | 23,606 | 100.0 | 30.7 | 45.1 | 11.8 | 12.4 |
| 1973 | 24,158 | 100.0 | 28.4 | 45.9 | 12.4 | 13.3 |
| 1974 | 25,203 | 100.0 | 26.7 | 45.3 | 13.4 | 14.6 |
| 1975 | 26,146 | 100.0 | 26.5 | 45.5 | 13.9 | 14.1 |
| 1976 | 27,166 | 100.0 | 24.0 | 45.1 | 14.7 | 16.2 |
| 1977 | 28,369 | 100.0 | 22.8 | 45.1 | 15.2 | 16.9 |
| 1978 | 29,738 | 100.0 | 22.0 | 44.9 | 16.1 | 17.0 |
| 1979 | 31,151 | 100.0 | 20.1 | 45.0 | 17.1 | 17.8 |
| 1980 | 32,593 | 100.0 | 18.4 | 45.4 | 17.4 | 18.7 |
| 1981 | 33,910 | 100.0 | 17.4 | 46.1 | 17.9 | 18.6 |
| 1982 | 34,870 | 100.0 | 16.6 | 45.6 | 18.3 | 19.5 |
| 1983 | 35,712 | 100.0 | 15.6 | 44.8 | 18.8 | 20.9 |
| 1984 | 37,234 | 100.0 | 14.5 | 44.9 | 18.9 | 21.7 |
| 1985 | 38,779 | 100.0 | 13.7 | 44.4 | 19.9 | 22.0 |
| 1986 | 39,767 | 100.0 | 13.2 | 44.3 | 20.3 | 22.2 |
| 1987 | 41,105 | 100.0 | 12.5 | 44.0 | 20.7 | 22.8 |
| 1988 | 42,254 | 100.0 | 12.4 | 43.3 | 21.2 | 23.1 |
| 1989 | 43,650 | 100.0 | 11.9 | 42.9 | 20.9 | 24.3 |
| 1990 | 44,699 | 100.0 | 11.3 | 42.4 | 21.9 | 24.5 |
| 1991 | 45,315 | 100.0 | 10.9 | 41.6 | 22.2 | 25.2 |

| Year | Civilian labor force (thousands) | Total | Less than a high school diploma | High school graduates, no college[a] | Some college or associate's degree | Bachelor's degree and higher[b] |
|------|------|------|------|------|------|------|
| 1992 | 46,589 | 100.0 | 10.3 | 37.4 | 27.3 | 25.0 |
| 1993 | 47,245 | 100.0 | 9.3 | 36.6 | 28.4 | 25.7 |
| 1994 | 48,405 | 100.0 | 9.0 | 35.0 | 29.8 | 26.2 |
| 1995 | 49,247 | 100.0 | 8.8 | 34.1 | 30.2 | 26.9 |
| 1996 | 50,240 | 100.0 | 8.8 | 33.6 | 29.9 | 27.8 |
| 1997 | 51,261 | 100.0 | 8.7 | 33.5 | 29.4 | 28.4 |
| 1998 | 51,678 | 100.0 | 8.8 | 32.7 | 29.4 | 29.2 |
| 1999 | 52,525 | 100.0 | 8.5 | 32.1 | 29.5 | 29.9 |
| 2000 | 53,749 | 100.0 | 8.5 | 31.6 | 29.8 | 30.1 |
| 2001 | 54,229 | 100.0 | 8.4 | 31.0 | 30.2 | 30.4 |
| 2002 | 54,710 | 100.0 | 8.1 | 30.6 | 29.9 | 31.3 |
| 2003 | 55,596 | 100.0 | 7.9 | 30.0 | 29.9 | 32.2 |
| 2004 | 55,616 | 100.0 | 7.7 | 29.4 | 30.2 | 32.6 |
| 2005 | 56,322 | 100.0 | 7.7 | 28.7 | 30.2 | 33.3 |
| 2006 | 57,201 | 100.0 | 7.6 | 28.3 | 30.2 | 33.9 |
| 2007 | 57,791 | 100.0 | 7.1 | 27.9 | 30.1 | 34.9 |
| 2008 | 58,465 | 100.0 | 6.9 | 27.2 | 30.4 | 35.6 |
| 2009 | 58,787 | 100.0 | 7.0 | 26.7 | 30.3 | 36.0 |
| 2010 | 58,808 | 100.0 | 6.8 | 26.4 | 30.3 | 36.4 |
| 2011 | 58,520 | 100.0 | 6.7 | 25.8 | 30.4 | 37.1 |
| 2012 | 59,031 | 100.0 | 6.5 | 25.0 | 30.4 | 38.1 |
| 2013 | 58,812 | 100.0 | 6.3 | 24.6 | 30.1 | 39.0 |
| 2014 | 58,983 | 100.0 | 6.1 | 24.1 | 29.8 | 40.0 |
| 2015 | 59,252 | 100.0 | 6.1 | 23.2 | 29.6 | 41.1 |

[a]Includes people with a high school diploma or equivalent.
[b]Includes people with bachelor's, master's, and doctoral degrees.
Note: Data from 1970–1991 are from the March Current Population Survey. The educational attainment categories for these years were based on the number of years of school completed. Data beginning in 1992 are annual averages, and the educational attainment categories are based on the highest diploma or degree received.

SOURCE: Adapted from "Table 9A. Percent Distribution of the Civilian Labor Force, 25 to 64 Years of Age, by Educational Attainment and Gender, 1970–2015," and "Table 9B. Percent Distribution of the Civilian Labor Force, 25 to 64 Years of Age, by Educational Attainment and Gender, 1970–2015," in *Women in the Labor Force: A Databook*, US Bureau of Labor Statistics, April 2017, https://www.bls.gov/opub/reports/womens-databook/2016/pdf/home.pdf (accessed January 19, 2018)

slower population growth, the aging of the US population, the leveling off of the labor force participation rate, and other demographic factors point to a future in which the labor force is expected to grow more slowly between 2016 and 2060 than it has in previous decades.

Toossi notes that declines in labor force participation since 2000 are evident across many demographic categories. Since peaking at 60% in 1999, women's labor force participation rate has been declining slowly and is projected to stand at 51.9% in 2060. (See Figure 3.1.) Men's labor force participation rate has been steadily declining

**FIGURE 3.1**

**Labor force participation rate, by sex, 1950–2060**

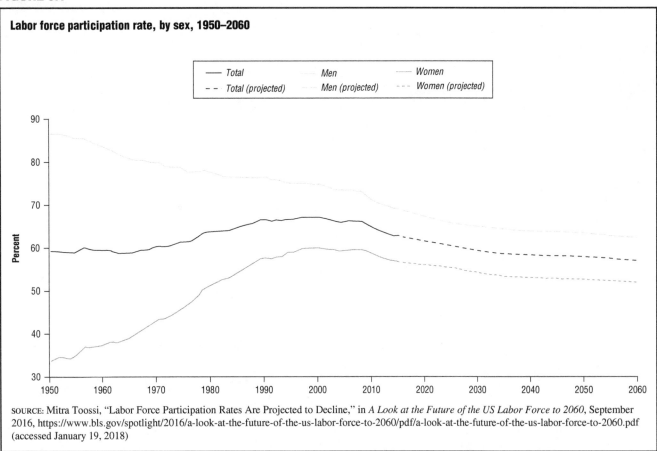

SOURCE: Mitra Toossi, "Labor Force Participation Rates Are Projected to Decline," in *A Look at the Future of the US Labor Force to 2060*, September 2016, https://www.bls.gov/spotlight/2016/a-look-at-the-future-of-the-us-labor-force-to-2060/pdf/a-look-at-the-future-of-the-us-labor-force-to-2060.pdf (accessed January 19, 2018)

since 1950, when it stood at 86.4%; by 2060 it is expected to reach 62.3%. Whereas the labor force grew more rapidly than the overall population (which itself grew rapidly) between 1960 and 2000, between 2000 and 2060 the labor force is expected to grow at a slower rate than the overall population (which is also expected to grow more slowly than in previous decades). By 2060 those aged 55 years and older are expected to make up 26.8% of the labor force, up from 22.2% in 2015, and the gap between male and female labor force participation is expected to continue narrowing as it has done since World War II.

# CHAPTER 4
## WOMEN'S OCCUPATIONS

Until the second half of the 20th century, women's occupations outside of the home were restricted primarily to a few selected fields in which women would be unlikely to compete with men. Thus, women were often household servants and nannies, farmworkers, shop girls, seamstresses, laundresses, barmaids, and waitresses. Well into the 20th century, employers were able to use labor laws and court rulings to justify not hiring women for certain jobs or for restricting their hours and paying them less than men. Women's rights in the workplace were significantly advanced by the Civil Rights Act of 1964, as Title VII of the law forbids workplace discrimination on the basis of race, color, religion, sex, or national origin. Although women were legally entitled to enter nearly any occupation, the law still left room for employers to treat them differently than their male coworkers, and even bar them from certain jobs, on the basis of their reproductive functions.

The US Supreme Court even legitimized the idea that women's workplace rights did not include their reproductive rights in the case of *General Electric Co. v. Gilbert* (429 US 125 [1976]), when it ruled that employers should not be required to pay disability benefits to women who were temporarily unable to work because of pregnancy or childbirth. In essence, the court's opinion stated that pregnancy discrimination was not necessarily sex discrimination. Two years later, Congress effectively overruled the Supreme Court decision by passing the Pregnancy Discrimination Act of 1978. The law amended Title VII of the Civil Rights Act of 1964 by stipulating that the prohibition against sex discrimination included any discrimination or differential treatment on the basis of pregnancy, childbirth, and related medical conditions. The law states that employers must treat "women affected by pregnancy... the same for all employment-related purposes... as other persons not so affected but similar in their ability or inability to work." It explicitly covers all aspects and terms of employment, including hiring, firing, training, job assignments, wages, promotions, layoffs, and fringe benefits, such as leave and health insurance.

Although the Pregnancy Discrimination Act went a long way toward clarifying the definition and parameters of what constitutes sex discrimination, some employers continued to test the limits of the law. For example, in 1982 Johnson Controls adopted a policy that barred all women, regardless of age, from jobs involving contact with lead in its car battery manufacturing plant, unless the women had medical proof of sterility. As a result, women were kept out of some of the highest paying jobs at the plant. In 1991 the US Supreme Court ruled in *United Automobile Workers v. Johnson Controls* (499 US 187) that the Civil Rights Act of 1964 prohibited companies from barring women from jobs that might jeopardize a developing fetus. The court noted that "decisions about the welfare of future children be left to the parents who conceive, bear, support, and raise them, rather than to the employers who hire those parents."

Unofficial forms of systematic equal-rights violations in the workplace continued well into the 21st century. One prominent case involving such discrimination was a 2001 class-action lawsuit, *Dukes v. Wal-Mart Stores Inc.* (WL 1902806 [N.D. Cal. 2001]), in which 1.6 million female employees of Wal-Mart and affiliated Sam's Club stores claimed that in the absence of any companywide system for protecting women from sex discrimination, individual managers routinely showed preferential treatment to male workers when it came to pay and promotion. The dispute began with a discrimination claim by Stephanie Odle, a Sam's Club assistant manager in California. The claim was certified as a class-action suit by the US District Court for the Northern District of California after the plaintiffs' expert witnesses testified that discriminatory conditions similar to those experienced by Odle prevailed in all 46 regions where Wal-Mart operated.

Wal-Mart appealed to the US Supreme Court to stop the suit from proceeding. The Supreme Court addressed only the technical issue of whether the 1.6 million plaintiffs, whose suit amounted to the largest employee discrimination case in US history, could legally constitute a class. The court ruled in *Wal-Mart v. Dukes* (No. 10-277 [2011]) that the plaintiffs did not constitute a class and did not have the standing (right to file a lawsuit) to sue. Although the ruling was a victory for Wal-Mart, the original plaintiffs—including Betty Dukes, for whom the case was named, and four other female Wal-Mart employees—did not drop their case, and ongoing claims of gender discrimination continued to generate negative publicity for Wal-Mart in the years that followed. In July 2016 Wal-Mart reached a private settlement with the original plaintiffs in exchange for their agreement to drop their individual claims of gender bias. The following year, in November 2017, a different group of women, who had been part of the original 2001 class action, filed a new class-action suit, *Forbes v. Wal-Mart Stores Inc.*, focusing on alleged patterns of gender discrimination in the company's southeastern US stores. Jordyn Holman reports in "Wal-Mart Female Employees Try Again for Sex-Bias Class Action" (Bloomberg.com, November 7, 2017) that the US Equal Employment Opportunity Commission had received some 2,000 claims of gender discrimination in pay and promotions at Wal-Mart since the original class action was dismissed in 2011. As of April 2018, the case was still ongoing.

The issue of pregnancy discrimination made national news again in 2015 with the Supreme Court ruling in *Young v. United Parcel Service, Inc.* (No. 12-1226). The case involved Peggy Young, a United Parcel Service (UPS) driver whose doctor advised her not to lift anything heavier than 20 pounds (9 kg) after she became pregnant. Although UPS drivers are normally expected to lift up to 70 pounds (32 kg), employees who are injured can be temporarily assigned to light-duty work. Nevertheless, instead of offering such an accommodation to Young, the company put her on unpaid leave, which led to the loss of her employee medical coverage. Young sued the company for back pay and damages. After lower courts dismissed the case, it went to the Supreme Court, which ruled 6–3 that, under the Pregnancy Discrimination Act, employers could not use the issue of cost or inconvenience to justify denying pregnant workers the same accommodations that were already available to workers injured on the job. The ruling was widely hailed as a significant precedent that expanded the social safety net for working women. In "Young v. United Parcel Service: For Conservative Reasons, Supreme Court Rules for Pregnant Women—and against Corporations" (DailyBeast.com,

March 25, 2015), Jay Michaelson states that "for women who want to keep their jobs, even if they become pregnant, *Young v. UPS* is clearly a step forward.... *Young* stands for the principle that, according to a literal reading of the Pregnancy [Discrimination] Act, if some disabilities are accommodated, pregnancy must be accommodated."

## TRADITIONAL FEMALE OCCUPATIONS

Although formal restrictions barring women from many occupations have for the most part disappeared, most women in the US labor force still work in what may be considered traditional female occupations, such as teachers, nurses, and secretaries. (See Figure 4.1.) Indeed, according to the US Bureau of Labor Statistics (BLS), in *Women in the Labor Force: A Databook* (April 2017, https://www.bls.gov/opub/reports/womens-data book/2016/pdf/home.pdf), in 2015 an overwhelming proportion of child care workers (94.9%), secretaries and administrative assistants (94.5%), teacher assistants (91.4%), receptionists and information clerks (90.6%), bookkeeping, accounting, and auditing clerks (89.8%), and registered nurses (89.4%) were women. Whereas 94.5% of secretaries and administrative assistants were women, only 27.9% of chief executive officers were women.

In 2016 nearly half (48.1%) of women who worked full time on a wage or salary basis were in either management, business, and financial operations occupations (17.8%) or professional and related occupations (30.3%). (See Figure 4.2.) One-fifth (20.2%) worked in office and administrative support occupations, 16.1% worked in service occupations, and 8.6% worked in sales and related occupations. The rest were in production, transportation, and material moving occupations (6%) or natural resources, construction, and maintenance occupations (0.9%). Roughly equal proportions of males and females worked in management and sales, but there was a much lower percentage of male professionals (19.4%) and male office and administrative support staff (6.4%), and a slightly lower percentage of men in service occupations (12.9%). A much higher proportion of men worked in occupations involving physical labor, including natural resources, construction, and maintenance occupations (17%) and production, transportation, and material moving occupations (18.8%). In general, male workers were more spread out among the five major occupational groups than were female workers, who were concentrated in the management, professional, service, sales, and office occupations.

Among all employed women (including part-time and self-employed workers) in 2017, Asian American women were the most likely to hold relatively high-paid management, professional, and related jobs: 49.7% of Asian American women held these positions, compared with 45.1% of white women, 35.6% of African American women, and 27.6% of Hispanic women. (See Table 4.1.)

FIGURE 4.1

**Most common occupations for employed women, 2015**

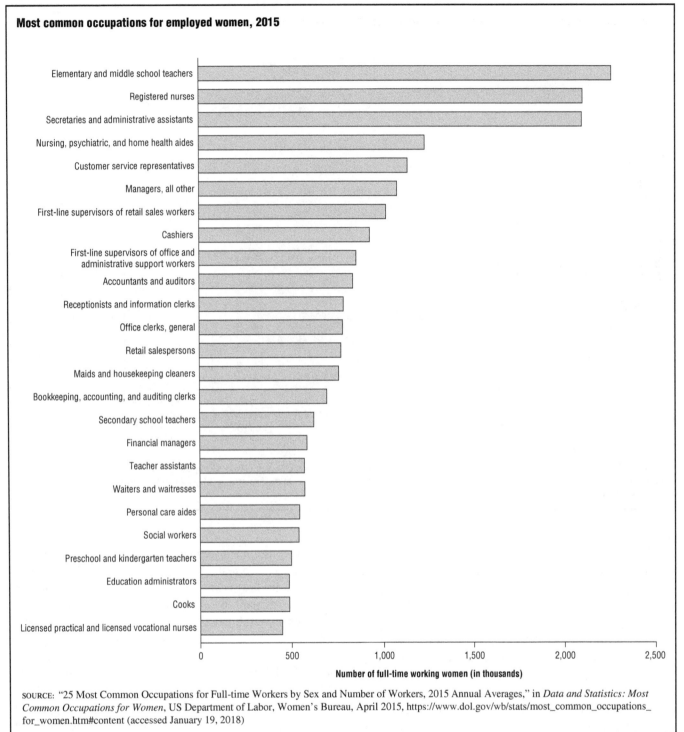

SOURCE: "25 Most Common Occupations for Full-time Workers by Sex and Number of Workers, 2015 Annual Averages," in *Data and Statistics: Most Common Occupations for Women*, US Department of Labor, Women's Bureau, April 2015, https://www.dol.gov/wb/stats/most_common_occupations_for_women.htm#content (accessed January 19, 2018)

A greater proportion of women than men were professionals (28.1% versus 18.8%), whereas a greater proportion of men than women were in management, business, and financial operations occupations (17.5% versus 15.5%).

Approximately 15.2 million (21.4%) American female workers aged 16 years and older were in service occupations (many of which pay less, on average, than professional and managerial jobs) in 2016, compared with 11.6 million (14.4%) male workers. (See Table 3.6

in Chapter 3 and Table 4.1.) A lower proportion of Asian American women (20.3%) and white women (20%) were employed in service occupations than African American women (28.8%) or Hispanic women (32.2%). Among those in service occupations, a far greater proportion of men than women were in protective service occupations, whereas most workers in health care support and personal care and service occupations were women. (See Table 3.6 in Chapter 3.) Among food preparation service occupations, women outnumbered men more modestly.

**FIGURE 4.2**

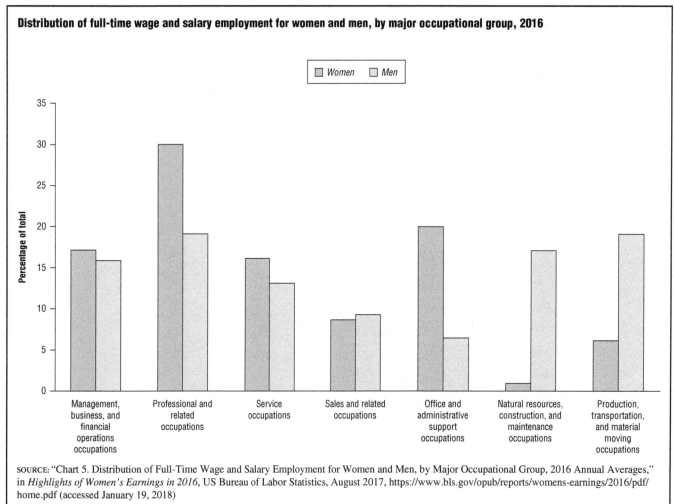

Distribution of full-time wage and salary employment for women and men, by major occupational group, 2016

SOURCE: "Chart 5. Distribution of Full-Time Wage and Salary Employment for Women and Men, by Major Occupational Group, 2016 Annual Averages," in *Highlights of Women's Earnings in 2016*, US Bureau of Labor Statistics, August 2017, https://www.bls.gov/opub/reports/womens-earnings/2016/pdf/home.pdf (accessed January 19, 2018)

## NEW OCCUPATIONS FOR WOMEN

Although most women continue to work in occupations that traditionally have been considered female, women have made impressive inroads into other occupations. Nontraditional occupations for women are those in which women make up 25% or less of the total employment. Many occupations that were nontraditional for women during the 1970s and 1980s are no longer considered so, among them physicians, chemists, lawyers, and postal service mail carriers. Other jobs, especially those involving heavy industry and physical labor, remain dominated by men. Between these two categories of jobs are a number of occupations that continue to be considered nontraditional but in which the proportion of women has begun to approach 25%, such as farmers and ranchers, architects, detectives and criminal investigators, computer programmers, and butchers. (See Table 4.2.)

### Law

According to the American Bar Association (ABA; April 2013, http://www.americanbar.org/content/dam/aba/administrative/legal_education_and_admissions_to_the_bar/statistics/enrollment_degrees_awarded.authcheckdam.pdf), only 1,739 women (3.7% of the total 46,666) were enrolled in law school during the 1963–64 academic year. Enrollment by women grew significantly in the decades that followed, peaking at 50.4% (64,644 of a total 128,212 students) in 1992–93, but has since hovered between 45% and 49%. In 2012–13 women accounted for 47% (65,387 of the total 139,055) of all US law students. Although women have almost achieved parity with men in law school enrollment, a much smaller proportion goes on to practice law. In "A Current Glance at Women in the Law" (January 2017, https://www.americanbar.org/content/dam/aba/marketing/women/current_glance_statistics_january2017.pdf), the ABA indicates that women made up only 36% of the legal profession in 2016.

Men also continue to hold most of the prestige and financial power in the profession. The ABA notes that women accounted for 45% of associates (lawyers at the salaried introductory level in a firm), but only 18% of all law partners (those who have an ownership stake in a firm as well as a salary and therefore make significantly more money than associates). Women were employed at

TABLE 4.1

## Employed persons by occupation, race and Hispanic origin, and sex, 2016–17

[Percent distribution]

| Occupation, race, and Hispanic or Latino ethnicity | Total | | Men | | Women | |
|---|---|---|---|---|---|---|
| | 2016 | 2017 | 2016 | 2017 | 2016 | 2017 |
| **Total** | | | | | | |
| Total, 16 years and over (in thousands) | 151,436 | 153,337 | 80,568 | 81,402 | 70,868 | 71,936 |
| Percent of total employed | 100.0 | 100.0 | 100.0 | 100.0 | 100.0 | 100.0 |
| Management, professional, and related occupations | 39.2 | 39.7 | 35.8 | 36.2 | 43.2 | 43.7 |
| Management, business, and financial operations occupations | 16.5 | 16.6 | 17.4 | 17.5 | 15.4 | 15.5 |
| Professional and related occupations | 22.8 | 23.2 | 18.4 | 18.8 | 27.8 | 28.1 |
| Service occupations | 17.7 | 17.4 | 14.4 | 14.3 | 21.4 | 21.0 |
| Sales and office occupations | 22.1 | 21.9 | 16.2 | 15.9 | 28.9 | 28.6 |
| Sales and related occupations | 10.5 | 10.3 | 10.0 | 9.9 | 11.0 | 10.8 |
| Office and administrative support occupations | 11.7 | 11.6 | 6.1 | 6.1 | 18.0 | 17.8 |
| Natural resources, construction, and maintenance occupations | 9.2 | 9.3 | 16.4 | 16.6 | 0.9 | 1.0 |
| Farming, fishing, and forestry occupations | 0.7 | 0.8 | 1.1 | 1.1 | 0.3 | 0.4 |
| Construction and extraction occupations | 5.2 | 5.2 | 9.5 | 9.6 | 0.3 | 0.3 |
| Installation, maintenance, and repair occupations | 3.2 | 3.2 | 5.8 | 5.9 | 0.2 | 0.3 |
| Production, transportation, and material moving occupations | 11.7 | 11.7 | 17.2 | 17.0 | 5.5 | 5.7 |
| Production occupations | 5.6 | 5.5 | 7.5 | 7.4 | 3.4 | 3.4 |
| Transportation and material moving occupations | 6.1 | 6.2 | 9.6 | 9.6 | 2.2 | 2.3 |
| **White** | | | | | | |
| Total, 16 years and over (in thousands) | 119,313 | 120,176 | 64,612 | 65,000 | 54,701 | 55,176 |
| Percent of total employed | 100.0 | 100.0 | 100.0 | 100.0 | 100.0 | 100.0 |
| Management, professional, and related occupations | 40.0 | 40.6 | 36.3 | 36.7 | 44.4 | 45.1 |
| Management, business, and financial operations occupations | 17.3 | 17.5 | 18.4 | 18.5 | 16.0 | 16.3 |
| Professional and related occupations | 22.7 | 23.0 | 17.9 | 18.2 | 28.4 | 28.8 |
| Service occupations | 16.5 | 16.2 | 13.5 | 13.2 | 20.0 | 19.7 |
| Sales and office occupations | 22.1 | 21.9 | 15.9 | 15.9 | 29.5 | 29.0 |
| Sales and related occupations | 10.6 | 10.5 | 10.3 | 10.2 | 11.0 | 10.9 |
| Office and administrative support occupations | 11.5 | 11.4 | 5.6 | 5.7 | 18.5 | 18.2 |
| Natural resources, construction, and maintenance occupations | 10.1 | 10.3 | 17.9 | 18.1 | 1.0 | 1.1 |
| Farming, fishing, and forestry occupations | 0.8 | 0.9 | 1.2 | 1.2 | 0.4 | 0.5 |
| Construction and extraction occupations | 5.9 | 5.9 | 10.5 | 10.5 | 0.4 | 0.4 |
| Installation, maintenance, and repair occupations | 3.5 | 3.5 | 6.2 | 6.3 | 0.2 | 0.3 |
| Production, transportation, and material moving occupations | 11.3 | 11.1 | 16.4 | 16.1 | 5.1 | 5.1 |
| Production occupations | 5.5 | 5.4 | 7.5 | 7.4 | 3.1 | 3.1 |
| Transportation and material moving occupations | 5.7 | 5.7 | 8.9 | 8.7 | 2.0 | 2.0 |
| **Black or African American** | | | | | | |
| Total, 16 years and over (in thousands) | 17,982 | 18,587 | 8,471 | 8,742 | 9,511 | 9,845 |
| Percent of total employed | 100.0 | 100.0 | 100.0 | 100.0 | 100.0 | 100.0 |
| Management, professional, and related occupations | 30.1 | 30.8 | 24.9 | 25.4 | 34.8 | 35.6 |
| Management, business, and financial operations occupations | 11.3 | 11.2 | 11.0 | 10.8 | 11.6 | 11.4 |
| Professional and related occupations | 18.8 | 19.6 | 13.9 | 14.5 | 23.2 | 24.1 |
| Service occupations | 25.1 | 24.2 | 20.9 | 21.1 | 28.8 | 27.0 |
| Sales and office occupations | 23.5 | 23.4 | 18.2 | 17.1 | 28.3 | 29.0 |
| Sales and related occupations | 9.7 | 9.4 | 8.5 | 8.2 | 10.8 | 10.5 |
| Office and administrative support occupations | 13.8 | 13.9 | 9.7 | 8.9 | 17.5 | 18.5 |
| Natural resources, construction, and maintenance occupations | 5.7 | 5.6 | 11.2 | 11.3 | 0.7 | 0.6 |
| Farming, fishing, and forestry occupations | 0.3 | 0.3 | 0.5 | 0.5 | 0.2 | 0.1 |
| Construction and extraction occupations | 3.0 | 3.0 | 6.1 | 6.1 | 0.2 | 0.2 |
| Installation, maintenance, and repair occupations | 2.4 | 2.3 | 4.7 | 4.6 | 0.3 | 0.3 |
| Production, transportation, and material moving occupations | 15.6 | 16.0 | 24.8 | 25.2 | 7.4 | 7.9 |
| Production occupations | 6.1 | 6.1 | 8.4 | 8.2 | 4.0 | 4.2 |
| Transportation and material moving occupations | 9.5 | 9.9 | 16.4 | 16.9 | 3.4 | 3.7 |
| **Asian** | | | | | | |
| Total, 16 years and over (in thousands) | 9,213 | 9,448 | 4,915 | 4,989 | 4,298 | 4,458 |
| Percent of total employed | 100.0 | 100.0 | 100.0 | 100.0 | 100.0 | 100.0 |
| Management, professional, and related occupations | 52.3 | 52.0 | 53.4 | 54.1 | 51.0 | 49.7 |
| Management, business, and financial operations occupations | 17.9 | 17.2 | 18.0 | 18.0 | 17.8 | 16.3 |
| Professional and related occupations | 34.4 | 34.8 | 35.4 | 36.1 | 33.2 | 33.5 |
| Service occupations | 16.1 | 16.8 | 12.4 | 12.9 | 20.3 | 21.1 |
| Sales and office occupations | 18.9 | 17.9 | 16.1 | 14.6 | 22.1 | 21.5 |
| Sales and related occupations | 9.8 | 9.3 | 10.0 | 9.1 | 9.6 | 9.6 |
| Office and administrative support occupations | 9.1 | 8.5 | 6.1 | 5.5 | 12.5 | 11.9 |

lower rates as corporate general counsels than in private practice, accounting for 24.8% of all general counsels for *Fortune* 500 companies (the largest 500 US companies, as ranked by *Fortune* magazine).

Women have made great strides in the judiciary, but they have not achieved full parity. The ABA notes that women held 27.1% of all federal and state judgeships and three of nine positions (33.3%) on the US Supreme Court.

**TABLE 4.1**

**Employed persons by occupation, race and Hispanic origin, and sex, 2016–17** [CONTINUED]

[Percent distribution]

| Occupation, race, and Hispanic or Latino ethnicity | Total | | Men | | Women | |
|---|---|---|---|---|---|---|
| | 2016 | 2017 | 2016 | 2017 | 2016 | 2017 |
| Natural resources, construction, and maintenance occupations | 3.4 | 3.3 | 5.7 | 5.6 | 0.7 | 0.7 |
|     Farming, fishing, and forestry occupations | 0.2 | 0.2 | 0.2 | 0.2 | 0.2 | 0.2 |
|     Construction and extraction occupations | 1.5 | 1.4 | 2.5 | 2.4 | 0.2 | 0.2 |
|     Installation, maintenance, and repair occupations | 1.7 | 1.7 | 3.0 | 3.0 | 0.2 | 0.3 |
| Production, transportation, and material moving occupations | 9.3 | 10.0 | 12.3 | 12.8 | 5.9 | 6.9 |
|     Production occupations | 5.4 | 5.5 | 6.2 | 5.8 | 4.6 | 5.2 |
|     Transportation and material moving occupations | 3.9 | 4.5 | 6.2 | 7.0 | 1.2 | 1.7 |
| **Hispanic or Latino ethnicity** | | | | | | |
| Total, 16 years and over (in thousands) | **25,249** | **25,938** | **14,563** | **14,874** | **10,686** | **11,064** |
| Percent of total employed | 100.0 | 100.0 | 100.0 | 100.0 | 100.0 | 100.0 |
|     Management, professional, and related occupations | 22.0 | 22.5 | 18.3 | 18.6 | 27.0 | 27.6 |
|       Management, business, and financial operations occupations | 9.7 | 9.8 | 9.5 | 9.2 | 10.0 | 10.5 |
|       Professional and related occupations | 12.3 | 12.7 | 8.8 | 9.4 | 17.0 | 17.1 |
|     Service occupations | 25.4 | 24.8 | 20.3 | 19.5 | 32.2 | 31.9 |
|     Sales and office occupations | 20.8 | 20.6 | 14.3 | 14.3 | 29.6 | 29.1 |
|       Sales and related occupations | 9.8 | 9.7 | 8.2 | 8.1 | 12.1 | 11.9 |
|       Office and administrative support occupations | 10.9 | 10.9 | 6.1 | 6.2 | 17.5 | 17.2 |
|     Natural resources, construction, and maintenance occupations | 16.3 | 16.8 | 26.8 | 27.6 | 2.1 | 2.3 |
|       Farming, fishing, and forestry occupations | 2.0 | 2.0 | 2.6 | 2.5 | 1.1 | 1.4 |
|       Construction and extraction occupations | 10.7 | 11.1 | 18.0 | 19.0 | 0.7 | 0.6 |
|       Installation, maintenance, and repair occupations | 3.7 | 3.6 | 6.2 | 6.1 | 0.3 | 0.3 |
|     Production, transportation, and material moving occupations | 15.6 | 15.4 | 20.3 | 20.0 | 9.1 | 9.2 |
|       Production occupations | 7.5 | 7.5 | 8.7 | 8.7 | 5.7 | 5.9 |
|       Transportation and material moving occupations | 8.1 | 7.9 | 11.6 | 11.3 | 3.4 | 3.3 |

Note: Estimates for the above race groups (white, black or African American, and Asian) do not sum to totals because data are not presented for all races. Persons whose ethnicity is identified as Hispanic or Latino may be of any race. Updated population controls are introduced annually with the release of January data.

SOURCE: "10. Employed Persons by Occupation, Race, Hispanic or Latino Ethnicity, and Sex," in *Labor Force Statistics from the Current Population Survey*, US Bureau of Labor Statistics, February 8, 2017, https://www.bls.gov/cps/cpsaat10.pdf (accessed January 19, 2018)

In 1981 Sandra Day O'Connor (1930–) became the first woman to be appointed as one of the nine justices of the US Supreme Court. She was joined on the court in 1993 by Justice Ruth Bader Ginsburg (1933–). O'Connor retired in 2006, leaving Ginsburg as the only female Supreme Court justice. When Justice David H. Souter (1939–) announced his retirement in 2009, President Barack Obama (1961–) nominated the federal appellate judge Sonia Sotomayor (1954–). Following her confirmation by the US Senate, she became the first Hispanic and third female to sit on the court. In May 2010 Obama nominated his US solicitor general, Elena Kagan (1960–) for another vacancy on the Supreme Court. She was confirmed by the Senate and sworn in as the 112th Supreme Court justice in August of that year.

### Women in the Corporate World

In 2016, 30.6 million (51.5%) of the nation's 59.4 million managers and professionals were women aged 16 years and older. (See Table 3.6 in Chapter 3.) Women are more likely to be managers and executives in industries with more female employees at lower levels, such as in the insurance, banking, and retail trades. Women also appear to advance more rapidly in fast-growing industries such as business services and direct marketing, and in industries that are undergoing changes such as deregulation and restructuring. Women managers and executives are much less common in the communications, transportation, and utilities industries. The Equal Employment Opportunity Commission reports in "2015 Job Patterns for Minorities and Women in Private Industry" (2018, https://www1.eeoc.gov/eeoc/statistics/employment/jobpat-eeo1/2015/index.cfm#select_label) that in 2015 women accounted for 1.9 million (39.2%) of the total 4.9 million first- and mid-level officials and managers in private industry and 252,567 (29.7%) of the total 849,503 executive- and senior-level officials and managers.

Although women hold more executive positions than in previous eras, men continue to dominate the higher reaches of the corporate world, holding an overwhelming majority of the most important and lucrative positions with the largest corporations. According to Catalyst, a nonprofit organization that is devoted to expanding opportunities for women in business, in "Women in S&P 500 Companies" (2018, http://www.catalyst.org/knowledge/women-sp-500-companies), women occupied 26.5% of executive officer jobs and 21.2% of board seats among *Fortune* 500 companies. Meanwhile, only 5.2% of chief executive officers at any of those companies were women. In "Women CEOs of the S&P 500" (March 13, 2018, http://www.catalyst.org/knowledge/women-ceos-sp-500), Catalyst lists the top women of *Fortune* 500

TABLE 4.2

## Nontraditional occupations for women, 2014

| Occupations | Total number of workers (in thousands) | Women as a percentage of total employed in the occupation | Women's median weekly earnings* | Men's median weekly earnings* | Women's earnings as a percentage of men's* |
|---|---|---|---|---|---|
| Total workers, all occupations | 146,305 | 46.9% | $719 | $871 | 82.5% |
| Cement masons, concrete finishers, and terrazzo workers | 58 | 0.0% | — | — | — |
| Derrick, rotary drill, and service unit operators, oil, gas, and mining | 54 | 0.0% | — | $1,187 | — |
| Crane and tower operators | 74 | 0.2% | — | $959 | — |
| Bus and truck mechanics and diesel engine specialists | 323 | 0.3% | — | $811 | — |
| Miscellaneous vehicle and mobile equipment mechanics, installers, and repairers | 93 | 0.3% | — | $559 | — |
| Roofers | 206 | 0.5% | — | $620 | — |
| Heavy vehicle and mobile equipment service technicians and mechanics | 211 | 0.5% | — | $886 | — |
| Brickmasons, blockmasons, and stonemasons | 142 | 0.7% | — | $656 | — |
| Heating, air conditioning, and refrigeration mechanics and installers | 378 | 1.2% | — | $773 | — |
| Tool and die makers | 67 | 1.3% | — | $1,025 | — |
| Automotive service technicians and mechanics | 883 | 1.4% | — | $737 | — |
| Locomotive engineers and operators | 55 | 1.4% | — | $1,197 | — |
| Highway maintenance workers | 123 | 1.5% | — | $794 | — |
| Mining machine operators | 68 | 1.5% | — | $1,047 | — |
| Other extraction workers | 92 | 1.5% | — | $1,126 | — |
| Pipelayers, plumbers, pipefitters, and steamfitters | 564 | 1.6% | — | $916 | — |
| Automotive body and related repairers | 133 | 1.6% | — | $668 | — |
| Carpenters | 1,282 | 1.7% | — | $699 | — |
| Operating engineers and other construction equipment operators | 336 | 1.8% | — | $862 | — |
| Structural iron and steel workers | 52 | 2.0% | — | — | — |
| Stationary engineers and boiler operators | 96 | 2.0% | — | $1,051 | — |
| Drywall installers, ceiling tile installers, and tapers | 162 | 2.1% | — | $595 | — |
| Small engine mechanics | 50 | 2.1% | — | — | — |
| Carpet, floor, and tile installers and finishers | 170 | 2.3% | — | $687 | — |
| First-line supervisors of construction trades and extraction workers | 696 | 2.4% | — | $1,033 | — |
| Electricians | 769 | 2.4% | — | $884 | — |
| Construction laborers | 1,686 | 2.5% | — | $605 | — |
| Industrial and refractory machinery mechanics | 454 | 2.8% | — | $876 | — |
| Electrical power-line installers and repairers | 115 | 3.0% | — | $1,018 | — |
| Maintenance and repair workers, general | 471 | 3.2% | — | $812 | — |
| Aircraft mechanics and service technicians | 127 | 3.3% | — | $1,062 | — |
| Pest control workers | 80 | 3.7% | — | $653 | — |
| Telecommunications line installers and repairers | 184 | 4.4% | — | $877 | — |
| Machinists | 391 | 4.5% | — | $770 | — |
| Water and wastewater treatment plant and system operators | 72 | 4.5% | — | $835 | — |
| Helpers, construction trades | 57 | 4.7% | — | — | — |
| First-line supervisors of landscaping, lawn service, and groundskeeping workers | 210 | 4.8% | — | $716 | — |
| First-line supervisors of mechanics, installers, and repairers | 284 | 4.8% | — | $1,040 | — |
| Welding, soldering, and brazing workers | 615 | 4.8% | — | $733 | — |
| Sheet metal workers | 110 | 5.2% | — | $857 | — |
| Other installation, maintenance, and repair workers | 224 | 5.2% | — | $811 | — |
| Logging workers | 71 | 5.4% | — | — | — |
| Home appliance repairers | 51 | 5.6% | — | — | — |
| Firefighters | 300 | 5.7% | — | $1,142 | — |
| Chemical processing machine setters, operators, and tenders | 63 | 5.8% | — | $831 | — |
| Driver/sales workers and truck drivers | 3,406 | 5.8% | $545 | $739 | 73.7% |
| Painters, construction and maintenance | 561 | 6.0% | — | $562 | — |
| Grounds maintenance workers | 1,389 | 6.3% | — | $454 | — |
| Aircraft pilots and flight engineers | 133 | 7.2% | — | $1,446 | — |
| Construction managers | 711 | 7.4% | — | $1,332 | — |
| Radio and telecommunications equipment installers and repairers | 134 | 7.4% | — | $846 | — |
| Industrial truck and tractor operators | 564 | 7.4% | — | $595 | — |
| Security and fire alarm systems installers | 58 | 7.5% | — | — | — |
| Automotive and watercraft service attendants | 97 | 7.5% | — | $518 | — |
| Architectural and engineering managers | 122 | 7.6% | — | $1,975 | — |
| First-line supervisors of firefighting and prevention workers | 58 | 7.8% | — | $1,448 | — |
| Computer control programmers and operators | 71 | 8.1% | — | $790 | — |
| Refuse and recyclable material collectors | 84 | 8.6% | — | $564 | — |
| Mechanical engineers | 303 | 8.8% | — | $1,453 | — |
| Motor vehicle operators, all other | 61 | 8.9% | — | — | — |
| Surveying and mapping technicians | 77 | 9.7% | — | $882 | — |
| Cabinetmakers and bench carpenters | 51 | 9.9% | — | — | — |
| Parking lot attendants | 78 | 10.5% | — | $441 | — |
| Engineers, all other | 406 | 11.7% | — | $1,488 | — |
| Crushing, grinding, polishing, mixing, and blending workers | 69 | 11.7% | — | $694 | — |

TABLE 4.2

**Nontraditional occupations for women, 2014** [CONTINUED]

| Occupations | Total number of workers (in thousands) | Women as a percentage of total employed in the occupation | Women's median weekly earnings* | Men's median weekly earnings* | Women's earnings as a percentage of men's* |
|---|---|---|---|---|---|
| Construction and building inspectors | 78 | 12.2% | — | $1,028 | — |
| Electrical and electronics engineers | 271 | 12.3% | — | $1,568 | — |
| Computer network architects | 123 | 12.4% | — | $1,650 | — |
| Police and sheriff's patrol officers | 680 | 12.4% | $743 | $1,043 | 71.2% |
| Cleaners of vehicles and equipment | 375 | 12.4% | — | $480 | — |
| Painting workers | 156 | 12.7% | — | $703 | — |
| Taxi drivers and chauffeurs | 383 | 12.7% | — | $609 | — |
| Chemical engineers | 79 | 13.0% | — | $1,570 | — |
| Broadcast and sound engineering technicians and radio operators | 108 | 13.0% | — | $958 | — |
| Computer, automated teller, and office machine repairers | 265 | 13.3% | — | $889 | — |
| Cost estimators | 105 | 13.7% | — | $1,074 | — |
| Precision instrument and equipment repairers | 85 | 14.2% | — | $836 | — |
| Computer hardware engineers | 84 | 15.3% | — | $1,795 | — |
| Parts salespersons | 93 | 15.3% | — | $643 | — |
| Aerospace engineers | 147 | 15.6% | — | $1,727 | — |
| First-line supervisors of police and detectives | 126 | 15.9% | — | $1,149 | — |
| Industrial engineers, including health and safety | 194 | 16.0% | — | $1,464 | — |
| Couriers and messengers | 233 | 16.0% | — | $737 | — |
| Civil engineers | 349 | 16.5% | $1,275 | $1,406 | 90.7% |
| Barbers | 110 | 16.8% | — | — | — |
| Industrial production managers | 273 | 17.8% | — | $1,383 | — |
| Information security analysts | 68 | 18.1% | — | — | — |
| Drafters | 138 | 18.1% | — | $986 | — |
| Television, video, and motion picture camera operators and editors | 72 | 18.1% | — | — | — |
| Supervisors of transportation and material moving workers | 199 | 18.3% | — | $925 | — |
| Laborers and freight, stock, and material movers, hand | 1,867 | 18.3% | $476 | $546 | 87.2% |
| Clergy | 433 | 18.6% | $763 | $1,007 | 75.8% |
| First-line supervisors of production and operating workers | 789 | 18.6% | $659 | $942 | 70.0% |
| Network and computer systems administrators | 205 | 19.1% | — | $1,286 | — |
| Printing press operators | 187 | 19.6% | — | $686 | — |
| Software developers, applications and systems software | 1,235 | 19.8% | $1,457 | $1,736 | 83.9% |
| Baggage porters, bellhops, and concierges | 85 | 20.2% | — | $664 | — |
| Miscellaneous agricultural workers | 739 | 20.2% | $369 | $437 | 84.4% |
| Metal workers and plastic workers, all other | 342 | 20.4% | $511 | $647 | 79.0% |
| Engineering technicians, except drafters | 369 | 20.5% | $785 | $1,066 | 73.6% |
| First-line supervisors of protective service workers, all other | 91 | 20.9% | — | $1,004 | — |
| Detectives and criminal investigators | 164 | 21.0% | — | $1,183 | — |
| Dishwashers | 246 | 21.2% | — | $364 | — |
| Computer programmers | 509 | 21.4% | $1,253 | $1,447 | 86.6% |
| Chefs and head cooks | 430 | 21.4% | $531 | $601 | 88.4% |
| Transportation, storage, and distribution managers | 260 | 21.6% | $836 | $1,014 | 82.4% |
| Cutting workers | 60 | 21.9% | — | — | — |
| Chiropractors | 66 | 22.4% | — | — | — |
| Security guards and gaming surveillance officers | 899 | 22.6% | $514 | $589 | 87.3% |
| Computer occupations, all other | 512 | 23.1% | $984 | $1,122 | 87.7% |
| Butchers and other meat, poultry, and fish processing workers | 331 | 23.5% | $457 | $537 | 85.1% |
| Farmers, ranchers, and other agricultural managers | 941 | 23.8% | — | $818 | — |
| Cutting, punching, and press machine setters, operators, and tenders, metal and plastic | 85 | 24.2% | — | $663 | — |
| Environmental scientists and geoscientists | 91 | 24.5% | — | $1,388 | — |
| Production workers, all other | 947 | 24.7% | $492 | $676 | 72.8% |
| Helpers–production workers | 54 | 25.1% | — | — | — |
| Architects, except naval | 178 | 25.3% | — | $1,391 | — |

*Median weekly earnings are 2014 annual averages based on full-time wage and salary workers only.
—Indicates no data or base is less than 50,000.
Notes: Nontraditional or male-dominated occupations are those in which women represent 25 percent or less of total employed. Occupations include those with a sample size of at least 50,000 people employed. Total number of workers and women as a percentage of total employed are 2014 annual averages for all people employed (includes part-time and self-employed).

SOURCE: "Nontraditional (Male-Dominated) Occupations, 2014 Annual Averages," in *Data and Statistics: Traditional and Nontraditional Occupations*, US Department of Labor, Women's Bureau, 2015, https://www.dol.gov/wb/stats/Nontraditional%20Occupations.pdf (accessed January 19, 2018)

companies, including Indra K. Nooyi (1955–) of PepsiCo, Inc.; Adena Friedman (1969–) of Nasdaq; Virginia Rometty (1957–) of International Business Machines Corp.; and Mary T. Barra (1961–) of General Motors Company.

**THE GLASS CEILING.** The term *glass ceiling* is commonly used to describe the invisible barrier women encounter in their attempts to achieve high management positions. Although more women and minorities have professional occupations than ever before, they are usually confined to the lower levels of management. The US Department of Labor defined in *A Report on the Glass Ceiling Initiative* (1991) the glass ceiling as "artificial barriers based on attitudinal or organizational bias that prevent qualified individuals from advancing upward in their organization into management level positions."

As a result of the report, the Civil Rights Act of 1991 established the Glass Ceiling Commission. In *Good for Business: Making Full Use of the Nation's Human Capital* (March 1995, https://www.dol.gov/oasam/programs/history/reich/reports/ceiling.pdf), the commission found three types of artificial barriers to the advancement of women and minorities in the private sector: societal barriers, such as barriers related to educational opportunity and attainment; internal structure barriers, such as alienating corporate climates; and governmental barriers, including inconsistent monitoring and enforcement of antidiscrimination legislation.

In *A Solid Investment: Making Full Use of the Nation's Human Capital* (November 1995, https://www.dol.gov/oasam/programs/history/reich/reports/ceiling2.pdf), the Glass Ceiling Commission offered several recommendations for companies:

- Demonstrate commitment to change from the highest level (chief executive officers)
- Include diversity in strategic business plans
- Use affirmative action as a tool
- Select, promote, and train qualified workers
- Prepare minorities and women for senior positions in the corporate ranks
- Initiate family friendly policies

The commission stated that the government should lead by example and make equal opportunity a reality, strengthen enforcement of antidiscrimination laws, improve data collection, and increase disclosure of diversity data.

In 2013 Sheryl Sandberg (1969–), the chief operating officer of the social media giant Facebook, renewed the national conversation about the glass ceiling with her book (cowritten with Nell Scovell) *Lean In: Women, Work, and the Will to Lead*, a manifesto arguing that women should address barriers to workplace equality head-on, whether these barriers are blatant, extremely subtle, or even subconscious or self-created. She encourages women to "lean in" to workplace challenges by working harder, refusing to compromise on career goals in anticipation of having children, demanding that their spouse contribute equally to household chores, and forming "lean in circles" in which like-minded women can share ideas relating to their lives and careers. Underpinning Sandberg's argument is the idea that increasing numbers of women in leadership positions

in business and the public sector will expand opportunities for all women.

In "100 Women: 'Why I Invented the Glass Ceiling Phrase'" (BBC.com, December 13, 2017), the management consultant Marilyn Loden notes that women have made significant gains since she coined the phrase "glass ceiling" in 1978, and yet "the metaphor continues to symbolise an enduring barrier to gender equality—one that has been normalised in many organisations where there is now a sense of complacency about the lack of women at the top." Far from being an inevitable condition, Loden argues, the glass ceiling will be shattered when institutions acknowledge and eradicate the embedded cultural biases that value men (and stereotypically masculine work styles) more than women (and work styles that are thought of as feminine) in the workplace. Loden explains, "I am referring to the biases that assume men are 'born leaders,' that working mothers are not committed to their careers, that women are too emotional, that sexual harassment is not a problem, and that there is no room on the executive floor for people who speak softly, have a high degree of emotional intelligence and favour participative leadership over autocratic management."

During the early 21st century the case of Lilly Ledbetter (1938–) became emblematic of the complex ways in which discrimination often operates in the workplace. Ledbetter, who had worked at the Alabama Goodyear Tire and Rubber Company for nearly 20 years, discovered just before she retired that she was making substantially less money than her male coworkers who did the same job. She had lost more than $200,000 in salary and even more in Social Security and pension benefits, which are pegged to salary levels throughout a worker's lifetime. A jury initially awarded Ledbetter $3.3 million, but in May 2007 the US Supreme Court ruled in *Ledbetter v. Goodyear Tire & Rubber Co., Inc.* (550 US 618) that according to the Civil Rights Act of 1964 women who believe they are being denied equal pay have only 180 days from their first discriminatory paycheck to file suit.

In dissenting with the court's majority ruling, Justice Ginsburg pointed out that the requirement to file suit immediately after discriminatory paychecks are issued ignores the actual workings of discrimination, which does not always occur in easy-to-identify forms such as wrongful termination, failure to promote, or refusal to hire (which were clearly covered under Title VII of the Civil Rights Act of 1964): "Pay disparities often occur, as they did in Ledbetter's case, in small increments; cause to suspect that discrimination is at work develops only over time. Comparative pay information, moreover, is often hidden from the employee's view. Employers may keep under wraps the pay differentials maintained among supervisors, no less [than] the reasons for those differentials." Ginsburg thus argued that the majority opinion represented an artificially narrow reading of Title VII and suggested that Congress should act to correct her colleagues' ruling.

Accordingly, one of Obama's first acts as president was to sign the Lilly Ledbetter Fair Pay Act in January 2009, which amended the Civil Rights Act to state that the 180-day statute of limitations on filing pay-discrimination claims would reset with each new paycheck that was affected by discriminatory practices. Thus, in a case such as Ledbetter's, in which she found out about the discrimination she had faced toward the end of her career, she would have been entitled to seek redress for all of the preceding instances of pay discrimination.

**SEXUAL HARASSMENT IN THE WORKPLACE.** In late 2017 the question of sexual harassment in the workplace became a topic of heated national discussion, following explosive revelations about the prominent Hollywood film producer Harvey Weinstein (1952–), who was accused of sexually harassing and assaulting dozens of female actors and employees over a period of decades. Jodi Kantor and Megan Twohey report in "Harvey Weinstein Paid Off Sexual Harassment Accusers for Decades" (NYTimes.com, October 5, 2017) that Weinstein used his enormous power in the film industry to coerce the women he targeted, promising to help or ruin their careers, depending on how they responded to his sexual advances. According to Nadia Khomami, in "#MeToo: How a Hashtag Became a Rallying Cry against Sexual Harassment" (TheGuardian.com, October 20, 2017), the Weinstein scandal catalyzed a cultural uprising of sorts, when the actor Alyssa Milano (1972–), an outspoken critic of Weinstein, issued a call on Twitter, saying: "If all the women who have been sexually harassed or assaulted wrote 'Me too' as a status, we might give people a sense of the magnitude of the problem." Millions of women (some famous, some not) responded on social media platforms such as Twitter and Facebook, sharing their stories of sexual victimization by powerful men in other industries and professions, including sports, entertainment, academia, restaurants, and even Congress. The public outcry, which became known as the #MeToo movement, highlighted how widespread and commonplace men's sexual misconduct is in the American workplace and the extent to which it hinders women's ability to realize their full career potential.

## Science, Technology, Engineering, and Mathematics

In recent years there has been increasing focus on the persistent underrepresentation of women in science, technology, engineering, and mathematical (STEM) professions. The BLS (January 19, 2018, http://www.bls.gov/cps/cpsaat11.htm) indicates that in 2017 women accounted for only 16.2% of the labor force in architecture and

engineering and 25.5% of the labor force in computer and mathematical occupations. Specifically, women were particularly outnumbered by men among computer programmers (only 21.2% were female) and software developers (18.7%), occupations that are at the forefront of technological and cultural change. Women had made inroads in some areas of science, mainly in the life sciences: 68.9% of psychologists, 54.4% of biological scientists, and 52.1% of medical scientists were women. By comparison, only 38.3% of chemists and material scientists and 35.8% of environmental scientists and geoscientists were women.

**THE NATIONAL SCIENCE FOUNDATION REPORT.** Every two years the National Science Foundation publishes a congressionally mandated report on the status of women and minorities in science and engineering. In *Women, Minorities, and Persons with Disabilities in Science and Engineering: 2017* (December 2016, https://www.nsf.gov/statistics/2017/nsf17310/static/downloads/nsf17310-digest.pdf), the National Science Foundation indicates that in 2015, 49% of all scientists and engineers working in science and engineering occupations were white men. White women (18%) were the second-largest demographic group in science and engineering occupations, followed by Asian American men (14%) and Asian American women (7%). African American men, African American women, Hispanic men, and Hispanic women each accounted for 4% or fewer of all working scientists and engineers. In all, minority women accounted for approximately one out of 10 employed scientists and engineers.

The National Science Foundation (September 2014, https://www.nsf.gov/statistics/2017/nsf17310/static/data/tab9-25.pdf) also notes that female scientists and engineers in academia have significant ground to cover before reaching parity with men. As of 2013, women with science, engineering, and health doctorates held less than a quarter of all full-time full professorships in these fields. Nonetheless, women have made steady progress in this arena since 1993, when only 10% of all full-time full professorships in these fields were held by women. Underrepresented minorities held slightly more than 5% of all science and engineering full professorships in 2013, and this percentage had been rising far more slowly than that of women. The situation for minority female scientists and engineers in academia was, accordingly, significantly less hopeful than that of women in general.

**UNDERSTANDING THE STEM GENDER GAP.** In January 2005 Lawrence H. Summers (1954–), then the president of Harvard University, set off a firestorm of controversy when he suggested that females have less innate math and science ability than males. In a speech he delivered before the National Bureau of Economic Research, Summers posited that the lack of high-ranking women in science and engineering was due to the choice of working mothers to work fewer hours than their male colleagues and to women's lesser innate mathematic and scientific ability. Widely criticized for his remarks, which failed to sufficiently account for the significant impact of socialization and discrimination in steering women away from STEM professions, Summers left his position as president of the university the following year.

The Summers debacle prompted new research to determine why women are underrepresented in STEM professions and how they can be encouraged to increase their participation in these fields. In *Why So Few? Women in Science, Technology, Engineering, and Mathematics* (February 2010, https://www.aauw.org/files/2013/02/Why-So-Few-Women-in-Science-Technology-Engineering-and-Mathematics.pdf), Catherine Hill, Christianne Corbett, and Andresse St. Rose of the American Association of University Women present findings drawn from a large and diverse body of research indicating that the gender gap in STEM fields is largely a product of social and environmental factors. For example, negative stereotypes about girls' abilities in math and science can undermine their confidence, hinder their test performance, and ultimately squelch their interest in these subjects. Conversely, positive messaging from educators about the equal ability and learning potential of girls and boys can help foster girls' achievement and career aspirations in STEM fields. Similarly, implicit biases continue to reinforce the idea that STEM fields are inherently masculine, even among people who outwardly support gender equity. Efforts to increase awareness of these unconscious assumptions can help men and women alike develop a more inclusive image of STEM professions. At the college and university level, small changes to the curriculum and culture of STEM departments, such as broader introductory courses and better mentoring programs, can improve recruitment of female students and faculty.

These findings are echoed by Sapna Cheryan et al., in "Why Are Some STEM Fields More Gender Balanced Than Others?" (*Psychological Bulletin*, vol. 143, no. 1, January 2017), a study that focuses particularly on computer science, engineering, and physics, the academic fields where gender gaps remain most pronounced. The researchers find that, even before girls get to college, they are deterred from computer science, engineering, and physics courses because of the overtly masculine culture that surrounds them—that is, a culture that is characterized by "stereotypes of the field that are incompatible with the way that many women see themselves, negative stereotypes and perceived bias, and few role models for women." Cheryan et al. suggest that broadening the image of these fields to be more inclusive of girls' interests is the key to engaging girls in STEM studies.

### Women in the Military

In 1973, when the male military draft was replaced by an all-volunteer force, the number of women joining the military began increasing. According to the US Department of Defense, in 2017 there were 169,988 women on active duty in the armed services, accounting for 16% of the total military. (See Table 4.3.) Among all active-duty armed forces branches, the largest number of women served in the US Army (54,078), whereas

**TABLE 4.3**

**Number of women serving in the military, 2017**

| | Females | | | | | DoD total | Pct females |
|---|---|---|---|---|---|---|---|
| | Army | Navy | Marine Corps | Air Force | Total | | |
| **Officer total** | **15,787** | **10,017** | **1,611** | **12,887** | **40,302** | **228,100** | **17.67%** |
| E09 | 281 | 173 | 56 | 402 | 912 | 10,147 | 9.0% |
| E08 | 1,286 | 609 | 204 | 1,036 | 3,135 | 26,200 | 12.0% |
| E07 | 4,223 | 2,667 | 488 | 5,129 | 12,507 | 89,185 | 14.0% |
| E06 | 6,232 | 6,394 | 1,117 | 7,325 | 21,068 | 154,670 | 13.6% |
| E05 | 9,712 | 11,981 | 2,492 | 11,233 | 35,418 | 217,150 | 16.3% |
| E04 | 16,790 | 11,547 | 3,107 | 9,743 | 41,187 | 249,318 | 16.5% |
| E03 | 7,561 | 12,228 | 3,601 | 11,355 | 34,745 | 189,555 | 18.3% |
| E02 | 4,410 | 3,047 | 2,000 | 1,858 | 11,315 | 69,024 | 16.4% |
| E01 | 3,583 | 3,055 | 878 | 2,185 | 9,701 | 58,756 | 16.5% |
| **Enlisted total** | **54,078** | **51,701** | **13,943** | **50,266** | **169,988** | **1,064,005** | **15.98%** |
| **Total DoD officer & enlisted (Excl cadets/midshipmen)** | **69,865** | **61,718** | **15,554** | **63,153** | **210,290** | **1,292,105** | **16.27%** |
| Military academy cadets & midshipmen | 1,008 | 1,201 | N/A | 1,101 | 3,310 | 13,201 | 25.07% |
| **Grand total (Officers, enlisted and cadets/midshipmen)** | **70,873** | **62,919** | **15,554** | **64,254** | **213,600** | **1,305,306** | **16.36%** |

Note: DoD = Department of Defense.

SOURCE: Adapted from "Table of Active Duty Females by Rank/Grade and Service, June 2015," in *DoD Personnel, Workforce Reports & Publications*, Department of Defense, 2017, https://www.dmdc.osd.mil/appj/dwp/rest/download?fileName=rg1711_female.pdf&groupName=milRankGrade (accessed January 19, 2017)

only a quarter as many women served in the US Marine Corps (13,943).

In *Women in the Military: Where They Stand* (8th ed., February 2013, http://wrei.org/WIM2013e.pdf), the Women's Research and Education Institute notes that women played a greater role in the two wars launched in the wake of the September 11, 2001, attacks—Operation Enduring Freedom (OEF; commonly known as the War in Afghanistan, which began in 2001 and officially ended in 2014) and Operation Iraqi Freedom (OIF; commonly known as the Iraq War, which began in 2003 and officially ended in 2010)—than in any previous US wars or operations. As of 2013, when the United States began drawing down troops in Afghanistan, women had served more than 285,000 tours of duty (because many women served more than one tour of duty, this number is not equivalent to the number of women who served) in these wars. In spite of official armed forces policies restricting women's ability to engage enemy ground forces, women in fact regularly fought in ground engagements in these wars. More than 865 women had been awarded Purple Hearts for wounds received during enemy action, and at least two had received the Silver Star for heroism, one in each conflict. According to the Defense Manpower Data Center, which serves the Department of Defense, as of February 2018, 50 US servicewomen had died in the OEF (https://dcas.dmdc .osd.mil/dcas/pages/report_oef_deaths.xhtml) and 110 had died in the OIF (https://dcas.dmdc.osd.mil/dcas/pages/report_ oif_all.xhtml).

Women were officially banned, both before and during these wars, from ground combat and from the front lines of military engagements. Nevertheless, because there were no conventional front lines in Iraq and Afghanistan, women were exposed to the same dangers as men, and their performance altered the debate about the combat ban. The Women's Research and Education Institute states:

> OEF and OIF have provided ample empirical data on and observations of women's performance under fire. Prior to these operations, one could only speculate on how women might perform. Many of these speculations were voiced by those who felt that women's presence was softening the military: that, in combat, women would destroy the important unit bond; that women would not have the physical strength to remove wounded comrades to safety; that female casualties would excessively upset male soldiers; and that the American public would find the loss of women soldiers too unbearable to continue the fighting. None of these speculations has held up under the real-world tests of OEF and OIF.

The combat ban not only diminished the credit female soldiers received for serving their country bravely during war but also prevented them from working in certain units and holding certain jobs and thereby constrained their ability to advance in rank because many promotions occur as a result of accomplishments in combat. In January 2013 the outgoing US secretary of defense Leon Panetta (1938–), who served during the first Obama administration, announced that the Department of Defense intended to end the combat ban and open all service units and military occupations to women beginning in January 2016. During the transitional period that followed, the leaders of each branch of the armed forces were tasked to devise a process for integrating women into previously closed positions. They were also responsible for assessing and recommending whether any of the most physically intense and deadly units, such as the navy SEALs or the army's Delta Force, should remain off limits to women. Requests for exceptions (positions from which women should still be excluded) were to be substantiated by factual data pertaining to the skills, knowledge, and abilities required to succeed in a given unit. Any such requests were to be submitted to the Department of Defense by October 1, 2015.

Dan Lamothe reports in "In Historic Decision, Pentagon Chief Opens All Jobs in Combat Units to Women" (WashingtonPost.com, December 3, 2015) that although top leaders in the army, navy, air force, and US Special Operations Command recommended that all combat units in their divisions be open to women, General Joseph F. Dunford Jr. (1955–), the top officer for the marines, recommended that women should be restricted from holding certain positions in marine infantry and reconnaissance units. Dunford's recommendation followed the release in September 2015 of results from a yearlong study of women in marine combat units, which found that all-male units consistently outperformed mixed-gender units. Supporters of gender integration called attention to flaws in the study. Among the study's most prominent critics was the US secretary of the navy Ray Mabus (1948–), who noted that the research reflected only on the performance of the average woman in combat, rather than on the abilities of elite individuals.

On December 2, 2016, the US secretary of defense Ashton Carter (1954–) announced his decision to open all military combat positions to women, without exception. Accordingly, women would be eligible to join elite special operations units such as the navy SEALs, the army Special Forces, and the marine infantry. Quoted by Lamothe, Mabus affirmed the historic decision, predicting that it would maximize the combat effectiveness of the US Navy and US Marine Corps alike: "Our process and studies showed that as long as someone can meet operationally relevant, occupation-specific, gender-neutral individual standards, that person is qualified to serve. Gender does not define the Service of a United States Sailor or Marine—instead, it is their character, selflessness, and abilities."

In recent years, progress toward equality in the military has advanced on another front as well. In 2010 President Obama signed legislation that repealed the Don't Ask, Don't Tell policy signed into law in 1993 by President Bill Clinton (1946–) and enforced by President George W. Bush (1946–). The policy had allowed gay, lesbian, and bisexual men and women to serve in the armed forces only if they kept their sexual orientation secret. The 2010 repeal allowed gay, lesbian, and bisexual service members to serve openly, without fear of reprisals or discrimination. The new policy went into effect in September 2011.

During this period one of the greatest obstacles to gender equality in the military was the epidemic—as it was characterized by many service members and media reports—of sexual assaults on women in the armed forces. According to the Department of Defense, in *Department of Defense Annual Report on Sexual Assault in the Military, Fiscal Year 2012, Volume I* (April 2013, http://www.sapr .mil/public/docs/reports/FY12_DoD_SAPRO_Annual_ Report_on_Sexual_Assault-VOLUME_ONE.pdf), an estimated 26,000 active-duty service members experienced unwanted sexual contact in 2012, but only 3,374 reports of sexual assault involving service members were filed. A small number of both reported and unreported assaults were committed against men, but the overwhelming majority of victims were women. The dismal levels of reporting were believed to stem largely from fears of retaliation and a military culture in which male officers protected one another at the expense of victims. Numerous high-profile cases surfaced in which commanding officers absolved offenders of blame or those charged with investigating sexual crimes were themselves accused of sexual crimes. The ensuing public outcry led to congressional hearings and the implementation of new rules and sexual assault prevention initiatives by Chuck Hagel (1946–), the US secretary of defense at that time.

In November 2014 Hagel released *Report to the President of the United States on Sexual Assault Prevention and Response* (http://sapr.mil/public/docs/reports/ FY14_POTUS/FY14_DoD_Report_to_POTUS_Full_Report .pdf), which detailed the progress of new and enhanced efforts to prevent, respond to, and effectively adjudicate sexual assault crimes within the armed services. The report reflected a significant reduction in sexual assaults—down from 26,000 in fiscal year 2012 to 19,000 in fiscal year 2014. Furthermore, a 63% increase over the same period in the number of service members who chose to report assaults seemed to indicate service members' increased confidence in the department's ability to support victims and hold assailants accountable. Two years later, in *Department of Defense Annual Report on Sexual Assault in the Military, Fiscal Year 2016* (May 2017, http://www.sapr.mil/public/docs/reports/

FY16_Annual/FY16_SAPRO_Annual_Report.pdf), the Department of Defense illustrated more progress on this issue. In 2016 the estimated number of service members experiencing unwanted sexual contact dropped to 14,900. Moreover, the rate of reporting these incidents had increased to 32%—nearly triple the report rate in 2012.

In spite of apparent progress, in late 2017, as the #MeToo movement drew national attention to the pervasiveness of sexual harassment in the workplace, the Department of Defense continued to draw criticism from those who charged that it was not doing enough to prevent and punish sexual misconduct in the military. In "Congress Advances New Sexual Assault, Harassment Rules for the Military" (MilitaryTimes.com, November 26, 2017), Leo Shane III notes that the US senator Kirsten Gillibrand (1966–; D-NY) was among the most vocal of these critics, leading a group of 13 US senators who were pushing to establish an independent legal process— outside the military chain of command—for adjudicating sexual assault crimes. Gillibrand objected to existing legal procedures on the grounds that they enabled military leaders to dismiss accusations of assault and harassment, thereby discouraging victims from reporting traumatic incidents. Furthermore, in November 2017 Congress included items in the annual defense authorization bill that pressed military leaders to expand their Sexual Assault Prevention and Response Program and enact stricter rules against sexual misconduct by service members. Widely noted among the new additions to the budget bill was a provision that outlawed "the non-consensual sharing of intimate images" by military personnel, which was a response to scandals earlier that year involving active-duty marines who shared nude pictures of female colleagues on the internet.

## Women Entrepreneurs

Recent years have shown dynamic growth for women's entrepreneurship, according to *The 2017 State of Women-Owned Businesses Report* (November 2017, http://about.americanexpress.com/news/docs/2017-State- of-Women-Owned-Businesses-Report.pdf), a report commissioned by American Express OPEN and based on research provided by Womenable, an organization dedicated to promoting women's entrepreneurship worldwide. The report finds that as of January 2017, there were approximately 11.6 million women-owned businesses in the United States. These businesses employed nearly 9 million people and generated more than $1.7 trillion in annual revenues.

Between 1997 and 2017 the number of all new US businesses grew 44%, whereas new women-owned businesses saw a much greater increase of 114%. Over this 20-year period, an average of 849 women-owned businesses were started every day. The average rose from 588 new businesses per day in 1997–2002 to 714 per day in 2002–07. The growth of women-owned businesses spiked to 1,143 per day in 2007–12, as high unemployment during this period of economic recession and recovery led more people to become "necessity entrepreneurs." According to *2017 State of Women-Owned Businesses Report*, a necessity entrepreneur is an individual who cannot find quality employment or is unemployed and whose only viable employment option is to start a business. Even as unemployment declined and fewer women were turning to entrepreneurship out of necessity, the growth rate for new women-owned businesses remained strong in 2016–17, with 827 new women-owned businesses per day.

Between 1997 and 2017 entrepreneurship was particularly strong among minority women. Although women-owned businesses as a whole increased 114% during this period, firms owned by African American women grew 605%, followed by 493% for Native Hawaiian/Pacific Islander women, 491% for Hispanic women, 314% for Asian American women, and 201% for Native American/Alaskan Native women. In 2017 nonminority women owned 53.5% of all women-owned businesses, followed by African American women (19%), Hispanic women (17.2%), and Asian American women (8.6%). In spite of the high rates of new business growth for Native American/Alaskan Native and Native Hawaiian/Pacific Islander women, these groups only accounted for 1.4% and 0.3%, respectively, of all women-owned businesses in 2017.

Amy Haimerl reports in "The Fastest-Growing Group of Entrepreneurs in America" (Fortune.com, June 29, 2015) on the steep rise in entrepreneurship among women of color. Reflecting on the reasons for this trend, Margot Dorfman, the chief executive officer of the US Women's Chamber of Commerce, was quoted as saying: "We attribute the growth in women-owned firms to the lack of fair pay, fair promotion, and family-friendly policies found in corporate America. Women of color, when you look at the statistics, are impacted more significantly by all of the negative factors that women face. It's not surprising that they have chosen to invest in themselves."

## OBSTACLES REMAIN

Despite equal-opportunity laws and regulations and affirmative action policies, various personnel practices, including the wording of job descriptions and the structure of the corporate hierarchy, can keep women from entering male-dominated occupations. Women starting out in new fields lack the seniority that is necessary for advancing in their career. Women entering male-dominated occupations may face suspicion, distrust, or outright hostility. Off-color comments or jokes, gossip, sexual harassment, or the refusal of help by coworkers may make the workplace inhospitable for women.

Women consistently identify mentoring as a crucial factor for success. Because most senior positions are occupied by men, it may be difficult for a female to find a mentor. As more women achieve higher-echelon jobs, more mentors will be available for younger women. Isolation and exclusion from "old-boys' networks" are also cited as important obstacles for women moving into new occupations. Nonetheless, as more women make their way up to more influential positions, this may begin to change as well.

# CHAPTER 5
# MONEY, INCOME, AND POVERTY

## INCOME INEQUALITY

Chad Stone et al. of the Center on Budget and Policy Priorities (CBPP) note in *A Guide to Statistics on Historical Trends in Income Inequality* (February 16, 2018, https://www.cbpp.org/sites/default/files/atoms/files/11-28-11 pov_0.pdf) that the years from the end of World War II (1939–1945) through the 1970s marked a period during which the US economy grew and prosperity was shared broadly among people at all income levels. Since the 1970s the economy has grown more slowly, and income has become concentrated among the top earners to a degree not seen since the 1920s. These trends continued during and after the so-called Great Recession (which lasted from late 2007 to mid-2009), which left many lower- and middle-class Americans unemployed and indebted while those at the upper end of the income scale were much less affected. According to Jessica L. Semega, Kayla R. Fontenot, and Melissa A. Kollar of the US Census Bureau, in *Income and Poverty in the United States: 2016* (September 2017, https://www.census.gov/content/dam/Census/library/publications/2017/demo/P60-259.pdf), the top 20% of earners took home 51.5% of all income generated in 2016, and the top 5% received 22.6% of all income. These numbers had been gradually climbing over the course of the preceding decade, and they were markedly higher than in 1990 (when the top 20% earned 46.6% of all income, and the top 5% claimed 18.5%) and 1980 (when the top 20% earned 44.1%, and the top 5% claimed 16.5%).

These trends impact women disproportionately because on average women earn less money than men, have fewer assets, and are far more likely to live in poverty. Historically, women entered the labor market by filling the lowest-paying jobs and mirroring the work they customarily did at home: cleaning, cooking, sewing, and child care. In those rare cases where women and men did the same work prior to the civil rights and women's movements, women were paid less as a matter of course.

In *The American Woman: Her Changing Social, Economic, and Political Roles, 1920–1970* (1972), William Henry Chafe examines the dimensions of the challenges women faced in seeking equality in the workplace, noting that a wage survey taken in 1833 in Philadelphia, Pennsylvania, found that most women workers in local textile factories received less for working 78 hours per week than men were getting for one 10-hour day.

Women had closed that earnings gap dramatically by the early 21st century. The American Association of University Women (AAUW) reports in *The Simple Truth about the Gender Pay Gap* (March 2018, https://www.aauw.org/aauw_check/pdf_download/show_pdf.php?file=The-Simple-Truth) that in 2016 it was typical for women working full time in the United States to be paid 80% of what men were paid for the same work (meaning that the earnings gap was 20%). If the pay gap continues to close at the same rate that was seen between 1960 and 2016, women can expect to reach pay equity with men in 2059. The AAUW finds that, however, since 2001 the gap has been narrowing at a slower rate. If this rate persists, women will not reach pay equity with men until 2119.

## THE EARNINGS GAP

Women's median pay (the middle value; half are paid more and half are paid less) remains substantially lower than men's in the 21st century. Experts cite numerous factors that contribute to this disparity. Many women leave the workforce to stay at home while their children are young. Discrimination against female employees also contributes, at least in part, to the wage gap. In addition, women are more likely to be in low-paying, entry-level jobs, and they often work fewer hours and have fewer job skills than men. Because women have historically been excluded from many professions, older women are less likely to be highly experienced at their job than men; the most experienced and highest-paid workers in many industries are men.

As women in the aggregate have accumulated job experience and approached numerical parity among workers in individual professions, their wages have approached those of their male counterparts. Women's educational attainment has likewise increased dramatically since the mid-20th century. Women with degrees tend to earn more money and work for more years than women without degrees, and their salaries typically increase as they move up the professional ladder. As Figure 5.1 shows, the gap between women's and men's median earnings has narrowed over time, but progress has not been steady. Between 1960 and 2013 there were periods during which the earnings ratio (an expression of women's earnings as a percentage of men's) remained flat and periods that saw faster or slower movement toward equality. The earnings ratio hovered near 60% from 1960 through the early 1980s, when it began to climb rapidly. The ratio grew from 60.2% in 1980 to 71.6% in 1990, but then over the following two decades growth in women's earnings relative to men's was slower. (See Table 5.1.) By 2000 the ratio was 73.7%, and by 2016 it was 80.5%. In 2016 men who worked full time, year round had median earnings of $51,640 annually, whereas women who worked full time, year round had median earnings of $41,554. (See Figure 5.1.)

Weekly earnings may be a more accurate measure of the earnings gap because many women do not work year round. Some women leave the workforce to care for children, and others leave the workforce during the summer months when their children are out of school. Therefore, annual figures may not provide an accurate measure of women's earnings relative to the work they have done. In 2017 the median weekly earnings for women aged 16 years and older was $770, compared with $941 for men of the same age. (See Table 5.2.) The resulting ratio of women's to men's earnings was 81.8%

## Race and Hispanic Origin

The gap between women's and men's weekly earnings was higher among some racial and ethnic groups than others in 2017. White women earned a median of $795 per week, whereas white men earned $971; the resulting ratio of women's to men's earnings was 81.9%. (See Table 5.2.) Asian American women earned a median of $903 per week, compared with $1,207 for Asian American men (who had the highest median income of all demographic groups), for an earnings ratio of 74.8%. The gaps between the wages of African American women and men and Hispanic women and men were

**FIGURE 5.1**

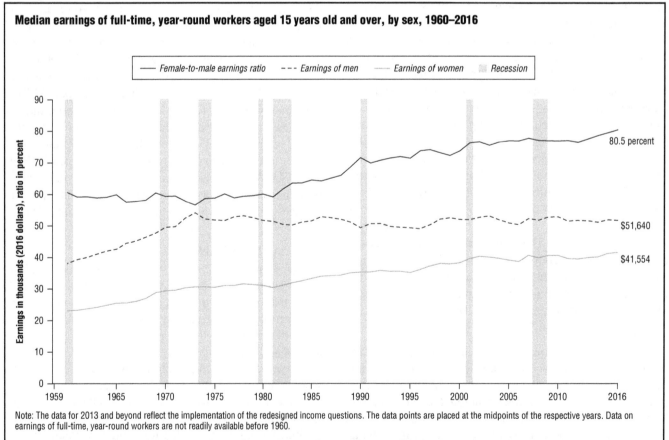

Median earnings of full-time, year-round workers aged 15 years old and over, by sex, 1960–2016

Note: The data for 2013 and beyond reflect the implementation of the redesigned income questions. The data points are placed at the midpoints of the respective years. Data on earnings of full-time, year-round workers are not readily available before 1960.

SOURCE: Jessica L. Semega, Kayla R. Fontenot, and Melissa A. Kollar, "Figure 2. Female-to-Male Earnings Ratio and Median Earnings of Full-Time, Year-Round Workers 15 Years and Older by Sex: 1960 to 2016," in *Income and Poverty in the United States: 2016*, US Census Bureau, September 2017, https://www.census.gov/content/dam/Census/library/publications/2017/demo/P60-259.pdf (accessed January 19, 2018)

**TABLE 5.1**

## Women's earnings as a percentage of men's earnings, by race and Hispanic origin, 1960–2016

[Based on median earnings of full-time, year-round workers 15 years old and over as of March of the following year. Before 1989, earnings are for civilian workers only.]

| Year | All races | White alone | White | White alone, not Hispanic | White, not Hispanic | Black A.O.I.C. |
|------|-----------|-------------|-------|---------------------------|---------------------|----------------|
| 2016 | 80.5 | 80.6 | NA | 79.0 | NA | 87.5 |
| 2015 | 79.6 | 79.5 | NA | 75.3 | NA | 88.1 |
| 2014 | 78.6 | 79.3 | NA | 75.4 | NA | 81.7 |
| 2013 | 77.6 | 79.3 | NA | 74.8 | NA | 82.9 |
| 2013 | 78.3 | 79.6 | NA | 77.4 | NA | 84.1 |
| 2012 | 76.5 | 77.4 | NA | 77.9 | NA | 87.7 |
| 2011 | 77.0 | 75.3 | NA | 77.1 | NA | 85.4 |
| 2010 | 76.9 | 74.5 | NA | 77.5 | NA | 87.4 |
| 2009 | 77.0 | 75.4 | NA | 75.0 | NA | 85.1 |
| 2008 | 77.1 | 76.4 | NA | 73.0 | NA | 84.6 |
| 2007 | 77.8 | 77.2 | NA | 73.0 | NA | 86.0 |
| 2006 | 76.9 | 76.5 | NA | 73.8 | NA | 87.1 |
| 2005 | 77.0 | 76.6 | NA | 73.5 | NA | 90.0 |
| 2004 | 76.6 | 76.1 | NA | 71.4 | NA | 88.8 |
| 2003 | 75.5 | 75.6 | NA | 71.6 | NA | 83.7 |
| 2002 | 76.6 | 75.4 | NA | 73.9 | NA | 85.6 |
| 2001 | 76.3 | NA | 75.1 | NA | 73.9 | NA |
| 2000 | 73.7 | NA | 73.1 | NA | 72.3 | NA |
| 1999 | 72.3 | NA | 71.6 | NA | 67.8 | NA |
| 1998 | 73.2 | NA | 72.6 | NA | 71.2 | NA |
| 1997 | 74.2 | NA | 72.0 | NA | 70.8 | NA |
| 1996 | 73.8 | NA | 73.3 | NA | 70.2 | NA |
| 1995 | 71.4 | NA | 71.2 | NA | 68.8 | NA |
| 1994 | 72.0 | NA | 71.6 | NA | 71.1 | NA |
| 1993 | 71.5 | NA | 70.8 | NA | 70.0 | NA |
| 1992 | 70.8 | NA | 70.0 | NA | 69.0 | NA |
| 1991 | 69.9 | NA | 68.7 | NA | 67.9 | NA |
| 1990 | 71.6 | NA | 69.4 | NA | 67.6 | NA |
| 1989 | 68.7 | NA | 66.3 | NA | 64.2 | NA |
| 1988 | 66.0 | NA | 65.4 | NA | 64.1 | NA |
| 1987 | 65.2 | NA | 64.4 | NA | 63.5 | NA |
| 1986 | 64.3 | NA | 63.3 | NA | NA | NA |
| 1985 | 64.6 | NA | 63.0 | NA | NA | NA |
| 1984 | 63.7 | NA | 62.2 | NA | NA | NA |
| 1983 | 63.6 | NA | 62.7 | NA | NA | NA |
| 1982 | 61.7 | NA | 60.9 | NA | NA | NA |
| 1981 | 59.2 | NA | 58.5 | NA | NA | NA |
| 1980 | 60.2 | NA | 58.9 | NA | NA | NA |
| 1979 | 59.7 | NA | 58.8 | NA | NA | NA |
| 1978 | 59.4 | NA | 58.9 | NA | NA | NA |
| 1977 | 58.9 | NA | 57.6 | NA | NA | NA |
| 1976 | 60.2 | NA | 59.0 | NA | NA | NA |
| 1975 | 58.8 | NA | 57.6 | NA | NA | NA |
| 1974 | 58.8 | NA | 57.9 | NA | NA | NA |
| 1973 | 56.6 | NA | 55.9 | NA | NA | NA |
| 1972 | 57.9 | NA | 56.6 | NA | NA | NA |
| 1971 | 59.5 | NA | 58.5 | NA | NA | NA |
| 1970 | 59.4 | NA | 58.7 | NA | NA | NA |
| 1969 | 58.9 | NA | 58.1 | NA | NA | NA |
| 1968 | 58.2 | NA | 58.2 | NA | NA | NA |
| 1967 | 57.8 | NA | 57.9 | NA | NA | NA |
| 1966 | 57.6 | NA | NA | NA | NA | NA |
| 1965 | 59.9 | NA | NA | NA | NA | NA |
| 1964 | 59.1 | NA | NA | NA | NA | NA |
| 1963 | 58.9 | NA | NA | NA | NA | NA |
| 1962 | 59.3 | NA | NA | NA | NA | NA |
| 1961 | 59.2 | NA | NA | NA | NA | NA |
| 1960 | 60.7 | NA | NA | NA | NA | NA |

| Year | Black alone | Black | Asian A.O.I.C. | Asian alone | Asian or Pacific Islander | Hispanic (any race) |
|------|-------------|-------|----------------|-------------|---------------------------|---------------------|
| 2016 | 87.7 | N/A | 76.9 | 77.2 | N/A | 84.4 |
| 2015 | 88.1 | N/A | 78.3 | 78.2 | N/A | 87.2 |
| 2014 | 82.4 | N/A | 81.9 | 81.4 | N/A | 87.7 |
| 2013 | 82.9 | N/A | 77.9 | 79.1 | N/A | 95.6 |
| 2013 | 83.4 | N/A | 75.1 | 73.5 | N/A | 93.5 |
| 2012 | 88.0 | N/A | 79.5 | 77.6 | N/A | 88.2 |
| 2011 | 84.8 | N/A | 74.9 | 74.2 | N/A | 91.1 |

significantly lower, but that was a function more of comparatively low male earnings than of high female earnings. African American women made $657 per week, compared with $710 for men, for a ratio of 92.5%.

**TABLE 5.1**

**Women's earnings as a percentage of men's earnings, by race and Hispanic origin, 1960–2016** [CONTINUED]

[Based on median earnings of full-time, year-round workers 15 years old and over as of March of the following year. Before 1989, earnings are for civilian workers only.]

| Year | Black alone | Black | Asian A.O.I.C. | Asian alone | Asian or Pacific Islander | Hispanic (any race) |
|------|-------------|-------|----------------|-------------|---------------------------|----------------------|
| 2010 | 87.7 | NA | 79.9 | 79.8 | NA | 89.2 |
| 2009 | 84.9 | NA | 82.1 | 81.8 | NA | 86.6 |
| 2008 | 84.4 | NA | 82.5 | 82.2 | NA | 86.7 |
| 2007 | 86.0 | NA | 79.7 | 79.6 | NA | 88.1 |
| 2006 | 87.3 | NA | 77.3 | 76.4 | NA | 86.7 |
| 2005 | 89.7 | NA | 76.4 | 75.1 | NA | 90.5 |
| 2004 | 88.6 | NA | 78.5 | 78.3 | NA | 88.1 |
| 2003 | 83.6 | NA | 71.9 | 71.5 | NA | 85.7 |
| 2002 | 85.6 | NA | 75.4 | 75.1 | NA | 84.4 |
| 2001 | NA | 84.8 | NA | NA | 73.3 | 85.7 |
| 2000 | NA | 83.3 | NA | NA | 75.1 | 86.9 |
| 1999 | NA | 81.5 | NA | NA | 77.4 | 86.5 |
| 1998 | NA | 83.7 | NA | NA | 77.7 | 86.3 |
| 1997 | NA | 83.4 | NA | NA | 80.1 | 87.8 |
| 1996 | NA | 81.3 | NA | NA | 74.2 | 88.6 |
| 1995 | NA | 84.6 | NA | NA | 78.8 | 84.3 |
| 1994 | NA | 83.9 | NA | NA | 76.3 | 86.5 |
| 1993 | NA | 86.1 | NA | NA | 78.8 | 83.2 |
| 1992 | NA | 88.2 | NA | NA | 74.7 | 87.4 |
| 1991 | NA | 84.8 | NA | NA | 70.2 | 82.2 |
| 1990 | NA | 85.4 | NA | NA | 79.7 | 81.9 |
| 1989 | NA | 85.1 | NA | NA | 75.9 | 85.3 |
| 1988 | NA | 81.2 | NA | NA | 71.3 | 83.2 |
| 1987 | NA | 82.4 | NA | NA | NA | 83.3 |
| 1986 | NA | 80.3 | NA | NA | NA | 82.3 |
| 1985 | NA | 81.9 | NA | NA | NA | 76.6 |
| 1984 | NA | 82.5 | NA | NA | NA | 74.1 |
| 1983 | NA | 78.6 | NA | NA | NA | 72.1 |
| 1982 | NA | 78.3 | NA | NA | NA | 72.2 |
| 1981 | NA | 76.0 | NA | NA | NA | 72.9 |
| 1980 | NA | 78.8 | NA | NA | NA | 71.4 |
| 1979 | NA | 74.6 | NA | NA | NA | 68.2 |
| 1978 | NA | 71.5 | NA | NA | NA | 68.8 |
| 1977 | NA | 77.5 | NA | NA | NA | 69.7 |
| 1976 | NA | 75.7 | NA | NA | NA | 68.0 |
| 1975 | NA | 74.6 | NA | NA | NA | 68.3 |
| 1974 | NA | 75.3 | NA | NA | NA | 66.7 |
| 1973 | NA | 69.6 | NA | NA | NA | NA |
| 1972 | NA | 70.5 | NA | NA | NA | NA |
| 1971 | NA | 75.2 | NA | NA | NA | NA |
| 1970 | NA | 69.8 | NA | NA | NA | NA |
| 1969 | NA | 68.2 | NA | NA | NA | NA |
| 1968 | NA | 65.6 | NA | NA | NA | NA |
| 1967 | NA | 66.9 | NA | NA | NA | NA |

NA = Not available.
A.O.I.C. = alone or in combincation (with other races).

SOURCE: "Table P-40. Women's Earnings as a Percentage of Men's Earnings by Race and Hispanic Origin: 1960 to 2016," in *Historical Income Tables: People,* US Census Bureau, September 2014, https://www2.census.gov/programs-surveys/cps/tables/time-series/historical-income-people/p40.xls (accessed January 19, 2018)

Hispanic women made $603 per week, compared with $690 for men, for a ratio of 87.4%.

## Occupation

The earnings gap varies dramatically by occupation, but lower pay for women who do the same work as men is a constant in almost all occupations. Some of the most striking earnings disparities exist in higher-paid positions. For example, female personal financial advisers made 59.4% of what their male counterparts made in 2015. (See Table 5.3.) Significant differences also exist among accountants and auditors (73.5%), financial analysts (69.7%), and financial managers (65.2%). Many

other high-paying and high-status occupations are also characterized by significant pay disparities. Female chief executives made only 81.6% of what male chief executives made in 2015, female postsecondary teachers (e.g., college professors) made only 81.4% of what male postsecondary teachers made, and female physicians and surgeons made only 80.1% of what male physicians and surgeons made.

Unsurprisingly, the most educated and highly skilled women earned the highest salaries in 2015. Chief executives ($1,836), pharmacists ($1,811), lawyers ($1,717), computer and information systems managers ($1,563), physicians and surgeons ($1,533), and nurse practitioners

TABLE 5.2

**Median weekly earnings of full-time wage and salary workers, by sex, age, and race and Hispanic origin, 2016–17**

| Characteristic | Number of workers (in thousands) | | Median weekly earnings | |
|---|---|---|---|---|
| | 2016 | 2017 | 2016 | 2017 |
| **Sex and age** | | | | |
| Total, 16 years and over | **111,091** | **113,272** | **$832** | **$860** |
| Men, 16 years and over | 61,930 | 62,980 | 915 | 941 |
| 16 to 24 years | 5,646 | 5,791 | 512 | 547 |
| 25 years and over | 56,284 | 57,190 | 969 | 996 |
| Women, 16 years and over | 49,161 | 50,291 | 749 | 770 |
| 16 to 24 years | 4,430 | 4,490 | 486 | 499 |
| 25 years and over | 44,731 | 45,801 | 784 | 810 |
| **Race and Hispanic or Latino ethnicity** | | | | |
| White | 86,474 | 87,730 | 862 | 890 |
| Men | 49,310 | 50,003 | 942 | 971 |
| Women | 37,163 | 37,727 | 766 | 795 |
| Black or African American | 13,963 | 14,521 | 678 | 682 |
| Men | 6,728 | 6,928 | 718 | 710 |
| Women | 7,235 | 7,593 | 641 | 657 |
| Asian | 7,030 | 7,320 | 1,021 | 1,043 |
| Men | 3,888 | 4,014 | 1,151 | 1,207 |
| Women | 3,142 | 3,306 | 902 | 903 |
| Hispanic or Latino ethnicity | 18,950 | 19,615 | 624 | 655 |
| Men | 11,666 | 11,896 | 663 | 690 |
| Women | 7,284 | 7,719 | 586 | 603 |

Note: Estimates for the above race groups (white, black or African American, and Asian) do not sum to totals because data are not presented for all races. Persons whose ethnicity is identified as Hispanic or Latino may be of any race. Updated population controls are introduced annually with the release of January data.

SOURCE: "37. Median Weekly Earnings of Full-Time Wage and Salary Workers by Selected Characteristics," in *Labor Force Statistics from the Current Population Survey*, US Bureau of Labor Statistics, February 8, 2017, https://www.bls.gov/cps/cpsaat37.pdf (accessed January 19, 2018)

($1,522) had the highest median weekly earnings among women. (See Table 5.3.) The lowest-paying jobs for women were clustered in food preparation and serving occupations. Food preparation workers ($388), hostesses at restaurants, lounges, and coffee shops ($397), and maids and housekeeping cleaners ($407) had some of the lowest median weekly earnings among all workers; these were also jobs in which the majority of employees were women. Child care workers, almost all of whom were women, also had one of the lowest median weekly earnings ($430) of all employed people. Women working in agriculture were also poorly paid: graders and sorters of agricultural products were paid a median of $468 per week, and miscellaneous agricultural workers were paid a median of $398 per week.

## Education

Although women are becoming more educated and therefore earning more in aggregate than in previous decades, they continue to earn less at each level of educational attainment than men do. In 2015 female high school graduates with no college credits earned a median weekly wage of $586, compared with a median weekly wage of $759 earned by male high school graduates with

no college credits. (See Table 5.4) Women with some college or an associate's degree earned a median of $664 per week, compared with $883 for men with the same level of education. Women with bachelor's degrees had median weekly earnings of $975, whereas men with the same educational attainment had median earnings of $1,304. At the master's ($1,160 versus $1,566), professional ($1,451 versus $1,888), and doctoral levels ($1,442 versus $1,758), women continued to have lower median earnings than their male counterparts.

Nonetheless, women's median weekly earnings had either declined less or grown more than men's at all educational levels between 1979 and 2016. (See Figure 5.2.) Men without a high school diploma lost 29% in constant (inflation-adjusted) dollar earnings during this period, whereas women lost 10%. Male high school graduates with no college credits saw their median weekly earnings fall 19% over the same period, whereas their female counterparts saw their earnings rise 5%. Men with some college or an associate's degree saw their earnings fall 12%, whereas their female counterparts saw their earnings rise 6%. Among those with a bachelor's degree or higher, women's earnings grew 35%, a rate almost double that of men's earnings (20%).

## Marital Status and Children

In spite of changing attitudes about the roles of men and women, the burden of child-rearing continues to fall more heavily on women than on men, and it falls particularly heavily on single women. In 2016 married women living with their spouse and working full time had higher median weekly earnings ($838) than did women who had never married, were divorced or separated, or were widowed ($671). (See Table 5.5.) Married women with children under the age of 18 years earned slightly more ($870) than married childless women ($815), but single women with children earned much less ($607) than their childless counterparts ($697). Single women with children under the age of six years earned the least ($524) among all women workers. Married men with children, like married women with children, earned slightly more ($1,071) than their childless counterparts ($1,053). Although single men, like single women, made significantly less per week than married men, the presence of children did not correlate as strongly with lower incomes: childless single men earned only slightly more ($733) than single men with children under the age of 18 years ($719). There were more single childless men (23 million) than single childless women (18.4 million) in 2016, but there were more than twice as many single women with children under the age of 18 years (6 million) than single men with children under the age of 18 years (2.7 million).

## Age

The earnings gap varies with age. As Table 5.6 shows, women's weekly earnings grow fairly steadily

TABLE 5.3

**Median weekly earnings of full-time wage and salary workers by occupation and gender, 2015**

[Numbers in thousands]

| Occupation | Total | | Women | | Men | | Women's earnings as a percentage of men's |
|---|---|---|---|---|---|---|---|
| | Number of workers | Median weekly earnings | Number of workers | Median weekly earnings | Number of workers | Median weekly earnings | |
| Total, full-time wage and salary workers | 109,080 | $809 | 48,334 | $726 | 60,746 | $895 | 81.1 |
| Management, professional, and related occupations | 44,844 | 1,158 | 23,038 | 996 | 21,807 | 1,383 | 72.0 |
| Management, business, and financial operations occupations | 18,422 | 1,258 | 8,404 | 1,073 | 10,018 | 1,436 | 74.7 |
| Management occupations | 12,480 | 1,351 | 5,147 | 1,139 | 7,332 | 1,486 | 76.6 |
| Chief executives | 1,046 | 2,041 | 283 | 1,836 | 763 | 2,251 | 81.6 |
| General and operations managers | 823 | 1,260 | 202 | 1,002 | 621 | 1,347 | 74.4 |
| Legislators | 8 | — | 4 | — | 5 | — | — |
| Advertising and promotions managers | 55 | 1,050 | 26 | — | 29 | — | — |
| Marketing and sales managers | 948 | 1,462 | 378 | 1,258 | 570 | 1,603 | 78.5 |
| Public relations and fundraising managers | 59 | 1,557 | 35 | — | 24 | — | — |
| Administrative services managers | 170 | 1,191 | 73 | 981 | 96 | 1,451 | 67.6 |
| Computer and information systems managers | 636 | 1,728 | 169 | 1,563 | 466 | 1,817 | 86.0 |
| Financial managers | 1,124 | 1,408 | 573 | 1,130 | 551 | 1,732 | 65.2 |
| Compensation and benefits managers | 23 | — | 16 | — | 7 | — | — |
| Human resources managers | 254 | 1,365 | 186 | 1,274 | 68 | 1,495 | 85.2 |
| Training and development managers | 37 | — | 20 | — | 17 | — | — |
| Industrial production managers | 267 | 1,485 | 45 | — | 221 | 1,528 | — |
| Purchasing managers | 193 | 1,348 | 84 | 1,226 | 109 | 1,404 | 87.3 |
| Transportation, storage, and distribution managers | 276 | 966 | 52 | 749 | 224 | 1,006 | 74.5 |
| Farmers, ranchers, and other agricultural managers | 129 | 769 | 23 | — | 106 | 847 | — |
| Construction managers | 471 | 1,329 | 42 | — | 429 | 1,357 | — |
| Education administrators | 778 | 1,423 | 496 | 1,252 | 282 | 1,585 | 79.0 |
| Architectural and engineering managers | 110 | 1,899 | 10 | — | 101 | 1,892 | — |
| Food service managers | 763 | 742 | 374 | 680 | 389 | 820 | 82.9 |
| Funeral service managers | 13 | — | 2 | — | 10 | — | — |
| Gaming managers | 19 | — | 6 | — | 13 | — | — |
| Lodging managers | 123 | 985 | 68 | 902 | 54 | 1,171 | 77.0 |
| Medical and health services managers | 592 | 1,210 | 438 | 1,156 | 154 | 1,422 | 81.3 |
| Natural sciences managers | 24 | — | 13 | — | 11 | — | — |
| Postmasters and mail superintendents | 20 | — | 10 | — | 10 | — | — |
| Property, real estate, and community association managers | 401 | 914 | 230 | 823 | 171 | 1,137 | 72.4 |
| Social and community service managers | 305 | 1,022 | 200 | 965 | 105 | 1,142 | 84.5 |
| Emergency management directors | 9 | — | 3 | — | 6 | — | — |
| Managers, all other | 2,803 | 1,408 | 1,085 | 1,213 | 1,717 | 1,525 | 79.5 |
| Business and financial operations occupations | 5,942 | 1,137 | 3,256 | 1,004 | 2,686 | 1,327 | 75.7 |
| Agents and business managers of artists, performers, and athletes | 27 | — | 14 | — | 13 | — | — |
| Buyers and purchasing agents, farm products | 11 | — | 2 | — | 9 | — | — |
| Wholesale and retail buyers, except farm products | 142 | 926 | 69 | 985 | 73 | 886 | 111.2 |
| Purchasing agents, except wholesale, retail, and farm products | 260 | 1,009 | 124 | 986 | 136 | 1,020 | 96.7 |
| Claims adjusters, appraisers, examiners, and investigators | 317 | 963 | 176 | 824 | 141 | 1,134 | 72.7 |
| Compliance officers | 235 | 1,198 | 109 | 1,025 | 126 | 1,375 | 74.5 |
| Cost estimators | 95 | 1,232 | 12 | — | 83 | 1,264 | — |
| Human resources workers | 592 | 1,002 | 441 | 984 | 151 | 1,158 | 85.0 |
| Compensation, benefits, and job analysis specialists | 63 | 998 | 50 | 898 | 12 | — | — |
| Training and development specialists | 107 | 990 | 65 | 1,037 | 42 | — | — |
| Logisticians | 111 | 1,028 | 44 | — | 66 | 1,075 | — |
| Management analysts | 529 | 1,431 | 237 | 1,348 | 291 | 1,519 | 88.7 |
| Meeting, convention, and event planners | 117 | 859 | 90 | 840 | 27 | — | — |
| Fundraisers | 62 | 1,136 | 48 | — | 14 | — | — |
| Market research analysts and marketing specialists | 203 | 1,284 | 118 | 1,239 | 85 | 1,411 | 87.8 |
| Business operations specialists, all other | 186 | 1,090 | 112 | 969 | 74 | 1,461 | 66.3 |
| Accountants and auditors | 1,464 | 1,132 | 846 | 988 | 618 | 1,345 | 73.5 |
| Appraisers and assessors of real estate | 42 | — | 21 | — | 21 | — | — |
| Budget analysts | 44 | — | 28 | — | 17 | — | — |
| Credit analysts | 17 | — | 9 | — | 8 | — | — |
| Financial analysts | 295 | 1,426 | 127 | 1,171 | 168 | 1,680 | 69.7 |
| Personal financial advisors | 407 | 1,419 | 159 | 1,033 | 248 | 1,738 | 59.4 |
| Insurance underwriters | 106 | 1,149 | 63 | 956 | 44 | — | — |
| Financial examiners | 17 | — | 8 | — | 9 | — | — |
| Credit counselors and loan officers | 313 | 997 | 166 | 906 | 146 | 1,186 | 76.4 |
| Tax examiners and collectors, and revenue agents | 59 | 1,051 | 39 | — | 20 | — | — |
| Tax preparers | 56 | 892 | 37 | — | 19 | — | — |
| Financial specialists, all other | 66 | 1,162 | 40 | — | 25 | — | — |
| Professional and related occupations | 26,423 | 1,112 | 14,634 | 963 | 11,789 | 1,343 | 71.7 |
| Computer and mathematical occupations | 4,009 | 1,428 | 973 | 1,245 | 3,036 | 1,503 | 82.8 |
| Computer and information research scientists | 28 | — | 5 | — | 23 | — | — |

with age, before falling after the age of 55 years. Women make a weekly median of $388 at ages 16 to 19 years, $500 at 20 to 24 years, $705 at 25 to 34 years, $839 at 35 to 44 years, $836 at 45 to 54 years. and $812 at 55 to

TABLE 5.3

**Median weekly earnings of full-time wage and salary workers by occupation and gender, 2015** [CONTINUED]

[Numbers in thousands]

| Occupation | Total | | Women | | Men | | Women's earnings as a percentage of men's |
|---|---|---|---|---|---|---|---|
| | Number of workers | Median weekly earnings | Number of workers | Median weekly earnings | Number of workers | Median weekly earnings | |
| Computer systems analysts | 499 | 1,389 | 173 | 1,256 | 325 | 1,462 | 85.9 |
| Information security analysts | 67 | 1,538 | 11 | — | 56 | 1,562 | — |
| Computer programmers | 450 | 1,438 | 93 | 1,302 | 357 | 1,501 | 86.7 |
| Software developers, applications and systems software | 1,287 | 1,682 | 232 | 1,415 | 1,054 | 1,751 | 80.8 |
| Web developers | 151 | 1,165 | 53 | 1,026 | 98 | 1,233 | 83.2 |
| Computer support specialists | 396 | 1,079 | 105 | 908 | 291 | 1,135 | 80.0 |
| Database administrators | 90 | 1,536 | 32 | — | 58 | 1,829 | — |
| Network and computer systems administrators | 208 | 1,242 | 28 | — | 179 | 1,266 | — |
| Computer network architects | 115 | 1,552 | 15 | — | 100 | 1,577 | — |
| Computer occupations, all other | 490 | 1,227 | 116 | 1,145 | 374 | 1,252 | 91.5 |
| Actuaries | 24 | — | 6 | — | 18 | — | — |
| Mathematicians | 6 | — | 0 | — | 6 | — | — |
| Operations research analysts | 122 | 1,441 | 63 | 1,325 | 59 | 1,574 | 84.2 |
| Statisticians | 76 | 1,275 | 39 | — | 37 | — | — |
| Miscellaneous mathematical science occupations | 1 | — | 0 | — | 1 | — | — |
| Architecture and engineering occupations | 2,656 | 1,424 | 383 | 1,257 | 2,272 | 1,452 | 86.6 |
| Architects, except naval | 138 | 1,441 | 31 | — | 106 | 1,492 | — |
| Surveyors, cartographers, and photogrammetrists | 29 | — | 6 | — | 23 | — | — |
| Aerospace engineers | 140 | 1,662 | 18 | — | 122 | 1,668 | — |
| Agricultural engineers | 5 | — | 0 | — | 5 | — | — |
| Biomedical engineers | 12 | — | 2 | — | 10 | — | — |
| Chemical engineers | 79 | 1,532 | 10 | — | 69 | 1,583 | — |
| Civil engineers | 316 | 1,460 | 41 | — | 275 | 1,474 | — |
| Computer hardware engineers | 72 | 1,876 | 10 | — | 62 | 1,871 | — |
| Electrical and electronics engineers | 283 | 1,778 | 37 | — | 246 | 1,819 | — |
| Environmental engineers | 35 | — | 9 | — | 26 | — | — |
| Industrial engineers, including health and safety | 205 | 1,447 | 37 | — | 168 | 1,430 | — |
| Marine engineers and naval architects | 9 | — | 0 | — | 9 | — | — |
| Materials engineers | 36 | — | 4 | — | 33 | — | — |
| Mechanical engineers | 316 | 1,534 | 23 | — | 294 | 1,550 | — |
| Mining and geological engineers, including mining safety engineers | 15 | — | 0 | — | 15 | — | — |
| Nuclear engineers | 5 | — | 2 | — | 3 | — | — |
| Petroleum engineers | 43 | — | 3 | — | 39 | — | — |
| Engineers, all other | 393 | 1,527 | 54 | 1,448 | 339 | 1,537 | 94.2 |
| Drafters | 114 | 977 | 23 | — | 91 | 977 | — |
| Engineering technicians, except drafters | 352 | 963 | 68 | 827 | 284 | 984 | 84.0 |
| Surveying and mapping technicians | 58 | 1,012 | 4 | — | 54 | 1,031 | — |
| Life, physical, and social science occupations | 1,176 | 1,206 | 514 | 1,067 | 662 | 1,379 | 77.4 |
| Agricultural and food scientists | 22 | — | 10 | — | 12 | — | — |
| Biological scientists | 74 | 1,233 | 28 | — | 46 | — | — |
| Conservation scientists and foresters | 23 | — | 7 | — | 16 | — | — |
| Medical scientists | 151 | 1,250 | 84 | 1,082 | 68 | 1,362 | 79.4 |
| Life scientists, all other | 1 | — | 0 | — | 1 | — | — |
| Astronomers and physicists | 14 | — | 3 | — | 11 | — | — |
| Atmospheric and space scientists | 8 | — | 1 | — | 8 | — | — |
| Chemists and materials scientists | 93 | 1,432 | 33 | — | 61 | 1,496 | — |
| Environmental scientists and geoscientists | 90 | 1,423 | 25 | — | 65 | 1,740 | — |
| Physical scientists, all other | 189 | 1,553 | 68 | 1,170 | 121 | 1,770 | 66.1 |
| Economists | 29 | — | 12 | — | 17 | — | — |
| Survey researchers | 0 | — | 0 | — | 0 | — | — |
| Psychologists | 114 | 1,367 | 83 | 1,189 | 31 | — | — |
| Sociologists | 0 | — | 0 | — | 0 | — | — |
| Urban and regional planners | 22 | — | 9 | — | 13 | — | — |
| Miscellaneous social scientists and related workers | 37 | — | 19 | — | 19 | — | — |
| Agricultural and food science technicians | 28 | — | 7 | — | 21 | — | — |
| Biological technicians | 20 | — | 10 | — | 10 | — | — |
| Chemical technicians | 75 | 944 | 32 | — | 43 | — | — |
| Geological and petroleum technicians | 22 | — | 4 | — | 18 | — | — |
| Nuclear technicians | 2 | — | 0 | — | 2 | — | — |
| Social science research assistants | 3 | — | 3 | — | 0 | — | — |
| Miscellaneous life, physical, and social science technicians | 157 | 846 | 78 | 780 | 79 | 1,001 | 77.9 |
| Community and social service occupations | 2,143 | 889 | 1,367 | 845 | 776 | 973 | 86.8 |
| Counselors | 635 | 904 | 451 | 902 | 184 | 908 | 99.3 |
| Social workers | 677 | 877 | 549 | 862 | 127 | 943 | 91.4 |
| Probation officers and correctional treatment specialists | 85 | 967 | 43 | — | 42 | — | — |
| Social and human service assistants | 173 | 676 | 149 | 673 | 23 | — | — |

64 years. The US Bureau of Labor Statistics (BLS), which is part of the US Department of Labor, indicates in *Highlights of Women's Earnings in 2016* (August 2017, https://www.bls.gov/opub/reports/womens-earnings/2016/

TABLE 5.3

**Median weekly earnings of full-time wage and salary workers by occupation and gender, 2015** [CONTINUED]

[Numbers in thousands]

| Occupation | Total | | Women | | Men | | Women's earnings as a percentage of men's |
|---|---|---|---|---|---|---|---|
| | Number of workers | Median weekly earnings | Number of workers | Median weekly earnings | Number of workers | Median weekly earnings | |
| Miscellaneous community and social service specialists, including health educators and community health workers | 92 | 831 | 63 | 728 | 29 | — | — |
| Clergy | 376 | 1,002 | 60 | 924 | 316 | 1,021 | 90.5 |
| Directors, religious activities and education | 62 | 929 | 31 | — | 31 | — | — |
| Religious workers, all other | 44 | — | 21 | — | 23 | — | — |
| Legal occupations | 1,346 | 1,391 | 722 | 1,135 | 624 | 1,877 | 60.5 |
| Lawyers | 803 | 1,886 | 300 | 1,717 | 503 | 1,914 | 89.7 |
| Judicial law clerks | 11 | — | 10 | — | 1 | — | — |
| Judges, magistrates, and other judicial workers | 54 | 1,952 | 20 | — | 33 | — | — |
| Paralegals and legal assistants | 341 | 927 | 294 | 910 | 47 | — | — |
| Miscellaneous legal support workers | 136 | 770 | 97 | 746 | 40 | — | — |
| Education, training, and library occupations | 6,884 | 956 | 5,034 | 907 | 1,849 | 1,144 | 79.3 |
| Postsecondary teachers | 917 | 1,258 | 401 | 1,144 | 516 | 1,405 | 81.4 |
| Preschool and kindergarten teachers | 517 | 616 | 506 | 618 | 11 | — | — |
| Elementary and middle school teachers | 2,806 | 974 | 2,262 | 957 | 543 | 1,077 | 88.9 |
| Secondary school teachers | 1,048 | 1,066 | 610 | 1,006 | 438 | 1,149 | 87.6 |
| Special education teachers | 297 | 987 | 258 | 990 | 38 | — | — |
| Other teachers and instructors | 378 | 896 | 199 | 817 | 179 | 1,024 | 79.8 |
| Archivists, curators, and museum technicians | 38 | — | 20 | — | 18 | — | — |
| Librarians | 130 | 991 | 102 | 966 | 27 | — | — |
| Library technicians | 18 | — | 15 | — | 4 | — | — |
| Teacher assistants | 614 | 541 | 565 | 530 | 48 | — | — |
| Other education, training, and library workers | 123 | 1,001 | 95 | 1,031 | 28 | — | — |
| Arts, design, entertainment, sports, and media occupations | 1,643 | 1,001 | 713 | 942 | 930 | 1,088 | 86.6 |
| Artists and related workers | 58 | 1,166 | 20 | — | 39 | — | — |
| Designers | 593 | 993 | 291 | 918 | 301 | 1,099 | 83.5 |
| Actors | 12 | — | 4 | — | 8 | — | — |
| Producers and directors | 120 | 1,270 | 53 | 1,234 | 67 | 1,340 | 92.1 |
| Athletes, coaches, umpires, and related workers | 147 | 780 | 39 | — | 108 | 818 | — |
| Dancers and choreographers | 11 | — | 9 | — | 2 | — | — |
| Musicians, singers, and related workers | 42 | — | 9 | — | 33 | — | — |
| Entertainers and performers, sports and related workers, all other | 14 | — | 3 | — | 11 | — | — |
| Announcers | 25 | — | 5 | — | 21 | — | — |
| News analysts, reporters and correspondents | 56 | 1,218 | 27 | — | 29 | — | — |
| Public relations specialists | 120 | 1,211 | 71 | 971 | 49 | — | — |
| Editors | 108 | 1,148 | 50 | 1,125 | 58 | 1,205 | 93.4 |
| Technical writers | 52 | 1,158 | 30 | — | 22 | — | — |
| Writers and authors | 79 | 1,232 | 42 | — | 36 | — | — |
| Miscellaneous media and communication workers | 46 | — | 30 | — | 16 | — | — |
| Broadcast and sound engineering technicians and radio operators | 83 | 954 | 7 | — | 77 | 937 | — |
| Photographers | 45 | — | 21 | — | 24 | — | — |
| Television, video, and motion picture camera operators and editors | 30 | — | 1 | — | 28 | — | — |
| Media and communication equipment workers, all other | 2 | — | 0 | — | 2 | — | — |
| Healthcare practitioners and technical occupations | 6,566 | 1,041 | 4,928 | 991 | 1,639 | 1,272 | 77.9 |
| Chiropractors | 22 | — | 7 | — | 15 | — | — |
| Dentists | 59 | 1,656 | 20 | — | 39 | — | — |
| Dietitians and nutritionists | 79 | 886 | 69 | 879 | 9 | — | — |
| Optometrists | 19 | — | 13 | — | 6 | — | — |
| Pharmacists | 206 | 1,920 | 108 | 1,811 | 98 | 2,117 | 85.5 |
| Physicians and surgeons | 740 | 1,824 | 283 | 1,533 | 457 | 1,915 | 80.1 |
| Physician assistants | 57 | 1,368 | 40 | — | 17 | — | — |
| Podiatrists | 9 | — | 4 | — | 5 | — | — |
| Audiologists | 8 | — | 6 | — | 1 | — | — |
| Occupational therapists | 74 | 1,210 | 64 | 1,199 | 10 | — | — |
| Physical therapists | 178 | 1,265 | 123 | 1,215 | 56 | 1,347 | 90.2 |
| Radiation therapists | 12 | — | 7 | — | 5 | — | — |
| Recreational therapists | 6 | — | 4 | — | 2 | — | — |
| Respiratory therapists | 99 | 1,000 | 67 | 937 | 32 | — | — |
| Speech-language pathologists | 108 | 1,147 | 106 | 1,148 | 1 | — | — |
| Exercise physiologists | 3 | — | 0 | — | 3 | — | — |
| Therapists, all other | 132 | 944 | 101 | 951 | 31 | — | — |
| Veterinarians | 55 | 1,455 | 39 | — | 16 | — | — |
| Registered nurses | 2,382 | 1,116 | 2,104 | 1,098 | 278 | 1,222 | 89.9 |
| Nurse anesthetists | 23 | — | 12 | — | 11 | — | — |
| Nurse midwives | 6 | — | 6 | — | 0 | — | — |
| Nurse practitioners | 115 | 1,532 | 103 | 1,522 | 11 | — | — |
| Health diagnosing and treating practitioners, all other | 2 | — | 2 | — | 0 | — | — |

pdf/home.pdf) that as a proportion of men's earnings, women's earnings come closest to parity between ages 20 and 24 years, when they are 95.6% of men's. In their peak earning years, however, women's wages

**TABLE 5.3**

**Median weekly earnings of full-time wage and salary workers by occupation and gender, 2015** [CONTINUED]

[Numbers in thousands]

| Occupation | Total | | Women | | Men | | Women's earnings as a percentage of men's |
|---|---|---|---|---|---|---|---|
| | Number of workers | Median weekly earnings | Number of workers | Median weekly earnings | Number of workers | Median weekly earnings | |
| Clinical laboratory technologists and technicians | 270 | 901 | 201 | 796 | 69 | 1,089 | 73.1 |
| Dental hygienists | 86 | 914 | 80 | 953 | 6 | — | — |
| Diagnostic related technologists and technicians | 253 | 964 | 177 | 908 | 76 | 1,106 | 82.1 |
| Emergency medical technicians and paramedics | 175 | 811 | 49 | — | 126 | 899 | — |
| Health practitioner support technologists and technicians | 487 | 636 | 389 | 633 | 99 | 652 | 97.1 |
| Licensed practical and licensed vocational nurses | 508 | 743 | 459 | 737 | 48 | — | — |
| Medical records and health information technicians | 174 | 740 | 157 | 723 | 17 | — | — |
| Opticians, dispensing | 44 | — | 23 | — | 21 | — | — |
| Miscellaneous health technologists and technicians | 99 | 671 | 66 | 642 | 32 | — | — |
| Other healthcare practitioners and technical occupations | 78 | 1,128 | 38 | — | 40 | — | — |
| Service occupations | 15,279 | 509 | 7,650 | 463 | 7,629 | 585 | 79.1 |
| Healthcare support occupations | 2,395 | 498 | 2,074 | 490 | 320 | 577 | 84.9 |
| Nursing, psychiatric, and home health aides | 1,400 | 467 | 1,237 | 457 | 163 | 526 | 86.9 |
| Occupational therapy assistants and aides | 17 | — | 12 | — | 4 | — | — |
| Physical therapist assistants and aides | 53 | 742 | 35 | — | 18 | — | — |
| Massage therapists | 37 | — | 22 | — | 16 | — | — |
| Dental assistants | 188 | 531 | 175 | 522 | 14 | — | — |
| Medical assistants | 422 | 539 | 387 | 530 | 35 | — | — |
| Medical transcriptionists | 28 | — | 26 | — | 3 | — | — |
| Pharmacy aides | 22 | — | 18 | — | 4 | — | — |
| Veterinary assistants and laboratory animal caretakers | 21 | — | 17 | — | 4 | — | — |
| Phlebotomists | 91 | 551 | 76 | 534 | 15 | — | — |
| Miscellaneous healthcare support occupations, including medical equipment preparers | 115 | 524 | 71 | 511 | 44 | — | — |
| Protective service occupations | 2,729 | 796 | 547 | 655 | 2,181 | 851 | 77.0 |
| First-line supervisors of correctional officers | 57 | 856 | 16 | — | 41 | — | — |
| First-line supervisors of police and detectives | 114 | 1,427 | 17 | — | 97 | 1,425 | — |
| First-line supervisors of fire fighting and prevention workers | 42 | — | 3 | — | 39 | — | — |
| First-line supervisors of protective service workers, all other | 72 | 808 | 16 | — | 56 | 825 | — |
| Firefighters | 260 | 1,033 | 16 | — | 245 | 1,052 | — |
| Fire inspectors | 18 | — | 3 | — | 15 | — | — |
| Bailiffs, correctional officers, and jailers | 453 | 754 | 112 | 686 | 341 | 779 | 88.1 |
| Detectives and criminal investigators | 141 | 1,159 | 41 | — | 100 | 1,265 | — |
| Fish and game wardens | 6 | — | 1 | — | 5 | — | — |
| Parking enforcement workers | 9 | — | 3 | — | 6 | — | — |
| Police and sheriff's patrol officers | 655 | 1,002 | 86 | 1,009 | 569 | 1,001 | 100.8 |
| Transit and railroad police | 3 | — | 0 | — | 3 | — | — |
| Animal control workers | 4 | — | 2 | — | 2 | — | — |
| Private detectives and investigators | 85 | 843 | 36 | — | 49 | — | — |
| Security guards and gaming surveillance officers | 708 | 567 | 153 | 515 | 555 | 592 | 87.0 |
| Crossing guards | 26 | — | 13 | — | 13 | — | — |
| Transportation security screeners | 33 | — | 11 | — | 22 | — | — |
| Lifeguards and other recreational, and all other protective service workers | 42 | — | 18 | — | 24 | — | — |
| Food preparation and serving related occupations | 4,124 | 441 | 1,991 | 414 | 2,133 | 481 | 86.1 |
| Chefs and head cooks | 340 | 619 | 55 | 492 | 285 | 656 | 75.0 |
| First-line supervisors of food preparation and serving workers | 378 | 498 | 222 | 458 | 156 | 621 | 73.8 |
| Cooks | 1,302 | 416 | 494 | 400 | 808 | 427 | 93.7 |
| Food preparation workers | 366 | 402 | 192 | 388 | 174 | 414 | 93.7 |
| Bartenders | 252 | 521 | 142 | 493 | 110 | 569 | 86.6 |
| Combined food preparation and serving workers, including fast food | 173 | 391 | 107 | 380 | 67 | 401 | 94.8 |
| Counter attendants, cafeteria, food concession, and coffee shop | 56 | 354 | 28 | — | 28 | — | — |
| Waiters and waitresses | 868 | 451 | 563 | 411 | 305 | 501 | 82.0 |
| Food servers, nonrestaurant | 93 | 509 | 62 | 485 | 31 | — | — |
| Dining room and cafeteria attendants and bartender helpers | 107 | 403 | 48 | — | 59 | 389 | — |
| Dishwashers | 117 | 398 | 19 | — | 98 | 401 | — |
| Hosts and hostesses, restaurant, lounge, and coffee shop | 66 | 400 | 58 | 397 | 8 | — | — |
| Food preparation and serving related workers, all other | 6 | — | 3 | — | 4 | — | — |
| Building and grounds cleaning and maintenance occupations | 3,605 | 486 | 1,275 | 419 | 2,330 | 517 | 81.0 |
| First-line supervisors of housekeeping and janitorial workers | 172 | 620 | 64 | 571 | 108 | 700 | 81.6 |
| First-line supervisors of landscaping, lawn service, and groundskeeping workers | 80 | 649 | 1 | — | 79 | 653 | — |
| Janitors and building cleaners | 1,536 | 507 | 425 | 429 | 1,111 | 547 | 78.4 |
| Maids and housekeeping cleaners | 876 | 416 | 742 | 407 | 134 | 475 | 85.7 |
| Pest control workers | 77 | 585 | 3 | — | 74 | 591 | — |
| Grounds maintenance workers | 862 | 469 | 39 | — | 824 | 473 | — |
| Personal care and service occupations | 2,427 | 498 | 1,763 | 475 | 664 | 597 | 79.6 |

fall substantially as a proportion of men's. Women's earnings reach 83.3% of men' earnings at ages 35 to 44 years, 77.8% at 45 to 54 years, and 73.7% at 55 to 64 years.

[Numbers in thousands]

| Occupation | Total | | Women | | Men | | Women's earnings as a percentage of men's |
|---|---|---|---|---|---|---|---|
| | Number of workers | Median weekly earnings | Number of workers | Median weekly earnings | Number of workers | Median weekly earnings | |
| First-line supervisors of gaming workers | 117 | 769 | 52 | 680 | 65 | 900 | 75.6 |
| First-line supervisors of personal service workers | 60 | 608 | 35 | — | 25 | — | — |
| Animal trainers | 26 | — | 8 | — | 19 | — | — |
| Nonfarm animal caretakers | 100 | 505 | 68 | 501 | 32 | — | — |
| Gaming services workers | 69 | 676 | 39 | — | 30 | — | — |
| Motion picture projectionists | 3 | — | 0 | — | 3 | — | — |
| Ushers, lobby attendants, and ticket takers | 9 | — | 4 | — | 5 | — | — |
| Miscellaneous entertainment attendants and related workers | 69 | 485 | 28 | — | 42 | — | — |
| Embalmers and funeral attendants | 2 | — | 0 | — | 2 | — | — |
| Morticians, undertakers, and funeral directors | 23 | — | 7 | — | 17 | — | — |
| Barbers | 46 | — | 12 | — | 33 | — | — |
| Hairdressers, hairstylists, and cosmetologists | 253 | 461 | 229 | 463 | 23 | — | — |
| Miscellaneous personal appearance workers | 191 | 501 | 159 | 497 | 32 | — | — |
| Baggage porters, bellhops, and concierges | 75 | 608 | 12 | — | 63 | 606 | — |
| Tour and travel guides | 21 | — | 9 | — | 11 | — | — |
| Childcare workers | 407 | 437 | 393 | 430 | 14 | — | — |
| Personal care aides | 680 | 462 | 552 | 441 | 128 | 537 | 82.1 |
| Recreation and fitness workers | 185 | 555 | 107 | 526 | 78 | 684 | 76.9 |
| Residential advisors | 24 | — | 16 | — | 8 | — | — |
| Personal care and service workers, all other | 67 | 499 | 32 | — | 35 | — | — |
| Sales and office occupations | 23,620 | 673 | 14,236 | 627 | 9,384 | 777 | 80.7 |
| Sales and related occupations | 9,725 | 716 | 4,303 | 578 | 5,423 | 880 | 65.7 |
| First-line supervisors of retail sales workers | 2,326 | 711 | 1,030 | 614 | 1,296 | 825 | 74.4 |
| First-line supervisors of non-retail sales workers | 835 | 1,028 | 280 | 896 | 556 | 1,140 | 78.6 |
| Cashiers | 1,342 | 415 | 931 | 405 | 411 | 471 | 86 |
| Counter and rental clerks | 73 | 594 | 37 | — | 35 | — | — |
| Parts salespersons | 92 | 601 | 11 | — | 82 | 600 | — |
| Retail salespersons | 1,918 | 590 | 759 | 494 | 1,159 | 694 | 71.2 |
| Advertising sales agents | 161 | 925 | 83 | 729 | 78 | 1,155 | 63.1 |
| Insurance sales agents | 427 | 815 | 232 | 717 | 194 | 1,028 | 69.7 |
| Securities, commodities, and financial services sales agents | 211 | 1,155 | 65 | 767 | 146 | 1,461 | 52.5 |
| Travel agents | 62 | 711 | 53 | 685 | 9 | — | — |
| Sales representatives, services, all other | 406 | 966 | 139 | 699 | 268 | 1,147 | 60.9 |
| Sales representatives, wholesale and manufacturing | 1,138 | 1,020 | 295 | 917 | 843 | 1,066 | 86.0 |
| Models, demonstrators, and product promoters | 15 | — | 11 | — | 4 | — | — |
| Real estate brokers and sales agents | 463 | 837 | 266 | 735 | 197 | 1,052 | 69.9 |
| Sales engineers | 33 | — | 2 | — | 31 | — | — |
| Telemarketers | 39 | — | 21 | — | 17 | — | — |
| Door-to-door sales workers, news and street vendors, and related workers | 28 | — | 18 | — | 9 | — | — |
| Sales and related workers, all other | 158 | 916 | 70 | 727 | 89 | 1,088 | 66.8 |
| Office and administrative support occupations | 13,894 | 656 | 9,933 | 646 | 3,961 | 693 | 93.2 |
| First-line supervisors of office and administrative support workers | 1,297 | 812 | 863 | 781 | 434 | 878 | 89.0 |
| Switchboard operators, including answering service | 17 | — | 10 | — | 7 | — | — |
| Telephone operators | 22 | — | 18 | — | 4 | — | — |
| Communications equipment operators, all other | 5 | — | 3 | — | 2 | — | — |
| Bill and account collectors | 152 | 657 | 98 | 648 | 54 | 674 | 96.1 |
| Billing and posting clerks | 406 | 657 | 366 | 664 | 39 | — | — |
| Bookkeeping, accounting, and auditing clerks | 769 | 692 | 682 | 692 | 87 | 690 | 100.3 |
| Gaming cage workers | 11 | — | 10 | — | 2 | — | — |
| Payroll and timekeeping clerks | 128 | 757 | 111 | 751 | 17 | — | — |
| Procurement clerks | 35 | — | 21 | — | 15 | — | — |
| Tellers | 264 | 514 | 231 | 516 | 33 | — | — |
| Financial clerks, all other | 61 | 767 | 32 | — | 30 | — | — |
| Brokerage clerks | 3 | — | 1 | — | 1 | — | — |
| Correspondence clerks | 3 | — | 2 | — | 1 | — | — |
| Court, municipal, and license clerks | 60 | 755 | 51 | 743 | 9 | — | — |
| Credit authorizers, checkers, and clerks | 42 | — | 29 | — | 12 | — | — |
| Customer service representatives | 1,760 | 621 | 1,149 | 604 | 611 | 690 | 87.5 |
| Eligibility interviewers, government programs | 67 | 781 | 50 | 805 | 17 | — | — |
| File clerks | 145 | 634 | 120 | 627 | 25 | — | — |
| Hotel, motel, and resort desk clerks | 127 | 481 | 69 | 467 | 58 | 486 | 96.1 |
| Interviewers, except eligibility and loan | 105 | 615 | 89 | 617 | 16 | — | — |
| Library assistants, clerical | 35 | — | 28 | — | 7 | — | — |
| Loan interviewers and clerks | 134 | 710 | 109 | 722 | 25 | — | — |
| New accounts clerks | 20 | — | 17 | — | 3 | — | — |
| Order clerks | 74 | 599 | 48 | — | 26 | — | — |

| Occupation | Total | | Women | | Men | | Women's earnings as a percentage of men's |
|---|---|---|---|---|---|---|---|
| | Number of workers | Median weekly earnings | Number of workers | Median weekly earnings | Number of workers | Median weekly earnings | |
| Human resources assistants, except payroll and timekeeping | 50 | 737 | 40 | — | 11 | — | — |
| Receptionists and information clerks | 852 | 575 | 781 | 569 | 72 | 619 | 91.9 |
| Reservation and transportation ticket agents and travel clerks | 95 | 713 | 61 | 680 | 34 | — | — |
| Information and record clerks, all other | 100 | 618 | 78 | 616 | 22 | — | — |
| Cargo and freight agents | 20 | — | 9 | — | 12 | — | — |
| Couriers and messengers | 153 | 752 | 19 | — | 134 | 750 | — |
| Dispatchers | 250 | 698 | 141 | 655 | 109 | 759 | 86.3 |
| Meter readers, utilities | 39 | — | 4 | — | 34 | — | — |
| Postal service clerks | 127 | 927 | 51 | 833 | 76 | 974 | 85.5 |
| Postal service mail carriers | 302 | 954 | 115 | 854 | 187 | 1,021 | 83.6 |
| Postal service mail sorters, processors, and processing machine operators | 53 | 828 | 26 | — | 27 | — | — |
| Production, planning, and expediting clerks | 256 | 838 | 141 | 732 | 116 | 978 | 74.8 |
| Shipping, receiving, and traffic clerks | 502 | 591 | 148 | 566 | 354 | 604 | 93.7 |
| Stock clerks and order fillers | 1,027 | 520 | 376 | 506 | 651 | 537 | 94.2 |
| Weighers, measurers, checkers, and samplers, recordkeeping | 59 | 629 | 31 | — | 29 | — | — |
| Secretaries and administrative assistants | 2,223 | 687 | 2,099 | 683 | 124 | 786 | 86.9 |
| Computer operators | 58 | 751 | 33 | — | 25 | — | — |
| Data entry keyers | 223 | 619 | 169 | 638 | 55 | 589 | 108.3 |
| Word processors and typists | 68 | 650 | 62 | 639 | 6 | — | — |
| Desktop publishers | 1 | — | 0 | — | 1 | — | — |
| Insurance claims and policy processing clerks | 259 | 689 | 203 | 675 | 56 | 762 | 88.6 |
| Mail clerks and mail machine operators, except postal service | 63 | 563 | 39 | — | 24 | — | — |
| Office clerks, general | 929 | 620 | 773 | 622 | 156 | 609 | 102.1 |
| Office machine operators, except computer | 31 | — | 16 | — | 14 | — | — |
| Proofreaders and copy markers | 2 | — | 2 | — | 0 | — | — |
| Statistical assistants | 15 | — | 10 | — | 5 | — | — |
| Office and administrative support workers, all other | 391 | 745 | 298 | 718 | 93 | 852 | 84.3 |
| Natural resources, construction, and maintenance occupations | 10,834 | 761 | 453 | 580 | 10,381 | 770 | 75.3 |
| Farming, fishing, and forestry occupations | 810 | 464 | 174 | 437 | 637 | 477 | 91.6 |
| First-line supervisors of farming, fishing, and forestry workers | 42 | — | 10 | — | 32 | — | — |
| Agricultural inspectors | 12 | — | 6 | — | 7 | — | — |
| Animal breeders | 2 | — | 0 | — | 2 | — | — |
| Graders and sorters, agricultural products | 83 | 486 | 51 | 468 | 32 | — | — |
| Miscellaneous agricultural workers | 613 | 445 | 102 | 398 | 511 | 460 | 86.5 |
| Fishers and related fishing workers | 11 | — | 0 | — | 11 | — | — |
| Hunters and trappers | 0 | — | 0 | — | 0 | — | — |
| Forest and conservation workers | 15 | — | 5 | — | 10 | — | — |
| Logging workers | 31 | — | 0 | — | 31 | — | — |
| Construction and extraction occupations | 5,722 | 749 | 137 | 704 | 5,586 | 751 | 93.7 |
| First-line supervisors of construction trades and extraction workers | 560 | 1,040 | 20 | — | 540 | 1,047 | — |
| Boilermakers | 21 | — | 0 | — | 21 | — | — |
| Brickmasons, blockmasons, and stonemasons | 122 | 652 | 0 | — | 122 | 652 | — |
| Carpenters | 802 | 687 | 10 | — | 792 | 687 | — |
| Carpet, floor, and tile installers and finishers | 89 | 637 | 1 | — | 89 | 634 | — |
| Cement masons, concrete finishers, and terrazzo workers | 44 | — | 0 | — | 44 | — | — |
| Construction laborers | 1,181 | 639 | 25 | — | 1,155 | 642 | — |
| Paving, surfacing, and tamping equipment operators | 10 | — | 0 | — | 10 | — | — |
| Pile-driver operators | 2 | — | 0 | — | 2 | — | — |
| Operating engineers and other construction equipment operators | 324 | 856 | 6 | — | 318 | 859 | — |
| Drywall installers, ceiling tile installers, and tapers | 121 | 596 | 2 | — | 119 | 595 | — |
| Electricians | 651 | 888 | 19 | — | 632 | 891 | — |
| Glaziers | 33 | — | 0 | — | 32 | — | — |
| Insulation workers | 43 | — | 3 | — | 41 | — | — |
| Painters, construction and maintenance | 344 | 585 | 14 | — | 330 | 587 | — |
| Paperhangers | 0 | — | 0 | — | 0 | — | — |
| Pipelayers, plumbers, pipefitters, and steamfitters | 456 | 863 | 2 | — | 455 | 862 | — |
| Plasterers and stucco masons | 20 | — | 1 | — | 19 | — | — |
| Reinforcing iron and rebar workers | 9 | — | 0 | — | 9 | — | — |
| Roofers | 171 | 584 | 2 | — | 170 | 580 | — |
| Sheet metal workers | 106 | 766 | 6 | — | 100 | 776 | — |
| Structural iron and steel workers | 54 | 869 | 2 | — | 52 | 864 | — |
| Solar photovoltaic installers | 8 | — | 0 | — | 8 | — | — |
| Helpers, construction trades | 47 | — | 0 | — | 47 | — | — |
| Construction and building inspectors | 67 | 939 | 9 | — | 58 | 965 | — |
| Elevator installers and repairers | 23 | — | 0 | — | 23 | — | — |
| Fence erectors | 33 | — | 0 | — | 33 | — | — |

**TABLE 5.3**

**Median weekly earnings of full-time wage and salary workers by occupation and gender, 2015** [CONTINUED]

[Numbers in thousands]

| Occupation | Total Number of workers | Total Median weekly earnings | Women Number of workers | Women Median weekly earnings | Men Number of workers | Men Median weekly earnings | Women's earnings as a percentage of men's |
|---|---|---|---|---|---|---|---|
| Hazardous materials removal workers | 39 | — | 5 | — | 35 | — | — |
| Highway maintenance workers | 91 | 754 | 0 | — | 91 | 755 | — |
| Rail-track laying and maintenance equipment operators | 9 | — | 0 | — | 9 | — | — |
| Septic tank servicers and sewer pipe cleaners | 8 | — | 0 | — | 8 | — | — |
| Miscellaneous construction and related workers | 25 | — | 2 | — | 23 | — | — |
| Derrick, rotary drill, and service unit operators, oil, gas, and mining | 28 | — | 1 | — | 27 | — | — |
| Earth drillers, except oil and gas | 30 | — | 0 | — | 30 | — | — |
| Explosives workers, ordnance handling experts, and blasters | 5 | — | 0 | — | 5 | — | — |
| Mining machine operators | 68 | 1,106 | 2 | — | 65 | 1,098 | — |
| Roof bolters, mining | 3 | — | 0 | — | 3 | — | — |
| Roustabouts, oil and gas | 7 | — | 0 | — | 7 | — | — |
| Helpers—extraction workers | 6 | — | 0 | — | 6 | — | — |
| Other extraction workers | 61 | 900 | 3 | — | 58 | 918 | — |
| Installation, maintenance, and repair occupations | 4,301 | 839 | 143 | 761 | 4,159 | 842 | 90.4 |
| First-line supervisors of mechanics, installers, and repairers | 270 | 1,032 | 18 | — | 252 | 1,033 | — |
| Computer, automated teller, and office machine repairers | 194 | 856 | 28 | — | 166 | 865 | — |
| Radio and telecommunications equipment installers and repairers | 139 | 862 | 13 | — | 126 | 879 | — |
| Avionics technicians | 4 | — | 0 | — | 4 | — | — |
| Electric motor, power tool, and related repairers | 22 | — | 1 | — | 20 | — | — |
| Electrical and electronics installers and repairers, transportation equipment | 2 | — | 0 | — | 2 | — | — |
| Electrical and electronics repairers, industrial and utility | 18 | — | 0 | — | 17 | — | — |
| Electronic equipment installers and repairers, motor vehicles | 17 | — | 0 | — | 17 | — | — |
| Electronic home entertainment equipment installers and repairers | 30 | — | 2 | — | 28 | — | — |
| Security and fire alarm systems installers | 67 | 911 | 2 | — | 65 | 913 | — |
| Aircraft mechanics and service technicians | 133 | 1,025 | 7 | — | 125 | 1,032 | — |
| Automotive body and related repairers | 120 | 846 | 2 | — | 118 | 849 | — |
| Automotive glass installers and repairers | 21 | — | 1 | — | 20 | — | — |
| Automotive service technicians and mechanics | 710 | 722 | 16 | — | 694 | 724 | — |
| Bus and truck mechanics and diesel engine specialists | 327 | 831 | 0 | — | 327 | 830 | — |
| Heavy vehicle and mobile equipment service technicians and mechanics | 206 | 928 | 0 | — | 206 | 928 | — |
| Small engine mechanics | 39 | — | 0 | — | 39 | — | — |
| Miscellaneous vehicle and mobile equipment mechanics, installers, and repairers | 66 | 592 | 1 | — | 65 | 591 | — |
| Control and valve installers and repairers | 23 | — | 0 | — | 23 | — | — |
| Heating, air conditioning, and refrigeration mechanics and installers | 341 | 806 | 4 | — | 337 | 810 | — |
| Home appliance repairers | 36 | — | 0 | — | 36 | — | — |
| Industrial and refractory machinery mechanics | 394 | 895 | 11 | — | 383 | 894 | — |
| Maintenance and repair workers, general | 469 | 773 | 10 | — | 459 | 771 | — |
| Maintenance workers, machinery | 31 | — | 1 | — | 30 | — | — |
| Millwrights | 49 | — | 1 | — | 48 | — | — |
| Electrical power-line installers and repairers | 113 | 1,105 | 0 | — | 112 | 1,105 | — |
| Telecommunications line installers and repairers | 157 | 882 | 9 | — | 148 | 880 | — |
| Precision instrument and equipment repairers | 64 | 996 | 4 | — | 60 | 1,009 | — |
| Wind turbine service technicians | 3 | — | 0 | — | 3 | — | — |
| Coin, vending, and amusement machine servicers and repairers | 38 | — | 4 | — | 34 | — | — |
| Commercial divers | 1 | — | 0 | — | 1 | — | — |
| Locksmiths and safe repairers | 12 | — | 0 | — | 12 | — | — |
| Manufactured building and mobile home installers | 4 | — | 1 | — | 4 | — | — |
| Riggers | 7 | — | 0 | — | 7 | — | — |
| Signal and track switch repairers | 9 | — | 0 | — | 9 | — | — |
| Helpers—installation, maintenance, and repair workers | 17 | — | 0 | — | 17 | — | — |
| Other installation, maintenance, and repair workers | 150 | 792 | 6 | — | 144 | 810 | — |
| Production, transportation, and material moving occupations | 14,504 | 656 | 2,958 | 512 | 11,546 | 704 | 72.7 |
| Production occupations | 7,551 | 663 | 2,003 | 519 | 5,548 | 729 | 71.2 |
| First-line supervisors of production and operating workers | 783 | 875 | 133 | 623 | 650 | 924 | 67.4 |
| Aircraft structure, surfaces, rigging, and systems assemblers | 15 | — | 4 | — | 11 | — | — |
| Electrical, electronics, and electromechanical assemblers | 123 | 554 | 64 | 544 | 59 | 566 | 96.1 |
| Engine and other machine assemblers | 14 | — | 2 | — | 12 | — | — |
| Structural metal fabricators and fitters | 31 | — | 3 | — | 28 | — | — |
| Miscellaneous assemblers and fabricators | 950 | 581 | 377 | 512 | 573 | 637 | 80.4 |
| Bakers | 150 | 505 | 80 | 475 | 69 | 570 | 83.3 |
| Butchers and other meat, poultry, and fish processing workers | 247 | 542 | 60 | 463 | 187 | 582 | 79.6 |
| Food and tobacco roasting, baking, and drying machine operators and tenders | 9 | — | 1 | — | 7 | — | — |
| Food batchmakers | 79 | 500 | 54 | 489 | 25 | — | — |

TABLE 5.3

**Median weekly earnings of full-time wage and salary workers by occupation and gender, 2015 [CONTINUED]**

[Numbers in thousands]

| Occupation | Total | | Women | | Men | | Women's earnings as a percentage of men's |
|---|---|---|---|---|---|---|---|
| | Number of workers | Median weekly earnings | Number of workers | Median weekly earnings | Number of workers | Median weekly earnings | |
| Food cooking machine operators and tenders | 7 | — | 2 | — | 5 | — | — |
| Food processing workers, all other | 132 | 594 | 50 | 508 | 82 | 679 | 74.8 |
| Computer control programmers and operators | 83 | 833 | 2 | — | 81 | 857 | — |
| Extruding and drawing machine setters, operators, and tenders, metal and plastic | 8 | — | 1 | — | 7 | — | — |
| Forging machine setters, operators, and tenders, metal and plastic | 6 | — | 0 | — | 6 | — | — |
| Rolling machine setters, operators, and tenders, metal and plastic | 15 | — | 3 | — | 12 | — | — |
| Cutting, punching, and press machine setters, operators, and tenders, metal and plastic | 78 | 633 | 15 | — | 62 | 674 | — |
| Drilling and boring machine tool setters, operators, and tenders, metal and plastic | 5 | — | 1 | — | 5 | — | — |
| Grinding, lapping, polishing, and buffing machine tool setters, operators, and tenders, metal and plastic | 41 | — | 3 | — | 39 | — | — |
| Lathe and turning machine tool setters, operators, and tenders, metal and plastic | 12 | — | 1 | — | 11 | — | — |
| Milling and planing machine setters, operators, and tenders, metal and plastic | 1 | — | 0 | — | 1 | — | — |
| Machinists | 338 | 834 | 17 | — | 320 | 840 | — |
| Metal furnace operators, tenders, pourers, and casters | 29 | — | 1 | — | 28 | — | — |
| Model makers and patternmakers, metal and plastic | 6 | — | 3 | — | 3 | — | — |
| Molders and molding machine setters, operators, and tenders, metal and plastic | 47 | — | 9 | — | 39 | — | — |
| Multiple machine tool setters, operators, and tenders, metal and plastic | 1 | — | 0 | — | 1 | — | — |
| Tool and die makers | 49 | — | 0 | — | 49 | — | — |
| Welding, soldering, and brazing workers | 568 | 760 | 23 | — | 545 | 767 | — |
| Heat treating equipment setters, operators, and tenders, metal and plastic | 4 | — | 0 | — | 4 | — | — |
| Layout workers, metal and plastic | 4 | — | 1 | — | 4 | — | — |
| Plating and coating machine setters, operators, and tenders, metal and plastic | 24 | — | 0 | — | 24 | — | — |
| Tool grinders, filers, and sharpeners | 7 | — | 0 | — | 7 | — | — |
| Metal workers and plastic workers, all other | 351 | 639 | 72 | 581 | 278 | 678 | 85.7 |
| Prepress technicians and workers | 14 | — | 2 | — | 12 | — | — |
| Printing press operators | 160 | 707 | 26 | — | 134 | 729 | — |
| Print binding and finishing workers | 16 | — | 6 | — | 9 | — | — |
| Laundry and dry-cleaning workers | 133 | 466 | 80 | 460 | 53 | 487 | 94.5 |
| Pressers, textile, garment, and related materials | 21 | — | 12 | — | 9 | — | — |
| Sewing machine operators | 147 | 493 | 105 | 476 | 42 | — | — |
| Shoe and leather workers and repairers | 5 | — | 1 | — | 4 | — | — |
| Shoe machine operators and tenders | 1 | — | 1 | — | 0 | — | — |
| Tailors, dressmakers, and sewers | 37 | — | 27 | — | 9 | — | — |
| Textile bleaching and dyeing machine operators and tenders | 2 | — | 0 | — | 2 | — | — |
| Textile cutting machine setters, operators, and tenders | 9 | — | 2 | — | 7 | — | — |
| Textile knitting and weaving machine setters, operators, and tenders | 8 | — | 4 | — | 3 | — | — |
| Textile winding, twisting, and drawing out machine setters, operators, and tenders | 7 | — | 2 | — | 5 | — | — |
| Extruding and forming machine setters, operators, and tenders, synthetic and glass fibers | 0 | — | 0 | — | 0 | — | — |
| Fabric and apparel patternmakers | 4 | — | 1 | — | 3 | — | — |
| Upholsterers | 29 | — | 7 | — | 21 | — | — |
| Textile, apparel, and furnishings workers, all other | 16 | — | 4 | — | 12 | — | — |
| Cabinetmakers and bench carpenters | 40 | — | 2 | — | 38 | — | — |
| Furniture finishers | 6 | — | 0 | — | 6 | — | — |
| Model makers and patternmakers, wood | 0 | — | 0 | — | 0 | — | — |
| Sawing machine setters, operators, and tenders, wood | 26 | — | 4 | — | 22 | — | — |
| Woodworking machine setters, operators, and tenders, except sawing | 23 | — | 1 | — | 21 | — | — |
| Woodworkers, all other | 17 | — | 3 | — | 14 | — | — |
| Power plant operators, distributors, and dispatchers | 35 | — | 1 | — | 34 | — | — |
| Stationary engineers and boiler operators | 84 | 996 | 3 | — | 81 | 1,012 | — |
| Water and wastewater treatment plant and system operators | 82 | 880 | 3 | — | 79 | 868 | — |
| Miscellaneous plant and system operators | 35 | — | 3 | — | 33 | — | — |
| Chemical processing machine setters, operators, and tenders | 62 | 1,052 | 5 | — | 57 | 1,082 | — |
| Crushing, grinding, polishing, mixing, and blending workers | 82 | 652 | 7 | — | 75 | 668 | — |
| Cutting workers | 51 | 685 | 9 | — | 41 | — | — |
| Extruding, forming, pressing, and compacting machine setters, operators, and tenders | 31 | — | 6 | — | 25 | — | — |

TABLE 5.3

**Median weekly earnings of full-time wage and salary workers by occupation and gender, 2015** [CONTINUED]

[Numbers in thousands]

| Occupation | Total Number of workers | Total Median weekly earnings | Women Number of workers | Women Median weekly earnings | Men Number of workers | Men Median weekly earnings | Women's earnings as a percentage of men's |
|---|---|---|---|---|---|---|---|
| Furnace, kiln, oven, drier, and kettle operators and tenders | 6 | — | 0 | — | 5 | — | — |
| Inspectors, testers, sorters, samplers, and weighers | 701 | 710 | 260 | 583 | 440 | 844 | 69.1 |
| Jewelers and precious stone and metal workers | 19 | — | 7 | — | 11 | — | — |
| Medical, dental, and ophthalmic laboratory technicians | 86 | 648 | 42 | — | 44 | — | — |
| Packaging and filling machine operators and tenders | 239 | 518 | 120 | 482 | 118 | 605 | 79.7 |
| Painting workers | 129 | 708 | 18 | — | 110 | 733 | — |
| Photographic process workers and processing machine operators | 26 | — | 14 | — | 12 | — | — |
| Semiconductor processors | 1 | — | 0 | — | 1 | — | — |
| Adhesive bonding machine operators and tenders | 9 | — | 4 | — | 5 | — | — |
| Cleaning, washing, and metal pickling equipment operators and tenders | 4 | — | 1 | — | 2 | — | — |
| Cooling and freezing equipment operators and tenders | 4 | — | 0 | — | 3 | — | — |
| Etchers and engravers | 12 | — | 4 | — | 8 | — | — |
| Molders, shapers, and casters, except metal and plastic | 14 | — | 2 | — | 12 | — | — |
| Paper goods machine setters, operators, and tenders | 27 | — | 5 | — | 22 | — | — |
| Tire builders | 8 | — | 0 | — | 8 | — | — |
| Helpers—production workers | 24 | — | 7 | — | 18 | — | — |
| Production workers, all other | 846 | 625 | 203 | 501 | 643 | 666 | 75.2 |
| Transportation and material moving occupations | 6,953 | 646 | 955 | 494 | 5,998 | 679 | 72.8 |
| Supervisors of transportation and material moving workers | 186 | 894 | 33 | — | 153 | 898 | — |
| Aircraft pilots and flight engineers | 114 | 1,735 | 9 | — | 104 | 1,830 | — |
| Air traffic controllers and airfield operations specialists | 32 | — | 8 | — | 24 | — | — |
| Flight attendants | 63 | 846 | 43 | — | 20 | — | — |
| Ambulance drivers and attendants, except emergency medical technicians | 18 | — | 4 | — | 14 | — | — |
| Bus drivers | 323 | 615 | 138 | 572 | 184 | 681 | 84.0 |
| Driver/sales workers and truck drivers | 2,687 | 747 | 105 | 632 | 2,582 | 751 | 84.2 |
| Taxi drivers and chauffeurs | 253 | 585 | 38 | — | 216 | 600 | — |
| Motor vehicle operators, all other | 21 | — | 3 | — | 18 | — | — |
| Locomotive engineers and operators | 44 | — | 2 | — | 42 | — | — |
| Railroad brake, signal, and switch operators | 5 | — | 0 | — | 5 | — | — |
| Railroad conductors and yardmasters | 55 | 1,117 | 4 | — | 52 | 1,137 | — |
| Subway, streetcar, and other rail transportation workers | 15 | — | 3 | — | 12 | — | — |
| Sailors and marine oilers | 10 | — | 0 | — | 9 | — | — |
| Ship and boat captains and operators | 29 | — | 1 | — | 28 | — | — |
| Ship engineers | 5 | — | 1 | — | 4 | — | — |
| Bridge and lock tenders | 4 | — | 0 | — | 4 | — | — |
| Parking lot attendants | 57 | 492 | 8 | — | 49 | — | — |
| Automotive and watercraft service attendants | 63 | 452 | 5 | — | 58 | 470 | — |
| Transportation inspectors | 21 | — | 7 | — | 14 | — | — |
| Transportation attendants, except flight attendants | 17 | — | 8 | — | 9 | — | — |
| Other transportation workers | 39 | — | 4 | — | 35 | — | — |
| Conveyor operators and tenders | 7 | — | 0 | — | 7 | — | — |
| Crane and tower operators | 75 | 988 | 4 | — | 71 | 1,016 | — |
| Dredge, excavating, and loading machine operators | 25 | — | 0 | — | 25 | — | — |
| Hoist and winch operators | 5 | — | 0 | — | 5 | — | — |
| Industrial truck and tractor operators | 579 | 609 | 37 | — | 541 | 612 | — |
| Cleaners of vehicles and equipment | 222 | 485 | 22 | — | 200 | 498 | — |
| Laborers and freight, stock, and material movers, hand | 1,433 | 526 | 219 | 455 | 1,214 | 547 | 83.2 |
| Machine feeders and offbearers | 30 | — | 9 | — | 21 | — | — |
| Packers and packagers, hand | 385 | 438 | 227 | 424 | 158 | 462 | 91.8 |
| Pumping station operators | 18 | — | 1 | — | 17 | — | — |
| Refuse and recyclable material collectors | 72 | 501 | 6 | — | 66 | 496 | — |
| Mine shuttle car operators | 0 | — | 0 | — | 0 | — | — |
| Tank car, truck, and ship loaders | 6 | — | 0 | — | 6 | — | — |
| Material moving workers, all other | 37 | — | 5 | — | 32 | — | — |

Note: Women's earnings as a percentage of men's are not shown where employment for either women or men is less than 50,000. Median earnings are not shown where employment is less than 50,000. Dash indicates no data or data that do not meet publication criteria.

SOURCE: "Table 18. Median Usual Weekly Earnings of Full-Time Wage and Salary Workers, by Detailed Occupation and Gender, 2015 Annual Averages (Numbers in Thousands)," in *Women in the Labor Force: A Databook*, US Bureau of Labor Statistics, April 2017, https://www.bls.gov/opub/reports/womens-databook/2016/pdf/home.pdf (accessed January 19, 2018).

## Location

Disparities in women's and men's wages vary by state. As Table 5.7 shows, women's salaries as a proportion of men's salaries in 2016 were highest in Vermont (90.2%), California (88%), New Mexico (88%), the District of Columbia (87.7%), and Oregon (87.5%). The states with the largest gender gaps were Utah, where women made only 69.9% of what men made per week,

**TABLE 5.4**

**Median weekly earnings of full-time wage and salary workers aged 25 years and older, by educational attainment and gender, 2015**

| Educational attainment and gender | Total employed (in thousands) | Median weekly earnings |
|---|---|---|
| **Total** | | |
| Total | 99,291 | $860 |
| Less than high school diploma | 7,289 | 493 |
| High school graduate or more | 92,001 | 900 |
| High school graduate, no college | 25,221 | 678 |
| Some college or associate's degree | 26,801 | 762 |
| Some college, no degree | 15,894 | 738 |
| Associate's degree | 10,908 | 798 |
| Occupational program | 4,684 | 785 |
| Academic program | 6,224 | 809 |
| Bachelor's degree and higher | 39,979 | 1,230 |
| Bachelor's degree | 25,043 | 1,137 |
| Master's degree | 11,106 | 1,341 |
| Professional degree | 1,752 | 1,730 |
| Doctoral degree | 2,080 | 1,623 |
| **Women** | | |
| Total | 44,020 | 761 |
| Less than high school diploma | 2,255 | 418 |
| High school graduate or more | 41,766 | 787 |
| High school graduate, no college | 9,905 | 586 |
| Some college or associate's degree | 12,692 | 664 |
| Some college, no degree | 7,153 | 637 |
| Associate's degree | 5,539 | 703 |
| Occupational program | 2,199 | 678 |
| Academic program | 3,340 | 723 |
| Bachelor's degree and higher | 19,169 | 1,064 |
| Bachelor's degree | 11,748 | 975 |
| Master's degree | 5,885 | 1,160 |
| Professional degree | 721 | 1,451 |
| Doctoral degree | 814 | 1,442 |
| **Men** | | |
| Total | 55,270 | $947 |
| Less than high school diploma | 5,035 | 520 |
| High school graduate or more | 50,236 | 1,001 |
| High school graduate, no college | 15,316 | 759 |
| Some college or associate's degree | 14,109 | 883 |
| Some college, no degree | 8,741 | 850 |
| Associate's degree | 5,368 | 931 |
| Occupational program | 2,485 | 915 |
| Academic program | 2,883 | 950 |
| Bachelor's degree and higher | 20,811 | 1,420 |
| Bachelor's degree | 13,295 | 1,304 |
| Master's degree | 5,220 | 1,566 |
| Professional degree | 1,030 | 1,888 |
| Doctoral degree | 1,266 | 1,758 |

Note: Data exclude all self-employed people, both those with incorporated and unincorporated businesses.

SOURCE: "Table 17. Median Usual Weekly Earnings of Full-Time Wage and Salary Workers 25 Years and Older, by Educational Attainment and Gender, 2015 Annual Averages," in *Women in the Labor Force: A Databook,* US Bureau of Labor Statistics, April 2017, https://www.bls.gov/opub/reports/womens-databook/2016/pdf/home.pdf (accessed January 19, 2018)

Wyoming (72.1%), New Hampshire (75.2%), and Connecticut (75.3%).

## Unions

In 2016 women who belonged to unions earned a weekly median of $955 per week, women who were represented by unions without being members earned a median of $942 per week, and women without union representation made $723 per week. (See Table 5.8.)

Although union representation did not eliminate the earnings gap, it did ameliorate it somewhat. Women who were members of unions earned 91% of what their male counterparts were paid, compared with 90.4% for women who were represented by unions and 81.2% for women without union representation.

## Part-Time Status

Women are substantially more likely than men to work part time or for part of the year. Semega, Fontenot, and Kollar indicate that an estimated 74.8% of working men were employed full time, year round in 2016, compared with 62.2% of working women. If taken over a woman's life span, the cumulative effect on earnings of periodic absences from the labor force or part-time work to balance work and family responsibilities is extensive. Nevertheless, women who worked part time had slightly higher median earnings than their male counterparts. As Table 5.9 shows, women working part time in 2017 had median weekly earnings of $265, compared with $250 for male part-time workers. Reducing the number of hours per week in the workforce as a way to balance work and family responsibilities is considered more acceptable for women than for men. This may account for why women part-time workers had higher median wages than did men.

## Equal Pay Laws

The Equal Pay Act of 1963 made it illegal to pay women less than men working at the same job. However, pay discrimination is often much more difficult to identify than more visible forms of discrimination involving hiring, firing, and promotions, as illustrated by the Lilly Ledbetter (1938–) case. (See Chapter 4.) Moreover, Gwen Moran reports in "Here's What It Takes to Sue for Gender Pay Discrimination—and Win" (Fortune.com, April 12, 2016) that gender pay discrimination is also difficult to prove. Although the Equal Pay Act broadly stipulates that women and men should be paid equally for doing the same work, the law permits exceptions if the employer can prove that differential pay is justified as the result of a seniority system, a merit system, a pay system based on quantity or quality of output, or any other factor other than sex. Debra Lawrence, a regional attorney in the US Equal Employment Opportunity Commission's Philadelphia District Office, explained to Moran that although the first three exceptions are clear and concrete, the "any other factor" exception allows the employer to cite a wide range of justifications for differential pay, including that the male employee has more experience or training or even that he negotiated more effectively for his higher salary. Statistics illustrate the difficulty of building a gender pay discrimination case. Moran reports that during fiscal year 2015, the Equal Employment Opportunity Commission received 973 equal wage discrimination complaints

**FIGURE 5.2**

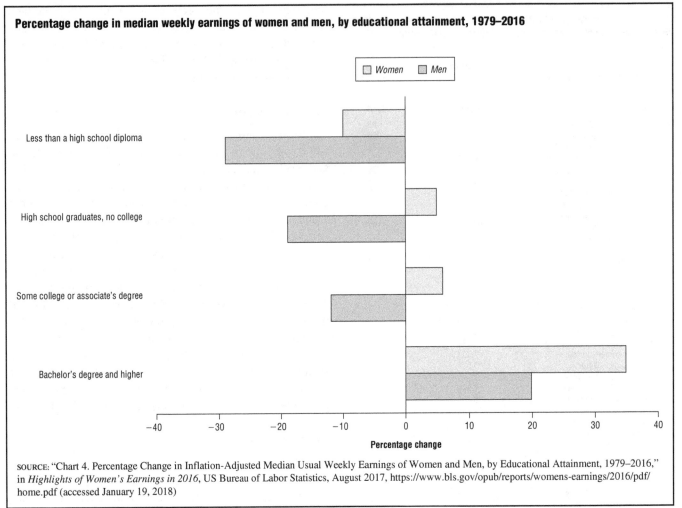

Percentage change in median weekly earnings of women and men, by educational attainment, 1979–2016

☐ Women  ☐ Men

Less than a high school diploma

High school graduates, no college

Some college or associate's degree

Bachelor's degree and higher

−40   −30   −20   −10   0   10   20   30   40

Percentage change

SOURCE: "Chart 4. Percentage Change in Inflation-Adjusted Median Usual Weekly Earnings of Women and Men, by Educational Attainment, 1979–2016," in *Highlights of Women's Earnings in 2016*, US Bureau of Labor Statistics, August 2017, https://www.bls.gov/opub/reports/womens-earnings/2016/pdf/home.pdf (accessed January 19, 2018)

(a number that has remained roughly the same since 1997), but 64% of these complaints were found to have "no reasonable cause" for action.

Notable among the successful gender pay discrimination cases in recent years was the 2012 victory of Heidi Wilson against Citicorp North America. When Wilson was promoted to manage a Citicorp service center in Tampa, Florida, she was paid $75,329. Wilson sued after she discovered that her male predecessor had been paid more than $129,000 the year before. In 2012 the court ordered Citicorp to pay Wilson nearly $340,000 in back wages. Wilson's lawyer Ryan D. Barack explained to Moran that this case was unusual in its clarity, given that Wilson's job was identical to the one held by her predecessor. When the wage disparity was revealed, Citicorp's violation of the Equal Pay Act was indisputable. According to Barack, job equivalency is rarely so easy to prove. Moreover, proving job equivalency gets increasingly more difficult in cases of higher skilled jobs. Lawrence explained to Moran, "When you have somebody in a factory making widgets, [proving] the equality is going to be easier. When you have professors of different subject matters within the same department of a university, that's going to be harder."

Likewise, equal pay for equal work laws have little effect when the workplace is gender-segregated. In *Separate and Not Equal? Gender Segregation in the Labor Market and the Gender Wage Gap* (September 2010, https://iwpr.org/wp-content/uploads/wpallimport/files/iwpr-export/publications/C377.pdf), Ariane Hegewisch et al. note that when ranking jobs into a three-tiered schema of low-skilled, medium-skilled, and high-skilled jobs, most workers fall into an occupation where at least 75% are of one gender. The researchers find that at each skill level, the median earnings are highest in male-dominated occupations and lowest in female-dominated occupations. Hegewisch and Heidi Hartmann consider these skill categories in a more recent report, *Occupational Segregation and the Gender Wage Gap: A Job Half Done* (January 2014, https://iwpr.org/wp-content/uploads/wpallimport/files/iwpr-export/publications/C419.pdf), finding that "the earnings penalty for working in predominantly female compared to predominantly male occupations is proportionately highest for both women and men working

TABLE 5.5

**Median weekly earnings of full-time wage and salary workers, by sex, marital status, and presence and age of own children under 18 years old, 2016**

| Characteristic | Number of workers (thousands) | Median weekly earnings |
|---|---|---|
| **Women** | | |
| **Total, all marital statuses** | **49,161** | **$749** |
| With children under 18 years old | 17,288 | 756 |
| With children 6 to 17, none younger | 10,517 | 772 |
| With children under 6 years old | 6,771 | 730 |
| With no children under 18 years old | 31,873 | 746 |
| **Total, married, spouse present[1]** | **24,849** | **838** |
| With children under 18 years old | 11,327 | 870 |
| With children 6 to 17, none younger | 6,810 | 857 |
| With children under 6 years old | 4,516 | 885 |
| With no children under 18 years old | 13,523 | 815 |
| **Total, other marital statuses[2]** | **24,312** | **671** |
| With children under 18 years old | 5,961 | 607 |
| With children 6 to 17, none younger | 3,706 | 662 |
| With children under 6 years old | 2,255 | 524 |
| With no children under 18 years old | 18,350 | 697 |
| **Men** | | |
| **Total, all marital statuses** | **61,930** | **915** |
| With children under 18 years old | 22,021 | 1,013 |
| With children 6 to 17, none younger | 11,953 | 1,085 |
| With children under 6 years old | 10,068 | 952 |
| With no children under 18 years old | 39,909 | 861 |
| **Total, married, spouse present[a]** | **36,195** | **1,062** |
| With children under 18 years old | 19,297 | 1,071 |
| With children 6 to 17, none younger | 10,623 | 1,134 |
| With children under 6 years old | 8,674 | 1,013 |
| With no children under 18 years old | 16,898 | 1,053 |
| **Total, other marital statuses[b]** | **25,736** | **732** |
| With children under 18 years old | 2,724 | 719 |
| With children 6 to 17, none younger | 1,330 | 813 |
| With children under 6 years old | 1,394 | 652 |
| With no children under 18 years old | 23,011 | 733 |

[a]Refers to people in opposite-sex married couples only.
[b]Includes people who are never married; widowed; divorced; separated; and married, spouse absent.
Note: "Children" refers to "own" children and includes sons, daughters, stepchildren, and adopted children under age 18 who live in the household. Not included are other related children, such as grandchildren, nieces, nephews, and cousins, as well as unrelated children in the household.

SOURCE: Adapted from "Table 7. Median Usual Weekly Earnings of Full-Time Wage and Salary Workers, by Marital Status and Presence and Age of Own Children under 18 Years Old, 2016 Annual Averages," in *Highlights of Women's Earnings in 2016*, US Bureau of Labor Statistics, August 2017, https://www.bls.gov/opub/reports/womens-earnings/2016/pdf/home.pdf (accessed January 19, 2018).

Comparable worth laws provide for equal pay if men's and women's jobs are comparable rather than identical. Workers of both sexes in occupations that have traditionally been filled by women would gain from the implementation of comparable worth. Forty-six states have taken some action to implement comparable worth, and Congress adopted a comparable worth measure in the Civil Service Reform Act of 1978. The American Federation of State, County, and Municipal Employees has been particularly active in bargaining for comparable worth.

Activism continues on the federal level. The Paycheck Fairness Act, which passed the Democratic-controlled US House of Representatives in 2009 and was strongly supported by President Barack Obama (1961–), would strengthen the Equal Pay Act and make it more difficult for employers to pay women less than they pay men. The bill did not, however, have enough support to reach the US Senate floor for a vote. Reintroduced in both the House of Representatives and the Senate in 2011, the bill again stalled in the Senate under threat of a Republican filibuster (a tactic whereby a minority in the legislative body extends debate indefinitely, essentially killing a bill). A revised version of the Paycheck Fairness Act was introduced in March 2015 and again in April 2017; as of April 2018, it remained under consideration of the House and Senate committees to which it had been referred. Similarly, the US delegate Eleanor Holmes Norton (1937–; D-DC) and the US senator Tom Harkin (1939–; D-IA) introduced the Fair Pay Act in April 2015 and again in April 2017. The bill seeks to prohibit wage discrimination based on sex, race, or national origin among workers in "equivalent jobs." As of April 2018, this act was still in committee.

## POVERTY AND GENDER

The federal government defines poverty according to a poverty threshold, an income level that it determines yearly and that is used to calculate a variety of federal and state benefits. The poverty threshold depends on family size and the age of the householder. In 2018 a family of three was considered impoverished if its yearly income was less than $20,780 per year, and a family of five was considered impoverished if its yearly income was less than $29,420 per year. (See Table 5.10.)

The official poverty rate in 2016 was 12.7%. (See Table 5.11.) This number was only slightly higher than the rate in 2007 (12.5%), before the dramatic spike in poverty that accompanied the Great Recession and the long, slow economic recovery that followed. Poverty disproportionately affects women. As Table 5.12 shows, 14% of women were living below the poverty line in 2016, compared with 11.3% of men. The number of women and men classified as impoverished has fluctuated over

in occupations that require at least a four-year college or university degree." Indeed, women in highly skilled "women's jobs" make only 71% of median hourly earnings of women who work in highly skilled "men's jobs."

To improve equity in female-dominated jobs, one school of thought advocates replacing equal pay laws with laws that provide for pay equity or comparable worth for men and women. Comparable worth recognizes that some occupations traditionally done by women are underpaid simply because they are done by women.

TABLE 5.6

**Median weekly earnings of full-time wage and salary workers by age, 2016**

| Characteristic | Total | | Women | | Men | | Women's earnings as a percentage of men's |
|---|---|---|---|---|---|---|---|
| | Number of workers (thousands) | Median weekly earnings | Number of workers (thousands) | Median weekly earnings | Number of workers (thousands) | Median weekly earnings | |
| **Age** | | | | | | | |
| Total, 16 years and older | 111,091 | $832 | 49,161 | $749 | 61,930 | $915 | 81.9 |
| 16 to 24 years | 10,076 | 501 | 4,430 | 486 | 5,646 | 512 | 94.9 |
| 16 to 19 years | 1,289 | 405 | 545 | 388 | 745 | 419 | 92.6 |
| 20 to 24 years | 8,786 | 513 | 3,885 | 500 | 4,901 | 523 | 95.6 |
| 25 years and older | 101,015 | 885 | 44,731 | 784 | 56,284 | 969 | 80.9 |
| 25 to 34 years | 27,456 | 751 | 11,972 | 705 | 15,484 | 794 | 88.8 |
| 35 to 44 years | 25,284 | 934 | 10,900 | 839 | 14,383 | 1,007 | 83.3 |
| 45 to 54 years | 25,652 | 955 | 11,555 | 836 | 14,097 | 1,075 | 77.8 |
| 55 to 64 years | 18,496 | 952 | 8,504 | 812 | 9,992 | 1,102 | 73.7 |
| 65 years and older | 4,128 | 866 | 1,800 | 749 | 2,328 | 992 | 75.5 |

SOURCE: Adapted from "Table 1. Median Usual Weekly Earnings of Full-Time Wage and Salary Workers, by Selected Characteristics, 2016 Annual Averages," in *Highlights of Women's Earnings in 2016*, US Bureau of Labor Statistics, August 2017, https://www.bls.gov/opub/reports/womens-earnings/2016/pdf/home.pdf (accessed January 19, 2018)

the decades, in keeping with economic cycles and statistical anomalies such as those discussed earlier in this chapter, but the percentage of women living in poverty has consistently outpaced that of men living in poverty since the 1960s. Likewise, families headed by women are far more likely than other families to be impoverished. Among all families, the poverty rate was 10.7% in 2016, but among families headed by a woman with no spouse present, the poverty rate was 28.8%. (See Table 5.11.) This disparity has also been consistent over the course of all the decades during which the Census Bureau has been tracking poverty.

Children are more likely to live in poverty than adults, in large part due to the prevalence of poverty among households headed by single mothers. According to the Census Bureau, in *Historical Poverty Tables: People and Families—1959 to 2016* (September 8, 2017, https://www.census.gov/data/tables/time-series/demo/income-poverty/historical-poverty-people.html), 18% of all children under the age of 18 years lived below the poverty threshold in 2016. This number was especially high among African American children, 30.8% of whom lived below the poverty line, and among Hispanic children, 26.6% of whom lived below the poverty line. In 2016 approximately 12.8 million related children under the age of 18 years lived below the poverty line, and more than 7.6 million (59.5%) of them were in female-headed households.

**The Working Poor**

In *A Profile of the Working Poor, 2015* (April 2017, https://www.bls.gov/opub/reports/working-poor/2015/pdf/home.pdf), the BLS notes that of the 43.1 million people living below the poverty line in 2015, 8.6 million were

categorized as the "working poor." The working poor are those who remain below the poverty line in spite of having spent at least 27 weeks in the labor force (either working or looking for work) during a given year. This number was down from 9.5 million in 2014, but it was still higher than pre-recession levels. The ratio of the working poor to all individuals in the labor force was 5.6% in 2015, down slightly from 6.3% the previous year but still higher than the working-poor rate of 5.1% in 2007. Women were more likely than men to be among the working poor. Approximately 4.5 million women were categorized as working poor in 2015, for a working-poor rate of 6.3%, compared with 4.1 million men, whose working-poor rate was 5%.

According to the BLS, 4 million families with at least one member in the labor force for half the year or more lived in poverty in 2015. Among married-couple families with only one member in the labor force for at least half of the year, 8.5% were poor. Among nonmarital families, 9.6% of households maintained by men and 18.3% of households maintained by women numbered among the working poor.

**Government Benefits**

There are two principal categories of government benefit programs: those that are means-tested, in which benefits are given to the poor based on an individual's or household's income in relation to the poverty threshold, and those that provide benefits regardless of an individual's or household's income. The primary programs in the first category are Temporary Assistance for Needy Families (TANF; a program that provides cash payments to the poorest Americans on a temporary basis), the Supplemental Nutrition Assistance Program

TABLE 5.7

**Median weekly earnings of full-time wage and salary workers, by state, 2016**

| State | Total | | Women | | Men | | Women's earnings as a percentage of men's |
|---|---|---|---|---|---|---|---|
| | Number of workers (thousands) | Median weekly earnings | Number of workers (thousands) | Median weekly earnings | Number of workers (thousands) | Median weekly earnings | |
| United States | 111,091 | $832 | 49,161 | $749 | 61,930 | $915 | 81.9 |
| Alabama | 1,580 | 743 | 715 | 651 | 865 | 856 | 76.1 |
| Alaska | 245 | 932 | 113 | 841 | 133 | 1,014 | 82.9 |
| Arizona | 2,213 | 829 | 947 | 768 | 1,266 | 890 | 86.3 |
| Arkansas | 1,014 | 716 | 459 | 638 | 555 | 769 | 83.0 |
| California | 12,862 | 879 | 5,383 | 814 | 7,479 | 925 | 88.0 |
| Colorado | 1,995 | 894 | 841 | 812 | 1,154 | 967 | 84.0 |
| Connecticut | 1,232 | 1,014 | 555 | 876 | 677 | 1,164 | 75.3 |
| Delaware | 357 | 831 | 166 | 775 | 191 | 902 | 85.9 |
| District of Columbia | 306 | 1,198 | 152 | 1,117 | 154 | 1,274 | 87.7 |
| Florida | 6,799 | 750 | 3,158 | 701 | 3,641 | 805 | 87.1 |
| Georgia | 3,581 | 771 | 1,654 | 721 | 1,927 | 839 | 85.9 |
| Hawaii | 494 | 794 | 218 | 718 | 276 | 869 | 82.6 |
| Idaho | 540 | 759 | 220 | 645 | 320 | 843 | 76.5 |
| Illinois | 4,513 | 887 | 1,979 | 775 | 2,534 | 978 | 79.2 |
| Indiana | 2,402 | 762 | 1,079 | 702 | 1,322 | 829 | 84.7 |
| Iowa | 1,143 | 763 | 528 | 684 | 614 | 895 | 76.4 |
| Kansas | 1,026 | 762 | 460 | 692 | 566 | 851 | 81.3 |
| Kentucky | 1,413 | 761 | 650 | 711 | 763 | 828 | 85.9 |
| Louisiana | 1,517 | 757 | 704 | 659 | 813 | 863 | 76.4 |
| Maine | 438 | 820 | 194 | 754 | 244 | 900 | 83.8 |
| Maryland | 2,386 | 987 | 1,120 | 915 | 1,266 | 1,048 | 87.3 |
| Massachusetts | 2,504 | 1,019 | 1,114 | 932 | 1,390 | 1,105 | 84.3 |
| Michigan | 3,260 | 841 | 1,438 | 742 | 1,822 | 932 | 79.6 |
| Minnesota | 2,035 | 946 | 901 | 849 | 1,134 | 1,020 | 83.2 |
| Mississippi | 941 | 702 | 452 | 624 | 490 | 778 | 80.2 |
| Missouri | 2,199 | 793 | 1,021 | 703 | 1,178 | 885 | 79.4 |
| Montana | 314 | 781 | 138 | 705 | 176 | 866 | 81.4 |
| Nebraska | 706 | 766 | 318 | 697 | 388 | 855 | 81.5 |
| Nevada | 996 | 754 | 414 | 681 | 582 | 828 | 82.2 |
| New Hampshire | 524 | 904 | 230 | 762 | 294 | 1,013 | 75.2 |
| New Jersey | 3,324 | 998 | 1,448 | 894 | 1,877 | 1,113 | 80.3 |
| New Mexico | 621 | 730 | 280 | 679 | 341 | 772 | 88.0 |
| New York | 6,837 | 916 | 3,145 | 840 | 3,692 | 975 | 86.2 |
| North Carolina | 3,533 | 761 | 1,598 | 704 | 1,935 | 836 | 84.2 |
| North Dakota | 299 | 805 | 131 | 713 | 168 | 930 | 76.7 |
| Ohio | 3,927 | 806 | 1,717 | 713 | 2,210 | 899 | 79.3 |
| Oklahoma | 1,248 | 724 | 534 | 651 | 714 | 824 | 79.0 |
| Oregon | 1,327 | 857 | 554 | 791 | 772 | 904 | 87.5 |
| Pennsylvania | 4,453 | 857 | 1,984 | 741 | 2,468 | 956 | 77.5 |
| Rhode Island | 385 | 839 | 179 | 765 | 206 | 907 | 84.3 |
| South Carolina | 1,623 | 779 | 773 | 687 | 851 | 884 | 77.7 |
| South Dakota | 309 | 778 | 137 | 670 | 172 | 876 | 76.5 |
| Tennessee | 2,252 | 747 | 983 | 666 | 1,269 | 821 | 81.1 |
| Texas | 9,801 | 780 | 4,197 | 707 | 5,603 | 860 | 82.2 |
| Utah | 997 | 833 | 358 | 668 | 640 | 955 | 69.9 |
| Vermont | 228 | 850 | 104 | 801 | 124 | 888 | 90.2 |
| Virginia | 3,025 | 902 | 1,376 | 809 | 1,649 | 1,013 | 79.9 |
| Washington | 2,506 | 929 | 1,065 | 814 | 1,441 | 1,056 | 77.1 |
| West Virginia | 565 | 762 | 248 | 688 | 316 | 846 | 81.3 |
| Wisconsin | 2,098 | 843 | 947 | 737 | 1,152 | 940 | 78.4 |
| Wyoming | 199 | 848 | 82 | 699 | 117 | 970 | 72.1 |

Note: Comparisons of state estimates should be made with caution. Data shown are based on workers' state of residence; workers' reported earnings, however, may or may not be from a job located in the same state.

SOURCE: "Table 3. Median Usual Weekly Earnings of Full-Time Wage and Salary Workers, by State, 2016 Annual Averages," in *Highlights of Women's Earnings in 2016*, US Bureau of Labor Statistics, August 2017, https://www.bls.gov/opub/reports/womens-earnings/2016/pdf/home.pdf (accessed January 19, 2018)

(SNAP; also known as the food stamp program), Supplemental Security Income (SSI; a program that provides cash assistance to the disabled), Medicaid (a state and federal health insurance program for low-income people), and the Earned Income Tax Credit (a program that provides tax refunds to those earning below certain amounts annually). The primary programs in the second category are Social Security (a program that provides retirement income and health care for older adults), Medicare (a federal health insurance program for people aged 65 years and older and people with disabilities), and unemployment insurance (a program that provides cash payments on a temporary basis to those who have lost their job).

**TABLE 5.8**

**Median weekly earnings of full-time wage and salary workers by union representation, 2016**

| Characteristic | Total | | Women | | Men | | Women's earnings as a percentage of men's |
|---|---|---|---|---|---|---|---|
| | Number of workers (thousands) | Median weekly earnings | Number of workers (thousands) | Median weekly earnings | Number of workers (thousands) | Median weekly earnings | |
| Menbers of a union[a] | 13,119 | 1,004 | 5,697 | 955 | 7,421 | 1,050 | 91.0 |
| Represented by unions[b] | 14,593 | 995 | 6,429 | 942 | 8,163 | 1,042 | 90.4 |
| Not represented by a union | 96,498 | 802 | 42,731 | 723 | 53,767 | 890 | 81.2 |

[a]Members of a labor union or an employee association similar to a union.
[b]Union members and workers who report no union affiliation but whose jobs are covered by a union or an employee association contract.

SOURCE: Adapted from "Table 1. Median Usual Weekly Earnings of Full-Time Wage and Salary Workers, by Selected Characteristics, 2016 Annual Averages," in *Highlights of Women's Earnings in 2016*, US Bureau of Labor Statistics, August 2017, https://www.bls.gov/opub/reports/womens-earnings/2016/pdf/home .pdf (accessed January 19, 2018)

**TABLE 5.9**

**Median weekly earnings of part-time wage and salary workers, by sex, age, and race and Hispanic origin, 2016–17**

| Characteristic | Number of workers (in thousands) | | Median weekly earnings | |
|---|---|---|---|---|
| | 2016 | 2017 | 2016 | 2017 |
| **Sex and age** | | | | |
| Total, 16 years and over | 24,832 | 24,433 | $252 | $260 |
| Men, 16 years and over | 8,573 | 8,378 | 245 | 250 |
| 16 to 24 years | 3,758 | 3,683 | 196 | 201 |
| 25 years and over | 4,815 | 4,696 | 292 | 301 |
| Women, 16 years and over | 16,259 | 16,054 | 255 | 265 |
| 16 to 24 years | 4,698 | 4,771 | 193 | 199 |
| 25 years and over | 11,561 | 11,284 | 291 | 302 |
| **Race and Hispanic or Latino ethnicity** | | | | |
| White | 19,536 | 19,235 | 254 | 264 |
| Men | 6,623 | 6,454 | 244 | 253 |
| Women | 12,913 | 12,781 | 259 | 269 |
| Black or African American | 3,033 | 2,953 | 236 | 243 |
| Men | 1,116 | 1,095 | 238 | 237 |
| Women | 1,917 | 1,858 | 234 | 247 |
| Asian | 1,305 | 1,237 | 264 | 275 |
| Men | 478 | 439 | 260 | 275 |
| Women | 827 | 798 | 267 | 276 |
| Hispanic or Latino ethnicity | 4,115 | 4,024 | 247 | 262 |
| Men | 1,449 | 1,436 | 250 | 265 |
| Women | 2,667 | 2,588 | 246 | 260 |

Note: Estimates for the above race groups (white, black or African American, and Asian) do not sum to totals because data are not presented for all races. Persons whose ethnicity is identified as Hispanic or Latino may be of any race. Updated population controls are introduced annually with the release of January data.

SOURCE: "38. Median Weekly Earnings of Part-Time Wage and Salary Workers by Selected Characteristics," in *Labor Force Statistics from the Current Population Survey*, US Bureau of Labor Statistics, February 8, 2017, https://www.bls.gov/cps/cpsaat38.pdf (accessed January 19, 2018)

## Means-Tested Programs

Robert Greenstein of the CBPP considers in *Commentary: How Effective Is the Safety Net?* (February 6, 2013, https://www.cbpp.org/sites/default/files/atoms/files/2-6-13pov.pdf) the effectiveness of means-tested programs for the poor. Using a widely accepted National Academy of Sciences measure of poverty (which many advocates for the poor contend is more effective than the

**TABLE 5.10**

**Poverty guidelines, 2018**

| Persons in family/household | Poverty guideline |
|---|---|
| 1 | $12,140 |
| 2 | 16,460 |
| 3 | 20,780 |
| 4 | 25,100 |
| 5 | 29,420 |
| 6 | 33,740 |
| 7 | 38,060 |
| 8 | 42,380 |

SOURCE: "2018 Poverty Guidelines for the 48 Contiguous States and the District of Columbia," in "Annual Update of the HHS Poverty Guidelines," *Federal Register*, vol. 83, no. 12, January 18, 2018, https://www.gpo.gov/fdsys/pkg/FR-2018-01-18/pdf/2018-00814.pdf (accessed January 19, 2018)

official government measure), Greenstein finds that "if the safety net hadn't existed in 2010, nearly 29 percent of Americans would have been poor, nearly twice the actual figure of about 15 percent." Greenstein also notes that safety-net programs go beyond the straightforward reduction of poverty, pointing out that prior to the introduction of the food stamp program, malnutrition was as prevalent in some areas of the United States (such as the Mississippi delta, parts of Appalachia, and coastal South Carolina) as in developing countries. After the introduction of the food stamp program, symptoms of malnutrition virtually disappeared in the United States, and further research shows that food stamp participation in childhood leads to better health outcomes in adulthood. Additionally, research shows that participation in Medicaid correlates with better health, improved mortality statistics, and decreased levels of household debt and that the Earned Income Tax Credit spurs significant numbers of poor single parents to seek employment, leading to better outcomes for their children in school and later in life.

Nevertheless, many advocates for the poor point out that TANF has lost much of the power that its predecessor program, Aid to Families with Dependent Children

**TABLE 5.11**

## Poverty status of people by family relationship, 1959–2016

[All races]

| Year | All people Total | All people Below poverty Number | All people Below poverty Percent | All families Total | All families Below poverty Number | All families Below poverty Percent | People in families – Families with female householder No husband present Total | Below poverty Number | Below poverty Percent | Unrelated individuals Total | Below poverty Number | Below poverty Percent |
|---|---|---|---|---|---|---|---|---|---|---|---|---|
| 2016 | 319,911 | 40,616 | 12.7 | 259,863 | 27,762 | 10.7 | 48,243 | 13,914 | 28.8 | 58,839 | 12,336 | 21.0 |
| 2015 | 318,454 | 43,123 | 13.5 | 258,121 | 29,893 | 11.6 | 48,497 | 14,719 | 30.4 | 58,988 | 12,671 | 21.5 |
| 2014 | 315,804 | 46,657 | 14.8 | 256,308 | 32,615 | 12.7 | 48,019 | 15,905 | 33.1 | 57,937 | 13,374 | 23.1 |
| 2013[a] | 313,096 | 46,269 | 14.8 | 256,070 | 32,786 | 12.8 | 49,951 | 17,170 | 34.4 | 55,400 | 12,707 | 22.9 |
| 2013[b] | 312,965 | 45,318 | 14.5 | 254,988 | 31,530 | 12.4 | 47,007 | 15,606 | 33.2 | 56,564 | 13,181 | 23.3 |
| 2012 | 310,648 | 46,496 | 15.0 | 252,863 | 33,198 | 13.1 | 47,085 | 15,957 | 33.9 | 56,185 | 12,558 | 22.4 |
| 2011 | 308,456 | 46,247 | 15.0 | 252,316 | 33,126 | 13.1 | 48,103 | 16,451 | 34.2 | 54,517 | 12,416 | 22.8 |
| 2010[c] | 306,130 | 46,343 | 15.1 | 250,200 | 33,120 | 13.2 | 46,454 | 15,911 | 34.3 | 54,250 | 12,449 | 22.9 |
| 2009 | 303,820 | 43,569 | 14.3 | 249,384 | 31,197 | 12.5 | 45,315 | 14,746 | 32.5 | 53,079 | 11,678 | 22.0 |
| 2008 | 301,041 | 39,829 | 13.2 | 248,301 | 28,564 | 11.5 | 44,027 | 13,812 | 31.4 | 51,534 | 10,710 | 20.8 |
| 2007 | 298,699 | 37,276 | 12.5 | 245,443 | 26,509 | 10.8 | 43,961 | 13,478 | 30.7 | 51,740 | 10,189 | 19.7 |
| 2006 | 296,450 | 36,460 | 12.3 | 245,199 | 25,915 | 10.6 | 43,223 | 13,199 | 30.5 | 49,884 | 9,977 | 20.0 |
| 2005 | 293,135 | 36,950 | 12.6 | 242,389 | 26,068 | 10.8 | 42,244 | 13,153 | 31.1 | 49,526 | 10,425 | 21.1 |
| 2004[d] | 290,617 | 37,040 | 12.7 | 240,754 | 26,544 | 11.0 | 42,053 | 12,832 | 30.5 | 48,609 | 9,926 | 20.4 |
| 2003 | 287,699 | 35,861 | 12.5 | 238,903 | 25,684 | 10.8 | 41,311 | 12,413 | 30.0 | 47,594 | 9,713 | 20.4 |
| 2002 | 285,317 | 34,570 | 12.1 | 236,921 | 24,534 | 10.4 | 40,529 | 11,657 | 28.8 | 47,156 | 9,618 | 20.4 |
| 2001 | 281,475 | 32,907 | 11.7 | 233,911 | 23,215 | 9.9 | 39,261 | 11,223 | 28.6 | 46,392 | 9,226 | 19.9 |
| 2000[e] | 278,944 | 31,581 | 11.3 | 231,909 | 22,347 | 9.6 | 38,375 | 10,926 | 28.5 | 45,624 | 8,653 | 19.0 |
| 1999[f] | 276,208 | 32,791 | 11.9 | 230,789 | 23,830 | 10.3 | 38,580 | 11,764 | 30.5 | 43,977 | 8,400 | 19.1 |
| 1998 | 271,059 | 34,476 | 12.7 | 227,229 | 25,370 | 11.2 | 39,000 | 12,907 | 33.1 | 42,539 | 8,478 | 19.9 |
| 1997 | 268,480 | 35,574 | 13.3 | 225,369 | 26,217 | 11.6 | 38,412 | 13,494 | 35.1 | 41,672 | 8,687 | 20.8 |
| 1996 | 266,218 | 36,529 | 13.7 | 223,955 | 27,376 | 12.2 | 38,584 | 13,796 | 35.8 | 40,727 | 8,452 | 20.8 |
| 1995 | 263,733 | 36,425 | 13.8 | 222,792 | 27,501 | 12.3 | 38,908 | 14,205 | 36.5 | 39,484 | 8,247 | 20.9 |
| 1994 | 261,616 | 38,059 | 14.5 | 221,430 | 28,985 | 13.1 | 37,253 | 14,380 | 38.6 | 38,538 | 8,287 | 21.5 |
| 1993[g] | 259,278 | 39,265 | 15.1 | 219,489 | 29,927 | 13.6 | 37,861 | 14,636 | 38.7 | 38,038 | 8,388 | 22.1 |
| 1992[h] | 256,549 | 38,014 | 14.8 | 217,936 | 28,961 | 13.3 | 36,446 | 14,205 | 39.0 | 36,842 | 8,075 | 21.9 |
| 1991[i] | 251,192 | 35,708 | 14.2 | 212,723 | 27,143 | 12.8 | 34,795 | 13,824 | 39.7 | 36,845 | 7,773 | 21.1 |
| 1990 | 248,644 | 33,585 | 13.5 | 210,967 | 25,232 | 12.0 | 33,795 | 12,578 | 37.2 | 36,056 | 7,446 | 20.7 |
| 1989 | 245,992 | 31,528 | 12.8 | 209,515 | 24,066 | 11.5 | 32,525 | 11,668 | 35.9 | 35,185 | 6,760 | 19.2 |
| 1988 | 243,530 | 31,745 | 13.0 | 208,056 | 24,048 | 11.6 | 32,164 | 11,972 | 37.2 | 34,340 | 7,070 | 20.6 |
| 1987[j] | 240,982 | 32,221 | 13.4 | 206,877 | 24,725 | 12.0 | 31,893 | 12,148 | 38.1 | 32,992 | 6,857 | 20.8 |
| 1986 | 238,554 | 32,370 | 13.6 | 205,459 | 24,754 | 12.0 | 31,152 | 11,944 | 38.3 | 31,679 | 6,846 | 21.6 |
| 1985 | 236,594 | 33,064 | 14.0 | 203,963 | 25,729 | 12.6 | 30,878 | 11,600 | 37.6 | 31,351 | 6,725 | 21.5 |
| 1984 | 233,816 | 33,700 | 14.4 | 202,288 | 26,458 | 13.1 | 30,844 | 11,831 | 38.4 | 30,268 | 6,609 | 21.8 |
| 1983[k] | 231,700 | 35,303 | 15.2 | 201,338 | 27,933 | 13.9 | 30,049 | 12,072 | 40.2 | 29,158 | 6,740 | 23.1 |
| 1982 | 229,412 | 34,398 | 15.0 | 200,385 | 27,349 | 13.6 | 28,834 | 11,701 | 40.6 | 27,908 | 6,458 | 23.1 |
| 1981[l] | 227,157 | 31,822 | 14.0 | 198,541 | 24,850 | 12.5 | 28,587 | 11,051 | 38.7 | 27,714 | 6,490 | 23.4 |
| 1980 | 225,027 | 29,272 | 13.0 | 196,963 | 22,601 | 11.5 | 27,565 | 10,120 | 36.7 | 27,133 | 6,227 | 22.9 |
| 1979[m] | 222,903 | 26,072 | 11.7 | 195,860 | 19,964 | 10.2 | 26,927 | 9,400 | 34.9 | 26,170 | 5,743 | 21.9 |
| 1978 | 215,656 | 24,497 | 11.4 | 191,071 | 19,062 | 10.0 | 26,032 | 9,269 | 35.6 | 24,585 | 5,435 | 22.1 |
| 1977 | 213,867 | 24,720 | 11.6 | 190,757 | 19,505 | 10.2 | 25,404 | 9,205 | 36.2 | 23,110 | 5,216 | 22.6 |
| 1976 | 212,303 | 24,975 | 11.8 | 190,844 | 19,632 | 10.3 | 24,204 | 9,029 | 37.3 | 21,459 | 5,344 | 24.9 |
| 1975 | 210,864 | 25,877 | 12.3 | 190,630 | 20,789 | 10.9 | 23,580 | 8,846 | 37.5 | 20,234 | 5,088 | 25.1 |
| 1974[n] | 209,362 | 23,370 | 11.2 | 190,436 | 18,817 | 9.9 | 23,165 | 8,462 | 36.5 | 18,926 | 4,553 | 24.1 |
| 1973 | 207,621 | 22,973 | 11.1 | 189,361 | 18,299 | 9.7 | 21,823 | 8,178 | 37.5 | 18,260 | 4,674 | 25.6 |
| 1972 | 206,004 | 24,460 | 11.9 | 189,193 | 19,577 | 10.3 | 21,264 | 8,114 | 38.2 | 16,811 | 4,883 | 29.0 |
| 1971[o] | 204,554 | 25,559 | 12.5 | 188,242 | 20,405 | 10.8 | 20,153 | 7,797 | 38.7 | 16,311 | 5,154 | 31.6 |
| 1970 | 202,183 | 25,420 | 12.6 | 186,692 | 20,330 | 10.9 | 19,673 | 7,503 | 38.1 | 15,491 | 5,090 | 32.9 |
| 1969 | 199,517 | 24,147 | 12.1 | 184,891 | 19,175 | 10.4 | 17,995 | 6,879 | 38.2 | 14,626 | 4,972 | 34.0 |
| 1968 | 197,628 | 25,389 | 12.8 | 183,825 | 20,695 | 11.3 | 18,048 | 6,990 | 38.7 | 13,803 | 4,694 | 34.0 |
| 1967[p] | 195,672 | 27,769 | 14.2 | 182,558 | 22,771 | 12.5 | 17,788 | 6,898 | 38.8 | 13,114 | 4,998 | 38.1 |
| 1966 | 193,388 | 28,510 | 14.7 | 181,117 | 23,809 | 13.1 | 17,240 | 6,861 | 39.8 | 12,271 | 4,701 | 38.3 |
| 1965 | 191,413 | 33,185 | 17.3 | 179,281 | 28,358 | 15.8 | 16,371 | 7,524 | 46.0 | 12,132 | 4,827 | 39.8 |
| 1964 | 189,710 | 36,055 | 19.0 | 177,653 | 30,912 | 17.4 | NA | 7,297 | 44.4 | 12,057 | 5,143 | 42.7 |
| 1963 | 187,258 | 36,436 | 19.5 | 176,076 | 31,498 | 17.9 | NA | 7,646 | 47.7 | 11,182 | 4,938 | 44.2 |
| 1962 | 184,276 | 38,625 | 21.0 | 173,263 | 33,623 | 19.4 | NA | 7,781 | 50.3 | 11,013 | 5,002 | 45.4 |
| 1961 | 181,277 | 39,628 | 21.9 | 170,131 | 34,509 | 20.3 | NA | 7,252 | 48.1 | 11,146 | 5,119 | 45.9 |
| 1960 | 179,503 | 39,851 | 22.2 | 168,615 | 34,925 | 20.7 | NA | 7,247 | 48.9 | 10,888 | 4,926 | 45.2 |
| 1959 | 176,557 | 39,490 | 22.4 | 165,858 | 34,562 | 20.8 | NA | 7,014 | 49.4 | 10,699 | 4,928 | 46.1 |

(AFDC), had to reduce poverty among families. As part of the Personal Responsibility and Work Opportunity Reconciliation Act of 1996, which transformed the AFDC into TANF, states were granted broad control in administering TANF benefits, and TANF benefits were tied to adults' work participation. Thus, states whose elected representatives seek to limit government spending on behalf of the needy have been able to significantly

NA—Not available.

[a]The 2014 Current Population Survey Annual Social and Economic Supplement (CPS ASEC) included redesigned questions for income and health insurance coverage. All of the approximately 98,000 addresses were eligible to receive the redesigned set of health insurance coverage questions. The redesigned income questions were implemented to a subsample of these 98,000 addresses using a probability split panel design. Approximately 68,000 addresses were eligible to receive a set of income questions similar to those used in the 2013 CPS ASEC and the remaining 30,000 addresses were eligible to receive the redesigned income questions. The source of data for this table is the portion of the CPS ASEC sample which received the redesigned income questions, approximately 30,000 addresses.

[b]Data are based on the CPS ASEC sample of 68,000 addresses. The 2014 CPS ASEC included redesigned questions for income and health insurance coverage. All of the approximately 98,000 addresses were eligible to receive the redesigned set of health insurance coverage questions. The redesigned income questions were implemented to a subsample of these 98,000 addresses using a probability split panel design. Approximately 68,000 addresses were eligible to receive a set of income questions similar to those used in the 2013 CPS ASEC and the remaining 30,000 addresses were eligible to receive the redesigned income questions. The source of the 2013 data for this table is the portion of the CPS ASEC sample which received the income questions consistent with the 2013 CPS ASEC, approximately 68,000 addresses.

[c]Implementation of Census 2010-based population controls.

[d]The 2004 data have been revised to reflect a correction to the weights in the 2005 ASEC.

[e]Implementation of Census 2000 based population controls and sample expanded by 28,000 households.

[f]Implementation of Census 2000 based population controls.

[g]Data collection method changed from paper and pencil to computer- assisted interviewing. In addition, the March 1994 income supplement was revised to allow for the coding of different income amounts on selected questionnaire items. Limits either increased or decreased in the following categories: earnings increased to $999,999; Social Security increased to $49,999; Supplemental Security Income and Public Assistance increased to $24,999; Veterans' Benefits increased to $99,999; Child Support and Alimony decreased to $49,999.

[h]Implementation of 1990 census population controls.

[i]CPS file for March 1992 (1991 data) was corrected after the release of the 1991 Income and Poverty reports. Weights for nine person records were omitted on the original file.

[j]Implementation of a new March CPS processing system.

[k]Implementation of Hispanic population weighting controls.

[l]Implemented three technical changes to the poverty definition.

[m]Implementation of 1980 census population controls. Questionnaire expanded to show 27 possible values from 51 possible sources of income.

[n]Implementation of a new March CPS processing system. Questionnaire expanded to ask eleven income questions.

[o]Implementation of 1970 census population controls.

[p]Implementation of a new March CPS processing system.

Note: Numbers in thousands. People as of March of the following year.

SOURCE: Adapted from "Table 2. Poverty Status of People by Family Relationship, Race, and Hispanic Origin: 1959 to 2016," in *Historical Poverty Tables: People and Families—1959 to 2016*, US Census Bureau, September 2017, https://www2.census.gov/programs-surveys/cps/tables/time-series/historical-poverty-people/hstpov2.xls (accessed January 18, 2018)

reduce TANF benefit levels over time. Meanwhile, because a household head's ability to collect benefits depends on his or her actively looking for and eventually finding a job, TANF fails to help those whose inability to find work is caused by conditions of high unemployment, such as during the Great Recession.

According to Ife Floyd, Ladonna Pavetti, and Liz Schott of the CBPP, in *TANF Reaching Few Poor Families* (December 13, 2017, https://www.cbpp.org/sites/default/files/atoms/files/6-16-15tanf.pdf), the annual TANF budget has been frozen since 1996, such that benefits have not even kept pace with inflation. To address the crisis of the Great Recession, President Obama signed the American Recovery and Reinvestment Act (ARRA) of 2009, which allocated $5 billion for a TANF emergency fund for fiscal years 2009 and 2010. When the emergency fund expired, however, in September 2010, TANF funding returned to its original level.

Floyd, Pavetti, and Schott note that in 2015 TANF provided cash assistance for only 23 of every 100 families in poverty, which was a marked decrease from 1996, the year TANF was first enacted, when 68 of every 100 families in poverty received these benefits. Furthermore, the researchers explain that TANF has been far less successful than the AFDC at helping families climb out of deep poverty. In 1995 the AFDC lifted 2.5 million children out of deep poverty. By comparison, in 2014 TANF lifted only 420,000 children out of deep poverty.

Also, because SNAP is available to almost all individuals and families whose gross and net incomes fall below certain thresholds and who have assets below certain limits, this program responded more effectively to the Great Recession. Participation in SNAP climbed sharply during the severe economic downturn, and the ARRA increased SNAP benefits for all households by 13.6% between 2009 and 2011. Following smaller increases in 2012 and 2013, the SNAP benefit increases provided by the ARRA expired in November 2013.

In "Supplemental Nutrition Assistance Program Participation and Costs" (April 6, 2018, http://www.fns.usda.gov/pd/supplemental-nutrition-assistance-program-snap), the US Department of Agriculture's Food and Nutrition Service, the agency responsible for overseeing SNAP, reports that approximately 26.3 million people were served by the program in fiscal year (FY) 2007. During the Great Recession, as long-term unemployment became widespread, the SNAP rolls expanded dramatically, from 33.5 million SNAP participants in FY 2009 to a peak of 47.6 million in FY 2013. As Table 5.13 shows, 23.1 million households accessed SNAP benefits in FY 2013, and the average value of each household's monthly benefit was $274.98. Both participation and benefits declined in the years that followed. In FY 2017, 20.9 million households accessed SNAP, receiving an average monthly benefit of $254.38.

**TABLE 5.12**

## Poverty of people by sex, 1966–2016

[Numbers in thousands. People as of March of the following year.]

| | | Male | | | Female | | |
|---|---|---|---|---|---|---|---|
| | | Total | | | Total | | |
| | | | Below poverty | | | Below poverty | |
| Year | Total | Total | Number | Percent | Total | Number | Percent |
| 2016 | 319,911 | 156,677 | 17,685 | 11.3 | 163,234 | 22,931 | 14.0 |
| 2015 | 318,454 | 156,009 | 19,037 | 12.2 | 162,445 | 24,086 | 14.8 |
| 2014 | 315,804 | 154,639 | 20,708 | 13.4 | 161,164 | 25,949 | 16.1 |
| 2013 | 313,096 | 153,465 | 20,294 | 13.2 | 159,630 | 25,975 | 16.3 |
| 2013 | 312,965 | 153,361 | 20,119 | 13.1 | 159,605 | 25,199 | 15.8 |
| 2012 | 310,648 | 152,058 | 20,656 | 13.6 | 158,590 | 25,840 | 16.3 |
| 2011 | 308,456 | 150,990 | 20,501 | 13.6 | 157,466 | 25,746 | 16.3 |
| 2010 | 306,130 | 149,737 | 20,893 | 14.0 | 156,394 | 25,451 | 16.3 |
| 2009 | 303,820 | 149,237 | 19,475 | 13.0 | 154,582 | 24,094 | 15.6 |
| 2008 | 301,041 | 147,862 | 17,698 | 12.0 | 153,179 | 22,131 | 14.4 |
| 2007 | 298,699 | 146,655 | 16,302 | 11.1 | 152,044 | 20,973 | 13.8 |
| 2006 | 296,450 | 145,486 | 16,000 | 11.0 | 150,964 | 20,460 | 13.6 |
| 2005 | 293,135 | 143,803 | 15,950 | 11.1 | 149,331 | 21,000 | 14.1 |
| 2004 | 290,617 | 142,433 | 16,399 | 11.5 | 148,183 | 20,641 | 13.9 |
| 2003 | 287,699 | 140,931 | 15,783 | 11.2 | 146,768 | 20,078 | 13.7 |
| 2002 | 285,317 | 139,558 | 15,162 | 10.9 | 145,759 | 19,408 | 13.3 |
| 2001 | 281,475 | 137,558 | 14,327 | 10.4 | 143,917 | 18,580 | 12.9 |
| 2000 | 278,944 | 136,274 | 13,536 | 9.9 | 142,670 | 18,045 | 12.6 |
| 1999 | 276,208 | 134,823 | 14,079 | 10.4 | 141,385 | 18,712 | 13.2 |
| 1998 | 271,059 | 132,408 | 14,712 | 11.1 | 138,652 | 19,764 | 14.3 |
| 1997 | 268,480 | 131,376 | 15,187 | 11.6 | 137,105 | 20,387 | 14.9 |
| 1996 | 266,218 | 130,353 | 15,611 | 12.0 | 135,865 | 20,918 | 15.4 |
| 1995 | 263,733 | 128,852 | 15,683 | 12.2 | 134,880 | 20,742 | 15.4 |
| 1994 | 261,616 | 127,838 | 16,316 | 12.8 | 133,778 | 21,744 | 16.3 |
| 1993 | 259,278 | 126,668 | 16,900 | 13.3 | 132,610 | 22,365 | 16.9 |
| 1992 | 256,549 | 125,288 | 16,222 | 12.9 | 131,261 | 21,792 | 16.6 |
| 1991 | 251,192 | 122,418 | 15,082 | 12.3 | 128,774 | 20,626 | 16.0 |
| 1990 | 248,644 | 121,073 | 14,211 | 11.7 | 127,571 | 19,373 | 15.2 |
| 1989 | 245,992 | 119,704 | 13,366 | 11.2 | 126,288 | 18,162 | 14.4 |
| 1988 | 243,530 | 118,399 | 13,599 | 11.5 | 125,131 | 18,146 | 14.5 |
| 1987 | 240,982 | 117,108 | 13,781 | 11.8 | 123,874 | 18,439 | 14.9 |
| 1986 | 238,554 | 115,915 | 13,721 | 11.8 | 122,640 | 18,649 | 15.2 |
| 1985 | 236,594 | 114,970 | 14,140 | 12.3 | 121,624 | 18,923 | 15.6 |
| 1984 | 233,816 | 113,391 | 14,537 | 12.8 | 120,425 | 19,163 | 15.9 |
| 1983 | 231,700 | 112,310 | 15,296 | 13.6 | 119,390 | 20,006 | 16.8 |
| 1982 | 229,412 | 111,175 | 14,842 | 13.4 | 118,237 | 19,556 | 16.5 |
| 1981 | 227,157 | 110,010 | 13,360 | 12.1 | 117,147 | 18,462 | 15.8 |
| 1980 | 225,027 | 108,990 | 12,207 | 11.2 | 116,037 | 17,065 | 14.7 |
| 1979 | 222,903 | 108,005 | 10,861 | 10.1 | 114,898 | 15,211 | 13.2 |
| 1978 | 215,656 | 104,480 | 10,017 | 9.6 | 111,175 | 14,480 | 13.0 |
| 1977 | 213,867 | 103,629 | 10,340 | 10.0 | 110,238 | 14,381 | 13.0 |
| 1976 | 212,303 | 102,955 | 10,373 | 10.1 | 109,348 | 14,603 | 13.4 |
| 1975 | 210,864 | 102,211 | 10,908 | 10.7 | 108,652 | 14,970 | 13.8 |
| 1974 | 209,362 | 101,561 | 9,945 | 9.8 | 107,801 | 13,429 | 12.5 |
| 1973 | 207,621 | 100,694 | 9,642 | 9.6 | 106,898 | 13,316 | 12.5 |
| 1972 | 206,004 | 99,804 | 10,190 | 10.2 | 106,168 | 14,258 | 13.4 |
| 1971 | 204,554 | 99,232 | 10,708 | 10.8 | 105,298 | 14,841 | 14.1 |
| 1970 | 202,489 | 98,228 | 10,879 | 11.1 | 104,248 | 14,632 | 14.0 |
| 1969 | 199,848 | 96,802 | 10,292 | 10.6 | 103,037 | 13,978 | 13.6 |
| 1968 | 197,618 | 95,681 | 10,793 | 11.3 | 101,919 | 14,578 | 14.3 |
| 1967 | 195,677 | 94,796 | 11,813 | 12.5 | 100,861 | 15,951 | 15.8 |
| 1966 | 193,390 | 93,718 | 12,225 | 13.0 | 99,637 | 16,265 | 16.3 |

SOURCE: Adapted from "Table 7. Poverty of People, by Sex: 1966 to 2016," in *Historical Poverty Tables—People*, US Census Bureau, September 2017, https://www2.census.gov/programs-surveys/cps/tables/time-series/historical-poverty-people/hstpov7.xls (accessed January 19, 2018)

Dorothy Rosenbaum and Brynne Keith-Jennings of the CBPP indicate in *SNAP Caseload and Spending Declines Accelerated in 2016* (January 27, 2017, https://www.cbpp.org/sites/default/files/atoms/files/7-29-16fa.pdf) that although the decline in SNAP caseloads was attributable in large part to economic recovery, many people were also being cut from the program due to the reinstatement of a three-month time limit on benefits, which had been waived in many states when unemployment was at its highest. When the cutoff took effect again in April 2016, an estimated 500,000 adults lost their SNAP benefits. Rosenbaum and Keith-Jennings explain, "To the extent that recent and future SNAP caseload declines reflect improving economic circumstances among low-income households, they are welcome. However, the large declines seen in April 2016... are troublesome. The loss

**TABLE 5.13**

## Summary of federal Food and Nutrition Service programs, 2013–17

[Data as of January 05, 2018]

| | Fiscal year 2013 | Fiscal year 2014 | Fiscal year 2015 | Fiscal year 2016 | Fiscal year 2017 |
|---|---|---|---|---|---|
| **Supplemental Nutrition Assistance Program**[a] | | | | | |
| People participating (thous.) | 47,636 | 46,664 | 45,767 | 44,219 | 42,138 |
| Households participating (thous.) | 23,052 | 22,744 | 22,522 | 21,778 | 20,871 |
| Value of benefits (mil. $) | 76,066 | 69,999 | 69,645 | 66,539 | 63,710 |
| Average monthly benefit per person ($) | 133.07 | 125.01 | 126.81 | 125.40 | 125.99 |
| Average monthly benefit per household ($) | 274.98 | 256.47 | 257.69 | 254.61 | 254.38 |
| **Total cost (mil. $)** | **79,859** | **74,062** | **73,946** | **70,922** | **67,960** |
| Puerto Rico grant (mil. $)[b] | 2,001 | 1,903 | 1,951 | 1,959 | 1,449 |
| **National school lunch program**[c] | | | | | |
| Children participating (thous.) | 30,683 | 30,459 | 30,475 | 30,355 | 29,963 |
| Total lunches served (mil.) | 5,098 | 5,020 | 5,005 | 5,052 | 4,887 |
| Percent free (%) | 62.1 | 63.6 | 65.4 | 66.6 | 67.1 |
| Percent reduced-price (%) | 8.3 | 8.0 | 7.2 | 6.7 | 6.5 |
| Total afterschool snacks served (mil.) | 220 | 221 | 221 | 211 | 206 |
| Cash payments (mil. $) | 11,058 | 11,356 | 11,696 | 12,257 | 12,236 |
| Commodity costs (mil. $) | 1,163 | 1,302 | 1,307 | 1,311 | 1,394 |
| **Total cost (mil. $)** | **12,221** | **12,658** | **13,004** | **13,568** | **13,630** |
| **School breakfast program**[c] | | | | | |
| Children participating (thous.) | 13,203 | 13,636 | 14,037 | 14,562 | 14,648 |
| Total breakfasts served (mil.) | 2,223 | 2,274 | 2,334 | 2,448 | 2,411 |
| Percent free or reduced price (%) | 84.8 | 84.9 | 85.2 | 85.1 | 85.0 |
| **Total cost (mil. $)** | **3,514** | **3,685** | **3,892** | **4,212** | **4,247** |
| **Special milk program**[d] | | | | | |
| Total half-pints served (mil.) | 55 | 50 | 47 | 45 | 41 |
| **Total cost (mil. $)** | **11** | **10** | **11** | **9** | **8** |
| **Child/adult care food program**[e] | | | | | |
| Average daily attendance (thous.) | 3,681 | 3,897 | 4,182 | 4,405 | 4,439 |
| Total meals served (mil.) | 1,957 | 1,979 | 2,019 | 2,082 | 2,046 |
| Child care centers (mil.) | 1,337 | 1,371 | 1,419 | 1,494 | 1,483 |
| Day care homes (mil.) | 551 | 537 | 526 | 511 | 484 |
| Adult care centers (mil.) | 70 | 71 | 74 | 77 | 78 |
| Percent free or reduced price (%) | 81.7 | 81.8 | 81.8 | 81.7 | 81.4 |
| Cash payments (mil. $) | 2,720 | 2,849 | 3,009 | 3,217 | 3,235 |
| Commodity costs (mil. $) | 124 | 134 | 148 | 155 | 147 |
| **Total costs (mil. $)** | **2,994** | **3,131** | **3,308** | **3,518** | **3,521** |
| **Summer food service program**[f] | | | | | |
| Average daily attendance (thous.) | 2,425 | 2,663 | 2,570 | 2,822 | 2,610 |
| Total meals served (mil.) | 151 | 160 | 163 | 154 | 151 |
| **Total cost (mil.)** | **426** | **466** | **488** | **478** | **474** |
| Child nutrition state admin (mil. $)[g] | 225 | 237 | 256 | 270 | 248 |
| **WIC (special supplemental food)**[h] | | | | | |
| Women-infants-children participating (thous.) | 8,663 | 8,258 | 8,024 | 7,696 | 7,286 |
| Food cost (mil. $) | 4,497 | 4,324 | 4,176 | 3,949 | 3,604 |
| Avg. monthly food cost per person ($) | 43.26 | 43.64 | 43.37 | 42.76 | 41.22 |
| **Total cost (mil. $)** | **6,502** | **6,354** | **6,223** | **5,979** | **5,639** |
| **Commodity supplemental food**[i] | | | | | |
| Total participation (thous.) | 580 | 574 | 572 | 585 | 630 |
| **Total cost (mil. $)** | **203** | **198** | **193** | **183** | **198** |
| **Food distribution on Indian reserve**[i] | | | | | |
| Total participation (thous.) | 76 | 85 | 89 | 93 | 90 |
| **Total cost (mil. $)** | **100** | **110** | **119** | **122** | **121** |
| **NSIP (elderly feeding)**[j] | | | | | |
| Total meals served (mil.) | NA | NA | NA | NA | NA |
| **Total cost (mil. $)** | **2.5** | **1.8** | **2.5** | **2.5** | **3.2** |

of benefits will likely cause serious hardship among many, since the average income of those potentially affected is less than 20 percent of the poverty line while they're receiving SNAP."

**TABLE 5.13**

## Summary of federal Food and Nutrition Service programs, 2013–17 [CONTINUED]

[Data as of January 05, 2018]

| | Fiscal year 2013 | Fiscal year 2014 | Fiscal year 2015 | Fiscal year 2016 | Fiscal year 2017 |
|---|---|---|---|---|---|
| **TEFAP (emergency food assistance)**[k] | | | | | |
| Total pounds distributed (mil.) | 840 | 757 | 671 | 811 | 830 |
| Total food cost (mil. $) | 629 | 560 | 451 | 586 | 583 |
| **Total cost (mil. $)** | **693** | **629** | **525** | **664** | **662** |
| **Other food distribution programs** | | | | | |
| Disaster feeding (mil. $)[l] | 0.000 | 0.000 | 0.000 | 0.000 | 0.000 |
| Charitable institutes (mil. $)[m] | 0.000 | 0.000 | 0.000 | 0.000 | 0.000 |

NSIP = Nutrition Services Incentive Program.
WIC = Women, Infants, and Children.
TEFAP = The Emergency Food Assistance Program.
[a]Participation data are 12-month averages. Total cost includes benefits, the federal share of state administrative expenses, and other federal costs (e.g., printing and processing stamps). The Supplemental Nutrition Assistance Program (SNAP) formerly known as the Food Stamp Program prior to fiscal year 2009.
[b]Puerto Rico's Nutrition Assistance Grant provides benefits analogous to SNAP. Smaller outlying areas with similar grants include American Samoa ($6.5 million in FY 2008) and the Northern Marianas ($16.2 million).
[c]National School Lunch and School Breakfast participation data are 9-month averages (summer months are excluded). They represent average daily meals served adjusted by an attendance factor. School Lunch costs include cash payments, entitlement commodities, bonus commodities (surplus foods donated by the Dept. of Agriculture), and cash-in-lieu of commodities. School breakfast costs are cash payments. Cash payments are federal reimbursements to state agencies based on meals served multiplied by reimbursement rates which are adjusted annually to reflect changes in food costs. Free and reduced-price meals served to needy children are reimbursed at much higher rates than full-price meals.
[d]Special milk costs are cash payments based on an annually determined reimbursement rate and the actual cost of free milk (a small portion of the total—less than 7% for all years).
[e]Total costs include cash payments, entitlement and bonus commodities, cash-in-lieu of commodities, sponsor administrative costs, start-up costs and audits.
[f]Average daily attendance is reported only for July, the peak month of activity. Costs include cash payments, entitlement and bonus commodities, and the federal share of state and sponsor administrative costs. The decline in meals served since fiscal year 2001 is largely attributable to alternative summer meal service in the National School Lunch and School Breakfast Program under Seamless Waiver provisions which eased reporting requirements for sponsors.
[g]The federal share of state administrative costs for the National School Lunch, School Breakfast, and Child and Adult Food Care Programs.
[h]Total costs include food benefits, nutrition services and administrative funds, the Farmers' Market Nutrition Program, infrastructure, breastfeeding promotion and peer counseling, program evaluation, and technical assistance.
[i]Includes commodity distribution costs (entitlement and bonus), the federal share of state administrative expenses, and other costs (such as storage and transportation, food losses and demo projects—national level only, unavailable prior to fiscal year 1996).
[j]The Nutrition Services Incentive Program was formerly called Nutrition Program for the Elderly. As of fiscal year 2002, meals served are reported to the Agency on Aging (DHHS) rather than FNS. *In fiscal year 2003, administration of cash grants was transferred to the Agency on Aging, and FNS costs were limited to the value of commodities distributed.*
[k]Total cost includes commodities distributed (entitlement and bonus) and the federal share of state admin. expenses. Emergency food assistance is food made available to hunger relief organizations such as food banks and soup kitchens. It is not disaster relief.
[l]Most disaster relief is provided through SNAP.
[m]Includes summer camps.
Notes: Data are provided by Federal fiscal year (October through September). Commodity costs reflect the value of food distributed to participants (Food Distribution on Indian Reservations and Commodity Supplemental Food Program) or delivered to State warehouses (all other programs). Fiscal year 2017 data are preliminary and all data are subject to revision.

SOURCE: "Annual Summary of Food and Nutrition Service Programs," in *Program Data: Overview*, US Department of Agriculture, Food and Nutrition Service, January 2018, http://www.fns.usda.gov/sites/default/files/pd/annual.xls (accessed January 19, 2018)

Families that lack access to adequate food and nutrition are classified as "food insecure." The Food and Nutrition Service subdivides all food-insecure households into those that experience low food security (those that struggle to provide enough food for the entire household during the year) and very low food security (those in which some household members may be forced to reduce their food intake due to insufficient financial resources).

In 2016, 12.3% (15.6 million) of all households in the United States were food insecure. (See Table 5.14.) Households with children were more likely to be food insecure than those without: 16.5% of households with children under the age of 18 years were food insecure in 2016, compared with 10.5% of households with no children. Single-parent households were significantly more likely to be food insecure than married-couple households, and female-headed single-parent households were more often food insecure than those headed by males. Among married-couple households, the rate of food insecurity was 9.9%. Whereas 21.7% of male-headed households with no spouse present experienced food insecurity in 2016, 31.6% of all such female-headed households were food insecure in the same year, with more than one out of 10 (10.5%) reporting very low food security.

The Food and Nutrition Service oversees other important but much smaller means-tested food programs, including the National School Lunch Program, which provides free and reduced-price lunches to children based on household income. In FY 2017, 30 million children accessed the program, 67.1% of whom were given free lunches and 6.5% of whom were given reduced-price lunches. (See Table 5.13.) Because of the prevalence of poverty and food insecurity in female-headed single-parent households, this program offers a particularly important resource for women.

The Special Supplemental Nutrition Program for Women, Infants, and Children (WIC) is also a vital resource for low-income women and their children. WIC provides low-income pregnant, postpartum, and

TABLE 5.14

**Households by food security status and selected household characteristics, 2016**

| Category | Total[a] 1,000 | Food secure 1,000 | Food secure Percent | Food insecure — All 1,000 | Food insecure — All Percent | Food insecure — With low food security 1,000 | Food insecure — With low food security Percent | Food insecure — With very low food security 1,000 | Food insecure — With very low food security Percent |
|---|---|---|---|---|---|---|---|---|---|
| All households | 126,401 | 110,850 | 87.7 | 15,551 | 12.3 | 9,413 | 7.4 | 6,138 | 4.9 |
| **Household composition:** | | | | | | | | | |
| With children <18 yrs | 38,400 | 32,059 | 83.5 | 6,341 | 16.5 | 4,501 | 11.7 | 1,840 | 4.8 |
| With children <6 yrs | 16,571 | 13,820 | 83.4 | 2,751 | 16.6 | 1,923 | 11.6 | 828 | 5.0 |
| Married-couple families | 25,031 | 22,560 | 90.1 | 2,471 | 9.9 | 1,843 | 7.4 | 628 | 2.5 |
| Female head, no spouse | 9,780 | 6,692 | 68.4 | 3,088 | 31.6 | 2,061 | 21.1 | 1,027 | 10.5 |
| Male head, no spouse | 3,070 | 2,403 | 78.3 | 667 | 21.7 | 509 | 16.6 | 158 | 5.1 |
| Other household with child[b] | 519 | 404 | 77.8 | 115 | 22.2 | NA | NA | NA | NA |
| With no children <18 yrs | 88,001 | 78,792 | 89.5 | 9,209 | 10.5 | 4,911 | 5.6 | 4,298 | 4.9 |
| More than one adult | 52,353 | 48,162 | 92.0 | 4,191 | 8.0 | 2,411 | 4.6 | 1,780 | 3.4 |
| Women living alone | 19,649 | 16,910 | 86.1 | 2,739 | 13.9 | 1,420 | 7.2 | 1,319 | 6.7 |
| Men living alone | 15,999 | 13,719 | 85.7 | 2,280 | 14.3 | 1,080 | 6.8 | 1,200 | 7.5 |
| With elderly | 36,335 | 33,496 | 92.2 | 2,839 | 7.8 | 1,786 | 4.9 | 1,053 | 2.9 |
| Elderly living alone | 13,529 | 12,326 | 91.1 | 1,203 | 8.9 | 733 | 5.4 | 470 | 3.5 |
| **Race/ethnicity of households:** | | | | | | | | | |
| White, non-Hispanic | 84,087 | 76,271 | 90.7 | 7,816 | 9.3 | 4,591 | 5.5 | 3,225 | 3.8 |
| Black, non-Hispanic | 15,940 | 12,346 | 77.5 | 3,594 | 22.5 | 2,048 | 12.8 | 1,546 | 9.7 |
| Hispanic[c] | 17,054 | 13,907 | 81.5 | 3,147 | 18.5 | 2,152 | 12.7 | 995 | 5.8 |
| Other, non-Hispanic | 9,319 | 8,325 | 89.3 | 994 | 10.7 | 622 | 6.7 | 372 | 4.0 |
| **Household income-to-poverty ratio:** | | | | | | | | | |
| Under 1.00 | 13,929 | 8,598 | 61.7 | 5,331 | 38.3 | 2,920 | 21.0 | 2,411 | 17.3 |
| Under 1.30 | 18,522 | 11,917 | 64.3 | 6,605 | 35.7 | 3,725 | 20.2 | 2,880 | 15.5 |
| Under 1.85 | 29,025 | 19,860 | 68.4 | 9,165 | 31.6 | 5,319 | 18.3 | 3,846 | 13.3 |
| 1.85 and over | 67,785 | 64,001 | 94.4 | 3,784 | 5.6 | 2,499 | 3.7 | 1,285 | 1.9 |
| Income unknown | 29,590 | 26,988 | 91.2 | 2,602 | 8.8 | 1,595 | 5.4 | 1,007 | 3.4 |
| **Area of residence:[d]** | | | | | | | | | |
| Inside metropolitan area | 108,118 | 95,315 | 88.2 | 12,803 | 11.8 | 7,868 | 7.2 | 4,935 | 4.6 |
| In principal cities[e] | 37,176 | 31,879 | 85.8 | 5,297 | 14.2 | 3,117 | 8.3 | 2,180 | 5.9 |
| Not in principal cities | 54,399 | 49,222 | 90.5 | 5,177 | 9.5 | 3,286 | 6.0 | 1,891 | 3.5 |
| Outside metropolitan area | 18,283 | 15,535 | 85.0 | 2,748 | 15.0 | 1,545 | 8.4 | 1,203 | 6.6 |
| **Census geographic region:** | | | | | | | | | |
| Northeast | 22,669 | 20,217 | 89.2 | 2,452 | 10.8 | 1,594 | 7.0 | 858 | 3.8 |
| Midwest | 27,307 | 23,976 | 87.8 | 3,331 | 12.2 | 1,871 | 6.9 | 1,460 | 5.3 |
| South | 47,966 | 41,476 | 86.5 | 6,490 | 13.5 | 3,890 | 8.1 | 2,600 | 5.4 |
| West | 28,458 | 25,180 | 88.5 | 3,278 | 11.5 | 2,057 | 7.2 | 1,221 | 4.3 |

NA = Not reported; fewer than 10 households in the survey with this characteristic had very low food security.

[a]Totals exclude households for which food security status is unknown because household respondents did not give a valid response to any of the questions in the food security scale. In 2016, these exclusions represented 408,000 households (0.3 percent of all households).

[b]Households with children in complex living arrangements, e.g., children of other relatives or unrelated roommate or boarder.

[c]Hispanics may be of any race.

[d]Metropolitan area residence is based on 2013 Office of Management and Budget delineation. Prevalence rates by area of residence are comparable with those for 2014 and 2015 but are not precisely comparable with those of earlier years.

[e]Households within incorporated areas of the largest cities in each metropolitan area. Residence inside or outside of principal cities is not identified for about 15 percent of households in metropolitan statistical areas.

SOURCE: Alisha Coleman-Jensen et al., "Table 2. Households by Food Security Status and Selected Household Characteristics, 2016," in *Household Food Security in the United States in 2016*, US Department of Agriculture, Economic Research Service, September 2017, https://www.ers.usda.gov/webdocs/publications/84973/err-237.pdf?v=42979 (accessed January 19, 2018)

breast-feeding women and children up to the age of five years with food, nutrition education, and health care consultation. In FY 2017 the program served 7.3 million individuals, adding an average monthly supplement of $41.22 to their food budget. (See Table 5.13.)

In February 2018, as President Donald Trump (1946–) unveiled his proposed federal budget for FY 2019, it appeared that TANF, SNAP, and other means-tested assistance programs were facing drastic cuts. According to Sharon Parrott et al. of the CBPP, in "Trump Budget

Deeply Cuts Health, Housing, Other Assistance for Low- and Moderate-Income Families" (February 14, 2018, https://www.cbpp.org/sites/default/files/atoms/files/2-14-18bud.pdf), the proposed budget included cuts to TANF and SNAP amounting to $21 billion and $213 billion, respectively, over the coming decade. The researchers warn, "The cuts would affect a broad range of low- and moderate-income people, including parents, children, seniors, and people with disabilities. Taken together, the cuts are far deeper than any ever enacted and would deepen poverty and hardship and swell the ranks of the uninsured." Although the final details of the budget were subject to negotiation by Congress in the weeks and months that followed, the Republican president's proposal signaled his intention to radically limit these programs.

## Elderly Women

Poverty among older Americans has declined since the establishment of Medicare in 1965 and the subsequent increases in Social Security benefits (the Social Security program was originally established in 1935). In addition, SSI has become available to more disabled people, many of whom are elderly. According to Semega, Fontenot, and Kollar, the poverty rate for people aged 65 years and older was 9.3% in 2016, which was slightly higher than the year before. (See Table 5.15.) As in past years, this figure was significantly lower than the poverty rates for children under the age of 18 years (18%) and adults aged 18 to 64 years (11.6%).

Elderly women are more likely than elderly men to live in poverty for a variety of reasons. Women typically earn less than men (as the gender wage gap illustrates) and take more time out of the paid workforce to raise children. In turn, they accumulate less retirement savings than men and receive smaller pensions. They also live longer, are more likely to be widowed and thus to live alone, and are more likely than elderly men to raise their grandchildren in place of parents. According to Semega, Fontenot, and Kollar, 10.6% of women aged 65 years and older lived in poverty in 2016, compared with 7.6% of men the same age.

## Social Security

Social Security protects senior citizens from a drastic reduction in income at retirement. It was originally intended to be supplemented by other sources of income, such as pensions and income from assets, but over the

**TABLE 5.15**

**People in poverty by selected characteristics, 2015–16**

[Numbers in thousands. People as of March of the following year.]

| | 2015 | | | 2016 | | | Change in poverty (2016 less 2015)[a] | |
| | | Below poverty | | | Below poverty | | | |
| Characteristic | Total | Number | Percent | Total | Number | Percent | Number | Percent |
|---|---|---|---|---|---|---|---|---|
| **People** | | | | | | | | |
| Total | 318,454 | 43,123 | 13.5 | 319,911 | 40,616 | 12.7 | −2,507 | −0.8 |
| **Family status** | | | | | | | | |
| In families | 258,121 | 29,893 | 11.6 | 259,863 | 27,762 | 10.7 | −2,132 | −0.9 |
| Householder | 82,199 | 8,589 | 10.4 | 82,854 | 8,081 | 9.8 | −508 | −0.7 |
| Related children under age 18 | 72,558 | 13,962 | 19.2 | 72,674 | 12,803 | 17.6 | −1,159 | −1.6 |
| Related children under age 6 | 23,459 | 4,923 | 21.0 | 23,531 | 4,586 | 19.5 | −337 | −1.5 |
| In unrelated subfamilies | 1,344 | 559 | 41.6 | 1,208 | 519 | 43.0 | −40 | 1.4 |
| Reference person | 563 | 231 | 41.0 | 496 | 202 | 40.6 | −29 | −0.3 |
| Children under age 18 | 701 | 321 | 45.9 | 622 | 298 | 48.0 | −23 | 2.1 |
| Unrelated individuals | 58,988 | 12,671 | 21.5 | 58,839 | 12,336 | 21.0 | −336 | −0.5 |
| **Race[b] and Hispanic origin** | | | | | | | | |
| White | 245,536 | 28,566 | 11.6 | 245,985 | 27,113 | 11.0 | −1,453 | −0.6 |
| White, not Hispanic | 195,450 | 17,786 | 9.1 | 195,221 | 17,263 | 8.8 | −523 | −0.3 |
| Black | 41,625 | 10,020 | 24.1 | 41,962 | 9,234 | 22.0 | −786 | −2.1 |
| Asian | 18,241 | 2,078 | 11.4 | 18,879 | 1,908 | 10.1 | −170 | −1.3 |
| Hispanic (any race) | 56,780 | 12,133 | 21.4 | 57,556 | 11,137 | 19.4 | −996 | −2.0 |
| **Sex** | | | | | | | | |
| Male | 156,009 | 19,037 | 12.2 | 156,677 | 17,685 | 11.3 | −1,351 | −0.9 |
| Female | 162,445 | 24,086 | 14.8 | 163,234 | 22,931 | 14.0 | −1,156 | −0.8 |
| **Age** | | | | | | | | |
| Under age 18 | 73,647 | 14,509 | 19.7 | 73,586 | 13,253 | 18.0 | −1,255 | −1.7 |
| Aged 18 to 64 | 197,260 | 24,414 | 12.4 | 197,051 | 22,795 | 11.6 | −1,619 | −0.8 |
| Aged 65 and older | 47,547 | 4,201 | 8.8 | 49,274 | 4,568 | 9.3 | 367 | 0.4 |

[a]Details may not sum to totals because of rounding.
[b]Federal surveys give respondents the option of reporting more than one race. Therefore, two basic ways of defining a race group are possible. A group such as Asian may be defined as those who reported Asian and no other race (the race-alone or single-race concept) or as those who reported Asian regardless of whether they also reported another race (the race-alone-or-in-combination concept). This table shows data using the first approach (race alone). The use of the single-race population does not imply that it is the preferred method of presenting or analyzing data. The Census Bureau uses a variety of approaches. Information on people who reported more than one race, such as white **and** American Indian and Alaska Native or Asian **and** black or African American, is available from the 2010 Census through American FactFinder. About 2.9 percent of people reported more than one race in the 2010 Census. Data for American Indians and Alaska Natives, Native Hawaiians and other Pacific Islanders, and those reporting two or more races are not shown separately.

SOURCE: Adapted from Jessica L. Semega, Kayla R. Fontenot, and Melissa A. Kollar, "Table 3. People in Poverty by Selected Characteristics: 2015 and 2016," in *Income and Poverty in the United States: 2016*, US Census Bureau, September 2017, https://www.census.gov/content/dam/Census/library/publications/2017/demo/P60-259.pdf (accessed January 19, 2018)

decades Social Security has become a bigger share of many older Americans' incomes. According to the CBPP, in *Policy Basics: Top Ten Facts about Social Security* (August 14, 2017, https://www.cbpp.org/sites/default/files/atoms/files/8-8-16socsec.pdf), Social Security benefits lifted 22.1 million Americans out of poverty in 2015. In the absence of Social Security, an estimated 40.5% of Americans over the age of 65 years would live below the poverty line. (These CBPP estimates are based on 2016 census figures.) The percentage is even higher for elderly women, 44.3% of whom would live in poverty if not for Social Security benefits. In 2016 women in their 60s and 70s represented 54% of Social Security beneficiaries, while women in their 80s made up 60% of beneficiaries and those in their 90s made up 70%. Significantly too, because women are much more likely to outlive their spouses, they made up 97% of Social Security survivor beneficiaries in 2016.

### Private Pensions

With the decline of private pension programs for retirees in the 21st century, elderly Americans may become more likely to live in poverty in the future. In previous decades employers typically offered defined-benefit pension plans, which were funded by some combination of worker and employer contributions and provided fixed payments based on years of service to the company and other factors. In the 21st century private pensions are more commonly defined-contribution plans, in which payments are based on the total amount of money contributed by the worker and/or employer and on the success of the plan's investment strategy in the stock and bond markets. Not only are employers generally contributing less money to pension plans but also retirees are much less able to count on a set amount of income from private pensions, due to the ups and downs of the stock market.

In *Shortchanged in Retirement: Continuing Challenges to Women's Financial Future* (March 2016, https://www.nirsonline.org/wp-content/uploads/2017/06/final_short changed_retirement_report_2016.pdf), Jennifer Erin Brown et al. of the National Institute on Retirement Security report that women have been participating in employer-sponsored retirement plans at the same rate as men since 2006. In 2012 this participation rate was 46%. Even so, women continue to accumulate less retirement wealth over the course of their careers, due to the gender pay gap. The researchers indicate that in 2010 men received $17,856 in median retirement income from a pension, whereas women received $12,000 (33% less).

### Child Support

Children living in single-parent households are far more likely to be poor than children living in two-parent households. Timothy S. Grall of the Census Bureau notes in *Custodial Mothers and Fathers and Their Child Support: 2015* (January 2018, https://www.census.gov/content/dam/Census/library/publications/2018/demo/P60-262.pdf) that in 2015 there were 13.6 million parents who had custody of children under the age of 21 years while the other parent lived elsewhere. Mothers accounted for 80.4% of all custodial parents and were nearly twice as likely as custodial fathers to have incomes below the poverty line (29.2%, compared with 16.7%). Half (50.2%, or 6.8 million) of the 13.6 million custodial parents had either a legal or an informal child support agreement with the other parent, usually requiring the noncustodial parent to make payments to the custodial parent. The total amount owed in child support payments in 2015 was $33.7 billion, but only 59.8% was received. Among those who received child support payments, the average amount received for the year was $3,447, or $287 per month. The proportion of custodial parents who were owed child support and who received the full amount owed was 43.5%. Among custodial parents living below the poverty line who received the full amount of child support owed, these payments represented 58% of their average income.

### Homeless Women

Homelessness is difficult to measure, but the US Department of Housing and Urban Development (HUD) attempts to do so by conducting counts of the homeless population simultaneously across the country on one night each January. In *The 2016 Annual Homeless Assessment Report to Congress—Part 2: Estimates of Homelessness in the United States* (December 2017, https://www.hudex change.info/resources/documents/2016-AHAR-Part-2.pdf), which is based on these point-in-time counts and on data from shelters and other service providers, HUD notes that 1.4 million individuals used an emergency shelter or transitional housing in 2016. Women are underrepresented in this count, however, because it does not factor in women in domestic violence shelters. On the night when the point-in-time count was conducted, approximately 37.1% of the sheltered homeless population was female and 62.9% was male. In 2016 an estimated 481,410 people (about one-third of all people experiencing sheltered homelessness) used an emergency shelter or a transitional housing program as part of a family with children. Among this group, more than three-quarters (77.6%) of the adults were women.

## CHAPTER 6
## WOMEN'S HEALTH

In *Health, United States, 2016* (May 2017, https://www.cdc.gov/nchs/data/hus/hus16.pdf), the National Center for Health Statistics (NCHS) notes that in 2015 the life expectancy at birth was 81.2 years for US females and 76.3 years for US males. In every major racial group, women had a longer life expectancy than their male counterparts. Among African Americans, women had a life expectancy of 78.5 years, compared with 72.2 years for men. White women had a life expectancy of 81.3 years, compared with 76.6 years for white men. Among Hispanics, women had a life expectancy of 84.3 years, whereas men had a life expectancy of 79.3 years. The US Census Bureau (May 9, 2017, https://www2.census.gov/programs-surveys/popproj/tables/2014/2014-summary-tables/np2014-t17.xls) projects that by 2060 female life expectancy at birth will be 87.1 years, compared with 84 years for men, and that disparities among racial and ethnic groups will narrow considerably.

Women smoke and drink less than men, and they are not nearly as likely to die from complications of childbirth as they were in past centuries. Women, however, are more likely than men to suffer from chronic illnesses, both because they live longer and because their higher rates of poverty often mean they have less access to preventive medicine and advanced medical treatments.

Since the beginning of the 21st century the death rates for both females and males have declined for most major diseases and other causes of death. The age-adjusted death rate for men declined 18.1%, from 1,053.8 per 100,000 population in 2000 to 863.2 in 2015, compared with a 14.7% decline, from 731.4 per 100,000 to 624.2 over the same period, for women. As Table 6.1 shows, women's age-adjusted death rate from cerebrovascular diseases (strokes and hemorrhages) decreased 37.6%, from 59.1 per 100,000 population in 2000 to 36.9 in 2015; their rate of death from heart disease decreased 36.7%, from 210.9 per 100,000

population to 133.6; and their rate of death from malignant neoplasms (cancer) decreased 18.9%, from 167.6 per 100,000 to 135.9.

By contrast, rates of death from Alzheimer's disease increased for both sexes during the same period. Men's deaths from Alzheimer's increased 55.9%, from 15.2 per 100,000 population in 2000 to 23.7 in 2015; women's deaths from Alzheimer's increased 69.9%, from 19.3 per 100,000 to 32.8. Increased longevity is believed to be behind some portion of these increases, as is increased awareness of the disease itself. Before the 1980s symptoms now associated with Alzheimer's were considered a normal consequence of aging. Some research suggests that a possible link between estrogen levels and Alzheimer's may account for the higher prevalence of the disease among women; so far, however, no conclusive link has been established.

## WOMEN'S ACCESS TO HEALTH CARE
### Sources of Health Care

The NCHS notes in *Health, United States, 2016* that in 2014–15, 12.4% of women aged 18 to 64 years had no usual source of health care, compared with 22.3% of men the same age. Women made far more health care visits than men. Only 10.8% of women made no visits to doctors' offices or emergency departments or had no home visits from a health care provider in 2015, compared with 19.5% of men. Nearly half of both men (49.8%) and women (47.1%) reported between one and three health care visits, but women were more likely than men to report between four and nine visits (26.9% versus 20.3%) and 10 or more visits (15.2% versus 10.5%). Women were also more likely than men to have made emergency department visits in 2015: 20.6% of women had made at least one emergency department visit, and 8.1% of women had made at least two visits, compared with 16.9% and 5.7%, respectively, for men.

TABLE 6.1

## Age-adjusted death rates for selected causes of death for all ages, by sex, 1950–2015

[Data are based on death certificates]

| Sex, race, Hispanic origin, and cause of death[a] | 1950[b, c] | 1960[b, c] | 1970[c] | 1980[c] | 1990[c] | 2000[d] | 2005[d] | 2010[d] | 2014[d] | 2015[d] |
|---|---|---|---|---|---|---|---|---|---|---|
| **All persons** | | | | | Age-adjusted death rate per 100,000 population[e] | | | | | |
| All causes | 1,446.0 | 1,339.2 | 1,222.6 | 1,039.1 | 938.7 | 869.0 | 815.0 | 747.0 | 724.6 | 733.1 |
| Diseases of heart | 588.8 | 559.0 | 492.7 | 412.1 | 321.8 | 257.6 | 216.8 | 179.1 | 167.0 | 168.5 |
| Ischemic heart disease | — | — | — | 345.2 | 249.6 | 186.8 | 148.2 | 113.6 | 98.8 | 97.2 |
| Cerebrovascular diseases | 180.7 | 177.9 | 147.7 | 96.2 | 65.3 | 60.9 | 48.0 | 39.1 | 36.5 | 37.6 |
| Malignant neoplasms | 193.9 | 193.9 | 198.6 | 207.9 | 216.0 | 199.6 | 185.1 | 172.8 | 161.2 | 158.5 |
| Trachea, bronchus, and lung | 15.0 | 24.1 | 37.1 | 49.9 | 59.3 | 56.1 | 52.7 | 47.6 | 42.1 | 40.5 |
| Colon, rectum, and anus | — | 30.3 | 28.9 | 27.4 | 24.5 | 20.8 | 17.7 | 15.8 | 14.3 | 14.2 |
| Chronic lower respiratory diseases[f] | — | — | — | 28.3 | 37.2 | 44.2 | 43.9 | 42.2 | 40.5 | 41.6 |
| Influenza and pneumonia[g] | 48.1 | 53.7 | 41.7 | 31.4 | 36.8 | 23.7 | 21.0 | 15.1 | 15.1 | 15.2 |
| Chronic liver disease and cirrhosis | 11.3 | 13.3 | 17.8 | 15.1 | 11.1 | 9.5 | 8.9 | 9.4 | 10.4 | 10.8 |
| Diabetes mellitus[h] | 23.1 | 22.5 | 24.3 | 18.1 | 20.7 | 25.0 | 24.9 | 20.8 | 20.9 | 21.3 |
| Alzheimer's disease | — | — | — | † | † | 18.1 | 24.0 | 25.1 | 25.4 | 29.4 |
| Human immunodeficiency virus (HIV) disease | … | … | … | … | 10.2 | 5.2 | 4.2 | 2.6 | 2.0 | 1.9 |
| Unintentional injuries | 78.0 | 62.3 | 60.1 | 46.4 | 36.3 | 34.9 | 39.5 | 38.0 | 40.5 | 43.2 |
| Motor vehicle-related injuries | 24.6 | 23.1 | 27.6 | 22.3 | 18.5 | 15.4 | 15.2 | 11.3 | 10.8 | 11.4 |
| Poisoning | 2.5 | 1.7 | 2.8 | 1.9 | 2.3 | 4.5 | 8.0 | 10.6 | 13.1 | 14.8 |
| Nephritis, nephrotic syndrome, and nephrosis[h] | — | — | — | 9.1 | 9.3 | 13.5 | 14.7 | 15.3 | 13.2 | 13.4 |
| Suicide[i] | 13.2 | 12.5 | 13.1 | 12.2 | 12.5 | 10.4 | 10.9 | 12.1 | 13.0 | 13.3 |
| Homicide[j] | 5.1 | 5.0 | 8.8 | 10.4 | 9.4 | 5.9 | 6.1 | 5.3 | 5.1 | 5.7 |
| **Male** | | | | | | | | | | |
| All causes | 1,674.2 | 1,609.0 | 1,542.1 | 1,348.1 | 1,202.8 | 1,053.8 | 971.9 | 887.1 | 855.1 | 863.2 |
| Diseases of heart | 699.0 | 687.6 | 634.0 | 538.9 | 412.4 | 320.0 | 268.2 | 225.1 | 210.9 | 211.8 |
| Ischemic heart disease | — | — | — | 459.7 | 328.2 | 241.4 | 192.3 | 151.3 | 133.5 | 131.2 |
| Cerebrovascular diseases | 186.4 | 186.1 | 157.4 | 102.2 | 68.5 | 62.4 | 48.4 | 39.3 | 36.9 | 37.8 |
| Malignant neoplasms | 208.1 | 225.1 | 247.6 | 271.2 | 280.4 | 248.9 | 227.2 | 209.9 | 192.9 | 189.2 |
| Trachea, bronchus, and lung | 24.6 | 43.6 | 67.5 | 85.2 | 91.1 | 76.7 | 69.1 | 60.3 | 51.7 | 49.5 |
| Colon, rectum, and anus | — | 31.8 | 32.3 | 32.8 | 30.4 | 25.1 | 21.2 | 19.0 | 16.9 | 16.8 |
| Prostate | 28.6 | 28.7 | 28.8 | 32.8 | 38.4 | 30.4 | 25.3 | 21.9 | 19.0 | 18.8 |
| Chronic lower respiratory diseases[f] | — | — | — | 49.9 | 55.4 | 55.8 | 52.2 | 48.7 | 45.4 | 46.0 |
| Influenza and pneumonia[g] | 55.0 | 65.8 | 54.0 | 42.1 | 47.8 | 28.9 | 24.9 | 18.2 | 17.8 | 17.7 |
| Chronic liver disease and cirrhosis | 15.0 | 18.5 | 24.8 | 21.3 | 15.9 | 13.4 | 12.4 | 12.9 | 14.1 | 14.5 |
| Diabetes mellitus[h] | 18.8 | 19.9 | 23.0 | 18.1 | 21.7 | 27.8 | 28.8 | 24.9 | 25.6 | 26.2 |
| Alzheimer's disease | — | — | — | † | † | 15.2 | 19.5 | 21.0 | 20.6 | 23.7 |
| Human immunodeficiency virus (HIV) disease | … | … | … | … | 18.5 | 7.9 | 6.3 | 3.8 | 3.0 | 2.8 |
| Unintentional injuries | 101.8 | 85.5 | 87.4 | 69.0 | 52.9 | 49.3 | 55.0 | 51.5 | 54.6 | 58.7 |
| Motor vehicle-related injuries | 38.5 | 35.4 | 41.5 | 33.6 | 26.5 | 21.7 | 21.9 | 16.2 | 15.8 | 16.7 |
| Poisoning | 3.3 | 2.3 | 3.9 | 2.7 | 3.5 | 6.6 | 10.8 | 13.8 | 17.3 | 19.8 |
| Nephritis, nephrotic syndrome, and nephrosis[h] | — | — | — | 12.2 | 12.1 | 16.9 | 18.1 | 18.7 | 16.2 | 16.3 |
| Suicide[i] | 21.2 | 20.0 | 19.8 | 19.9 | 21.5 | 17.7 | 18.1 | 19.8 | 20.7 | 21.1 |
| Homicide[j] | 7.9 | 7.5 | 14.3 | 16.6 | 14.8 | 9.0 | 9.7 | 8.4 | 8.0 | 9.1 |
| **Female** | | | | | | | | | | |
| All causes | 1,236.0 | 1,105.3 | 971.4 | 817.9 | 750.9 | 731.4 | 692.3 | 634.9 | 616.7 | 624.2 |
| Diseases of heart | 486.6 | 447.0 | 381.6 | 320.8 | 257.0 | 210.9 | 177.5 | 143.3 | 131.8 | 133.6 |
| Ischemic heart disease | — | — | — | 263.1 | 193.9 | 146.5 | 115.0 | 84.9 | 71.6 | 70.5 |
| Cerebrovascular diseases | 175.8 | 170.7 | 140.0 | 91.7 | 62.6 | 59.1 | 47.0 | 38.3 | 35.6 | 36.9 |
| Malignant neoplasms | 182.3 | 168.7 | 163.2 | 166.7 | 175.7 | 167.6 | 156.7 | 146.7 | 138.1 | 135.9 |
| Trachea, bronchus, and lung | 5.8 | 7.5 | 13.1 | 24.4 | 37.1 | 41.3 | 40.6 | 38.1 | 34.7 | 33.5 |
| Colon, rectum, and anus | — | 29.1 | 26.5 | 23.8 | 20.6 | 17.7 | 15.0 | 13.3 | 12.1 | 12.1 |
| Breast | 31.9 | 31.7 | 32.1 | 31.9 | 33.3 | 26.8 | 24.2 | 22.1 | 20.6 | 20.3 |
| Chronic lower respiratory diseases[f] | — | — | — | 14.9 | 26.6 | 37.4 | 38.7 | 38.0 | 37.1 | 38.6 |
| Influenza and pneumonia[g] | 41.9 | 43.8 | 32.7 | 25.1 | 30.5 | 20.7 | 18.6 | 13.1 | 13.2 | 13.5 |
| Chronic liver disease and cirrhosis | 7.8 | 8.7 | 11.9 | 9.9 | 7.1 | 6.2 | 5.8 | 6.2 | 7.1 | 7.6 |
| Diabetes mellitus[h] | 27.0 | 24.7 | 25.1 | 18.0 | 19.9 | 23.0 | 21.9 | 17.6 | 17.2 | 17.3 |
| Alzheimer's disease | — | — | — | † | † | 19.3 | 26.2 | 27.3 | 28.3 | 32.8 |
| Human immunodeficiency virus (HIV) disease | … | … | … | … | 2.2 | 2.5 | 2.3 | 1.4 | 1.1 | 1.0 |
| Unintentional injuries | 54.0 | 40.0 | 35.1 | 26.1 | 21.5 | 22.0 | 25.3 | 25.6 | 27.3 | 28.7 |
| Motor vehicle-related injuries | 11.5 | 11.7 | 14.9 | 11.8 | 11.0 | 9.5 | 8.9 | 6.5 | 6.1 | 6.4 |
| Poisoning | 1.7 | 1.1 | 1.8 | 1.3 | 1.2 | 2.5 | 5.1 | 7.5 | 9.1 | 9.8 |
| Nephritis, nephrotic syndrome, and nephrosis[h] | — | — | — | 7.3 | 7.7 | 11.5 | 12.6 | 13.0 | 11.1 | 11.3 |
| Suicide[i] | 5.6 | 5.6 | 7.4 | 5.7 | 4.8 | 4.0 | 4.4 | 5.0 | 5.8 | 6.0 |
| Homicide[j] | 2.4 | 2.6 | 3.7 | 4.4 | 4.0 | 2.8 | 2.5 | 2.3 | 2.1 | 2.2 |

## The Health Care Needs of Women

The health care needs and medical concerns of women are often different from those of men. After the onset of menarche (the first menstrual period, usually between the ages of about nine and 13 years), women's health issues are often heavily focused on their reproductive system, as they deal with issues related to fertility, contraception, pregnancy, abortion, and childbearing. Women often experience difficulties related to their menstrual cycles, and various complications associated with

[Data are based on death certificates]

— Data not available.

† Data for Alzheimer's disease are only presented for data years 1999 and beyond due to large differences in death rates caused by changes in the International Classification of Diseases (ICD) coding of the causes of death between ICD–9 and ICD–10.

. . . Category not applicable.

ªUnderlying cause of death code numbers are based on the applicable revision of the ICD for data years shown.

ᵇIncludes deaths of persons who were not residents of the 50 states and the District of Columbia (D.C.).

ᶜUnderlying cause of death was coded according to the 6th Revision of the ICD in 1950, 7th Revision in 1960, 8th Revision in 1970, and 9th Revision in 1980–1998.

ᵈStarting with 1999 data, cause of death is coded according to ICD–10.

ᵉAge-adjusted rates are calculated using the year 2000 standard population. Prior to 2001, age-adjusted rates were calculated using standard million proportions based on rounded population numbers. Starting with 2001 data, unrounded population numbers are used to calculate age-adjusted rates.

ᶠBetween 1998 and 1999, the cause of death title for Chronic obstructive pulmonary diseases in the ICD–9 was renamed to Chronic lower respiratory diseases (CLRD) in ICD–10.

ᵍ Starting with 1999 data, the rules for selecting CLRD and Pneumonia as the underlying cause of death changed, resulting in an increase in the number of deaths for CLRD and a decrease in the number of deaths for pneumonia. Therefore, trend data for these two causes of death should be interpreted with caution.

ʰStarting with 2011 data, the rules for selecting Renal failure as the underlying cause of death were changed, affecting the number of deaths in the Nephritis, nephrotic syndrome, and nephrosis and Diabetes categories. These changes directly affect deaths with mention of Renal failure and other associated conditions, such as Diabetes mellitus with renal complications. The result is a decrease in the number of deaths for Nephritis, nephrotic syndrome, and nephrosis and an increase in the number of deaths for Diabetes mellitus. Therefore, trend data for these two causes of death should be interpreted with caution.

ⁱFigures for 2001 include September 11-related deaths for which death certificates were filed as of October 24, 2002.

Notes: Starting with *Health, United States, 2003*, rates for 1991–1999 were revised using intercensal population estimates based on the 1990 and 2000 censuses. For 2000, population estimates are bridged-race April 1 census counts. Starting with *Health, United States, 2012*, rates for 2001–2009 were revised using intercensal population estimates based on the 2000 and 2010 censuses. For 2010, population estimates are bridged-race April 1 census counts. Rates for 2011 and beyond were computed using 2010-based postcensal estimates. Starting with 2003 data, some states began to collect information on more than one race on the death certificate, according to 1997 Office of Management and Budget (OMB) standards. The multiple-race data for these states were bridged to the single-race categories of the 1977 OMB standards, for comparability with other states. Data for additional years are available. Some data have been revised and differ from previous editions of *Health, United States*.

SOURCE: Adapted from "Table 17. Age-Adjusted Death Rates for Selected Causes of Death by Sex, Race, and Hispanic Origin: United States, Selected Years 1950–2015," in *Health, United States, 2016: With Chartbook on Long-term Trends in Health*, Centers for Disease Control and Prevention, National Center for Health Statistics, May 2017, https://www.cdc.gov/nchs/data/hus/hus16.pdf (accessed January 17, 2018)

pregnancy and its aftermath. Women in their 40s or 50s enter menopause, a significant hormonal change that brings multiple symptoms and may require major medical and lifestyle adjustments. Many women are affected by diseases or abnormalities of the reproductive system, and hundreds of thousands of women have hysterectomies (removal of the uterus) every year. The unique health concerns of women make their health care more expensive than that of men, presenting significant costs that must be borne both by their insurers and themselves. As Figure 6.1 shows, women were more likely than men to be unable to seek needed treatment due to cost. During the first half of 2017, 6.7% of women aged 18 to 64 years failed to obtain needed medical care due to cost, compared with 5.4% of men.

**Health Insurance**

Access to health care is highly dependent on whether an individual is covered by a health insurance policy. Women are more likely than men to have health insurance. In 2015, 9.3% of women under the age of 65 years had no health insurance, compared with 12% of men. (See Table 6.2.) People between the ages of 18 and 44 years were far more likely than younger or older Americans to be without insurance: 15.9% of those in this age group had no insurance, compared with 4.5% of those under the age of 18 years and 9% of those aged 45 to 64 years. Largely due to Medicare, almost all adults aged 65 years and older had health insurance. Many children whose families cannot afford health insurance are likewise covered through Medicaid (a state

and federal health insurance program for low-income people) and the Children's Health Insurance Program, which provides free and subsidized coverage for approximately 8.9 million children nationally. The total number of Americans without health insurance in 2015 was 28.7 million, or 10.6% of the population. These figures showed a marked improvement since 2010, when 48.3 million Americans (18.2% of the population) had no health insurance.

According to the NCHS, in *Health, United States, 2016*, 71.4% of Americans had health care coverage through their employer in 1978, and employer-based coverage numbers remained high through the 1990s. In 2000, 68.8% of Americans still had employer-based coverage, but these numbers dropped sharply over the course of the following decade. By 2010 only 58.9% of people had employer-provided coverage. The primary reason for this decline was the skyrocketing cost of health care, which made it increasingly difficult for employers to bear the cost of health insurance for their employees.

Meanwhile, as the number of people under the age of 65 years living in poverty increased during this same period, the Medicaid rolls expanded. The NCHS notes that the percentage of adults aged 18 to 64 years that were covered by Medicaid increased from 5.2% in 2000 to 13.2% in 2015. Additionally, the aging of the baby boom generation (people born between 1946 and 1964) meant that Medicare (a federal health insurance program for people aged 65 years and older and people with disabilities) was also rapidly expanding, both in terms

**FIGURE 6.1**

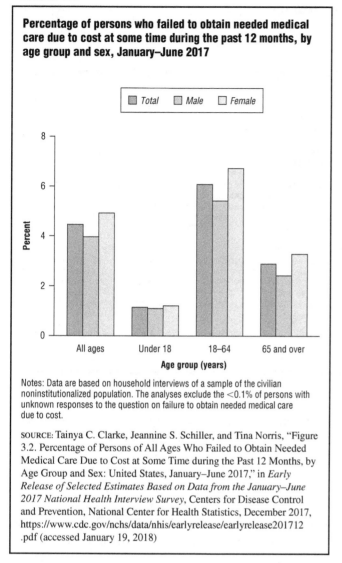

**Percentage of persons who failed to obtain needed medical care due to cost at some time during the past 12 months, by age group and sex, January–June 2017**

Notes: Data are based on household interviews of a sample of the civilian noninstitutionalized population. The analyses exclude the <0.1% of persons with unknown responses to the question on failure to obtain needed medical care due to cost.

SOURCE: Tainya C. Clarke, Jeannine S. Schiller, and Tina Norris, "Figure 3.2. Percentage of Persons of All Ages Who Failed to Obtain Needed Medical Care Due to Cost at Some Time during the Past 12 Months, by Age Group and Sex: United States, January–June 2017," in *Early Release of Selected Estimates Based on Data from the January–June 2017 National Health Interview Survey*, Centers for Disease Control and Prevention, National Center for Health Statistics, December 2017, https://www.cdc.gov/nchs/data/nhis/earlyrelease/earlyrelease201712 .pdf (accessed January 19, 2018)

of enrollee numbers and total government expenditures on the program. In 1970, 20.4 million people over the age of 65 years were enrolled in Medicare, and total expenditures were $7.5 billion. By 2000 there were 39.7 million enrollees, at a cost of $221.8 billion. By 2015 there were 55.3 million elderly Americans enrolled in Medicare, at a cost to the federal government of $647.6 billion.

### The Affordable Care Act

President Barack Obama (1961–) made reform of the health care system a major priority early in his first administration, and during the spring of 2010 he and his Democratic allies in Congress pushed through the Patient Protection and Affordable Care Act (also known as the Affordable Care Act [ACA] or Obamacare), over fierce Republican opposition. The law, which was designed to go into effect in stages between 2010 and 2014, survived a challenge that was heard by the US Supreme Court in 2012. Full implementation of the ACA began on January 1, 2014.

The ACA included a number of provisions directed at improving health outcomes for women. It outlawed the practice of denying health insurance to people with pre-existing medical conditions, including pregnancy and infertility; it ended the practice of charging different premiums based on gender; and it mandated free preventive services for all women, including mammograms (a low-dose x-ray examination that can detect small cancers), wellness visits to the doctor, and birth control. The law also required insurers to cover breastfeeding support and equipment for working mothers to ease the transition back to work after giving birth and increase the proportion of women who continued to breastfeed after their children were six months old.

Within a year of the ACA's full implementation, its benefits to women were becoming clear. Adelle Simmons, Katherine Warren, and Kellyann McClain of the US Department of Health and Human Services report in *The Affordable Care Act: Advancing the Health of Women and Children* (January 9, 2015, https://aspe.hhs .gov/system/files/pdf/77191/ib_mch.pdf) that the uninsured rate among women aged 18 to 64 years had declined 5.5% since October 2013. Of the total number of Americans who had selected a marketplace plan during the 2015 open enrollment period, more than half (56%) were women. Also through the ACA, 48.5 million women gained access to preventive services with no out-of-pocket costs.

During his first year in office, President Donald Trump (1946–) made a concerted effort to fulfill one of his central campaign promises to repeal and replace the ACA, but the Republican-controlled Congress was unable to pass legislation that would implement such a sweeping overhaul. Still, the Trump administration used its authority to address one of the most controversial provisions of the ACA: the mandate that employer-provided health insurance must include coverage for at least one form of contraception that was approved by the US Food and Drug Administration. In October 2017 the US Department of Health and Human Services issued an interim final rule that significantly broadened the scope of insurers and employers who did not want to provide contraception coverage on the basis of religious or moral beliefs. In "Trump Administration Narrows Affordable Care Act's Contraception Mandate" (WashingtonPost.com, October 6, 2017), Amy Goldstein, Juliet Eilperin, and William Wan note that many Republican lawmakers and social conservatives hailed the policy change as a victory for religious liberty, while women's advocacy and civil liberties groups vigorously objected, warning that it would leave millions of American women without access to contraception and thereby vulnerable to unintended pregnancies.

## LEADING CAUSES OF DEATH AMONG WOMEN

The NCHS indicates in *Health, United States, 2016* that the age-adjusted death rate for females of all ages in

**TABLE 6.2**

## Persons under age 65 with no health insurance coverage by selected characteristics, selected years 1984–2015

[Data are based on household interviews of a sample of the civilian noninstitutionalized population]

| Characteristic | 1984[a] | 1997 | 2000[b] | 2005[c] | 2010[c] | 2012[c] | 2013[c] | 2014[c] | 2015[c] |
|---|---|---|---|---|---|---|---|---|---|
| | | | | | Number, in millions | | | | |
| Total[d] | 29.8 | 41.0 | 41.4 | 42.1 | 48.3 | 45.2 | 44.6 | 35.7 | 28.7 |
| | | | | | Percent of population | | | | |
| Total[d] | 14.5 | 17.5 | 17.0 | 16.4 | 18.2 | 16.9 | 16.7 | 13.3 | 10.6 |
| **Age** | | | | | | | | | |
| Under 19 years | 14.1 | 14.4 | 12.9 | 9.7 | 8.3 | 7.0 | 7.1 | 5.7 | 4.8 |
| Under 6 years | 14.9 | 12.5 | 11.8 | 7.7 | 6.3 | 4.6 | 5.0 | 4.1 | 3.3 |
| 6–18 years | 13.8 | 15.2 | 13.4 | 10.6 | 9.2 | 8.1 | 8.0 | 6.5 | 5.5 |
| Under 18 years | 13.9 | 14.0 | 12.6 | 9.3 | 7.8 | 6.6 | 6.6 | 5.4 | 4.5 |
| 6–17 years | 13.4 | 14.7 | 13.0 | 10.1 | 8.6 | 7.6 | 7.4 | 6.1 | 5.1 |
| 18–64 years | 14.8 | 19.0 | 18.9 | 19.3 | 22.3 | 20.9 | 20.5 | 16.3 | 13.0 |
| 18–44 years | 17.1 | 22.4 | 22.4 | 23.5 | 27.1 | 24.8 | 24.2 | 19.7 | 15.9 |
| 18–24 years | 25.0 | 30.1 | 30.4 | 29.1 | 31.4 | 24.5 | 24.6 | 18.1 | 14.6 |
| 19–25 years | 25.1 | 31.5 | 32.3 | 31.7 | 33.8 | 26.3 | 26.7 | 19.7 | 16.0 |
| 25–34 years | 16.2 | 23.8 | 23.3 | 25.6 | 28.3 | 28.1 | 27.1 | 22.7 | 18.0 |
| 35–44 years | 11.2 | 16.7 | 16.9 | 17.9 | 22.6 | 21.7 | 21.0 | 17.7 | 14.6 |
| 45–64 years | 9.6 | 12.4 | 12.6 | 12.9 | 15.7 | 15.6 | 15.4 | 11.8 | 9.0 |
| 45–54 years | 10.5 | 12.8 | 12.8 | 14.2 | 17.9 | 17.7 | 17.1 | 13.7 | 10.2 |
| 55–64 years | 8.7 | 11.8 | 12.4 | 11.1 | 12.8 | 13.2 | 13.5 | 9.7 | 7.7 |
| **Sex** | | | | | | | | | |
| Male | 15.3 | 18.7 | 18.1 | 17.9 | 20.3 | 18.5 | 18.1 | 14.7 | 12.0 |
| Female | 13.8 | 16.3 | 15.9 | 15.0 | 16.1 | 15.4 | 15.2 | 11.9 | 9.3 |
| **Sex and marital status**[e] | | | | | | | | | |
| Male: | | | | | | | | | |
| Married | 11.1 | 13.9 | 14.1 | 14.4 | 17.2 | 16.2 | 15.9 | 12.6 | 10.6 |
| Divorced, separated, widowed | 24.9 | 28.8 | 25.8 | 28.6 | 31.4 | 29.3 | 28.1 | 23.2 | 20.0 |
| Never married | 22.4 | 27.9 | 27.2 | 27.6 | 31.1 | 27.5 | 26.9 | 21.9 | 17.4 |
| Female: | | | | | | | | | |
| Married | 11.2 | 13.0 | 13.3 | 13.0 | 14.7 | 14.6 | 14.6 | 11.6 | 8.8 |
| Divorced, separated, widowed | 19.2 | 23.2 | 21.3 | 22.1 | 23.6 | 24.2 | 22.8 | 17.7 | 13.4 |
| Never married | 16.3 | 20.5 | 21.1 | 20.0 | 21.9 | 19.6 | 19.6 | 15.1 | 12.1 |
| **Race**[f] | | | | | | | | | |
| White only | 13.6 | 16.4 | 15.4 | 15.9 | 17.6 | 16.7 | 16.3 | 13.3 | 10.7 |
| Black or African American only | 19.9 | 20.1 | 19.5 | 18.4 | 20.6 | 18.0 | 18.9 | 13.7 | 11.3 |
| American Indian or Alaska Native only | 22.5 | 38.1 | 38.4 | 32.2 | 44.0 | 27.0 | 29.4 | 28.3 | 21.4 |
| Asian only | 18.5 | 19.5 | 17.6 | 17.1 | 17.1 | 16.8 | 14.2 | 10.8 | 7.5 |
| Native Hawaiian or other Pacific Islander only | — | — | * | * | * | * | * | * | * |
| 2 or more races | — | — | 16.8 | 16.5 | 15.8 | 14.5 | 15.3 | 10.1 | 9.5 |
| **Hispanic origin and race**[f] | | | | | | | | | |
| Hispanic or Latino | 29.5 | 34.5 | 35.6 | 33.0 | 32.0 | 30.4 | 30.7 | 25.5 | 21.1 |
| Mexican | 33.8 | 39.4 | 39.9 | 36.0 | 34.8 | 33.2 | 33.4 | 27.2 | 23.5 |
| Puerto Rican | 18.3 | 19.0 | 16.4 | 16.3 | 13.7 | 14.4 | 15.6 | 13.0 | 9.6 |
| Cuban | 21.6 | 21.1 | 25.4 | 23.2 | 26.5 | 24.3 | 26.6 | 19.4 | 14.2 |
| Other Hispanic or Latino | 27.4 | 33.0 | 33.4 | 32.6 | 32.4 | 30.1 | 28.8 | 26.2 | 19.7 |
| Not Hispanic or Latino | 13.2 | 15.2 | 14.0 | 13.4 | 15.2 | 13.9 | 13.4 | 10.5 | 8.2 |
| White only | 11.9 | 13.8 | 12.5 | 12.0 | 13.7 | 12.7 | 12.2 | 9.7 | 7.5 |
| Black or African American only | 19.7 | 20.0 | 19.5 | 18.3 | 20.7 | 17.8 | 18.8 | 13.5 | 11.2 |
| **Age and percent of poverty level**[g] | | | | | | | | | |
| Under 65 years: | | | | | | | | | |
| Below 100% | 33.9 | 33.7 | 34.2 | 30.6 | 30.3 | 28.2 | 28.0 | 23.0 | 18.2 |
| 100%–199% | 21.8 | 30.6 | 31.0 | 28.6 | 32.4 | 29.3 | 29.3 | 23.4 | 18.3 |
| 100%–133% | 28.8 | 36.6 | 35.7 | 30.1 | 34.9 | 31.1 | 30.4 | 25.0 | 18.4 |
| 134%–199% | 18.7 | 27.7 | 28.7 | 27.8 | 31.0 | 28.4 | 28.6 | 22.4 | 18.1 |
| 200%–399% | 7.6 | 14.2 | 15.4 | 15.7 | 17.4 | 16.2 | 16.1 | 12.6 | 11.1 |
| 400% or more | 3.2 | 6.1 | 5.9 | 6.3 | 5.6 | 4.9 | 4.8 | 3.8 | 3.3 |
| Under 19 years: | | | | | | | | | |
| Below 100% | 29.0 | 23.8 | 22.6 | 15.2 | 11.3 | 8.3 | 8.9 | 6.7 | 5.4 |
| 100%–199% | 18.0 | 23.7 | 22.1 | 15.6 | 13.5 | 11.1 | 11.7 | 9.3 | 7.4 |
| 100%–133% | 24.4 | 28.2 | 26.5 | 15.6 | 15.9 | 9.6 | 11.6 | 9.4 | 7.7 |
| 134%–199% | 14.9 | 21.4 | 19.7 | 15.6 | 12.0 | 12.0 | 11.7 | 9.3 | 7.2 |
| 200%–399% | 5.1 | 9.7 | 9.6 | 8.2 | 7.4 | 6.8 | 6.7 | 5.7 | 5.4 |
| 400% or more | 1.8 | 4.0 | 3.5 | 3.3 | 2.3 | 2.2 | 1.9 | 1.7 | 1.6 |

**TABLE 6.2**

**Persons under age 65 with no health insurance coverage by selected characteristics, selected years 1984–2015** [CONTINUED]

[Data are based on household interviews of a sample of the civilian noninstitutionalized population]

| Characteristic | 1984[a] | 1997 | 2000[b] | 2005[c] | 2010[c] | 2012[c] | 2013[c] | 2014[c] | 2015[c] |
|---|---|---|---|---|---|---|---|---|---|
| | | | | | Percent of population | | | | |
| Under 18 years: | | | | | | | | | |
|   Below 100% | 28.9 | 23.2 | 22.0 | 14.3 | 10.6 | 7.6 | 8.2 | 6.4 | 4.9 |
|   100%–199% | 17.5 | 23.2 | 21.7 | 15.0 | 12.7 | 10.4 | 11.1 | 8.7 | 6.9 |
|     100%–133% | 24.0 | 28.1 | 26.4 | 15.1 | 15.1 | 9.0 | 11.2 | 8.9 | 7.3 |
|     134%–199% | 14.4 | 20.7 | 19.1 | 15.0 | 11.3 | 11.3 | 11.1 | 8.5 | 6.7 |
|   200%–399% | 4.9 | 9.4 | 9.3 | 7.8 | 7.0 | 6.7 | 6.3 | 5.5 | 5.2 |
|   400% or more | 1.8 | 3.9 | 3.3 | 3.2 | 2.1 | 2.1 | 1.8 | 6.1* | 1.6 |
| 18–64 years: | | | | | | | | | |
|   Below 100% | 37.6 | 41.2 | 42.4 | 40.9 | 42.7 | 40.5 | 40.0 | 32.9 | 26.2 |
|   100%–199% | 24.4 | 34.7 | 36.4 | 35.9 | 42.1 | 38.6 | 37.8 | 30.5 | 23.9 |
|     100%–133% | 31.9 | 41.7 | 41.7 | 38.9 | 45.7 | 42.2 | 40.4 | 33.9 | 24.5 |
|     134%–199% | 21.1 | 31.5 | 34.0 | 34.4 | 40.3 | 36.5 | 36.4 | 28.7 | 23.6 |
|   200%–399% | 8.9 | 16.4 | 18.2 | 19.0 | 21.3 | 19.8 | 19.7 | 15.3 | 13.3 |
|   400% or more | 3.4 | 6.7 | 6.6 | 7.1 | 6.5 | 5.6 | 5.6 | 4.3 | 3.8 |
| **Disability measure among adults 18–64 years**[h] | | | | | | | | | |
| Any basic actions difficulty or complex activity limitation | — | 20.1 | 17.6 | 19.6 | 20.8 | 20.4 | 20.4 | 16.2 | 11.6 |
| Any basic actions difficulty | — | 20.1 | 17.6 | 19.8 | 20.9 | 20.3 | 20.4 | 16.3 | 11.8 |
| Any complex activity limitation | — | 20.2 | 16.1 | 16.9 | 17.2 | 18.3 | 17.1 | 12.5 | 9.2 |
| No disability | — | 17.6 | 18.5 | 19.5 | 21.6 | 20.4 | 19.9 | 16.3 | 13.1 |
| **Geographic region** | | | | | | | | | |
| Northeast | 10.2 | 13.5 | 12.2 | 11.3 | 12.4 | 11.5 | 11.2 | 9.3 | 6.8 |
| Midwest | 11.3 | 13.2 | 12.3 | 11.9 | 14.1 | 13.6 | 13.1 | 10.3 | 8.2 |
| South | 17.7 | 20.9 | 20.5 | 21.0 | 21.9 | 20.3 | 19.9 | 16.9 | 14.2 |
| West | 18.2 | 20.6 | 20.7 | 18.4 | 20.6 | 19.0 | 18.9 | 13.3 | 10.1 |
| **Location of residence**[i] | | | | | | | | | |
| Within MSA | 13.6 | 16.9 | 16.6 | 16.1 | 17.8 | 16.4 | 16.2 | 13.0 | 10.3 |
| Outside MSA | 16.6 | 19.8 | 18.6 | 17.8 | 20.4 | 19.9 | 19.3 | 15.2 | 12.8 |

— Data not available.

*Estimates are considered unreliable.

[a]Data prior to 1997 are not strictly comparable with data for later years due to the 1997 questionnaire redesign.

[b]Estimates for 2000–2002 were calculated using 2000-based sample weights and may differ from estimates in other reports that used 1990-based sample weights for 2000–2002 estimates.

[c]Beginning in quarter 3 of the 2004 National Health Interview Survey (NHIS), persons under age 65 with no reported coverage were asked explicitly about Medicaid coverage. Estimates were calculated without and with the additional information from this question in the columns labeled 2004(1) and 2004(2), respectively, and estimates were calculated with the additional information starting with 2005 data.

[d]Includes all other races not shown separately, those with unknown marital status, unknown disability status, and, in 1984 and 1989, persons with unknown poverty level.

[e]Includes persons aged 14–64.

[f]The race groups, white, black, American Indian or Alaska Native, Asian, Native Hawaiian or other Pacific Islander, and 2 or more races, include persons of Hispanic and non-Hispanic origin. Persons of Hispanic origin may be of any race. Starting with 1999 data, race-specific estimates are tabulated according to the 1997 *Revisions to the Standards for the Classification of Federal Data on Race and Ethnicity* and are not strictly comparable with estimates for earlier years. The five single-race categories plus multiple-race categories shown in the table conform to the 1997 Standards. Starting with 1999 data, race-specific estimates are for persons who reported only one racial group; the category 2 or more races includes persons who reported more than one racial group. Prior to 1999, data were tabulated according to the 1977 Standards with four racial groups, and the Asian only category included Native Hawaiian or other Pacific Islander. Estimates for single-race categories prior to 1999 included persons who reported one race or, if they reported more than one race, identified one race as best representing their race. Starting with 2003 data, race responses of other race and unspecified multiple race were treated as missing, and then race was imputed if these were the only race responses. Almost all persons with a race response of other race were of Hispanic origin.

[g]Percent of poverty level is based on family income and family size and composition using US Census Bureau poverty thresholds. Poverty level was unknown for 10%–11% of persons under age 65 in 1984 and 1989. Missing family income data were imputed for 1995 and beyond.

[h]Any basic actions difficulty or complex activity limitation is defined as having one or more of the following limitations or difficulties: movement difficulty, emotional difficulty, sensory (seeing or hearing) difficulty, cognitive difficulty, self-care (activities of daily living or instrumental activities of daily living) limitation, social limitation, or work limitation. Starting with 2007 data, the hearing question, a component of the basic actions difficulty measure, was revised. Consequently, data prior to 2007 are not comparable with data for 2007 and beyond.

[i]MSA is metropolitan statistical area. Starting with 2006 data, MSA status is determined using 2000 census data and the 2000 standards for defining MSAs.

Notes: Persons not covered by private insurance, Medicaid, Children's Health Insurance Program (CHIP), public assistance (through 1996), state-sponsored or other government-sponsored health plans (starting in 1997), Medicare, or military plans are considered to have no health insurance coverage. Persons with only Indian Health Service coverage are considered to have no health insurance coverage. Health insurance coverage is at the time of interview. The number of persons with no health insurance coverage was calculated by multiplying the percentage with no coverage by the number of persons under age 65 in the civilian noninstitutionalized US population, which was determined from the post-stratification Census control total for each survey year. Percentages of persons without coverage were calculated with unknown values excluded from denominators.

SOURCE: "Table 105. No Health Insurance Coverage among Persons under Age 65, by Selected Characteristics: United States, Selected Years 1984–2015," in *Health, United States, 2016: With Chartbook on Long-term Trends in Health*, Centers for Disease Control and Prevention, National Center for Health Statistics, May 2017, https://www.cdc.gov/nchs/data/hus/hus16.pdf (accessed January 17, 2018)

2015 was 624.2 per 100,000 people, compared with a male death rate of 863.2 per 100,000 people. This represented a dramatic decline in the death rate since 1950, when the female death rate from all causes was 1,236 per 100,000 people and the male rate was 1,674.2 per 100,000 people. In 2015 the leading causes of death among women were heart disease, malignant neoplasms (cancer), chronic lower respiratory diseases, cerebrovascular diseases, Alzheimer's disease, and unintentional injuries. (See Table 6.3.)

TABLE 6.3

**Leading causes of death and numbers of deaths among women, by race and Hispanic origin, 1980 and 2015**

[Data are based on death certificates]

| Sex, race, Hispanic origin, and rank order | 1980 | | 2015 | |
|---|---|---|---|---|
| | Cause of death | Deaths | Cause of death | Deaths |
| **Female** | | | | |
| Rank | All causes | 914,763 | All causes | 1,339,226 |
| 1 | Diseases of heart | 355,424 | Diseases of heart | 298,840 |
| 2 | Malignant neoplasms | 190,561 | Malignant neoplasms | 282,112 |
| 3 | Cerebrovascular diseases | 100,252 | Chronic lower respiratory diseases[a, b] | 82,543 |
| 4 | Unintentional injuries | 31,538 | Cerebrovascular diseases | 82,035 |
| 5 | Pneumonia and influenza[b] | 27,045 | Alzheimer's disease | 76,871 |
| 6 | Diabetes mellitus | 20,526 | Unintentional injuries | 53,652 |
| 7 | Atherosclerosis | 17,848 | Diabetes mellitus[c] | 36,412 |
| 8 | Chronic obstructive pulmonary diseases[a] | 17,425 | Influenza and pneumonia[b] | 30,159 |
| 9 | Chronic liver disease and cirrhosis | 10,815 | Nephritis, nephrotic syndrome, and nephrosis[c] | 24,518 |
| 10 | Certain conditions originating in the perinatal period | 9,815 | Septicemia | 21,388 |
| **White female** | | | | |
| Rank | All causes | 804,729 | All causes | 1,142,685 |
| 1 | Diseases of heart | 318,668 | Diseases of heart | 254,973 |
| 2 | Malignant neoplasms | 169,974 | Malignant neoplasms | 237,728 |
| 3 | Cerebrovascular diseases | 88,639 | Chronic lower respiratory diseases[a, b] | 76,086 |
| 4 | Unintentional injuries | 27,159 | Alzheimer's disease | 69,156 |
| 5 | Pneumonia and influenza[b] | 24,559 | Cerebrovascular diseases | 69,075 |
| 6 | Diabetes mellitus | 16,743 | Unintentional injuries | 46,886 |
| 7 | Atherosclerosis | 16,526 | Diabetes mellitus[c] | 27,639 |
| 8 | Chronic obstructive pulmonary diseases[a] | 16,398 | Influenza and pneumonia[b] | 26,083 |
| 9 | Chronic liver disease and cirrhosis | 8,833 | Nephritis, nephrotic syndrome, and nephrosis[c] | 18,876 |
| 10 | Certain conditions originating in the perinatal period | 6,512 | Septicemia | 17,282 |
| **Black or African American female** | | | | |
| Rank | All causes | 102,997 | All causes | 155,402 |
| 1 | Diseases of heart | 35,079 | Diseases of heart | 35,924 |
| 2 | Malignant neoplasms | 19,176 | Malignant neoplasms | 34,139 |
| 3 | Cerebrovascular diseases | 10,941 | Cerebrovascular diseases | 9,915 |
| 4 | Unintentional injuries | 3,779 | Diabetes mellitus[c] | 6,960 |
| 5 | Diabetes mellitus | 3,534 | Alzheimer's disease | 5,973 |
| 6 | Certain conditions originating in the perinatal period | 3,092 | Chronic lower respiratory diseases[a, b] | 5,147 |
| 7 | Pneumonia and influenza[b] | 2,262 | Unintentional injuries | 4,966 |
| 8 | Homicide | 1,898 | Nephritis, nephrotic syndrome, and nephrosis[c] | 4,769 |
| 9 | Chronic liver disease and cirrhosis | 1,770 | Septicemia | 3,549 |
| 10 | Nephritis, nephrotic syndrome, and nephrosis | 1,722 | Essential hypertension and hypertensive renal disease | 3,175 |
| **American Indian or Alaska Native female** | | | | |
| Rank | All causes | 2,730 | All causes | 8,565 |
| 1 | Diseases of heart | 577 | Malignant neoplasms | 1,577 |
| 2 | Malignant neoplasms | 362 | Diseases of heart | 1,454 |
| 3 | Unintentional injuries | 344 | Unintentional injuries | 714 |
| 4 | Chronic liver disease and cirrhosis | 171 | Diabetes mellitus[c] | 514 |
| 5 | Cerebrovascular diseases | 159 | Chronic lower respiratory diseases[a, b] | 475 |
| 6 | Diabetes mellitus | 124 | Chronic liver disease and cirrhosis | 463 |
| 7 | Pneumonia and influenza[b] | 109 | Cerebrovascular diseases | 368 |
| 8 | Certain conditions originating in the perinatal period | 92 | Alzheimer's disease | 218 |
| 9 | Nephritis, nephrotic syndrome, and nephrosis | 56 | Nephritis, nephrotic syndrome, and nephrosis[c] | 186 |
| 10 | Homicide | 55 | Septicemia | 167 |

## Cardiovascular Disease

Cardiovascular disease (CVD) includes both diseases of the heart and cerebrovascular diseases (disorders of the brain that are commonly caused by high blood pressure and result in strokes or hemorrhages). According to the American Heart Association (AHA), in "Heart Disease and Stroke Statistics—2017 Update" (*Circulation*, vol. 135, no. 10, March 7, 2017), an average of one American dies every 40 seconds from CVD. For both women and men the incidence of CVD increases with age. Of the estimated 92.1 million adults who have one or more types of CVD, approximately 46.7 million are aged 60 years or older. Between 2005 and 2013 the average annual rate of having a diagnosed heart attack or fatal coronary heart disease for men aged 35 to 44 years was 25 per 1,000 men, and for men aged 75 to 84 years it was 130 per 1,000 men. For women comparable rates of heart attack and coronary heart disease fatality were observed among those a decade older: 40 per 1,000 women aged 45 to 54 years and 120 per 1,000 over the age of 85 years.

TABLE 6.3

**Leading causes of death and numbers of deaths among women, by race and Hispanic origin, 1980 and 2015** [CONTINUED]

[Data are based on death certificates]

| Sex, race, Hispanic origin, and rank order | 1980 | | 2015 | |
| --- | --- | --- | --- | --- |
| | Cause of death | Deaths | Cause of death | Deaths |
| **Asian or Pacific Islander female** | | | | |
| Rank | All causes | 4,262 | All causes | 32,574 |
| 1 | Diseases of heart | 1,091 | Malignant neoplasms | 8,668 |
| 2 | Malignant neoplasms | 1,037 | Diseases of heart | 6,489 |
| 3 | Cerebrovascular diseases | 507 | Cerebrovascular diseases | 2,677 |
| 4 | Unintentional injuries | 254 | Alzheimer's disease | 1,524 |
| 5 | Diabetes mellitus | 124 | Diabetes mellitus[c] | 1,299 |
| 6 | Certain conditions originating in the perinatal period | 118 | Unintentional injuries | 1,086 |
| 7 | Pneumonia and influenza[b] | 115 | Influenza and pneumonia[b] | 1,069 |
| 8 | Congenital anomalies | 104 | Chronic lower respiratory diseases[a, b] | 835 |
| 9 | Suicide | 90 | Nephritis, nephrotic syndrome, and nephrosis[c] | 687 |
| 10 | Homicide | 60 | Essential hypertension and hypertensive renal disease | 635 |
| **Hispanic or Latina female** | | | | |
| Rank | — | — | All causes | 81,287 |
| 1 | — | — | Malignant neoplasms | 17,957 |
| 2 | — | — | Diseases of heart | 16,176 |
| 3 | — | — | Cerebrovascular diseases | 5,251 |
| 4 | — | — | Alzheimer's disease | 4,409 |
| 5 | — | — | Diabetes mellitus[c] | 3,852 |
| 6 | — | — | Unintentional injuries | 3,739 |
| 7 | — | — | Chronic lower respiratory diseases[a, b] | 2,553 |
| 8 | — | — | Chronic liver disease and cirrhosis | 1,909 |
| 9 | — | — | Influenza and pneumonia[b] | 1,762 |
| 10 | — | — | Nephritis, nephrotic syndrome, and nephrosis[c] | 1,744 |

—Data not available. Complete coverage of all states for the Hispanic origin variable began in 1997.

[a]Between 1998 and 1999, the cause of death title for Chronic obstructive pulmonary diseases in the International Classification of Diseases, 9th Revision (ICD–9) was renamed to Chronic lower respiratory diseases (CLRD) in ICD–10.

[b]Starting with 1999 data, the rules for selecting CLRD and Pneumonia as the underlying cause of death changed, resulting in an increase in the number of deaths for CLRD and a decrease in the number of deaths for pneumonia. Therefore, trend data for these two causes of death should be interpreted with caution.

[c]Starting with 2011 data, the rules for selecting Renal failure as the underlying cause of death were changed, affecting the number of deaths in the Nephritis, nephrotic syndrome, and nephrosis and Diabetes categories. These changes directly affect deaths with mention of Renal failure and other associated conditions, such as Diabetes mellitus with renal complications. The result is a decrease in the number of deaths for Nephritis, nephrotic syndrome, and nephrosis and an increase in the number of deaths for Diabetes mellitus. Therefore, trend data for these two causes of death should be interpreted with caution.

Notes: Starting with 2003 data, some states began to collect information on more than ane race on the death certificate, according to 1997 Office of Management and Budget (OMB) standards. The multiple-race data for these states were bridged to the single-race categories of the 1977 OMB standards, for comparability with other states. The race groups, white, black, Asian or Pacific Islander, and American Indian or Alaska Native, include persons of Hispanic and non-Hispanic origin. Persons of Hispanic origin may be of any race.

SOURCE: Adapted from "Table 19. Leading Causes of Death and Numbers of Deaths, by Sex, Race, and Hispanic Origin: United States, 1980 and 2015," in *Health, United States, 2016: With Chartbook on Long-term Trends in Health*, Centers for Disease Control and Prevention, National Center for Health Statistics, May 2017, https://www.cdc.gov/nchs/data/hus/hus16.pdf (accessed January 17, 2018)

Research suggests that the delay of CVD incidence in women may be attributable to premenopausal women's production of estrogen, which appears to help protect them from CVD. Although women first experience cardiovascular events about 10 years later than men, this gender gap decreases with age as women's estrogen levels drop at menopause.

Smoking, a diet high in fat, being overweight or obese, lack of exercise, high cholesterol, and high blood pressure are all risk factors for developing CVD. The use of oral contraceptives, especially if combined with smoking, also increases the risk factor for women.

**DISEASES OF THE HEART.** Heart disease, which includes all diseases of the heart such as coronary heart disease and angina, was the leading cause of death among American women in 2015, killing 298,840 women that

year and accounting for 22.3% of all female deaths. (See Table 6.3.) Diseases of the heart were the leading cause of death among white and African American women; by contrast, cancer claimed a slightly greater number of lives among Native American/Alaskan Native, Asian or Pacific Islander, and Hispanic women in 2015. Diseases of the heart were also the leading cause of death among women in 1980, but at that time it accounted for both a higher number of female deaths (355,424) and a larger percentage of all female deaths (38.9%). The decline in heart disease mortality corresponds to decreases in unhealthy behaviors such as smoking and to medical and pharmaceutical advances.

Coronary heart disease is the most common form of heart disease; it often results in heart attacks, approximately 15% of which are fatal. According to the AHA, in "Heart Disease and Stroke Statistics—2017 Update," the average age for a first heart attack is 65.3 years for men and 71.8 years for women. Among those aged 45 years and older who have had a first heart attack, 23% of women and 18% of men typically die within a year. Because women tend to experience heart attacks at older ages than men, they are more likely to die within a few weeks. Within five years of a first heart attack, 47% of women aged 45 years and older and 36% of men the same age typically die. The median (the middle value) survival time after a first heart attack is 5.5 years for women over the age of 45 years and 8.2 years for men the same age. Medicare claims data indicate that only 13.9% of Medicare beneficiaries undergo cardiac rehabilitation after a heart attack, and the rate of enrollment is even lower for women.

CEREBROVASCULAR DISEASES. Cerebrovascular diseases are a group of brain disorders generally related to high blood pressure (hypertension), which over time damages blood vessels so that changes in blood pressure can lead to strokes (intracranial hemorrhages). Cerebrovascular diseases were the fourth-leading cause of death among females as a group in 2015, accounting for 82,035 deaths (6.1% of all deaths), but there was variation among racial and ethnic groups. (See Table 6.3.) Among white women cerebrovascular diseases were the fifth-leading cause of death, whereas among African American, Asian or Pacific Islander, and Hispanic women they were the third-leading cause of death. Among Native American/Alaskan Native women cerebrovascular diseases were the seventh-leading cause of death, eclipsed by unintentional injuries, diabetes, chronic lower respiratory diseases, and liver disease, in addition to cancer and heart disease. As with heart disease, both the number (100,252) and the percentage (11%) of female deaths from cerebrovascular diseases were much higher in 1980 but have fallen due to healthier lifestyles and medical advancements.

In "Heart Disease and Stroke Statistics—2017 Update," the AHA notes that because women live longer than men, they have a higher lifetime risk of stroke than men (one out of five versus one out of six). Women constituted 58.3% of all US stroke deaths in 2014. Women are less likely than men to have high blood pressure, the most important cause of cerebrovascular diseases, until the age of 64 years. The AHA notes that between the ages of 65 and 74 years, 65.8% of women and 63.6% of men have high blood pressure. After the age of 75 years, 81.2% of women and 73.4% of men have high blood pressure. Non-Hispanic African American women have a much higher incidence of high blood pressure than do either non-Hispanic white women or Hispanic women. Oral contraceptive use has been linked to high blood pressure, particularly among older and obese women.

## Cancer

Malignant neoplasms were the second-leading cause of death among all women in 2015, accounting for 282,112 deaths, or 21.1% of the total. (See Table 6.3.) Cancer prevalence varied among women of different racial and ethnic groups. It was the second-leading cause of death among white and African American women, and it was the leading cause of death among Native American/Alaskan Native, Asian or Pacific Islander, and Hispanic women. Cancer was also the second-leading cause of death among all women in 1980.

According to the American Cancer Society (ACS), in *Cancer Facts and Figures, 2018* (January 2018, https://www.cancer.org/content/dam/cancer-org/research/cancer-facts-and-statistics/annual-cancer-facts-and-figures/2018/cancer-facts-and-figures-2018.pdf), an estimated 878,980 new cases of cancer would be diagnosed among women in 2018, compared with an estimated 856,370 new cases in men. The ACS estimates that 286,010 women and 323,630 men would die from cancer in 2018.

Breast cancer is the most common type of cancer in females, while prostate cancer is the most common form in males (although lung cancer is the deadliest cancer for both sexes). Cancer of the lung and bronchus are the second-most common cancers among both men and women, followed by cancer of the colon and rectum.

BREAST CANCER. The ACS projects in *Cancer Facts and Figures, 2018* that 266,120 new cases of invasive breast cancer would be diagnosed in women in 2018, accounting for about 30% of all newly diagnosed cancers in women. Men contract breast cancer with extreme rarity; women were expected to account for 99% of newly diagnosed breast cancers over the course of 2018. In *Breast Cancer Facts and Figures 2017–2018* (2017, https://www.cancer.org/content/dam/cancer-org/research/cancer-facts-and-statistics/breast-cancer-facts-and-figures/breast-cancer-facts-and-figures-2017-2018.pdf), the ACS observes that there was a sharp (nearly 7%) decrease in breast cancer incidence between 2002 and 2003 following the widespread discontinuation of menopausal hormone therapy (or hormone replacement therapy), which was found to be linked to breast cancer and heart disease. Overall, breast cancer incidence rates have been stable since 2000 among women aged 50 years and older and since 2007 among younger women. The ACS also expects that another 63,960 cases of in situ breast cancer (cancerous tissue that has not yet become invasive) would be diagnosed in 2018. The increase in the diagnosis rate of this type of cancer during the last quarter of the 20th century is attributed to the growth in the use of mammography screening.

Risk factors for breast cancer include a family history of the disease, early menarche and/or late menopause, childlessness or having a first child after the age of 30, use of oral contraceptives or hormone replacement therapy, lack of exercise, smoking, obesity, alcohol consumption, and high breast tissue density. Although there is concern that environmental pollutants are linked to rising breast cancer incidence, no studies have yet found a connection.

The ACS expects that 40,920 women would die of breast cancer in 2018. Although breast cancer remained the second-most deadly form of cancer for women, after lung cancer, death rates from breast cancer have been declining since 1989, especially for younger women, largely due to an increase in early detection and advances in treatment effectiveness. In 1987 only 29% of women aged 40 years and older had had a mammogram in the previous two years, compared with 64% in 2015. (See Table 6.4) The rate of mammography screening varies according to poverty, access to health insurance, and education level. In 2015, 52.2% of women over the age of 40 years living below the poverty level received a mammogram, compared with 54.9% of women living at or up to 199% of poverty; this rate rose steadily, too, as incomes rose. Among women who had been uninsured for more than 12 months, only 23.9% received screening, compared with 70.6% of women who had been insured continuously over the preceding 12 months. Among women who had not graduated from high school, 51.7% received a mammogram in 2015, compared with 70.5% of women who had at least some college.

Although most major health organizations agree that mammography saves many women's lives each year by increasing early detection of breast cancer, there is debate about the age at which women should begin receiving routine mammograms and the extent to which mammography may contribute to overdiagnosis and overtreatment of breast cancer, especially ductal carcinoma in situ (DCIS) and small, slow-growing invasive breast cancers that might remain harmless if left undetected and untreated. In "Weighing the Benefits and Risks of Mammography" (August 17, 2017, http://ww5.komen.org/BreastCancer/TheMammographyDebate.html), the Susan G. Komen Foundation, a leading nonprofit organization in the fight against breast cancer, cites data estimating that about 19% of DCIS and invasive breast cancers identified in mammograms may be overdiagnosed. Researchers are looking for ways to differentiate between cases of DCIS and small, invasive breast cancer that are more likely to progress and those that are not. The foundation notes, "This would allow treatment to be targeted to those who are at higher risk and might allow some people to avoid treatment."

In 2009 the US Preventive Services Task Force, an independent, government-appointed panel of medical experts, issued a controversial recommendation that, for women considered to be at normal risk for breast cancer,

routine screening should begin at age 50, rather than at 40, as had long been the accepted standard. The recommendation was based on the task force's findings that mammograms saved too few lives among women between the ages of 40 and 49 years, compared with the disproportionate overdiagnosis and overtreatment of breast cancer for women in this age bracket. Although some advocacy groups, including the National Breast Cancer Coalition, welcomed the task force's recommendations, the ACS rejected the task force's recommendation, maintaining that women should have the option to begin regular mammography screening at age 40 if they choose, and should begin regular screenings at age 45, given that the potential benefits of such early breast cancer detection still outweighs the risks. Under the ACA, both Medicare and private insurance plans are required to cover the full cost of mammogram screening for women aged 40 years and older.

LUNG CANCER. In *Cancer Facts and Figures, 2018*, the ACS estimates that there would be 112,350 new cases of lung cancer diagnosed among women in 2015, accounting for 12.8% of all new cancer diagnoses in women. The lung cancer incidence rate for women is lower than it is for men, who are projected to have 121,680 newly diagnosed cases of the disease in 2018. The incidence rate for men, however, has been declining since the mid-1980s, whereas women's incidence rates did not begin to decline until the middle of the first decade of the 21st century. Between 2010 and 2014 women had a lung cancer incidence rate of 52.8 per 100,000 population, compared with a rate of 73 per 100,000 population for men.

Lung cancer has long been the deadliest form of cancer for both women and men. In 2018 it was projected to account for 70,500, or 24.6%, of all cancer deaths among women. As with incidence rates, the yearly death rates from lung cancer for women (35.4 deaths per every 100,000 women in 2011–15) are significantly lower than those for men (53.8 deaths per every 100,000 men in 2011–15). Smoking is by far the leading cause of lung cancer, and gender differences in incidence and death rates are commonly attributed to historical differences in men's and women's patterns of smoking uptake and cessation. Other causes of lung cancer include exposure to industrial materials such as arsenic, organic chemicals such as radon and asbestos, radiation, and air pollution and secondhand smoke.

## SEXUALLY TRANSMITTED DISEASES AND INFECTIONS
### HIV/AIDS

HIV/AIDS is much more prevalent in men than it is in women, owing to the fact that the disease is most commonly transmitted through male-to-male sexual contact. According to the Centers for Disease Control and

TABLE 6.4

**Use of mammography among women aged 40 years and older, by selected characteristics, selected years 1987–2015**

[Data are based on household interviews of a sample of the civilian noninstitutionalized population]

| Characteristic | 1987 | 1993 | 1994 | 2000 | 2005 | 2008 | 2010 | 2013 | 2015 |
|---|---|---|---|---|---|---|---|---|---|
| | Percent of women having a mammogram within the past 2 years[a] | | | | | | | | |
| 40 years and over, age-adjusted[b, c] | 29.0 | 59.7 | 61.0 | 70.4 | 66.6 | 67.1 | 66.5 | 65.7 | 64.0 |
| 40 years and over, crude[b] | 28.7 | 59.7 | 60.9 | 70.4 | 66.8 | 67.6 | 67.1 | 66.8 | 65.3 |
| 50 years and over, age-adjusted[b, c] | 27.3 | 59.7 | 60.9 | 73.7 | 68.2 | 70.3 | 68.8 | 69.1 | 67.2 |
| 50 years and over, crude[b] | 27.4 | 59.7 | 60.6 | 73.6 | 68.4 | 70.5 | 69.2 | 69.5 | 67.8 |
| **Age** | | | | | | | | | |
| 40–49 years | 31.9 | 59.9 | 61.3 | 64.3 | 63.5 | 61.5 | 62.3 | 59.6 | 58.3 |
| 50–64 years | 31.7 | 65.1 | 66.5 | 78.7 | 71.8 | 74.2 | 72.6 | 71.4 | 71.3 |
| 65 years and over | 22.8 | 54.2 | 55.0 | 67.9 | 63.8 | 65.5 | 64.4 | 66.9 | 63.3 |
| 65–74 years | 26.6 | 64.2 | 63.0 | 74.0 | 72.5 | 72.6 | 71.9 | 75.3 | 72.2 |
| 75 years and over | 17.3 | 41.0 | 44.6 | 61.3 | 54.7 | 57.9 | 55.7 | 56.5 | 51.5 |
| **Race[d]** | | | | | | | | | |
| 40 years and over, crude: | | | | | | | | | |
| White only | 29.6 | 60.0 | 60.6 | 71.4 | 67.4 | 67.9 | 67.4 | 66.8 | 65.3 |
| Black or African American only | 24.0 | 59.1 | 64.3 | 67.8 | 64.9 | 68.0 | 67.9 | 67.1 | 69.8 |
| American Indian or Alaska Native only | * | 49.8 | 65.8 | 47.4 | 72.8 | 62.7 | 71.2 | 62.6 | 51.5 |
| Asian only | * | 55.1 | 55.8 | 53.5 | 54.6 | 66.1 | 62.4 | 66.6 | 59.7 |
| Native Hawaiian or other Pacific Islander only | — | — | — | * | * | * | * | * | * |
| 2 or more races | — | — | — | 69.2 | 63.7 | 55.2 | 51.4 | 65.4 | 62.7 |
| **Hispanic origin and race[d]** | | | | | | | | | |
| 40 years and over, crude: | | | | | | | | | |
| Hispanic or Latina | 18.3 | 50.9 | 51.9 | 61.2 | 58.8 | 61.2 | 64.2 | 61.4 | 60.9 |
| Not Hispanic or Latina | 29.4 | 60.3 | 61.5 | 71.1 | 67.5 | 68.3 | 67.4 | 67.5 | 65.9 |
| White only | 30.3 | 60.6 | 61.3 | 72.2 | 68.3 | 68.7 | 67.8 | 67.6 | 65.8 |
| Black or African American only | 23.8 | 59.2 | 64.4 | 67.9 | 65.2 | 68.3 | 67.4 | 67.2 | 69.7 |
| **Age and Hispanic origin and race[d]** | | | | | | | | | |
| 40–49 years: | | | | | | | | | |
| Hispanic or Latina | 15.3* | 52.6 | 47.5 | 54.1 | 54.2 | 54.1 | 59.8 | 56.4 | 50.3 |
| Not Hispanic or Latina: | | | | | | | | | |
| White only | 34.3 | 61.6 | 62.0 | 67.2 | 65.5 | 64.1 | 62.6 | 60.3 | 58.8 |
| Black or African American only | 27.8 | 55.6 | 67.2 | 60.9 | 62.1 | 59.5 | 63.5 | 59.4 | 67.8 |
| 50–64 years: | | | | | | | | | |
| Hispanic or Latina | 23.0 | 59.2 | 60.1 | 66.5 | 61.5 | 71.3 | 68.6 | 65.6 | 71.6 |
| Not Hispanic or Latina: | | | | | | | | | |
| White only | 33.6 | 66.2 | 67.5 | 80.6 | 73.5 | 74.1 | 73.5 | 72.1 | 71.4 |
| Black or African American only | 26.4 | 65.5 | 63.6 | 77.7 | 71.6 | 76.7 | 74.0 | 71.7 | 73.5 |
| 65 years and over: | | | | | | | | | |
| Hispanic or Latina | * | 35.7* | 48.0 | 68.3 | 63.8 | 59.0 | 65.2 | 63.2 | 60.9 |
| Not Hispanic or Latina: | | | | | | | | | |
| White only | 24.0 | 54.7 | 54.9 | 68.3 | 64.7 | 66.1 | 65.0 | 67.3 | 63.9 |
| Black or African American only | 14.1 | 56.3 | 61.0 | 65.5 | 60.5 | 66.4 | 60.9 | 68.8 | 65.2 |
| **Age and percent of poverty level[e]** | | | | | | | | | |
| 40 years and over, crude: | | | | | | | | | |
| Below 100% | 14.6 | 41.1 | 44.2 | 54.8 | 48.5 | 51.4 | 51.4 | 49.9 | 52.2 |
| 100%–199% | 20.9 | 47.5 | 48.6 | 58.1 | 55.3 | 55.8 | 53.8 | 56.7 | 54.9 |
| 200%–399% | 29.7 | 63.2 | 65.0 | 68.8 | 67.2 | 64.4 | 66.2 | 66.0 | 63.4 |
| 400% or more | 42.9 | 74.1 | 74.1 | 81.5 | 76.6 | 79.0 | 78.1 | 77.2 | 74.7 |
| 40–49 years: | | | | | | | | | |
| Below 100% | 18.6 | 36.1 | 43.0 | 47.4 | 42.5 | 46.6 | 48.1 | 43.3 | 45.8 |
| 100%–199% | 18.4 | 47.8 | 47.6 | 43.6 | 49.8 | 46.5 | 46.2 | 52.0 | 47.5 |
| 200%–399% | 31.2 | 63.0 | 64.5 | 60.2 | 61.8 | 56.8 | 59.2 | 58.5 | 55.6 |
| 400% or more | 44.1 | 69.6 | 69.9 | 75.8 | 73.6 | 72.5 | 73.6 | 69.0 | 68.2 |
| 50–64 years: | | | | | | | | | |
| Below 100% | 14.6 | 47.3 | 46.2 | 61.7 | 50.4 | 57.5 | 54.7 | 55.0 | 56.9 |
| 100%–199% | 24.2 | 47.0 | 49.0 | 68.3 | 58.8 | 58.9 | 57.3 | 57.2 | 60.5 |
| 200%–399% | 29.7 | 66.1 | 69.6 | 75.1 | 70.7 | 69.8 | 70.7 | 69.5 | 69.0 |
| 400% or more | 44.7 | 78.7 | 78.0 | 86.9 | 80.6 | 84.3 | 82.8 | 80.9 | 79.2 |
| 65 years and over: | | | | | | | | | |
| Below 100% | 13.1 | 40.4 | 43.9 | 54.8 | 52.3 | 49.1 | 50.6 | 49.8 | 52.7 |
| 100%–199% | 19.9 | 47.6 | 48.8 | 60.3 | 56.1 | 59.4 | 55.5 | 59.3 | 54.4 |
| 200%–399% | 27.7 | 60.3 | 61.0 | 71.1 | 68.6 | 65.0 | 67.2 | 68.1 | 63.3 |
| 400% or more | 34.7 | 71.3 | 73.0 | 81.9 | 72.6 | 78.3 | 74.5 | 79.0 | 73.1 |

Prevention (CDC), in *HIV Surveillance Report: Diagnoses of HIV Infection in the United States and Dependent Areas, 2016* (November 2017, https://www.cdc.gov/hiv/pdf/library/reports/surveillance/cdc-hiv-surveillance-report-2016-vol-28.pdf), 232,692 females aged 13 years and older and 738,832 males the same age were living with

TABLE 6.4

**Use of mammography among women aged 40 years and older, by selected characteristics, selected years 1987–2015** [CONTINUED]

[Data are based on household interviews of a sample of the civilian noninstitutionalized population]

| Characteristic | 1987 | 1993 | 1994 | 2000 | 2005 | 2008 | 2010 | 2013 | 2015 |
|---|---|---|---|---|---|---|---|---|---|
| Health insurance status at the time of interview[f] | | Percent of women having a mammogram within the past 2 years[a] | | | | | | | |
| 40–64 years: | | | | | | | | | |
| Insured | — | 66.2 | 68.3 | 76.0 | 72.5 | 73.4 | 74.1 | 72.1 | 69.7 |
| Private | — | 67.1 | 69.4 | 77.1 | 74.5 | 74.2 | 75.6 | 73.4 | 72.2 |
| Medicaid | — | 51.9 | 54.5 | 61.7 | 55.6 | 64.2 | 64.4 | 63.5 | 57.7 |
| Uninsured | — | 36.0 | 34.0 | 40.7 | 38.1 | 39.7 | 36.0 | 37.3 | 30.0 |
| Health insurance status prior to interview[f] | | | | | | | | | |
| 40–64 years: | | | | | | | | | |
| Insured continuously all 12 months | — | 66.6 | 68.6 | 76.8 | 73.1 | 74.1 | 74.7 | 72.7 | 70.6 |
| Uninsured for any period up to 12 months | — | 49.4 | 49.9 | 53.0 | 51.3 | 55.3 | 57.3 | 54.5 | 50.0 |
| Uninsured more than 12 months | — | 28.4 | 26.6 | 34.0 | 32.9 | 34.6 | 30.0 | 32.8 | 23.9 |
| Age and education[g] | | | | | | | | | |
| 40 years and over, crude: | | | | | | | | | |
| No high school diploma or GED | 17.8 | 46.4 | 48.2 | 57.7 | 52.8 | 53.8 | 53.0 | 53.6 | 51.7 |
| High school diploma or GED | 31.3 | 59.0 | 61.0 | 69.7 | 64.9 | 65.2 | 64.4 | 63.4 | 60.1 |
| Some college or more | 37.7 | 69.5 | 69.7 | 76.2 | 72.7 | 73.4 | 72.1 | 71.6 | 70.5 |
| 40–49 years: | | | | | | | | | |
| No high school diploma or GED | 15.1 | 43.6 | 50.4 | 46.8 | 51.2 | 46.9 | 44.9 | 46.9 | 43.8 |
| High school diploma or GED | 32.6 | 56.6 | 55.8 | 59.0 | 58.8 | 57.2 | 58.4 | 51.8 | 47.5 |
| Some college or more | 39.2 | 66.1 | 68.7 | 70.6 | 68.3 | 66.3 | 66.5 | 64.3 | 64.0 |
| 50–64 years: | | | | | | | | | |
| No high school diploma or GED | 21.2 | 51.4 | 51.6 | 66.5 | 56.9 | 64.9 | 56.7 | 58.2 | 58.1 |
| High school diploma or GED | 33.8 | 62.4 | 67.8 | 76.6 | 70.1 | 70.4 | 69.9 | 66.9 | 67.0 |
| Some college or more | 40.5 | 78.5 | 74.7 | 84.2 | 77.0 | 78.5 | 77.0 | 75.7 | 75.3 |
| 65 years and over: | | | | | | | | | |
| No high school diploma or GED | 16.5 | 44.2 | 45.6 | 57.4 | 50.7 | 49.2 | 54.1 | 53.4 | 50.8 |
| High school diploma or GED | 25.9 | 57.4 | 59.1 | 71.8 | 64.3 | 65.7 | 62.5 | 66.5 | 60.0 |
| Some college or more | 32.3 | 64.8 | 64.3 | 74.1 | 73.0 | 75.6 | 70.9 | 73.6 | 69.8 |
| Disability measure[h] | | | | | | | | | |
| 40 years and over, crude: | | | | | | | | | |
| Any basic actions difficulty or complex activity limitation | — | — | — | 67.8 | 63.5 | 63.9 | 63.3 | 63.5 | 62.2 |
| Any basic actions difficulty | — | — | — | 67.9 | 63.5 | 63.9 | 63.3 | 63.8 | 62.4 |
| Any complex activity limitation | — | — | — | 64.1 | 59.9 | 60.2 | 58.2 | 58.4 | 56.1 |
| No disability | — | — | — | 72.6 | 69.8 | 71.1 | 70.8 | 69.8 | 68.0 |

*Estimates are considered unreliable.
—Data not available.
[a]Questions concerning use of mammography differed slightly on the National Health Interview Survey across survey years. Data prior to 1997 are not strictly comparable with data for later years due to the 1997 questionnaire redesign.
[b]Includes all other races not shown separately, unknown poverty level in 1987, unknown health insurance status, unknown education level, and unknown disability status.
[c]Estimates for women aged 40 and over are age-adjusted to the year 2000 standard population using four age groups: 40–49 years, 50–64 years, 65–74 years, and 75 years and over. Estimates for women 50 years of age and over are age-adjusted using three age groups.
[d]The race groups, white, black, American Indian or Alaska Native, Asian, Native Hawaiian or other Pacific Islander, and 2 or more races, include persons of Hispanic and non-Hispanic origin. Persons of Hispanic origin may be of any race. Starting with 1999 data, race-specific estimates are tabulated according to the 1997 Revisions to the Standards for the Classification of Federal Data on Race and Ethnicity and are not strictly comparable with estimates for earlier years. The five single-race categories plus multiple-race categories shown in the table conform to the 1997 Standards. Starting with 1999 data, race-specific estimates are for persons who reported only one racial group; the category 2 or more races includes persons who reported more than one racial group. Prior to 1999, data were tabulated according to the 1977 Standards with four racial groups, and the Asian only category included Native Hawaiian or other Pacific Islander. Estimates for single-race categories prior to 1999 included persons who reported one race or, if they reported more than one race, identified one race as best representing their race. Starting with 2003 data, race responses of other race and unspecified multiple race were treated as missing, and then race was imputed if these were the only race responses. Almost all persons with a race response of other race were of Hispanic origin.
[e]Percent of poverty level is based on family income and family size and composition using US Census Bureau poverty thresholds. Poverty level was unknown for 11% of women aged 40 and over in 1987. Missing family income data were imputed for 1997 and beyond.
[f]Health insurance categories are mutually exclusive. Persons who reported both Medicaid and private coverage are classified as having private coverage. Starting with 1997 data, state-sponsored health plan coverage is included as Medicaid coverage. Starting with 1999 data, coverage by the Children's Health Insurance Program (CHIP) is included with Medicaid coverage. In addition to private and Medicaid, the insured category also includes military plans, other government-sponsored health plans, and Medicare, not shown separately. Persons not covered by private insurance, Medicaid, CHIP, public assistance (through 1996), state-sponsored or other government-sponsored health plans (starting in 1997), Medicare, or military plans are considered to have no health insurance coverage. Persons with only Indian Health Service coverage are considered to have no health insurance coverage.
[g]Education categories shown are for 1998 and subsequent years. GED is General Educational Development high school equivalency diploma. In years prior to 1998, the following categories based on number of years of school completed were used: less than 12 years, 12 years, 13 years or more.
[h]Any basic actions difficulty or complex activity limitation is defined as having one or more of the following limitations or difficulties: movement difficulty, emotional difficulty, sensory (seeing or hearing) difficulty, cognitive difficulty, self-care (activities of daily living or instrumental activities of daily living) limitation, social limitation, or work limitation. Starting with 2007 data, the hearing question, a component of the basic actions difficulty measure, was revised. Consequently, data prior to 2007 are not comparable with 2007 data and beyond.
Notes: Data starting in 1997 are not strictly comparable with data for earlier years due to the 1997 questionnaire redesign.

SOURCE: "Table 70. Use of Mammography among Women Aged 40 and over, by Selected Characteristics: United States, Selected Years 1987–2015," in *Health, United States, 2016: With Chartbook on Long-term Trends in Health*, Centers for Disease Control and Prevention, National Center for Health Statistics, May 2017, https://www.cdc.gov/nchs/data/hus/hus16.pdf (accessed January 17, 2018)

the human immunodeficiency virus (HIV) in the United States in 2015. The prevalence rate of females living with the virus was 169.7 per 100,000, compared with 563.9 per 100,000 for males. An estimated 123,707 (90.2

per 100,000) females were living with Stage 3 HIV, or acquired immunodeficiency syndrome (AIDS), compared with 398,300 males (304 per 100,000).

The rate of new HIV diagnoses in 2016 was estimated at 5.4 per 100,000 female adults and adolescents and 24.3 per 100,000 male adults and adolescents. (See Table 6.5.) As Figure 6.2 shows, among heterosexual women, African American women are far more likely than Hispanic and white women to be diagnosed with HIV. The CDC notes that 4,142 African American heterosexual women were diagnosed with HIV in 2015, which was more than four times the number of Hispanic heterosexual women (1,010) and white heterosexual women (968). African American heterosexual women also accounted for more than twice as many HIV diagnoses as African American heterosexual men (1,926) in 2015. By far the leading cause of infection among females was heterosexual contact with an infected partner, which accounted for 6,541 (86.9%) of the 7,529 new diagnoses in 2016. (See Table 6.5.) Males were much less likely to be infected via heterosexual contact.

The rate of new AIDS diagnoses in 2016 was estimated at 3.1 per 100,000 female adults and adolescents and 10.5 per 100,000 male adults and adolescents. (See Table 6.6.) The CDC indicates in *HIV Surveillance in Women* (November 2017, https://www.cdc.gov/hiv/pdf/library/slidesets/cdc-hiv-surveillance-women-2016.pdf) that the percentage of female adult and adolescent AIDS cases among all AIDS cases increased steadily from 8% in 1985 to a peak of more than 25% in 2007. Since then, the percentage of female adult and adolescent AIDS cases among all AIDS cases has gradually declined, reaching 24% in 2015. The number of cases peaked during the mid-1990s and has since declined steadily with the success of new drug therapies for those diagnosed with HIV. From the beginning of the AIDS epidemic during the early 1980s to 2016, females accounted for 251,653 (20.4%) of the total 1,232,346 AIDS cases. (See Table 6.6.)

Between the beginning of the AIDS epidemic and 2015, an estimated 126,525 female adults and adolescents died from the disease. (See Table 6.7.) The number of people who die each year from AIDS has been steadily declining since the introduction of effective drug therapies during the 1990s. In 2015 an estimated 12,497 people in the United States died of AIDS, down from 13,556 in 2011. Of the 12,497 AIDS deaths in 2015, an estimated 3,042 (24.3%) were female adults and adolescents.

Infected women may transmit HIV to their newborns during childbirth. In *HIV Surveillance Report: Diagnoses of HIV Infection in the United States and Dependent Areas, 2016*, the CDC estimates that of the 2,322 children under the age of 13 years who were living with HIV in 2015, 1,872 (80.6%) of them had been infected via their mother with HIV infection. Planned cesarean deliveries combined with antiretroviral drug therapy throughout

**TABLE 6.5**

Diagnoses of HIV infection, by transmission category, 2011–16

| Transmission category[b] | 2011 No. | 2011 Rate[a] | 2012 No. | 2012 Rate[a] | 2013 No. | 2013 Rate[a] | 2014 No. | 2014 Rate[a] | 2015 No. | 2015 Rate[a] | 2016 No. | 2016 Rate[a] |
|---|---|---|---|---|---|---|---|---|---|---|---|---|
| **Male adult or adolescent** | | | | | | | | | | | | |
| Male-to-male sexual contact | 26,052 | — | 26,254 | — | 25,719 | — | 26,642 | — | 26,459 | — | 26,570 | — |
| Injection drug use | 1,666 | — | 1,489 | — | 1,396 | — | 1,297 | — | 1,343 | — | 1,285 | — |
| Male-to-male sexual contact and injection drug use | 1,455 | — | 1,407 | — | 1,288 | — | 1,271 | — | 1,270 | — | 1,201 | — |
| Heterosexual contact[c] | 3,745 | — | 3,461 | — | 3,323 | — | 3,223 | — | 3,187 | — | 3,037 | — |
| Other[d] | 46 | — | 59 | — | 46 | — | 44 | — | 46 | — | 38 | — |
| **Subtotal** | 32,964 | 26.1 | 32,671 | 25.6 | 31,772 | 24.7 | 32,476 | 25.0 | 32,306 | 24.7 | 32,131 | 24.3 |
| **Female adult or adolescent** | | | | | | | | | | | | |
| Injection drug use | 1,262 | — | 1,147 | — | 1,002 | — | 933 | — | 1,004 | — | 939 | — |
| Heterosexual contact[c] | 7,517 | — | 7,071 | — | 6,640 | — | 6,653 | — | 6,401 | — | 6,541 | — |
| Other[d] | 43 | — | 40 | — | 52 | — | 35 | — | 30 | — | 49 | — |
| **Subtotal** | 8,822 | 6.7 | 8,257 | 6.2 | 7,694 | 5.7 | 7,620 | 5.6 | 7,435 | 5.4 | 7,529 | 5.4 |
| **Total** | 41,984 | 13.5 | 41,168 | 13.1 | 39,652 | 12.5 | 40,276 | 12.6 | 39,876 | 12.4 | 39,782 | 12.3 |

[a]Rates are per 100,000 population. Rates are not calculated by transmission category because of the lack of denominator data.
[b]Data have been statistically adjusted to account for missing transmission category; therefore, values may not sum to column subtotals and total.
[c]Heterosexual contact with a person known to have, or to be at high risk for, human immunodeficiency virus (HIV) infection.
[d]Includes hemophilia, blood transfusion, perinatal exposure, and risk factor not reported or not identified.
Note. Data for the year 2016 are preliminary (subject to change) because they are based on only a 6-month reporting delay. Data for the year 2016 should not be used when assessing trends.

SOURCE: Adapted from "Table 1a. Diagnoses of HIV Infection, by Year of Diagnosis and Selected Characteristics, 2011–2016—United States," in "Diagnoses of HIV Infection in the United States and Dependent Areas, 2016," *HIV Surveillance Report*, vol. 28, Centers for Disease Control and Prevention, November 2017, https://www.cdc.gov/hiv/pdf/library/reports/surveillance/cdc-hiv-surveillance-report-2016-vol-28.pdf (accessed January 31, 2017)

FIGURE 6.2

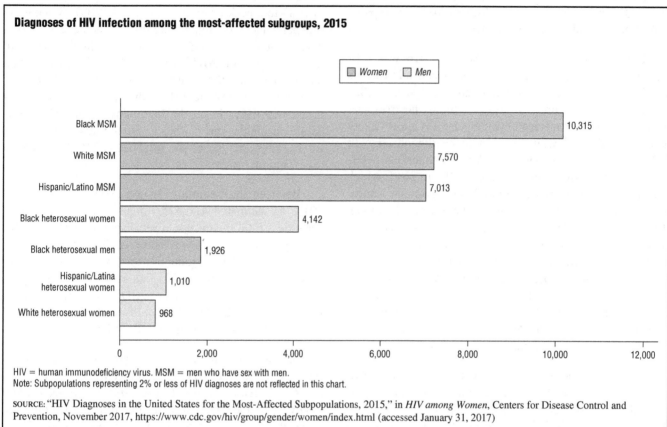

Diagnoses of HIV infection among the most-affected subgroups, 2015

HIV = human immunodeficiency virus. MSM = men who have sex with men.
Note: Subpopulations representing 2% or less of HIV diagnoses are not reflected in this chart.

SOURCE: "HIV Diagnoses in the United States for the Most-Affected Subpopulations, 2015," in *HIV among Women*, Centers for Disease Control and Prevention, November 2017, https://www.cdc.gov/hiv/group/gender/women/index.html (accessed January 31, 2017)

pregnancy lower the chances of an HIV-positive mother delivering an HIV-positive baby. In 2016 only 99 children of HIV-positive mothers in the United States were diagnosed with HIV.

**Other Sexually Transmitted Infections**

The CDC provides in *Sexually Transmitted Disease Surveillance 2016* (September 2017, https://www .cdc.gov/std/stats16/CDC_2016_STDS_Report-for508Web Sep21_2017_1644.pdf) data on HIV and seven other common sexually transmitted infections (STIs): chlamydia, gonorrhea, hepatitis B virus, herpes simplex virus type 2 (HSV-2), human papillomavirus (HPV), syphilis, and trichomoniasis. According to CDC estimates, there are nearly 20 million new STIs reported in the United States every year, about 50% of which occur in young people aged 15 to 24 years. Although young women and young men contract STIs at roughly the same rate, the consequences of untreated STIs are frequently more serious for women than for men. Chlamydia, gonorrhea, syphilis, and trichomoniasis infections typically have no symptoms, so they often go undetected and untreated. Untreated chlamydia and gonorrhea can lead to chronic pelvic pain, infertility, and life-threatening ectopic pregnancy in women. HPV, the most common type of STI, typically resolves without complication in one year. Some types of HPV, however, cause cervical cancer,

and other types cause genital warts, Papanicolaou test (Pap smear) abnormalities, and, in rare cases, respiratory problems in infants born to mothers with the infection.

In the fact sheet "Genital HPV Infection" (July 2017, https://www.cdc.gov/std/hpv/HPV-FS-July-2017.pdf), the CDC estimates that HPV accounts for about 14 million (70%) of the 20 million new STIs per year. The second most common STI among new cases is chlamydia, which accounted for 1.6 million (8%) new cases in 2016. Chlamydia appears to be far more prevalent in women than in men. In *Sexually Transmitted Disease Surveillance 2016*, the CDC notes that although the rate of chlamydia cases for women (657.3 per 100,000) was nearly twice the rate for men (330.5 per 100,000) in 2016, this disparity is largely influenced by the higher rate of screening for women. (See Figure 6.3.)

Most STIs are either treatable or curable. HPV has long been treatable, and in recent years it has become largely preventable. An HPV vaccine was licensed for US females in 2006, and for males in 2009. The CDC recommends the vaccines, which protect against the types of HPV that cause cervical cancer, anal cancer, and genital warts, and which are most effective if administered before the individual becomes sexually active, for all boys through age 21 and all girls through age 26. The CDC recommends screening for chlamydia, gonorrhea,

**TABLE 6.6**

## AIDS diagnoses, by transmission category, 2011–16

| Transmission category[c] | 2011 No. | 2011 Rate[b] | 2012 No. | 2012 Rate[b] | 2013 No. | 2013 Rate[b] | 2014 No. | 2014 Rate[b] | 2015 No. | 2015 Rate[b] | 2016 No. | 2016 Rate[b] | Cumulative[a] No. |
|---|---|---|---|---|---|---|---|---|---|---|---|---|---|
| **Male adult or adolescent** | | | | | | | | | | | | | |
| Male-to-male sexual contact | 13,493 | — | 13,212 | — | 12,997 | — | 10,413 | — | 10,067 | — | 10,075 | — | 599,230 |
| Injection drug use | 1,657 | — | 1,557 | — | 1,348 | — | 1,159 | — | 1,010 | — | 952 | — | 185,414 |
| Male-to-male sexual contact and injection drug use | 1,256 | — | 1,185 | — | 1,006 | — | 782 | — | 786 | — | 751 | — | 87,872 |
| Heterosexual contact[d] | 2,822 | — | 2,666 | — | 2,550 | — | 2,157 | — | 1,989 | — | 1,992 | — | 86,911 |
| Other[e] | 123 | — | 109 | — | 127 | — | 80 | — | 99 | — | 80 | — | 11,694 |
| **Subtotal** | **19,350** | **15.3** | **18,729** | **14.7** | **18,028** | **14.0** | **14,591** | **11.2** | **13,951** | **10.6** | **13,851** | **10.5** | **971,120** |
| **Female adult or adolescent** | | | | | | | | | | | | | |
| Injection drug use | 1,285 | — | 1,176 | — | 1,023 | — | 840 | — | 786 | — | 728 | — | 91,021 |
| Heterosexual contact[d] | 5,049 | — | 4,882 | — | 4,560 | — | 3,820 | — | 3,625 | — | 3,434 | — | 154,584 |
| Other[e] | 127 | — | 103 | — | 139 | — | 87 | — | 78 | — | 109 | — | 6,048 |
| **Subtotal** | **6,461** | **4.9** | **6,160** | **4.6** | **5,721** | **4.2** | **4,747** | **3.5** | **4,489** | **3.3** | **4,271** | **3.1** | **251,653** |
| **Total[f]** | **25,829** | **8.3** | **24,900** | **7.9** | **23,758** | **7.5** | **19,409** | **6.1** | **18,480** | **5.8** | **18,160** | **5.6** | **1,232,346** |

[a]From the beginning of the epidemic through 2016.
[b]Rates are per 100,000 population. Rates are not calculated by transmission category because of the lack of denominator data.
[c]Data have been statistically adjusted to account for missing transmission category; therefore, values may not sum to column subtotals and total.
[d]Heterosexual contact with a person known to have, or to be at high risk for, HIV infection.
[e]Includes hemophilia, blood transfusion, perinatal exposure, and risk factor not reported or not identified.
[f]Cumulative total includes 92 persons whose race/ethnicity is unknown.
Note: Data for the year 2016 are preliminary (subject to change) because they are based on only a 6-month reporting delay. Data for the year 2016 should not be used when assessing trends. Numbers less than 12, and rates and trends based on these numbers, should be interpreted with caution. AIDS = acquired immune deficiency syndrome.

SOURCE: Adapted from "Table 2a. Stage 3 (AIDS), by Year of Diagnosis and Selected Characteristics, 2011–2016 and Cumulative—United States," in "Diagnoses of HIV Infection in the United States and Dependent Areas, 2016," *HIV Surveillance Report*, vol. 28, Centers for Disease Control and Prevention, November 2017, https://www.cdc.gov/hiv/pdf/library/reports/surveillance/cdc-hiv-surveillance-report-2016-vol-28.pdf (accessed January 31, 2017)

TABLE 6.7

**Deaths of persons with diagnosed HIV infection ever classified as AIDS, by transmission category, 2011–15**

| Transmission category[c] | 2011 No. | 2011 Rate[b] | 2012 No. | 2012 Rate[b] | 2013 No. | 2013 Rate[b] | 2014 No. | 2014 Rate[b] | 2015 No. | 2015 Rate[b] | Cumulative[a] No. |
|---|---|---|---|---|---|---|---|---|---|---|---|
| **Male adult or adolescent** | | | | | | | | | | | |
| Male-to-male sexual contact | 5,248 | — | 5,188 | — | 5,228 | — | 5,269 | — | 5,180 | — | 325,330 |
| Injection drug use | 2,179 | — | 2,097 | — | 2,032 | — | 2,032 | — | 1,869 | — | 134,466 |
| Male-to-male sexual contact and injection drug use | 1,125 | — | 1,105 | — | 1,119 | — | 1,137 | — | 1,124 | — | 53,521 |
| Heterosexual contact[d] | 1,373 | — | 1,317 | — | 1,290 | — | 1,268 | — | 1,192 | — | 38,727 |
| Perinatal | 34 | — | 40 | — | 32 | — | 28 | — | 26 | — | 463 |
| Other[e] | 74 | — | 65 | — | 60 | — | 55 | — | 62 | — | 8,789 |
| Subtotal | 10,032 | 7.9 | 9,812 | 7.7 | 9,762 | 7.6 | 9,789 | 7.5 | 9,453 | 7.2 | 561,296 |
| **Female adult or adolescent** | | | | | | | | | | | |
| Injection drug use | 1,341 | — | 1,243 | — | 1,267 | — | 1,198 | — | 1,090 | — | 59,438 |
| Heterosexual contact[d] | 2,113 | — | 2,117 | — | 2,025 | — | 2,086 | — | 1,885 | — | 62,839 |
| Perinatal | 44 | — | 43 | — | 31 | — | 30 | — | 45 | — | 592 |
| Other[e] | 26 | — | 30 | — | 26 | — | 25 | — | 22 | — | 3,655 |
| Subtotal | 3,524 | 2.7 | 3,433 | 2.6 | 3,349 | 2.5 | 3,340 | 2.5 | 3,042 | 2.2 | 126,525 |
| Total[f] | 13,556 | 4.3 | 13,246 | 4.2 | 13,112 | 4.1 | 13,129 | 4.1 | 12,497 | 3.9 | 692,789 |

[a]From the beginning of the epidemic through 2015.
[b]Rates are per 100,000 population. Rates are not calculated by transmission category because of the lack of denominator data.
[c]Data have been statistically adjusted to account for missing transmission category; therefore, values may not sum to column subtotals and total.
[d]Heterosexual contact with a person known to have, or to be at high risk for, HIV infection.
[e]Includes hemophilia, blood transfusion, and risk factor not reported or not identified.
[f]Includes persons whose race/ethnicity is unknown.
Note: Deaths of persons with a diagnosis of HIV infection may be due to any cause. Numbers less than 12, and rates and trends based on these numbers, should be interpreted with caution. HIV = human immunodeficiency virus. AIDS = acquired immune deficiency syndrome.

SOURCE: Adapted from "Table 17a. Deaths of Persons with Diagnosed HIV Infection Ever Classified as Stage 3 (AIDS), by Year of Death and Selected Characteristics, 2011–2015 and Cumulative—United States," in "Diagnoses of HIV Infection in the United States and Dependent Areas, 2016," *HIV Surveillance Report*, vol. 28, Centers for Disease Control and Prevention, November 2017, https://www.cdc.gov/hiv/pdf/library/reports/surveillance/cdc-hiv-surveillance-report-2016-vol-28.pdf (accessed January 31, 2017)

syphilis, and trichomoniasis, which are treatable but often asymptomatic (showing no symptoms). HSV-2 (genital herpes), like HIV, is treatable, but it is a lifelong infection for which there is no cure.

## OSTEOPOROSIS

Osteoporosis (the loss of bone mass and deterioration of bone tissue) is a serious concern for many elderly Americans, and for women in particular. The National Osteoporosis Foundation estimates in "What Women Need to Know" (2018, https://www.nof.org/preventing-fractures/general-facts/what-women-need-to-know/) that about 80% of the 10 million people in the United States with osteoporosis are women. The condition predisposes those who have it to debilitating bone fractures, loss of height and degradation of posture due to the collapse of the spine, and decreased mobility, among other problems. Approximately one out of two women over the age of 50 years typically break a bone—most commonly a hip, vertebra, or wrist—due to osteoporosis. The risk of breaking a hip is roughly equal to the combined risk of developing breast and ovarian cancer.

According to the National Osteoporosis Foundation, older women are most at risk for osteoporosis because menopause causes a sharp decrease in estrogen levels, which can lead to bone loss. Indeed, a woman can lose up to 20% of her bone density in the five to seven years following menopause. Although women experience menopause as an inevitable part of aging, they can reduce the risk of osteoporosis by maintaining a diet that is rich in calcium and vitamin D, as well as in fruits and vegetables; by moderating caffeine, alcohol, protein, and sodium intake; by maintaining an active lifestyle; and by not smoking or losing too much weight. Bone density tests, which can detect osteoporosis, are recommended for postmenopausal women and elderly men.

## MENTAL HEALTH

According to the NCHS, in *Early Release of Selected Estimates Based on Data from the National Health Interview Survey, January–June 2017* (December 2017, https://www.cdc.gov/nchs/data/nhis/earlyrelease/earlyrelease201712.pdf), at the time they were interviewed 2.9% of American adults aged 18 to 44 years, 4.3% of adults aged 45 to 64 years, and 2.4% of adults aged 65 years and older had suffered from serious psychological distress during the past 30 days based on a variety of symptoms and interview responses. (See Figure 6.4.) Females in every age group were more likely than their male peers to have experienced serious psychological distress.

**FIGURE 6.3**

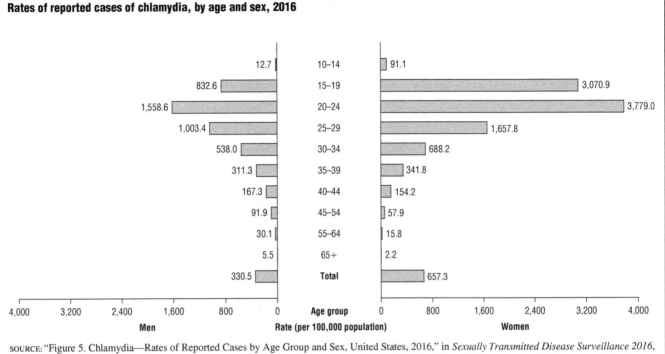

Rates of reported cases of chlamydia, by age and sex, 2016

| Men | Age group | Women |
|---|---|---|
| 12.7 | 10–14 | 91.1 |
| 832.6 | 15–19 | 3,070.9 |
| 1,558.6 | 20–24 | 3,779.0 |
| 1,003.4 | 25–29 | 1,657.8 |
| 538.0 | 30–34 | 688.2 |
| 311.3 | 35–39 | 341.8 |
| 167.3 | 40–44 | 154.2 |
| 91.9 | 45–54 | 57.9 |
| 30.1 | 55–64 | 15.8 |
| 5.5 | 65+ | 2.2 |
| 330.5 | Total | 657.3 |

Rate (per 100,000 population)

SOURCE: "Figure 5. Chlamydia—Rates of Reported Cases by Age Group and Sex, United States, 2016," in *Sexually Transmitted Disease Surveillance 2016*, Centers for Disease Control and Prevention, September 2017, https://www.cdc.gov/std/stats16/CDC_2016_STDS_Report-for508WebSep21_2017_1644 .pdf (accessed January 31, 2018)

## Depression

Hormonal factors, including menstrual cycle changes, pregnancy, miscarriage, the postpartum period, perimenopause, and menopause, can bring about depression in women. Childhood experiences of trauma or abuse, and various stresses during adulthood, can also increase the risk of depression. Both reproductive hormones and stress hormones have been linked to depression in women. Some types of depression include major depression; dysthymia, a long-term chronic but less severe depression; seasonal affective disorder; and bipolar disorder (manic-depressive illness), which is characterized by extreme highs and lows.

In *Depression in Women* (2018, https://www.nimh .nih.gov/health/publications/depression-in-women/tr-16-4779_153310.pdf), the National Institute of Mental Health (NIMH) explains that the symptoms of depression include persistent feelings of sadness, anxiety, and hopelessness; feelings of guilt or worthlessness; loss of interest in previously pleasurable activities; fatigue; difficulty concentrating; changes in sleep patterns; changes in eating patterns; thoughts of suicide or suicide attempts; and persistent physical aches and pains that do not lessen even with treatment. Treatment for depression might include the use of antidepressants, psychotherapy, and counseling.

## Eating Disorders

The most common eating disorders are anorexia nervosa, binge eating disorder, and bulimia nervosa. Anorexia is severe weight loss to at least 15% below normal body weight. Anorexics see themselves as overweight even when they are dangerously thin. Binge eating disorder involves recurrent episodes of dramatic overeating, during which the sufferer feels his or her eating to be out of control. Those with binge eating disorder tend to be overweight or obese. Bulimics binge eat as well, but they also purge (induce vomiting), fast (abstain from eating food), or exercise excessively to compensate for their caloric intake. Bulimics, like anorexics, tend to fear weight gain and are extremely critical of their body size and type, but unlike anorexics, they can fall on the normal spectrum of weight for their height. Eating disorders are frequently experienced by those with other psychiatric disorders, such as depression, anxiety disorders, and/or substance abuse. Furthermore, they correlate with higher mortality and can create a variety of additional health problems.

The NIMH reports in "Eating Disorders" (November 2017, https://www.nimh.nih.gov/health/statistics/eating-disorders.shtml) that the lifetime prevalence of anorexia among females is 0.9%, compared with 0.3% for males. The average age of onset for anorexia is 18 years old. Women also outpace men in their lifetime prevalence of binge eating disorder. The NIMH indicates that the prevalence of binge eating disorder among women is 1.6%, compared with 0.8% for men. Bulimia is less prevalent among both women and men, but women are five times more likely to suffer from the disorder. According to the

FIGURE 6.4

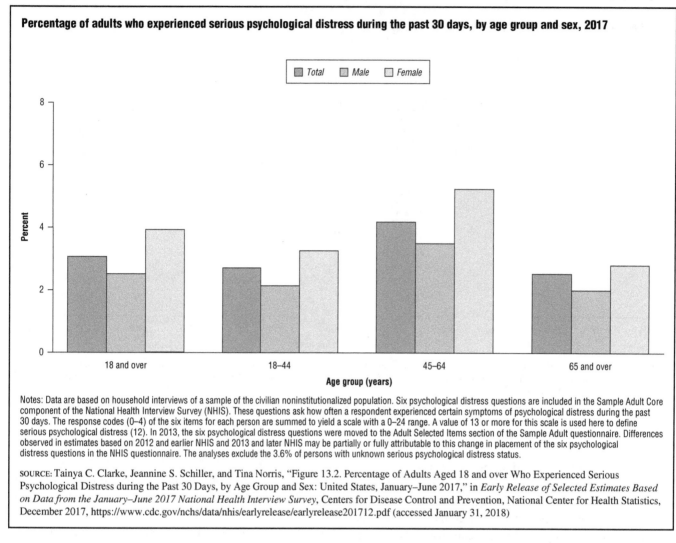

**Percentage of adults who experienced serious psychological distress during the past 30 days, by age group and sex, 2017**

Notes: Data are based on household interviews of a sample of the civilian noninstitutionalized population. Six psychological distress questions are included in the Sample Adult Core component of the National Health Interview Survey (NHIS). These questions ask how often a respondent experienced certain symptoms of psychological distress during the past 30 days. The response codes (0–4) of the six items for each person are summed to yield a scale with a 0–24 range. A value of 13 or more for this scale is used here to define serious psychological distress (12). In 2013, the six psychological distress questions were moved to the Adult Selected Items section of the Sample Adult questionnaire. Differences observed in estimates based on 2012 and earlier NHIS and 2013 and later NHIS may be partially or fully attributable to this change in placement of the six psychological distress questions in the NHIS questionnaire. The analyses exclude the 3.6% of persons with unknown serious psychological distress status.

SOURCE: Tainya C. Clarke, Jeannine S. Schiller, and Tina Norris, "Figure 13.2. Percentage of Adults Aged 18 and over Who Experienced Serious Psychological Distress during the Past 30 Days, by Age Group and Sex: United States, January–June 2017," in *Early Release of Selected Estimates Based on Data from the January–June 2017 National Health Interview Survey*, Centers for Disease Control and Prevention, National Center for Health Statistics, December 2017, https://www.cdc.gov/nchs/data/nhis/earlyrelease/earlyrelease201712.pdf (accessed January 31, 2018)

NIMH, the prevalence of the condition among women is 0.5%, compared with 0.1% for men.

## PREVENTION

Disease prevention through healthy lifestyle choices has had a profound effect on women's health in the late 20th and early 21st centuries. Prevention remains an extremely important factor in keeping women physically and mentally healthy.

### Smoking

In *The Health Consequences of Smoking: 50 Years of Progress* (2014, https://www.surgeongeneral.gov/library/reports/50-years-of-progress/full-report.pdf), the US surgeon general observes, "The disease risks from smoking by women have risen sharply over the last 50 years and are now equal to those for men for lung cancer, chronic obstructive pulmonary disease, and cardiovascular diseases." The ACS notes in *Cancer Facts and Figures, 2018* that as of 2018, women smokers were about 25 times more likely to develop lung cancer than women who never smoked. Cancer of the bladder, cervix, esophagus, kidneys,

larynx, mouth, pancreas, and stomach and leukemia have all been linked to cigarette smoking. Approximately, one-third of all cancer deaths in the United States are caused by cigarette smoking.

According to the NCHS, in *Health, United States, 2016*, 13.8% of all women over the age of 18 years smoked in 2015, compared with 16.8% of men the same age. (See Table 6.8.) This was down dramatically from 1965, when 33.7% of women and 51.2% of men smoked. White females (14.8%) were more likely than African American females (13.2%) to smoke.

The percentage of smokers decreased as the level of educational attainment increased beyond a high school diploma. Among those women with a high school diploma or GED in 2015, the NCHS reports that 21.2% were smokers, compared with 17.2% of women with some college but no bachelor's degree and 5.3% of those with a bachelor's degree or higher.

### Alcohol

As Table 6.9 shows, 47.4% of females aged 12 years and older were alcohol users in 2015, compared with

**TABLE 6.8**

## Current cigarette smoking among adults, by sex, race, and age, selected years 1965–2015

[Data are based on household interviews of a sample of the civilian noninstitutionalized population]

| Sex, race, and age | 1965[a] | 1979[a] | 1985[a] | 1990[a] | 2000 | 2005 | 2010 | 2012 | 2013 | 2014 | 2015 |
|---|---|---|---|---|---|---|---|---|---|---|---|
| **18 years and over, age-adjusted[b]** | | | | | Percent of adults who were current cigarette smokers[c] | | | | | | |
| All persons | 41.9 | 33.3 | 29.9 | 25.3 | 23.1 | 20.8 | 19.3 | 18.2 | 17.9 | 17.0 | 15.3 |
| Male | 51.2 | 37.0 | 32.2 | 28.0 | 25.2 | 23.4 | 21.2 | 20.6 | 20.5 | 19.0 | 16.8 |
| Female | 33.7 | 30.1 | 27.9 | 22.9 | 21.1 | 18.3 | 17.5 | 15.9 | 15.5 | 15.1 | 13.8 |
| White male[d] | 50.4 | 36.4 | 31.3 | 27.6 | 25.4 | 23.3 | 21.4 | 20.7 | 20.5 | 18.8 | 16.8 |
| Black or African American male[d] | 58.8 | 43.9 | 40.2 | 32.8 | 25.7 | 25.9 | 23.3 | 22.0 | 21.8 | 21.7 | 20.3 |
| White female[d] | 33.9 | 30.3 | 27.9 | 23.5 | 22.0 | 19.1 | 18.3 | 16.9 | 16.3 | 16.0 | 14.8 |
| Black or African American female[d] | 31.8 | 30.5 | 30.9 | 20.8 | 20.7 | 17.1 | 16.6 | 14.2 | 14.9 | 13.4 | 13.2 |
| **18 years and over, crude** | | | | | | | | | | | |
| All persons | 42.4 | 33.5 | 30.1 | 25.5 | 23.2 | 20.9 | 19.3 | 18.1 | 17.8 | 16.8 | 15.1 |
| Male | 51.9 | 37.5 | 32.6 | 28.4 | 25.6 | 23.9 | 21.5 | 20.5 | 20.5 | 18.8 | 16.7 |
| Female | 33.9 | 29.9 | 27.9 | 22.8 | 20.9 | 18.1 | 17.3 | 15.8 | 15.3 | 14.8 | 13.6 |
| White male[d] | 51.1 | 36.8 | 31.7 | 28.0 | 25.7 | 23.6 | 21.4 | 20.3 | 20.3 | 18.5 | 16.5 |
| Black or African American male[d] | 60.4 | 44.1 | 39.9 | 32.5 | 26.2 | 26.5 | 24.3 | 22.0 | 21.9 | 21.8 | 20.6 |
| White female[d] | 34.0 | 30.1 | 27.7 | 23.4 | 21.4 | 18.7 | 17.9 | 16.6 | 15.9 | 15.5 | 14.3 |
| Black or African American female[d] | 33.7 | 31.1 | 31.0 | 21.2 | 20.8 | 17.3 | 17.0 | 14.7 | 15.1 | 13.5 | 13.1 |
| **All males** | | | | | | | | | | | |
| 18–44 years | 57.9 | 40.4 | 35.2 | 31.4 | 29.2 | 27.1 | 23.9 | 24.0 | 22.9 | 21.7 | 18.5 |
| 18–24 years | 54.1 | 35.0 | 28.0 | 26.6 | 28.1 | 28.0 | 22.8 | 20.1 | 21.9 | 18.5 | 15.0 |
| 25–34 years | 60.7 | 43.9 | 38.2 | 31.6 | 28.9 | 27.7 | 26.1 | 28.0 | 24.4 | 23.7 | 21.3 |
| 35–44 years | 58.2 | 41.8 | 37.6 | 34.5 | 30.2 | 26.0 | 22.5 | 22.8 | 22.1 | 22.0 | 18.3 |
| 45–64 years | 51.9 | 39.3 | 33.4 | 29.3 | 26.4 | 25.2 | 23.2 | 20.2 | 21.9 | 19.4 | 17.9 |
| 45–54 years | 55.9 | 42.0 | 34.9 | 32.1 | 28.8 | 28.1 | 25.2 | 21.4 | 21.4 | 19.9 | 18.3 |
| 55–64 years | 46.6 | 36.4 | 31.9 | 25.9 | 22.6 | 21.1 | 20.7 | 18.8 | 22.6 | 18.8 | 17.5 |
| 65 years and over | 28.5 | 20.9 | 19.6 | 14.6 | 10.2 | 8.9 | 9.7 | 10.6 | 10.6 | 9.8 | 9.7 |
| **White male[d]** | | | | | | | | | | | |
| 18–44 years | 57.1 | 40.0 | 34.6 | 31.3 | 30.2 | 27.7 | 24.6 | 24.8 | 23.4 | 21.7 | 18.9 |
| 18–24 years | 53.0 | 34.3 | 28.4 | 27.4 | 30.4 | 29.7 | 23.8 | 21.9 | 23.5 | 20.0 | 15.6 |
| 25–34 years | 60.1 | 43.6 | 37.3 | 31.6 | 29.7 | 27.7 | 26.6 | 28.4 | 24.6 | 23.4 | 20.9 |
| 35–44 years | 57.3 | 41.3 | 36.6 | 33.5 | 30.6 | 26.3 | 23.1 | 23.3 | 21.9 | 21.2 | 19.1 |
| 45–64 years | 51.3 | 38.3 | 32.1 | 28.7 | 25.8 | 24.5 | 22.5 | 19.4 | 21.7 | 19.0 | 17.3 |
| 45–54 years | 55.3 | 40.9 | 33.7 | 31.3 | 28.0 | 27.4 | 24.5 | 20.7 | 21.2 | 19.7 | 17.8 |
| 55–64 years | 46.1 | 35.3 | 30.5 | 25.6 | 22.5 | 20.4 | 20.1 | 17.9 | 22.2 | 18.2 | 16.9 |
| 65 years and over | 27.7 | 20.5 | 18.9 | 13.7 | 9.8 | 7.9 | 9.6 | 10.3 | 10.0 | 9.4 | 9.3 |
| **Black or African American male[d]** | | | | | | | | | | | |
| 18–44 years | 66.3 | 45.2 | 39.6 | 32.9 | 25.5 | 25.1 | 22.6 | 21.3 | 20.9 | 22.2 | 20.2 |
| 18–24 years | 62.8 | 40.2 | 27.2 | 21.3 | 20.9 | 21.6 | 18.8 | 13.2 | 13.2* | 13.9* | 15.9* |
| 25–34 years | 68.4 | 47.5 | 45.6 | 33.8 | 23.2 | 29.8 | 25.7 | 24.9 | 24.8 | 28.0 | 26.0 |
| 35–44 years | 67.3 | 48.6 | 45.0 | 42.0 | 30.7 | 23.3 | 22.6 | 24.7 | 24.0 | 24.0 | 17.9 |
| 45–64 years | 57.9 | 50.0 | 46.1 | 36.7 | 32.2 | 32.4 | 31.8 | 24.6 | 25.7 | 24.0 | 22.8 |
| 45–54 years | 62.4 | 51.5 | 47.7 | 42.0 | 35.6 | 33.9 | 33.2 | 23.3 | 25.7 | 22.5 | 20.5 |
| 55–64 years | 51.8 | 47.9 | 44.4 | 30.2 | 26.3 | 29.8 | 29.6 | 26.4 | 25.6 | 25.9 | 25.5 |
| 65 years and over | 36.4 | 26.2 | 27.7 | 21.5 | 14.2 | 16.8 | 10.0 | 17.4 | 15.5 | 13.9 | 16.0 |
| **All females** | | | | | | | | | | | |
| 18–44 years | 42.1 | 34.7 | 31.4 | 25.6 | 24.5 | 21.2 | 19.1 | 16.9 | 16.6 | 16.6 | 14.5 |
| 18–24 years | 38.1 | 33.8 | 30.4 | 22.5 | 24.9 | 20.7 | 17.4 | 14.5 | 15.4 | 14.8 | 11.0 |
| 25–34 years | 43.7 | 33.7 | 32.0 | 28.2 | 22.3 | 21.5 | 20.6 | 19.4 | 17.9 | 17.5 | 15.0 |
| 35–44 years | 43.7 | 37.0 | 31.5 | 24.8 | 26.2 | 21.3 | 19.0 | 16.1 | 16.3 | 17.0 | 16.5 |
| 45–64 years | 32.0 | 30.7 | 29.9 | 24.8 | 21.7 | 18.8 | 19.1 | 18.9 | 18.1 | 16.8 | 16.1 |
| 45–54 years | 37.5 | 32.6 | 32.4 | 28.5 | 22.2 | 20.9 | 21.3 | 21.3 | 20.6 | 18.7 | 18.4 |
| 55–64 years | 25.0 | 28.6 | 27.4 | 20.5 | 20.9 | 16.1 | 16.5 | 16.2 | 15.2 | 14.8 | 13.7 |
| 65 years and over | 9.6 | 13.2 | 13.5 | 11.5 | 9.3 | 8.3 | 9.3 | 7.5 | 7.5 | 7.5 | 7.3 |
| **White female[d]** | | | | | | | | | | | |
| 18–44 years | 42.2 | 35.1 | 31.6 | 26.5 | 26.5 | 22.6 | 20.5 | 18.6 | 17.8 | 17.8 | 15.7 |
| 18–24 years | 38.4 | 34.5 | 31.8 | 25.4 | 28.5 | 22.6 | 18.4 | 16.9 | 17.0 | 16.5 | 11.2 |
| 25–34 years | 43.4 | 34.1 | 32.0 | 28.5 | 24.9 | 23.1 | 22.0 | 20.7 | 19.2 | 18.6 | 16.3 |
| 35–44 years | 43.9 | 37.2 | 31.0 | 25.0 | 26.6 | 22.2 | 20.5 | 17.6 | 17.0 | 18.0 | 18.3 |
| 45–64 years | 32.7 | 30.6 | 29.7 | 25.4 | 21.4 | 18.9 | 19.5 | 19.4 | 18.4 | 17.6 | 17.1 |
| 45–54 years | 38.2 | 32.5 | 32.4 | 29.1 | 21.9 | 21.0 | 22.4 | 22.7 | 21.2 | 19.9 | 20.2 |
| 55–64 years | 25.7 | 28.5 | 27.2 | 21.2 | 20.6 | 16.2 | 15.9 | 15.8 | 15.5 | 15.3 | 14.0 |
| 65 years and over | 9.8 | 13.8 | 13.3 | 11.5 | 9.1 | 8.4 | 9.4 | 7.5 | 7.9 | 7.6 | 7.5 |

56.2% of males. The NCHS further reports that an estimated 20.5% of females and 29.6% of males were binge drinkers (having five or more drinks on one occasion in the past 30 days), and 4.2% of females and 8.9% of males were heavy drinkers (having five or more drinks on at least five occasions in the past 30 days). Among teens, alcohol use varied less by gender: 9.9% of girls and 9.3% of boys aged 12 to 17 years reported alcohol use, girls

TABLE 6.8

**Current cigarette smoking among adults, by sex, race, and age, selected years 1965–2015** [CONTINUED]

[Data are based on household interviews of a sample of the civilian noninstitutionalized population]

| Sex, race, and age | 1965[a] | 1979[a] | 1985[a] | 1990[a] | 2000 | 2005 | 2010 | 2012 | 2013 | 2014 | 2015 |
|---|---|---|---|---|---|---|---|---|---|---|---|
| **Black or African American female[d]** | | | | | Percent of adults who were current cigarette smokers[c] | | | | | | |
| 18–44 years | 42.9 | 34.7 | 33.5 | 22.8 | 20.8 | 16.9 | 17.1 | 12.3 | 15.1 | 13.9 | 13.3 |
| 18–24 years | 37.1 | 31.8 | 23.7 | 10.0 | 14.2 | 14.2 | 14.2 | 7.4* | 11.8 | 9.3* | 8.6* |
| 25–34 years | 47.8 | 35.2 | 36.2 | 29.1 | 15.5 | 16.9 | 19.3 | 17.3 | 16.4 | 15.1 | 14.9 |
| 35–44 years | 42.8 | 37.7 | 40.2 | 25.5 | 30.2 | 19.0 | 17.2 | 11.2 | 16.4 | 16.4 | 15.4 |
| 45–64 years | 25.7 | 34.2 | 33.4 | 22.6 | 25.6 | 21.0 | 19.8 | 20.4 | 18.8 | 15.0 | 14.5 |
| 45–54 years | 32.3 | 36.2 | 36.4 | 26.5 | 26.5 | 22.2 | 20.4 | 20.1 | 22.2 | 15.7 | 14.7 |
| 55–64 years | 16.5 | 31.9 | 29.8 | 17.6 | 24.2 | 19.1 | 18.9 | 20.8 | 14.8 | 14.2 | 14.3 |
| 65 years and over | 7.1 | *8.5 | 14.5 | 11.1 | 10.2 | 10.0 | 9.4 | 9.1 | 6.5 | 8.1 | 9.7 |

*Estimates are considered unreliable.

[a]Data prior to 1997 are not strictly comparable with data for later years due to the 1997 questionnaire redesign.

[b]Estimates are age-adjusted to the year 2000 standard population using five age groups: 18–24 years, 25–34 years, 35–44 years, 45–64 years, and 65 years and over. Age-adjusted estimates in this table may differ from other age-adjusted estimates based on the same data and presented elsewhere if different age groups are used in the adjustment procedure.

[c]Starting with 1993 data, current cigarette smokers were defined as ever smoking 100 cigarettes in their lifetime and smoking now every day or some days.

[d]The race groups, white and black, include persons of Hispanic and non-Hispanic origin. Starting with 1999 data, race-specific estimates are tabulated according to the 1997 Revisions to the Standards for the Classification of Federal Data on Race and Ethnicity and are not strictly comparable with estimates for earlier years. The single-race categories shown in the table conform to the 1997 Standards. Starting with 1999 data, race-specific estimates are for persons who reported only one racial group. Prior to 1999, data were tabulated according to the 1977 Standards. Estimates for single-race categories prior to 1999 included persons who reported one race or, if they reported more than one race, identified one race as best representing their race. Starting with 2003 data, race responses of other race and unspecified multiple race were treated as missing, and then race was imputed if these were the only race responses. Almost all persons with a race response of other race were of Hispanic origin.

SOURCE: "Table 47. Current Cigarette Smoking among Adults Aged 18 and over, by Sex, Race, and Age: United States, Selected Years 1965–2015," in *Health, United States, 2016: With Chartbook on Long-term Trends in Health,* Centers for Disease Control and Prevention, National Center for Health Statistics, May 2017, https://www.cdc.gov/nchs/data/hus/hus16.pdf (accessed January 17, 2018)

and boys reported binge drinking equally (5.8%), and 0.7% of girls and 1.1% of boys reported heavy drinking.

Women are at greater risk of developing chronic alcohol-related diseases than men due to their increased sensitivity to alcohol and their smaller body size. Women are at risk for developing cirrhosis of the liver with lower levels of alcohol consumption and at earlier ages than men. Alcohol can cause cancers of the oral cavity, esophagus, and larynx, particularly in combination with smoking. Alcohol consumption also increases the risk of breast cancer.

**Other Substance Abuse**

As with cigarettes and alcohol, women are less likely than men to engage in illicit drug use. (Illicit drugs are both illegal drugs and controlled substances that are used illegally.) In 2015, 7.9% of females aged 12 years and older and 12.5% of males had used an illicit drug within the past month. (See Table 6.9.) Among those aged 12 to 17 years, 8.8% of both girls and boys had used illicit drugs.

In "Youth Risk Behavior Surveillance—United States, 2015" (*Morbidity and Mortality Weekly Report,* vol. 65, no. 6, June 10, 2016), the CDC finds that among high school students, 37.5% of females and 39.8% of males had tried marijuana at some point during their lifetime, and 20.1% of females and 23.2% of males reported current marijuana use. Fewer students had tried inhalants (6.6% of females and 7.2% of males), ecstasy (3.9% of females and 6% of males), cocaine (3.8% of females and 6.3% of males), and hallucinogenic drugs (4.6% of females and 8% of males). Only 1.2% of female

and 2.7% of male high school students had used heroin, and only 2.3% of female and 3.6% of male high school students had used methamphetamines.

**Overweight and Obesity**

According to the CDC, in "Defining Adult Overweight and Obesity" (June 16, 2016, https://www.cdc.gov/obesity/adult/defining.html), healthy weight for adults is defined as having a body mass index (BMI; a measure of body fat based on height and weight) between 18.5 and 24.9. People with a BMI of 25 or higher are considered overweight, while those with a BMI of 30 or higher are considered obese. Research shows that as individuals reach the overweight and obese levels of BMI, the risks for each of the following conditions increases: cancer (especially breast, colon, and endometrial cancers), elevated cholesterol and triglyceride levels, heart disease, hypertension, liver and gallbladder disease, osteoarthritis, sleep apnea and respiratory problems, stroke, type 2 diabetes, and gynecological problems including abnormal menses and infertility.

The percentage of overweight and obese women and men among the total US population has increased steadily in recent decades. In 1988–94, 51.4% of women and 60.9% of men aged 20 years and older were overweight or obese; by 2011–14, 66.2% of women and 73% of men aged 20 years and older were overweight or obese. (See Table 6.10.) More than four out of five (82%) non-Hispanic African American women were overweight and over half (56.5%) were obese. Overweight levels were similar for Mexican American women (80.3%), and obesity

TABLE 6.9

## Use of selected substances in the past month among people 12 years of age and over, by age, sex, race, and Hispanic origin, 2002–15

[Data are based on household interviews of a sample of the civilian noninstitutionalized population aged 12 and over]

| Age, sex, race, and Hispanic origin | Any illicit drug[a] | | | Marijuana | | | Misuse of prescription psychotherapeutic drugs[b] | | |
|---|---|---|---|---|---|---|---|---|---|
| | 2002 | 2014 | 2015 | 2002 | 2014 | 2015 | 2002 | 2014 | 2015 |
| | | | | | Percent of population | | | | |
| 12 years and over | — | — | 10.1 | 6.2 | 8.4 | 8.3 | — | — | 2.4 |
| **Age** | | | | | | | | | |
| 12–13 years | — | — | 2.6 | 1.4 | 1.1 | 0.8 | — | — | 0.9 |
| 14–15 years | — | — | 7.2 | 7.6 | 5.5 | 5.7 | — | — | 1.7 |
| 16–17 years | — | — | 16.3 | 15.7 | 15.0 | 14.2 | — | — | 3.3 |
| 18–25 years | — | — | 22.3 | 17.3 | 19.6 | 19.8 | — | — | 5.1 |
| 26–34 years | — | — | 15.4 | 7.7 | 12.7 | 12.9 | — | — | 3.7 |
| 35 years and over | — | — | 6.6 | 3.1 | 5.2 | 5.1 | — | — | 1.6 |
| **Sex** | | | | | | | | | |
| Male | — | — | 12.5 | 8.1 | 10.9 | 10.6 | — | — | 2.6 |
| Female | — | — | 7.9 | 4.4 | 6.0 | 6.2 | — | — | 2.2 |
| **Age and sex** | | | | | | | | | |
| 12–17 years | — | — | 8.8 | 8.2 | 7.4 | 7.0 | — | — | 2.0 |
| Male | — | — | 8.8 | 9.1 | 7.9 | 7.5 | — | — | 1.7 |
| Female | — | — | 8.8 | 7.2 | 6.8 | 6.5 | — | — | 2.3 |
| **Hispanic origin and race[c]** | | | | | | | | | |
| Not Hispanic or Latino: | | | | | | | | | |
| White only | — | — | 10.2 | 6.5 | 8.7 | 8.4 | — | — | 2.6 |
| Black or African American only | — | — | 12.5 | 7.4 | 10.3 | 10.7 | — | — | 1.8 |
| American Indian or Alaska Native only | — | — | 14.2 | 6.7 | 11.8 | 11.2 | — | — | 2.6 |
| Native Hawaiian or other Pacific Islander only | — | — | 9.8 | 4.4 | 12.1 | 9.2 | — | — | 1.7 |
| Asian only | — | — | 4.0 | 1.8 | 2.8 | 3.0 | — | — | 0.7 |
| 2 or more races | — | — | 17.2 | 9.0 | 12.4 | 13.4 | — | — | 4.8 |
| Hispanic or Latino | — | — | 9.2 | 4.3 | 6.7 | 7.2 | — | — | 2.3 |

| Age, sex, race, and Hispanic origin | Alcohol use | | | Binge alcohol use[d] | | | Heavy alcohol use[e] | | |
|---|---|---|---|---|---|---|---|---|---|
| | 2002 | 2014 | 2015 | 2002 | 2014 | 2015 | 2002 | 2014 | 2015 |
| | | | | | Percent of population | | | | |
| 12 years and over | 51.0 | 52.7 | 51.7 | — | — | 24.9 | — | — | 6.5 |
| **Age** | | | | | | | | | |
| 12–13 years | 4.3 | 2.1 | 1.3 | — | — | 0.7 | — | — | 0.0 |
| 14–15 years | 16.6 | 8.5 | 7.4 | — | — | 3.8 | — | — | 0.3 |
| 16–17 years | 32.6 | 23.3 | 19.7 | — | — | 12.6 | — | — | 2.3 |
| 18–25 years | 60.5 | 59.6 | 58.3 | — | — | 39.0 | — | — | 10.9 |
| 26–34 years | 61.4 | 66.0 | 65.0 | — | — | 38.3 | — | — | 9.7 |
| 35 years and over | 52.1 | 54.4 | 53.5 | — | — | 21.8 | — | — | 5.6 |
| **Sex** | | | | | | | | | |
| Male | 57.4 | 57.3 | 56.2 | 31.2 | 30.0 | 29.6 | 10.8 | 9.3 | 8.9 |
| Female | 44.9 | 48.4 | 47.4 | — | — | 20.5 | — | — | 4.2 |
| **Age and sex** | | | | | | | | | |
| 12–17 years | 17.6 | 11.5 | 9.6 | — | — | 5.8 | — | — | 0.9 |
| Male | 17.4 | 10.8 | 9.3 | 11.4 | 6.4 | 5.8 | 3.1 | 1.2 | 1.1 |
| Female | 17.9 | 12.3 | 9.9 | — | — | 5.8 | — | — | 0.7 |
| **Hispanic origin and race[c]** | | | | | | | | | |
| Not Hispanic or Latino: | | | | | | | | | |
| White only | 55.0 | 57.7 | 57.0 | — | — | 26.0 | — | — | 7.6 |
| Black or African American only | 39.9 | 44.2 | 43.8 | — | — | 23.4 | — | — | 4.8 |
| American Indian or Alaska Native only | 44.7 | 42.3 | 37.9 | — | — | 24.1 | — | — | 4.7 |
| Native Hawaiian or other Pacific Islander only | * | 37.9 | 33.8 | — | — | 17.8 | — | — | 3.0 |
| Asian only | 37.1 | 38.7 | 39.7 | — | — | 14.0 | — | — | 2.2 |
| 2 or more races | 49.9 | 49.5 | 42.8 | — | — | 22.9 | — | — | 6.8 |
| Hispanic or Latino | 42.8 | 44.4 | 42.4 | — | — | 25.7 | — | — | 4.8 |

levels were slightly lower (49.6%). More than three out of five (63.5%) non-Hispanic white females were over-weight and more than one-third (35.3%) were obese.

Only 31.7% of women and 26% of men reported a healthy weight in 2011–14, compared with 45% of women and 37.9% of men in 1988–94.

**TABLE 6.9**

**Use of selected substances in the past month among people 12 years of age and over, by age, sex, race, and Hispanic origin, 2002–15** [CONTINUED]

Data are based on household interviews of a sample of the civilian noninstitutionalized population aged 12 and over]

| Age, sex, race, and Hispanic origin | Any tobacco[f] | | | Cigarettes | | | Cigars | | |
|---|---|---|---|---|---|---|---|---|---|
| | 2002 | 2014 | 2015 | 2002 | 2014 | 2015 | 2002 | 2014 | 2015 |
| | Percent of population | | | | | | | | |
| 12 years and over | 30.4 | 25.2 | 23.9 | 26.0 | 20.8 | 19.4 | 5.4 | 4.5 | 4.7 |
| **Age** | | | | | | | | | |
| 12–13 years | 3.8 | 1.1 | 0.6 | 3.2 | 0.7 | 0.5 | 0.7 | 0.3 | 0.2 |
| 14–15 years | 13.4 | 5.1 | 4.6 | 11.2 | 3.4 | 3.1 | 3.8 | 1.5 | 1.2 |
| 16–17 years | 29.0 | 14.4 | 12.4 | 24.9 | 10.2 | 8.7 | 9.3 | 4.4 | 4.8 |
| 18–25 years | 45.3 | 35.0 | 33.0 | 40.8 | 28.4 | 26.7 | 11.0 | 9.7 | 8.9 |
| 26–34 years | 38.2 | 34.8 | 35.1 | 32.7 | 29.4 | 29.3 | 6.6 | 6.8 | 7.8 |
| 35 years and over | 27.9 | 23.7 | 22.1 | 23.4 | 19.7 | 17.9 | 4.1 | 3.3 | 3.5 |
| **Sex** | | | | | | | | | |
| Male | 37.0 | 31.1 | 29.6 | 28.7 | 23.2 | 21.8 | 9.4 | 7.5 | 7.6 |
| Female | 24.3 | 19.7 | 18.5 | 23.4 | 18.6 | 17.1 | 1.7 | 1.7 | 2.0 |
| **Age and sex** | | | | | | | | | |
| 12–17 years | 15.2 | 7.0 | 6.0 | 13.0 | 4.9 | 4.2 | 4.5 | 2.1 | 2.1 |
| Male | 16.0 | 8.2 | 7.0 | 12.3 | 5.1 | 4.6 | 6.2 | 2.7 | 2.6 |
| Female | 14.4 | 5.8 | 4.9 | 13.6 | 4.6 | 3.8 | 2.7 | 1.5 | 1.5 |
| **Hispanic origin and race[e]** | | | | | | | | | |
| Not Hispanic or Latino: | | | | | | | | | |
| White only | 32.0 | 27.6 | 25.9 | 26.9 | 22.3 | 20.7 | 5.5 | 4.6 | 4.5 |
| Black or African American only | 28.8 | 26.6 | 26.0 | 25.3 | 22.5 | 21.3 | 6.8 | 6.5 | 8.0 |
| American Indian or Alaska Native only | 44.3 | 37.8 | 37.0 | 37.1 | 32.5 | 29.5 | 5.2 | 4.2 | 6.4 |
| Native Hawaiian or other Pacific Islander only | * | 30.6 | 19.2 | * | 25.4 | 16.3 | 4.1 | 3.2 | 4.2 |
| Asian only | 18.6 | 10.2 | 11.4 | 17.7 | 9.2 | 10.0 | 1.1 | 1.2 | 2.2 |
| 2 or more races | 38.1 | 29.5 | 31.9 | 35.0 | 24.4 | 26.8 | 5.5 | 6.5 | 5.9 |
| Hispanic or Latino | 25.2 | 18.8 | 17.7 | 23.0 | 16.7 | 15.3 | 5.0 | 3.7 | 3.7 |

*Estimates are considered unreliable.
—Data not available.
[a]Any illicit drug includes marijuana, cocaine (including crack), heroin, hallucinogens (including LSD, PCP, peyote, mescaline, psilocybin mushrooms, "Ecstasy," ketamine, DMT/AMT/ "Foxy," and Salvia divinorum), inhalants, methamphetamine, or the misuse of prescription pain relievers, tranquilizers, stimulants, and sedatives.
[b]Misuse of prescription psychotherapeutic drugs is defined as use in any way not directed by a doctor, including use without a prescription of one's own; use in greater amounts, more often, or longer than told to take a drug; or use in any other way not directed by a doctor.
[c]Persons of Hispanic origin may be of any race. Data on race and Hispanic origin were collected using the 1997 Revisions to the Standards for the Classification of Federal Data on Race and Ethnicity. Single-race categories shown include persons who reported only one racial group. The category 2 or more races includes persons who reported more than one racial group.
[d]Binge alcohol use for men is defined as drinking five or more drinks on the same occasion on at least 1 day in the past 30 days. Starting in 2015, binge alcohol use for women is defined as drinking four or more drinks on the same occasion on a least 1 day in the past 30 days. Occasion is defined as at the same time or within a couple of hours of each other.
[e]Heavy alcohol use is defined as drinking five or more drinks on the same occasion on each of 5 or more days in the past 30 days. By definition, all heavy alcohol users are also binge alcohol users.
[f]Any tobacco product includes cigarettes, smokeless tobacco (such as snuff, dip, chewing tobacco, or "snus"), cigars, or pipe tobacco.
Notes: The National Survey on Drug Use & Health (NSDUH), formerly called the National Household Survey on Drug Abuse (NHSDA), began a new baseline in 2002 and cannot be compared with previous years. The NSDUH questionnaire underwent a partial redesign in 2015, including changes to some questions. Consequently, for some categories, data for prior years are not comparable to 2015 estimates and are not shown in this table. Starting with 2011 data, 2010-census based control totals were used in the weighting process. Because of methodological differences among the National Survey on Drug Use & Health, the Monitoring the Future (MTF) Study, and the Youth Risk Behavior Survey (YRBS), rates of substance use measured by these surveys are not directly comparable.

SOURCE: "Table 50. Use of Selected Substances in the Past Month among Persons Aged 12 and over, by Age, Sex, Race, and Hispanic Origin: United States, Selected Years 2002–2015," in *Health, United States, 2016: With Chartbook on Long-term Trends in Health*, Centers for Disease Control and Prevention, National Center for Health Statistics, May 2017, https://www.cdc.gov/nchs/data/hus/hus16.pdf (accessed January 17, 2018).

Problems with weight often begin in childhood. Table 6.11 shows that among schoolchildren aged six to 11 years in 2011–14, 17.5% of girls and 17.6% of boys were obese. These proportions were up dramatically from 1988–94, when 11% of girls and 11.6% of boys the same age were obese. Among children aged 12 to 19 years in 2011–14, 21% of girls and 20.1% of boys were obese, up from 9.7% of girls and 11.3% of boys in 1988–94. As with adults, obesity levels of children varied among racial and ethnic groups.

Among girls aged six to 11 years in 2011–14, 14.4% of non-Hispanic whites, 21.6% of non-Hispanic African Americans, and 25.3% of Mexican Americans were obese. Among girls aged 12 to 19 years, 20.4% of non-Hispanic whites, 24.4% of non-Hispanic African Americans, and 24.2% of Mexican Americans were obese.

**Exercise**

Only a minority of Americans, and fewer women than men, meet the federal Physical Activity Guidelines for Americans, which were issued in October 2008 (https://health.gov/paguidelines/pdf/paguide.pdf). The aerobic activity guidelines call for 150 minutes of moderate-intensity aerobic physical activity or 75 minutes

**TABLE 6.10**

**Normal weight, overweight, and obesity rates among adults aged 20 years and older, by selected characteristics, selected years 1988–94 through 2011–14**

[Data are based on measured height and weight of a sample of the civilian noninstitutionalized population]

| Sex, age, race and Hispanic origin[a], and percent of poverty level | Normal weight (BMI from 18.5 to 24.9)[b] | | | | |
|---|---|---|---|---|---|
| | 1988–1994 | 1999–2002 | 2003–2006 | 2007–2010 | 2011–2014 |
| 20 years and over, age-adjusted[c] | Percent of population | | | | |
| Both sexes[d] | 41.6 | 33.0 | 31.6 | 29.8 | 28.9 |
| Male | 37.9 | 30.2 | 26.6 | 25.7 | 26.0 |
| Female | 45.0 | 35.7 | 36.5 | 33.7 | 31.7 |
| Not Hispanic or Latino: | | | | | |
| White only | 43.1 | 34.6 | 33.2 | 31.4 | 30.0 |
| White only, male | 37.3 | 29.6 | 26.8 | 25.5 | 25.6 |
| White only, female | 48.7 | 39.5 | 39.6 | 36.9 | 34.3 |
| Black or African American only | 33.9 | 27.6 | 22.7 | 22.7 | 22.0 |
| Black or African American only, male | 40.1 | 34.7 | 27.0 | 28.5 | 29.0 |
| Black or African American only, female | 29.2 | 21.6 | 19.2 | 17.9 | 16.0 |
| Asian only | — | — | — | — | 55.7 |
| Asian only, male | — | — | — | — | 50.2 |
| Asian only, female | — | — | — | — | 60.5 |
| Hispanic or Latino | — | — | — | 21.1 | 20.9 |
| Hispanic or Latino, male | — | — | — | 19.0 | 19.5 |
| Hispanic or Latina, female | — | — | — | 23.5 | 22.3 |
| Mexican origin | 30.1 | 26.9 | 24.4 | 19.6 | 17.7 |
| Mexican origin, male | 30.2 | 26.5 | 23.8 | 18.5 | 16.5 |
| Mexican origin, female | 29.8 | 27.5 | 25.1 | 21.3 | 19.1 |
| Percent of poverty level:[e] | | | | | |
| Below 100% | 37.5 | 32.7 | 32.1 | 27.3 | 28.1 |
| 100%–199% | 39.3 | 30.5 | 31.3 | 27.6 | 24.6 |
| 200%–399% | 41.8 | 29.6 | 29.7 | 29.7 | 27.5 |
| 400% or more | 45.5 | 36.5 | 33.7 | 32.1 | 33.4 |
| | Overweight or obese (BMI greater than or equal to 25.0)[b] | | | | |
| 20 years and over, age-adjusted[c] | Percent of population | | | | |
| Both sexes[d] | 56.0 | 65.1 | 66.7 | 68.5 | 69.5 |
| Male | 60.9 | 68.8 | 72.1 | 73.3 | 73.0 |
| Female | 51.4 | 61.6 | 61.3 | 63.9 | 66.2 |
| Not Hispanic or Latino: | | | | | |
| White only | 54.4 | 63.3 | 64.8 | 66.8 | 68.5 |
| White only, male | 61.6 | 69.4 | 71.8 | 73.6 | 73.7 |
| White only, female | 47.5 | 57.2 | 57.9 | 60.3 | 63.5 |
| Black or African American only | 63.7 | 70.5 | 76.1 | 75.5 | 76.3 |
| Black or African American only, male | 57.8 | 62.6 | 71.6 | 70.0 | 69.6 |
| Black or African American only, female | 68.2 | 77.2 | 79.8 | 80.0 | 82.0 |
| Asian only | — | — | — | — | 40.3 |
| Asian only, male | — | — | — | — | 46.9 |
| Asian only, female | — | — | — | — | 34.4 |
| Hispanic or Latino | — | — | — | 78.4 | 78.4 |
| Hispanic or Latino, male | — | — | — | 80.6 | 79.6 |
| Hispanic or Latina, female | — | — | — | 75.7 | 77.1 |
| Mexican origin | 68.9 | 72.3 | 75.0 | 79.9 | 81.6 |
| Mexican origin, male | 68.9 | 73.2 | 75.8 | 81.3 | 82.7 |
| Mexican origin, female | 68.9 | 71.2 | 73.9 | 78.0 | 80.3 |
| Percent of poverty level:[e] | | | | | |
| Below 100% | 59.6 | 64.7 | 65.7 | 69.7 | 69.1 |
| 100%–199% | 58.0 | 67.3 | 66.5 | 70.5 | 73.9 |
| 200%–399% | 56.0 | 68.6 | 69.0 | 68.6 | 71.6 |
| 400% or more | 52.4 | 62.2 | 64.7 | 66.9 | 65.6 |

of vigorous-intensity aerobic physical activity spread throughout the week. The muscle-building guidelines call for moderate- or high-intensity muscle-strengthening activities that involve all major muscle groups on two or more days per week.

Just over half (53.9%) of all US adults aged 18 years and older met the federal physical activity guidelines for aerobic activity during the first half of 2017, and women (50.1%) lagged behind men (57.9%) in meeting the guidelines. (See Figure 6.5.) Those aged 18 to 24 years

were the most likely to meet the guidelines, although the gender disparity was also greatest in this age group, as 68.3% of males met the guidelines, compared with 57.4% of females. In the older age groups, participation decreased over time for both women and men.

These patterns carry over from high school, when boys are more likely than girls to be physically active. As Table 6.12 shows, 17.5% of female high school students did not participate in at least 60 minutes of physical activity on any day during the seven days prior to being

TABLE 6.10

**Normal weight, overweight, and obesity rates among adults aged 20 years and older, by selected characteristics, selected years 1988–94 through 2011–14** [CONTINUED]

[Data are based on measured height and weight of a sample of the civilian noninstitutionalized population]

| Sex, age, race and Hispanic origin[a], and percent of poverty level | Obesity (BMI greater than or equal to 30.0)[b] | | | | |
|---|---|---|---|---|---|
| | 1988–1994 | 1999–2002 | 2003–2006 | 2007–2010 | 2011–2014 |
| **20 years and over, age-adjusted[c]** | Percent of population | | | | |
| Both sexes[d] | 22.9 | 30.4 | 33.4 | 34.7 | 36.4 |
| Male | 20.2 | 27.5 | 32.4 | 33.9 | 34.5 |
| Female | 25.5 | 33.2 | 34.3 | 35.5 | 38.1 |
| Not Hispanic or Latino: | | | | | |
| White only | 21.6 | 29.4 | 32.0 | 33.3 | 34.6 |
| White only, male | 20.2 | 28.0 | 32.4 | 34.1 | 34.0 |
| White only, female | 22.9 | 30.7 | 31.6 | 32.5 | 35.3 |
| Black or African American only | 30.7 | 39.2 | 45.5 | 47.0 | 48.0 |
| Black or African American only, male | 20.9 | 27.8 | 35.7 | 38.3 | 37.9 |
| Black or African American only, female | 38.3 | 48.6 | 53.4 | 54.0 | 56.5 |
| Asian only | — | — | — | — | 11.8 |
| Asian only, male | — | — | — | — | 11.3 |
| Asian only, female | — | — | — | — | 11.9 |
| Hispanic or Latino | — | — | — | 38.9 | 42.6 |
| Hispanic or Latino, male | — | — | — | 35.7 | 39.1 |
| Hispanic or Latina, female | — | — | — | 42.1 | 45.6 |
| Mexican origin | 29.3 | 32.7 | 35.3 | 40.3 | 46.4 |
| Mexican origin, male | 23.8 | 27.8 | 29.5 | 36.3 | 43.3 |
| Mexican origin, female | 35.2 | 38.0 | 41.8 | 44.6 | 49.6 |
| Percent of poverty level:[e] | | | | | |
| Below 100% | 28.1 | 34.7 | 35.0 | 37.2 | 39.2 |
| 100%–199% | 26.1 | 34.1 | 35.9 | 37.3 | 42.6 |
| 200%–399% | 22.7 | 32.1 | 35.7 | 36.8 | 38.8 |
| 400% or more | 18.7 | 25.5 | 28.9 | 31.3 | 29.7 |
| **20 years and over, age-adjusted[c]** | Grade 1 obesity (BMI from 30.0 to 34.9)[b] | | | | |
| | Percent of population | | | | |
| Both sexes[d] | 14.8 | 17.9 | 19.8 | 19.9 | 20.6 |
| Male | 14.9 | 18.2 | 21.8 | 22.3 | 22.0 |
| Female | 14.7 | 17.6 | 17.9 | 17.6 | 19.3 |
| Not Hispanic or Latino: | | | | | |
| White only | 14.0 | 17.6 | 19.3 | 19.2 | 19.6 |
| White only, male | 14.9 | 18.9 | 21.6 | 22.7 | 21.4 |
| White only, female | 13.2 | 16.2 | 17.0 | 15.9 | 17.9 |
| Black or African American only | 17.3 | 19.0 | 23.1 | 23.0 | 23.5 |
| Black or African American only, male | 14.2 | 16.1 | 22.4 | 20.8 | 22.0 |
| Black or African American only, female | 19.6 | 21.6 | 23.8 | 24.8 | 24.9 |
| Asian only | — | — | — | — | 9.3 |
| Asian only, male | — | — | — | — | 9.4 |
| Asian only, female | — | — | — | — | 8.9 |
| Hispanic or Latino | — | — | — | 23.7 | 25.6 |
| Hispanic or Latino, male | — | — | — | 23.9 | 27.2 |
| Hispanic or Latina, female | — | — | — | 23.5 | 24.1 |
| Mexican origin | 20.3 | 21.1 | 22.8 | 24.8 | 26.9 |
| Mexican origin, male | 18.9 | 19.5 | 22.0 | 24.7 | 29.7 |
| Mexican origin, female | 22.0 | 22.9 | 23.6 | 24.9 | 23.8 |
| Percent of poverty level:[e] | | | | | |
| Below 100% | 16.6 | 17.3 | 19.3 | 19.8 | 20.7 |
| 100%–199% | 16.1 | 17.7 | 20.6 | 19.8 | 21.7 |
| 200%–399% | 14.5 | 19.8 | 21.6 | 20.2 | 22.7 |
| 400% or more | 13.3 | 16.6 | 18.0 | 19.4 | 18.2 |

surveyed by the CDC in 2015, and only 39.1% were physically active at least 60 minutes per day on five or more days in the preceding week. By contrast, only 11.1% of male high school students did not participate in at least 60 minutes of physical activity on any day during the seven days prior to being surveyed, and 57.8% were physically active at least 60 minutes per day. Furthermore, girls are now as likely as boys to spend excessive amounts of sedentary time each day watching television or using a computer for something other than schoolwork.

In "Youth Risk Behavior Surveillance—United States, 2011" (*Morbidity and Mortality Weekly Report*, vol. 61, no. 4, June 8, 2012), the CDC reports that in 2011, 26.6% of female high school students used a computer for three or more hours per day, compared with 35.3% of male high school students; and 31.6% of female students watched television for three or more hours per day, compared with 33.3% of their male peers. The CDC notes in "Youth Risk Behavior Surveillance—United States, 2015" that in 2015 computer time had increased more sharply for girls than for boys:

**TABLE 6.10**

**Normal weight, overweight, and obesity rates among adults aged 20 years and older, by selected characteristics, selected years 1988–94 through 2011–14** [CONTINUED]

[Data are based on measured height and weight of a sample of the civilian noninstitutionalized population]

| Sex, age, race and Hispanic origin[a], and percent of poverty level | Grade 2 obesity (BMI from 35.0 to 39.9)[b] | | | | |
|---|---|---|---|---|---|
| | 1988–1994 | 1999–2002 | 2003–2006 | 2007–2010 | 2011–2014 |
| **20 years and over, age-adjusted[c]** | Percent of population | | | | |
| Both sexes[d] | 5.2 | 7.6 | 8.2 | 8.9 | 8.8 |
| Male | 3.5 | 5.9 | 7.1 | 7.4 | 7.6 |
| Female | 6.8 | 9.2 | 9.3 | 10.3 | 9.9 |
| Not Hispanic or Latino: | | | | | |
| White only | 4.9 | 7.4 | 7.8 | 8.6 | 8.5 |
| White only, male | 3.5 | 5.8 | 7.2 | 7.3 | 7.8 |
| White only, female | 6.3 | 9.0 | 8.4 | 9.9 | 9.1 |
| Black or African American only | 7.8 | 11.2 | 12.0 | 12.0 | 12.3 |
| Black or African American only, male | 4.1 | 8.3 | 7.6 | 10.2 | 8.9 |
| Black or African American only, female | 10.7 | 13.6 | 15.4 | 13.4 | 15.1 |
| Asian only | — | — | — | — | 1.9 |
| Asian only, male | — | — | — | — | * |
| Asian only, female | — | — | — | — | 2.1* |
| Hispanic or Latino | — | — | — | 9.8 | 10.6 |
| Hispanic or Latino, male | — | — | — | 7.8 | 7.3 |
| Hispanic or Latina, female | — | — | — | 12.0 | 13.5 |
| Mexican origin | 6.1 | 7.4 | 8.0 | 9.8 | 12.4 |
| Mexican origin, male | 3.8 | 5.4 | 5.1 | 7.2 | 8.3 |
| Mexican origin, female | 8.4 | 9.4 | 11.2 | 12.9 | 16.6 |
| Percent of poverty level:[e] | | | | | |
| Below 100% | 6.8 | 9.6 | 8.6 | 10.0 | 10.1 |
| 100%–199% | 6.5 | 9.7 | 9.0 | 9.4 | 11.0 |
| 200%–399% | 5.2 | 7.5 | 8.8 | 10.3 | 9.4 |
| 400% or more | 3.6 | 5.7 | 6.7 | 7.6 | 6.5 |
| | Grade 3 obesity (BMI greater than or equal to 40.0)[b] | | | | |
| **20 years and over, age-adjusted[c]** | Percent of population | | | | |
| Both sexes[d] | 2.9 | 4.9 | 5.4 | 6.0 | 6.9 |
| Male | 1.7 | 3.3 | 3.5 | 4.2 | 4.9 |
| Female | 4.0 | 6.4 | 7.2 | 7.6 | 8.9 |
| Not Hispanic or Latino: | | | | | |
| White only | 2.7 | 4.4 | 4.9 | 5.4 | 6.5 |
| White only, male | 1.8* | 3.3 | 3.5 | 4.0 | 4.7 |
| White only, female | 3.5 | 5.5 | 6.3 | 6.7 | 8.2 |
| Black or African American only | 5.6 | 8.9 | 10.4 | 11.9 | 12.1 |
| Black or African American only, male | 2.5 | 3.4 | 5.6 | 7.3 | 7.0 |
| Black or African American only, female | 8.0 | 13.4 | 14.2 | 15.8 | 16.5 |
| Asian only | — | — | — | — | * |
| Asian only, male | — | — | — | — | * |
| Asian only, female | — | — | — | — | * |
| Hispanic or Latino | — | — | — | 5.3 | 6.4 |
| Hispanic or Latino, male | — | — | — | 4.0 | 4.7 |
| Hispanic or Latina, female | — | — | — | 6.6 | 8.1 |
| Mexican origin | 2.9 | 4.2 | 4.6 | 5.6 | 7.1 |
| Mexican origin, male | * | 2.9* | 2.4* | 4.4 | 5.3 |
| Mexican origin, female | 4.9 | 5.7 | 6.9 | 6.8 | 9.2 |
| Percent of poverty level:[e] | | | | | |
| Below 100% | 4.7 | 7.8 | 7.0 | 7.5 | 8.5 |
| 100%–199% | 3.6 | 6.7 | 6.3 | 8.1 | 9.8 |
| 200%–399% | 3.0 | 4.8 | 5.2 | 6.3 | 6.7 |
| 400% or more | 1.9 | 3.2 | 4.2 | 4.4 | 5.0 |

42.8% of female high school students spent three or more hours per day in front of the computer, compared with 40.6% of male students. (See Table 6.13.) Female and male high school students, however, had reduced their time in front of the television; the percentage of those who watched three or more hours per day of television was nearly the same (24.4% for girls versus 25% for boys).

**TABLE 6.10**

**Normal weight, overweight, and obesity rates among adults aged 20 years and older, by selected characteristics, selected years 1988–94 through 2011–14** [CONTINUED]

[Data are based on measured height and weight of a sample of the civilian noninstitutionalized population]

— Data not available.

*Estimates are considered unreliable.

[a]Persons of Hispanic and Mexican origin may be of any race. Starting with 1999 data, race-specific estimates are tabulated according to the 1997 *Revisions to the Standards for the Classification of Federal Data on Race and Ethnicity* and are not strictly comparable with estimates for earlier years. The non-Hispanic race categories shown in the table conform to the 1997 Standards. Starting with 1999 data, race-specific estimates are for persons who reported only one racial group. Prior to data year 1999, estimates were tabulated according to the 1977 Standards. Estimates for single-race categories prior to 1999 included persons who reported one race or, if they reported more than one race, identified one race as best representing their race.

[b]Body mass index (BMI) equals weight in kilograms divided by height in meters squared. In *Health, United States* the NHANES variable, Body Mass Index, is used to assign persons to BMI categories.

[c]Estimates are age-adjusted to the year 2000 standard population using five age groups: 20–34 years, 35–44 years, 45–54 years, 55–64 years, and 65 years and over. Age-adjusted estimates in this table may differ from other age-adjusted estimates based on the same data and presented elsewhere if different age groups are used in the adjustment procedure.

[d]Includes persons of all races and Hispanic origins, not just those shown separately.

[e]Percent of poverty level was calculated by dividing family income by the US Department of Health and Human Services' poverty guideline specific to family size, as well as the appropriate year, and state. Persons with unknown percent of poverty level are excluded (6% in 2011–2014).

Notes: Percents do not sum to 100 because the percentage of persons with BMI less than normal weight (18.5 kilograms per meters squared) is not shown and the percentage of persons with obesity is a subset of the percentage with overweight. Height was measured without shoes. Excludes pregnant women.

SOURCE: Adapted from "Table 58. Normal Weight, Overweight, and Obesity among Adults Aged 20 and over, by Selected Characteristics: United States, Selected Years 1988–1994 through 2011–2014," in *Health, United States, 2016: With Chartbook on Long-term Trends in Health*, Centers for Disease Control and Prevention, National Center for Health Statistics, May 2017, https://www.cdc.gov/nchs/data/hus/hus16.pdf (accessed January 17, 2018)

TABLE 6.11

## Obesity rates among children and adolescents aged 2–19 years, by selected characteristics, selected years 1988–94 through 2011–14

[Data are based on measured height and weight of a sample of the civilian noninstitutionalized population]

| Sex, age, race and Hispanic origin[a], and percent of poverty level | 1988–1994 | 1999–2002 | 2003–2006 | 2007–2010 | 2011–2014 |
|---|---|---|---|---|---|
| 2–5 years | | | Percent of population | | |
| Both sexes[b] | 7.2 | 10.3 | 12.5 | 11.1 | 8.9 |
| Not Hispanic or Latino: | | | | | |
| White only | 5.2 | 8.7 | 10.8 | 9.0 | 5.2* |
| Black or African American only | 7.8 | 8.8 | 14.9 | 15.0 | 10.4 |
| Asian only | — | — | — | — | * |
| Hispanic or Latino | — | — | — | 15.3 | 15.6 |
| Mexican origin | 12.3 | 13.1 | 16.7 | 14.6 | 15.3 |
| Boys | 6.2 | 10.0 | 12.8 | 11.9 | 9.2 |
| Not Hispanic or Latino: | | | | | |
| White only | 4.5* | 8.2* | 11.1 | 8.8 | * |
| Black or African American only | 7.9 | 8.0* | 13.3 | 15.7 | 9.0* |
| Asian only | — | — | — | — | * |
| Hispanic or Latino | — | — | — | 17.7 | 16.7 |
| Mexican origin | 12.4 | 14.1 | 18.8 | 19.1 | 14.5* |
| Girls | 8.2 | 10.6 | 12.2 | 10.2 | 8.6 |
| Not Hispanic or Latina: | | | | | |
| White only | 5.9 | 9.0* | 10.4 | 9.2* | 4.4* |
| Black or African American only | 7.6 | 9.6 | 16.6 | 14.2* | 11.9 |
| Asian only | — | — | — | — | * |
| Hispanic or Latina | — | — | — | 12.7 | 14.6 |
| Mexican origin | 12.3 | 12.2* | 14.5 | 9.9* | 16.1* |
| Percent of poverty level:[c] | | | | | |
| Below 100% | 9.7 | 10.9 | 14.3 | 13.2 | 11.6 |
| 100%–199% | 7.3 | 13.8* | 12.7 | 11.8 | 10.2 |
| 200%–399% | 5.6 | 7.6* | 11.9 | 13.9 | 7.7* |
| 400% or more | * | * | 10.0* | 5.8* | * |
| 6–11 years | | | | | |
| Both sexes[b] | 11.3 | 15.9 | 17.0 | 18.8 | 17.5 |
| Not Hispanic or Latino: | | | | | |
| White only | 10.2 | 13.6 | 15.0 | 16.4 | 13.6 |
| Black or African American only | 14.6 | 19.8 | 21.3 | 23.9 | 21.4 |
| Asian only | — | — | — | — | 9.8* |
| Hispanic or Latino | — | — | — | 23.8 | 25.0 |
| Mexican origin | 16.4 | 21.8 | 23.7 | 23.3 | 25.3 |
| Boys | 11.6 | 16.9 | 18.0 | 20.7 | 17.6 |
| Not Hispanic or Latino: | | | | | |
| White only | 10.7 | 14.0 | 15.5 | 18.6 | 13.0 |
| Black or African American only | 12.3 | 17.0 | 18.6 | 23.3 | 21.2 |
| Asian only | — | — | — | — | 14.7* |
| Hispanic or Latino | — | — | — | 26.0 | 25.8 |
| Mexican origin | 17.5 | 26.5 | 27.5 | 24.3 | 25.3 |
| Girls | 11.0 | 14.7 | 15.8 | 16.9 | 17.5 |
| Not Hispanic or Latina: | | | | | |
| White only | 9.8* | 13.1 | 14.4 | 14.0 | 14.4 |
| Black or African American only | 17.0 | 22.8 | 24.0 | 24.5 | 21.6 |
| Asian only | — | — | — | — | * |
| Hispanic or Latina | — | — | — | 21.5 | 24.1 |
| Mexican origin | 15.3 | 17.1 | 19.7 | 22.4 | 25.3 |
| Percent of poverty level:[c] | | | | | |
| Below 100% | 11.4 | 19.1 | 22.0 | 22.2 | 21.5 |
| 100%–199% | 11.1 | 16.4 | 19.2 | 20.7 | 20.4 |
| 200%–399% | 11.7 | 15.3 | 16.7 | 18.9 | 15.7 |
| 400% or more | * | 12.9* | 9.2* | 12.5* | 12.2* |

**TABLE 6.11**

**Obesity rates among children and adolescents aged 2–19 years, by selected characteristics, selected years 1988–94 through 2011–14** [CONTINUED]

[Data are based on measured height and weight of a sample of the civilian noninstitutionalized population]

| Sex, age, race and Hispanic origin[a], and percent of poverty level | 1988–1994 | 1999–2002 | 2003–2006 | 2007–2010 | 2011–2014 |
|---|---|---|---|---|---|
| **12–19 years** | | | Percent of population | | |
| Both sexes[b] | 10.5 | 16.0 | 17.6 | 18.2 | 20.5 |
| Not Hispanic or Latino: | | | | | |
| White only | 10.3 | 13.7 | 16.0 | 15.9 | 19.6 |
| Black or African American only | 13.4 | 21.1 | 22.9 | 24.1 | 22.6 |
| Asian only | — | — | — | — | 9.4 |
| Hispanic or Latino | — | — | — | 22.5 | 22.8 |
| Mexican origin | 13.8 | 22.3 | 21.1 | 23.1 | 23.5 |
| Boys | 11.3 | 16.7 | 18.2 | 19.4 | 20.1 |
| Not Hispanic or Latino: | | | | | |
| White only | 11.6 | 14.6 | 17.3 | 17.1 | 18.7 |
| Black or African American only | 10.7 | 18.8 | 18.4 | 21.2 | 20.9 |
| Asian only | — | — | — | — | 12.9 |
| Hispanic or Latino | — | — | — | 26.0 | 22.7 |
| Mexican origin | 14.1 | 24.7 | 22.1 | 27.9 | 22.8 |
| Girls | 9.7 | 15.3 | 16.8 | 16.9 | 21.0 |
| Not Hispanic or Latina: | | | | | |
| White only | 8.9 | 12.6 | 14.5 | 14.6 | 20.4 |
| Black or African American only | 16.3 | 23.5 | 27.7 | 27.1 | 24.4 |
| Asian only | — | — | — | — | 5.7* |
| Hispanic or Latina | — | — | — | 18.7 | 22.8 |
| Mexican origin | 13.4* | 19.6 | 19.9 | 18.0 | 24.2 |
| Percent of poverty level:[c] | | | | | |
| Below 100% | 15.8 | 19.8 | 19.3 | 24.3 | 22.4 |
| 100%–199% | 11.2 | 15.1 | 18.4 | 20.1 | 25.7 |
| 200%–399% | 9.4 | 15.7 | 19.3 | 16.3 | 19.7 |
| 400% or more | * | 13.9 | 12.6 | 14.0 | 13.7* |

—Data not available.

*Estimates are considered unreliable.

[a]Persons of Hispanic and Mexican origin may be of any race. Starting with 1999 data, race-specific estimates are tabulated according to the 1997 *Revisions to the Standards for the Classification of Federal Data on Race and Ethnicity* and are not strictly comparable with estimates for earlier years. The non-Hispanic race categories shown in the table conform to the 1997 Standards. Starting with 1999 data, race-specific estimates are for persons who reported only one racial group. Prior to data year 1999, estimates were tabulated according to the 1977 Standards. Estimates for single-race categories prior to 1999 included persons who reported one race or, if they reported more than one race, identified one race as best representing their race.

[b]Includes persons of all races and Hispanic origins, not just those shown separately.

[c]Percent of poverty level was calculated by dividing family income by the US Department of Health and Human Services' poverty guideline specific to family size, as well as the appropriate year, and state. Persons with unknown percent of poverty level are excluded (6% in 2011–2014).

Notes: Obesity is defined as body mass index (BMI) at or above the sex- and age-specific 95th percentile from the 2000 CDC Growth Charts: United States. In Health, United States the NHANES variable, body mass index, is used to assign persons to BMI categories. Age is at time of examination at the mobile examination center. Crude rates, not age-adjusted rates, are shown. Height was measured without shoes. Excludes pregnant females.

SOURCE: "Table 59. Obesity among Children and Adolescents Aged 2–19 Years, by Selected Characteristics: United States, Selected Years 1988–1994 through 2011–2014," in *Health, United States, 2016: With Chartbook on Long-term Trends in Health*, Centers for Disease Control and Prevention, National Center for Health Statistics, May 2017, https://www.cdc.gov/nchs/data/hus/hus16.pdf (accessed January 17, 2018)

**FIGURE 6.5**

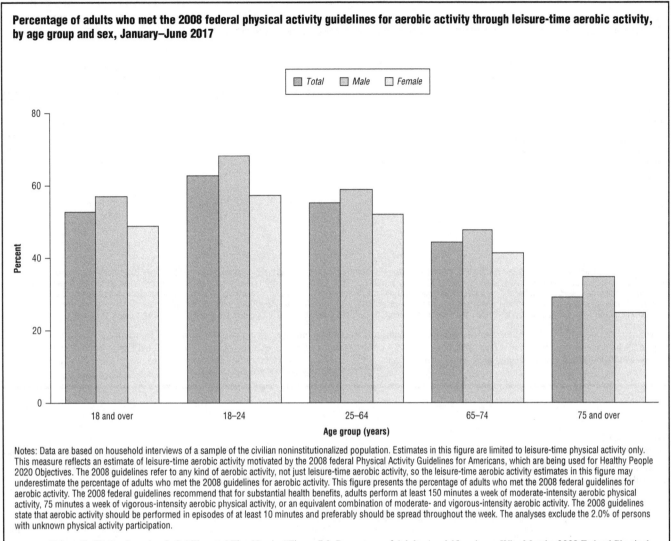

**Percentage of adults who met the 2008 federal physical activity guidelines for aerobic activity through leisure-time aerobic activity, by age group and sex, January–June 2017**

Notes: Data are based on household interviews of a sample of the civilian noninstitutionalized population. Estimates in this figure are limited to leisure-time physical activity only. This measure reflects an estimate of leisure-time aerobic activity motivated by the 2008 federal Physical Activity Guidelines for Americans, which are being used for Healthy People 2020 Objectives. The 2008 guidelines refer to any kind of aerobic activity, not just leisure-time aerobic activity, so the leisure-time aerobic activity estimates in this figure may underestimate the percentage of adults who met the 2008 guidelines for aerobic activity. This figure presents the percentage of adults who met the 2008 federal guidelines for aerobic activity. The 2008 federal guidelines recommend that for substantial health benefits, adults perform at least 150 minutes a week of moderate-intensity aerobic physical activity, 75 minutes a week of vigorous-intensity aerobic physical activity, or an equivalent combination of moderate- and vigorous-intensity aerobic activity. The 2008 guidelines state that aerobic activity should be performed in episodes of at least 10 minutes and preferably should be spread throughout the week. The analyses exclude the 2.0% of persons with unknown physical activity participation.

SOURCE: Tainya C. Clarke, Jeannine S. Schiller, and Tina Norris, "Figure 7.2. Percentage of Adults Aged 18 and over Who Met the 2008 Federal Physical Activity Guidelines for Aerobic Activity through Leisure-Time Aerobic Activity, by Age Group and Sex: United States, January–June 2017," in *Early Release of Selected Estimates Based on Data from the January–June 2017 National Health Interview Survey*, Centers for Disease Control and Prevention, National Center for Health Statistics, December 2017, https://www.cdc.gov/nchs/data/nhis/earlyrelease/earlyrelease201712.pdf (accessed January 31, 2018)

**TABLE 6.12**

**Percentage of high school students who did not participate in at least 60 minutes of physical activity on at least one day and percentage who were physically active at least 60 minutes per day on 5 or more days, by sex, race/ethnicity, and grade, 2015**

| Category | Did not participate in at least 60 minutes of physical activity on at least 1 day | | | Physically active at least 60 minutes/day on 5 or more days | | |
|---|---|---|---|---|---|---|
| | Female | Male | Total | Female | Male | Total |
| | % | % | % | % | % | % |
| **Race/ethnicity** | | | | | | |
| White* | 14.3 | 8.8 | 11.6 | 43.5 | 62.0 | 52.7 |
| Black* | 25.2 | 16.2 | 20.4 | 33.4 | 52.2 | 43.5 |
| Hispanic | 19.2 | 11.9 | 15.6 | 33.1 | 53.5 | 43.4 |
| **Grade** | | | | | | |
| 9 | 14.7 | 9.5 | 12.0 | 43.9 | 62.3 | 53.7 |
| 10 | 15.8 | 10.4 | 13.1 | 41.9 | 58.7 | 50.2 |
| 11 | 18.2 | 12.4 | 15.5 | 36.6 | 56.3 | 46.5 |
| 12 | 21.4 | 12.4 | 16.9 | 33.4 | 53.3 | 43.5 |
| **Total** | **17.5** | **11.1** | **14.3** | **39.1** | **57.8** | **48.6** |

* Non-Hispanic.

Notes: Because of changes in question context starting in 2011, national Youth Risk Behavior Survey (YRBS) prevalence estimates derived from the 60 minutes of physical activity question in 2011, 2013, and 2015 are not comparable to those reported in 2009 or earlier. On the 2005–2009 national YRBS questionnaire, physical activity was assessed with three questions (in the following order) that asked the number of days students participated in 1) at least 20 minutes of vigorous physical activity; 2) at least 30 minutes of moderate physical activity; and 3) at least 60 minutes of aerobic (moderate and vigorous) physical activity. On the 2011, 2013, and 2015 national YRBS questionnaires, only the 60 minutes of aerobic physical activity question was included. Physical activity is such that it would increase their heart rate and make them breathe hard some of the time during the 7 days before the survey.

SOURCE: Adapted from "Table 105. Percentage of High School Students Who Did Not Participate in at Least 60 Minutes of Physical Activity on at Least One Day and Who Were Physically Active at Least 60 Minutes/Day on 5 or More Days, by Sex, Race/Ethnicity, and Grade—United States, Youth Risk Behavior Survey, 2015," in "Youth Risk Behavior Surveillance—United States, 2015," *Morbidity and Mortality Weekly Report*, vol. 65, no. 6, June 10, 2016, https://www.cdc.gov/healthyyouth/data/yrbs/pdf/2015/ss6506_updated.pdf (accessed January 31, 2018)


**TABLE 6.13**

**Percentage of high school students who played video or computer games or used a computer for three or more hours per day and percentage who watched three or more hours per day of television, by sex, race/ethnicity, and grade, 2015**

| Category | Used computers 3 or more hours/day | | | Watched television 3 or more hours/day | | |
|---|---|---|---|---|---|---|
| | Female | Male | Total | Female | Male | Total |
| | % | % | % | % | % | % |
| **Race/ethnicity** | | | | | | |
| White* | 38.3 | 38.9 | 38.6 | 18.8 | 21.4 | 20.0 |
| Black* | 48.4 | 41.2 | 44.6 | 41.5 | 37.0 | 39.2 |
| Hispanic | 47.4 | 45.1 | 46.2 | 29.2 | 27.4 | 28.2 |
| **Grade** | | | | | | |
| 9 | 48.7 | 42.5 | 45.4 | 25.3 | 26.3 | 25.7 |
| 10 | 43.3 | 43.4 | 43.4 | 24.1 | 24.6 | 24.5 |
| 11 | 38.1 | 36.1 | 37.2 | 22.4 | 24.6 | 23.6 |
| 12 | 40.4 | 40.8 | 40.5 | 25.9 | 24.4 | 25.1 |
| **Total** | **42.8** | **40.6** | **41.7** | **24.4** | **25.0** | **24.7** |

* Non-Hispanic.

Notes: Using a computer for something that was not school work, on an average school day.

SOURCE: Adapted from "Table 109. Percentage of High School Students Who Played Video or Computer Games or Used a Computer for 3 or More Hours/Day and Who Watched 3 or More Hours/Day of Television, by Sex, Race/Ethnicity, and Grade—United States, Youth Risk Behavior Survey, 2015," in "Youth Risk Behavior Surveillance—United States, 2015," *Morbidity and Mortality Weekly Report*, vol. 65, no. 6, June 10, 2016, https://www.cdc.gov/healthyyouth/data/yrbs/pdf/2015/ss6506_updated.pdf (accessed January 31, 2018)

# CHAPTER 7
# CHILDBEARING, CONTRACEPTION, AND REPRODUCTIVE RIGHTS

Although more women are joining the workforce and pursuing educational opportunities and new careers, raising children remains a significant priority for many. The development of effective methods of contraception (including birth control pills), increased condom use for contraception and to combat the spread of the human immunodeficiency virus and other sexually transmitted infections, and the legalization of abortion and the morning-after pill have contributed to falling fertility and birth rates and have enabled women to time their childbearing. Increases in maternal age, in single motherhood, and in labor force participation by women have affected many aspects of women's relationships with their children. Likewise, pregnancy and parenting have profound effects on women's work lives.

## FERTILITY AND BIRTH RATES

American women are having fewer children than in the past. The fertility rate is defined as the total number of live births per 1,000 women aged 15 to 44 years in a given year. According to Joyce A. Martin et al. of the Centers for Disease Control and Prevention (CDC), in "Births: Final Data for 2015" (*National Vital Statistics Reports*, vol. 66, no. 1, January 5, 2017), during the baby boom (1946–1964) that followed World War II (1939–1945), the fertility rate (the number of births per 1,000 women aged 15 to 44) increased dramatically, from 85.9 in 1946 to 118 in 1960. The increase was attributable in large part to low (relative to wartime) female labor force participation and a trend toward larger families that accompanied the strong postwar economy. These trends shifted during the 1970s, as the availability of effective birth control and the movement of women in large numbers into the workforce corresponded with a significant drop in the fertility rate. The total number of live births per 1,000 women aged 15 to 44 years dropped below 70 in 1973 and—with the exception of a brief spike in 1990—has not regained this level since. (See Figure 7.1.) After

generally increasing between 1998 and 2007, the fertility rate declined almost every year thereafter. Martin et al. report in "Births: Final Data for 2016" (*National Vital Statistics Reports*, vol. 67, no. 1, January 31, 2018), that the fertility rate declined from 62.5 per 1,000 women aged 15 to 44 years in 2015 to 62 per 1,000 in 2016, the lowest rate ever reported in the United States.

Another way to measure fertility is by birth rates. Birth rates are the number of live births per 1,000 of a given population in a particular year. The 2016 national birth rate of 12.2 was, like the fertility rate, the lowest on record. (See Table 7.1.) This rate represented a dramatic drop of more than 20% from the 1980s, when the birth rate ranged between 15.6 and 16.4 annually (See Table 7.2; note that this table shows birth numbers and rates by race and excludes birth numbers and rates by Hispanic origin because Hispanic people may be of any race. The data for women of Hispanic origin are presented in Table 7.3.)

Birth and fertility rates vary by demographic characteristics of the mother. Native Hawaiian/Other Pacific Islander women had the highest birth (16.8) and fertility (72.9) rates in 2016. (See Table 7.1.) Hispanic women also had higher birth (16) and fertility (70.6) rates in 2016 than African American women, with a birth rate of 14 and a fertility rate of 63.3, Asian American women, 14.6 and 61.1, Native American/Alaskan Native women, 13.3 and 62.7, and white women, 10.5 and 58.8.

Although Hispanic women were more fertile than other demographic subgroups, their birth and fertility rates had been falling faster than all other groups except Native American/Alaskan Native women. Between 1989 and 2015 the birth rate among Native American/Alaskan Native women fell by 10 (from 19.7 to 9.7) and their fertility rate fell by 35.1 (from 79 to 43.9). During the same period Hispanic women's birth rate fell by 9.9 (from 26.2 to 16.3) and their fertility rate fell by 33.2

**FIGURE 7.1**

**Live births and fertility rates, 1970–2016**

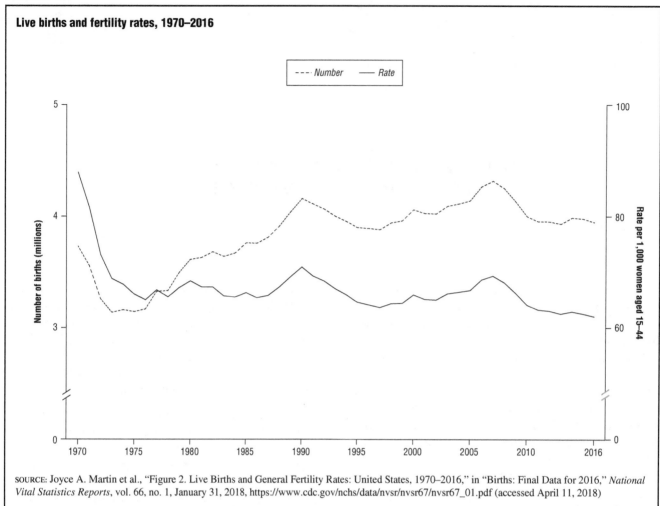

SOURCE: Joyce A. Martin et al., "Figure 2. Live Births and General Fertility Rates: United States, 1970–2016," in "Births: Final Data for 2016," *National Vital Statistics Reports*, vol. 66, no. 1, January 31, 2018, https://www.cdc.gov/nchs/data/nvsr/nvsr67/nvsr67_01.pdf (accessed April 11, 2018)

(from 104.9 to 71.7). The birth and fertility rates for African American women fell by 8 and 22.2, respectively; the rates for Asian or Pacific Islander women fell by 4.7 and 9.7, respectively; and the rates for white women fell by 3.4 and 3.3, respectively. (See Table 7.2 and Table 7.3.)

Declines in births among women in their teens and 20s, coupled with increases in births among women in their 30s, have raised the average age of mothers at the birth of their first child substantially since the 1970s. In 1970 women were most likely to give birth between the ages of 20 and 24 years, but by the 1980s, 25- to 29-year-olds were the most fertile age group, and by 2009, 30- to 34-year-olds had a higher birth rate than 20- to 24-year-olds. (See Table 7.4.) Between 1970 and 2015 the birth rate for women aged 15 to 19 years dropped from 68.3 to 22.3; the birth rate for women aged 20 to 24 years dropped from 167.8 to 76.8; and the birth rate for women aged 25 to 29 years dropped from 145.1 to 104.3. Meanwhile, the birth rate for women aged 30 to 34 years rose from 73.3 to 101.5, and the birth rate for women aged 35 to 39 years rose from 31.7 to 51.8. The birth rate for

women aged 40 to 44 years also grew substantially during these years, climbing from a low of 3.9 in the early 1980s to 11 in 2015.

Martin et al. report in "Births: Final Data for 2015" that the average age of mothers at first birth has been steadily rising for decades from 21.4 in 1970 to 22.7 in 1980, 24.2 in 1990, 24.9 in 2000, and 25.4 in 2010. According to Martin et al., in "Births: Final Data for 2016," the average age of a mother at the birth of her first child was a record high of 26.6 in 2016. The average age at which women gave birth to their first child varied by race and Hispanic-origin from a low of 23.2 years for Native American/Alaskan Native women to 30.1 years for Asian American women. The average age at first birth for Hispanic women was 24.8 years; for non-Hispanic African Americans it was 24.8, and for non-Hispanic white women it was 27.4.

The sustained decline in the birth and fertility rates that began in 2007 was likely linked to the Great Recession (2007–2009), which resulted in high unemployment for years after its official end in 2009 and caused many individuals and couples to delay their plans to have

TABLE 7.1

**Births and birth rates, 2010–16, and by race and Hispanic origin, 2016**

[Birth rates are births per 1,000 population in specified group. Fertility rates are births per 1,000 women aged 15–44 in specified group. Populations based on counts enumerated as of April 1 for census years and estimated as of July 1 for all other years]

| Race and Hispanic origin and year | Number | Birth rate | Fertility rate |
|---|---|---|---|
| **All races and origins[a]** | | | |
| 2016 | 3,945,875 | 12.2 | 62.0 |
| 2015 | 3,978,497 | 12.4 | 62.5 |
| 2014 | 3,988,076 | 12.5 | 62.9 |
| 2013 | 3,932,181 | 12.4 | 62.5 |
| 2012 | 3,952,841 | 12.6 | 63.0 |
| 2011 | 3,953,590 | 12.7 | 63.2 |
| 2010 | 3,999,386 | 13.0 | 64.1 |
| **Non-Hispanic, single race[b]** | | | |
| 2016: | | | |
| White | 2,056,332 | 10.5 | 58.8 |
| Black | 558,622 | 14.0 | 63.3 |
| American Indian or Alaska Native | 31,452 | 13.3 | 62.7 |
| Asian | 254,471 | 14.6 | 61.1 |
| Native Hawaiian or Other Pacific Islander | 9,342 | 16.8 | 72.9 |
| **Hispanic[c]** | | | |
| 2016 | 918,447 | 16.0 | 70.6 |

[a]Includes births to race and origin groups not shown separately, such as Hispanic single-race white, Hispanic single-race black, and non-Hispanic multiple-race women, as well as births with origin not stated.
[b]Race and Hispanic origin are reported separately on birth certificates; persons of Hispanic origin may be of any race. In this table, non-Hispanic women are classified by race. Race categories are consistent with 1997 Office of Management and Budget standards. Single race is defined as only one race reported on the birth certificate.
[c]Includes all persons of Hispanic origin of any race.

SOURCE: Joyce A. Martin et al., "Table 1. Births and Birth Rates: United States, 2010–2016, and by Race and Hispanic Origin, 2016," in "Births: Final Data for 2016," *National Vital Statistics Reports*, vol. 67, no. 1, January 31, 2018, https://www.cdc.gov/nchs/data/nvsr/nvsr67/nvsr67_01.pdf (accessed April 11, 2018)

children. Still, in 2017, when birth and fertility rates continued to decline despite the stronger economy, it appeared that other factors were also influencing women's childbearing choices. Ariana Eunjung Cha reports in "The U.S. Fertility Rate Just Hit a Record Low: Why Some Demographers Are Freaking Out" (WashingtonPost.com, June 30, 2017) that 2016 population data from the CDC showed a 1% drop in the number of US births in 2016, which brought the general fertility rate to 62 births per 1,000 women ages 15 to 44. The trend was driven by a decline in birth rates for teens and women in their 20s, and increased birth rates for women in their 30s and 40s were not enough to make up for the lower numbers among younger women. Demographers noted that US fertility rates in the coming years would be largely determined by millennials (the generation usually defined as being born between 1983 and 1999), who ranged between 18 and 34 years old in 2017. It remained to be seen whether the women of this generation were simply delaying pregnancy or choosing not to have children at all.

## CHARACTERISTICS OF MOTHERS

In "Fertility of Women in the United States: 2016—Detailed Tables" (May 4, 2017, https://www.census.gov/data/tables/2016/demo/fertility/women-fertility.html), the US Census Bureau provides a snapshot of American women who were mothers in 2016. Of the 75.9 million American women between the ages of 15 and 50 in 2016, 43 million (56.6%) were mothers. Among all American mothers, 33.9 million (78.8%) were native born, and 9.1 million (21.2%) were foreign born. Concerning the marital status of mothers, 6.4% of those under 20 years old were married at the time of their first birth, compared with 22.4% of those ages 20 to 25 and 33.7% of those over the age of 25. Meanwhile, 6.3% of those under 20 years old were living with an unmarried partner at the time of their first birth, compared with 10% of those ages 20 to 25 and 4.2% of those over the age of 25. Furthermore, 7.4% of those under 20 years old were neither married nor living with an unmarried partner at the time of their first birth, compared with 7.5% of those ages 20 to 25 and 2.2% of those over the age of 25. Of the 3.9 million women who gave birth in 2016, roughly 3.2 million were living above the federal poverty line ($24,300 for a family of four in 2016), compared with 736,700 who were living in poverty.

### Childless Women

It has become increasingly common for American women to remain childless. As of 2018, the percentage of childless women between the ages of 15 and 44 years had been growing since 1976, and the increased percentage of childless women was especially pronounced among women aged 25 years and older. (See Table 7.5.) More than half (53.8%) of women aged 25 to 29 years were childless in 2016, compared with 30.8% in 1976; 30.8% of women aged 30 to 34 years were childless in 2016, compared with 15.6% in 1976; 18.5% of women aged 35 to 39 years were childless in 2016, compared with 10.5% in 1976; and 14.4% of women aged 40 to 44 years were childless, compared with 10.2% in 1976.

### FAMILY SIZE

In *America's Families and Living Arrangements: 2017* (November 2017, https://www2.census.gov/programs-surveys/demo/tables/families/2017/cps-2017/tabavg3.xls), the Census Bureau reports that the average number of children in families with their own children under the age of 18 years was 1.9. Family households headed by women averaged slightly more children (1.82) than family households headed by men (1.63), although neither averaged as many as married-couple households (1.96). There was some variation in family size among different racial and ethnic groups. Hispanic families averaged 2.09 children, compared with 1.94 children for non-Hispanic African

# TABLE 7.2

## Births and birth rates, by race, 1980–2015

[Birth rates are births per 1,000 population in specified group. Fertility rates are births per 1,000 women aged 15–44 in specified group. Populations based on counts enumerated as of April 1 for census years and estimated as of July 1 for all other years. Beginning with 1970, excludes births to nonresidents of the United States.]

| Year | Number: All races[a] | White | Black | American Indian or Alaska Native | Asian or Pacific Islander | Birth rate: All races[a] | White | Black | American Indian or Alaska Native | Asian or Pacific Islander | Fertility rate: All races[a] | White | Black | American Indian or Alaska Native | Asian or Pacific Islander |
|---|---|---|---|---|---|---|---|---|---|---|---|---|---|---|---|
| **Registered births** | | | | | | | | | | | | | | | |
| | | | | | | Race of mother | | | | | | | | | |
| 2015 | 3,978,497 | 3,012,855 | 640,079 | 44,299 | 281,264 | 12.4 | 12.0 | 14.3 | 9.7 | 14.0 | 62.5 | 63.1 | 64.0 | 43.9 | 58.5 |
| 2014 | 3,988,076 | 3,019,863 | 640,562 | 44,928 | 282,723 | 12.5 | 12.0 | 14.5 | 9.9 | 14.6 | 62.9 | 63.2 | 64.6 | 44.8 | 60.7 |
| 2013 | 3,932,181 | 2,985,757 | 634,760 | 45,991 | 265,673 | 12.4 | 12.0 | 14.5 | 10.3 | 14.3 | 62.5 | 62.7 | 64.7 | 46.4 | 59.2 |
| 2012 | 3,952,841 | 2,999,820 | 634,126 | 46,093 | 272,802 | 12.6 | 12.1 | 14.7 | 10.5 | 15.1 | 63.0 | 63.0 | 65.1 | 47.0 | 62.2 |
| 2011 | 3,953,590 | 3,020,355 | 632,901 | 46,419 | 253,915 | 12.7 | 12.2 | 14.8 | 10.7 | 14.5 | 63.2 | 63.4 | 65.5 | 47.7 | 59.9 |
| 2010 | 3,999,386 | 3,069,315 | 636,425 | 46,760 | 246,886 | 13.0 | 12.5 | 15.1 | 11.0 | 14.5 | 64.1 | 64.4 | 66.3 | 48.6 | 59.2 |
| 2009 | 4,130,665 | 3,173,293 | 657,618 | 48,665 | 251,089 | 13.5 | 13.0 | 15.8 | 11.8 | 15.1 | 66.2 | 66.4 | 68.8 | 51.6 | 61.3 |
| 2008 | 4,247,694 | 3,274,163 | 670,809 | 49,537 | 253,185 | 14.0 | 13.5 | 16.3 | 12.4 | 15.7 | 68.1 | 68.3 | 70.6 | 54.0 | 63.3 |
| 2007 | 4,316,233 | 3,336,626 | 675,676 | 49,443 | 254,488 | 14.3 | 13.8 | 16.7 | 12.9 | 16.4 | 69.3 | 69.4 | 71.7 | 55.5 | 65.3 |
| 2006 | 4,265,555 | 3,310,308 | 666,481 | 47,721 | 241,045 | 14.3 | 13.8 | 16.7 | 12.9 | 16.0 | 68.6 | 68.7 | 71.4 | 55.3 | 63.7 |
| 2005 | 4,138,349 | 3,229,294 | 633,134 | 44,813 | 231,108 | 14.0 | 13.6 | 16.1 | 12.6 | 15.9 | 66.7 | 66.8 | 68.5 | 53.6 | 63.0 |
| 2004 | 4,112,052 | 3,222,928 | 616,074 | 43,927 | 229,123 | 14.0 | 13.6 | 15.9 | 12.8 | 16.4 | 66.4 | 66.5 | 67.2 | 54.2 | 64.5 |
| 2003 | 4,089,950 | 3,225,848 | 599,847 | 43,052 | 221,203 | 14.1 | 13.7 | 15.7 | 13.0 | 16.4 | 66.1 | 66.4 | 66.0 | 54.8 | 64.2 |
| 2002 | 4,021,726 | 3,174,760 | 593,691 | 42,368 | 210,907 | 14.0 | 13.6 | 15.7 | 13.2 | 16.3 | 65.0 | 65.1 | 65.7 | 55.7 | 63.3 |
| 2001 | 4,025,933 | 3,177,626 | 606,156 | 41,872 | 200,279 | 14.1 | 13.7 | 16.3 | 13.5 | 16.1 | 65.1 | 65.0 | 67.5 | 56.8 | 62.5 |
| 2000 | 4,058,814 | 3,194,005 | 622,598 | 41,668 | 200,543 | 14.4 | 13.9 | 17.0 | 14.0 | 17.1 | 65.9 | 65.3 | 70.0 | 58.7 | 65.8 |
| 1999 | 3,959,417 | 3,132,501 | 605,970 | 40,170 | 180,776 | 14.2 | 13.7 | 16.8 | 14.2 | 15.9 | 64.4 | 64.0 | 68.5 | 59.0 | 60.9 |
| 1998 | 3,941,553 | 3,118,727 | 609,902 | 40,272 | 172,652 | 14.3 | 13.8 | 17.1 | 14.8 | 15.9 | 64.3 | 63.6 | 69.4 | 61.3 | 60.1 |
| 1997 | 3,880,894 | 3,072,640 | 599,913 | 38,572 | 169,769 | 14.2 | 13.7 | 17.1 | 14.7 | 16.2 | 63.6 | 62.8 | 69.0 | 60.8 | 61.3 |
| 1996 | 3,891,494 | 3,093,057 | 594,781 | 37,880 | 165,776 | 14.4 | 13.9 | 17.3 | 14.9 | 16.5 | 64.1 | 63.3 | 69.2 | 61.8 | 62.3 |
| 1995 | 3,899,589 | 3,098,885 | 603,139 | 37,278 | 160,287 | 14.6 | 14.1 | 17.8 | 15.3 | 16.7 | 64.6 | 63.6 | 71.0 | 63.0 | 62.6 |
| 1994 | 3,952,767 | 3,121,004 | 636,391 | 37,740 | 157,632 | 15.0 | 14.3 | 19.1 | 16.0 | 17.1 | 65.9 | 64.2 | 75.9 | 65.8 | 63.9 |
| 1993 | 4,000,240 | 3,149,833 | 658,875 | 38,732 | 152,800 | 15.4 | 14.6 | 20.2 | 17.0 | 17.3 | 67.0 | 64.9 | 79.6 | 69.7 | 64.3 |
| 1992 | 4,065,014 | 3,201,678 | 673,633 | 39,453 | 150,250 | 15.8 | 15.0 | 21.1 | 17.9 | 17.9 | 68.4 | 66.1 | 82.4 | 73.1 | 66.1 |
| 1991 | 4,110,907 | 3,241,273 | 682,602 | 38,841 | 145,372 | 16.2 | 15.3 | 21.8 | 18.3 | 18.3 | 69.3 | 66.7 | 84.8 | 73.9 | 67.1 |
| 1990 | 4,158,212 | 3,290,273 | 684,336 | 39,051 | 141,635 | 16.7 | 15.8 | 22.4 | 18.9 | 19.0 | 70.9 | 68.3 | 86.8 | 76.2 | 69.6 |
| 1989 | 4,040,958 | 3,192,355 | 673,124 | 39,478 | 133,075 | 16.4 | 15.4 | 22.3 | 19.7 | 18.7 | 69.2 | 66.4 | 86.2 | 79.0 | 68.2 |
| 1988 | 3,909,510 | 3,102,083 | 638,562 | 37,088 | 129,035 | 16.0 | 15.0 | 21.5 | 19.3 | 19.2 | 67.3 | 64.5 | 82.6 | 76.8 | 70.2 |
| 1987 | 3,809,394 | 3,043,828 | 611,173 | 35,322 | 116,560 | 15.7 | 14.9 | 20.8 | 19.1 | 18.4 | 65.8 | 63.3 | 80.1 | 75.6 | 67.1 |
| 1986 | 3,756,547 | 3,019,175 | 592,910 | 34,169 | 107,797 | 15.6 | 14.8 | 20.5 | 19.2 | 18.0 | 65.4 | 63.1 | 78.9 | 75.9 | 66.0 |
| 1985 | 3,760,561 | 3,037,913 | 581,824 | 34,037 | 104,606 | 15.8 | 15.0 | 20.4 | 19.8 | 18.7 | 66.3 | 64.1 | 78.8 | 78.6 | 68.4 |
| 1984[b] | 3,669,141 | 2,967,100 | 568,138 | 33,256 | 98,926 | 15.6 | 14.8 | 20.1 | 20.1 | 18.8 | 65.5 | 63.2 | 78.2 | 79.8 | 69.2 |
| 1983[b] | 3,638,933 | 2,946,468 | 562,624 | 32,881 | 95,713 | 15.6 | 14.8 | 20.2 | 20.6 | 19.5 | 65.7 | 63.4 | 78.7 | 81.8 | 71.7 |
| 1982[b] | 3,680,537 | 2,984,817 | 568,506 | 32,436 | 93,193 | 15.9 | 15.1 | 20.7 | 21.1 | 20.3 | 67.3 | 64.8 | 80.9 | 83.6 | 74.8 |
| 1981[b] | 3,629,238 | 2,947,679 | 564,955 | 29,688 | 84,553 | 15.8 | 15.0 | 20.8 | 20.0 | 20.1 | 67.3 | 64.8 | 82.0 | 79.6 | 73.7 |
| 1980[b] | 3,612,258 | 2,936,351 | 568,080 | 29,389 | 74,355 | 15.9 | 15.1 | 21.3 | 20.7 | 19.9 | 68.4 | 65.6 | 84.7 | 82.7 | 73.2 |

—Data not available.

[a]For 1960–1991, includes births to races not shown separately. For 1992 and later years, unknown race of mother is imputed.

[b]Based on 100% of births in selected states and a 50% sample of births in all other states.

Notes: Race and Hispanic origin are reported separately on birth certificates. Race categories are consistent with 1977 Office of Management and Budget standards. Forty-nine states and the District of Columbia reported multiple-race data for 2015 that were bridged to single-race categories for comparability with other states. Multiple-race reporting areas vary for 2003–2015. In this table, all women, including Hispanic women, are classified only according to their race.

SOURCE: Adapted from Joyce A. Martin et al., "Table 1. Births and Birth Rates, by Race: United States, Specified Years 1940–1955 and Each Year, 1960–2015," in "Births: Final Data for 2015," *National Vital Statistics Reports*, vol. 66, no. 1, January 5, 2017, https://www.cdc.gov/nchs/data/nvsr/nvsr66/nvsr66_01.pdf (accessed January 17, 2018)

**TABLE 7.3**

**Births and birth rates, by race/ethnicity of mother, 1989–2015**

| Measure and year | All origins^a | Hispanic | | | | | Non-Hispanic | | | |
|---|---|---|---|---|---|---|---|---|---|---|
| | | Total | Mexican | Puerto Rican | Cuban | Central and South American | Other and unknown Hispanic | Total^b | White | Black |
| **Number** | | | | | | | | | | |
| 2015 | 3,978,497 | 924,048 | 546,169 | 70,987 | 21,107 | 142,249 | 143,536 | 3,021,999 | 2,130,279 | 589,047 |
| 2014 | 3,988,076 | 914,065 | 545,977 | 69,879 | 20,163 | 136,656 | 141,390 | 3,043,519 | 2,149,302 | 588,891 |
| 2013 | 3,932,181 | 901,033 | 545,202 | 68,302 | 18,854 | 131,305 | 137,370 | 3,003,556 | 2,129,196 | 583,834 |
| 2012 | 3,952,841 | 907,677 | 555,823 | 67,182 | 17,396 | 131,794 | 135,482 | 3,014,314 | 2,134,044 | 583,489 |
| 2011 | 3,953,590 | 918,129 | 566,699 | 67,018 | 17,131 | 136,221 | 131,060 | 3,008,200 | 2,146,566 | 582,345 |
| 2010 | 3,999,386 | 945,180 | 598,317 | 66,368 | 16,882 | 142,692 | 120,921 | 3,026,614 | 2,162,406 | 589,808 |
| 2009 | 4,130,665 | 999,548 | 645,297 | 68,486 | 16,641 | 148,647 | 120,477 | 3,101,330 | 2,212,552 | 609,584 |
| 2008 | 4,247,694 | 1,041,239 | 684,883 | 69,015 | 16,718 | 155,578 | 115,045 | 3,173,629 | 2,267,817 | 623,029 |
| 2007 | 4,316,233 | 1,062,779 | 722,055 | 68,488 | 16,981 | 169,851 | 85,404 | 3,222,460 | 2,310,333 | 627,191 |
| 2006 | 4,265,555 | 1,039,077 | 718,146 | 66,932 | 16,936 | 165,321 | 71,742 | 3,196,082 | 2,308,640 | 617,247 |
| 2005 | 4,138,349 | 985,505 | 693,197 | 63,340 | 16,064 | 151,201 | 61,703 | 3,123,005 | 2,279,768 | 583,759 |
| 2004 | 4,112,052 | 946,349 | 677,621 | 61,221 | 14,943 | 143,520 | 49,044 | 3,133,125 | 2,296,683 | 578,772 |
| 2003 | 4,089,950 | 912,329 | 654,504 | 58,400 | 14,867 | 135,586 | 48,972 | 3,149,034 | 2,321,904 | 576,033 |
| 2002 | 4,021,726 | 876,642 | 627,505 | 57,465 | 14,232 | 125,981 | 51,459 | 3,119,944 | 2,298,156 | 578,335 |
| 2001 | 4,025,933 | 851,851 | 611,000 | 57,568 | 14,017 | 121,365 | 47,901 | 3,149,572 | 2,326,578 | 589,917 |
| 2000 | 4,058,814 | 815,868 | 581,915 | 58,124 | 13,429 | 113,344 | 49,056 | 3,199,994 | 2,362,968 | 604,346 |
| 1999 | 3,959,417 | 764,339 | 540,674 | 57,138 | 13,088 | 103,307 | 50,132 | 3,147,580 | 2,346,450 | 588,981 |
| 1998 | 3,941,553 | 734,661 | 516,011 | 57,349 | 13,226 | 98,226 | 49,849 | 3,158,975 | 2,361,462 | 593,127 |
| 1997 | 3,880,894 | 709,767 | 499,024 | 55,450 | 12,887 | 97,405 | 45,001 | 3,115,174 | 2,333,363 | 581,431 |
| 1996 | 3,891,494 | 701,339 | 489,666 | 54,863 | 12,613 | 97,888 | 46,309 | 3,133,484 | 2,358,989 | 578,099 |
| 1995 | 3,899,589 | 679,768 | 469,615 | 54,824 | 12,473 | 94,996 | 47,860 | 3,160,495 | 2,382,638 | 587,781 |
| 1994 | 3,952,767 | 665,026 | 454,536 | 57,240 | 11,889 | 93,485 | 47,876 | 3,245,115 | 2,438,855 | 619,198 |
| 1993 | 4,000,240 | 654,418 | 443,733 | 58,102 | 11,916 | 92,371 | 48,296 | 3,295,345 | 2,472,031 | 641,273 |
| 1992^c | 4,049,012 | 643,271 | 432,047 | 59,569 | 11,472 | 89,031 | 51,152 | 3,365,862 | 2,527,207 | 657,450 |
| 1991^c | 4,094,566 | 623,085 | 411,233 | 59,833 | 11,058 | 86,908 | 54,053 | 3,434,464 | 2,589,878 | 666,758 |
| 1990^d | 4,092,994 | 595,073 | 385,640 | 58,807 | 11,311 | 83,008 | 56,307 | 3,457,417 | 2,626,500 | 661,701 |
| 1989^e | 3,903,012 | 532,249 | 327,233 | 56,229 | 10,842 | 72,443 | 65,502 | 3,297,493 | 2,526,367 | 611,269 |
| **Birth rate** | | | | | | | | | | |
| 2015^f | 12.4 | 16.3 | — | — | — | — | ^f | 11.5 | 10.7 | 14.2 |
| 2014^f | 12.5 | 16.5 | 15.5 | 13.3 | 9.9 | 22.0 | ^f | 11.7 | 10.8 | 14.4 |
| 2013^f | 12.4 | 16.7 | 15.8 | 13.3 | 9.4 | 21.9 | ^f | 11.6 | 10.7 | 14.4 |
| 2012^f | 12.6 | 17.1 | 16.3 | 13.5 | 8.9 | 22.3 | ^f | 11.7 | 10.7 | 14.6 |
| 2011^f | 12.7 | 17.6 | 16.9 | 13.7 | 9.1 | 23.0 | ^f | 11.7 | 10.8 | 14.7 |
| 2010^f | 13.0 | 18.7 | 18.2 | 14.1 | 9.0 | 23.4 | ^f | 11.8 | 10.9 | 15.1 |
| 2009^f | 13.5 | 20.3 | 19.8 | 15.5 | 9.5 | 25.5 | ^f | 12.2 | 11.2 | 15.7 |
| 2008^f | 14.0 | 21.8 | 21.7 | 16.4 | 10.1 | 26.1 | ^f | 12.5 | 11.5 | 16.3 |
| 2007^f | 14.3 | 23.0 | 23.9 | 17.1 | 10.2 | 24.6 | ^f | 12.8 | 11.7 | 16.6 |
| 2006^f | 14.3 | 23.3 | 24.6 | 17.5 | 10.4 | 23.8 | ^f | 12.7 | 11.7 | 16.5 |
| 2005^f | 14.0 | 22.9 | 24.5 | 17.0 | 10.2 | 22.7 | ^f | 12.5 | 11.6 | 15.8 |
| 2004^f | 14.0 | 22.8 | 24.8 | 16.0 | 9.3 | 22.1 | ^f | 12.6 | 11.7 | 15.8 |
| 2003^f | 14.1 | 22.8 | 24.6 | 15.0 | 10.0 | 23.0 | ^f | 12.7 | 11.8 | 15.9 |
| 2002^f | 14.0 | 22.7 | 24.3 | 16.5 | 10.1 | 22.5 | ^f | 12.6 | 11.7 | 16.1 |
| 2001^f | 14.1 | 22.9 | 24.7 | 17.7 | 10.3 | 21.7 | ^f | 12.8 | 11.9 | 16.6 |
| 2000^f | 14.4 | 23.1 | 25.0 | 18.1 | 9.7 | 21.8 | ^f | 13.2 | 12.2 | 17.3 |
| 1999^f | 14.2 | 22.5 | 24.2 | 18.0 | 9.4 | 21.7 | ^f | 13.0 | 12.1 | 17.1 |
| 1998^f | 14.3 | 22.7 | 24.6 | 17.9 | 9.7 | 21.7 | ^f | 13.2 | 12.2 | 17.5 |
| 1997^f | 14.2 | 23.0 | 25.3 | 17.2 | 10.0 | 21.3 | ^f | 13.1 | 12.2 | 17.4 |
| 1996^f | 14.4 | 23.8 | 26.2 | 17.2 | 10.6 | 22.5 | ^f | 13.3 | 12.3 | 17.6 |
| 1995^f | 14.6 | 24.1 | 25.8 | 19.0 | 10.8 | 24.2 | ^f | 13.5 | 12.5 | 18.2 |
| 1994^f | 15.0 | 24.7 | 26.1 | 20.8 | 10.7 | 24.9 | ^f | 13.9 | 12.8 | 19.5 |
| 1993^f | 15.4 | 25.4 | 26.8 | 21.5 | 10.5 | 26.3 | ^f | 14.3 | 13.1 | 20.7 |
| 1992^c, f | 15.8 | 26.1 | 27.4 | 22.9 | 10.1 | 27.5 | ^f | 14.8 | 13.4 | 21.6 |
| 1991^c, f | 16.2 | 26.5 | 27.6 | 23.3 | 9.8 | 28.3 | ^f | 15.2 | 13.9 | 22.4 |
| 1990^d, f | 16.7 | 26.7 | 28.7 | 21.6 | 10.9 | 27.5 | ^f | 15.7 | 14.4 | 23.0 |
| 1989^e, f | 16.3 | 26.2 | 25.7 | 23.7 | 10.0 | 28.3 | ^f | 15.4 | 14.2 | 22.8 |

American families, 1.91 children for non-Hispanic white families, and 1.67 children for Asian American families.

## Multiple Births

Increasing maternal age and the corresponding likelihood that women seek fertility treatments such as in-vitro fertilization and ovulation-induction medications have been largely responsible for the growth in multiple birth rates since the 1980s. Martin et al. report in "Births: Final Data for 2016" that the rate of twin births rose 76% (to 33.2 from 18.9 per 1,000) between 1980 and 2009. After holding fairly stable for a few years, it reached a record high of 33.9 in 2014, before declining slightly to 33.5 in 2015 and 33.4 in 2016. Among the total of approximately 3.9 million live births in 2016, 131,723 infants were born as twins. The highest rate of increase in

**TABLE 7.3**

**Births and birth rates, by race/ethnicity of mother, 1989–2015** [CONTINUED]

| | | Hispanic | | | | | | Non-Hispanic | | |
|---|---|---|---|---|---|---|---|---|---|---|
| Measure and year | All origins[a] | Total | Mexican | Puerto Rican | Cuban | Central and South American | Other and unknown Hispanic | Total[b] | White | Black |
| **Fertility rate** | | | | | | | | | | |
| 2015[f] | 62.5 | 71.7 | — | — | — | — | [f] | 60.2 | 59.3 | 64.1 |
| 2014[f] | 62.9 | 72.1 | 67.0 | 57.5 | 52.1 | 94.9 | [f] | 60.7 | 59.5 | 64.5 |
| 2013[f] | 62.5 | 72.9 | 68.4 | 57.8 | 48.0 | 94.4 | [f] | 59.9 | 58.7 | 64.6 |
| 2012[f] | 63.0 | 74.4 | 70.7 | 58.2 | 45.4 | 94.9 | [f] | 60.3 | 58.6 | 65.0 |
| 2011[f] | 63.2 | 76.2 | 73.0 | 59.6 | 46.1 | 96.3 | [f] | 60.1 | 58.7 | 65.4 |
| 2010[f] | 64.1 | 80.2 | 78.2 | 59.7 | 46.4 | 97.1 | [f] | 60.4 | 58.7 | 66.6 |
| 2009[f] | 66.2 | 86.5 | 84.8 | 63.7 | 46.0 | 107.5 | [f] | 61.6 | 59.6 | 68.9 |
| 2008[f] | 68.1 | 92.7 | 92.6 | 67.0 | 50.1 | 109.1 | [f] | 62.7 | 60.5 | 70.8 |
| 2007[f] | 69.3 | 97.4 | 102.8 | 70.3 | 47.6 | 100.1 | [f] | 63.3 | 61.0 | 71.4 |
| 2006[f] | 68.6 | 98.3 | 105.6 | 71.6 | 47.9 | 95.6 | [f] | 62.5 | 60.3 | 70.7 |
| 2005[f] | 66.7 | 96.4 | 104.5 | 69.8 | 49.1 | 90.5 | [f] | 60.8 | 59.0 | 67.2 |
| 2004[f] | 66.4 | 95.7 | 104.5 | 66.8 | 52.2 | 87.4 | [f] | 60.8 | 58.9 | 67.1 |
| 2003[f] | 66.1 | 95.2 | 103.7 | 60.6 | 60.8 | 89.7 | [f] | 60.7 | 58.9 | 67.1 |
| 2002[f] | 65.0 | 94.7 | 103.0 | 65.6 | 59.3 | 86.5 | [f] | 59.8 | 57.6 | 67.5 |
| 2001[f] | 65.1 | 95.4 | 105.0 | 71.7 | 56.4 | 82.2 | [f] | 60.0 | 57.7 | 69.1 |
| 2000[f] | 65.9 | 95.9 | 105.1 | 73.5 | 49.3 | 85.1 | [f] | 61.1 | 58.5 | 71.4 |
| 1999[f] | 64.4 | 93.0 | 101.5 | 71.1 | 47.0 | 84.8 | [f] | 60.0 | 57.7 | 69.9 |
| 1998[f] | 64.3 | 93.2 | 103.2 | 69.7 | 46.5 | 83.5 | [f] | 60.0 | 57.6 | 70.9 |
| 1997[f] | 63.6 | 94.2 | 106.6 | 65.8 | 53.1 | 80.6 | [f] | 59.3 | 56.8 | 70.3 |
| 1996[f] | 64.1 | 97.5 | 110.7 | 66.5 | 55.1 | 84.2 | [f] | 59.6 | 57.1 | 70.7 |
| 1995[f] | 64.6 | 98.8 | 109.9 | 71.3 | 52.2 | 89.1 | [f] | 60.2 | 57.5 | 72.8 |
| 1994[f] | 65.9 | 100.7 | 109.9 | 78.2 | 53.6 | 93.2 | [f] | 61.6 | 58.2 | 77.5 |
| 1993[f] | 67.0 | 103.3 | 110.9 | 79.8 | 53.9 | 101.5 | [f] | 62.7 | 58.9 | 81.5 |
| 1992[c, f] | 68.4 | 106.1 | 113.3 | 87.9 | 49.4 | 104.7 | [f] | 64.2 | 60.0 | 84.5 |
| 1991[c, f] | 69.3 | 106.9 | 114.9 | 87.9 | 47.6 | 105.5 | [f] | 65.2 | 60.9 | 87.0 |
| 1990[d, f] | 71.0 | 107.7 | 118.9 | 82.9 | 52.6 | 102.7 | [f] | 67.1 | 62.8 | 89.0 |
| 1989[e, f] | 69.2 | 104.9 | 106.6 | 86.6 | 49.8 | 95.8 | [f] | 65.7 | 60.5 | 84.8 |

—Data not available.
[a]Includes origin not stated.
[b]Includes races other than white and black.
[c]Excludes data for New Hampshire, which did not report Hispanic origin.
[d]Excludes data for New Hampshire and Oklahoma, which did not report Hispanic origin.
[e]Excludes data for Louisiana, New Hampshire, and Oklahoma, which did not report Hispanic origin.
[f]Rates for the Central and South American population include other and unknown Hispanic.
Notes: Race and Hispanic origin are reported separately on birth certificates. Race categories are consistent with 1977 Office of Management and Budget standards. Forty-nine states and the District of Columbia reported multiple-race data for 2015 that were bridged to single-race categories for comparability with other states. Multiple-race reporting areas vary for 2003–2015. Persons of Hispanic origin may be of any race. In this table, Hispanic women are classified only by place of origin; non-Hispanic women are classified by race. This table will be updated to include rates for specified Hispanic-origin groups when 2015 population data for these groups are available.

SOURCE: Joyce A. Martin et al., "Table 5. Births and Birth Rates, by Hispanic Origin of Mother, and by Race for Mothers of Non-Hispanic Origin: United States, 1989–2015," in "Births: Final Data for 2015," *National Vital Statistics Reports*, vol. 66, no. 1, January 5, 2017, https://www.cdc.gov/nchs/data/nvsr/nvsr66/nvsr66_01.pdf (accessed January 17, 2018).

twin births over the decades has occurred among non-Hispanic white women. The twin birth rate for this group increased by 62% between 1990 and 2009, compared with 42% for non-Hispanic African American women and 25% for Hispanic women.

The triplet and higher-order multiple birth rate rose even more dramatically than the twin birth rate between 1980 and 1998, increasing by more than 400% (although the total number of such births has always remained comparatively small). Since peaking in 1998, however, the triplet and higher-order multiple birth rate has decreased by more than a third. This decrease is largely a function of the refinement of fertility treatment techniques and of improved guidelines for the practitioners who employ them. Multiple-birth infants are more likely than single infants to be born prematurely, and their chances for survival are not as good, so health care providers attempt to limit the chances of

multiple-child pregnancies. Martin et al. report in "Births: Final Data for 2016" that the 4,003 triplet or higher-order multiple births in 2016 was the lowest number reported since 1992. In 2016 triplet and higher-order multiple births included 2,755 triplets, 217 quadruplets, and 31 quintuplets and higher-order multiple births.

**UNMARRIED CHILDBEARING**

According to the National Center for Health Statistics (NCHS), in *Health, United States, 2016* (May 2017, https://www.cdc.gov/nchs/data/hus/hus16.pdf), increasing percentages of women of all ages, races, and ethnicities have been giving birth outside of marriage since the 1970s. In 1970 only 10.7% of all live births were to unmarried mothers. (See Table 7.6.) This proportion had more than tripled by 2000, when it was 33.2%. Four out of 10 (40.3%) live births were to unmarried women in 2015.

TABLE 7.4

## Birth rates, by maternal age, 1970–2015

[Total fertility rates are sums of birth rates for 5-year age groups multiplied by 5. Birth rates are births per 1,000 women in specified group. Populations based on counts enumerated as of April 1 for census years and estimated as of July 1 for all other years.]

| Year and race | Total fertility rate | 10–14 | 15–19 Total | 15–17 | 18–19 | 20–24 | 25–29 | 30–34 | 35–39 | 40–44 | 45–49[a] |
|---|---|---|---|---|---|---|---|---|---|---|---|
| **All races[b]** | | | | | | | | | | | |
| 2015 | 1,843.5 | 0.2 | 22.3 | 9.9 | 40.7 | 76.8 | 104.3 | 101.5 | 51.8 | 11.0 | 0.8 |
| 2014 | 1,862.5 | 0.3 | 24.2 | 10.9 | 43.8 | 79.0 | 105.8 | 100.8 | 51.0 | 10.6 | 0.8 |
| 2013 | 1,857.5 | 0.3 | 26.5 | 12.3 | 47.1 | 80.7 | 105.5 | 98.0 | 49.3 | 10.4 | 0.8 |
| 2012 | 1,880.5 | 0.4 | 29.4 | 14.1 | 51.4 | 83.1 | 106.5 | 97.3 | 48.3 | 10.4 | 0.7 |
| 2011 | 1,894.5 | 0.4 | 31.3 | 15.4 | 54.1 | 85.3 | 107.2 | 96.5 | 47.2 | 10.3 | 0.7 |
| 2010 | 1,931.0 | 0.4 | 34.2 | 17.3 | 58.2 | 90.0 | 108.3 | 96.5 | 45.9 | 10.2 | 0.7 |
| 2009 | 2,002.0 | 0.5 | 37.9 | 19.6 | 64.0 | 96.2 | 111.5 | 97.5 | 46.1 | 10.0 | 0.7 |
| 2008 | 2,072.0 | 0.6 | 40.2 | 21.1 | 68.2 | 101.8 | 115.0 | 99.4 | 46.8 | 9.9 | 0.7 |
| 2007 | 2,120.0 | 0.6 | 41.5 | 21.7 | 71.7 | 105.4 | 118.1 | 100.6 | 47.6 | 9.6 | 0.6 |
| 2006 | 2,108.0 | 0.6 | 41.1 | 21.6 | 71.2 | 105.5 | 118.0 | 98.9 | 47.5 | 9.4 | 0.6 |
| 2005 | 2,057.0 | 0.6 | 39.7 | 21.1 | 68.4 | 101.8 | 116.5 | 96.7 | 46.4 | 9.1 | 0.6 |
| 2004 | 2,051.5 | 0.6 | 40.5 | 21.8 | 68.7 | 101.5 | 116.5 | 96.2 | 45.5 | 9.0 | 0.5 |
| 2003 | 2,047.5 | 0.6 | 41.1 | 22.2 | 69.6 | 102.3 | 116.7 | 95.7 | 43.9 | 8.7 | 0.5 |
| 2002 | 2,020.5 | 0.7 | 42.6 | 23.1 | 72.2 | 103.1 | 114.7 | 92.6 | 41.6 | 8.3 | 0.5 |
| 2001 | 2,030.5 | 0.8 | 45.0 | 24.5 | 75.5 | 105.6 | 113.8 | 91.8 | 40.5 | 8.1 | 0.5 |
| 2000 | 2,056.0 | 0.9 | 47.7 | 26.9 | 78.1 | 109.7 | 113.5 | 91.2 | 39.7 | 8.0 | 0.5 |
| 1999 | 2,007.5 | 0.9 | 48.8 | 28.2 | 79.1 | 107.9 | 111.2 | 87.1 | 37.8 | 7.4 | 0.4 |
| 1998 | 1,999.0 | 1.0 | 50.3 | 29.9 | 80.9 | 108.4 | 110.2 | 85.2 | 36.9 | 7.4 | 0.4 |
| 1997 | 1,971.0 | 1.1 | 51.3 | 31.4 | 82.1 | 107.3 | 108.3 | 83.0 | 35.7 | 7.1 | 0.4 |
| 1996 | 1,976.0 | 1.2 | 53.5 | 33.3 | 84.7 | 107.8 | 108.6 | 82.1 | 34.9 | 6.8 | 0.3 |
| 1995 | 1,978.0 | 1.3 | 56.0 | 35.5 | 87.7 | 107.5 | 108.8 | 81.1 | 34.0 | 6.6 | 0.3 |
| 1994 | 2,001.5 | 1.4 | 58.2 | 37.2 | 90.2 | 109.2 | 111.0 | 80.4 | 33.4 | 6.4 | 0.3 |
| 1993 | 2,019.5 | 1.4 | 59.0 | 37.5 | 91.1 | 111.3 | 113.2 | 79.9 | 32.7 | 6.1 | 0.3 |
| 1992 | 2,046.0 | 1.4 | 60.3 | 37.6 | 93.6 | 113.7 | 115.7 | 79.6 | 32.3 | 5.9 | 0.3 |
| 1991 | 2,062.5 | 1.4 | 61.8 | 38.6 | 94.0 | 115.3 | 117.2 | 79.2 | 31.9 | 5.5 | 0.2 |
| 1990 | 2,081.0 | 1.4 | 59.9 | 37.5 | 88.6 | 116.5 | 120.2 | 80.8 | 31.7 | 5.5 | 0.2 |
| 1989 | 2,014.0 | 1.4 | 57.3 | 36.4 | 84.2 | 113.8 | 117.6 | 77.4 | 29.9 | 5.2 | 0.2 |
| 1988 | 1,934.0 | 1.3 | 53.0 | 33.6 | 79.9 | 110.2 | 114.4 | 74.8 | 28.1 | 4.8 | 0.2 |
| 1987 | 1,872.0 | 1.3 | 50.6 | 31.7 | 78.5 | 107.9 | 111.6 | 72.1 | 26.3 | 4.4 | 0.2 |
| 1986 | 1,837.5 | 1.3 | 50.2 | 30.5 | 79.6 | 107.4 | 109.8 | 70.1 | 24.4 | 4.1 | 0.2 |
| 1985 | 1,844.0 | 1.2 | 51.0 | 31.0 | 79.6 | 108.3 | 111.0 | 69.1 | 24.0 | 4.0 | 0.2 |
| 1984[c] | 1,806.5 | 1.2 | 50.6 | 31.0 | 77.4 | 106.8 | 108.7 | 67.0 | 22.9 | 3.9 | 0.2 |
| 1983[c] | 1,799.0 | 1.1 | 51.4 | 31.8 | 77.4 | 107.8 | 108.5 | 64.9 | 22.0 | 3.9 | 0.2 |
| 1982[c] | 1,827.5 | 1.1 | 52.4 | 32.3 | 79.4 | 111.6 | 111.0 | 64.1 | 21.2 | 3.9 | 0.2 |
| 1981[c] | 1,812.0 | 1.1 | 52.2 | 32.0 | 80.0 | 112.2 | 111.5 | 61.4 | 20.0 | 3.8 | 0.2 |
| 1980[c] | 1,839.5 | 1.1 | 53.0 | 32.5 | 82.1 | 115.1 | 112.9 | 61.9 | 19.8 | 3.9 | 0.2 |
| 1979[c] | 1,808.0 | 1.2 | 52.3 | 32.3 | 81.3 | 112.8 | 111.4 | 60.3 | 19.5 | 3.9 | 0.2 |
| 1978[c] | 1,760.0 | 1.2 | 51.5 | 32.2 | 79.8 | 109.9 | 108.5 | 57.8 | 19.0 | 3.9 | 0.2 |
| 1977[c] | 1,789.5 | 1.2 | 52.8 | 33.9 | 80.9 | 112.9 | 111.0 | 56.4 | 19.2 | 4.2 | 0.2 |
| 1976[c] | 1,738.0 | 1.2 | 52.8 | 34.1 | 80.5 | 110.3 | 106.2 | 53.6 | 19.0 | 4.3 | 0.2 |
| 1975[c] | 1,774.0 | 1.3 | 55.6 | 36.1 | 85.0 | 113.0 | 108.2 | 52.3 | 19.5 | 4.6 | 0.3 |
| 1974[c] | 1,835.0 | 1.2 | 57.5 | 37.3 | 88.7 | 117.7 | 111.5 | 53.8 | 20.2 | 4.8 | 0.3 |
| 1973[c] | 1,879.0 | 1.2 | 59.3 | 38.5 | 91.2 | 119.7 | 112.2 | 55.6 | 22.1 | 5.4 | 0.3 |
| 1972[c] | 2,010.0 | 1.2 | 61.7 | 39.0 | 96.9 | 130.2 | 117.7 | 59.8 | 24.8 | 6.2 | 0.4 |
| 1971[d] | 2,266.5 | 1.1 | 64.5 | 38.2 | 105.3 | 150.1 | 134.1 | 67.3 | 28.7 | 7.1 | 0.4 |
| 1970[d] | 2,480.0 | 1.2 | 68.3 | 38.8 | 114.7 | 167.8 | 145.1 | 73.3 | 31.7 | 8.1 | 0.5 |

[a]Beginning in 1997, birth rates are computed by relating births to women aged 45 and over to women aged 45–49.
[b]For 1970–1991, includes births to races not shown separately. For 1992 and later years, unknown race of mother is imputed.
[c]Based on 100% of births in selected states and on a 50% sample of births in all other states.
[d]Based on a 50% sample of births.

SOURCE: Adapted from Joyce A. Martin et al., "Table 4. Birth Rates, by Age of Mother: United States, 1970–2015, and by Age and Race of Mother: United States, 1980–2015" in "Births: Final Data for 2015," *National Vital Statistics Reports*, vol. 66, no. 1, January 5, 2017, https://www.cdc.gov/nchs/data/nvsr/nvsr66/nvsr66_01.pdf (accessed January 17, 2018)

The likelihood that a pregnant woman will marry before giving birth has declined sharply since the early 1960s. There are several reasons for this change. Unmarried women are more sexually active than in the past, and many of them have put their education and careers ahead of marriage. The stigma that was formerly attached to unmarried motherhood has largely disappeared. In addition, many women feel that being single is preferable to living in an unhappy, unstable, or abusive marriage, and some prefer to raise their children by themselves. Furthermore, many women who are having children without being married live with their partner in families that may be traditional in every way except for the marriage license. Also, prior to recent gains in marriage equality, which were solidified by the 2015 Supreme Court ruling in *Obergefell v. Hodges* (No. 14-556), mothers in same-sex

TABLE 7.5

**Percentage of childless women, by age group, selected years 1976–2016**

[Years ending in June.]

| | Age of women | | | | | | | | |
|---|---|---|---|---|---|---|---|---|---|
| Year | 15 to 44 years | 15 to 50 years | 15 to 19 years | 20 to 24 years | 25 to 29 years | 30 to 34 years | 35 to 39 years | 40 to 44 years | 45 to 50 years |
| **Percent childless** | | | | | | | | | |
| 2016 | 48.6 | 43.4 | 96.2 | 75.8 | 53.8 | 30.8 | 18.5 | 14.4 | 17.1 |
| 2014 | 47.6 | 42.4 | 95.9 | 75.2 | 49.6 | 28.9 | 18.5 | 15.3 | 16.7 |
| 2012[a] | 46.5 | 41.3 | 94.9 | 71.4 | 49.4 | 28.2 | 17.2 | 15.1 | 16.8 |
| 2010 | 47.1 | N | 94.6 | 70.5 | 47.6 | 29.7 | 19.7 | 18.8 | N |
| 2008 | 45.7 | N | 93.7 | 70.6 | 46.2 | 26.8 | 19.4 | 17.8 | N |
| 2006 | 45.1 | N | 93.3 | 68.6 | 45.6 | 26.2 | 18.9 | 20.4 | N |
| 2004 | 44.6 | N | 93.3 | 68.9 | 44.2 | 27.6 | 19.6 | 19.3 | N |
| 2002[b] | 43.8 | N | 91.1 | 67.2 | 45.5 | 27.7 | 20.3 | 18.0 | N |
| 2000 | 42.8 | N | 90.5 | 63.6 | 44.2 | 28.1 | 20.1 | 19.0 | N |
| 1998 | 42.2 | N | 90.1 | 64.0 | 43.5 | 27.4 | 19.8 | 19.0 | N |
| 1995 | 41.8 | N | 90.7 | 64.3 | 43.8 | 26.7 | 19.7 | 17.5 | N |
| 1994 | 42.0 | N | 91.6 | 65.3 | 43.6 | 26.3 | 19.6 | 17.5 | N |
| 1992 | 41.2 | N | 92.7 | 65.9 | 41.3 | 26.1 | 18.8 | 15.7 | N |
| 1990 | 41.6 | N | 91.9 | 64.6 | 42.1 | 25.7 | 17.7 | 16.0 | N |
| 1988 | 38.0[c] | N | N | 74.2[d] | 42.2 | 25.1 | 17.7 | 14.7 | N |
| 1987 | 36.6[c] | N | N | 71.7[d] | 39.3 | 23.6 | 16.7 | 14.2 | N |
| 1986 | 37.3[c] | N | N | 71.8[d] | 40.7 | 23.9 | 16.6 | 13.2 | N |
| 1985 | 38.1[c] | N | N | 71.4[d] | 41.5 | 26.2 | 16.7 | 11.4 | N |
| 1984 | 37.6[c] | N | N | 71.4[d] | 39.9 | 23.5 | 15.4 | 11.1 | N |
| 1983 | 37.7[c] | N | N | 71.4[d] | 39.5 | 22.9 | 14.6 | 10.1 | N |
| 1982 | 38.2[c] | N | N | 72.2[d] | 38.8 | 22.5 | 14.4 | 11.0 | N |
| 1981 | 36.7[c] | N | N | 69.7[d] | 37.2 | 20.6 | 12.3 | 9.5 | N |
| 1980 | 36.7[c] | N | N | 70.0[d] | 36.8 | 19.8 | 12.1 | 10.1 | N |
| 1976 | 35.1[c] | N | N | 69.0[d] | 30.8 | 15.6 | 10.5 | 10.2 | N |

[a]Changes were made to data processing in 2012 which affected estimates of childlessness.
[b]Counts for 2002 were corrected September 8, 2014.
[c]18 to 44 years old.
[d]18 to 24 years old
N = Not available.

SOURCE: Adapted from "Historical Table 1. Percent Childless and Births per 1,000 Women in the Last 12 Months: Selected Years, 1976–2016," in *Fertility—Historical Time Series Tables*, US Census Bureau, April 9, 2014, https://www2.census.gov/programs-surveys/demo/tables/fertility/time-series/his-cps/h1.xlsx (accessed January 31, 2018)

couples who conceived a child with a male friend or by artificial insemination with sperm from a sperm bank (a facility that collects and stores human sperm) could not legally marry their female partners.

Part of the increase in unmarried childbearing as a percentage of all childbearing is attributable to the decrease in the birth rate for married women; in other words, the proportion of births to unmarried women has increased faster than the number of births and the birth rate for unmarried women. As Table 7.5 shows, the birth rate for unmarried women peaked above 47 between 2005 and 2010, but by 2015 it had dipped to 43.4, slightly below the 1990 level.

**Teenage Motherhood**

The declines in the unmarried birth rate during the early 21st century are due in part to the falling birth rate for teenage mothers. At one time, unmarried motherhood was nearly synonymous with teen motherhood. In 1970, 50.1% of births to unmarried mothers were to unmarried mothers under the age of 20 years. (See Table 7.5.) By 2015 only 12.9% of nonmarital births were to teenagers.

Over the same period, births to women aged 20 to 24 years as a percentage of all nonmarital births remained comparatively constant: after an upsurge from 31.8% in 1970 to 35.6% in 1980 and 38.3% in 2005, rates have generally hovered between 35% and 37%. Meanwhile, the percentage of all nonmarital births to women over the age of 25 years grew dramatically, from 18.1% in 1970 to 52.1% in 2015.

The birth rate for teenagers aged 15 to 19 years fell from 59.9 per 1,000 in 1990 to a low of 24.2 in 2015. (See Figure 7.2.) Among young girls aged 10 to 14 years the rate declined by 86% between 1991 and 2015, and among girls aged 15 to 19 years the rate declined by 64%. (See Table 7.7.) The declines occurred across all demographic categories, but disparities among demographic subgroups remained, especially within the 15- to 19-year-old age group. Among girls aged 15 to 19 years the birth rate in 2015 was lowest for Asian or Pacific Islanders (6.9 per 1,000) and non-Hispanic whites (16) and highest for Hispanics (34.9) and non-Hispanic African Americans (31.8).

According to the CDC, in "About Teen Pregnancy" (May 9, 2017, https://www.cdc.gov/teenpregnancy/about/

TABLE 7.6

**Nonmarital childbearing, by race and Hispanic origin and age of mother, selected years 1970–2015**

[Data are based on birth certificates]

| Maternal race, Hispanic origin, and age | 1970 | 1980 | 1990 | 1995 | 2000 | 2005 | 2010 | 2013 | 2014 | 2015 |
|---|---|---|---|---|---|---|---|---|---|---|
| | Live births per 1,000 unmarried women aged 15–44[a] | | | | | | | | | |
| All races and origins | 26.4 | 29.4 | 43.8 | 44.3 | 44.1 | 47.2 | 47.5 | 44.3 | 43.9 | 43.4 |
| White[b] | 13.9 | 18.1 | 32.9 | 37.0 | 38.2 | 43.2 | 44.5 | 40.8 | 40.6 | 40.4 |
| Black or African American[b] | 95.5 | 81.1 | 90.5 | 74.5 | 70.5 | 67.2 | 65.3 | 61.7 | 61.5 | 59.6 |
| Asian or Pacific Islander | — | — | — | — | 20.9 | 22.8 | 22.3 | 21.8 | 21.7 | 20.4 |
| Hispanic or Latina[c] | — | — | 89.6 | 88.8 | 87.2 | 96.2 | 80.6 | 69.9 | 68.5 | 67.4 |
| White, not Hispanic or Latina[c] | — | — | 24.4 | 28.1 | 28.0 | 30.4 | 32.9 | 31.7 | 31.8 | 31.6 |
| | Percent of live births to unmarried mothers | | | | | | | | | |
| All races and origins | 10.7 | 18.4 | 28.0 | 32.2 | 33.2 | 36.9 | 40.8 | 40.6 | 40.2 | 40.3 |
| White | 5.5 | 11.2 | 20.4 | 25.3 | 27.1 | 31.7 | 35.9 | 35.8 | 35.7 | 35.8 |
| Black or African American | 37.5 | 56.1 | 66.5 | 69.9 | 68.5 | 69.3 | 72.1 | 71.0 | 70.4 | 70.1 |
| American Indian or Alaska Native | 22.4 | 39.2 | 53.6 | 57.2 | 58.4 | 63.5 | 65.6 | 66.4 | 65.7 | 65.8 |
| Asian or Pacific Islander[d] | — | 7.3 | 13.2 | 16.3 | 14.8 | 16.2 | 17.0 | 17.0 | 16.4 | 16.4 |
| Hispanic or Latina[c] | — | 23.6 | 36.7 | 40.8 | 42.7 | 48.0 | 53.4 | 53.2 | 52.9 | 53.0 |
|    Mexican | — | 20.3 | 33.3 | 38.1 | 40.7 | 46.7 | 52.0 | 51.9 | 51.6 | 51.5 |
|    Puerto Rican | — | 46.3 | 55.9 | 60.0 | 59.6 | 61.7 | 65.2 | 64.6 | 63.9 | 64.2 |
|    Cuban | — | 10.0 | 18.2 | 23.8 | 27.3 | 36.4 | 47.0 | 50.1 | 49.8 | 50.7 |
|    Central and South American | — | 27.1 | 41.2 | 44.1 | 44.7 | 49.2 | 51.8 | 50.1 | 50.4 | 51.0 |
|    Other and unknown Hispanic or Latina | — | 22.4 | 37.2 | 44.0 | 46.2 | 48.6 | 56.3 | 56.1 | 55.5 | 55.1 |
| Not Hispanic or Latina:[c] | | | | | | | | | | |
|    White | — | 9.5 | 16.9 | 21.2 | 22.1 | 25.3 | 29.0 | 29.3 | 29.2 | 29.2 |
|    Black or African American | — | 57.2 | 66.7 | 70.0 | 68.7 | 69.9 | 72.5 | 71.5 | 70.9 | 70.5 |
| | Number of live births, in thousands | | | | | | | | | |
| Live births to unmarried mothers | 399 | 666 | 1,165 | 1,254 | 1,347 | 1,527 | 1,633 | 1,596 | 1,605 | 1,602 |
| | Percent distribution of live births to unmarried mothers | | | | | | | | | |
| **Maternal age** | | | | | | | | | | |
| Under 20 years | 50.1 | 40.8 | 30.9 | 30.9 | 28.0 | 23.1 | 20.1 | 15.4 | 13.9 | 12.9 |
| 20–24 years | 31.8 | 35.6 | 34.7 | 34.5 | 37.4 | 38.3 | 36.8 | 36.8 | 36.1 | 35.0 |
| 25 years and over | 18.1 | 23.5 | 34.4 | 34.7 | 34.6 | 38.7 | 43.1 | 47.9 | 50.0 | 52.1 |

—Data not available.

[a]Rates computed by dividing births to unmarried mothers, regardless of age of mother, by the population of unmarried women aged 15–44. Population data for unmarried American Indian or Alaska Native women are not available for rate calculations. Prior to 2000, population data for unmarried Asian or Pacific Islander women were not available for rate calculations.

[b]For 1970 and 1975 (shown in spreadsheet version), birth rates are by race of child.

[c]Prior to 1993, data from states that did not report Hispanic origin on the birth certificate were excluded. Data for non-Hispanic white and non-Hispanic black women for years prior to 1989 are not nationally representative and are provided solely for comparison with Hispanic data.

[d]Estimates are not available for Asian or Pacific Islander subgroups because not all states have adopted the 2003 revision of the US Standard Certificate of Live Birth.

Notes: National estimates for 1970 and 1975 for unmarried mothers are based on births occurring in states reporting marital status of mother. Changes in reporting procedures for marital status occurred in some states during the 1990s. Data for states in which marital status was not reported have been inferred and included with data from the remaining states. Interpretation of trend data for Hispanic births should take into consideration expansion of reporting areas. The race groups, white, black, American Indian or Alaska Native, and Asian or Pacific Islander, include persons of Hispanic and non-Hispanic origin. Persons of Hispanic origin may be of any race. Starting with 2003 data, some states reported multiple-race data. The multiple-race data for these states were bridged to the single-race categories of the 1977 Office of Management and Budget standards, for comparability with other states. Starting with *Health, United States, 2003*, rates for 1991–1999 were revised using intercensal population estimates based on the 1990 and 2000 censuses. Rates for 2000 were based on bridged-race April 1, 2000 census counts. Starting with *Health, United States, 2012*, rates for 2001–2009 were revised using intercensal population estimates based on the 2000 and 2010 censuses. Rates for 2010 were based on 2010 bridged-race April 2010 census counts. Rates for 2011 and beyond were computed using 2010-based postcensal estimates.

SOURCE: "Table 4. Nonmarital Childbearing, by Detailed Race and Hispanic Origin of Mother, and Maternal Age: United States, Selected Years 1970–2015," in *Health, United States, 2016: With Chartbook on Long-term Trends in Health*, Centers for Disease Control and Prevention, National Center for Health Statistics, May 2017, https://www.cdc.gov/nchs/data/hus/hus16.pdf (accessed January 17, 2018).

index.htm), the reasons for the decline in teen pregnancy are still being investigated. Possible explanations include the fact that teens appear to be less sexually active than in the past, as well as the fact that among sexually active teens, the use of birth control is more common.

**SEXUALLY ACTIVE TEENAGERS.** In "Youth Risk Behavior Surveillance—United States, 2015" June 10, 2016, https://www.cdc.gov/healthyyouth/data/yrbs/pdf/2015/ss6506_updated.pdf), the CDC notes that between 1991 and 2013 the percentage of high school students who reported ever having sexual intercourse dropped significantly, from 54.1% to 46.8%. By 2015 the figure had fallen further still, to 41.2%. (See Table 7.8.) In 2015, 30.1% of all high school students reported that they were currently sexually active, and 11.5% reported that they had had four or more sex partners during their lifetime. (See Table 7.9.) More than half (56.9%) of sexually active students reported using a condom during their last sexual intercourse, and 18.2% reported birth control pill use before their last sexual intercourse. (See Table 7.10.)

Early sexual activity results in many unintended pregnancies. In "Trends in Teen Pregnancy and Childbearing" (2016, https://www.hhs.gov/ash/oah/adolescent-development/reproductive-health-and-teen-pregnancy/teen-pregnancy-and-childbearing/trends/index.html), the US Department of Health and Human Services (HHS) Office of

**FIGURE 7.2**

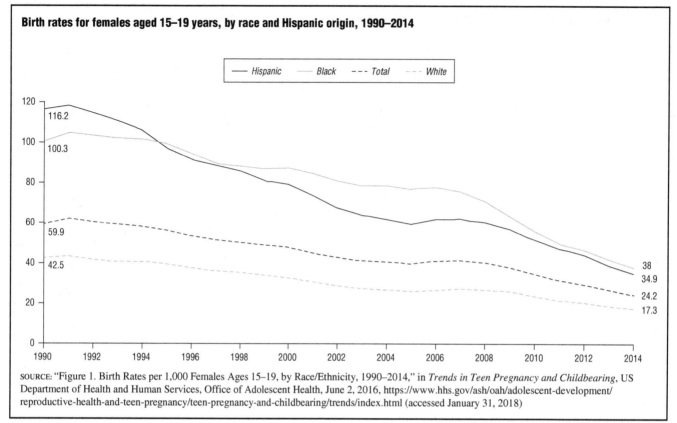

Birth rates for females aged 15–19 years, by race and Hispanic origin, 1990–2014

SOURCE: "Figure 1. Birth Rates per 1,000 Females Ages 15–19, by Race/Ethnicity, 1990–2014," in *Trends in Teen Pregnancy and Childbearing*, US Department of Health and Human Services, Office of Adolescent Health, June 2, 2016, https://www.hhs.gov/ash/oah/adolescent-development/reproductive-health-and-teen-pregnancy/teen-pregnancy-and-childbearing/trends/index.html (accessed January 31, 2018)

Adolescent Health estimates that 77% of teen pregnancies are unplanned. In "Pregnancies, Births and Abortions among Adolescents and Young Women in the United States, 2013: National and State Trends by Age, Race and Ethnicity" (September 2017, https://www.guttmacher.org/sites/default/files/report_pdf/us-adolescent-pregnancy-trends-2013.pdf), Kathryn Kost, Isaac Maddow-Zimet, and Alex Arpaia of the Guttmacher Institute report that the downward trend in teen birth rates has been paralleled by a corresponding decline in teen abortions. Between 1990 and 2013 the teen abortion rate fell 74.2% from 41.1 per 1,000 to 10.6

SOCIAL CONSEQUENCES OF TEEN CHILDBEARING. Children born to teen mothers face a host of disadvantages that make them disproportionately likely to grow up in poverty and have diminished prospects for their own future well-being. Teen mothers frequently must discontinue their education to care for their children, and households headed by adults without a high school education are far more likely than other households to live in poverty. Children born to teen mothers are more likely to score poorly on measures of well-being, and they are more likely to end up in prison than are children born into more mature families. According to Power to Decide: The Campaign to Prevent Unplanned Pregnancy, in "National Cost Savings Fact Sheet" (January 2018, https://powertodecide.org/sites/default/files/media/savings-fact-sheet-national.pdf), the public cost of teen pregnancy

is about $16,000 per birth, including the cost of prenatal, labor and delivery, and postpartum care for the mother, one year of infant care, and receipt of social assistance during pregnancy and infancy for those who participate. The organization calculates that the decline in teen pregnancy rates led to 428,000 fewer teen births in 2015, effectively saving US taxpayers $4.4 billion.

## HEALTH ISSUES DURING PREGNANCY, CHILDBIRTH, AND INFANCY

### Tobacco and Alcohol Use

Smoking tobacco while pregnant has been conclusively linked to increased risks of miscarriage, problems with the placenta (the tissue that serves as the source of fetal nutrition), premature birth, low birth weight, birth defects, and sudden infant death syndrome. Growing awareness of these risks, along with broad declines in the numbers of women who smoke, has resulted in dramatic reductions in the number of pregnant women who smoke since the mid-20th century. Nevertheless, smoking while pregnant remains a serious public health issue. The CDC estimates that 10.7% of pregnant women smoked in 2010. (See Table 7.11.) More than a quarter (26%) of Native American/Alaskan Native women smoked while pregnant that year, as did 14.3% of non-Hispanic white pregnant women and 8.9% of non-Hispanic African American women. By contrast, the percentages of Asian

**TABLE 7.7**

**Birth rates for women aged 10–19 years, by age and race and Hispanic origin, 1991, 2007, 2014, and 2015**

[Rates per 1,000 women in specified age and race and Hispanic-origin group. Population estimated as of July 1.]

| Age and race and Hispanic origin of mother | Year | | | | Percent change | | |
|---|---|---|---|---|---|---|---|
| | 2015 | 2014 | 2007 | 1991[a] | 2014–2015 | 2007–2015 | 1991–2015 |
| **10–14** | | | | | | | |
| All races and origins[b] | 0.2 | 0.3 | 0.6 | 1.4 | −33 | −67 | −86 |
| Non-Hispanic white[c] | 0.1 | 0.1 | 0.2 | 0.5 | † | −50 | −80 |
| Non-Hispanic black[c] | 0.6 | 0.6 | 1.4 | 4.9 | † | −57 | −88 |
| American Indian or Alaska Native total[c, d] | 0.3 | 0.3 | 0.7 | 1.6 | † | −57 | −81 |
| Asian or Pacific Islander total[c, d] | 0.1 | 0.1 | 0.2 | 0.8 | † | −50 | −88 |
| Hispanic[e] | 0.4 | 0.4 | 1.2 | 2.4 | † | −67 | −83 |
| **15–19** | | | | | | | |
| All races and origins[b] | 22.3 | 24.2 | 41.5 | 61.8 | −8 | −46 | −64 |
| Non-Hispanic white[c] | 16.0 | 17.3 | 27.2 | 43.4 | −8 | −41 | −63 |
| Non-Hispanic black[c] | 31.8 | 34.9 | 62.0 | 118.2 | −9 | −49 | −73 |
| American Indian or Alaska Native total[c, d] | 25.7 | 27.3 | 49.3 | 84.1 | −6 | −48 | −69 |
| Asian or Pacific Islander total[c, d] | 6.9 | 7.7 | 14.8 | 27.3 | −10 | −53 | −75 |
| Hispanic[e] | 34.9 | 38.0 | 75.3 | 104.6 | −8 | −54 | −67 |
| **15–17** | | | | | | | |
| All races and origins[b] | 9.9 | 10.9 | 21.7 | 38.6 | −9 | −54 | −74 |
| Non-Hispanic white[c] | 6.0 | 6.7 | 11.9 | 23.6 | −10 | −50 | −75 |
| Non-Hispanic black[c] | 15.3 | 16.6 | 34.6 | 86.1 | −8 | −56 | −82 |
| American Indian or Alaska Native total[c, d] | 12.7 | 13.2 | 26.1 | 51.9 | † | −51 | −76 |
| Asian or Pacific Islander total[c, d] | 2.7 | 3.3 | 7.4 | 16.3 | −18 | −64 | −83 |
| Hispanic[e] | 17.4 | 19.3 | 44.4 | 69.2 | −10 | −61 | −75 |
| **18–19** | | | | | | | |
| All races and origins[b] | 40.7 | 43.8 | 71.7 | 94.0 | −7 | −43 | −57 |
| Non-Hispanic white[c] | 30.6 | 32.9 | 50.4 | 70.6 | −7 | −39 | −57 |
| Non-Hispanic black[c] | 56.7 | 61.5 | 105.2 | 162.2 | −8 | −46 | −65 |
| American Indian or Alaska Native total[c, d] | 45.8 | 48.6 | 86.3 | 134.2 | −6 | −47 | −66 |
| Asian or Pacific Islander total[c, d] | 12.8 | 13.9 | 24.9 | 42.2 | −8 | −48 | −70 |
| Hispanic[e] | 61.9 | 66.1 | 124.7 | 155.5 | −6 | −50 | −60 |

[†]Difference not statistically significant at p = 0.05.
[a]Excludes data for New Hampshire, which did not report Hispanic origin.
[b]Includes births to race and Hispanic-origin groups not shown separately, such as white Hispanic and black Hispanic women, and births with origin not stated.
[c]Race and Hispanic origin are reported separately on birth certificates. Persons of Hispanic origin may be of any race. Race categories are consistent with the 1977 Office of Management and Budget (OMB) standards. Forty-nine states and the District of Columbia reported multiple-race data in 2015 that were bridged to the single-race categories of the 1977 OMB standards for comparability with other states. Multiple-race reporting areas vary for 2007, 2014, and 2015.
[d]Includes persons of Hispanic and non-Hispanic origin and origin not stated, according to the mother's reported race.
[e]Includes all persons of Hispanic origin of any race.
Note: Comparisons are made with 2007 and 1991 because these years represent recent and longer-term highs in teenage birth rates.

SOURCE: Joyce A. Martin et al., "Table A. Birth Rates for Women Aged 10–19, by Age and Race and Hispanic Origin of Mother: United States, 1991, 2007, 2014, and 2015," in "Births: Final Data for 2015," *National Vital Statistics Reports*, vol. 66, no. 1, January 5, 2017, https://www.cdc.gov/nchs/data/nvsr/nvsr66/nvsr66_01.pdf (accessed January 17, 2018)

or Pacific Islander women (2.1%) and Hispanic women (3.4%) who smoked while pregnant were much lower.

The dangers of alcohol consumption during pregnancy are also well known. These dangers include elevated risk levels for low birth weight and birth defects. Excessive consumption of alcohol by pregnant women can lead to fetal alcohol syndrome, a condition that may include mental retardation and growth deficiencies in the child. Nevertheless, many women continue to drink while they are pregnant. In *Results from the 2016 National Survey on Drug Use and Health: Summary of National Findings* (September 2017, https://www.samhsa.gov/data/sites/default/files/NSDUH-DetTabs-2016/NSDUH-DetTabs-2016.pdf), the Substance Abuse and Mental Health Services Administration indicates that in 2016, 8.3% of pregnant women aged 15 to 44 years who were polled reported currently using alcohol, 4.3% reported

binge drinking ("having five or more drinks on the same occasion" at least once in the 30 days prior to the survey), and 0.9% reported heavy drinking ("binge drinking on at least 5 days in the past 30 days."

**Prenatal Care**

Women are more likely to avoid or manage pregnancy complications and ensure the health of their infants when they receive prenatal care, which consists of regular visits to a health care provider starting soon after conception. During a woman's course of prenatal visits, the provider will regularly perform physical exams and provide advice and guidance about diet, risk avoidance, and the effects of the mother's existing health conditions on the developing fetus's health. Over the course of the pregnancy the provider will likely perform blood or urine analyses and at least one ultrasound as a means of monitoring

**TABLE 7.8**

**Percentage of high school students who ever had sexual intercourse and who had sexual intercourse for the first time before 13 years old, by sex, race and Hispanic origin, and grade, 2015**

| Category | Ever had sexual intercourse | | | Had first sexual intercourse before age 13 years | | |
|---|---|---|---|---|---|---|
| | Female | Male | Total | Female | Male | Total |
| | % | % | % | % | % | % |
| Race/ethnicity | | | | | | |
| White* | 40.3 | 39.5 | 39.9 | 1.6 | 3.5 | 2.5 |
| Black* | 37.4 | 58.8 | 48.5 | 4.3 | 12.1 | 8.3 |
| Hispanic | 39.8 | 45.1 | 42.5 | 3.1 | 6.8 | 5.0 |
| Grade | | | | | | |
| 9 | 20.7 | 27.3 | 24.1 | 2.5 | 4.6 | 3.6 |
| 10 | 33.5 | 37.9 | 35.7 | 2.7 | 6.8 | 4.7 |
| 11 | 48.2 | 51.2 | 49.6 | 1.6 | 4.8 | 3.2 |
| 12 | 57.2 | 59.0 | 58.1 | 1.7 | 5.5 | 3.6 |
| **Total** | **39.2** | **43.2** | **41.2** | **2.2** | **5.6** | **3.9** |

*Non-Hispanic.

SOURCE: Adapted from "Table 69. Percentage of High School Students Who Ever Had Sexual Intercourse and Who Had Sexual Intercourse for the First Time before Age 13 Years, by Sex, Race/Ethnicity, and Grade—United States, Youth Risk Behavior Survey, 2015," in "Youth Risk Behavior Surveillance—United States, 2015," *Morbidity and Mortality Weekly Report*, vol. 65, no. 6, June 10, 2016, https://www.cdc.gov/healthyyouth/data/yrbs/pdf/2015/ss6506_updated.pdf (accessed January 31, 2018)

---

**TABLE 7.9**

**Percentage of high school students who had sexual intercourse with four or more persons during their life and who were currently sexually active, by sex, race and Hispanic origin, and grade, 2015**

| Category | Had sexual intercourse with four or more persons during their life | | | Currently sexually active | | |
|---|---|---|---|---|---|---|
| | Female | Male | Total | Female | Male | Total |
| | % | % | % | % | % | % |
| Race/ethnicity | | | | | | |
| White* | 9.2 | 10.6 | 9.9 | 31.4 | 29.1 | 30.3 |
| Black* | 9.2 | 28.2 | 19.0 | 25.7 | 40.0 | 33.1 |
| Hispanic | 6.7 | 15.3 | 11.0 | 30.1 | 30.5 | 30.3 |
| Grade | | | | | | |
| 9 | 3.0 | 6.7 | 4.9 | 14.0 | 17.3 | 15.7 |
| 10 | 6.0 | 12.1 | 9.0 | 24.7 | 26.4 | 25.5 |
| 11 | 10.7 | 16.0 | 13.4 | 36.7 | 34.5 | 35.5 |
| 12 | 16.1 | 22.4 | 19.2 | 46.5 | 45.4 | 46.0 |
| **Total** | **8.8** | **14.1** | **11.5** | **29.8** | **30.3** | **30.1** |

*Non-Hispanic.
Note: Sexually active refers to having had sexual intercourse with at least one person during the 3 months before the survey.

SOURCE: Adapted from "Table 71. Percentage of High School Students Who Had Sexual Intercourse with Four or More Persons during Their Life and Who Were Currently Sexually Active, by Sex, Race/Ethnicity, and Grade—United States, Youth Risk Behavior Survey, 2015," in "Youth Risk Behavior Surveillance—United States, 2015," *Morbidity and Mortality Weekly Report*, vol. 65, no. 6, June 10, 2016, https://www.cdc.gov/healthyyouth/data/yrbs/pdf/2015/ss6506_updated.pdf (accessed January 31, 2018)

---

fetal health and development. As Figure 7.3 shows, 84.8% of women who gave birth in 2011 received adequate prenatal care (defined as receiving at least 80% of expected visits given the timing of when prenatal care began and gestational age of the fetus at delivery). Native American/Alaskan Native mothers (76.7%), Native Hawaiian/Other Pacific Islander mothers (77.9%) non-Hispanic African American mothers (80.8%), and Hispanic mothers (83.3%) were less likely than non-Hispanic white mothers (86.8%) and Asian American mothers (86.4%) to have received adequate prenatal care.

In *Child Health USA 2014*, the Maternal and Child Health Bureau of the HHS reports that in 2012 non-Hispanic white women (79%) and Asian American women (78%) initiated prenatal care during the first trimester of their pregnancies at a higher rate than other racial or ethnic groups. By comparison, 70.7% of multiple race women, 69% of Hispanic women, 63.6% of non-Hispanic African American women, 59.4% of Native American/Alaskan Native women, and 54.7% of Native Hawaiian/Other Pacific Islander women received prenatal care during the first trimester of their pregnancies in

**TABLE 7.10**

**Percentage of high school students who used a condom during last sexual intercourse and who used birth control pills before last sexual intercourse, by sex, race and Hispanic origin, and grade, 2015**

| | Condom use | | | Birth control pill use | | |
|---|---|---|---|---|---|---|
| | Female | Male | Total | Female | Male | Total |
| Category | % | % | % | % | % | % |
| **Race/ethnicity** | | | | | | |
| White* | 55.9 | 58.1 | 56.8 | 25.4 | 21.4 | 23.5 |
| Black* | 46.7 | 73.6 | 63.4 | 9.0 | 9.0 | 9.0 |
| Hispanic | 48.3 | 62.5 | 55.6 | 15.4 | 8.1 | 11.8 |
| **Grade** | | | | | | |
| 9 | 56.7 | 63.3 | 60.5 | 11.2 | 10.8 | 10.9 |
| 10 | 54.0 | 65.6 | 59.9 | 20.2 | 11.6 | 15.9 |
| 11 | 52.9 | 62.5 | 57.7 | 23.9 | 19.1 | 21.5 |
| 12 | 48.8 | 57.4 | 52.9 | 23.2 | 16.9 | 20.1 |
| **Total** | **52.0** | **61.5** | **56.9** | **21.3** | **15.2** | **18.2** |

*Non-Hispanic.
Notes: Among the 30.1% of students nationwide who were currently sexually active. Birth control pills were used to prevent pregnancy.

SOURCE: Adapted from "Table 73. Percentage of High School Students Who Used a Condom during Last Sexual Intercourse and Who Used Birth Control Pills before Last Sexual Intercourse, by Sex, Race/Ethnicity, and Grade—United States, Youth Risk Behavior Survey, 2015," in "Youth Risk Behavior Surveillance—United States, 2015," *MMWR*, vol. 65, no. 6, June 10, 2016, https://www.cdc.gov/healthyyouth/data/yrbs/pdf/2015/ss6506_updated.pdf (accessed January 31, 2018)

**TABLE 7.11**

**Mothers who smoked cigarettes before, during, and after pregnancy and who quit smoking during pregnancy, by selected characteristics, 2010**

[Pregnancy Risk Assessment Monitoring System, United States, 27 sites[a]]

| Maternal characteristic | Smoked before pregnancy[b] Unweighted Population = 9,808 % | Smoked during pregnancy[c] Unweighted Population = 6,097 % | Quit smoking during pregnancy[d] Unweighted Population = 4,712 % | Smoked after delivery[e] Unweighted Population = 7,023 % |
|---|---|---|---|---|
| **Total** | **23.2** | **10.7** | **54.3** | **15.9** |
| **Age group (yrs)** | | | | |
| <20 | 32.2 | 13.6 | 59.3 | 24.3 |
| 20–24 | 34.7 | 17.6 | 50.0 | 25.5 |
| 25–34 | 19.8 | 8.8 | 55.9 | 12.8 |
| ≥35 | 12.5 | 5.7 | 54.7 | 7.6 |
| **Race/ethnicity** | | | | |
| White, non-Hispanic | 29.3 | 14.3 | 51.5 | 20.1 |
| Black, non-Hispanic | 19.7 | 8.9 | 55.9 | 16.2 |
| Hispanic | 11.8 | 3.4 | 71.2 | 6.5 |
| American Indian/Alaska Native | 55.1 | 26.0 | 53.1 | 40.1 |
| Asian/Pacific Islander | 7.5 | 2.1 | 72.0 | 3.6 |
| Other | 24.4 | 13.9 | 43.1 | 17.8 |
| **Education (yrs)** | | | | |
| <12 | 28.1 | 17.4 | 39.1 | 22.9 |
| 12 | 32.6 | 16.4 | 50.2 | 24.5 |
| >12 | 17.3 | 5.9 | 65.7 | 9.7 |

PRAMS = Pregnancy Risk Assessment Monitoring System.
[a]Data aggregated for 27 PRAMS sites (Alaska, Arkansas, Colorado, Delaware, Georgia, Hawaii, Maine, Maryland, Massachusetts, Michigan, Minnesota, Missouri, Nebraska, New Jersey, New York, New York City, Ohio, Oklahoma, Oregon, Pennsylvania, Rhode Island, Texas, Utah, Vermont, Washington, West Virginia, and Wyoming) with data available for 2010.
[b]Smoking before pregnancy was defined as smoking during the 3 months before pregnancy on the basis of the PRAMS survey.
[c]Smoking during pregnancy was defined as smoking in the last 3 months of pregnancy on the basis of the PRAMS survey.
[d]Quitting smoking was defined as no smoking during the last 3 months of pregnancy among women who smoked 3 months before pregnancy on the basis of the PRAMS survey.
[e]Smoking after delivery was defined as smoking approximately 4 months after delivery on the basis of the PRAMS survey.

SOURCE: Adapted from "Table 2. Prevalence of Smoking before, during, and after Pregnancy and Quit Smoking during Pregnancy by Selected Maternal Characteristics—Pregnancy Risk Assessment Monitoring System, United States, 27 Sites, 2010," in "Trends in Smoking before, during, and after Pregnancy—Pregnancy Risk Assessment Monitoring System, United States, 40 Sites, 2000–2010," *Morbidity and Mortality Weekly Report* vol. 62, no. 6, November 8, 2013, https://www.cdc.gov/mmwr/pdf/ss/ss6206.pdf (accessed January 31, 2018)

FIGURE 7.3

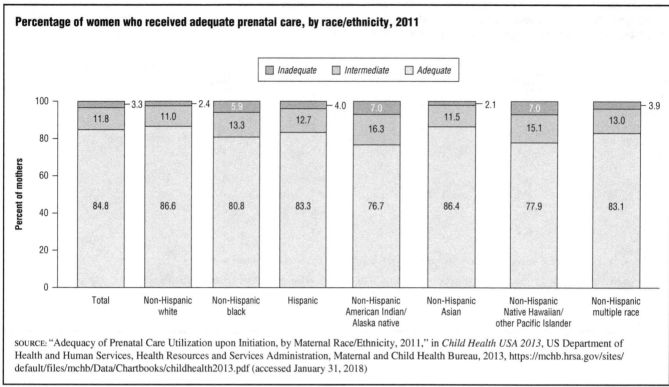

**Percentage of women who received adequate prenatal care, by race/ethnicity, 2011**

SOURCE: "Adequacy of Prenatal Care Utilization upon Initiation, by Maternal Race/Ethnicity, 2011," in *Child Health USA 2013*, US Department of Health and Human Services, Health Resources and Services Administration, Maternal and Child Health Bureau, 2013, https://mchb.hrsa.gov/sites/default/files/mchb/Data/Chartbooks/childhealth2013.pdf (accessed January 31, 2018)

2012. Overall, 74.1% of pregnant women sought prenatal care during the first trimester of their pregnancies that year, 19.9% received care during the second trimester, and 6% received care during the third trimester only or received no prenatal care at all. The likelihood of first-trimester prenatal care increased with educational attainment in 2012, with 86.1% of those with a bachelor's degree or higher education receiving first-trimester care, compared with 68.6% of those with a high school diploma or equivalent education, and 58.5% of pregnant women who had not completed high school. Conversely, women with the least education were the most likely to have received care only during the third trimester or no care at all during their pregnancies (11.4%), compared with 7.2% of those who had a high school diploma, and 2.7% of college graduates.

**Cesarean Births**

In *Child Health USA 2013* (October 2013, https://mchb.hrsa.gov/sites/default/files/mchb/Data/Chartbooks/childhealth2013.pdf), the Maternal and Child Health Bureau reports that the rate at which cesarean deliveries (births accomplished via abdominal surgery on the mother) were performed in the United States increased dramatically from about 21% of all births in 1996 to nearly 33% in 2009. Although the proportion of cesarean deliveries remained stable at about one in three births between 2009 and 2013, it was more than double the upper limit of 15% advised by the World Health Organization. As Figure 7.4 shows, cesarean rates for first

births are significantly higher among older mothers; more than half (51.6%) of women aged 40 years and over had cesarean deliveries in 2011. In 2016 the total cesarean rate was 31.9%, with some variation among racial and ethnic groups. (See Table 7.12.)

Cesarean delivery consists of major abdominal surgery and results in more frequent complications for both the mother and the baby than does vaginal delivery, so many health practitioners, researchers, and women's advocates questioned whether the increased rate of cesarean delivery was in fact resulting in improved health outcomes for mothers and babies. Cesareans are frequently performed in response to clear clinical indications, such as the baby being in a breech (feet-first) position or the existence of placenta previa (in which the placenta is too close to the cervix). Cesareans are also performed for more subjective reasons, such as the slow progress of a labor or concerns about the baby's heart rate.

**Low Birth Weight and Preterm Births**

As Table 7.12 shows, 8.2% of all babies born in 2016 were low birth weight (infants weighing less than 5 pounds 8 ounces [2,500 grams (g)] at birth). Martin et al. report in "Births: Final Data for 2016" that this figure had increased by nearly 20% between 1990 and 2006, before slowly decreasing (by 3%) between 2007 and 2012. The low birth weight percentage among non-Hispanic African American mothers was much higher than average, at 13.7%, whereas the percentages among non-Hispanic white and Hispanic mothers were 7% and

**FIGURE 7.4**

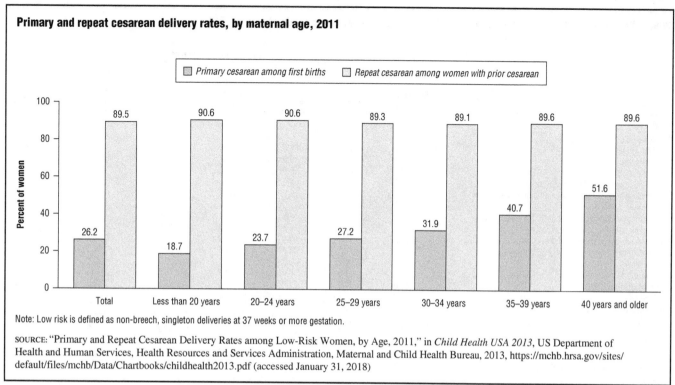

**Primary and repeat cesarean delivery rates, by maternal age, 2011**

Note: Low risk is defined as non-breech, singleton deliveries at 37 weeks or more gestation.

SOURCE: "Primary and Repeat Cesarean Delivery Rates among Low-Risk Women, by Age, 2011," in *Child Health USA 2013*, US Department of Health and Human Services, Health Resources and Services Administration, Maternal and Child Health Bureau, 2013, https://mchb.hrsa.gov/sites/default/files/mchb/Data/Chartbooks/childhealth2013.pdf (accessed January 31, 2018)

7.3%, respectively. Non-Hispanic African American mothers also had a higher incidence of very low birth weight babies (infants weighing less than 3 pounds, 4 ounces [1,500 g] at birth), at 3%, compared with 1.1% for non-Hispanic white mothers and 1.2% for Hispanic mothers.

The rate of preterm births, or those that occurred prior to the 37th week of gestation (39 to 40 weeks is considered full term), was 9.9% in 2016. (See Table 7.12.) This figure represented a 2% increase from 9.6% in 2015. Preterm birth rates had risen between 1990 and 2006, before falling (by 10.4%) between 2007 and 2014. According to Martin et al., in "Births: Final Data for 2016," as with low birth weight, preterm rates were higher among non-Hispanic African American women, 13.8% of whom gave birth before the 37th of week of gestation, compared with 9% of non-Hispanic white women and 9.5% of Hispanic women.

**Breastfeeding**

In the widely cited report *Breastfeeding and Maternal and Infant Health Outcomes in Developed Countries* (April 2007, https://archive.ahrq.gov/downloads/pub/evidence/pdf/brfout/brfout.pdf), the Agency for Healthcare Research and Quality surveyed 400 studies on the effects of breastfeeding on maternal and infant health and found that breastfeeding had positive effects for both infants and mothers. Breastfed infants had reduced risks of asthma, childhood leukemia, diabetes, gastroenteritis, obesity, respiratory tract infections, and sudden infant death syndrome. Mothers had a reduced risk of breast and ovarian cancer, postpartum depression, and type 2

diabetes. The American Academy of Pediatrics recommends that infants be exclusively breastfed, with no added liquids or solids, for the first six months.

The CDC, however, reports in "Breastfeeding among U.S. Children Born 2002–2014, CDC National Immunization Survey" (December 1, 2017, https://www.cdc.gov/breastfeeding/data/nis_data/results.html) that few American women actually follow these breastfeeding recommendations. Although the rates for any amount of breastfeeding were relatively high during the early postpartum period, climbing from 71.4% of all infants born in 2002 to 82.5% of those born in 2014, these rates were dramatically lower at six months of age, when 37.9% of infants born in 2002 and 55.3% of infants born in 2014 were breastfed. (See Figure 7.5.) Exclusive breastfeeding rates were far lower at all stages of infant life. Only 29.6% of babies born in 2003 were exclusively breastfed for the first three months of life, and only 46.6% of those born in 2014 were exclusively breastfed for three months. At six months of age, exclusive breastfeeding rates were 10.3% for babies born in 2003 and 24.9% for babies born in 2014.

Employment is a major obstacle to exclusive breastfeeding. According to Robert Drago, Jeffrey Hayes, and Youngmin Yi, in *Better Health for Mothers and Children: Breastfeeding Accommodations under the Affordable Care Act* (December 2010, https://iwpr.org/publications/better-health-for-mothers-and-children-breastfeeding-accommodations-under-the-affordable-care-act/), breastfeeding rates are much lower in the United States than in

**TABLE 7.12**

**Selected medical and health characteristics of births, by race and Hispanic origin of mother, 2016**

| Characteristic | All races and origins[b] | Non-Hispanic, single race[a] White | Black | American Indian or Alaska Native | Asian | Native Hawaiian or Other Pacific Islander | Hispanic[c] |
|---|---|---|---|---|---|---|---|
| **Mother** | | | | | | | |
| Prenatal care initiation: | | | | | | | |
| First trimester | 77.1 | 82.3 | 66.5 | 63.0 | 80.6 | 51.9 | 72.0 |
| Late or no care | 6.2 | 4.3 | 10.0 | 12.5 | 5.4 | 19.2 | 7.7 |
| Smoked during pregnancy | 7.2 | 10.5 | 6.0 | 16.7 | 0.6 | 4.5 | 1.8 |
| Pregnancy resulted from infertility treatment | 1.7 | 2.4 | 0.6 | 0.4 | 2.8 | 0.4 | 0.6 |
| Mother received WIC food for herself during this pregnancy | 39.6 | 26.2 | 59.6 | 58.3 | 23.2 | 48.2 | 61.4 |
| Diabetes: | | | | | | | |
| Prepregnancy (diagnosis prior to this pregnancy) | 0.9 | 0.7 | 1.2 | 2.1 | 0.9 | 1.8 | 1.0 |
| Gestational (diagnosis in this pregnancy) | 6.0 | 5.3 | 4.8 | 9.2 | 11.1 | 8.4 | 6.6 |
| Overweight or obese (BMI of 25.0 or over) | 52.2 | 48.7 | 63.2 | 65.6 | 29.6 | 72.7 | 59.0 |
| Induction of labor | 24.5 | 27.6 | 23.1 | 25.6 | 19.1 | 18.3 | 20.2 |
| CNM delivery[d] | 8.8 | 1.2 | 0.2 | 0.3 | 0.2 | 0.3 | 0.3 |
| Home births | 1.0 | 1.5 | 0.4 | 0.6 | 0.3 | 0.5 | 0.3 |
| Cesarean delivery (total) | 31.9 | 30.9 | 35.9 | 28.0 | 33.3 | 30.5 | 31.7 |
| Low-risk[e] | 25.7 | 24.7 | 30.3 | 21.2 | 27.5 | 26.7 | 25.1 |
| Source of payment for the delivery: | | | | | | | |
| Medicaid | 42.6 | 30.3 | 65.6 | 66.9 | 24.9 | 53.7 | 59.8 |
| Private | 49.4 | 63.3 | 27.7 | 19.7 | 65.4 | 27.8 | 28.4 |
| Self-pay | 4.1 | 2.9 | 3.2 | 1.9 | 6.7 | 6.5 | 7.0 |
| Other[f] | 3.9 | 3.5 | 3.5 | 11.6 | 3.0 | 12.0 | 4.8 |
| Infant was being breastfed at discharge[g] | 83.1 | 84.4 | 70.8 | 74.8 | 91.0 | 82.3 | 87.3 |
| **Infant** | | | | | | | |
| Gestational age: | | | | | | | |
| Preterm[h] | 9.85 | 9.04 | 13.77 | 11.39 | 8.63 | 11.52 | 9.45 |
| Early preterm[i] | 2.76 | 2.33 | 4.93 | 2.98 | 2.13 | 3.12 | 2.53 |
| Late preterm[j] | 7.09 | 6.72 | 8.84 | 8.41 | 6.50 | 8.40 | 6.92 |
| Birthweight: | | | | | | | |
| Very low birthweight[k] | 1.40 | 1.07 | 2.95 | 1.39 | 1.09 | 1.47 | 1.24 |
| Low birthweight[l] | 8.17 | 6.97 | 13.68 | 7.77 | 8.43 | 7.67 | 7.32 |
| Twin births[m] | 33.4 | 35.7 | 39.9 | 28.2 | 30.6 | 24.4 | 24.6 |
| Triplet or higher-order births[n] | 101.4 | 121.7 | 112.4 | 12.7 | 74.3 | 32.1 | 58.6 |

[a]Race and Hispanic origin are reported separately on birth certificates; persons of Hispanic origin may be of any race. In this table, non-Hispanic women are classified by race. Race categories are consistent with 1997 Office of Management and Budget standards. Single race is defined as only one race reported on the birth certificate.
[b]Includes births to race and origin groups not shown separately, such as Hispanic single-race white, Hispanic single-race black, and non-Hispanic multiple-race women, as well as births with origin not stated.
[c]Includes all persons of Hispanic origin of any race.
[b]Births delivered by certified nurse midwives (CNMs).
[e]Low-risk cesarean rate is the number of singleton, term (37 weeks or more of gestation based on the obstetric estimate), cephalic, cesarean deliveries to women having a first birth per 100 women delivering singleton, term, cephalic births.
[f]Includes Indian Health Service, CHAMPUS or TRICARE, other government (federal, state, or local), or charity.
[g]Excludes data for California, which did not report infant was being breastfed at discharge. Also excludes Michigan, for which item wording for Michigan is not consistent with national standard.
[h]Born prior to 37 completed weeks of gestation based on the obstetric estimate.
[i]Born prior to 34 completed weeks of gestation based on the obstetric estimate.
[j]Born between 34 and 36 completed weeks of gestation based on the obstetric estimate.
[k]Less than 1,500 grams (3 lb 4 oz).
[l]Less than 2,500 grams (5 lb 8 oz).
[m]Live births in twin deliveries per 1,000 live births.
[n]Live births in triplet and other higher-order multiple deliveries per 100,000 live births.
Note: WIC is Special Supplemental Nutrition Program for Women, Infants, and Children; BMI is body mass index.

SOURCE: Adapted from Joyce A. Martin et al., "Table 13. Selected Medical and Health Characteristics of Births, by Race and Hispanic Origin of Mother: United States, 2016," in "Births: Final Data for 2016," *National Vital Statistics Reports*, vol. 67, no. 1, January 31, 2018, https://www.cdc.gov/nchs/data/nvsr/nvsr67/nvsr67_01.pdf (accessed April 11, 2018)

many other developed Western countries, and studies suggest that this is at least partly due to the lack of federal provisions for paid maternity leave in the United States. Women who must be away from their infants while working may use pumps to express their milk, and they must build up a supply of milk to leave with their children's daytime caregiver. Because the body produces milk in response to the amount expressed, women who do not express milk regularly throughout the day will see their milk supplies diminish, making exclusive breastfeeding impossible. Besides these challenges, many working women lack the privacy to express milk comfortably, the permission to take breaks to express milk, and the equipment necessary to store milk at work.

The Patient Protection and Affordable Care Act (ACA) of 2010 enacted revisions to the Fair Labor Standards Act that were meant to provide breastfeeding mothers

FIGURE 7.5

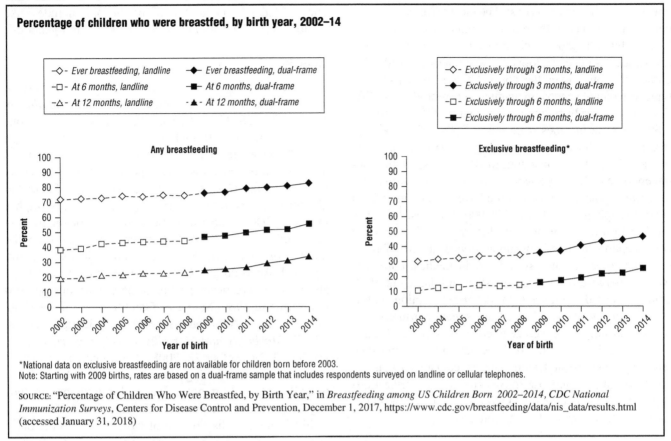

**Percentage of children who were breastfed, by birth year, 2002–14**

*National data on exclusive breastfeeding are not available for children born before 2003.
Note: Starting with 2009 births, rates are based on a dual-frame sample that includes respondents surveyed on landline or cellular telephones.

SOURCE: "Percentage of Children Who Were Breastfed, by Birth Year," in *Breastfeeding among US Children Born 2002–2014, CDC National Immunization Surveys*, Centers for Disease Control and Prevention, December 1, 2017, https://www.cdc.gov/breastfeeding/data/nis_data/results.html (accessed January 31, 2018)

with workplace rights and protections. As a result of the ACA, employers with 50 or more employees are now required to provide reasonable break time for women employees for up to one year after a child's birth for the purpose of expressing breast milk, and they are required to provide a private space other than a bathroom in which employees can express milk. The ACA also requires health insurance plans to cover the costs to mothers of breastfeeding support, supplies, and counseling. These provisions of the ACA were fully implemented in 2012. Drago, Hayes, and Yi estimate that in the first six years after taking effect, the ACA policies will encourage an additional 1 million mothers to breastfeed through their infants' first six months of life, raising the rate of breastfeeding at six months by approximately four percentage points. Data gauging the accuracy of these projections were not yet available as of April 2018. However, as reported by the CDC in "Breastfeeding among U.S. Children Born 2002–2014, CDC National Immunization Survey" and shown in Figure 7.5, the rates of breastfeeding in general and exclusive breastfeeding had both shown increases during the early years of the ACA.

## ALTERNATIVES TO CHILDBEARING
### Contraceptive Use

The Guttmacher Institute reports in "Contraceptive Use in the United States" (September 2016, https://www .guttmacher.org/sites/default/files/factsheet/fb_contr_use_ 0.pdf) that there are 61 million women of childbearing age (aged 15 to 44 years), 43 million (70%) of whom are sexually active but do not want to become pregnant. In the absence of contraception, a sexually active couple has roughly an 85% chance of bringing about a pregnancy in the course of any given year. Over 99% of women who have ever had sexual intercourse have used contraceptives of one kind or another, and about 62% of all women of childbearing age use contraceptives. Since 1982 birth control pills and female sterilization have been the two most common forms of contraception. In 2012, 9.7 million women, or 16% of all women aged 15 to 44 years, used the pill; and 9.4 million, or 15.5%, had undergone tubal sterilization. Male use of condoms was the next most popular contraceptive choice, used by 5.7 million (9.4%) women, followed by intrauterine devices (IUDs), vasectomy, and withdrawal.

Guttmacher Institute data illustrate the efficacy of modern contraception: the 68% of women at risk of unwanted pregnancy who use contraception consistently account for only 5% of all unwanted pregnancies; those who use contraception inconsistently (18%) account for 41% of unwanted pregnancies; and those who do not use contraception (14%) account for 54% of unwanted pregnancies. For many women who do not use contraception or who use ineffective or inconsistent forms of contraception, one of the main barriers is cost. The most effective forms of contraception, such as the pill and surgical intervention, can be prohibitively expensive, and even reliance on cheaper forms, such as male condoms, can amount to a considerable outlay of money over the course of the 30 years that a typical woman spends managing her reproductive life. The Guttmacher Institute indicates that in 2014, 20 million women whose incomes were below 250% of the poverty threshold or who were under the age of 20 years relied on publicly funded contraception. In 2014 access to this contraception enabled these women to prevent an estimated 2 million pregnancies, which would have resulted in perhaps 900,000 unplanned births and 700,000 abortions. The Guttmacher Institute estimates that for every dollar spent on contraception and family planning services in 2010, federal and state governments saved $7.09 in medical costs that would otherwise be covered by Medicaid. Nine out of 10 employer-based insurance plans cover prescription contraception, and as of July 2016, 28 states require insurers who provide prescription coverage to cover prescription contraception. Additionally, the ACA includes a federal mandate requiring most private health plans enacted after August 1, 2012, to cover all contraceptives (including sterilization) approved by the US Food and Drug Administration (FDA) for all women at no cost to the consumer.

Emergency contraception (drugs and devices that can be used within a few days of sexual intercourse that was unprotected or that involved contraceptive failure) has become increasingly accessible to women of all ages in recent years. It should be noted that emergency contraception has no effect on an established pregnancy and is therefore properly considered contraception rather than as a way of inducing abortion. (A different drug, mifepristone, marketed under the brand name Mifeprex—also known as the "abortion pill" and RU-486—terminates an established pregnancy of less than nine weeks and is discussed later in this chapter.) The most common form of emergency contraception is the so-called morning-after pill, which contains a concentrated dosage of the same hormones that are in birth control pills. The Guttmacher Institute indicates that as of 2010, one out of nine sexually active women of childbearing age had used emergency contraceptives. Availability of the morning-after pill was constrained for many years due to an ongoing legal dispute, particularly concerning age restrictions, between reproductive rights advocates, the Obama administration, and the FDA. A US District Court ruling in June 2013 settled the issue, making the most common morning-after pill, Plan B One Step, available over the counter, without a prescription, and with no age restrictions on purchasing the medication. A single pill containing 1.5 mg of levonorgestrel, Plan B One Step usually costs $40–$50. Although it is recommended for use within 72 hours of having unprotected sex, studies have shown that it can still be effective up to 120 hours after unprotected sex. Other brands of the pill include Take Action, Next Choice One-Dose, My Way, and generics.

## Abortion

Abortion has been a legal option for American women since the US Supreme Court ruling in *Roe v. Wade* (410 US 113 [1973]). The number of abortions generally increased from 1973 until they reached a high in 1990, when the CDC reported 1.4 million abortions and the Guttmacher Institute reported 1.6 million abortions. (See the CDC's *Health, United States, 2010*; the Guttmacher Institute's estimates are generally higher than the CDC's because some states do not report data on abortion to the CDC.) Between 1990 and 2006 the number of legal abortions in the United States generally declined. According to CDC estimates, the ratio of legal abortions to live births peaked at 35.9 abortions per 100 live births in 1980. Sonya B. Gamble et al. of the CDC indicate in "Abortion Surveillance—United States, 2005" (*Morbidity and Mortality Weekly Report*, vol. 57, no. SS-13, November 28, 2008) that a number of factors contributed to the falling abortion rate after 1980: "The overall declines . . . might reflect multiple factors, including a decrease in the number of unintended pregnancies; a shift in the age distribution of women toward the older and less fertile ages; reduced or limited access to abortion services, including the passage of abortion laws that affect adolescents (e.g., parental consent or notification laws and mandatory waiting periods); and changes in contraceptive practices, including increased use of contraceptives (e.g., condoms and, among young women, of long-acting hormonal contraceptive methods that were introduced in the early 1990s)."

By 2007 the ratio of abortions stood at 22.9 abortions per 100 births (or 229 per 1,000, as Table 7.13 shows), and after rising slightly in 2008, the ratio fell significantly to 20 abortions per 100 births (or 200 per 1,000) in 2013—the lowest rate since the procedure became legal in 1973. There were conflicting data on whether the declines showed signs of continuing to fall, of leveling off, or of rising again in response to the economic pressures that remained in the aftermath of the Great Recession. The Guttmacher Institute states in "Induced Abortion in the United States" (January 2018, https://www.guttmacher .org/sites/default/files/factsheet/fb_induced_abortion.pdf) that, based on 2014 abortion rates, "one in 20 women (5%) will have an abortion by age 20, one in five (19%) by age 30 and one in four (24%) by age 45."

According to the Guttmacher Institute, in 2014 teenagers accounted for 12% of all abortions, women aged 20 to 24 years accounted for 34% of all abortions, and women aged 25 to 29 years accounted for 27% of all abortions. Women who had never married and who were

TABLE 7.13

**Legal abortions and legal abortion rates, 2004–13**

[Data are based on reporting by state health departments and by hospitals and other medical facilities]

| Data provider | 2004 | 2005 | 2006 | 2007 | 2008 | 2009 | 2010 | 2011 | 2012 | 2013 |
|---|---|---|---|---|---|---|---|---|---|---|
| | Number of legal abortions reported, in thousands | | | | | | | | | |
| Centers for Disease Control and Prevention (CDC)[a] | 839 | 820 | 852 | 828 | 826 | 789 | 766 | 730 | 699 | 664 |
| Guttmacher Institute[b] | 1,222 | 1,206 | 1,242 | 1,210 | 1,212 | 1,152 | 1,103 | 1,059 | — | — |
| | CDC 47 continuous reporting areas[c] | | | | | | | | | |
| Number of legal abortions reported, in thousands | 818 | 808 | 835 | 819 | 817 | 779 | 755 | 720 | 688 | 653 |
| Number of legal abortions per 1,000 women aged 15–44 | 15.9 | 15.7 | 16.2 | 15.8 | 15.8 | 15.0 | 14.6 | 13.9 | 13.2 | 12.5 |
| Number of legal abortions per 1,000 live births | 241 | 236 | 237 | 229 | 232 | 227 | 227 | 219 | 210 | 200 |

— Data not available.

[a]Overall trends presented in this table should be interpreted with caution because of the different numbers of reporting areas that provided data to CDC in different years. The following states did not report abortion data to CDC in the specified year: California (2004–2013), Louisiana (2005), Maryland (2007–2013), New Hampshire (2004–2013), and West Virginia (2004). For 2006, the number of legal abortions is greater than reported in the 2006 report because of numbers subsequently provided by Louisiana. For 2009, the number of legal abortions is greater than reported in the 2009 report because of numbers subsequently provided by Delaware.
[b]No surveys were conducted in 2006 or 2009. Data for those years were estimated by interpolation.
[c]Because overall trends in abortion data are affected by the number of reporting areas that provide data to CDC on an annual basis, CDC also presents estimates for the 47 reporting areas that provided data for the entire period from 2004 to 2013. The 47 continuous reporting areas include all states except California, Louisiana, Maryland, New Hampshire, and West Virginia. The District of Columbia and New York City are included in the 47 continuous reporting areas.
Notes: Each year, CDC requests abortion data from the central health agencies of 52 reporting areas (the 50 states, the District of Columbia, and New York City). This information is provided voluntarily to CDC.

SOURCE: "Table 7. Legal Abortions, Legal Abortion Rates, and Legal Abortion Ratios: United States and 47 Continuous Reporting Areas, 2004–2013," in *Health, United States, 2016: With Chartbook on Long-term Trends in Health*, Centers for Disease Control and Prevention, National Center for Health Statistics, May 2017, https://www.cdc.gov/nchs/data/hus/hus16.pdf (accessed January 17, 2018)

not living with a partner accounted for 46% of abortions in 2014, and approximately 59% of abortions involved women who already had children. The link between abortion and economic stress is strong and well established. In 2014 poor and low-income women accounted for 75% of all abortion patients. Women with incomes below the poverty level accounted for 49% of abortions, and those with incomes between 100% and 199% of the poverty level accounted for 26% of abortions.

The Guttmacher Institute notes in "Induced Abortion in the United States" that most abortions arise as a result of faulty or inconsistently used contraception. In 2014 over half (51%) of abortion patients reported using contraceptives during the month they got pregnant, most commonly condoms (24%) or a hormonal method, such as the pill (13%). Citing 2013 data, the Guttmacher Institute indicates that 89% of abortions occur in the first trimester (the first 12 weeks) of pregnancy, when medical risks are extremely low. Teens are more likely than older women to delay having an abortion until after 15 weeks of pregnancy, when the medical risks associated with the procedure are much higher.

ABORTION DRUGS. Mifepristone (RU-486) is an abortion-inducing drug that has been used in Europe and China since the late 1980s. In September 2000 the FDA approved mifepristone for use in the United States. Mifepristone works by blocking the hormone progesterone, which is needed to sustain a pregnancy. In "Facts about

Mifepristone (RU-486)" (February 2008, http://www.prochoice.org/pubs_research/publications/downloads/about_abortion/facts_about_mifepristone.pdf), the National Abortion Federation indicates that mifepristone, when used in combination with the drug misoprostol, which causes the uterus to contract, is 95% to 98% effective in inducing abortion up to 63 days after the start of the last menstrual period. Some women are now choosing this method of "medical abortion," as opposed to surgical abortions. In "Induced Abortion in the United States," the Guttmacher Institute notes that medication abortions accounted for 31% of all nonhospital abortions in 2014 (up from 6% in 2001), and for 45% of abortions before nine weeks' gestation.

**Reproductive Rights**

More than 40 years after *Roe v. Wade*, abortion remains one of the most polarizing issues in the United States. Pro-choice activists argue that the freedom to terminate an unwanted pregnancy is part of a woman's fundamental civil right to make decisions about her own body, whereas pro-life activists insist abortion is a moral and religious abomination that violates the sanctity of the life of the unborn fetus. In this deeply divided and emotionally charged debate, activists and lawmakers have been largely unable, or unwilling, to compromise or find common ground.

Judicial rulings and congressional action since *Roe v. Wade* have weakened abortion rights at both the state and the federal levels, and many state legislatures have passed laws that make abortion services much harder to access. The 1992 Supreme Court decision in *Planned Parenthood v. Casey* (505 US 833) reaffirmed the right to abortion while leaving states the option to restrict it, and many states have acted aggressively to do so. In "An Overview of Abortion Laws" (April 1, 2018, https://www.guttmacher.org/state-policy/explore/overview-abortion-laws), the Guttmacher Institute notes that 43 states impose limits on how late in a pregnancy an abortion can be performed; 11 states limit the coverage of abortion in private health insurance plans; 45 states allow health care providers to refuse to conduct an abortion, and 42 states allow institutions to opt out of providing abortions; 18 states require women seeking an abortion to undergo counseling, including discussion of claims regarding links between abortion and breast cancer, abortion and mental health problems, and the ability of a fetus to feel pain; 27 states mandate a waiting period, typically of 24 hours, for women seeking an abortion; and 37 states require parental involvement when a minor is seeking an abortion.

Since 1977 Congress has blocked the use of federal funds to pay for abortions. This prohibition is not enshrined in permanent law but takes the form of the Hyde Amendment, which is attached each year to congressional appropriations bills (part of the larger federal budget). One result of the Hyde Amendment is that abortions are not covered by Medicaid except in cases of rape or incest or when the woman's life is in danger, leaving some of the women least able to afford children no option for terminating a pregnancy. According to the Guttmacher Institute, as of 2018 Medicaid recipients could access abortion services in 17 states where these states used state rather than federal funds for the purpose. The ACA maintains the prohibition on federal funding of abortion. As part of the law's passage, President Barack Obama (1961–) issued an executive order reinforcing the limits contained in the Hyde Amendment, and the law contains detailed instructions for the functioning of the state exchanges (where federally subsidized private insurance became available in 2014) to ensure that federal funds are not used to pay for abortions.

Over the years, antiabortion activists and policy makers have sought to take funding restrictions further at the state level by denying all public funding to family planning clinics or health care facilities that perform abortions or offer abortion referrals, even when these services account for only a fraction of the care they provide. Planned Parenthood, a nonprofit organization that is the nation's largest provider of reproductive health and family planning services, as well as the nation's largest abortion provider, has long been a primary target of these defunding efforts. In "The War on Planned Parenthood Is in the States" (Newsweek.com, August 3, 2015), Emily Cadei recounts instances in Wisconsin and Texas, for example, in which the state budgets passed in 2011 excluded Planned Parenthood from millions of state-level funding dollars that the organization normally allocated for contraception, treatment of STIs, and other reproductive health care. Cadei reports, "There is evidence that states' financial maneuvers against Planned Parenthood are limiting their female residents' access to reproductive health services. According to a study published in March in the *American Journal of Public Health*, a quarter of family planning clinics in Texas have closed since 2011 and the remaining clinics are able to serve 54% fewer women than were served before."

Antiabortion activism has also focused on the effort to ban late-term abortions, or those that occur after the 20th week of gestation. In "Induced Abortion in the United States," the Guttmacher Institute notes that late-term abortions are extremely rare. In 2013 only 1.3% of all abortions were performed after 20 weeks. Most providers do not even offer the procedure: in 2014, only 25% of abortion providers offered the procedure at 20 weeks, and only 10% offered abortions up to 24 weeks. Even so, the graphic details of how late-term abortions are performed, and the fact that a 20-week-old fetus has clearly recognizable human features, have fueled the claim that a 20-week-old fetus is capable of feeling pain and thus will suffer in the process of being aborted. Medical consensus rejects this claim, maintaining that the fetal nervous system is not sufficiently developed to feel pain before about 24 weeks. Nevertheless, pro-life groups remain determined to outlaw these procedures. Beginning with Nebraska in 2010, state legislatures have led the effort to enact 20-week abortion bans. By 2018, 20-week bans had been enacted in 17 states. At the federal level, in October 2017 the US House of Representatives passed the Pain-Capable Unborn Child Protection Act (H.R. 36) banning abortion after 20 weeks, but as of April 2018 the bill had not been passed in the US Senate.

In political discourse, late-term abortions are commonly known as "partial-birth" abortions, because the procedure involves removing the intact body of the fetus through the birth canal. Julie Rovner reports in "'Partial-Birth Abortion': Separating Fact from Spin" (NPR.org, February 21, 2006) that the term was coined during the mid-1990s by the National Right to Life Committee (NRLC), a pro-life group, to galvanize public opposition to these and all abortions. In 2003 President George W. Bush (1946–) signed into law the Partial Birth Abortion Ban Act, imposing the most significant federal restrictions on abortions rights since 1973; in April 2007 the Supreme Court upheld the law in *Gonzales v. Carhart* (550 US 124) and included no health exception.

The abortion debate made national headlines in July 2015, when an activist group called the Center for Medical Progress released an undercover video that appeared to implicate Planned Parenthood in the illegal practice of selling fetal tissue recovered from partial-birth abortions to medical researchers. Planned Parenthood's vice president of communications, Eric Ferrero, released a statement (July 14, 2015, https://www.plannedparenthood.org/about-us/newsroom/press-releases/statement-from-planned-parenthood-on-new-undercover-video#sthash.gn75qrhJ.dpuf) denying the allegations and explaining the organization's adherence to strict ethical and legal standards regarding fetal tissue donations (for which the there was no financial benefit to the organization). Moreover, as Jennifer Ludden reports in "Planned Parenthood Says Experts Found Misleading Edits in Videos" (NPR.org, August 27, 2015), the Center for Medical Progress was discredited when forensic experts hired by Planned Parenthood found "significant distortions and misleading edits" in the video. Still, the video created a national uproar and emboldened antiabortion lawmakers in the House of Representatives and Senate to push for a ban on federal funding for Planned Parenthood.

In the presidential election of 2016, Republican candidate Donald Trump (1946–) made defunding Planned Parenthood one of his key campaign promises. In December 2016, a month before President Trump took office, the HHS under outgoing President Obama issued a final rule (or federal guideline) to protect Planned Parenthood from being defunded. Kimberly Leonard reports in "Obama Administration Moves to Protect Planned Parenthood Funding" (USNews.com, December 14, 2016) that the regulation required that providers of family planning and preventive health care services could not be barred from receiving federal grant dollars for any reason other than those related to their "ability to deliver services to program beneficiaries in an effective manner." As such, Leonard explains, the rule stipulated that providing abortion services could not disqualify an organization from receiving funds.

Little more than a year later, however, in January 2018, the HHS under President Trump announced that it would revoke the Obama administration's guidance, opening the door for states to block Planned Parenthood from receiving Medicaid funding. At the same time, the HHS introduced a new regulation allowing health care workers to invoke religious or moral objections to refuse to provide abortion, euthanasia, sterilization, or other services. Marie Solis reports in "Trump Administration Targets Medicaid and Poor Women with New Attempt to Defund Planned Parenthood" (Newsweek.com, January 19, 2018) that the announcement was the latest in a series of measures by Trump to embolden states to defund Planned Parenthood. "By targeting Medicaid," Solis writes, "the Trump administration puts low-income women squarely in its crosshairs," given that half of Planned Parenthood's patients rely on Medicaid coverage to access the organization's reproductive health care services.

## Adoption

There are three primary forms of adoption in the United States: foster care adoption, private domestic adoption, and international adoption. Foster care adoption involves children who, prior to being adopted, have been removed from their birth families by public child welfare agencies and transferred into the foster care system. Some of these children are eventually reunited with their birth families, but in cases where this is not possible, adoption is generally considered the best outcome for them. Child welfare agencies usually oversee the adoption process with such children, but sometimes they work through private adoption agencies. Private domestic adoption involves children who are born in the United States and adopted through private agencies without ever being part of the foster care system. Some of these adoptions occur as a result of independent agreements between birth and adoptive parents, and some occur as a result of arrangements brokered by adoption agencies. International adoption involves children who are born outside of the United States. Private US adoption agencies typically coordinate these adoptions with foreign adoption agencies and other private and public entities in the children's birth country.

The circumstances influencing adoption in the United States, including changes in cultural attitudes and changes in federal and international law, are inherently unstable. Because of this, the proportion of children adopted through these respective channels is constantly changing, as are the overall numbers of adopted children and the demographic characteristics of adopted children and their families. For example, according to the US State Department, in "Adoption Statistics" (2018, https://travel.state.gov/content/travel/en/Intercountry-Adoption/adopt_ref/adoption-statistics.html), international adoption declined dramatically from a high of 22,989 in 2004 to 3,980 in 2016. In 2012, the most recent year reported by the State Department, the leading countries for international adoptions to the United States were China, Ethiopia, Russia, South Korea, and Ukraine. The top states for international adoptions that year were Texas, California, New York, Florida, and Illinois.

During the 1990s a number of private, state, and federal initiatives were introduced to increase the numbers of foster children who find permanent adoptive homes, with special attention being given to older foster children who have no prospects of reuniting with their birth family. Additionally, advances in fertility treatments for older women are believed to influence adoption numbers in the United States because adoption has historically been a primary alternative for women who want children but cannot conceive either because of their own or their partner's infertility. At the same time, it has become much rarer for unmarried women to relinquish newborn infants via adoption. In 1973, 8.7% of such births resulted in adoption, but by the 1990s this figure had fallen to 1%.

Sharon Vandivere, Karin Malm, and Laura Radel estimate in *Adoption USA: A Chartbook Based on the 2007 National Survey of Adoptive Parents* (October 2009, https://aspe.hhs.gov/report/adoption-usa-chartbook-based-2007-national-survey-adoptive-parents), the most recent statistical portrait of adoption in the United States as of April 2018, that among the almost 1.8 million adopted children living in the United States in 2007, 677,000 (38%) had been adopted through private domestic adoption, 661,000 (37%) had been adopted through foster care adoption, and 444,000 (25%) had been adopted through international adoption. Transracial adoptions (adoptions in which the child is of a different race, culture, or ethnicity than the adoptive parent or couple) represented 40% of all adoptions in 2007. More than one-third (37%) of adopted children were non-Hispanic white, whereas nearly three-quarters (73%) of adoptive parents were non-Hispanic white. The gender balance among adopted children was roughly even, but there was a sizable disparity in the gender breakdown among domestic versus international adoptions. As of 2007, a majority of children adopted through both foster care (57%) and private domestic adoptions (51%) were male, whereas 67% of internationally adopted children were female. Adopted children were roughly as likely to live in a married-couple household as were children as a whole (69% versus 71%), and internationally adopted children were significantly more likely (82%) to live in a married-couple household.

Since 1997 adoptive families have been able to take a federal tax credit to help cover adoption expenses. In addition, many employers offer adoption benefits to their employees, often in the form of cash to help cover medical costs for the birth mother and legal and other adoption fees. Employers also typically grant the same leaves to new adoptive parents that they grant to birth parents.

**NUMBERS AND RATES.** Jo Jones and Paul Placek of the National Council for Adoption report in *Adoption: By the Numbers* (February 2017, http://www.adoptioncouncil.org/publications/2017/02/adoption-by-the-numbers) that 110,373 adoptions took place in the United States in 2014. Of these, 41,023 (37%) were adoptions by relatives of the children, and 69,350 (63%) were unrelated adoptions. Among domestic adoptions in 2014, 18,239 adoptions were unrelated infant adoptions, representing 0.5% of live births that year and 1.1% of births to single mothers. The peak year for unrelated infant adoptions in National Council for Adoption surveys was 1992, when 26,672 infants were adopted by nonrelatives.

Most adoptions in 2014 were handled through public agencies (47,094), compared with 16,312 adoptions completed through private agencies and 5,944 adoptions arranged directly between individuals. Jones and Placek report that in 2014 there were 4.6 domestic infant adoptions per 1,000 live births in the United States, a ratio that means less than 0.5% of live births resulted in adoptions that year. Jones and Placek further report that there were 11.4 infant adoptions per 1,000 nonmarital live births, meaning that just 1.1% of unmarried mothers relinquished their infants for adoption in 2014.

**TRENDS.** Jones and Placek report adoption trends dating to the 1950s. In 1951 there were 72,000 total adoptions reported, of which 33,800 (47%) were unrelated adoptions. Adoption numbers rose throughout the 1960s, peaking in 1970 with 175,000 adoptions, 89,200 of which (51%) were unrelated adoptions. During the 1970s adoptions began a general decline, with 2007 (133,737 adoptions) representing the highest annual total since 1982. Of the total in 2007, 76,489 adoptions (57%) were by nonrelatives. The 69,350 unrelated adoptions in 2014, represented 63% of adoptions that year and was a record high in terms of percentage over the years reported by Jones and Placek.

Although adoptions in general had declined since the 1980s, adoptions of children with special needs (some of whom may be infants) had increased over the past three decades from 13,568 adoptions in 1986 to a high of 61,341 in 2014. Jones and Placek report that special needs children accounted for nearly nine out of 10 (88.5%) nonrelative adoptions in 2014.

# CHAPTER 8
# CHILD CARE AND ELDER CARE

Far more women than ever before, including mothers with infants and small children, have entered the labor force and are working full time outside of the home. Women are increasingly pursuing education and embarking on careers that may require long hours and extensive travel. Unprecedented numbers of women are raising children on their own. Nevertheless, one element of women's lives has not changed: Women remain the primary caregivers for children and elderly family members.

## WORKING MOTHERS AND CHILD CARE

In 2016, 25.4 million (70.5%) American women with children under the age of 18 years were in the labor force. (See Table 3.3 in Chapter 3.) Overall, 24.2 million (67.2%) women with children under the age of 18 years were employed, and 18.5 million (76.4%) of these employed women worked full time. More than 16.6 million married women and 8.8 million single women with children under the age of 18 years were in the labor force. Single women with children participated in the labor force at a higher rate than their married counterparts in 2016, and they were slightly more likely to be employed full time. Of the 16.1 million employed married women with children, 12.2 million (75.8%) worked full time; and of the 8.1 million employed single women with children, 6.2 million (76.5%) worked full time. Employment rates as a percentage of population were higher for women whose children were school-aged (six to 17 years old) than for women whose children were infants, toddlers, and preschoolers (under six years old), but even among these women with small children, the labor force participation rate was 64.7% and the employment-to-population rate was 61%, a fact that underscores the centrality of child care to American society.

Child care arrangements are a major concern for working mothers, at least until their children reach about the age of 12 years (full-time working mothers may need before- and after-school care for their school-aged children). Part-time workers and those with irregular working hours require child care arrangements that fit their work schedules and may often need to make last-minute arrangements. Child care arrangements must be made for school closures and vacations, and many mothers cannot take paid sick days to care for a sick child. According to the Institute for Women's Policy Research (IWPR), in "Paid Sick Days" (2018, https://iwpr.org/issue/work-family/paid-sick-days/), fewer than 60% of private-sector employees in the United States have access to paid sick days. Similarly, women who leave their jobs due to domestic violence or because they have no viable child care options have historically been ineligible for unemployment insurance.

Infant care poses special challenges for working mothers. As is discussed in Chapter 7, women who attempt to breastfeed their infants in compliance with the recommendations of health care professionals face a range of challenges in the workplace. Children at these ages are especially demanding even when breastfeeding is not an issue, and child care centers for young children are accordingly expensive, in some cases approaching the cost of college tuition. In 2016 mothers of children under the age of three years had a labor force participation rate of 61.8% and an employment-to-population rate of 58.3%, well below that of all mothers. (See Table 8.1.)

Single mothers with children under the age of three years were much more likely than other mothers to be unemployed. Although their labor force participation rate (67.1%) was significantly higher than that of married mothers with children under the age of three years (59.5%), single mothers of infants and toddlers had a high unemployment rate (10.5%). For many mothers of young children, stable, affordable child care arrangements can make the difference between employment and unemployment.

TABLE 8.1

**Employment status of mothers with own children under three years old, by age of youngest child and marital status, 2015–16**

[Numbers in thousands]

| Characteristic | 2015 With own children under 3 years old | | | | 2016 With own children under 3 years old | | | |
|---|---|---|---|---|---|---|---|---|
| | Total | 2 years | 1 year | Under 1 year | Total | 2 years | 1 year | Under 1 year |
| **Total mothers** | | | | | | | | |
| Civilian noninstitutional population | 9,308 | 2,920 | 3,254 | 3,134 | 9,158 | 2,850 | 3,322 | 2,985 |
| Civilian labor force | 5,714 | 1,869 | 2,024 | 1,821 | 5,662 | 1,858 | 2,055 | 1,749 |
| Participation rate | 61.4 | 64.0 | 62.2 | 58.1 | 61.8 | 65.2 | 61.9 | 58.6 |
| Employed | 5,336 | 1,741 | 1,897 | 1,698 | 5,343 | 1,764 | 1,933 | 1,645 |
| Full-time workers[a] | 3,882 | 1,280 | 1,370 | 1,232 | 3,870 | 1,312 | 1,392 | 1,165 |
| Part-time workers[b] | 1,455 | 462 | 526 | 466 | 1,473 | 452 | 540 | 480 |
| Employment-population ratio | 57.3 | 59.6 | 58.3 | 54.2 | 58.3 | 61.9 | 58.2 | 55.1 |
| Unemployed | 377 | 127 | 128 | 123 | 319 | 94 | 123 | 103 |
| Unemployment rate | 6.6 | 6.8 | 6.3 | 6.7 | 5.6 | 5.0 | 6.0 | 5.9 |
| **Married, spouse present[c]** | | | | | | | | |
| Civilian noninstitutional population | 6,341 | 1,974 | 2,252 | 2,114 | 6,335 | 1,964 | 2,302 | 2,069 |
| Civilian labor force | 3,772 | 1,198 | 1,356 | 1,218 | 3,768 | 1,210 | 1,367 | 1,191 |
| Participation rate | 59.5 | 60.7 | 60.2 | 57.6 | 59.5 | 61.6 | 59.4 | 57.6 |
| Employed | 3,628 | 1,149 | 1,300 | 1,179 | 3,648 | 1,171 | 1,321 | 1,156 |
| Full-time workers[a] | 2,698 | 864 | 961 | 873 | 2,691 | 876 | 966 | 849 |
| Part-time workers[b] | 931 | 285 | 339 | 306 | 957 | 294 | 356 | 307 |
| Employment-population ratio | 57.2 | 58.2 | 57.7 | 55.8 | 57.6 | 59.6 | 57.4 | 55.9 |
| Unemployed | 144 | 49 | 55 | 39 | 120 | 39 | 46 | 35 |
| Unemployment rate | 3.8 | 4.1 | 4.1 | 3.2 | 3.2 | 3.3 | 3.4 | 3.0 |
| **Other marital status[d]** | | | | | | | | |
| Civilian noninstitutional population | 2,967 | 946 | 1,001 | 1,020 | 2,823 | 886 | 1,020 | 917 |
| Civilian labor force | 1,942 | 670 | 669 | 603 | 1,894 | 648 | 689 | 557 |
| Participation rate | 65.4 | 70.9 | 66.8 | 59.1 | 67.1 | 73.1 | 67.5 | 60.8 |
| Employed | 1,708 | 592 | 596 | 519 | 1,695 | 594 | 612 | 489 |
| Full-time workers[a] | 1,184 | 415 | 409 | 359 | 1,179 | 436 | 427 | 316 |
| Part-time workers[b] | 524 | 177 | 187 | 160 | 516 | 158 | 185 | 173 |
| Employment-population ratio | 57.6 | 62.6 | 59.5 | 50.9 | 60.0 | 67.0 | 60.0 | 53.4 |
| Unemployed | 234 | 78 | 72 | 84 | 199 | 54 | 77 | 68 |
| Unemployment rate | 12.0 | 11.6 | 10.8 | 13.9 | 10.5 | 8.4 | 11.2 | 12.2 |

[a]Usually work 35 hours or more per week at all jobs.
[b]Usually work less than 35 hours per week at all jobs.
[c]Refers to persons in opposite-sex married couples only.
[d]Includes persons who are never married; widowed; divorced; separated; and married, spouse absent; as well as persons in same-sex marriages.
Note: Own children include sons, daughters, step-children, and adopted children. Not included are nieces, nephews, grandchildren, and other related and unrelated children. Detail may not sum to totals due to rounding. Updated population controls are introduced annually with the release of January data.

SOURCE: "Table 6. Employment Status of Mothers with Own Children under 3 Years Old by Single Year of Age of Youngest Child and Marital Status, 2015–2016 Annual Averages," in *Employment Characteristics of Families—2016*, US Bureau of Labor Statistics, April 20, 2017, https://www.bls.gov/news .release/pdf/famee.pdf (accessed January 31, 2018).

## CHILD CARE ARRANGEMENTS

### Types of Child Care Arrangements

The choice of child care arrangements depends on availability, work schedules, transportation, affordability, and the age of the child. Children in parental care are cared for regularly only by the parents. For infants and preschool-aged children with mothers who work, fathers may stay home full time or work a different shift to care for children. Because the average workday is longer than the average school day, many mothers need to find before- and after-school care for children aged six years and older who are enrolled in school. A significant portion of children are cared for at least part of the time by a grandparent or another family member in the person's home or in the child's home. Many studies reflect the importance of extended families for working mothers with young children.

Nonrelative child care takes place in a variety of settings. Some children have more than one type of regular nonparental care. Some working parents can afford to hire a babysitter or nanny to care for children in their own home; other parents rely on their friends for child care. Groups of parents may form a child care cooperative, using parent volunteers or a hired caregiver or preschool teacher.

However, most home-based or family day care is provided by an adult, usually a mother, who cares for several children in her own home. These home-based day care businesses are often more affordable than center-based day care, but unlike center-based day care, they are often unlicensed. Because there is no oversight of home-based day care, the quality and safety of the facilities and the care can be difficult for parents to ascertain.

Aside from individual care and relative care, center-based child care tends to offer the highest quality of care.

These programs include day care centers, nursery schools, preschools, Head Start programs, and other early childhood education and school-based programs such as prekindergarten. These child care facilities may operate as commercial businesses, private nonprofit organizations, or publicly funded programs (such as Head Start and public prekindergarten). Some businesses have child care facilities for their employees, and many schools and universities have child care facilities for students and staff. Some centers care for only one age group of children, whereas others care for all children from infancy through school age.

According to Karen E. Diamond et al. of the US Department of Education Institute of Education Sciences, in "Synthesis of IES Research on Early Intervention and Early-Childhood Education" (July 2013, https://ies.ed.gov/ncser/pubs/20133001/pdf/20133001.pdf), "A primary purpose of early childhood education is to promote children's acquisition of knowledge and skills linked to later social competence and academic success." There is also evidence to indicate that the quality of day care during children's early years is even more important for children whose learning may be challenged by poverty, who live in a non-English-speaking home, or who have identified disabilities. Diamond et al. conclude, "Early childhood education programs ... can be particularly important for

closing the gap in early skills among children experiencing risk factors relative to more-advantaged children." Similarly, Linda Bakken, Nola Brown, and Barry Downing, in "Early Childhood Education: The Long-Term Benefits" (*Journal of Research in Childhood Education*, vol. 31, no. 2, 2017), point to a growing body of research finding that "children who live in poverty and attend a quality preschool program experience long-lasting primary and secondary positive effects" in terms of their intellectual, social, emotional, and behavioral development.

## How Are Children Cared For?

**INFANTS AND PRESCHOOLERS.** The Federal Interagency Forum on Child and Family Statistics provides in *America's Children: Key National Indicators of Well-Being, 2017* (July 2017, https://www.childstats.gov/pdf/ac2017/ac_17.pdf) an overview of the child care arrangements of working mothers. In 2011 almost half (49%) of children aged four years and younger whose mothers were employed were primarily cared for by a relative: either a grandparent, the father, or the mother herself while she worked. (See Figure 8.1.) Among the children cared for by family members, 19.5% were cared for by their father, a percentage that had risen over the preceding decade and a half but was down from a high of 20% in 1991. The proportion of these children cared for

**FIGURE 8.1**

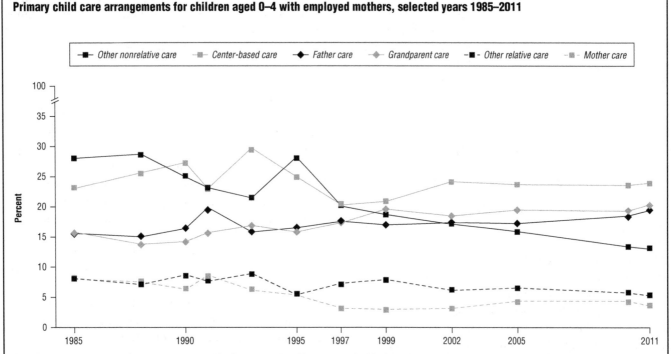

Primary child care arrangements for children aged 0–4 with employed mothers, selected years 1985–2011

Note: The primary arrangement is the arrangement used for the most number of hours per week while the mother worked. Mother and father care each refer to care while the mother worked.

SOURCE: "Indicator FAM3.A. Primary Child Care Arrangements for Children Ages 0–4 with Employed Mothers, Selected Years 1985–2011," in *America's Children: Key National Indicators of Well-Being, 2017*, Federal Interagency Forum on Child and Family Statistics, July 2017, https://www.childstats.gov/pdf/ac2017/ac_17.pdf (accessed January 31, 2018)

primarily by a grandparent had risen more or less steadily from 15.9% in 1985 to 20.5% in 2011. The proportion of these children cared for primarily by other relatives, at 5.3% in 2011, was down significantly from levels during the 1980s and 1990s, and the proportion cared for primarily by the working mother herself stood at 3.6%, down significantly from 8.1% in 1985.

Nearly a quarter (24%) of children aged zero to four years whose mothers worked were primarily cared for in a day care center, preschool, or Head Start facility in 2011. (See Figure 8.1.) This percentage had been fluctuating between 20.4% and 29.9%, without showing any clear movement up or down, since 1985. Another 13.1% of these young children were primarily cared for by nonrelatives in a home-based setting—formal or informal home-based day care businesses, in-home babysitters, and other providers working either out of the child's home or the provider's home. This percentage was down markedly from 1985, when it stood at 28.2%.

The Federal Interagency Forum on Child and Family Statistics notes that the distribution of child care arrangements among these children varied according to poverty level. Those children aged zero to four years who lived below the poverty line and whose mothers were employed in 2012 were less likely to be in center-based care, which tends to be more expensive than other forms of care, than were children whose families lived above the poverty line. Children from impoverished families were also substantially more likely to be cared for by a relative other than a father or grandparent. Among children between the ages of three and six years who were not yet in kindergarten in 2012, poverty was likewise a strong predictor of whether or not they had access to center-based care during their crucial preschool years. (See Figure 8.2.) Among children aged three to six years who were not in kindergarten yet and who lived below the poverty line, 45% attended day care centers, preschools, or Head Start in 2012, compared with 51% of children at 100% to 199% of the poverty line and 72% of children at 200% or more of the poverty line.

SCHOOL-AGED CHILDREN. The patterns for care of school-aged children whose mothers were employed and who needed care before and after school differed from the patterns of younger children. Children aged five to 11 years were the most likely to be cared for by their father, whereas children aged 12 to 14 years were the most likely to care for themselves. (See Figure 8.3.) Over a quarter (26.3%) of children aged five to eight years whose mothers worked were cared for by their father, and this proportion diminished with age, to 24.1% at ages nine to 11 years and 20.3% at ages 12 to 14 years. Meanwhile, self-care was rare among five- to eight-year-olds (2.4%), more common among nine- to 11-year-olds (10.2%), and most common among 12- to 14-year-olds (32.5%). Grandparent

care and enrichment activities were the other most common sources of before- and after-school care for those aged five to 11 years. Grandparent care was less common for children aged 12 to 14 years. Children over the age of 14 years typically care for themselves before and after school.

## Child Care Costs

Because the US economy depends not only on the ability of mothers and fathers to work but also on the healthy development of their children, who will one day assume their own place in the workforce, child care is essential to the emotional lives of families and children and to society at large. In spite of this fact, there is no comprehensive system for public financing of child care, as there is for elementary, secondary, and postsecondary education; and the cost of child care is prohibitively expensive even for many families with two wage earners. Child care costs, like the costs of many other goods and services necessary for families' daily functioning, have risen in recent decades, while wages have remained flat or declined, when adjusted for inflation.

In *Parents and the High Cost of Child Care* (2017, https://usa.childcareaware.org/wp-content/uploads/2017/12/2017_CCA_High_Cost_Report_FINAL.pdf), Child Care Aware of America reports that in 2017 the average cost of full-time center-based infant care was more than 10% of the

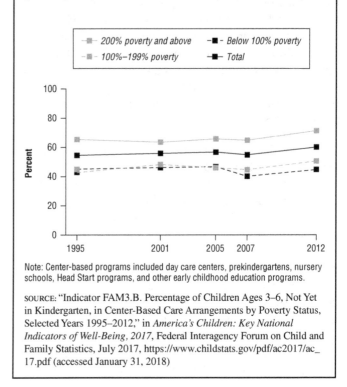

FIGURE 8.2

**Percentage of children aged 3–6, not yet in kindergarten, in center-based care arrangements by poverty level, selected years 1995–2012**

Note: Center-based programs included day care centers, prekindergartens, nursery schools, Head Start programs, and other early childhood education programs.

SOURCE: "Indicator FAM3.B. Percentage of Children Ages 3–6, Not Yet in Kindergarten, in Center-Based Care Arrangements by Poverty Status, Selected Years 1995–2012," in *America's Children: Key National Indicators of Well-Being, 2017*, Federal Interagency Forum on Child and Family Statistics, July 2017, https://www.childstats.gov/pdf/ac2017/ac_17.pdf (accessed January 31, 2018)

FIGURE 8.3

**Child care arrangements for grade school children aged 5–14 with employed mothers, 2011**

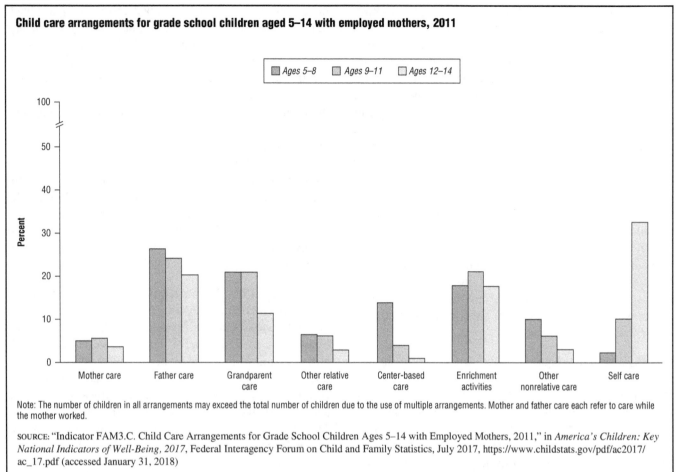

Note: The number of children in all arrangements may exceed the total number of children due to the use of multiple arrangements. Mother and father care each refer to care while the mother worked.

SOURCE: "Indicator FAM3.C. Child Care Arrangements for Grade School Children Ages 5–14 with Employed Mothers, 2011," in *America's Children: Key National Indicators of Well-Being, 2017*, Federal Interagency Forum on Child and Family Statistics, July 2017, https://www.childstats.gov/pdf/ac2017/ ac_17.pdf (accessed January 31, 2018)

median income (the middle value; half of all families earn less and half earn more) for a two-parent family in 41 states and the District of Columbia. Nationally, the average cost of full-time center-based infant care exceeded 27% of the median income for families headed by single parents. In 28 states and the District of Columbia, full-time center-based child care for an infant (the most expensive form of child care) cost more per year than tuition and fees at four-year public colleges.

Although child care is an essential and growing industry, and its workers are tasked with immense responsibility (overseeing the safety, health, and mental and emotional development of children), child care is one of the lowest-paying occupations in the US economy. According to Child Care Aware of America, center-based child care workers made an average of $10.18 per hour in 2016, or about $21,174 per year. This income fell below the federal poverty guidelines for a family of four and barely above the poverty guidelines for a family of three. Home-based child care workers made even less on average. Because wages account for approximately 80% of expenses for most child care centers, reducing them is the primary method the owners of such businesses have to hold costs down for families. With wages at such low

levels already, however, there is little chance that child care can become more affordable through the ordinary working of market forces.

**Government Assistance**

Although the majority of parents must pay market rates for child care, some public financing exists in the form of the federal Child Care and Development Block Grant (CCDBG). The federal government gives this money to the states, which use it to subsidize child care for low-income working families. Hannah Matthews and Christina Walker indicate in "Child Care and Development Block Grant Participation in 2014" (March 2016, https://www.clasp.org/sites/default/files/public/resources- and-publications/publication-1/CC-Spending-and-Partici pation-2014-1.pdf) that 1.4 million children received assistance through the CCDBG program in 2014, repre- senting a decrease of 364,000 children from 2006 and the lowest number since 1998. In 2014, 24 states served fewer children in than in 2013, and 29 states spent fewer CCDBG funds than the previous year. Moreover, many eligible low-income families did not receive CCDBG assistance. Matthews and Reeves estimate that 85% of potentially eligible children do not receive CCDBG- assisted child care.

In November 2014 President Barack Obama (1961–) signed into law the Child Care and Development Block Grant Act of 2014. Passed by Congress with strong bipartisan support, the law reauthorized the CCDBG program (the main source of federal funding for state-provided child care assistance for low-income families) for the first time since 1996. Included in the new law were important updates to protect the health and safety of children receiving child care, improve access to child care assistance for low-income families, and improve the overall quality of care. New provisions included requiring background checks for child care providers, stronger health and safety requirements for child care programs and providers, and regular on-site inspections of child care facilities. Changes to the law were modeled in part on the US Department of Defense's Child Development Program, which provides child care for military families. The Defense Department program is the largest employer-sponsored child care program in the country and is widely recognized for its superior quality of care, accountability, and oversight.

The only other significant form of federal assistance for child care available as of 2018 was the Child and Dependent Care Credit, a tax credit that allows parents to deduct up to $3,000 spent on child care for one child and up to $6,000 spent on two or more children from yearend income taxes. This tax credit primarily benefits working families well above the poverty level. Many low-income families do not make enough money to pay federal income taxes, so they are not able to take advantage of this credit.

## Family Leave

The Organisation for Economic Co-operation and Development (OECD), an international organization dedicated to promoting global economic development, conducts research regarding the national paid maternity leave policies of its 35 member countries. In "Length of Maternity Leave, Parental Leave and Paid Father-Specific Leave" (2016, http://www.oecd.org/gender/data/length-of-maternity-leave-parental-leave-and-paid-father-specific-leave.htm), the OECD reports that among its member countries, the average paid maternity leave time was just over 19 weeks in 2016. The United Kingdom ranked first, with a national policy providing up to a full year (52 weeks) of paid maternity leave; the US ranked last, making it the only developed country in the world that has no federally mandated paid maternity leave (zero weeks). Research shows that paid maternity leave correlates with lower infant mortality rates and higher rates of breastfeeding, which benefits the health of both mother and baby and therefore reduces the costs that are associated with illness and hospitalization.

President Bill Clinton (1946–) signed the landmark Family and Medical Leave Act (FMLA) in 1993, providing for up to 12 weeks of unpaid leave annually for illness, at the birth or adoption of a child or a foster-care placement, or to care for a seriously ill child, spouse, or parent. The law applies to all public agencies and all private companies with 50 or more employees and to employees who worked 1,250 hours in the previous year. Employers are required to maintain the employee's health coverage and to reinstate the returning employee in the same or an equivalent job. Many low-income families, however, do not have access to the unpaid leave the law offers because they often work for companies with fewer than 50 employees or have not met the 1,250-hour minimum. Additionally, parents whose families are struggling economically often cannot afford to take leave that will mean missing paychecks. An estimated 40% of US workers are believed to have no access to unpaid family leave, and paid leave is typically available only among professional and managerial workers.

As part of the Obama administration's ongoing effort to improve economic security for working families, the White House Council of Economic Advisers issued "The Economics of Paid and Unpaid Leave" (June 2014, https://obamawhitehouse.archives.gov/sites/default/files/docs/leave_report_final.pdf), a report that examines the composition of American workers with access to paid and unpaid, based on responses to the 2011 American Time Use Survey. As Table 8.2 shows, 59% of US workers had access to paid leave, and 77% had access to

**TABLE 8.2**

Access to paid and unpaid leave, by selected worker characteristics

| Leave type | Access to paid leave | Access to unpaid leave |
|---|---|---|
| **Total** | 59% | 77% |
| **Demographic characteristics** | | |
| Male | 60% | 75% |
| Female | 57% | 78% |
| White, non-Hispanic | 62% | 78% |
| Black, non-Hispanic | 61% | 77% |
| Asian, non-Hispanic | 62% | 72% |
| Hispanic | 43% | 71% |
| **Educational attainment (workers 25 and older)** | | |
| Less than high school | 35% | 70% |
| High school | 61% | 76% |
| Some college | 66% | 78% |
| Bachelor's degree or higher | 72% | 75% |
| **Weekly earnings** | | |
| $0–$540 | 50% | 78% |
| $541–$830 | 77% | 79% |
| $831–$1,230 | 81% | 75% |
| $1,230+ | 83% | 75% |
| **All workers** | | |
| Paid hourly | 56% | 80% |
| Salaried | 62% | 73% |

SOURCE: Adapted from "Table 2. Access to Leave by Selected Worker Characteristics," in *The Economics of Paid and Unpaid Leave*, White House Council of Economic Advisors, 2014, https://obamawhitehouse.archives.gov/sites/default/files/docs/leave_report_final.pdf (accessed January 31, 2018)

unpaid leave. These numbers varied according to worker characteristics such as level of education and weekly earnings, particularly in the category of paid leave. Among workers aged 25 years and older with a high school diploma but no college 61% had access to paid leave; among workers with a bachelor's degree or higher 72% had access to paid leave. Similarly, those with lower weekly earnings were also less likely to have access to paid leave. Most working women who give birth and fathers of newborns attempt to compensate for the lack of paid leave by combining vacation days, other forms of paid leave (such as sick leave), unpaid leave, and individual agreements with sympathetic employers. In general, the mothers least likely to enjoy paid maternity leave are those who need it most: less-educated, low-income workers who struggle to keep their families out of poverty even under normal circumstances.

Among those companies that provide paid leave, the maximum time off allowed new mothers and fathers is typically far lower than in other developed countries. In "In Paid Family Leave, U.S. Trails Most of the Globe" (NYTimes.com, February 22, 2013), Tara Siegel Bernard states that the average time off for mothers who received paid maternity leave in the United States in 2013 was seven weeks. By contrast, the OECD reports in "PF2.1: Key Characteristics of Parental Leave Systems" (October 26, 2017, https://www.oecd.org/els/soc/PF2_1_Parental_leave_systems.pdf) that as of 2016 paid leave for mothers in developed countries such as Germany (14 weeks), Japan (14 weeks), Canada (17 weeks), Australia (18 weeks), Italy (21.7 weeks), the United Kingdom (39 weeks), and Greece (43 weeks) far surpassed the US average.

Among all US economic sectors, the technology industry has led the way in extending paid family leave benefits to its workers. Elizabeth Trompeter reports in "50 Companies with Great Maternity Leave" (http://workplace.care.com/50-companies-with-great-maternity-leave, July 27, 2016) that in 2016, Netflix offered a full year of paid maternity leave, and other tech companies such as Adobe, Amazon, Cisco, eBay, Etsy, Microsoft, Spotify, and Twitter offered four or more months of this benefit. According to Trompeter, "To be a successful, forward-thinking company that is attractive to potential Millennial employees, competitive maternity leave is now a must." Indeed, comparatively generous family leave benefits in Silicon Valley appeared to be putting pressure on other industries to improve their benefits packages. Clare O'Connor reports in "These Companies All Boosted Paid Parental Leave in 2016" (Forbes.com, December 30, 2016) that 2016 saw significant expansion of family leave benefits by companies ranging from Swedish flat-pack furniture chain IKEA, to financial services giant American Express, to the top-selling Greek yogurt brand Chobani.

Throughout his presidency, President Obama made various efforts to expand FMLA coverage but failed to make significant headway due to opposition from the Republican-controlled Congress. During the 2016 presidential campaign, Republican candidate Donald Trump (1946–) proposed a plan for paid family leave that included six weeks of paid maternity leave for all mothers. Although this was a significant departure from the traditional stance of his party, which opposed mandating such benefits either through regulation or a government program, O'Connor reports that Trump's proposal was widely condemned by policy experts as "woefully inadequate" and "completely unserious." As of April 2018, more than a year into his presidency, Trump had not moved the proposal forward.

## ELDER CARE

If the creation of high-quality, affordable child care has not kept up with the needs of a changing workforce, issues surrounding elder care (the provision of care to someone over the age of 65 years who needs help because of conditions related to aging) have lagged even further behind. The elderly population in the United States is growing rapidly as a result of the aging of the baby boom generation (people born between 1946 and 1964). Meanwhile, most nonelderly men and women are in the labor force and therefore have limited time to care for their aged relatives. The elderly often need a wide variety of services, including not only intensive medical treatments but also psychological attention owing to the many challenges that come with aging and the loss of mobility and independence. Additionally, the needs of the elderly are in constant flux. Whereas children require less care as they get older, the elderly often need more care. Most elderly prefer to remain at home and avoid institutionalization, putting the burden of care on relatives. Typically, the burden of elder care falls more heavily on women than on men.

According to the US Bureau of Labor Statistics, in the press release "American Time Use Survey" (September 20, 2017, https://www.bls.gov/news.release/elcare.nr0.htm), 41.3 million Americans provided unpaid elder care in 2015–16, and 56.1% of these providers were women. Most elder care providers were between the ages of 45 and 54 years (21.4%) and 55 to 64 years (24.3%). Another 19.1% of elder care providers were 65 years and older. Of the total 41.3 million elder care providers in 2015–16, 8.7 million were also parents of at least one child under the age of 18 years in the household. Of these 8.7 million parents who also provided elder care, 81.1% were employed, and 63.8% were employed full time. Most elder care providers were caring for a parent (46.6%), a grandparent (22.7%), or another relative (27.1%); another 12.2% of providers were caring for a neighbor or friend. Women tend to live longer than men, which is one of the reasons wives are more likely than husbands to provide this form of elder care.

Besides being more likely than men to provide elder care, women also spent more time, on average, providing elder care. On days when elder care was provided, women typically spent 2.9 hours on the task, whereas men typically spent 2.8 hours. Of the average 2.84 hours that men and women spent providing elder care on the days they did so in 2016, more than half involved leisure activities (34%) and household activities (20.7%). (See Figure 8.4.) Elder care can consist of almost any activity, including assistance with hygiene and grooming, meal preparation, transportation to medical appointments, and simple companionship.

The FMLA allows for 12 weeks off to care for an ailing parent, a provision that may be used by that portion of elder care providers who work for companies with more than 50 employees and who care for their parents or spouse, as opposed to grandparents or other family members. Nonetheless, the proportion of employers who voluntarily allow elder care leave is relatively high. Kenneth Matos, Ellen Galinsky, and James T. Bond note in *National Study of Employers* (2017, https://www.shrm.org/hr-today/trends-and-forecasting/research-and-surveys/Documents/National%20Study%20of%20Employers.pdf) that 78% of US employers indicated that they authorize either paid or unpaid time off for workers to provide elder care. The researchers surmise that "this high prevalence of elder care leave may be indicative of the fact that decision makers in organizations are typically older and more likely to experience elder care issues than those not in decision-making positions, and, thus, the former may be more sensitive to providing help to others who have similar needs." In contrast to the employer provision of either paid or unpaid maternity leave, there was little disparity between the provision of elder care leave among small (50 to 99 employees) and large (1,000 or more employees) organizations. Large employers were, however, substantially more likely to offer Dependent Care Assistance Plans, which enable workers to pay for elder care (if they need to employ a nonrelative as a care provider) with pretax dollars.

The Older Americans Act Amendments of 2000 established the National Family Caregiver Support Program, a grant program to help states provide various caregiver services to those caring for people aged 60 years and older or children with disabilities aged 18 years and younger. The program provides caregivers with information, counseling, and training, and help gaining access to services, respite care, and supplemental caregiving services.

FIGURE 8.4

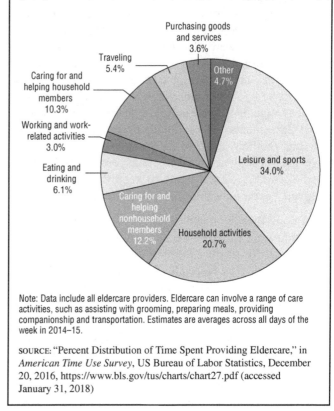

**Percentage distribution of time spent providing elder care, 2016**

[Average hours eldercare providers spent providing care on days they did so = 3.0]

- Purchasing goods and services 3.6%
- Traveling 5.4%
- Caring for and helping household members 10.3%
- Working and work-related activities 3.0%
- Eating and drinking 6.1%
- Other 4.7%
- Leisure and sports 34.0%
- Caring for and helping nonhousehold members 12.2%
- Household activities 20.7%

Note: Data include all eldercare providers. Eldercare can involve a range of care activities, such as assisting with grooming, preparing meals, providing companionship and transportation. Estimates are averages across all days of the week in 2014–15.

SOURCE: "Percent Distribution of Time Spent Providing Eldercare," in *American Time Use Survey*, US Bureau of Labor Statistics, December 20, 2016, https://www.bls.gov/tus/charts/chart27.pdf (accessed January 31, 2018)

The Older Americans Act Amendments of 2006 broadened the definition of a family caregiver to include caregivers of people aged 50 years and older with Alzheimer's disease. The program is small by the standards of federal initiatives, and funding has been falling rather than increasing in recent years. In "National Family Caregiver Support Program" (December 13, 2017, https://www.acl.gov/programs/support-caregivers/national-family-caregiver-support-program), the Administration for Community Living explains that funding for the program increased from $145.6 million in fiscal year (FY) 2015 to $150.6 million in FY 2016. In FY 2014 (the most recent year for which service data were available as of April 2018), the program provided services to more than 700,000 caregivers. These services included assistance with finding elder care help through private and nonprofit entities, counseling and training to help caregivers cope with the demands of elder care, and temporary elder care in moments when caregivers could not provide the care themselves.

# CHAPTER 9
# WOMEN IN US POLITICS

## THE POLITICAL POWER OF WOMEN

Between 1838 and 1910, 25 US states passed laws that allowed women to vote on school issues. In 1893 Colorado became the first state to allow full women's suffrage, and by 1920, 30 states, primarily in the West and Midwest, had granted women full suffrage. In August 1920 Tennessee became the 36th state to ratify the 19th Amendment to the US Constitution, and all American women were granted the right to vote. In the years since 1920, American women have exercised their right to vote, helped elect their government, influenced legislation, and helped determine the direction of the nation. Especially since the 1960s, women have increasingly shaped the nation by winning election to office themselves.

### A Note on the Sources of Data on Women's Political Activity

Important data on voting patterns in the United States are collected by the US Census Bureau. However, much information specific to women's involvement in voting and other political behaviors is compiled only by private nonprofit organizations. The Center for American Women and Politics (CAWP), a unit of the Eagleton Institute of Politics of Rutgers University of New Jersey, collects more comprehensive data on women's involvement in politics than any other group. Besides Census Bureau data, much of the material in this chapter is based on CAWP publications.

## WOMEN VOTERS
### Registration and Voter Turnout

Any discussion of US elections is usually broken down into two categories: presidential elections and nonpresidential (or midterm) elections. Each takes place every four years, but in an alternating pattern, so that 2012 was a presidential election, 2014 a nonpresidential election, and 2016 another presidential election. Although congressional seats are contested in both types of elections, voting and

registration rates tend to increase during presidential elections, a fact that has a pronounced effect on the demographic characteristics of the electorate. Therefore, the Census Bureau generally compares nonpresidential elections with other nonpresidential elections and presidential elections with other presidential elections.

**PRESIDENTIAL ELECTIONS.** The voting rate of women aged 18 years and older has surpassed that of men in every presidential election since 1980. Before 1980 men were more likely to vote than women. Experts attribute this shift to cultural changes, including increases in educational attainment and labor force participation among women during the second half of the 20th century, both of which correlate strongly with voting.

With the presidential election of 2016, women broke new ground in American politics, as the Democratic candidate Hillary Rodham Clinton (1947–) became the first woman in US history to win the nomination of one of the two major political parties. Clinton ran unsuccessfully against the Republican nominee Donald Trump (1946–), a real estate developer and reality television star who had never held political office. In 2016 there were 245.5 million people over the age of 18 years living in the United States, 224.1 million of whom were citizens by birth or naturalization and therefore eligible to vote. (See Table 9.1.) Women outnumbered men 116.5 million to 107.6 million, respectively, among eligible voters and 83.8 million to 73.8 million, respectively, among registered voters.

Besides their raw numerical advantage, women also register to vote at higher rates than men do. In 2016, 72% of voting-age women were registered, compared with 68.6% of voting-age men. (See Table 9.1.) Likewise, women were more likely than men to cast their votes during the 2016 presidential election: 73.7 million women, or 63.3% of all voting-age women, reported voting, compared with 63.8 million (59.3%) men.

**TABLE 9.1**

**Reported voting and registration by sex, November 2016**

[In thousands]

| All races | Total population | Total citizen population | US citizen Reported registered Number | Percent | Reported not registered Number | Percent | No response to registration[a] Number | Percent | Reported voted Number | Percent | Reported did not vote Number | Percent | No response to voting[b] Number | Percent | Total population Reported registered Percent | Reported voted Percent |
|---|---|---|---|---|---|---|---|---|---|---|---|---|---|---|---|---|
| **Both sexes** | | | | | | | | | | | | | | | | |
| **Total, 18 years and over** | **245,502** | **224,059** | **157,596** | **70.3** | **32,622** | **14.6** | **33,841** | **15.1** | **137,537** | **61.4** | **53,860** | **24.0** | **32,662** | **14.6** | **64.2** | **56.0** |
| 18 to 24 years | 29,320 | 26,913 | 14,905 | 55.4 | 6,650 | 24.7 | 5,358 | 19.9 | 11,560 | 43.0 | 10,171 | 37.8 | 5,182 | 19.3 | 50.8 | 39.4 |
| 25 to 44 years | 83,698 | 72,610 | 48,629 | 67.0 | 12,467 | 17.2 | 11,514 | 15.9 | 40,994 | 56.5 | 20,682 | 28.5 | 10,933 | 15.1 | 58.1 | 49.0 |
| 45 to 64 years | 83,799 | 77,544 | 57,394 | 74.0 | 9,063 | 11.7 | 11,087 | 14.3 | 51,668 | 66.6 | 15,065 | 19.4 | 10,810 | 13.9 | 68.5 | 61.7 |
| 65 to 74 years | 28,832 | 27,839 | 21,908 | 78.7 | 2,502 | 9.0 | 3,429 | 12.3 | 20,219 | 72.6 | 4,239 | 15.2 | 3,381 | 12.1 | 76.0 | 70.1 |
| 75 years and over | 19,852 | 19,154 | 14,759 | 77.1 | 1,941 | 10.1 | 2,454 | 12.8 | 13,095 | 68.4 | 3,703 | 19.3 | 2,356 | 12.3 | 74.3 | 66.0 |
| **Male** | | | | | | | | | | | | | | | | |
| **Total, 18 years and over** | **118,488** | **107,554** | **73,761** | **68.6** | **17,068** | **15.9** | **16,724** | **15.5** | **63,801** | **59.3** | **27,681** | **25.7** | **16,071** | **14.9** | **62.3** | **53.8** |
| 18 to 24 years | 14,822 | 13,530 | 7,200 | 53.2 | 3,579 | 26.5 | 2,752 | 20.3 | 5,409 | 40.0 | 5,448 | 40.3 | 2,673 | 19.8 | 48.6 | 36.5 |
| 25 to 44 years | 41,264 | 35,431 | 22,718 | 64.1 | 6,733 | 19.0 | 5,980 | 16.9 | 18,783 | 53.0 | 11,021 | 31.1 | 5,628 | 15.9 | 55.1 | 45.5 |
| 45 to 64 years | 40,642 | 37,516 | 27,229 | 72.6 | 4,853 | 12.9 | 5,434 | 14.5 | 24,364 | 64.9 | 7,899 | 21.1 | 5,253 | 14.0 | 67.0 | 59.9 |
| 65 to 74 years | 13,428 | 13,018 | 10,245 | 78.7 | 1,211 | 9.3 | 1,561 | 12.0 | 9,473 | 72.8 | 2,003 | 15.4 | 1,541 | 11.8 | 76.3 | 70.5 |
| 75 years and over | 8,333 | 8,059 | 6,369 | 79.0 | 692 | 8.6 | 997 | 12.4 | 5,772 | 71.6 | 1,310 | 16.3 | 976 | 12.1 | 76.4 | 69.3 |
| **Female** | | | | | | | | | | | | | | | | |
| **Total, 18 years and over** | **127,013** | **116,505** | **83,835** | **72.0** | **15,553** | **13.3** | **17,117** | **14.7** | **73,735** | **63.3** | **26,179** | **22.5** | **16,591** | **14.2** | **66.0** | **58.1** |
| 18 to 24 years | 14,498 | 13,382 | 7,706 | 57.6 | 3,070 | 22.9 | 2,606 | 19.5 | 6,150 | 46.0 | 4,723 | 35.3 | 2,509 | 18.7 | 53.2 | 42.4 |
| 25 to 44 years | 42,435 | 37,178 | 25,911 | 69.7 | 5,734 | 15.4 | 5,533 | 14.9 | 22,212 | 59.7 | 9,662 | 26.0 | 5,305 | 14.3 | 61.1 | 52.3 |
| 45 to 64 years | 43,157 | 40,028 | 30,165 | 75.4 | 4,210 | 10.5 | 5,653 | 14.1 | 27,304 | 68.2 | 7,167 | 17.9 | 5,557 | 13.9 | 69.9 | 63.3 |
| 65 to 74 years | 15,404 | 14,821 | 11,663 | 78.7 | 1,291 | 8.7 | 1,868 | 12.6 | 10,746 | 72.5 | 2,236 | 15.1 | 1,840 | 12.4 | 75.7 | 69.8 |
| 75 years and over | 11,519 | 11,095 | 8,390 | 75.6 | 1,249 | 11.3 | 1,456 | 13.1 | 7,324 | 66.0 | 2,392 | 21.6 | 1,379 | 12.4 | 72.8 | 63.6 |

[a]"No response to registration" includes those who were not asked if they were registered as well as those who responded "don't know" and "refused."

[b]"No response to voting" includes those who were not asked if they voted as well as those who responded "don't know" and "refused."

SOURCE: "Table 2. Reported Voting and Registration, by Race, Hispanic Origin, Sex, and Age, for the United States: November 2016," in *Voting and Registration in the Election of November 2016*, US Census Bureau, January 2018, https://www2.census.gov/programs-surveys/cps/tables/p20/580/table02_1.xls (accessed January 31, 2018)

The tendency of women to register and vote in greater numbers and at higher rates persisted, to varying degrees, across all racial and ethnic groups in 2016. According to the Census Bureau, in "Voting and Registration in the Election of November 2016" (May 2017, https://www.census.gov/data/tables/time-series/demo/voting-and-registration/p20-580.html), 53.1 million non-Hispanic white women (or 66.8% of all voting-age non-Hispanic white women) reported voting, compared with 47.8 million (63.7%) non-Hispanic white men. Among African Americans, the disparity was larger: 10.1 million (63.7%) African American women reported voting, compared with 7 million (54.2%) men. Hispanic women outnumbered Hispanic men among voters, 6.9 million (50%) to 5.8 million (45%), respectively. Only among Asian Americans did women vote in lower proportions than men, with 2.7 million (48.4%) women reporting that they had voted, compared with 2.4 million (49.7%) men.

These disparities in registration and voting tend to narrow among those voting-age adults with high levels of educational attainment. (See Table 9.2.) Among adults whose highest level of education was ninth to 12th grade with no high school diploma, 43.3% of men were registered and 32.2% voted in 2016, whereas 50.9% of women with the same educational attainment were registered and 38.8% voted. Among adults with a high school diploma but no college, 60.2% of men were registered and 49.1% voted, whereas 64.9% of women were registered and 54.1% voted. Among those with some college or an associate's degree, 71.7% of men were registered and 61.4% voted, whereas 74.3% of women were registered and 64.9% voted. Among those with a bachelor's degree, 80.4% of men were registered and 73.6% voted, whereas 80.5% of women were registered and 74.7% voted. Finally, among those voting-age adults with advanced degrees, 84.3% of men were registered and 80% voted, whereas 84.9% of women were registered and 80.5% voted.

NONPRESIDENTIAL ELECTIONS. The Census Bureau notes in "Voting and Registration in the Election of November 2014" (July 2015, https://www.census.gov/data/tables/time-series/demo/voting-and-registration/p20-577.html) that during the 2014 nonpresidential (congressional) election, 49.2 million women voted, compared with 43 million men. A higher proportion of the female voting-age population (43%) voted than the male voting-age population (40.8%). In that year female registered voters (76 million) outnumbered male registered voters (66.1 million) by 9.9 million. Since 1986 the proportion of eligible female voters who voted has exceeded the proportion of eligible male voters who voted, and this disparity seems to be growing.

## The Gender Gap

Besides disparities in registration and voting rates, women and men typically have different agendas that affect their voting behaviors, which are thought to reflect differences in their lives. Women earn less, have fewer employee benefits, live longer than men on average, and are frequently the primary caregivers for children and the elderly. These lifestyle factors appear to correlate with the political preferences women state in opinion polls. According to "The Gender Gap: Attitudes on Public Policy Issues" (2012, http://cawp.rutgers.edu/sites/default/files/resources/gg_issuesattitudes-2012.pdf), the CAWP's most recent analysis of women's policy priorities as of April 2018, women who voted were more likely than men to favor an activist government, more likely to support programs that provide health care and social services, more in favor of restrictions on firearms, more in favor of same-sex marriage, and more in favor of legal abortion without restrictions.

These and other policy priorities have translated into a consistent gender gap in voting (a difference in the proportions of women and men who vote for a candidate), with women tending to vote in larger numbers for Democratic candidates in most national elections since 1980. Democratic presidential candidates have received a larger share of the female vote than Republican candidates in each presidential election since 1992, and in each election since 1980 women have been more likely than men have been to vote for the Democratic candidate. The CAWP indicates in "The Gender Gap: Voting Choices in Presidential Elections" (January 2017, http://www.cawp.rutgers.edu/sites/default/files/resources/ggpresvote.pdf) that a majority (54%) of women voted for Democratic candidate, Hillary Rodham Clinton, in 2016, whereas a smaller percentage (41%) of men did. Meanwhile, 41% of women and 52% of men voted for the Republican candidate, Donald Trump. This gender gap of 11 percentage points was the largest since 1996. Still, however, exit polls revealed significant racial disparities among women voters. Tara Golshan reports in "The Women Who Helped Trump Win" (January 21, 2017, https://www.vox.com/policy-and-politics/2017/1/20/14061660/women-march-washington-vote-trump) that among white women, less than half (47%) voted for Clinton, compared with African American and Hispanic women, more than 90% of whom voted for Clinton.

Concerning the 2014 election, the CAWP reports in "Gender Gaps Apparent in Almost All 2014 Senate and Gubernatorial Races; Unlike 2010, a Majority of Women Voted for the Democratic Candidate in US House Contests" (November 6, 2014, http://www.cawp.rutgers.edu/sites/default/files/resources/pressrelease_11-06-14-gendergap.pdf) that gender gaps were apparent in almost every US Senate, US House of Representatives, and gubernatorial race where exit polls were conducted by Edison Research. Consistently, women were more likely than men to support the Democratic candidate and less

# TABLE 9.2

## Reported voting and registration by sex and educational attainment, November 2016

[In thousands]

| 18 years and over | Total population | Total citizen population | US citizen — Reported registered Number | Percent | Reported not registered Number | Percent | No response to registration[a] Number | Percent | Reported voted Number | Percent | Reported did not vote Number | Percent | No response to voting[b] Number | Percent | Total population — Reported registered Percent | Reported voted Percent |
|---|---|---|---|---|---|---|---|---|---|---|---|---|---|---|---|---|
| **Both sexes** | | | | | | | | | | | | | | | | |
| **Total** | **245,502** | **224,059** | **157,596** | **70.3** | **32,622** | **14.6** | **33,841** | **15.1** | **137,537** | **61.4** | **53,860** | **24.0** | **32,662** | **14.6** | **64.2** | **56.0** |
| Less than 9th grade | 9,761 | 5,643 | 2,389 | 42.3 | 2,081 | 36.9 | 1,173 | 20.8 | 1,788 | 31.7 | 2,732 | 48.4 | 1,123 | 19.9 | 24.5 | 18.3 |
| 9th to 12th grade, no diploma | 17,727 | 14,715 | 6,906 | 46.9 | 4,862 | 33.0 | 2,947 | 20.0 | 5,202 | 35.3 | 6,746 | 45.8 | 2,767 | 18.8 | 39.0 | 29.3 |
| High school graduate | 71,322 | 65,518 | 40,983 | 62.6 | 13,520 | 20.6 | 11,015 | 16.8 | 33,774 | 51.5 | 21,365 | 32.6 | 10,379 | 15.8 | 57.5 | 47.4 |
| Some college or associate degree | 69,935 | 66,809 | 48,845 | 73.1 | 8,198 | 12.3 | 9,766 | 14.6 | 42,296 | 63.3 | 15,057 | 22.5 | 9,456 | 14.2 | 69.8 | 60.5 |
| Bachelor's degree | 49,526 | 46,317 | 37,270 | 80.5 | 2,974 | 6.4 | 6,073 | 13.1 | 34,364 | 74.2 | 5,862 | 12.7 | 6,091 | 13.2 | 75.3 | 69.4 |
| Advanced degree | 27,231 | 25,057 | 21,203 | 84.6 | 986 | 3.9 | 2,867 | 11.4 | 20,113 | 80.3 | 2,098 | 8.4 | 2,845 | 11.4 | 77.9 | 73.9 |
| **Male** | | | | | | | | | | | | | | | | |
| **Total** | **118,488** | **107,554** | **73,761** | **68.6** | **17,068** | **15.9** | **16,724** | **15.5** | **63,801** | **59.3** | **27,681** | **25.7** | **16,071** | **14.9** | **62.3** | **53.8** |
| Less than 9th grade | 4,870 | 2,719 | 1,179 | 43.4 | 976 | 35.9 | 563 | 20.7 | 899 | 33.1 | 1,277 | 47.0 | 543 | 20.0 | 24.2 | 18.5 |
| 9th to 12th grade, no diploma | 9,263 | 7,676 | 3,326 | 43.3 | 2,725 | 35.5 | 1,626 | 21.2 | 2,472 | 32.2 | 3,692 | 48.1 | 1,512 | 19.7 | 35.9 | 26.7 |
| High school graduate | 36,156 | 33,182 | 19,991 | 60.2 | 7,434 | 22.4 | 5,756 | 17.3 | 16,285 | 49.1 | 11,538 | 34.8 | 5,359 | 16.2 | 55.3 | 45.0 |
| Some college or associate degree | 31,856 | 30,348 | 21,755 | 71.7 | 3,969 | 13.1 | 4,624 | 15.2 | 18,629 | 61.4 | 7,242 | 23.9 | 4,477 | 14.8 | 68.3 | 58.5 |
| Bachelor's degree | 23,288 | 21,746 | 17,491 | 80.4 | 1,459 | 6.7 | 2,796 | 12.9 | 16,006 | 73.6 | 2,893 | 13.3 | 2,847 | 13.1 | 75.1 | 68.7 |
| Advanced degree | 13,055 | 11,883 | 10,020 | 84.3 | 504 | 4.2 | 1,359 | 11.4 | 9,510 | 80.0 | 1,040 | 8.7 | 1,333 | 11.2 | 76.7 | 72.8 |
| **Female** | | | | | | | | | | | | | | | | |
| **Total** | **127,013** | **116,505** | **83,835** | **72.0** | **15,553** | **13.3** | **17,117** | **14.7** | **73,735** | **63.3** | **26,179** | **22.5** | **16,591** | **14.2** | **66.0** | **58.1** |
| Less than 9th grade | 4,891 | 2,924 | 1,210 | 41.4 | 1,105 | 37.8 | 609 | 20.8 | 889 | 30.4 | 1,455 | 49.8 | 580 | 19.9 | 24.7 | 18.2 |
| 9th to 12th grade, no diploma | 8,464 | 7,039 | 3,580 | 50.9 | 2,138 | 30.4 | 1,322 | 18.8 | 2,730 | 38.8 | 3,054 | 43.4 | 1,256 | 17.8 | 42.3 | 32.2 |
| High school graduate | 35,165 | 32,336 | 20,992 | 64.9 | 6,085 | 18.8 | 5,259 | 16.3 | 17,489 | 54.1 | 9,828 | 30.4 | 5,020 | 15.5 | 59.7 | 49.7 |
| Some college or associate degree | 38,079 | 36,461 | 27,091 | 74.3 | 4,228 | 11.6 | 5,142 | 14.1 | 23,666 | 64.9 | 7,816 | 21.4 | 4,979 | 13.7 | 71.1 | 62.2 |
| Bachelor's degree | 26,238 | 24,571 | 19,779 | 80.5 | 1,515 | 6.2 | 3,277 | 13.3 | 18,358 | 74.7 | 2,969 | 12.1 | 3,244 | 13.2 | 75.4 | 70.0 |
| Advanced degree | 14,176 | 13,174 | 11,184 | 84.9 | 482 | 3.7 | 1,508 | 11.5 | 10,604 | 80.5 | 1,058 | 8.0 | 1,512 | 11.5 | 78.9 | 74.8 |

[a]"No response to registration" includes those who were not asked if they were registered as well as those who responded "don't know," and "refused."
[b]"No response to voting" includes those who were not asked if they voted as well as those who responded "don't know," and "refused."

SOURCE: "Table 5. Reported Voting and Registration, by Age, Sex, and Educational Attainment: November 2016," in *Voting and Registration in the Election of November 2016*, US Census Bureau, January 2018, https://www2.census.gov/programs-surveys/cps/tables/p20/580/table05_1.xls (accessed January 31, 2018)

likely to support the Republican candidate. According to Susan J. Carroll, a senior scholar at the CAWP, "Gender gaps were even larger than usual in many of the most contested statewide races this year with women notably more likely than men to vote for the Democratic candidate. Yet Republicans prevailed in most of these contests largely because men's votes were so heavily skewed toward Republican candidates. Men's preference for Republican candidates was simply stronger than women's preference for Democratic candidates."

## WOMEN AS ELECTED OFFICIALS
### US Congress

Many human rights advocates measure women's participation in the democratic process relative to the goals set out by the Beijing Platform for Action, a document that was drafted by delegates to the United Nations (UN) Fourth World Conference on Women in 1995. In articulating an agenda for women's empowerment, the Platform for Action suggests a goal of seeing women occupy 30% of decision-making positions at all levels of government worldwide. According to Jennifer E. Manning, Ida A. Brudnick, and Colleen J. Shogan, in *Women in Congress: Historical Overview, Tables, and Discussion* (April 29, 2015, https://www.fas.org/sgp/crs/misc/R43244.pdf), the

most recent analysis done by the Congressional Research Service as of April 2018, the United States, with women accounting for 19.4% of the congressional membership in 2015, lagged behind the global average of 22.1% and ranked 72nd worldwide in its rate of female representation in national legislatures. Among highly developed countries, the Nordic nations of Denmark, Finland, Iceland, Norway, and Sweden had the highest levels of female representation, at a collective 41.5%. The only nations with majority-female national legislatures were Andorra, Bolivia, and Rwanda.

Nevertheless, the United States has made substantial progress since the first woman, Jeannette Rankin (1880–1973; R-MT), was elected to the House of Representatives in 1917. Since Rankin's election to the 65th Congress, female representation has risen gradually over time, with the most dramatic increases coming during the 103rd Congress (1993–1994), which saw female representation increase from 32 to 54. Women have continued to make steady gains since that time. (See Figure 9.1.) According to the CAWP, in "Women in the U.S. Congress 2018" (2018, http://www.cawp.rutgers.edu/women-us-congress-2018), during the 115th Congress, which began in 2017, women accounted for 105 seats (19.6%)—22 (22%) in the Senate and 83 (19.1%) in the House of Representatives.

**FIGURE 9.1**

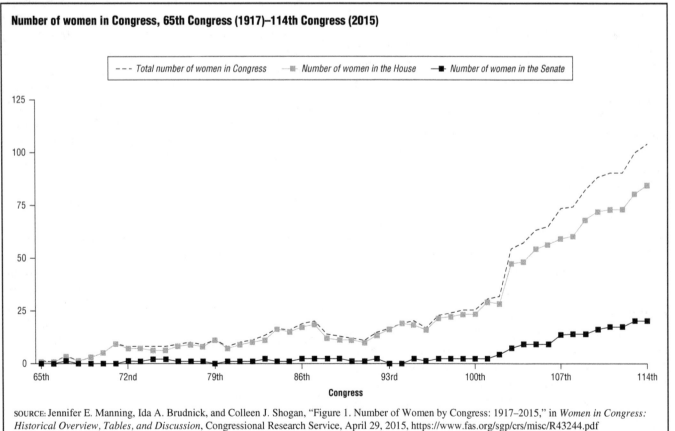

Number of women in Congress, 65th Congress (1917)–114th Congress (2015)

SOURCE: Jennifer E. Manning, Ida A. Brudnick, and Colleen J. Shogan, "Figure 1. Number of Women by Congress: 1917–2015," in *Women in Congress: Historical Overview, Tables, and Discussion*, Congressional Research Service, April 29, 2015, https://www.fas.org/sgp/crs/misc/R43244.pdf (accessed January 31, 2018)

The CAWP reports that as of 2018, 320 women (208 Democrats and 112 Republicans) had served in Congress. Of this total, 39 women (25 Democrats and 14 Republicans) had served in the Senate only, 269 women (174 Democrats and 95 Republicans) had served in the House of Representatives only, and 12 women (nine Democrats and three Republicans) had served in both the Senate and the House of Representatives. California, the most populous state in the United States and one of the most diverse, has sent more women to Congress (41) than any other, followed by New York (28). Mississippi and Vermont were the only states that had never elected a woman to Congress.

PIONEERING WOMEN IN CONGRESS. Manning, Brudnick, and Shogan note that Rankin, a women's suffragist prior to her political career and a lifelong pacifist, won election to the House of Representatives in November 1916 and served from 1917 to 1918. Famous as a pacifist, Rankin cast one of only 50 votes against US entry into World War I (1914–1918). When she served a second term in the House of Representatives from 1941 to 1942, she cast the only congressional vote against US entry into World War II (1939–1945). Rebecca Latimer Felton (1835–1930; D-GA) became the first female US senator in 1921, when she was appointed to serve out the term of an elected senator who died immediately after assuming office. The first woman elected to the Senate was Hattie Wyatt Caraway (1878–1950; D-AR). Caraway initially entered the Senate in 1931 by appointment, to serve out her late husband's term. After her initial term in office, she was elected to two six-year terms. As of 2018, the longest-serving woman in Congress was Senator Barbara A. Mikulski (1936–; D-MD), who was first elected to the House of Representatives in 1976. In 1986 she was elected to the Senate, becoming Maryland's first female senator, and in January 2011 she became the longest-serving female senator in US history, breaking the previous record of 23 years held by Margaret Chase Smith (1897–1995; R-ME), who served in the Senate from 1949 to 1972. In March 2012 Mikulski broke the record for length of service by any woman in Congress, when she surpassed Representative Edith Nourse Rogers's (1881–1960; R-MA) 35 years of service in the House of Representatives. Mikulski retired in January 2017.

WOMEN OF COLOR IN CONGRESS. According to the CAWP, in "History of Women of Color in U.S. Politics" (2018, http://www.cawp.rutgers.edu/history-women-color-us-politics), as of 2015, 64 women of color had served in Congress, 59 of them in the House of Representatives and five in the Senate. The first woman of color to serve in the Senate was Carol Moseley Braun (1947–; D-IL), an African American woman who was elected in 1992 and served one six-year term. Twenty years later, Mazie Hirono (1947–; D-HI), an Asian American woman, was elected

in 2012. Three women of color were elected to the Senate in 2016: Tammy Duckworth (1968– D-Illinois), who is Asian American; Catherine Cortez Masto (1964– D-NV), who is of Hispanic descent; and Kamala Harris (1964– D-CA), who, as the daughter of Jamaican and Indian immigrants, identifies as multiracial. Patsy T. Mink (1927–2002; D-HI) was the first woman of color and the first Asian American woman to serve in Congress. She served in the House of Representatives from 1965 to 1977 and later returned to Congress in 1990, where she continued to serve until her death in 2002. Shirley Chisholm (1924–2005; D-NY) was the first African American woman in Congress. She was elected to the House of Representatives in 1968 and served until 1982. Ileana Ros-Lehtinen (1952–; R-FL) was the first Hispanic woman to serve in Congress. The CAWP notes in "Women of Color in Elective Office 2018" (2018, http://www.cawp.rutgers.edu/women-color-elective-office-2018) that in the 115th Congress (2017–2019), 36.2% (38) of the 105 women in Congress and 7.1% of the total 535 members of Congress were women of color: 18 of these women were African Americans (17 Democrats and one Republican), nine were Asian or Pacific Islanders (all Democrats), 10 were of Hispanic origin (eight Democrats and two Republicans), and one was multiracial (a Democrat).

CONGRESSIONAL POSITIONS OF POWER. As of 2018, Representative Nancy Pelosi (1940–; D-CA) held the highest-ranking position in US politics of any woman in history. She became the 60th Speaker of the House of Representatives (the top position in the House) in 2007 and held the position until 2011, when Republicans retook control of the House and Pelosi became the House Minority Leader, a position she retained through the 115th Congress. As Speaker of the House, Pelosi was second in the line of succession for the presidency following Vice President Dick Cheney (1941–) during the presidency of George W. Bush (1946–) and Vice President Joseph R. Biden (1942–) during the presidency of Barack Obama (1961–).

According to the CAWP, in *Women in Congress: Leadership Roles and Committee Chairs* (2018, http://www.cawp.rutgers.edu/women-congress-leadership-committees), other female leaders in the 115th Congress included Senator Patty Murray (1950–; D-WA), who was assistant Democratic leader; Representative Cathy McMorris Rodgers (1969–; R-WA), who was the chair of the House Republican Conference; and Senator Lisa Murkowski (1957–; R-AK), who was the chair of the Energy and Natural Resources Committee.

## State Legislatures

Since the 1970s female politicians have made gains in state legislatures at rates that eclipse the gains made at the national level. As Figure 9.2 shows, the growth in

FIGURE 9.2

**Women in Congress and state legislatures, 92nd Congress (1971)–114th Congress (2015)**

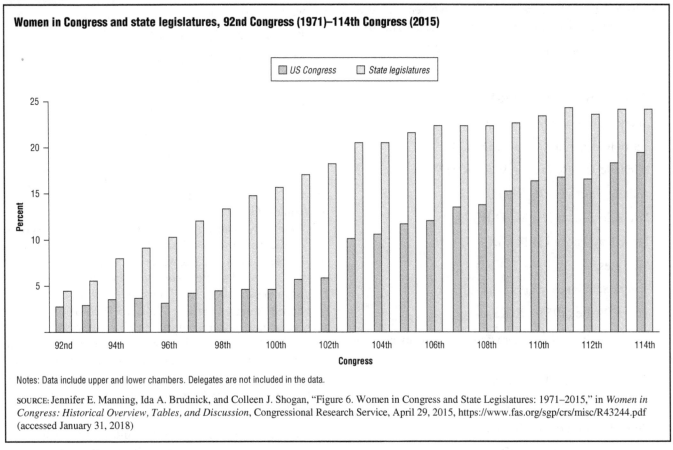

Notes: Data include upper and lower chambers. Delegates are not included in the data.

SOURCE: Jennifer E. Manning, Ida A. Brudnick, and Colleen J. Shogan, "Figure 6. Women in Congress and State Legislatures: 1971–2015," in *Women in Congress: Historical Overview, Tables, and Discussion*, Congressional Research Service, April 29, 2015, https://www.fas.org/sgp/crs/misc/R43244.pdf (accessed January 31, 2018)

female membership in state legislatures was significantly more rapid than at the national level beginning with the 92nd Congress (1971–1972). Manning, Brudnick, and Shogan report that the disparity between representation at the state and national levels peaked during the 102nd Congress (1991–1992), when women accounted for 18.3% of the membership in state legislatures and only 6% of the membership at the national level. These disparities began to narrow in the 21st century. In "Women in State Legislatures 2018" (2018, http://www.cawp.rutgers.edu/women-state-legislature-2018), the CAWP notes that the number of women serving in state legislatures has more than quintupled since 1971, with women accounting for 25.4% of the membership in state legislatures.

According to the CAWP, 1,875 of the 7,383 state legislative seats were held by women in 2018, including 447 (22.7%) of the 1,972 state senate seats and 1,428 (26.4%) of the 5,411 state house or assembly seats. The majority (60.9%) were Democrats, and 37.7% were Republicans. States with the highest percentages of women in state legislatures were Arizona and Vermont (where 40% of legislators were women), Nevada (38.1%), and Colorado (38%). Additionally, Alaska, Idaho, Illinois, Maine, Maryland, Minnesota, New Mexico, Oregon, Rhode Island, and Washington each surpassed the 30% level of female representation in their state legislatures. The states with

the lowest percentages of female legislators were Wyoming (11.1%), Oklahoma (14.1%), West Virginia (14.2%), Mississippi (14.9%), Alabama (15%), Louisiana (15.3%), South Carolina (15.9%) and Tennessee (15.9%).

The first women state legislators were three Republicans elected to the Colorado House of Representatives in 1894. The first female state senator was a Utah Democrat, Martha Hughes Cannon (1857–1932), who was elected in 1896.

**WOMEN OF COLOR.** The CAWP notes in "Women of Color in Elective Office 2018" that 450 (24%) of the 1,875 women in state legislatures in 2018 were women of color, constituting 6.1% of the total 7,383 state legislators nationwide. These legislators were overwhelmingly Democratic—423 were Democrats, 25 were Republicans, one belonged to the Working Families Party, and one was a Progressive. African American women held 276 seats in 43 state legislatures, including 69 state senate seats and 207 state house or assembly seats. Hispanic women held 112 seats in 27 state legislatures, including 27 state senate seats and 85 state house or assembly seats. Asian American or Pacific Islander women held 42 seats in 17 state legislatures, including 10 state senate seats and 32 state house or assembly seats. Native American women held 20 seats in nine state legislatures, including three state senate seats and 17 state house or assembly seats.

**LEADERSHIP POSITIONS.** In "Women in State Legislatures 2018," the CAWP reports that 12 women served as presidents or presidents pro tempore of state senates in 2018:

Laurie Monnes Anderson (1945–; D-OR)

Toni Atkins (1962–; D-CA)

Donna J. Boley (1935–; R-WV)

Sharon Carson (1957–;R-NH)

Harriette Chandler (1937–; D-MA)

Michelle L. Fischbach (1965–; R-MN)

Anitere Flores (1976–; R-FL)

Michelle Kidani (1948–; D-HI)

Mary Kay Papen (1932–; D-NM)

M. Teresa Ruiz (1974–; D-NJ)

Tonya Schuitmaker (1968–; R-MI)

Susan Wagle (1953–; R-KS)

Additionally, there were six female house speakers at the state level:

Crisanta Duran (1980–; D-CO)

Sara Gideon (1971–; D-ME)

Beth Harwell (1957–; R-TN)

Tina Kotek (1966–; D-OR)

Mitzi Johnson (1970–; D-VT)

Linda L. Upmeyer (1952–; R-IA)

## State Executive Offices

The rate at which women have held statewide elective executive offices (including positions such as governor, lieutenant governor, attorney general, and secretary of state, as well as lower-profile offices such as commissioner of insurance, corporation commissioner, and railroad commissioner) has, as with women's election to state legislatures, significantly outpaced the rate of female representation at the national level since the late 1970s. According to the CAWP, in "Women in Elective Office 2015" (2015, http://www.cawp.rutgers.edu/women-elective-office-2015), women held 11% of statewide elective executive offices in 1979, but by 1999 the figure had climbed to 27.6%, almost reaching the benchmark established by the Beijing Platform for Action. The CAWP notes in "Women in Statewide Elective Executive Office 2018" (2018, http://www.cawp.rutgers.edu/women-statewide-elective-executive-office-2018) that the proportion of women holding statewide executive offices has declined somewhat since then, to 22.8% in 2018.

According to the CAWP, women held 71 of the 312 available statewide elective executive office positions in 2018. Of these 71 female officeholders, 27 were Democrats, 43 were Republicans, and one had no party affiliation. Six women were governors:

Kate Brown (1960–; D-OR)

Mary Fallin (1954–; R-OK)

Kay Ivey (1944–; R-AL)

Susana Martinez (1959–; R-NM)

Gina Raimondo (1971–; D-RI)

Kim Reynolds (1959–; R-IA)

Since 1925, 39 women have held the office of governor in 28 states. According to the CAWP, in "History of Women Governors" (2018, http://www.cawp.rutgers.edu/history-women-governors), the first female governor was Nellie Tayloe Ross (1876–1977; D-WY), who won a special election in 1925 to succeed her husband after his death. Two weeks after Ross was inaugurated, Miriam Ferguson (1875–1961; D-TX) was elected to succeed her husband. Likewise, Lurleen Wallace (1926–1968; D-AL) succeeded her husband in 1967. Ella T. Grasso (1919–1981; D-CT) became the first woman to be elected governor on her own, rather than as a successor to her husband, serving from 1975 to 1980. The record number of women serving as governors simultaneously was nine in 2004 and 2007.

Women additionally held the following posts in 2018 (the number of women in each office is in parentheses):

Lieutenant governor (12)

Attorney general (7)

Secretary of state (11)

State treasurer (7)

State auditor (9)

State comptroller/controller (2)

Chief state education official (8)

Commissioner of labor (2)

Corporation commissioner (1)

Agriculture and commerce commissioner (1)

Public utilities commissioner (1)

Railroad commissioner (1)

Commissioner of public lands (1)

**MINORITY WOMEN.** According to the CAWP, in "Women of Color in Elective Office 2018," eight (11.3%) of the 71 women occupying statewide executive offices were women of color. Among these eight women was Susana Martinez of New Mexico, the first female Hispanic governor in US history. Other women of color in statewide executive offices included three lieutenant governors, one secretary of state, one state treasurer, one state controller, and one comptroller.

## Municipal Offices

In "Women Mayors in U.S. Cities 2018" (2018, http://cawp.rutgers.edu/levels_of_office/women-mayors-us-cities-2017), the CAWP reports that as of March 2018, 297 (21.6%) of the 1,365 mayors of cities with populations over 30,000 were women. Women were mayors in 10 of the 50-largest US cities (in population order):

Betsy Price (1949–), Fort Worth, Texas

Vi Alexander Lyles (1952–), Charlotte, North Carolina

Muriel Bowser (1972–), Washington, D.C.

Catherine E. Pugh (1950–), Baltimore, Maryland

Jenny A. Durkan (1958–), Seattle, Washington

Carolyn Goodman (1939–), Las Vegas, Nevada

Jean Stothert (1954–), Omaha, Nebraska

Keisha Lance Bottoms (1970–), Atlanta, Georgia

Nancy McFarlane (1956–), Raleigh, North Carolina

Libby Schaaf (1965–), Oakland, California

## PRESIDENTIAL AND VICE PRESIDENTIAL CANDIDATES

### Presidential Hopefuls

Although several first ladies, including Eleanor Roosevelt (1884–1962) and Hillary Rodham Clinton, have played important political roles during the presidency of their husband, no woman has yet served as president of the United States. The CAWP indicates in "Women Presidential and Vice Presidential Candidates: A Selected List" (2018, http://cawp.rutgers.edu/levels_of_office/women-presidential-and-vice-presidential-candidates-selected-list) that 14 women have received national attention in their bids for the presidency, and another five for the vice presidency. In 1872 Victoria C. Woodhull (1838–1927) ran against the Republican Ulysses S. Grant (1822–1885) and the Democrat Horace Greeley (1811–1872) as the candidate of the suffragist Equal Rights Party. Belva Ann Lockwood (1830–1917) was the Equal Rights Party presidential candidate in 1884 and 1888. She was also the first female lawyer to stand before the US Supreme Court.

In 1964 Margaret Chase Smith became the first woman to run in presidential primary elections. In 1972 Shirley Chisholm became the first African American woman to run in the presidential primaries. In 1988 Patricia Schroeder (1940–; D-CO) became the first woman to initiate a serious bid for the presidency, although she dropped out before the primaries due to a lack of money. In 1996 three female Democrats and six female Republicans entered presidential primaries; three third-party women also ran that year. Elizabeth H. Dole (1936–) initiated a bid for the Republican Party presidential nomination in 1999 but dropped out of the race before the primaries. Lenora Fulani (1950–) ran as the New Alliance Party presidential candidate during the 1992 general election, becoming the first African American and the first woman to appear on ballots in all 50 states. Carol Moseley Braun entered the race for the Democratic nomination for president in 2003. Braun's candidacy was endorsed by both the National Organization for Women and the National Women's Political Caucus. She withdrew from the race in early 2004.

MICHELLE BACHMANN AND CARLY FIORINA. In the 21st century, the two most serious Republican women candidates for the presidency were Michelle Bachman (1956–), who represented Minnesota's Sixth Congressional District from 2007 to 2015, and Carly Fiorina (1954–), a business executive whose most notable accomplishment was becoming the first female chief executive officer of Hewlett-Packard, a major technology company. Bachmann ran briefly as candidate for the Republican nomination in 2012 but withdrew from the primary race after a poor showing in the Iowa caucuses. Fiorina entered the race for the 2016 Republican nomination as the only woman in a crowded field of more than a dozen candidates. She suspended her campaign in February 2016 following weak results in the Iowa caucuses and the New Hampshire primary.

HILLARY RODHAM CLINTON. In 2016 Hillary Rodham Clinton came closer than any woman in US history to winning the presidency of the United States. In 2000 Clinton, the wife of the president Bill Clinton (1946–), became the only first lady in US history to be elected to public office, when she was elected to represent New York in the US Senate (she was reelected in 2006). Clinton was the early favorite to capture the Democratic nomination for president in 2008, but she narrowly lost the primary race to Barack Obama. After serving as US secretary of state during President Obama's first term, from 2009 to 2013, Clinton ran for president again in the 2016 election, surviving a serious challenge from Senator Bernie Sanders (1941–; I-VT) to become the Democratic nominee. With her long and distinguished career as a public servant, Clinton was widely considered the front-runner in the 2016 general election campaign against the Republican nominee Donald Trump, who had never held elected office or served in government. Gregory Krieg reports in "It's Official: Clinton Swamps Trump in Popular Vote" (CNN.com, December 22, 2016) that Clinton won the popular vote by almost 2.9 million votes, with 65,844,954 votes (48.2%) to Trump's 62,979,879 (46.1%). Nevertheless, Trump prevailed in the Electoral College, earning 306 electoral votes to Clinton's 232, and thereby winning the presidency.

### Vice Presidential Candidates

Frances Farenthold (1926–), the first woman to seek a major-party vice presidential nomination, received

400 votes at the 1972 Democratic National Convention, finishing second. In 1984 Geraldine A. Ferraro (1935–2011), a Democrat, became the first woman to run for vice president on a major-party ticket when Walter F. Mondale (1928–) picked her as his running mate. The Mondale-Ferraro ticket lost to Ronald Reagan (1911–2004) and George H. W. Bush (1924–), who won the election in a landslide. Besides these two women, the Libertarian Toni Nathan (1923–2014) won one electoral vote in 1972 when a Virginia elector voted for Richard M. Nixon (1913–1994) but would not support Nixon's running mate, Spiro T. Agnew (1918–1996). In 1996 and 2000 Winona LaDuke (1959–) of the White Earth Reservation in Minnesota was Ralph Nader's (1934–) running mate on the Green Party ticket. In 2008 the Alaska governor Sarah Palin (1964–) became the vice presidential running mate of John McCain (1936–) on the Republican ticket. A conservative Republican, Palin failed to attract significant numbers of women voters, who heavily favored Obama. McCain and Palin lost the 2008 election in a landslide.

## PRESIDENTIAL CABINETS

According to the CAWP, in "Women Appointed to Presidential Cabinets" (December 2017, http://www.cawp.rutgers.edu/sites/default/files/resources/womenapptdtoprescabinets.pdf), as of December 2017, 52 women had held 59 cabinet or cabinet-level posts. Of these women, 31 were appointed by Democratic presidents and 21 by Republican presidents. The first woman to serve in a cabinet post was Frances Perkins (1882–1965), who was appointed by President Franklin D. Roosevelt (1882–1945) as the US secretary of labor in 1933. She remained in that post until 1945, one of only two cabinet members to serve throughout the entire Roosevelt administration. Perkins was instrumental in the design and implementation of the New Deal legislation.

President Dwight D. Eisenhower (1890–1969) named Oveta Culp Hobby (1905–1995) as the secretary of the Department of Health, Education, and Welfare in 1953, and President Gerald R. Ford (1913–2006) named Carla A. Hills (1934–) as the secretary of the Department of Housing and Urban Development (HUD) in 1975. Since then many more women have been named to cabinet-level positions. Patricia Roberts Harris (1924–1985) was appointed by President Jimmy Carter (1924–) as the secretary of HUD in 1977 and as the secretary of the Department of Health and Human Services (HHS) in 1979. She was the first African American woman to serve in a presidential cabinet. Carter also appointed Shirley M. Hufstedler (1925–2016) as the secretary of education. President Reagan had four female cabinet members, including Elizabeth Dole, who was the secretary of transportation under Reagan and the secretary of labor under President George H. W. Bush. Reagan also named Jeane

Kirkpatrick (1926–2006) as the UN ambassador, and Bush named Hills as a special trade representative.

Under President Clinton, Hazel R. O'Leary (1937–) served as the secretary of energy, Carol Browner (1955–) was the head of the Environmental Protection Agency (EPA), Janet Reno (1938–2016) was the US attorney general, Donna E. Shalala (1941–) was the secretary of the HHS, and Alexis Herman (1947–) was the secretary of labor. Madeleine Albright (1937–) served under Clinton first as a UN ambassador and then as the secretary of state, the highest-ranking woman in the US government. Clinton also named women as chairs of the National Economic Council and the Council of Economic Advisers, as the US trade representative, and as the director of the Office of Personnel Management. Clinton appointed Alice M. Rivlin (1931–) as the director of the Office of Management and Budget in 1994 and named her to the Board of Governors of the Federal Reserve System in 1996. Aida Alvarez (1950–) became the administrator of the Small Business Administration in 1997, the first Hispanic woman to hold a cabinet-level position.

In 2001 President George W. Bush appointed Elaine Chao (1953–) as the secretary of labor, the first Asian American woman to hold a cabinet-level post. Bush also named Gale Norton (1954–) as the secretary of the interior, Condoleezza Rice (1954–) as the national security adviser, Ann Veneman (1949–) as the secretary of agriculture, and Christine Todd Whitman (1946–) as the administrator of the EPA. In 2005 Bush appointed Rice as the secretary of state and Margaret Spellings (1957–) as the secretary of education. In 2006 he appointed Mary E. Peters (1948–) as the secretary of transportation and Susan C. Schwab (1955–) as the US trade representative.

During President Obama's first term, the highest-profile female cabinet appointment was Hillary Rodham Clinton as the secretary of state. Obama also appointed Lisa P. Jackson (1962–) as the administrator of the EPA, Janet Napolitano (1957–) as the secretary of homeland security, Susan E. Rice (1964–) as the UN ambassador, Christina Romer (1958–) as the chair of the Council of Economic Advisers, Kathleen Sebelius (1948–) as the secretary of the HHS, and Hilda Solis (1957–) as the secretary of labor. In 2012, before the end of his first term, Obama appointed Karen G. Mills (1953–) as the administrator of the Small Business Administration.

Napolitano, Mills, and Sebelius left the Obama administration early during the president's second term, while seven more women joined the administration in cabinet or cabinet-level positions: Sally Jewell (1956–) as the secretary of the interior; Penny Pritzker (1959–) as the secretary of commerce; Sylvia Mathews Burwell (1965–) first as the director of the Office of Management and Budget and later as secretary of the HHS; Gina McCarthy (1954–) as the administrator of the EPA;

Samantha Power (1970–) as the UN ambassador; Maria Contreras-Sweet (1955–) as administrator of the Small Business Administration; and Loretta Lynch (1959–) as attorney general. Besides these cabinet-level appointments, in October 2013 Obama nominated Janet L. Yellen (1946–), the vice chair of the Board of Governors of the Federal Reserve System, to replace Ben Bernanke (1953–) as chair of the Federal Reserve. Upon being confirmed by the Senate in January 2014, Yellen became the first woman in US history to hold that position.

The CAWP notes in "Women Appointed to Presidential Cabinets" that at the end of 2017, the Trump administration included five women serving in cabinet or cabinet-level positions, including Kirstjen Nielsen (1972–) as secretary of homeland security; Betsy DeVos (1958–) as secretary of education; Nikki Haley (1972–) as UN ambassador; Elaine Chao as secretary of transportation; and Linda McMahon (1948–) as administrator of the Small Business Administration. These women represented 22% of Trump's cabinet or cabinet-level appointments. By comparison, women accounted for 35% of such positions during Obama's second term, and 30% during his first term.

## FINANCING WOMEN'S POLITICAL CAMPAIGNS

Political campaigns are expensive, and political action committees (PACs) are a major source of campaign financing. By far the most prominent PAC dedicated to increasing the numbers of women in electoral politics in 2018 was EMILY's List, a political network for pro-choice Democratic women founded in 1985. EMILY's List notes in "Women We Helped Elect" (January 2017, https://emilyslist.org/pages/entry/women-we-helped-elect) that it has provided money to successful women candidates to the US House of Representatives (116), the US Senate (23), gubernatorial offices (12), and state and local offices (over 800). Among the most prominent female politicians who have benefited from the support of EMILY's List are Hillary Rodham Clinton, Barbara Mikulski, Carol Moseley Braun, and Patsy Mink. EMILY's List was also instrumental in the election of the governors Ann Richards (1933–2006) of Texas, Kathleen Sebelius of Kansas, Janet Napolitano of Arizona, and Christine Gregoire (1947–) of Washington. EMILY's List expanded rapidly beginning in 2010, from a membership of 400,000 to 5 million in 2016. In "EMILY's List Announces Record Fundraising and Major Growth of Community in 2016 Cycle" (January 10, 2017; https://emilyslist.org/news/entry/emilys-list-announces-record-fundraising-and-major-growth-of-community), the organization announced that it had raised $90 million during the 2016 election cycle—surpassing its previous fundraising record by 50%.

The nonpartisan Women's Campaign Fund, founded in 1974, has also been a key player in increasing female representation at all levels of government since the 1980s. Committed to bringing about gender parity in public office, the organization provides financial support to candidates at all levels, from the local school board to the US Congress. The Women's Campaign Fund supports many of the same female politicians as EMILY's List, but it is not averse to supporting Republican candidates in the interest of increasing the number of women in government by all available means.

Although the most influential PACs devoted to women candidates are clustered on the left of the political spectrum, there are a number of conservative women's PACs as well. For example, Value in Electing Women Political Action Committee (2018, https://viewpac.org/about/), describes itself as being "exclusively dedicated to protecting and increasing the number of Republican women in the US House and US Senate." Founded in 1997, the organization has raised over $4.5 million to support Republican women candidates. Eliza Relman reports in "Both Conservative and Liberal Groups Are Hoping to Capitalize on Trump Backlash to Get Women Elected" (BusinessInsider.com, November 20, 2017) on the emergence of Winning for Women, a new PAC formed in anticipation of the 2018 election cycle, whose "primary objectives are to build a national membership base of conservative female activists, and advance a policy agenda focused on national security and free-market principles."

## GENDER POLITICS IN THE TRUMP ERA

The 2016 presidential election carried huge historical importance for American women, as Hillary Rodham Clinton appeared poised to break what many called "the ultimate glass ceiling" by becoming the first woman elected to the highest office in the United States. Kristin Jensen reports in "Clinton by 'Wide Margin' More Qualified Than Trump: Poll" (Bloomberg.com, September 16, 2016) that in the closing weeks of the campaign season, polling showed that 62% of likely voters believed Clinton was qualified to serve as president, compared with 38% of likely voters who believed Trump was qualified.

Besides his lack of political inexperience, Trump's fitness to serve as president was further called into question in the month before the election with the release of a tape from 2005 in which Trump (then the star of the reality television show, *The Apprentice*) apparently brags to a television interviewer about using his fame to make aggressive sexual advances toward women and to grope women without their consent. Ben Jacobs, Sabrina Siddiqui, and Scott Bixby report in "'You Can Do Anything': Trump Brags on Tape about Using Fame to Get Women" (TheGuardian.com, October 8, 2016) that Trump's lewd remarks prompted many Republican politicians to distance themselves from the candidate and "sent him plummeting to near-historic unfavorability ratings with female voters," as indicated by a poll from the Economist/YouGov in which 68% of female voters held either a somewhat unfavorable or very unfavorable view of Trump. Moreover, after the release of the tape, more than a dozen women came forward accusing Trump of various kinds of sexual misconduct over more than two decades. Trump dismissed these accusations as politically motivated attempts to bring down his campaign.

Nina Burleigh reports in "The Presidential Election Was a Referendum on Gender and Women Lost" (Newsweek.com, November 14, 2016) that Trump's election victory, in spite of these controversies, appeared to confirm that "men and women really did choose a presidential candidate this year based on their attitudes about what was acceptable behavior toward women." Many women were outraged that Trump's attitudes and conduct toward women did not disqualify him from serving as president. To express this outrage, to call attention to women's issues, and to voice opposition to multiple aspects of Trump's policy platform, millions of demonstrators participated in the Women's March in Washington, D.C., on January 21, 2017, the day after Trump's inauguration. In addition, protesters convened "sister marches" in hundreds of cities across the United States and throughout the world.

Although the Women's March was historic in its proportions, its organizers intended it as more than a one-day demonstration; rather, it was a call for women to become more politically engaged in the causes that affect their lives. Charlotte Alter reports in "Marchers Say They're Going to Stay Active in Politics" (Time.com, January 21, 2017), that many Women's March participants appeared to be embrace political activism: "Some will run for office. Some will register new voters. Some will badger their representatives. Some will speak up where they had previously been silent. But almost every one of the dozens of demonstrators *Time* interviewed at the Women's March in Washington D.C. Saturday agreed on one thing: even if the Women's March was their first action to resist Trump's presidency, it would not be their last."

A year later, this call to action appeared to be bearing fruit, as EMILY's List issued a press release (February 27, 2018; https://emilyslist.org/news/entry/over-34000-women-want-to-run-for-office) announcing that, since Trump's election, more than 34,000 women had contacted the organization to express their desire to run for office. This was up from 920 women who had contacted the organization during the 2016 election season—a number that had been record-breaking at the time. The president of EMILY's List, Stephanie Schriock, described women's unprecedented surge of interest in running for office as "a sea change moment in American politics."

Many cultural and political commentators also saw Trump's election as a catalyst for the #MeToo movement in 2017, during which countless women who had been victims of past sexual assault publicly accused their alleged assailants for the first time through social media and in the press. In an interview with Shankar Vedantam in "Why #MeToo Happened in 2017" (NPR.org, February 7, 2018), Ashwini Tambe of the University of Maryland Department of Women's Studies theorizes that "the election of Donald Trump has served as a trigger, and it has provoked a great deal of fury and impatience because he represents, for many people, the ultimate unpunished predator."

As of April 2018, President Trump continued to deny accusations of sexual misconduct against him. Even so, public #MeToo accusations had forced the resignation or retirement of half a dozen members of Congress, including Representative John Conyers (1929–; D-MI), Senator Al Franken (1951–; D-MN), and Representative Trent Franks (1957–; R-AZ). Still, Stephanie Akin reports in "Want to Know Who Else Has Been Accused of Sexual Harassment in Congress? Good Luck" (RollCall.com, December 7, 2017) that it was impossible to know the extent of sexual misconduct on Capitol Hill because of a secretive system of reporting and responding to sexual harassment complaints that had not been updated since 1995. Susan Tsui Grundmann, the executive director of the Office of Compliance, which oversees the response to sexual harassment complaints in Congress, explained, "The law doesn't allow us to release anything" pertaining to complaints that have been filed. Heather Caygle and Elana Schor report in "Congress nears Deal to Crack Down on Sexual Harassment" (Politico.com, March 12, 2018) that in March 2018, House and Senate negotiators were working on new legislation that would drastically overhaul Congressional protocols for addressing matters of sexual harassment. Besides greater protections for victims, the new legislation would require lawmakers found guilty of harassment to repay settlement costs out of their own pockets, rather than using taxpayer money, as had been done in the past.

# CHAPTER 10

# WOMEN AS VICTIMS OF CRIME

There are two primary authoritative sources for statistics on crime in the United States: the US Bureau of Justice Statistics' (BJS) National Crime Victimization Survey (NCVS), which measures crime from the point of view of victims, and the Federal Bureau of Investigation's (FBI) Uniform Crime Reporting (UCR) Program, which compiles statistics from law enforcement agencies. The US Census Bureau uses sampling techniques to collect data on behalf of the BJS for the NCVS, whereas the FBI's UCR Program presents total crime numbers reported to law enforcement agencies. The two data sources both provide detailed information regarding the incidence of rape, sexual assault, robbery, assault, theft, household burglary, and motor vehicle theft for the population as a whole, as well as for segments of the population, including women. Because of differences in the data sources and the methodology, the two programs frequently yield inconsistent results. One key difference in data and methodology is that the NCVS offers estimates of both reported and unreported crimes, whereas the UCR Program is limited to those crimes that are reported to law enforcement agencies. Nonetheless, the two data sources have rendered broadly consistent portraits of crime in the United States since the 1970s. BJS analyses of NCVS data are particularly central to this chapter given that some of the crimes that most disproportionately affect women, including sexual violence and violence committed by intimate partners, are less frequently reported to police than many other types of crime.

## CRIME RATES

According to Rachel E. Morgan and Grace Kena of the BJS, in *Criminal Victimization, 2016* (December 2017, https://www.bjs.gov/content/pub/pdf/cv16.pdf), the rates for both violent and property crime fluctuated, but saw an overall decrease between 2007 and 2016. As Figure 10.1 shows, incidences of violent crime fell 28.3%, from 27.2 victimizations per 1,000 people aged 12 years and older to 19.5 victimizations per 1,000 people aged 12 years

and older during that span. Property crime also declined significantly, falling from 154.9 victimizations per 1,000 people in 2007 to 113.9 per 1,000 in 2016, a decrease of 26.5%.

As Table 10.1 shows, men are slightly more likely than women to be the victims of violent crime, whereas women are more likely to be the victims of serious violent crime such as rape or sexual assault, robbery, and aggravated assault. In 2016 the violent victimization rate for men was 21.4 per 1,000 people aged 12 years and older, compared with 20.8 per 1,000 for women in the same age group. In the case of serious violent crime, however, women were victimized at a rate of 7.5 per 1,000, compared with 6.5 per 1,000 for men.

Assaults are historically the most common type of violent crime committed in the United States in a given year, and Morgan and Kena report that 2016 was no exception. The rate of assault was 18.1 per 1,000 people aged 12 years and older, with most of this figure consisting of simple assault (14.1) rather than aggravated assault (4 per 1,000; an unlawful attack of a severe nature intended to cause death or serious injury, usually involving a weapon). (See Table 10.2.) The victimization rates for those crimes committed primarily against women, such as rape and sexual assault (1.2 per 1,000 people) and intimate partner violence (2.2), were much lower, but there are reasons to be skeptical of such figures. The overall victimization rate for these crimes is low in part because of the presence of men in the survey sample (men also experience these crimes, but at much lower rates). Additionally, these crimes are much more likely to go unreported than are crimes that do not involve sex or domestic partners, as is discussed at greater length later in this chapter.

Victims of violent crime (especially robbery and assault) are often young, and the rates for these crimes decline sharply among older age groups. The violent victimization rate in 2016 was 30.9 per 1,000 among

FIGURE 10.1

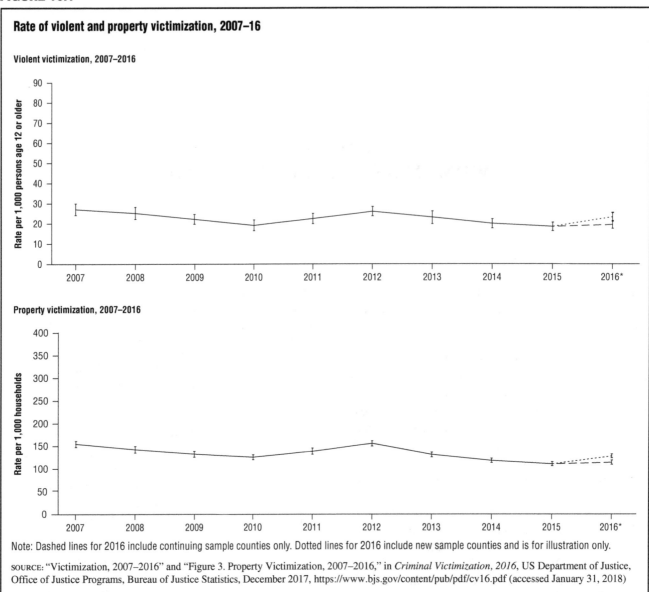

**Rate of violent and property victimization, 2007–16**

Violent victimization, 2007–2016

Property victimization, 2007–2016

Note: Dashed lines for 2016 include continuing sample counties only. Dotted lines for 2016 include new sample counties and is for illustration only.

SOURCE: "Victimization, 2007–2016" and "Figure 3. Property Victimization, 2007–2016," in *Criminal Victimization, 2016*, US Department of Justice, Office of Justice Programs, Bureau of Justice Statistics, December 2017, https://www.bjs.gov/content/pub/pdf/cv16.pdf (accessed January 31, 2018)

those aged 12 to 24 years and even higher (31.8 per 1,000) among those aged 25 to 34 years, but it dropped off considerably for people aged 35 and older. (See Table 10.1.) Married (12.4 per 1,000) and widowed (10.7 per 1,000) people were far less likely to be the victims of violent crime than were those who were separated (67.5 per 1,000), divorced (30.1 per 1,000), or never married (29.8 per 1,000). The rates of violent victimization also varied among different ethnic groups. The rates were notably higher for African Americans (24.1 per 1,000) and those of other races (23 per 1,000; including those who identify as Native American, Alaskan Native, Asian American, Native Hawaiian, or Pacific Islander, and people of two or more races) than for whites (20.5 per 1,000) and Hispanics (20.2 per 1,000).

**The Reporting of Crimes**

In general, property crimes are significantly less likely to be reported to police than are violent crimes.

In 2016 only 35.7% of property crimes were reported, compared with 42.1% of violent crimes. (See Table 10.3.) There were also consistent and pronounced disparities within certain subcategories. In 2016, for example, among violent crime types, serious violent crimes involving weapons (60.1%), aggravated assault (58.5%), and serious stranger violence (57.1%) were the most likely to be reported. Intimate partner violence (46.9%) was less likely to be reported, and simple assault (37.5%) was far less likely to be reported. Rape and sexual assault (22.9%) were the least likely of all violent crimes to be reported in 2016. Motor vehicle theft (79.9%) was the most likely type of crime victimization to be reported to police in 2016.

**HOMICIDE**

In *Homicide in the U.S. Known to Law Enforcement, 2011* (December 2013, https://www.bjs.gov/content/pub/

TABLE 10.1

**Rate of violent victimization and serious violent victimization and percentage of violent crimes reported to police, by demographic characteristics of victim, 2016**

| Victim demographic characteristic | Rate of total violence per 1,000 persons age 12 or older | | Percent of violence reported to police | |
|---|---|---|---|---|
| | Violent crime[a] | Serious violent crime[b] | Violent crime[a] | Serious violent crime[b] |
| **Total** | 21.1 | 7.0 | 42.1% | 51.3% |
| **Sex** | | | | |
| Male[c] | 21.4 | 6.5 | 44.3% | 60.5% |
| Female | 20.8 | 7.5 | 40.0 | 43.7 |
| **Race/Hispanic origin[d]** | | | | |
| White | 20.5 | 6.3 | 40.1% | 45.0% |
| Black[c] | 24.1 | 8.2 | 39.8 | 59.8 |
| Hispanic | 20.2 | 8.2 | 51.6 | 64.8 |
| Other[e] | 23.0 | 8.5 | 42.9 | 47.8 |
| **Age** | | | | |
| 12–17 | 30.9 | 8.6 | 27.7% | 48.1% |
| 18–24[c] | 30.9 | 11.0 | 35.7 | 51.5 |
| 25–34 | 31.8 | 12.8 | 38.9 | 37.8 |
| 35–49 | 22.9 | 6.8 | 49.8 | 58.6 |
| 50–64 | 16.1 | 5.2 | 49.1 | 65.2 |
| 65 or older | 4.4 | 1.1 | 60.4 | 62.0 |
| **Marital status** | | | | |
| Never married[c] | 29.8 | 10.7 | 33.5% | 45.8% |
| Married | 12.4 | 3.3 | 50.8 | 62.9 |
| Widowed | 10.7 | 2.6 | 48.1 | 60.5 |
| Divorced | 30.1 | 11.9 | 53.8 | 56.0 |
| Separated | 67.5 | 20.0 | 43.2 | 39.7 |
| **Household income** | | | | |
| Less than $10,000[c] | 35.8 | 13.0 | 47.3% | 37.3% |
| $10,000–$14,999 | 35.6 | 13.9 | 50.2 | 54.8 |
| $15,000–$24,999 | 32.9 | 14.0 | 45.3 | 52.0 |
| $25,000–$34,999 | 21.0 | 6.3 | 44.2 | 57.9 |
| $35,000–$49,999 | 20.4 | 6.8 | 34.0 | 43.9 |
| $50,000–$74,999 | 17.6 | 5.8 | 42.4 | 57.1 |
| $75,000 or more | 15.7 | 4.1 | 39.4 | 54.3 |

[a]Includes rape or sexual assault, robbery, aggravated assault, and simple assault. Excludes homicide because the NCVS is based on interviews with victims and cannot measure murder.
[b]In the National Crime Victimization Survey (NCVS), serious violent crime is a subset of violent crime and includes rape or sexual assault, robbery, and aggravated assault.
[c]Comparison group.
[d]White, black, and other race categories exclude persons of Hispanic or Latino origin.
[e]Includes American Indian or Alaska Native; Asian; Native Hawaiian, or other Pacific Islander; and persons of two or more races.
Note: Victimization rates are per 1,000 persons age 12 or older.

SOURCE: Rachel E. Morgan and Grace Kena, "Table 8. Rate of Violent Victimization and Serious Violent Victimization and Percent Reported to Police, by Demographic Characteristics of Victims, 2016," in *Criminal Victimization, 2016*, US Department of Justice, Office of Justice Programs, Bureau of Justice Statistics, December 2017, https://www.bjs.gov/content/pub/pdf/cv16.pdf (accessed January 31, 2018)

pdf/hus11.pdf), the most recent report of its kind as of April 2018, Erica L. Smith and Alexia Cooper of the BJS report that during the first decade of the 21st century the murder rate declined to levels not seen since the late 1960s. On average, between 1992 and 2011 the homicide rate for males was 3.6 times higher than that of females. In 2011 the homicide rate among men was 7.4 per 100,000, compared with 2 per 100,000 among women. Nearly three-quarters (73.1%) of all male homicide victims were killed by a firearm in 2011, compared with 49.3% of female homicide victims. By contrast, in 2011 female murder victims (22.2%) were more likely than male murder victims (15.8%) to be killed by a knife or blunt object, a personal weapon such as fists or feet (15.5% and 5%, respectively), or a nonpersonal weapon such as poison or fire (13% and 6.1%, respectively).

According to the FBI, in *Crime in the United States, 2016* (2017, https://ucr.fbi.gov/crime-in-the-u.s/2016/crime-in-the-u.s.-2016/tables/expanded-homicide-data-table-1.xls), females accounted for 3,208 (21.3%) of the 15,070 murder victims reported in 2016 for whom the sex was known. In the previous year's report, *Crime in the United States, 2015* (https://ucr.fbi.gov/crime-in-the-u.s/2015/crime-in-the-u.s.-2015), the FBI presents data on murder victims by age, sex, race, and ethnicity. (See Table 10.4.) In 2015 females accounted for 2,818 (20.9%) of the 13,455 murder victims reported. Most female victims (2,448, or 86.9%) were aged 18 years and older.

In *Crime in the United States, 2015*, the FBI also presents the most recent data on murder circumstances as of April 2018. Table 10.5 shows, that 370 (13.1%) of the 2,818 female victims for whom murder circumstances

**TABLE 10.2**

**Violent, serious violent, and property victimization, by type of crime, 2016**

| Type of crime | Number | Rate per 1,000[a] |
|---|---|---|
| **Violent crime[b]** | **5,749,330** | **21.1** |
| Rape or sexual assault | 323,450 | 1.2 |
| Robbery | 500,680 | 1.8 |
| Assault | 4,925,200 | 18.1 |
|    Aggravated assault | 1,084,340 | 4.0 |
|    Simple assault[c] | 3,840,860 | 14.1 |
| Domestic violence[d] | 1,109,610 | 4.1 |
|    Intimate partner violence[e] | 597,740 | 2.2 |
| Stranger violence | 2,232,260 | 8.2 |
| Violent crime involving injury | 1,366,250 | 5.0 |
| **Serious violent crime[f]** | **1,908,470** | **7.0** |
| Serious domestic violence[d] | 402,430 | 1.5 |
|    Serious intimate partner violence[e] | 272,380 | 1.0 |
| Serious stranger violence | 789,370 | 2.9 |
| Serious violent crime involving a weapon | 1,267,810 | 4.7 |
| Serious violent crime involving injury | 746,850 | 2.7 |
| **Property crime** | **15,917,430** | **119.4** |
| Burglary | 3,291,490 | 24.7 |
| Motor vehicle theft | 585,500 | 4.4 |
| Theft[g] | 12,040,440 | 90.3 |

[a]For violent and serious violent crime, rate is per 1,000 persons age 12 or older. For property crime, rate is per 1,000 households.
[b]Excludes homicide because the National Crime Victimization Survey (NCVS) is based on interviews with victims and cannot measure murder.
[c]Comparison group for violent crime. Simple assault is compared to rape or sexual assault, robbery, and aggravated assault.
[d]Includes victimization committed by intimate partners and family members.
[e]Includes victimization committed by current or former spouses, boyfriends or girlfriends.
[f]In the NCVS, serious violent crime is a subset of violent crime and includes rape or sexual assault, robbery, and aggravated assault.
[g]Comparison group for property crime.
Note: Violent crime classifications include rape or sexual assault, robbery, aggravated assault, and simple assault. Other violent crime categories in this table, including domestic violence and violent crime involving injury, are not mutually exclusive from these classifications. Detail may not sum to total due to rounding. Total population age 12 or older was 272,174,080 in 2016. Total number of households was 133,271,310 in 2016.

SOURCE: Rachel E. Morgan and Grace Kena, "Table 2. Violent and Property Victimization, by Type of Crime, 2016," in *Criminal Victimization, 2016*, US Department of Justice, Office of Justice Programs, Bureau of Justice Statistics, December 2017, https://www.bjs.gov/content/pub/pdf/cv16.pdf (accessed January 31, 2018)

**TABLE 10.3**

**Percentage of victimizations reported to the police, by type of crime, 2016**

| Type of crime | Percent |
|---|---|
| **Violent crime[a]** | **42.1%** |
| Rape or sexual assault | 22.9 |
| Robbery | 54.0 |
| Assault | 42.2 |
|    Aggravated assault | 58.5 |
|    Simple assault[b] | 37.5 |
| Domestic violence[c] | 49.1 |
|    Intimate partner violence[d] | 46.9 |
| Stranger violence | 44.7 |
| Violent crime involving injury | 47.4 |
| **Serious violent crime[e]** | **51.3%** |
| Serious domestic violence[c] | 52.6 |
|    Serious intimate partner violence[d] | 51.9 |
| Serious stranger violence | 57.1 |
| Serious violent crime involving weapons | 60.1 |
| Serious violent crime involving injury | 50.2 |
| **Property crime** | **35.7%** |
| Household burglary | 49.7 |
| Motor vehicle theft | 79.9 |
| Theft[f] | 29.7 |

[a]Excludes homicide because the National Crime Victimization Survey (NCVS) is based on interviews with victims and cannot measure murder.
[b]Comparison group for violent crime. Simple assault is compared to rape or sexual assault, robbery, and aggravated assault.
[c]Includes victimization committed by intimate partners and family members.
[d]Includes victimization committed by current or former spouses, boyfriends, or girlfriends.
[e]In the NCVS, serious violent crime is a subset of violent crime and includes rape or sexual assault, robbery, and aggravated assault.
[f]Comparison group for property crime.
Note: Violent crime classifications include rape or sexual assault, robbery, aggravated assault, and simple assault. Other violent crime categories in this table, including domestic violence and violent crime involving injury, are not mutually exclusive from these classifications.

SOURCE: Rachel E. Morgan and Grace Kena, "Table 5. Percent of Victimizations Reported to Police, by Type of Crime, 2016," in *Criminal Victimization, 2016,* US Department of Justice, Office of Justice Programs, Bureau of Justice Statistics, December 2017, https://www.bjs.gov/content/pub/pdf/cv16.pdf (accessed January 31, 2018)

were known in 2015 were murdered during the course of another felony—54 during robberies, 42 in connection with narcotics violations, 31 during burglaries, and 10 in connection with rape. In most cases (1,476, or 52.4%) in which women were victims, murder was the only felony committed. The most common circumstance in which women were killed was during an argument, which accounted for 822 murders, or 853 when arguments over money or property are included in the total.

## RAPE AND SEXUAL ASSAULT

Because of the cultural and social stigma associated with sexual assault, statistics gathered about rape and sexual assault must be approached with caution. It is likely that the number of sexual crimes reported to the police is only a small proportion of the total number of such crimes. Even NCVS data, which include information about both reported and unreported sexual assaults, are likely incomplete due to underreporting. Many women who have been the victims of sexual crimes resist disclosing these crimes. Women are often psychologically devastated by rape and sexual assault. They may be unwilling to talk about it, may feel responsible for it, or may believe that even if they do report it, they will court unwelcome scrutiny of their own lives, while nothing will happen to the offender. Because of historical insensitivity of the criminal justice system to rape victims, women may fear that they will be further victimized by law enforcement authorities if they report the crime. In still other cases, women may not identify a sexual assault, especially by an intimate partner, family member, or friend, as an assault at all.

The reporting of rape and sexual assaults is also dependent on the language that is used to inquire about and define these crimes. Victims frequently report different levels of sexual violence depending on how the questions and definitions are worded. In *Female Victims of*

TABLE 10.4

**Murder victims by age, sex, race, and ethnicity, 2015**

| Age | Total | Sex | | | Race | | | | Ethnicity | | |
|---|---|---|---|---|---|---|---|---|---|---|---|
| | | Male | Female | Unknown | White | Black or African American | Other[a] | Unknown | Hispanic or Latino | Not Hispanic or Latino | Unknown |
| Total | 13,455 | 10,608 | 2,818 | 29 | 5,854 | 7,039 | 366 | 196 | 2,028 | 7,971 | 2,224 |
| Percent distribution[b] | 100 | 78.8 | 20.9 | 0.2 | 43.5 | 52.3 | 2.7 | 1.5 | 16.6 | 65.2 | 18.2 |
| Under 18[c] | 1,093 | 761 | 329 | 3 | 504 | 544 | 26 | 19 | 193 | 611 | 189 |
| Under 22[c] | 2,624 | 2,135 | 487 | 2 | 954 | 1,598 | 44 | 28 | 488 | 1,484 | 443 |
| 18 and over[c] | 12,228 | 9,773 | 2,448 | 7 | 5,296 | 6,451 | 339 | 142 | 1,823 | 7,305 | 1,974 |
| Infant (under 1) | 168 | 104 | 63 | 1 | 89 | 65 | 8 | 6 | 24 | 104 | 28 |
| 1 to 4 | 260 | 153 | 106 | 1 | 130 | 117 | 6 | 7 | 32 | 160 | 58 |
| 5 to 8 | 91 | 49 | 42 | 0 | 58 | 30 | 1 | 2 | 12 | 57 | 16 |
| 9 to 12 | 56 | 35 | 20 | 1 | 30 | 22 | 3 | 1 | 9 | 30 | 6 |
| 13 to 16 | 282 | 218 | 64 | 0 | 110 | 167 | 4 | 1 | 62 | 141 | 49 |
| 17 to 19 | 996 | 870 | 126 | 0 | 325 | 647 | 16 | 8 | 191 | 546 | 159 |
| 20 to 24 | 2,431 | 2,102 | 329 | 0 | 764 | 1,596 | 45 | 26 | 414 | 1,398 | 368 |
| 25 to 29 | 2,071 | 1,733 | 338 | 0 | 717 | 1,290 | 48 | 16 | 321 | 1,201 | 331 |
| 30 to 34 | 1,647 | 1,340 | 307 | 0 | 650 | 927 | 49 | 21 | 266 | 974 | 254 |
| 35 to 39 | 1,263 | 1,021 | 241 | 1 | 539 | 666 | 45 | 13 | 200 | 728 | 223 |
| 40 to 44 | 925 | 701 | 222 | 2 | 467 | 428 | 23 | 7 | 150 | 545 | 158 |
| 45 to 49 | 781 | 586 | 194 | 1 | 399 | 330 | 33 | 19 | 118 | 485 | 115 |
| 50 to 54 | 737 | 568 | 169 | 0 | 428 | 282 | 17 | 10 | 84 | 468 | 120 |
| 55 to 59 | 580 | 425 | 154 | 1 | 363 | 183 | 27 | 7 | 57 | 389 | 102 |
| 60 to 64 | 360 | 250 | 109 | 1 | 226 | 114 | 12 | 8 | 36 | 231 | 54 |
| 65 to 69 | 235 | 168 | 67 | 0 | 166 | 59 | 6 | 4 | 14 | 168 | 41 |
| 70 to 74 | 159 | 93 | 65 | 1 | 113 | 33 | 9 | 4 | 11 | 100 | 33 |
| 75 and over | 279 | 118 | 161 | 0 | 226 | 39 | 13 | 1 | 15 | 191 | 48 |
| Unknown | 134 | 74 | 41 | 19 | 54 | 44 | 1 | 35 | 12 | 55 | 61 |

[a]Includes American Indian or Alaska Native, Asian, and Native Hawaiian or other Pacific Islander.
[b]Because of rounding, the percentages may not add to 100.0.
[c]Does not include unknown ages.

SOURCE: "Expanded Homicide Data Table 2. Murder Victims by Age, Sex, Race, and Ethnicity, 2015," in *Crime in the United States, 2015*, US Department of Justice, Federal Bureau of Investigation, 2016, https://ucr.fbi.gov/crime-in-the-u.s/2015/crime-in-the-u.s.-2015/tables/expanded_homicide_data_table_2_murder_victims_by_age_sex_and_race_2015.xls/output.xls (accessed January 31, 2018)

*Sexual Violence, 1994–2010* (March 2013, https://www.bjs.gov/content/pub/pdf/fvsv9410.pdf), the most recent analysis of data trends by the BJS as of April 2018, Michael Planty et al. provide the NCVS definitions of rape and sexual assault:

> Rape is the unlawful penetration of a person against the will of the victim, with use or threatened use of force, or attempting such an act. Rape includes psychological coercion and physical force, and forced sexual intercourse means vaginal, anal, or oral penetration by the offender. Rape also includes incidents where penetration is from a foreign object (e.g., a bottle), victimizations against male and female victims, and both heterosexual and homosexual rape. Attempted rape includes verbal threats of rape.
>
> Sexual assault is defined across a wide range of victimizations, separate from rape or attempted rape. These crimes include attacks or attempted attacks generally involving unwanted sexual contact between a victim and offender. Sexual assault may or may not involve force and includes grabbing or fondling. Sexual assault also includes verbal threats.

Although males are frequently the victims of sexual crimes, they represent a small fraction of the overall number of victims of rape and sexual assault. Planty et al. note that between 1995 and 2010 males accounted for approximately 9% of all rape and sexual assault victimizations reported in the NCVS. In 2010 males were sexually victimized at a rate of 0.1 per 1,000, compared with 2.1 per 1,000 for females. The rate of male victimization was higher at some points between 1995 and 2010, but it demonstrated no clear upward or downward trend.

By contrast, Planty et al. note that the total rate of sexual violence (including completed, attempted, or threatened rape or sexual assault) committed against women in the United States fell 64% between 1995 and 2005 and then remained unchanged between 2005 and 2010. The dramatic decrease in the total rate of sexual assault was due largely to a decline in completed rape or sexual assault, from 3.6 per 1,000 women aged 12 years and older in 1995 to 1.1 per 1,000 in 2010. (See Figure 10.2.) The rates of attempted or threatened rape or sexual assault remained flat over that 15-year period.

The rates of rape and sexual assault victimization are higher among women under the age of 34 years than among women aged 35 years and older. (See Table 10.6.) Girls aged 12 to 17 years were more likely to be the victims of rape or sexual assault (4.1 per 1,000) in 2005–10 than were women aged 18 to 34 years (3.7 per

**TABLE 10.5**

**Murder circumstances by sex of victim, 2015**

| Circumstances | Total murder victims | Male | Female | Unknown |
|---|---|---|---|---|
| **Total** | 13,455 | 10,608 | 2,818 | 29 |
| **Felony type total:** | 2,014 | 1,641 | 370 | 3 |
| Rape | 12 | 2 | 10 | 0 |
| Robbery | 595 | 541 | 54 | 0 |
| Burglary | 102 | 71 | 31 | 0 |
| Larceny-theft | 16 | 15 | 1 | 0 |
| Motor vehicle theft | 41 | 25 | 15 | 1 |
| Arson | 19 | 10 | 9 | 0 |
| Prostitution and commercialized vice | 6 | 2 | 4 | 0 |
| Other sex offenses | 15 | 8 | 7 | 0 |
| Narcotic drug laws | 468 | 426 | 42 | 0 |
| Gambling | 5 | 5 | 0 | 0 |
| Other-not specified | 735 | 536 | 197 | 2 |
| **Suspected felony type** | 117 | 85 | 32 | 0 |
| **Other than felony type total:** | 5,958 | 4,474 | 1,476 | 8 |
| Romantic triangle | 106 | 73 | 33 | 0 |
| Child killed by babysitter | 36 | 26 | 10 | 0 |
| Brawl due to influence of alcohol | 112 | 99 | 13 | 0 |
| Brawl due to influence of narcotics | 75 | 53 | 22 | 0 |
| Argument over money or property | 184 | 153 | 31 | 0 |
| Other arguments | 2,941 | 2,118 | 822 | 1 |
| Gangland killings | 188 | 178 | 10 | 0 |
| Juvenile gang killings | 604 | 584 | 20 | 0 |
| Institutional killings | 24 | 23 | 1 | 0 |
| Sniper attack | 5 | 4 | 1 | 0 |
| Other-not specified | 1,683 | 1,163 | 513 | 7 |
| **Unknown** | 5,366 | 4,408 | 940 | 18 |

SOURCE: "Expanded Homicide Data Table 13. Murder Circumstances by Sex of Victim, 2015," in *Crime in the United States, 2015*, US Department of Justice, Federal Bureau of Investigation, 2016, https://ucr.fbi.gov/crime-in-the-u.s/2015/crime-in-the-u.s.-2015/tables/expanded_homicide_data_table_13_murder_circumstances_by_sex_of_victim_2015.xls/output.xls (accessed January 31, 2018)

1,000). During the period analyzed by Planty et al., the rape and sexual assault victimization rate for girls aged 12 to 17 years fell more rapidly (from 11.3 per 1,000 in 1994–98) than for women aged 18 to 34 years (from 7 per 1,000 in 1994–98). The rates varied among racial and ethnic groups, but all groups had seen comparable declines since 1994–98. Native American and Alaskan Native females appeared to have significantly higher rates of rape and sexual assault victimization (4.5 per 1,000) than other groups in 2005–10, but Planty et al. note that the sample size for this group was insufficient and the resulting data unreliable. There were also sampling problems that rendered the reported rates among Asian or Pacific Islander females (0.7 per 1,000) suspect. Among those groups with reliable samples, Hispanic females had the lowest rate of rape and sexual assault victimization (1.4 per 1,000) in 2005–10, followed by non-Hispanic white females (2.2) and non-Hispanic African American females (2.8).

The rates of rape and sexual assault were strongly correlated with marital status and income across all the periods surveyed by Planty et al. Never-married females (4.1 per 1,000) and those who were divorced or separated (4.4) were far more likely to have been sexually victimized in 2005–10 than were married (0.6) or widowed (0.8) females. (See Table 10.6.) The rates for each of these groups had fallen by half or more since 1994–98, except for widowed women, whose rate of sexual victimization was flat between 1994 and 2010. Women with household incomes below $25,000 (3.5 per 1,000) were

**FIGURE 10.2**

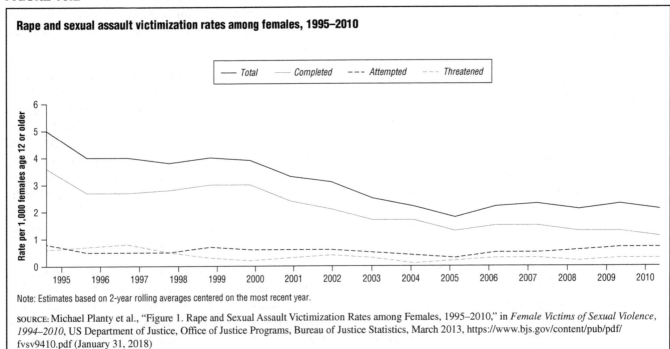

Rape and sexual assault victimization rates among females, 1995–2010

Note: Estimates based on 2-year rolling averages centered on the most recent year.

SOURCE: Michael Planty et al., "Figure 1. Rape and Sexual Assault Victimization Rates among Females, 1995–2010," in *Female Victims of Sexual Violence, 1994–2010*, US Department of Justice, Office of Justice Programs, Bureau of Justice Statistics, March 2013, https://www.bjs.gov/content/pub/pdf/fvsv9410.pdf (January 31, 2018)

TABLE 10.6

**Rape and sexual assault victimizations against females, by victim characteristics, 1994–98, 1999–2004, and 2005–10**

| Victim characteristic | Rate per 1,000 females age 12 or older | | |
|---|---|---|---|
| | 1994–1998 | 1999–2004 | 2005–2010 |
| Total | 4.2 | 3.1 | 2.1 |
| **Age** | | | |
| 12–17 | 11.3 | 7.6 | 4.1 |
| 18–34 | 7.0 | 5.3 | 3.7 |
| 35–64 | 2.3 | 1.8 | 1.5 |
| 65 or older | 0.1* | 0.2* | 0.2* |
| **Race/Hispanic origin** | | | |
| White[a] | 4.3 | 3.1 | 2.2 |
| Black[a] | 4.2 | 4.1 | 2.8 |
| Hispanic/Latina | 4.3 | 1.8 | 1.4 |
| American Indian/Alaska Native[a] | 6.4* | 4.8* | 4.5* |
| Asian/Pacific Islander[a] | 2.5 | 1.2 | 0.7* |
| Two or more races[a] | — | 6.6* | 5.1* |
| **Marital status[b]** | | | |
| Never married | 8.6 | 6.6 | 4.1 |
| Married | 1.3 | 0.7 | 0.6 |
| Widowed | 0.8 | 0.2* | 0.8 |
| Divorced or separated | 9.0 | 6.3 | 4.4 |
| **Household income** | | | |
| Less than $25,000 | 6.1 | 5.6 | 3.5 |
| $25,000–$49,999 | 3.3 | 2.7 | 1.9 |
| $50,000 or more | 2.9 | 2.0 | 1.8 |
| Unknown | 3.5 | 2.1 | 1.8 |
| **Location of residence** | | | |
| Urban | 5.1 | 4.0 | 2.2 |
| Suburban | 3.9 | 2.7 | 1.8 |
| Rural | 3.9 | 2.5 | 3.0 |

—Not applicable.

*Interpret with caution; estimate based on 10 or fewer sample cases, or coefficient of variation is greater than 50%.

[a]Excludes persons of Hispanic or Latino origin.

[b]The National Crime Victimization Survey (NCVS) collects information on respondent's marital status at the time of the interview, but it does not obtain marital status at the time of the incident or whether a change marital status occurred after the incident.

SOURCE: Michael Planty et al., "Table 1. Rape and Sexual Assault Victimizations against Females, by Victim Characteristics, 1994–1998, 1999–2004, and 2005–2010," in *Female Victims of Sexual Violence, 1994–2010*, US Department of Justice, Office of Justice Programs, Bureau of Justice Statistics, March 2013, https://www.bjs.gov/content/pub/pdf/fvsv9410.pdf (January 31, 2018)

TABLE 10.7

**Rape and sexual assault victimizations against females, by number of offenders and victim-offender relationship, 1994–98, 1999–2004, and 2005–10**

| Offender characteristic | 1994–1998 | 1999–2004 | 2005–2010 |
|---|---|---|---|
| **Number of offenders** | 100% | 100% | 100% |
| One | 93 | 91 | 90 |
| Two or more | 7 | 9 | 10 |
| **Victim-offender relationship[a]** | 100% | 100% | 100% |
| Stranger | 21 | 25 | 22 |
| Nonstranger | 79 | 75 | 78 |
| Intimate partner[b] | 28 | 30 | 34 |
| Relative | 9 | 3 | 6 |
| Well-known/casual acquaintance | 42 | 42 | 38 |

[a]Does not include a small percentage of victimizations in which the victim-offender relationship was unknown.

[b]Includes former or current spouse, boyfriend, or girlfriend.

Note: Detail may not sum to total due to rounding.

SOURCE: Michael Planty et al., "Table 3. Rape and Sexual Assault Victimizations against Females, by Number of Offenders and Victim-Offender Relationship, 1994–1998, 1999–2004, and 2005–2010," in *Female Victims of Sexual Violence, 1994–2010*, US Department of Justice, Office of Justice Programs, Bureau of Justice Statistics, March 2013, https://www.bjs.gov/content/pub/pdf/fvsv9410.pdf (January 31, 2018)

much more likely to be the victims of rape or sexual assault in 2005–10 than were women with household incomes of $25,000 to $49,999 (1.9) or $50,000 or more (1.8). Each of these groups had seen significant declines in victimization, although the declines were largest among women in under-$25,000 households, whose rate of victimization was 6.1 in 1994–98.

Women are far more likely to be sexually victimized by a family member, intimate partner, friend, or acquaintance than by a stranger. As Table 10.7 shows, at all periods between 1994 and 2010 more than 90% of rape and sexual assault victimizations involved one offender, and over 75% of all rapes and sexual assaults were committed by an intimate partner, a relative, a friend, or an acquaintance. In 2005–10, 78% of rape and sexual assault victimizations involved a non-stranger, and these

cases were split almost equally between intimate partners (34%) and well-known or casual acquaintances (38%). In another 6% of victimizations, the offender was a family member other than an intimate partner.

Rape was once believed to be a crime of sexual passion, but it is now recognized as a crime of anger and hate, driven by the desire for power over others. The Violence against Women Act of 1994 (VAWA) categorized rape as a gender-based hate crime, punishable under both federal civil rights laws and state criminal statutes. The act increased penalties for violence against women and provided funding to police, prosecutors, and the courts to help protect women from violence. It also established the Office on Violence against Women to administer grant programs established under the VAWA. The act was reauthorized and strengthened in 2000 and 2005. In 2013 the act was broadened to extend protections to same-sex couples, unauthorized immigrants, and Native Americans living on reservations.

## Sexual Victimization on College Campuses

Many experts believe that college women are particularly vulnerable to sexual assault and rape. In *Report on the AAU Campus Climate Survey on Sexual Assault and Sexual Misconduct* (October 20, 2017, https://www.aau.edu/sites/default/files/AAU-Files/Key-Issues/Campus-Safety/AAU-Campus-Climate-Survey-FINAL-10-20-17.pdf), David Cantor et al. present the results of a survey of more than 150,000 female students at 27 colleges and universities nationwide. Cantor et al. report that nearly one-quarter (23.6%) of all female undergraduate and graduate students had experienced some form of "nonconsensual sexual contact" (including penetration and unwelcome physical touching) while enrolled at school. This number included women who had experienced unwanted sexual contact by physical force, incapacitation due to alcohol or other substances, coercion (such as nonphysical threats or promises of rewards), or absence of explicit consent. According to Cantor et al., nearly one in five female students (18.1%) experienced nonconsensual sexual contact through physical force or incapacitation, both of which meet the legal definition of rape (in cases of penetration) or sexual assault (in cases of unwelcome sexual touching).

Cantor et al. note that incapacitation is a significant factor in many cases of nonconsensual sexual contact on college campuses. Of the nearly half (11.1%) of female students who reported having been raped while in college, roughly an equal number had experienced unwanted penetration due to incapacitation (5.4%) as due to physical force (5.7%). In "Incapacitated and Forcible Rape of College Women: Prevalence across the First Year" (*Journal of Adolescent Health*, vol. 56, 2015), Kate B. Carey et al. report that, in a survey of 483 first-year female students at a private college in the Northeast, 7.1% reported having been raped while incapacitated over the course of the academic year, compared with 5.2% who had been forcibly raped.

The federal government signaled its concern about the issue of campus sexual assault in 2011, when the US Department of Education's Office of Civil Rights sent a letter to all US colleges noting that they had obligations under Title IX to be more active in preventing and remedying sexual assaults. As is discussed in Chapter 2, however, in 2017 under the administration of President Donald Trump (1946–), Secretary of Education Betsy DeVos (1958–) rescinded the Obama-era directive and replaced it with new guidance, stating that the previous policy unfairly favored alleged assault victims over alleged perpetrators by denying them due process under the law. Advocates for sexual assault survivors and various women's rights groups strongly denounced the policy change.

## INTIMATE PARTNER VIOLENCE

Intimate partner violence, which affects women far more frequently than men, is difficult to quantify. Besides going unreported because of the private nature of the crimes and because of fear of reprisal, intimate partner violence can elude surveyors depending on the definitions of such crimes and/or the context in which questions are asked. In *Intimate Partner Violence: Attributes of Victimization, 1993–2011* (November 2013, https://www.bjs.gov/content/pub/pdf/ipvav9311.pdf), the most recent report of its kind, as of April 2018, Shannan Catalano of the BJS provides the following NCVS definition of the crime: "As defined in the NCVS, intimate

partner violence includes rape, sexual assault, robbery, aggravated assault, and simple assault committed by an offender who is the victim's current or former spouse, boyfriend, or girlfriend."

NCVS data are likely incomplete, but they are considered reliable in regard to trends over time. According to Catalano, the rate of intimate partner violence declined between 1994 and 2011 for both female and male victims. (See Figure 10.3.) Catalano reports that in 1994 the rate of intimate partner violence was 16.1 per 1,000 for females and 3 per 1,000 for males. By 2011 the rates of intimate partner violence had fallen to 4.7 per 1,000 women, and 1.5 per 1,000 men.

According to Catalano, the rate of serious intimate partner violence (i.e., rape or sexual assault, robbery, and aggravated assault) fell 74% for women and 64% for men between 1994 and 2011. As shown in Figure 10.3, among women, the number of victims of serious intimate partner violence dropped from 5.9 per 1,000 in 1994 to 1.6 per 1,000 in 2011. Over this span, the number of male victims of serious intimate partner violence fell from 1.1 in 1994 to 0.4 in 2011. Incidences of simple assault by intimate partners also saw a notable decline between

**FIGURE 10.3**

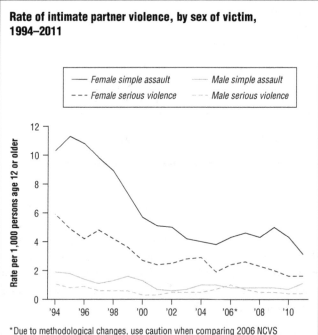

Rate of intimate partner violence, by sex of victim, 1994–2011

*Due to methodological changes, use caution when comparing 2006 NCVS (National Crime Victimization Study) criminal victimization estimates to other years.
Note: Estimates based on 2-year rolling averages beginning in 1993. Serious violent crime includes rape or sexual assault, robbery, and aggravated assault. Intimates include current or former spouses, boyfriends, and girlfriends.

SOURCE: Shannon Catalano, "Figure 1. Rate of Intimate Partner Violence, by Victim's Sex, 1994–2011," in *Intimate Partner Violence: Attributes of Victimization, 1993–2011*, US Department of Justice, Office of Justice Programs, Bureau of Justice Statistics, November 2013, https://www.bjs.gov/content/pub/pdf/ipvav9311.pdf (accessed January 31, 2018)

1994 and 2011. In 1994, 10.3 out of 1,000 women and 1.9 out of 1,000 men were victims of simple assault by an intimate partner. By 2011 these figures had fallen to 3.1 out of 1,000 women and 1.1 out of 1,000 men.

Catalano indicates that between 2002 and 2011 female victims of intimate partner violence were more likely than male victims to suffer injuries as a result of an incident. During this period, nearly half (49.7%) of all female victims of intimate partner violence were injured by their partner, compared with 43.5% of male victims. Female victims (13%) were more than twice as likely as male victims (5.4%) to suffer serious injuries as a result of intimate partner violence. Among female victims of intimate partner violence, 6.6% were victims of sexual violence compared with 0.7% of male victims. Women were also considerably more likely than men to be threatened before being attacked by an intimate partner. Between 2002 and 2011, more than half (51.8%) of female victims of intimate partner violence were threatened before suffering an attack, compared with less than one-third (31.4%) of male victims.

## Marital Rape

Only in recent decades has American society begun to accept that even in marriage sexual relations must be consensual. Yingyu Chen and Sarah E. Ullman find in "Women's Reporting of Sexual and Physical Assaults to Police in the National Violence against Women Survey" (*Violence against Women*, vol. 16, no. 3, March 2010) that rape victims are more likely to report incidents they see as examples of "real" rape: those perpetrated by strangers, with a high degree of physical force, weapons, and victim injury. The researchers state, "These findings suggest that the general public and women still need to be informed that sexual assault is a violent crime, even if committed by nonstrangers, without weapons, physical force, or physical injury."

Elaine K. Martin, Casey T. Taft, and Patricia A. Resick of the National Center for PTSD (post-traumatic stress disorder) find in "A Review of Marital Rape" (*Aggression and Violent Behavior*, vol. 12, no. 3, May–June 2007) that as many as 10% to 14% of all married women have experienced marital rape. Furthermore, 40% to 50% of women who are physically abused by their husband are also raped. The United Nations Entity for Gender Equality and the Empowerment of Women reports in *2011–12 Progress of the World's Women: In Pursuit of Justice* (2012, http://www .unwomen.org/~/media/headquarters/attachments/sections/ library/publications/2011/progressoftheworldswomen-2011-en.pdf?v=1&d=20150402T222835) that by 2011, 52 countries had passed legislation outlawing marital rape. The World Bank, however, reports in *Atlas of Sustainable Development Goals 2017* (2017, http://datatopics .worldbank.org/sdgatlas/SDG-05-gender-equality.html) that as of 2017, 112 countries still did not criminalize marital rape.

## Same-Sex versus Opposite-Sex Partners

Because same-sex partnerships have historically received little or no recognition from official government agencies or from the general public, and because male violence against women in heterosexual relationships is so prevalent, there is much less research concerning intimate partner violence (IPV) in same-sex relationships than there is in opposite-sex relationships. Therefore, the statistics on intimate partner violence in same-sex relationships are even more speculative than statistics on intimate partner violence in opposite-sex relationships. Nevertheless, according to the National Coalition of Antiviolence Programs (NCAVP), in *Lesbian, Gay, Bisexual, Transgender, Queer and HIV-Affected Intimate Partner Violence in 2016* (2017, http://avp.org/wp-content/uploads/ 2017/11/NCAVP-IPV-Report-2016.pdf), "research shows that LGBTQ people experience similar, if not higher, rates of IPV compared to their cisgender or heterosexual counterparts." In *The National Intimate Partner Violence and Sexual Violence Survey (NISVS): 2010 Findings on Victimization by Sexual Orientation* (January 2013, https:// www.cdc.gov/violenceprevention/pdf/nisvs_sofindings.pdf), Mikel L. Walters, Jieru Chen, and Matthew J. Breiding estimate that 44% of lesbian women, 61% of bisexual women, 26% of gay men, and 37% of bisexual men experience IPV at some point in their lives.

In *Lesbian, Gay, Bisexual, Transgender, Queer and HIV-Affected Intimate Partner Violence in 2016*, the NCAVP provides detailed data on incidents of lesbian, gay, bisexual, transgender, queer, and HIV-affected (LGBTQH) intimate partner violence that were reported to community organizations in 2016. Overall, there were 2,032 reported cases of LGBTQH intimate partner violence that year. The NCAVP notes that more than 80% of all victims and survivors of LGBTQH intimate partner violence identified as either cisgender (gender identity and gender expression that matches the sex assigned at birth) men (43%) or women (38%), whereas 15% identified as transgendered. (See Table 10.8.) The NCAVP reports that more than two in five (43%) of LGBTQH intimate partner violence victims identified their sexual orientation as gay; 16% identified as lesbian, 21% identified as heterosexual, and 10% identified as bisexual. Other sexual orientation categories reported by victims of LGBTQH intimate partner violence included queer (6%), self-identified (4%), and questioning/unsure (1%).

## The Prevalence and Role of Protection Orders

A victim in any state in the nation may go to court to obtain a protection order forbidding the abuser from harming her. Also known as restraining orders or injunctions, civil orders of protection are legally binding court orders

**TABLE 10.8**

**Survivors of intimate partner violence, by age, gender, sexual orientation, and race/ethnicity, 2016**

[Sample size = 2,032]

| | # of people | % |
|---|---|---|
| **Age (sample size = 1,322)** | | |
| 18 and younger | 20 | 1% |
| 19–29 years old | 418 | 32% |
| 30–39 years old | 429 | 32% |
| 40–49 years old | 243 | 18% |
| 50–59 years old | 161 | 12% |
| 60–69 years old | 43 | 3% |
| 70 years old and older | 8 | 1% |
| **Gender (sample size = 1,617)** | | |
| Transgender woman | 173 | 11% |
| Transgender man | 54 | 3% |
| Transgender non-binary | 14 | 1% |
| Cisgender man | 692 | 43% |
| Cisgender woman | 608 | 38% |
| Genderqueer | 8 | <1% |
| Gender non-conforming | 4 | <1% |
| Gender fluid | 8 | <1% |
| Self-identified/other | 56 | 3% |
| **Sexual orientation (sample size = 1,372)** | | |
| Bisexual | 137 | 10% |
| Gay | 584 | 43% |
| Heterosexual | 283 | 21% |
| Lesbian | 217 | 16% |
| Queer | 76 | 6% |
| Questioning/unsure | 16 | 1% |
| Self-identified | 59 | 4% |
| **Race & ethnicity\* (sample size = 1,418)** | | |
| Arab/Middle Eastern | 15 | 1% |
| Asian/Pacific Islander | 56 | 4% |
| Black/African American | 260 | 18% |
| Native American/American Indian | 24 | 2% |
| Latinx | 430 | 30% |
| Multiracial | 53 | 4% |
| White | 548 | 39% |
| Self-identified/other | 32 | 2% |

\*For this variable, survivors were able to choose more than one answer. The numbers and percentages reflect the total number of responses to this variable rather than respondents.

SOURCE: "Table 1. Description of Survivors Who Reported to NCAVP," in *Lesbian, Gay, Bisexual, Transgender, Queer, and HIV-Affected Intimate Partner Violence in 2016*, National Coalition of Anti-Violence Programs, 2017, http://avp.org/wp-content/uploads/2017/11/NCAVP-IPV-Report-2016.pdf (accessed January 31, 2018)

that prohibit an individual who has committed an act of domestic violence from further abusing the victim. Although the terms are often used interchangeably, restraining orders usually refer to short-term or temporary sanctions, whereas protection orders have longer duration and may be permanent. These orders generally prohibit harassment, contact, communication, and physical proximity to the victim. The availability as well as the nature of personal protection orders varies dramatically by state.

Protection orders give victims of intimate partner and other forms of domestic violence an option other than filing a criminal complaint. Issued immediately, usually within 24 hours, they provide safety for the victim by barring or evicting the abuser from the household.

However, this judicial protection has little meaning if the police do not maintain records and follow through with arrest should the abuser violate the order. Statutes in most states make violating a protection order a matter of criminal contempt, a misdemeanor, or even a felony.

Judy L. Postmus of Rutgers University notes in "Challenging the Negative Assumptions surrounding Civil Protection Orders: A Guide for Advocates" (*Affilia: Journal of Women and Social Work*, vol. 22, no. 4, Winter 2007) that many women, women's advocates, and law enforcement officers assume that protection orders are ineffective in deterring abusers and are not strictly enforced by law enforcement personnel. In a review of 20 years of research on the issue, Postmus rebuts these assumptions, showing that protection orders, while not preventing every single episode of further abuse, were effective in reducing future violence. She notes that in cases of severe abuse, protection orders proved less likely to reduce the frequency of violence, although in many cases they reduced its severity. When violations do occur, protection orders unfortunately do not guarantee that police will arrest abusers. In "Do Protection Orders Protect?" (*Journal of the American Academy of Psychiatry and the Law*, vol. 38, no. 3, 2010), Christopher T. Benitez, Dale E. McNiel, and Renée L. Binder of the University of California, San Francisco, arrive at a similar conclusion. The researchers find that although protection orders cannot fully protect victims of domestic violence, they do help manage the threat. In "State Progress in Record Reporting for Firearm-Related Background Checks: Protection Order Submissions" (April 2016, https://www.ncjrs.gov/pdffiles1/bjs/grants/249864.pdf), Becki Goggins and Anne Gallegos of the National Center for State Courts report that at the end of 2014 there were more than 2.1 million protection orders on file in state protection order databases.

## SEXUAL HARASSMENT

The US Equal Employment Opportunity Commission (EEOC), which enforces federal laws regarding discrimination in the workplace, outlines in "Sexual Harassment" (2018, https://www.eeoc.gov/laws/types/sexual_harassment.cfm) the federal laws pertaining to sexual harassment in the following way:

It is unlawful to harass a person (an applicant or employee) because of that person's sex. Harassment can include "sexual harassment" or unwelcome sexual advances, requests for sexual favors, and other verbal or physical harassment of a sexual nature.

Harassment does not have to be of a sexual nature, however, and can include offensive remarks about a person's sex. For example, it is illegal to harass a woman by making offensive comments about women in general.

Both victim and the harasser can be either a woman or a man, and the victim and harasser can be the same sex.

Although the law doesn't prohibit simple teasing, offhand comments, or isolated incidents that are not very serious, harassment is illegal when it is so frequent or severe that it creates a hostile or offensive work environment or when it results in an adverse employment decision (such as the victim being fired or demoted).

The harasser can be the victim's supervisor, a supervisor in another area, a co-worker, or someone who is not an employee of the employer, such as a client or customer.

Contemporary sexual harassment law has its roots in the landmark case *Meritor Savings Bank v. Vinson* (477 US 57 [1986]), in which the US Supreme Court ruled that sexual harassment is a violation of Title VII of the Civil Rights Act of 1964, which prohibits sexual discrimination. Mechelle Vinson claimed that her supervisor harassed her at work and outside of work and raped her. She did not file a complaint until a year after the harassment had ceased for fear of jeopardizing her employment. A lower court ruled against her, finding that sexual favors had not been a condition of her employment. The Supreme Court reversed the decision, ruling that "Title VII affords employees the right to work in an environment free from discriminatory intimidation, ridicule, and insult."

In 1998 the Supreme Court ruled in *Burlington Industries v. Ellerth* (524 US 742) that employers can be held liable when a supervisor threatens to demote or take other action against an employee who refuses a supervisor's sexual demands, even when the threats are not carried out. That same year the court ruled in *Faragher v. City of Boca Raton* (524 US 775) that companies are liable for the misconduct of their employees even if the company is unaware of the behavior. The high court's majority decision stated that employers can generally avoid liability for sexual harassment by showing that they have strong antiharassment programs, that the programs are communicated to all employees, and that systems are in place for submitting and reviewing complaints. Following these rulings, companies reexamined their sexual harassment policies and revised them to meet the court's tougher standards.

According to the EEOC, in "Charges Alleging Sexual Harassment, FY 2010–FY 2017" (2018, https://www.eeoc.gov/eeoc/statistics/enforcement/sexual_harassment_new.cfm), the commission received 6,696 charges of sexual harassment in FY 2017, down from 7,944 in FY 2010, a decline of 15.7%. Of the 7,511 cases resolved in FY 2017, more than half (4,206, or 56%) were found to be unwarranted (or without reasonable cause). In one-quarter (1,682, or 22.4%) of cases the EEOC found in favor of the person filing the charge.

As is discussed in Chapter 4, the emergence of the #MeToo movement in 2017 brought increased attention to the pervasive problem of sexual harassment in the workplace, forcing employers and employees in every industry to reexamine their assumptions about what constitutes acceptable workplace behavior and how to fairly and responsibly handle sexual harassment complaints. Nikki Graf reports in "Sexual Harassment at Work in the Era of #MeToo" (April 4, 2018, http://assets.pew research.org/wp-content/uploads/sites/3/2018/04/03161853/ Pew-Research-Center-Sexual-Harassment-Report-April-2018-FINAL.pdf) on a survey conducted during February–March 2018 by the Pew Research Center, in which 59% of women and 27% of men reported having received unwanted sexual advances or verbal or physical harassment of a sexual nature, either in or outside of work. With regard to how employers handle sexual harassment complaints, 52% of women thought that women not being believed is a major problem, compared with 39% of men. Asked whether men getting away with sexual harassment is a major problem, 55% of women and 44% of men responded that it is. Women and men were more closely aligned in their concerns over employers firing men who have been accused of sexual harassment without considering all of the facts, and women making false accusations of sexual harassment. As a whole, 34% of respondents thought premature firings were a serious problem, and 31% thought false claims were a serious problem. Asked about the impact of heightened scrutiny over interpersonal conduct in the workplace, more than half (51%) of those surveyed said the #MeToo movement had made it harder for men to know how to interact with women at work. Only 28% of survey respondents believed it would lead to increased opportunities for working women in the long run.

## Hate Crimes

Hate crimes are violent crimes or property crimes motivated by bias against a victim's race, ethnicity, sex, sexual orientation, religion, disability, or associations with others identified by these characteristics. A crime can be classified as a hate crime when police confirm that it was motivated by bias, but it can also be classified as a hate crime based on the victim's perception of bias as evidenced by the use of hate language or symbols. Women can be the victims of hate crimes motivated by biases against people identified by any of these categories, but they are far more likely than men to be the victims of hate crimes committed on the basis of gender.

Madeline Masucci and Lynn Langton of the BJS report in *Hate Crime Victimization, 2004–2015* (June 2017, https://www.bjs.gov/content/pub/pdf/hcv0415.pdf) that an estimated 207,880 nonfatal hate crime victimizations occurred in 2015. Of these, 192,020 were violent hate crimes, and 14,160 were hate crimes against property.

**FIGURE 10.4**

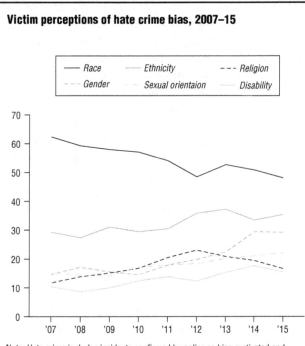

**Victim perceptions of hate crime bias, 2007–15**

Legend: Race — Ethnicity — Religion — — — | Gender — — — Sexual orientaion — Disability

Note: Hate crime includes incidents confirmed by police as bias-motivated and incidents perceived by victims to be bias-motivated because the offender used hate language or left behind hate symbols. Estimates based on 5-year rolling averages, centered on the most recent year. Detail may not sum to total due to victims reporting more than one type of bias motivating the hate-related victimizations.

SOURCE: Lynn Langton and Madeline Masucci, "Figure 3. Victims' Perception of Bias in Hate Crime Victimizations, 2007–2015," in *Hate Crime Victimization, 2004–2015*, US Department of Justice, Office of Justice Programs, Bureau of Justice Statistics, June 2017, https://www.bjs.gov/content/pub/pdf/hcv0415.pdf (accessed January 31, 2018)

Women accounted for slightly less than half (48.3%) of all hate crime victims during the period 2011 to 2015.

Of the 207,880 nonfatal hate crimes committed in 2015, 48.1% were believed to be motivated by race. (See Figure 10.4.) Hate crimes based on ethnicity were the second most-common form, accounting for 35.4% of all nonfatal hate crimes in 2015, Approximately 29.3% of hate crimes annually were believed to be motivated by gender, and 22.1% were believed to be motivated by sexual orientation. Religion and disability were motivating factors in 16.7% and 15.6% of hate crime cases, respectively.

# CHAPTER 11
# WOMEN AS CRIMINALS

## ARRESTS OF WOMEN

Violent crimes committed by women are often sensationalized far more than equivalent crimes committed by men, partly because of the way such crimes violate stereotypical notions of femininity. This is especially the case when women murder their children, a crime that happens with extreme rarity but that often results in national media coverage, and in cases involving the murder of a spouse or partner, which happens more frequently than other murders committed by women but that happens far less often than murders in which men kill their spouses or partners.

Women are less likely than men to commit almost every form of crime. As Table 11.1 shows, in both 2006 and 2015, men outnumbered women among those arrested for every crime the Federal Bureau of Investigation (FBI) tracks, with only two exceptions: embezzlement, in which female numbers were slightly higher in 2006, and prostitution and commercialized vice, in which female numbers significantly exceeded male numbers. The numbers of men arrested for violent and serious crimes typically dwarfed the numbers of women arrested by several multiples. Of the total 7,104 arrests for murder shown in Table 11.1 for 2006, 812 (11.4%) were female, and of the total 6,201 murder arrests shown for 2015, 738 (11.9%) were female. There were similar patterns for other crimes. Women accounted for 7,977 robbery arrests (11.7%) in 2006 and 7,943 arrests (14.7%) in 2015, 55,258 aggravated assault arrests (20.3%) in 2006 and 52,690 (22.7%) in 2015, 28,355 burglary arrests (15.1%) in 2006 and 26,049 (19.1%) in 2015, and 1,707 arson arrests (16.3%) in 2006 and 1,104 (19.2%) in 2015. (Note that 2015 is the most recent year for which the FBI reported arrests by sex as of April 2018.)

Men outnumbered women less dramatically among those arrested for certain nonviolent crimes, such as larceny-theft (the taking of property without force, violence, or fraud), forgery and counterfeiting, and fraud. Women accounted for 188 (1.3%) rape arrests in 2006 and 409 (2.9%) in 2015, and they accounted for 3,488 arrests for sex offenses (6.9%) other than rape and prostitution in 2006 and 2,494 (7.7%) in 2015. Overall, the percentage of women among those arrested for many crimes had risen between 2006 and 2015, but in most cases this was a function of sizable decreases in the number of men arrested, rather than any large increase in criminal activity among women.

The FBI reports in *Crime in the United States, 2015* (2016, https://ucr.fbi.gov/crime-in-the-u.s/2015/crime-in-the-u.s.-2015) that more than 2.2 million women were arrested in 2015. (See Table 11.2.) Arrest totals increased with age beginning in the teenage years and peaked at age 24. Teenagers and women aged 16 to 24 years (672,996 arrests) accounted for 30% of all female arrests, and arrest totals decreased steadily with age thereafter. Women aged 25 to 29 years accounted for another 384,567 (17,2%) of arrests, women aged 30 to 34 years accounted for 317,727 (14.2%) of arrests, and women aged 35 to 39 years accounted for 235,556 (10.5%) of arrests.

Among the 512,898 arrests of females shown in Table 11.2 for the most serious crimes the FBI tracks, 434,069 (84.6%) were for property crimes (burglary, larceny-theft, motor vehicle theft, and arson) and 78,829 (15.4%) for violent crimes (murder and nonnegligent manslaughter, rape, robbery, and aggravated assault) in 2015. The most common serious crime for which women were arrested was larceny, accounting for 388,520 arrests, or 17.4% of the total number of women arrested in 2015. The second most common serious charge for which women were arrested was aggravated assault, accounting for 66,822 arrests. Robbery (10,509) and motor vehicle theft (12,662) were a distant third and fourth among serious offenses in 2015, and even fewer numbers

**TABLE 11.1**

## Ten-year arrest trends by sex, 2006–15

[9,581 agencies; 2015 estimated population 199,921,204; 2006 estimated population 186,371,331]

| | Male | | | | | | Female | | | | | |
| | Total | | | Under 18 | | | Total | | | Under 18 | | |
| Offense charged | 2006 | 2015 | Percent change | 2006 | 2015 | Percent change | 2006 | 2015 | Percent change | 2006 | 2015 | Percent change |
|---|---|---|---|---|---|---|---|---|---|---|---|---|
| Total[a] | 6,605,457 | 4,913,199 | −25.6 | 922,499 | 405,325 | −56.1 | 2,070,999 | 1,826,164 | −11.8 | 357,696 | 173,213 | −51.6 |
| Murder and nonnegligent manslaughter | 6,292 | 5,463 | −13.2 | 612 | 394 | −35.6 | 812 | 738 | −9.1 | 30 | 27 | −10.0 |
| Rape[b] | 13,932 | 13,536 | — | 2,071 | 2,154 | — | 188 | 409 | — | 40 | 85 | — |
| Robbery | 60,460 | 46,060 | −23.8 | 16,413 | 8,658 | −47.2 | 7,977 | 7,943 | −0.4 | 1,788 | 1,095 | −38.8 |
| Aggravated assault | 216,482 | 179,138 | −17.3 | 27,741 | 13,273 | −52.2 | 55,258 | 52,690 | −4.6 | 8,243 | 4,444 | −46.1 |
| Burglary | 159,767 | 110,416 | −30.9 | 45,896 | 19,254 | −58.0 | 28,355 | 26,049 | −8.1 | 6,057 | 2,802 | −53.7 |
| Larceny–theft | 418,187 | 424,952 | +1.6 | 106,506 | 60,365 | −43.3 | 261,103 | 328,713 | +25.9 | 74,117 | 41,533 | −44.0 |
| Motor vehicle theft | 59,234 | 36,177 | −38.9 | 14,361 | 6,029 | −58.0 | 13,416 | 10,286 | −23.3 | 3,290 | 1,518 | −53.9 |
| Arson | 8,738 | 4,633 | −47.0 | 4,538 | 1,536 | −66.2 | 1,707 | 1,104 | −35.3 | 685 | 275 | −59.9 |
| Violent crime[c] | 297,166 | 244,197 | −17.8 | 46,837 | 24,479 | −47.7 | 64,235 | 61,780 | −3.8 | 10,101 | 5,651 | −44.1 |
| Property crime[c] | 645,926 | 576,178 | −10.8 | 171,301 | 87,184 | −49.1 | 304,581 | 366,152 | +20.2 | 84,149 | 46,128 | −45.2 |
| Other assaults | 592,204 | 486,355 | −17.9 | 101,366 | 52,882 | −47.8 | 199,974 | 192,182 | −3.9 | 51,030 | 30,807 | −39.6 |
| Forgery and counterfeiting | 41,028 | 22,493 | −45.2 | 1,513 | 470 | −68.9 | 27,291 | 12,418 | −54.5 | 775 | 162 | −79.1 |
| Fraud | 99,184 | 52,967 | −46.6 | 3,297 | 1,811 | −45.1 | 82,679 | 33,517 | −59.5 | 1,793 | 965 | −46.2 |
| Embezzlement | 6,101 | 4,850 | −20.5 | 517 | 220 | −57.4 | 6,907 | 5,073 | −26.6 | 432 | 171 | −60.4 |
| Stolen property; buying, receiving, possessing | 63,904 | 45,331 | −29.1 | 11,930 | 5,514 | −53.8 | 15,173 | 12,587 | −17.0 | 2,102 | 1,086 | −48.3 |
| Vandalism | 158,590 | 97,844 | −38.3 | 66,281 | 23,174 | −65.0 | 31,277 | 26,214 | −16.2 | 9,921 | 4,619 | −53.4 |
| Weapons; carrying, possessing, etc. | 105,054 | 78,496 | −25.3 | 25,051 | 10,331 | −58.8 | 9,050 | 7,947 | −12.2 | 2,656 | 1,283 | −51.7 |
| Prostitution and commercialized vice | 11,754 | 7,103 | −39.6 | 182 | 85 | −53.3 | 21,648 | 10,560 | −51.2 | 551 | 184 | −66.6 |
| Sex offenses (except rape and prostitution) | 47,168 | 29,862 | −36.7 | 9,029 | 4,914 | −45.6 | 3,488 | 2,494 | −28.5 | 919 | 729 | −20.7 |
| Drug abuse violations | 865,257 | 715,904 | −17.3 | 93,508 | 49,170 | −47.4 | 212,899 | 212,218 | −0.3 | 19,624 | 13,865 | −29.3 |
| Gambling | 2,366 | 1,272 | −46.2 | 279 | 121 | −56.6 | 441 | 385 | −12.7 | 13 | 12 | −7.7 |
| Offenses against the family and children | 60,217 | 41,552 | −31.0 | 2,070 | 1,379 | −33.4 | 19,351 | 16,825 | −13.1 | 1,278 | 829 | −35.1 |
| Driving under the influence | 738,512 | 508,633 | −31.1 | 9,943 | 3,251 | −67.3 | 187,306 | 167,327 | −10.7 | 3,004 | 1,043 | −65.3 |
| Liquor laws | 294,825 | 123,435 | −58.1 | 60,064 | 17,707 | −70.5 | 113,686 | 50,795 | −55.3 | 34,665 | 11,823 | −65.9 |
| Drunkenness | 310,500 | 202,628 | −34.7 | 8,281 | 2,503 | −69.8 | 57,771 | 48,796 | −15.5 | 2,812 | 1,025 | −63.5 |
| Disorderly conduct | 308,923 | 171,960 | −44.3 | 87,098 | 29,356 | −66.3 | 113,264 | 68,763 | −39.3 | 42,850 | 16,303 | −62.0 |
| Vagrancy | 13,876 | 11,847 | −14.6 | 2,390 | 457 | −80.9 | 4,230 | 3,170 | −25.1 | 1,085 | 141 | −87.0 |
| All other offenses (except traffic) | 1,902,249 | 1,477,329 | −22.3 | 180,909 | 77,354 | −57.2 | 575,732 | 520,470 | −9.6 | 67,920 | 29,896 | −56.0 |
| Suspicion | 869 | 384 | −55.8 | 157 | 95 | −39.5 | 256 | 96 | −62.5 | 46 | 32 | −30.4 |
| Curfew and loitering law violations | 40,653 | 12,963 | −68.1 | 40,653 | 12,963 | −68.1 | 20,016 | 6,491 | −67.6 | 20,016 | 6,491 | −67.6 |

[a]Does not include suspicion.
[b]The 2006 rape figures are based on the legacy definition, and the 2015 rape figures are aggregate totals based on both the legacy and revised Uniform Crime Reporting definitions. For this reason, a percent change is not provided.
[c]Violent crimes are offenses of murder and nonnegligent manslaughter, rape, robbery, and aggravated assault. Property crimes are offenses of burglary, larceny-theft, motor vehicle theft, and arson.

SOURCE: "Table 33. Ten-Year Arrest Trends by Sex, 2006–2015," in *Crime in the United States 2015*, US Department of Justice, Federal Bureau of Investigation, 2016, https://ucr.fbi.gov/crime-in-the-u.s/2015/crime-in-the-u.s.-2015/tables/table-33/table_33_ten_year_arrest_trends_by_sex_2015.xls/output.xls (accessed January 31, 2018)

of women were arrested for arson (1,342), murder and nonnegligent manslaughter (984), and rape (514). Among less-serious offenses, the most common crimes for which women were arrested in 2015 were drug abuse violations (257,999), assaults other than aggravated assault (233,684), driving under the influence (207,906), disorderly conduct (84,135), and liquor laws (59,427).

## More Women, Fewer Men Are Being Arrested

According to the FBI, in *Crime in the United States, 2015*, the violent crime rate in 1994 was 713.6 per 100,000 US inhabitants, and the property crime rate was 4,660.2 per 100,000. By 2016, the FBI reports in *Crime in the United States, 2016* (September 2017, https://ucr.fbi.gov/crime-in-the-u.s/2016/crime-in-the-u.s.-2016/cius-2016), the violent crime rate had fallen to 386.3 per 100,000 inhabitants, and the property crime rate had fallen to 2,450.7 per 100,000. There is no consensus among criminologists and other experts as to the reasons for this enormous decline in the crime rate. Some argue that the falling crime rate is explained by demographics: the baby boom (people born between 1946 and 1964) that followed World War II (1939–1945) resulted in a disproportionate number of 16- to 24-year-olds during the 1960s and 1970s, and this is the age group most likely to commit crimes. However, as birth rates returned to their postwar highs and the number of 16- to 24-year-olds rose again during the 1990s, crime rates declined. Others

**TABLE 11.2**

### Arrests of women by age, 2015

[12,706 agencies; 2015 estimated population 246,947,242]

| Offense charged | Total all ages | Ages under 15 | Ages under 18 | Ages 18 and over | Under 10 | 10–12 | 13–14 | 15 | 16 | 17 | 18 | 19 | 20 |
|---|---|---|---|---|---|---|---|---|---|---|---|---|---|
| Total | 2,238,335 | 59,947 | 207,853 | 2,030,482 | 908 | 11,846 | 47,193 | 41,096 | 50,315 | 56,495 | 72,355 | 78,315 | 79,147 |
| Total percent distribution[a] | 100.0 | 2.7 | 9.3 | 90.7 | * | 0.5 | 2.1 | 1.8 | 2.2 | 2.5 | 3.2 | 3.5 | 3.5 |
| Murder and nonnegligent manslaughter | 984 | 6 | 39 | 945 | 0 | 1 | 5 | 6 | 7 | 20 | 44 | 43 | 29 |
| Rape[b] | 514 | 58 | 108 | 406 | 1 | 13 | 44 | 19 | 15 | 16 | 17 | 22 | 10 |
| Robbery | 10,509 | 338 | 1,501 | 9,008 | 1 | 35 | 302 | 344 | 395 | 424 | 568 | 537 | 491 |
| Aggravated assault | 66,822 | 1,868 | 5,638 | 61,184 | 35 | 450 | 1,383 | 1,093 | 1,230 | 1,447 | 1,566 | 1,825 | 2,016 |
| Burglary | 31,545 | 1,138 | 3,672 | 27,873 | 40 | 237 | 861 | 763 | 830 | 941 | 1,091 | 1,160 | 1,070 |
| Larceny-theft | 388,520 | 11,826 | 48,831 | 339,689 | 115 | 2,357 | 9,354 | 9,173 | 12,844 | 14,988 | 17,514 | 16,183 | 14,426 |
| Motor vehicle theft | 12,662 | 559 | 1,994 | 10,668 | 4 | 50 | 505 | 497 | 494 | 444 | 446 | 441 | 472 |
| Arson | 1,342 | 186 | 332 | 1,010 | 9 | 68 | 109 | 70 | 41 | 35 | 21 | 25 | 43 |
| Violent crime[c] | 78,829 | 2,270 | 7,286 | 71,543 | 37 | 499 | 1,734 | 1,462 | 1,647 | 1,907 | 2,195 | 2,427 | 2,546 |
| Violent crime percent distribution[a] | 100.0 | 2.9 | 9.2 | 90.8 | * | 0.6 | 2.2 | 1.9 | 2.1 | 2.4 | 2.8 | 3.1 | 3.2 |
| Property crime[c] | 434,069 | 13,709 | 54,829 | 379,240 | 168 | 2,712 | 10,829 | 10,503 | 14,209 | 16,408 | 19,072 | 17,809 | 16,011 |
| Property crime percent distribution[a] | 100.0 | 3.2 | 12.6 | 87.4 | * | 0.6 | 2.5 | 2.4 | 3.3 | 3.8 | 4.4 | 4.1 | 3.7 |
| Other assaults | 233,684 | 14,248 | 37,045 | 196,639 | 182 | 3,274 | 10,792 | 7,578 | 7,993 | 7,226 | 6,418 | 6,567 | 7,196 |
| Forgery and counterfeiting | 15,085 | 27 | 207 | 14,878 | 2 | 2 | 23 | 27 | 46 | 107 | 310 | 454 | 636 |
| Fraud | 39,618 | 210 | 1,161 | 38,457 | 1 | 34 | 175 | 215 | 308 | 428 | 696 | 930 | 1,146 |
| Embezzlement | 6,154 | 10 | 191 | 5,963 | 0 | 2 | 8 | 7 | 56 | 118 | 288 | 391 | 337 |
| Stolen property; buying, receiving, possessing | 14,720 | 376 | 1,317 | 13,403 | 2 | 43 | 331 | 280 | 294 | 367 | 451 | 534 | 518 |
| Vandalism | 31,496 | 2,094 | 5,414 | 26,082 | 62 | 494 | 1,538 | 1,022 | 1,087 | 1,211 | 1,112 | 1,122 | 1,168 |
| Weapons; carrying, possessing, etc. | 9,950 | 629 | 1,602 | 8,348 | 13 | 177 | 439 | 279 | 335 | 359 | 338 | 323 | 339 |
| Prostitution and commercialized vice | 20,179 | 30 | 334 | 19,845 | 0 | 6 | 24 | 53 | 93 | 158 | 717 | 1,035 | 1,100 |
| Sex offenses (except rape and prostitution) | 3,032 | 416 | 851 | 2,181 | 15 | 100 | 301 | 160 | 160 | 115 | 97 | 93 | 94 |
| Drug abuse violations | 257,999 | 3,241 | 16,177 | 241,822 | 17 | 422 | 2,802 | 2,730 | 4,084 | 6,122 | 10,641 | 11,457 | 11,348 |
| Gambling | 724 | 1 | 32 | 692 | 0 | 0 | 1 | 4 | 10 | 17 | 14 | 24 | 19 |
| Offenses against the family and children | 20,820 | 366 | 980 | 19,840 | 62 | 63 | 241 | 167 | 212 | 235 | 287 | 325 | 395 |
| Driving under the influence | 207,906 | 38 | 1,251 | 206,655 | 3 | 0 | 35 | 64 | 319 | 830 | 2,433 | 3,875 | 4,738 |
| Liquor laws | 59,427 | 1,682 | 13,228 | 46,199 | 6 | 132 | 1,544 | 2,175 | 3,714 | 5,657 | 10,438 | 10,555 | 8,394 |
| Drunkenness | 61,291 | 216 | 1,210 | 60,081 | 4 | 18 | 194 | 208 | 307 | 479 | 1,334 | 1,467 | 1,490 |
| Disorderly conduct | 84,135 | 7,758 | 19,418 | 64,717 | 80 | 1,646 | 6,032 | 4,342 | 3,956 | 3,362 | 2,622 | 2,487 | 2,495 |
| Vagrancy | 4,334 | 56 | 207 | 4,127 | 2 | 11 | 43 | 55 | 52 | 44 | 102 | 124 | 134 |
| All other offenses (except traffic) | 645,061 | 9,719 | 35,497 | 609,564 | 204 | 1,664 | 7,851 | 7,436 | 8,784 | 9,558 | 12,780 | 16,312 | 19,036 |
| Suspicion | 243 | 10 | 37 | 206 | 1 | 2 | 7 | 7 | 11 | 9 | 10 | 4 | 7 |
| Curfew and loitering law violations | 9,579 | 2,841 | 9,579 | — | 47 | 545 | 2,249 | 2,322 | 2,638 | 1,778 | — | — | — |

| Offense charged | 21 | 22 | 23 | 24 | 25–29 | 30–34 | 35–39 | 40–44 | 45–49 | 50–54 | 55–59 | 60–64 | 65 and Over |
|---|---|---|---|---|---|---|---|---|---|---|---|---|---|
| Total | 80,774 | 83,464 | 85,502 | 86,629 | 384,567 | 317,727 | 235,566 | 172,973 | 140,846 | 108,616 | 59,405 | 26,168 | 18,428 |
| Total percent distribution[a] | 3.6 | 3.7 | 3.8 | 3.9 | 17.2 | 14.2 | 10.5 | 7.7 | 6.3 | 4.9 | 2.7 | 1.2 | 0.8 |
| Murder and nonnegligent manslaughter | 36 | 48 | 50 | 46 | 181 | 154 | 89 | 62 | 55 | 59 | 25 | 11 | 13 |
| Rape[b] | 16 | 11 | 12 | 20 | 59 | 78 | 58 | 46 | 25 | 11 | 16 | 4 | 1 |
| Robbery | 505 | 469 | 477 | 484 | 1,855 | 1,343 | 890 | 561 | 404 | 270 | 116 | 22 | 16 |
| Aggravated assault | 2,356 | 2,559 | 2,556 | 2,625 | 11,817 | 9,602 | 7,172 | 5,417 | 4,548 | 3,669 | 2,011 | 853 | 592 |
| Burglary | 1,219 | 1,187 | 1,251 | 1,205 | 5,568 | 4,691 | 3,279 | 2,214 | 1,694 | 1,215 | 622 | 251 | 156 |
| Larceny-theft | 13,674 | 13,767 | 13,480 | 13,629 | 61,302 | 51,844 | 37,602 | 27,318 | 22,559 | 17,469 | 10,129 | 5,070 | 3,723 |
| Motor vehicle theft | 510 | 527 | 509 | 515 | 2,457 | 1,937 | 1,216 | 734 | 494 | 260 | 105 | 25 | 20 |
| Arson | 32 | 22 | 32 | 26 | 169 | 152 | 125 | 101 | 82 | 92 | 52 | 17 | 19 |
| Violent crime[c] | 2,913 | 3,087 | 3,095 | 3,175 | 13,912 | 11,177 | 8,209 | 6,086 | 5,032 | 4,009 | 2,168 | 890 | 622 |
| Violent crime percent distribution[a] | 3.7 | 3.9 | 3.9 | 4.0 | 17.6 | 14.2 | 10.4 | 7.7 | 6.4 | 5.1 | 2.8 | 1.1 | 0.8 |
| Property crime[c] | 15,435 | 15,503 | 15,272 | 15,375 | 69,496 | 58,624 | 42,222 | 30,367 | 24,829 | 19,036 | 10,908 | 5,363 | 3,918 |
| Property crime percent distribution[a] | 3.6 | 3.6 | 3.5 | 3.5 | 16.0 | 13.5 | 9.7 | 7.0 | 5.7 | 4.4 | 2.5 | 1.2 | 0.9 |

argue that the most important factor in the declining crime rate is the implementation of new policing techniques, especially in major cities such as Los Angeles and New York, where the targeting of specific high-crime zones has yielded noticeable changes in neighborhods. Moreover, with falling crime urban centers have been repopulated by the affluent, leading to a broad decline in the prevalence of blighted properties, an influx of businesses, and other improvements that are believed to deter crime.

Whatever the explanation for the falling crime rate, much of the decline appears to be focused on male criminality. Although males continue to commit an overwhelming majority of all crime, the number of males arrested dropped substantially between 2006 and 2015, from 6.6 million to 4.9 million, for an 25.6% decline in arrests. (See Table 11.1.) By contrast, female arrests fell only 11.8% during the same period, from nearly 2.1 million in 2006 to more than 1.8 million in 2015.

**TABLE 11.2**

## Arrests of women by age, 2015 [CONTINUED]

[12,706 agencies; 2015 estimated population 246,947,242]

| Offense charged | 21 | 22 | 23 | 24 | 25–29 | 30–34 | 35–39 | 40–44 | 45–49 | 50–54 | 55–59 | 60–64 | 65 and Over |
|---|---|---|---|---|---|---|---|---|---|---|---|---|---|
| Other assaults | 8,230 | 8,386 | 8,622 | 8,504 | 36,429 | 29,919 | 22,729 | 17,349 | 14,192 | 11,341 | 6,069 | 2,701 | 1,987 |
| Forgery and counterfeiting | 501 | 571 | 601 | 641 | 3,156 | 2,660 | 1,991 | 1,365 | 956 | 613 | 266 | 99 | 58 |
| Fraud | 1,156 | 1,218 | 1,372 | 1,418 | 7,153 | 6,905 | 5,440 | 3,983 | 2,914 | 2,009 | 1,155 | 528 | 434 |
| Embezzlement | 304 | 300 | 294 | 252 | 1,033 | 814 | 603 | 481 | 350 | 262 | 151 | 69 | 34 |
| Stolen property; buying, receiving, possessing | 607 | 634 | 633 | 625 | 3,030 | 2,444 | 1,656 | 949 | 605 | 418 | 189 | 72 | 38 |
| Vandalism | 1,333 | 1,251 | 1,286 | 1,234 | 5,221 | 3,876 | 2,645 | 1,881 | 1,577 | 1,239 | 632 | 283 | 222 |
| Weapons; carrying, possessing, etc. | 370 | 392 | 411 | 404 | 1,690 | 1,368 | 911 | 644 | 450 | 343 | 223 | 69 | 73 |
| Prostitution and commercialized vice | 1,215 | 1,205 | 1,192 | 1,049 | 4,277 | 2,574 | 1,806 | 1,355 | 1,112 | 789 | 303 | 88 | 28 |
| Sex offenses (except rape and prostitution) | 88 | 99 | 105 | 81 | 349 | 314 | 271 | 180 | 177 | 118 | 65 | 29 | 21 |
| Drug abuse violations | 11,168 | 11,286 | 11,359 | 11,539 | 48,570 | 38,570 | 26,965 | 18,024 | 14,103 | 10,019 | 4,605 | 1,576 | 592 |
| Gambling | 9 | 13 | 11 | 14 | 73 | 84 | 69 | 64 | 87 | 71 | 66 | 44 | 30 |
| Offenses against the family and children | 566 | 698 | 773 | 845 | 4,367 | 4,309 | 2,991 | 1,789 | 1,156 | 729 | 338 | 166 | 106 |
| Driving under the influence | 8,493 | 8,982 | 9,396 | 9,371 | 37,851 | 29,149 | 22,850 | 19,299 | 17,623 | 15,266 | 9,504 | 4,621 | 3,204 |
| Liquor laws | 1,294 | 922 | 760 | 672 | 2,609 | 2,136 | 1,911 | 1,809 | 1,729 | 1,482 | 896 | 378 | 214 |
| Drunkenness | 2,175 | 2,016 | 2,052 | 2,136 | 9,077 | 8,451 | 7,167 | 6,435 | 6,282 | 5,420 | 2,958 | 1,083 | 538 |
| Disorderly conduct | 3,007 | 2,925 | 2,780 | 2,728 | 11,497 | 8,897 | 6,920 | 5,452 | 4,843 | 4,092 | 2,249 | 948 | 775 |
| Vagrancy | 85 | 104 | 154 | 114 | 573 | 481 | 539 | 498 | 413 | 388 | 257 | 105 | 56 |
| All other offenses (except traffic) | 21,811 | 23,864 | 25,318 | 26,448 | 124,165 | 104,945 | 77,654 | 54,941 | 42,406 | 30,963 | 16,399 | 7,055 | 5,467 |
| Suspicion | 14 | 8 | 16 | 4 | 39 | 30 | 17 | 22 | 10 | 9 | 4 | 1 | 11 |
| Curfew and loitering law violations | — | — | — | — | — | — | — | — | — | — | — | — | — |

aBecause of rounding, the percentages may not add to 100.0.
bThe rape figures in this table are aggregate totals of the data submitted based on both the legacy and revised Uniform Crime Reporting definitions.
cViolent crimes are offenses of murder and nonnegligent manslaughter, rape, robbery, and aggravated assault. Property crimes are offenses of burglary, larceny-theft, motor vehicle theft, and arson.
*Less than one-tenth of 1 percent.

SOURCE: "Table 40. Arrests: Females, by Age, 2015," in *Crime in the United States 2015*, US Department of Justice, Federal Bureau of Investigation, 2016, https://ucr.fbi.gov/crime-in-the-u.s/2015/crime-in-the-u.s.-2015/tables/table-40 (accessed January 31, 2018).

## WOMEN IN STATE AND FEDERAL PRISONS

According to E. Ann Carson of the US Bureau of Justice Statistics (BJS), in *Prisoners in 2016* (January 2018, https://www.bjs.gov/content/pub/pdf/p16.pdf), 1.5 million people were incarcerated in state and federal prisons in the United States in 2016. The number of people in US prisons had been roughly flat since 2006 even as the population grew, so the incarceration rate had been falling steadily since that time. The incarceration rate in 2016 was 450 inmates per 100,000 US residents.

The number of women in state or federal prisons in 2016 was 111,422, or 7.4% of the total incarcerated population, and it had been falling fairly steadily since 2008, when 114,612 women were incarcerated. (See Table 11.3.) The imprisonment rate for sentenced female prisoners in 2016, at 64 per 100,000 US residents, was similarly dwarfed by the imprisonment rate for men, at 847 per 100,000. (See Table 11.4.) Imprisonment rates had been falling for both men and women since 2008, but among men the rate fell further during this period, from 956, whereas the female rate fell from 69.

Carson notes that the imprisonment rate for women, like that for men, varies by race and ethnicity. In 2016 non-Hispanic white women (49 per 100,000) had a lower imprisonment rate than women in general (64), whereas Hispanic women (67) had a slightly higher than average imprisonment rate, and non-Hispanic African American women (96) had a rate 50% higher than the average for women and nearly twice the rate for non-Hispanic white women. (See Table 11.5.) For all races and ethnicities, female imprisonment rates were highest for women aged 30 to 34 years and dramatically lower for women aged 55 years and older.

Carson reports in *Prisoners in 2016* that as of December 31, 2015, 37% of sentenced female prisoners were incarcerated for violent crimes, 26.9% for property crimes, and 24.9% for drug crimes. By contrast, over half (55.9%) of sentenced male prisoners were incarcerated for violent crimes.

According to Carson, in 2016, 37,127 (35.2%) of the 105,489 sentenced female prisoners incarcerated in state and federal corrections facilities were in the four largest jurisdictions: the federal system (11,392), Texas (12,975), Florida (6,863), and California (5,897).

### Women in Jails

Jails differ from prisons in that they hold inmates for shorter sentences (usually less than one year). Jails also house inmates for federal, state, and other authorities due to overcrowding of those facilities. People awaiting trial, sentencing, and conviction are usually housed in jails, as are mentally ill individuals pending movement to an appropriate health care facility. Juveniles are temporarily detained in jail until they can be transferred to juvenile authorities, and individuals in the military are housed in

**TABLE 11.3**

**Prisoners under the jurisdiction of state and federal correctional authorities, yearend 2006–16**

| Year | Total | Federal[a] | State | Male | Female |
|------|-------|------------|-------|------|--------|
| 2006 | 1,568,674 | 193,046 | 1,375,628 | 1,456,366 | 112,308 |
| 2007 | 1,596,835 | 199,618 | 1,397,217 | 1,482,524 | 114,311 |
| 2008 | 1,608,282 | 201,280 | 1,407,002 | 1,493,670 | 114,612 |
| 2009 | 1,615,487 | 208,118 | 1,407,369 | 1,502,002 | 113,485 |
| 2010 | 1,613,803 | 209,771 | 1,404,032 | 1,500,936 | 112,867 |
| 2011 | 1,598,968 | 216,362 | 1,382,606 | 1,487,561 | 111,407 |
| 2012 | 1,570,397 | 217,815 | 1,352,582 | 1,461,625 | 108,772 |
| 2013 | 1,576,950 | 215,866 | 1,361,084 | 1,465,592 | 111,358 |
| 2014 | 1,562,319 | 210,567 | 1,351,752 | 1,449,291 | 113,028 |
| 2015 | 1,526,603 | 196,455 | 1,330,148 | 1,415,112 | 111,491 |
| 2016[b] | 1,505,397 | 189,192 | 1,316,205 | 1,393,975 | 111,422 |
| **Percent change** | | | | | |
| Average annual, 2006–2015 | −0.3% | 0.2% | −0.3% | −0.3% | −0.1% |
| 2015–2016 | −1.4 | −3.7 | −1.0 | −1.5 | −0.1 |

[a]Includes prisoners held in nonsecure, privately operated community corrections facilities and juveniles held in contract facilities.
[b]Total and state estimates include imputed counts for North Dakota and Oregon, which did not submit 2016 data to National Prisoner Statistics program.
Note: Jurisdiction refers to the legal authority of state or federal correctional officials over a prisoner, regardless of where the prisoner is held.

SOURCE: E. Ann Carson, "Table 1. Prisoners under the Jurisdiction of State or Federal Correctional Authorities, by Jurisdiction and Sex, December 31, 2006–2016," in *Prisoners in 2016*, US Department of Justice, Office of Justice Programs, Bureau of Justice Statistics, January 2018, https://www.bjs.gov/content/pub/pdf/p16.pdf (accessed January 31, 2018)

---

**TABLE 11.4**

**Imprisonment rates of sentenced prisoners under the jurisdiction of state or federal correctional authorities per 100,000 residents, by jurisdiction, sex, and race/ethnicity, yearend 2006–16**

| Year | Per 100,000 US residents of all ages | | | | | Per 100,000 US residents age 18 or older | | | | | |
|------|-------|---------|-------|------|--------|-------|------|--------|-------|-------|---------|
| | Total | Federal[b] | State | Male | Female | Total | Male | Female | White[c, d] | Black[c, d] | Hispanic[d] |
| 2006 | 501 | 58 | 443 | 948 | 68 | 666 | 1,275 | 89 | 324 | 2,261 | 1,073 |
| 2007 | 506 | 59 | 447 | 955 | 69 | 670 | 1,282 | 90 | 317 | 2,233 | 1,094 |
| 2008 | 506 | 60 | 447 | 956 | 69 | 669 | 1,279 | 90 | 316 | 2,196 | 1,057 |
| 2009 | 504 | 61 | 443 | 952 | 67 | 665 | 1,271 | 88 | 308 | 2,134 | 1,060 |
| 2010 | 500 | 61 | 439 | 948 | 66 | 656 | 1,260 | 86 | 307 | 2,059 | 1,014 |
| 2011 | 492 | 63 | 429 | 932 | 65 | 644 | 1,236 | 84 | 299 | 1,973 | 990 |
| 2012 | 480 | 62 | 417 | 910 | 63 | 626 | 1,201 | 82 | 293 | 1,873 | 949 |
| 2013 | 479 | 61 | 417 | 906 | 65 | 623 | 1,194 | 83 | 291 | 1,817 | 922 |
| 2014 | 471 | 60 | 412 | 890 | 65 | 612 | 1,170 | 84 | 289 | 1,754 | 893 |
| 2015 | 459 | 55 | 403 | 865 | 64 | 595 | 1,135 | 82 | 281 | 1,670 | 862 |
| 2016[a] | 450 | 53 | 397 | 847 | 64 | 582 | 1,108 | 82 | 274 | 1,608 | 856 |
| **Percent change** | | | | | | | | | | | |
| Average annual, 2006–2015 | −0.9% | −0.4% | −1.0% | −0.9% | −0.6% | −1.1% | −1.2% | −0.8% | −1.4% | −3.0% | −2.2% |
| 2015–2016 | −1.9 | −4.7 | −1.6 | −2.1 | −0.2 | −2.1 | −2.3 | −0.4 | −2.5 | −3.7 | −0.6 |

[a]Total and state estimates include imputed counts for North Dakota and Oregon, which did not submit 2016 National Prisoner Statistics (NPS) data.
[b]Includes prisoners held in nonsecure, privately operated community corrections facilities and juveniles held in contract facilities.
[c]Excludes persons of Hispanic or Latino origin and persons of two or more races.
[d]Race and Hispanic origin rates for all years have been reestimated using a different method and will not match previously published rates.
Note: Jurisdiction refers to the legal authority of state or federal correctional officials over a prisoner, regardless of where the prisoner is held. Counts are based on prisoners with sentences of more than 1 year.

SOURCE: E. Ann Carson, "Table 6. Imprisonment Rate of Sentenced Prisoners under Jurisdiction of State or Federal Correctional Authorities, by Jurisdiction and Demographic Characteristics, December 31, 2006–2016," in *Prisoners in 2016*, US Department of Justice, Office of Justice Programs, Bureau of Justice Statistics, January 2018, https://www.bjs.gov/content/pub/pdf/p16.pdf (accessed January 31, 2018)

---

jail for protective custody or while awaiting appearance as court witnesses.

Zhen Zeng of the BJS notes in *Jail Inmates in 2016* (February 2018, https://www.bjs.gov/content/pub/pdf/ji16.pdf) that males significantly outnumber females in jails. In 2016, 102,300 (14.5%) of the 704,500 inmates in local jails were female.

And yet, in recent decades, the number of women in jails has risen at a higher rate than the jail population as a whole. Elizabeth Swavola, Kristine Riley, and Ram Subramanian of the Vera Institute of Justice, an independent nonprofit national research and policy organization working to improve the US justice system, report in *Overlooked: Women and Jails in an Era of Reform* (August 2016,

TABLE 11.5

**Imprisonment rate of sentenced state and federal prisoners per 100,000 US residents, by sex, race/ethnicity, and age, yearend 2016**

| Age group | Total[a] | Male | | | | | Female | | | | |
|---|---|---|---|---|---|---|---|---|---|---|---|
| | | All male[a] | White[b] | Black[b] | Hispanic | Other[b] | All female[a] | White[b] | Black[b] | Hispanic | Other[b] |
| Total[c] | 450 | 847 | 400 | 2,415 | 1,092 | 1,305 | 64 | 49 | 96 | 67 | 118 |
| 18–19 | 130 | 244 | 72 | 853 | 298 | 338 | 11 | 8 | 25 | 11 | 21 |
| 20–24 | 653 | 1,191 | 453 | 3,371 | 1,417 | 1,831 | 85 | 61 | 141 | 85 | 168 |
| 25–29 | 998 | 1,801 | 803 | 4,725 | 2,249 | 2,485 | 167 | 136 | 216 | 170 | 271 |
| 30–34 | 1,091 | 1,981 | 960 | 5,334 | 2,450 | 3,006 | 186 | 155 | 232 | 193 | 312 |
| 35–39 | 1,053 | 1,944 | 934 | 5,435 | 2,359 | 2,791 | 164 | 136 | 214 | 161 | 263 |
| 40–44 | 886 | 1,655 | 820 | 4,645 | 1,975 | 2,430 | 129 | 108 | 181 | 114 | 213 |
| 45–49 | 710 | 1,333 | 688 | 3,781 | 1,611 | 2,106 | 100 | 79 | 158 | 90 | 150 |
| 50–54 | 575 | 1,093 | 572 | 3,087 | 1,359 | 1,756 | 75 | 56 | 124 | 69 | 133 |
| 55–59 | 377 | 733 | 376 | 2,142 | 1,016 | 1,208 | 40 | 28 | 72 | 41 | 79 |
| 60–64 | 220 | 439 | 229 | 1,246 | 739 | 683 | 19 | 13 | 33 | 22 | 35 |
| 65 or older | 76 | 165 | 97 | 430 | 319 | 321 | 5 | 4 | 8 | 8 | 9 |
| Number of sentenced prisoners[d] | 1,458,173 | 1,352,684 | 390,900 | 466,600 | 320,000 | 175,200 | 105,489 | 48,900 | 20,300 | 19,300 | 17,000 |

[a]Includes American Indians and Alaska Natives; Asians, Native Hawaiians, and other Pacific Islanders; and persons of two or more races.
[b]Excludes persons of Hispanic or Latino orgin.
[c]Includes persons age 17 or younger.
[d]Race and Hispanic origin totals are rounded to the nearest 100 to accommodate differences in data collection techniques between jurisdictions.
Note: Counts based on prisoners with sentences of more than 1 year under the jurisdiction of state or federal correctional officials. Imprisonment rate is the number of prisoners under state or federal jurisdiction with a sentence of more than 1 year per 100,000 US residents of corresponding sex, race, Hispanic origin, and age. Resident population estimates are from the US Census Bureau for January 1, 2016. Includes imputed counts for North Dakota and Oregon, which did not submit 2016 NPS data.

SOURCE: Ann E. Carson, "Table 10. Imprisonment Rate of Sentenced State and Federal Prisoners per 100,000 US Residents, by Sex, Race, Hispanic Origin, and Age, December 31, 2016," in *Prisoners in 2016*, US Department of Justice, Office of Justice Programs, Bureau of Justice Statistics, January 2018, http://www.bjs.gov/content/pub/pdf/p16.pdf (accessed January 31, 2018)

https://storage.googleapis.com/vera-web-assets/downloads/Publications/overlooked-women-and-jails-report/legacy_downloads/overlooked-women-and-jails-report-updated.pdf) that the number of people held in jail on any given day grew from 157,000 in 1970 to 745,000 in 2014—a nearly five-fold increase. Over the same period, the number of women in jail nationwide grew from under 8,000 to nearly 110,000—a nearly 14-fold increase. The authors note that in 1960, women accounted for 11% of all arrests; by 2014, this proportion had more than doubled to 26%.

Swavola, Riley, and Subramanian report that, like their male counterparts, women in jail are disproportionately people of color, poor and low-income, and survivors of violence and trauma. Women in jail also have high rates of substance use and physical and mental illness. Compared with their male counterparts, women in jail are more likely to be charged with low-level property and drug-related offenses, and they are less likely to have extensive criminal histories. Citing the need for policy reform that offers constructive alternatives to jail, the authors write, "Local jurisdictions should reserve jail incarceration as a last resort for women who are deemed a flight risk or a danger to public safety. Instead, they have allowed jails to become stopgap providers of social services, mental health and substance use assessment and treatment, and temporary housing for women caught up in the justice system—a catchall for those who have slipped through the net of community services, if any exist."

## Mothers in Prison

Lauren E. Glaze and Laura M. Maruschak of the BJS explain in *Parents in Prison and Their Minor Children* (March 2010, https://www.bjs.gov/content/pub/pdf/pptmc.pdf), the most recent report on this topic as of April 2018, that 2.3% of all minor children in the United States had a parent in prison in 2007. An estimated 357,300 households with children were missing a parent because of incarceration in that year. Approximately 65,600 mothers were incarcerated in 2007, a circumstance that separated them from their estimated 147,400 children. Nearly two-thirds (62%) of women in prison reported being a parent of a minor. Between 1991 and 2007 the number of children with a mother in prison increased by 131%, whereas the number of children with an imprisoned father increased by 77% during the same period.

Of the households in which a mother was incarcerated in state prison in 2007, Glaze and Maruschak note that 44.9% reported children were being raised by grandparents, 37% were with their father, 22.8% were with another relative, 7.8% were with a friend, and 10.9% were in foster care (this adds up to more than 100% because some prisoners had children in different homes). More than half (55.7%) of mothers in state prisons reported some type of weekly contact (visits, phone calls, or letters) with their children; 85% reported at least some contact with their minor children.

Some states have mother-infant programs within their prison systems to help prisoners care for their infants. The federal system has the Mothers and Infants Together program to help pregnant women and mothers with infants. However, most mothers in prison rely on relatives to care for their children. Additionally, many children of female prisoners are in foster care.

## Probation and Parole

Probationers are convicted criminals who have been sentenced to a period of supervision in the community rather than to incarceration. Parole is a period of conditional and supervised release after a period of incarceration. In *Probation and Parole in the United States, 2015* (February 2017, https://www.bjs.gov/content/pub/pdf/ppus15.pdf), Danielle Kaeble and Thomas P. Bonczar of the BJS report that the probation and parole population had been steadily declining, falling by 2015 to its lowest level since 2005. A quarter (25%) of adults on probation in 2015 were women, up from 23% in 2005. Women accounted for 13% of all parolees in 2015, up slightly from 12% in 2005.

## CAPITAL PUNISHMENT

Although executing prisoners for certain serious offenses was once a common feature of criminal justice systems worldwide, during the 20th century all Western industrialized nations except for the United States discontinued the practice on human rights grounds. Capital punishment remains legal at the federal level in the United States, but it is outlawed in 19 states, and its use in the states where it remains legal varies widely. For example, Tracy L. Snell of the BJS notes in *Capital Punishment, 2013—Statistical Tables* (December 2014, https://www.bjs.gov/content/pub/pdf/cp13st.pdf), the most recent report of its kind as of April 2018, that at yearend 2013 California had by far the most inmates on death row, 735, but the death penalty had been halted in the state since 2006 because of a court order, pending a judicial review of the execution chamber and methods of carrying out executions. Florida had 398 death-row inmates in 2013 and had executed seven that year; Texas had 273 death row inmates and had executed 16.

According to Snell, 2013 marked the 13th consecutive year of decreases in the number of prisoners being held under the sentence of death in the United States. There were 2,979 inmates in 35 states on death row at yearend 2013, and three states (California, Florida, and Texas) accounted for nearly half of all death-row prisoners. Just over half (56%) of death-row inmates were white, 42% were African American, and 14% were Hispanic. At yearend 2013, 83 inmates were placed on death row in 16 states, and 115 inmates were removed from death row in 22 states. Among those removed, 39 were executed, 31 died in prison but not from execution, and 45 were removed from death row due to overturned or commuted sentences. Those inmates executed in 2013 had been on death row for an average of 15.5 years.

Snell reports that at yearend 2013 there were 56 women on death row—38 of whom were white and 14 of whom were African American. (See Table 11.6.) Nearly half (27) were in state prisons in the South, including eight in Texas, five in Florida, and four in Alabama. Another 24 women on death row were in state prisons in the West—20 in California, two in Arizona, and one each in Idaho and Oregon. Only three women were on death row in the Northeast (all in Pennsylvania), and only one woman was on death row in the Midwest (in Indiana). There was also one woman, Lisa Montgomery (1968–), on death row in the federal prison system. One woman, Kimberly McCarthy (1961–2013), was executed in Texas in 2013.

The Death Penalty Information Center reports in "Women and the Death Penalty" (2018, https://deathpenaltyinfo.org/women-and-death-penalty#facts) that as of October 1, 2016, 54 women were on death row in the United States. These female prisoners constituted 1.9% of the death row population of 2,902 prisoners at that time. The center notes that more than 40 women have been executed in the United States since 1900, including 16 female prisoners executed between 1977 and April 2018. All of the executions took place in southern states, including six executions in Texas and three in Oklahoma. Twelve of the executed female prisoners were white, and four were African American. Their average age at execution was 47 years.

TABLE 11.6

## Female prisoners on death row, by region, jurisdiction, and race, 2012 and 2013

| Region and jurisdiction | Under sentence of death, 12/31/12[a] | | | Received under sentence of death, 2013 | Removed from death row (excluding executions), 2013 | | | Executed, 2013[b] | Under sentence of death, 12/31/13 | | |
|---|---|---|---|---|---|---|---|---|---|---|---|
| | All races[c] | White[d] | Black[d] | | All races[c] | White[d] | Black[d] | | All races[c] | White[d] | Black[d] |
| US total | 60 | 41 | 15 | 0 | 3 | 3 | 0 | 1 | 56 | 38 | 14 |
| Federal | 1 | 1 | 0 | 0 | 0 | 0 | 0 | 0 | 1 | 1 | 0 |
| State | 59 | 40 | 15 | 0 | 3 | 3 | 0 | 1 | 55 | 37 | 14 |
| Northeast | 3 | 1 | 2 | 0 | 0 | 0 | 0 | 0 | 3 | 1 | 2 |
| Pennsylvania | 3 | 1 | 2 | 0 | 0 | 0 | 0 | 0 | 3 | 1 | 2 |
| Midwest | 2 | 1 | 1 | 0 | 1 | 1 | 0 | 0 | 1 | 0 | 1 |
| Indiana | 1 | 0 | 1 | 0 | 0 | 0 | 0 | 0 | 1 | 0 | 1 |
| Ohio | 1 | 1 | 0 | 0 | 1 | 1 | 0 | 0 | 0 | 0 | 0 |
| South | 29 | 19 | 10 | 0 | 1 | 1 | 0 | 1 | 27 | 18 | 9 |
| Alabama | 4 | 3 | 1 | 0 | 0 | 0 | 0 | 0 | 4 | 3 | 1 |
| Florida | 5 | 2 | 3 | 0 | 0 | 0 | 0 | 0 | 5 | 2 | 3 |
| Georgia | 1 | 1 | 0 | 0 | 0 | 0 | 0 | 0 | 1 | 1 | 0 |
| Kentucky | 1 | 1 | 0 | 0 | 0 | 0 | 0 | 0 | 1 | 1 | 0 |
| Louisiana | 2 | 1 | 1 | 0 | 0 | 0 | 0 | 0 | 2 | 1 | 1 |
| Mississippi | 2 | 2 | 0 | 0 | 0 | 0 | 0 | 0 | 2 | 2 | 0 |
| North Carolina | 3 | 2 | 1 | 0 | 1 | 1 | 0 | 0 | 2 | 1 | 1 |
| Oklahoma | 1 | 1 | 0 | 0 | 0 | 0 | 0 | 0 | 1 | 1 | 0 |
| Tennessee | 1 | 1 | 0 | 0 | 0 | 0 | 0 | 0 | 1 | 1 | 0 |
| Texas | 9 | 5 | 4 | 0 | 0 | 0 | 0 | 1 | 8 | 5 | 3 |
| West | 25 | 19 | 2 | 0 | 1 | 1 | 0 | 0 | 24 | 18 | 2 |
| Arizona | 3 | 3 | 0 | 0 | 1 | 1 | 0 | 0 | 2 | 2 | 0 |
| California | 20 | 14 | 2 | 0 | 0 | 0 | 0 | 0 | 20 | 14 | 2 |
| Idaho | 1 | 1 | 0 | 0 | 0 | 0 | 0 | 0 | 1 | 1 | 0 |
| Oregon | 1 | 1 | 0 | 0 | 0 | 0 | 0 | 0 | 1 | 1 | 0 |

[a]Counts of female prisoners under sentence of death at yearend 2012 have been revised from those reported in *Capital Punishment, 2012—Statistical Tables* (NCJ 245789 BJS web, May 2014). The revised figures exclude 1 female inmate in Texas whose removal from under sentence of death occurred prior to 2012 but was not reported until the 2013 data collection.
[b]One black female inmate was executed in Texas in 2013.
[c]Includes American Indians or Alaska Natives; Asians, Native Hawaiians, or other Pacific Islander; and inmates of Hispanic or Latino origin for whom no other race was identified.
[d]Counts of white and black inmates include persons of Hispanic or Latino origin, which may differ from other tables in this report.

SOURCE: Tracy L. Snell, "Table 6. Female Prisoners under Sentence of Death, by Region, Jurisdiction, and Race, 2012 and 2013," in *Capital Punishment, 2013—Statistical Tables*, US Department of Justice, Office of Justice Programs, Bureau of Justice Statistics, December 2014, https://www.bjs.gov/content/pub/pdf/cp13st.pdf (accessed January 31, 2018).

# IMPORTANT NAMES
# AND ADDRESSES

**AARP (formerly American Association of Retired Persons)**
601 E St. NW
Washington, DC 20049
1-888-687-2277
Email: member@aarp.org
URL: https://www.aarp.org/

**American Association of University Women**
1310 L St. NW, Ste. 1000
Washington, DC 20005
(202) 785-7700
1-800-326-2289
Email: connect@aauw.org
URL: https://www.aauw.org/

**American Cancer Society**
250 Williams St. NW
Atlanta, GA 30303
1-800-227-2345
URL: https://www.cancer.org/

**American Heart Association**
7272 Greenville Ave.
Dallas, TX 75231
1-800-242-8721
URL: http://www.heart.org/

**Association for Women in Science**
1667 K Street NW, Ste. 800
Washington, DC 20006
(202) 588-8175
Email: awis@awis.org
URL: https://www.awis.org/

**Center for American Women and Politics**
**Eagleton Institute of Politics**
**Rutgers, the State University of**
**New Jersey**
191 Ryders Ln.
New Brunswick, NJ 08901-8557
(848) 932-9384
FAX: (848) 932-6778
Email: cawp.info@eagleton.rutgers.edu
URL: http://www.cawp.rutgers.edu/

**Center on Budget and Policy Priorities**
820 First St. NE, Ste. 510
Washington, DC 20002
(202) 408-1080
FAX: (202) 408-1056
Email: center@cbpp.org
URL: https://www.cbpp.org/

**Child Care Aware of America**
1515 N. Courthouse Rd., 3rd Fl.
Arlington, VA 22201
(703) 341-4100
FAX: (703) 341-4101
URL: https://usa.childcareaware.org/

**EMILY's List**
1800 M St. NW, Ste. 375N
Washington, DC 20036
(202) 326-1400
1-800-68-EMILY
URL: https://www.emilyslist.org/

**Families and Work Institute**
245 Fifth Ave., Ste. 1002
New York, NY 10016
(212) 465-2044
FAX: (212) 465-8637
Email: FWINews@familiesandwork.org
URL: http://www.familiesandwork.org/

**Feminist Majority Foundation**
1600 Wilson Blvd., Ste. 801
Arlington, VA 22209
(703) 522-2214
FAX: (703) 522-2219
URL: http://www.feminist.org/

**Guttmacher Institute**
125 Maiden Ln., 7th Fl.
New York, NY 10038
(212) 248-1111
1-800-355-0244
FAX: (212) 248-1951
URL: https://www.guttmacher.org/

**Henry J. Kaiser Family Foundation**
185 Berry St., Ste. 2000
San Francisco, CA 94107
(650) 854-9400
(650) 854-4800
URL: https://www.kff.org/

**Institute for Women's Policy Research**
1200 18th St. NW, Ste. 301
Washington, DC 20036
(202) 785-5100
Email: iwpr@iwpr.org
URL: https://www.iwpr.org/

**International Center for Research on Women**
1120 20th St. NW, Ste. 500N
Washington, DC 20036
(202) 797-0007
FAX: (202) 797-0020
Email: info@icrw.org
URL: https://www.icrw.org/

**National Abortion Federation**
1090 Vermont Ave. NW, Ste. 1000
Washington, DC 20005
(202) 667-5881
1-800-772-9100
FAX: (202) 667-5890
Email: naf@prochoice.org
URL: https://www.prochoice.org/

**National Association of Anorexia Nervosa and Associated Disorders**
220 N. Green St.
Chicago, IL 60607
(630) 577-1333
Helpline: (630)577-1330
Email: hello@anad.org
URL: http://www.anad.org/

**National Coalition against Domestic Violence**
One Broadway, Ste. B210
Denver, CO 80203

(303) 839-1852
URL: http://www.ncadv.org/

**National Coalition for the Homeless**
2201 P St. NW
Washington, DC 20037
(202) 462-4822
Email: info@nationalhomeless.org
URL: http://nationalhomeless.org/

**National Coalition of Girls' Schools**
PO Box 5729
Charlottesville, VA 22905
(434) 205-4496
Email: ncgs@ncgs.org
URL: https://www.ncgs.org/

**National Gay and Lesbian Task Force**
1325 Massachusetts Ave. NW, Ste. 600
Washington, DC 20005
(202) 393-5177
FAX: (202) 393-2241
URL: http://www.thetaskforce.org/

**National Organization for Women**
1100 H St. NW, Ste. 300
Washington, DC 20005

(202) 628-8669
URL: https://www.now.org/

**National Osteoporosis Foundation**
251 18th St. S, Ste. 630
Arlington, VA 22202
1-800-231-4222
Email: info@nof.org
URL: https://www.nof.org/

**Planned Parenthood Federation of America**
123 William St., 10th Fl.
New York, NY 10038
(212) 541-7800
FAX: (212) 245-1845
URL: https://www.plannedparenthood.org/

**Rape, Abuse, and Incest National Network**
1220 L St. NW, Ste. 505
Washington, DC 20005
(202) 544-1034
1-800-656-4673
Email: info@rainn.org
URL: https://www.rainn.org/

**Susan G. Komen Foundation**
5005 LBJ Fwy., Ste. 526
Dallas, TX 75244

1-877-465-6636
1-877-GO KOMEN
Email: helpline@komen.org
URL: https://ww5.komen.org/

**United Nations Entity for Gender Equality and the Empowerment of Women**
405 E. 42nd St.
New York, NY 10017
(646) 781-4400
FAX: (646) 781-4444
URL: http://www.unwomen.org/en/

**Urban Institute**
2100 M St. NW
Washington, DC 20037
(202) 833-7200
URL: https://www.urban.org/

**US Department of Health and Human Services, Office on Women's Health**
200 Independence Ave. SW, Rm. 712E
Washington, DC 20201
(202) 690-7650
1-800-994-9662
FAX: (202) 205-2631
URL: https://www.womenshealth.gov/

# RESOURCES

The US Census Bureau publishes the findings of its annual and ongoing surveys in a variety of publications and data tables. The Census releases that were of particular use in the preparation of this publication include *Age and Sex Composition in the United States: 2014* (August 2017), *America's Families and Living Arrangements: 2017* (November 2017), *Fertility—Historical Time Series Tables* (April 2014), *Historical Income Tables: People* (September 2014), *Historical Poverty Tables—People* (September 2014), *Historical Marriage Status Tables* (November 2017), *Income and Poverty in the United States: 2016* (Jessica L. Semega, Kayla R. Fontenot, and Melissa A. Kollar, September 2017), *School Enrollment: CPS October 2016—Detailed Tables* (August 2017), and *Voting and Registration in the Election of November 2016* (January 2018).

The National Center for Education Statistics provides detailed information on school enrollment, educational attainment, and other facets of women's educational experience in *Digest of Education Statistics: 2016* (March 2017) and in *Projections of Education Statistics to 2025* (William J. Hussar and Tabitha M. Bailey, September 2017).

The US Bureau of Labor Statistics (BLS) is the major source of statistical information on the nation's labor force. In *Labor Force Statistics from the Current Population Survey* (February 2017), the BLS provides important data on women's employment status, unemployment rates, employment in individual industries and occupations, and numerous other labor-force characteristics. Other BLS releases that were central to the preparation of this text were *American Time Use Survey* (December 2016), *Employment Characteristics of Families—2016* (April 2017), *Highlights of Women's Earnings in 2016* (August 2017), "Projections of the Labor Force to 2060: A Visual Essay" (Mitra Toossi, September 2016), and *Women in the Labor Force: A Databook* (April 2017), among others.

The US Department of Agriculture publishes information about government-funded nutritional programs and hunger via the Food Assistance and Nutrition Research Program. Particularly useful to this publication was *Household Food Security in the United States in 2016* (Alisha Coleman-Jensen et al., September 2017) and *Program Data: Overview* (January 2018).

The National Center for Health Statistics (NCHS), a division of the Centers for Disease Control and Prevention, publishes the *Morbidity and Mortality Weekly Report* and the *National Vital Statistics Reports*, which supplied important data on women's illness and health. The NCHS's annual overview of the health of the nation, *Health, United States, 2016* (May 2017), was also central to the compilation of this book. Other NCHS data came from *Early Release of Selected Estimates Based on Data from the January–June 2017 National Health Interview Survey* (December 2017).

Within the US Department of Justice, the Bureau of Justice Statistics (BJS) conducts an annual National Crime Victimization Survey, which forms the basis of numerous publications on specific criminal topics. The publications used in this volume include *Criminal Victimization, 2016* (Rachel E. Morgan and Grace Kena, December 2017), *Female Victims of Sexual Violence, 1994–2010* (Michael Planty et al., March 2013), *Hate Crime Victimization, 2004–2015* (Lynn Langton and Madeline Masucci, June 2017), *Intimate Partner Violence, 1993–2011* (Shannan Catalano, November 2013), and *Prisoners in 2016* (E. Ann Carson, January 2018). The Federal Bureau of Investigation also supplied important information about crimes reported to law enforcement agencies in the form of its annual data releases *Crime in the United States, 2015* (November 2016) and *Crime in the United States, 2016* (September 2017).

# INDEX

# U

UCR (Uniform Crime Reporting) Program, 167
UN (United Nations), 159, 164, 165, 175
Undocumented immigrants, 4
Unemployment
  by age, gender, race/ethnicity, marital status, and duration, 48*t*
  child care, 147
  demographics, 44*t*–45*t*
  duration, 47–49
  government benefits, 88
  marital status, 37
  mothers, 47
  rates, 46–47
  reasons for, 49
  trends, 36*t*
Uniform Crime Reporting (UCR) Program, 167
Uninsured persons, 98, 99*t*–100*t*
Unions, 81, 86(*t*5.8)
*United Automobile Workers v. Johnson Controls*, 53
United Kingdom, 152
United Nations (UN), 159, 164, 165, 175
*United Parcel Service, Inc., Young v.*, 54
*United States v. Windsor*, 9
Unmarried childbearing. *See* Single mothers
Unpaid family leave, 151–153, 152*t*, 154
Unpaid labor, 39, 42*t*
Upmeyer, Linda L., 162
US Bureau of Justice Statistics (BJS), 167
US Department of Defense, 63–65, 152
US Department of Education, 34, 174
US Department of Health and Human Services (HHS), 98
US Department of Housing and Urban Development (HUD), 94
US Food and Drug Administration (FDA), 98, 142
US Food and Nutrition Service, 91
US House of Representatives, 159–160, 159*f*, 165
US Preventive Services Task Force, 104

US Senate, 159*f*, 160, 165, 166
US Supreme Court, 57–58, 98
US Women's Chamber of Commerce, 66

# V

Vaccine, HPV, 108
Value in Electing Women Political Action Committee, 165
VAWA (Violence against Women Act), 173
Veneman, Ann, 164
Vice presidential candidates, 163–164
Victim-offender relationship, 173, 173(*t*10.7)
Victims of crime
  campus sexual victimization, 173–174
  crime rates, 167–168, 168*f*
  by crime type, 170(*t*10.2)
  hate crimes, 177–178, 178*f*
  homicide, 168–170, 171*t*
  intimate partner violence, 174–176, 174*f*, 176*t*
  rape and sexual assault, 170–174, 172*f*, 173*t*
  reporting of crimes, 168, 170(*t*10.3)
  sexual harassment, 176–177
  violent crime victims, by demographic characteristics, 169*t*
Vinson, Mechelle, 177
*Vinson, Meritor Savings Bank v.*, 177
Violence against Women Act (VAWA), 173
Violent crime
  arrests, 179, 180
  crime rates, 167–168, 168*f*
  homicide, 168–170, 171*t*, 172*t*
  intimate partner violence, 174–176, 174*f*, 176*t*
  rape and sexual assault, 170–174, 172*f*, 173*t*
  reporting of crimes, 168
  victims, 169*t*, 170*t*
Voting, 155, 156*t*, 157, 158*t*, 159

# W

*Wade, Roe v.*, 1, 142, 143–144
Wages. *See* Earnings gap; Income

Wagle, Susan, 162
Wallace, Lurleen, 162
Wal-Mart, 53–54
*Wal-Mart Stores Inc., Dukes v.*, 53–54
*Wal-Mart Stores Inc., Forbes v.*, 54
War in Afghanistan, 64
Weapons used in homicides, 169
Weinstein, Harvey, 62
White House Council of Economic Advisers, 152–153
Whitman, Christine Todd, 164
WIC (Special Supplemental Nutrition Program for Women, Infants, and Children), 91–92
Widowhood, 8
Wilson, Heidi, 82
Windsor, Edith, 9
*Windsor, United States v.*, 9
Winning for Women, 165
Wisconsin, 41
*Women, Minorities, and Persons with Disabilities in Science and Engineering* (National Science Foundation), 62
Women-owned businesses, 65–66
Women's Campaign Fund, 165
Women's Chamber of Commerce, 66
Women's March in Washington, 166
Women's Research and Education Institute, 64
Women's rights movement, 1, 35
Woodhull, Victoria C., 163
Working mothers. *See* Mothers
Working poor, 84
World Health Organization, 138
World War II, 35

# Y

Yellen, Janet L., 165
Young, Peggy, 54
*Young v. United Parcel Service, Inc.*, 54
"Youth Risk Behavior Surveillance," 114, 118–119, 133

OCT - - 2018

CPSIA information can be obtained
at www.ICGtesting.com
Printed in the USA
FFHW01n2300121018
48792253-52926FF

9 781410 325631